Ecocriticism

Ecocriticism: The Essential Reader charts the growth of this important field. The first-wave Ecocriticism section focuses on key readings from the 1960s to the 1990s. The second-wave Ecocriticism section goes on to consider a range of exciting contemporary trends, including environmental justice, aesthetics and philosophy, and globalization.

Readings include the work of:

- Raymond Williams
- Jonathan Bate
- Timothy Morton
- Ursula K. Heise
- Lawrence Buell
- Kate Soper
- Kate Rigby.

Containing seminal, representative, and contemporary work in the field, this volume and the editorial commentary is designed for use on both undergraduate and postgraduate ecocritical literature courses.

Ken Hiltner is a professor in the English Department at the University of California at Santa Barbara, where he was the inaugural Director of the Literature and the Environment Center 2007–11.

Routledge Literature Readers

Also available:

For further information on this series visit: www.routledge.com/books/series/RLR

Ecocriticism

The Essential Reader

Edited by

Ken Hiltner

Routledge
Taylor & Francis Group

LONDON AND NEW YORK

First published 2015
by Routledge
2 Park Square, Milton Park, Abingdon, Oxon OX14 4RN

and by Routledge
711 Third Avenue, New York, NY 10017

Routledge is an imprint of the Taylor & Francis Group, an informa business

British Library Cataloguing in Publication Data
A catalogue record for this book is available from the British Library

Library of Congress Cataloging in Publication Data
Ecocriticism : the essential reader / edited by Ken Hiltner.
  pages cm
  Includes bibliographical references and index.
  1. Ecocriticism.   2. Ecology in literature.   3. Environmental
  protection in literature.   I. Hiltner, Ken, editor of compilation.
  PN98.E36E39 2014
  809'.9336—dc23

                                                    2013050181

ISBN: 978-0-415-50859-9 (hbk)
ISBN: 978-0-415-50860-5 (pbk)

Typeset in Perpetua
by RefineCatch Limited, Bungay, Suffolk

Contents

Preface

H AVING TAUGHT QUITE a few courses over the years focusing on environmental issues, ranging from graduate seminars to lectures of 200 students, I have repeatedly found myself in need of a collection of essays containing seminal, representative, and contemporary critical work in the field. Unfortunately, no existing book fits the bill, though a few come close. *The Green Studies Reader*, which Routledge published in 2000, is a strong candidate, as it contains a number of classic ecocritical writings. However, as ecocriticism has in some sense been reinvented in the twenty-first century, *The Green Studies Reader* lacks chapters on such essential and timely issues as environmental justice and globalization. Conversely, more recent texts, such as *Environmental Criticism for the Twenty-First Century* (Routledge 2011), which I coedited, speak to newer trends, but are less invested in charting the history and growth of the field. Like many instructors, I need to reference classic and representative writings, as well as new, cutting-edge work.

This book fills that need by bringing together a range of works that defined the field of ecocriticism in its first few decades, as well as new writings that are helping to redefine it today.

Ecocriticism: The Essential Reader thus charts the growth of a field that has changed dramatically from its inception. In the 1970s through the 1990s, when ecocriticism began emerging as a movement, there was often a preoccupation with nature writing, wilderness, and texts celebrating pristine environments (or at least those imagined as pristine), such as those by Wordsworth and Thoreau. Given its October 2000 publication date, nearly all of the essays in *The Green Studies Reader* are in this vein. However, because concern over our present environmental crisis is now fueling ecocritical interests, twenty-first-century ecocritics (who sometimes refer to themselves as second- or even third-wave ecocritics) often see texts that romanticize untouched environments as offering limited insight into our present crisis. Consequently, eschewing potentially fetishized accounts of pristine wilderness, twenty-first-century ecocritics are often concerned with a variety of landscapes, including places like suburbs and cities, frequently directing themselves to sites of environmental devastation and texts that do the same. In addition, twenty-first-century ecocriticism has been profoundly influenced by a number of other factors and approaches, such as the environmental justice movement. One of the important advantages of these shifts in focus is that ecocriticism is now poised to have significant cultural and political relevance.

Acknowledgements

1: extract from Marx, Leo (1964) "Shakespeare's American Fable" (Chapter 2) in *The Machine in the Garden: Technology and the Pastoral Ideal in America*, pp. 34–72. Reprinted with permission of Oxford University Press.

2: Merchant, Carolyn (1980) "Nature as Female" (Chapter 1) in *The Death of Nature: Women, Ecology, and the Scientific Revolution*, pp. 1–41. Copyright © 1980 Carolyn Merchant. Reprinted with permission of HarperCollins Publishers.

3: Williams, Raymond (1975) "A Problem of Perspective" (Chapter 2) in *The Country and the City*, pp. 9–12. Published by Vintage. Reprinted with permission of The Random House Group Limited and Oxford University Press.

4: White Jr., Lynn (1967) "The Historical Roots of Our Ecological Crisis" in *Science* Vol. 155, No 3767, pp. 1203–7. Copyright © 1967 American Association for the Advancement of Science. Reprinted with permission of AAAS.

5: Naess, Arne (1986) "The Deep Ecological Movement: Some Philosophical Aspects" in *Philosophical Inquiry*, Vol. 8, Issue 1/2 (Winter 1986), pp. 10–31. Reprinted with permission of Professor D. Z. Andriopoulos, Editor of *Philosophical Inquiry* journal.

6: Shepard, Paul (1969) "Introduction: Ecology and Man—A Viewpoint" in *The Subversive Science: Essays Toward an Ecology of Man*, pp. 1–10. Boston: Houghton Mifflin Company.

7: extract from Snyder, Gary (1990) "The Place, the Region, and the Commons" in *The Practice of the Wild*, pp. 25–47. San Francisco: North Point Press. Copyright © 1990 Gary Snyder. Reprinted with permission of Gary Snyder and Counterpoint.

8: Bate, Jonathan (1991) "The Economy of Nature" (Chapter 2) in *Romantic Ecology: Wordsworth and the Environmental Tradition*, pp. 36–61. New York: Routledge. Reprinted with permission of Routledge Inc.

9: extract from Buell, Lawrence (1995) "Representing the Environment" in *The Environmental Imagination: Thoreau, Nature Writing, And The Formation Of American Culture*, pp. 83–114. Cambridge, Mass.: The Belknap Press of Harvard University Press. Copyright © 1995 President and Fellows of Harvard College. Reprinted with permission of the publisher.

10: Cronon, William (1995) "The Trouble with Wilderness; or, Getting Back to the Wrong Nature" in *Uncommon Ground*, edited by William Cronon. Copyright © 1995 William Cronon. Reprinted with permission of W. W. Norton & Company, Inc.

11: Glotfelty, Cheryll (1996) "Introduction: Literary Studies in an Age of Environmental Crisis" in *The Ecocriticism Reader: Landmarks in Literary Ecology*, pp. xv–xxxvii. Athens, GA: University of Georgia Press. Reprinted with permission of University of Georgia Press.

12: Adamson, Joni, Evans, Mei Mei, and Stein, Rachel (2002) "Introduction: Environmental Justice Politics, Poetics, and Pedagogy" in *The Environmental Justice Reader*. © 2002 The Arizona Board of Regents. Reprinted with permission of the University of Arizona Press.

13: Alaimo, Stacy and Heckman, Susan (2008) "Introduction: Emerging Models of Materiality in Feminist Theory" in *Material Feminisms*, pp. 1–19. © 2008 Indiana University Press. Reprinted with permission of Indiana University Press.

14: extract from Bullard, Robert (1990) "Race, Class, and the Politics of Place" (Chapter 2) in *Dumping in Dixie: Race, Class, and Environmental Quality*, pp. 25–43. Boulder, CO: Westview Press, pp 25–31, 124–26. Reprinted with permission of Westview Press.

15: extract from Mortimer-Sandilands, Catriona and Erickson, Bruce (2010) "Introduction: A Genealogy of Queer Ecologies" in *Queer Ecologies*, pp. 1–47. © 2010 Indiana University Press. Reprinted with permission of Indiana University Press.

16: Heise, Ursula K. (2006) "The Hitchhiker's Guide to Ecocriticism" in *PMLA*, pp. 503–16. Reprinted with permission of copyright owner, the Modern Language Association of America.

17: Huggan, Graham and Tiffin, Helen (2010) "Introduction" in *Postcolonial Ecocriticism: Literature, Animals, Environment*, pp. 1–24. New York: Routledge. Reprinted with permission of Routledge Inc.

18. Nixon, Rob (2005) "Environmentalism and Postcolonialism" in *Postcolonial Studies and Beyond*, Ania Loomba, Suvir Kaul, Matti Bunzl, Antoinette Burton and Jed Esty (eds), pp. 233–51. Copyright © 2005 Duke University Press, www.dukeupress.edu. All rights reserved. Reprinted with permission of the copyright holder.

19: Tsing, Anna Lowenhaupt (2005) "Natural Universals and the Global Scale" in *Friction*, pp. 88–112. Princeton University Press. Reprinted with permission of Princeton University Press.

20: Latour, Bruno (2004) "What is to be done? Political Ecology!" (Conclusion) in *Politics of Nature: How to Bring the Sciences into Democracy*, pp. 221–28. Cambridge, Mass: Harvard University Press. Copyright © 2004 President and Fellows of Harvard College. Reprinted with permission of the publisher.

21: Morton, Timothy "Imagining Ecology without Nature" in *Ecology Without Nature: Rethinking Environmental Aesthetics*, pp. 140–69. Cambridge, Mass: Harvard University Press. Copyright © 2007 President and Fellows of Harvard College. Reprinted with permission of the publisher.

22: extract from Philips, Dana (2003) "Expostulations and Replies" (Chapter 1) in *The Truth of Ecology: Nature, Culture and Literature in America*, pp. 3–41. Reprinted with permission of Oxford University Press.

23: Soper, Kate (1995) "The Discourse of Nature" (Chapter 1) in *What is Nature? Culture, Politics and the Non-Human*, pp. 15–36. Cambridge, Mass: Blackwell Publishing. Reprinted with permission of John Wiley & Sons Ltd / Blackwell Publishing.

24: Egan, Gabriel (2006) "Ecopolitics/Ecocriticism" (Chapter 1) in *Green Shakespeare: From Ecopolitics to Ecocriticism*, pp. 17–50. New York: Routledge. Reprinted with permission of Routledge Inc.

25: extract from Siewers, Alfred K. (2009) *Strange Beauty*. Palgrave Macmillan. Reprinted with permission of Palgrave Macmillan.

26: extract from Tobin, Beth (2005) "Introduction: Troping the Tropics and Aestheticizing Labor" in *Colonizing Nature: The Tropics in British Arts and Letters, 1760–1820*, pp. 1–31. Philadelphia: University of Pennsylvania Press. Reprinted with permission of the University of Pennsylvania Press.

27: extract from Watson, Robert (2006) "Ecology, Epistemology, Empiricism" (Chapter 1) in *Back to Nature: The Green and the Real in the Late Renaissance*, pp. 3–35. Philadelphia: University of Pennsylvania Press. Reprinted with permission of the University of Pennsylvania Press.

28: Chakrabarty, Dipesh (2009) "The Climate of History: Four Theses" in *Critical Inquiry*, Vol. 35, No. 2 (Winter 2009), pp. 197–222. Reprinted with permission of University of California Press and the author.

29: Le Guin, Ursula K. (1986) "The Carrier Bag Theory of Fiction" in *Dancing at the Edge of the World*. Copyright © 1989 Ursula K. Le Guin. Reprinted with permission of Grove/Atlantic, Inc. Any third party use of this material, outside of this publication, is prohibited.

30: Rigby, Kate (2006) "Writing after Nature" *Australian Humanities Review*, Issue 39–40 (September 2006), http://www.australianhumanitiesreview.org/archive/Issue-September-2006/rigby.html. Reprinted with permission of Australian Humanities Review.

Disclaimer

The publishers have made every effort to contact authors/copyright holders of works reprinted in *Ecocriticism: The Essential Reader* and to obtain permission to publish extracts. This has not been possible in every case, however, and we would welcome correspondence from those individuals/companies whom we have been unable to trace. Any omissions brought to our attention will be remedied in future editions.

General Introduction

KEN HILTNER

O VER THE YEARS, it has been my great fortune to encounter a range of bright, enthusiastic, and dedicated students who are deeply concerned about the present state of the planet, and moreover, want to do something about it. It is intensely rewarding to see the level of commitment that this emerging generation of environmentalists brings to the table. However, each of them has to personally confront an important question, as, I suppose, do we all: Environmentally, what can I do to help?

Make no mistake, this is a big, frightening question. The sheer enormity of it, as it reflects the enormity of our current environmental situation, has stopped more than a few individuals in their tracks. In general, big questions have a way of incapacitating us.

When most people think about doing their part for our planet (and I am thinking vocationally here—in practical terms, what sort of things they can major in at college, and, ultimately what sort of professions they can pursue) they often think about the sciences, such as geoscience, which can help us understand climate change, and biological sciences, which take up issues like species loss and biodiversity. In part, this is because when environmental studies programs first began appearing in American universities over forty years ago, interest in the subject more often than not came from the sciences.

Let me be very clear in saying that I am a staunch supporter of the environmental sciences and I have enormous respect for my colleagues working in those fields. However, perhaps because of the admirable gains made by the environmental sciences in the past few decades, when most people think about doing their part for our planet (and again, I mean by dedicating their lives to an environmental vocation), they often do not first think about art, literature, music, or the like.

That is, I think, a mistake—and a big one. The humanities, such as literary study, also have a major role to play in our shared challenge of forging an environmentally better future.

So, how can literature and the study of it help save the planet? To understand how, we need to separate the act of being a careful reader (i.e. being a literary critic, the profession of most of the thinkers anthologized here) from the activity of thoughtful writing. Although this book anthologizes works of literary criticism, let's first briefly take a look at writing.

If I were to ask a number of environmentalists, regardless of whether they represented the sciences or humanities, to provide a list of the top five most influential environmental works of the twentieth century, there is one work that would likely appear on almost everyone's list: Rachel Carson's *Silent Spring*, which was published in 1962.

For our purposes, it is noteworthy that Carson was not primarily a scientist and was never a professional research scientist. Although she did hold a Masters degree in zoology from Johns Hopkins University, Carson made her living as a writer. First, at the U.S. Bureau of Fisheries, she wrote brochures and other literature for the general public. She then moved to books, writing three award-winning books on the oceans, including *The Sea Around Us*, a bestseller that received the National Book Award. After decades of sharpening her skills as a writer, she produced her magnum opus, the great work of her life, *Silent Spring*.

What made this such a powerful and influential work was not just (or even mainly) Carson's training as a scientist, but her decades of experience and skill as a writer.

Michael Pollan is a more recent example. Unlike Carson, Pollan, in fact, has no special training in the sciences at all. Instead, he has an M.A. in English from Columbia University. Like Carson, he began as a professional writer, in his case as a journalist. As a contributing writer for the *New York Times Magazine*, he, again like Carson, cut his teeth on writing short, powerful pieces before authoring three early books. With his skills at research and writing honed for well over two decades, he was ready to write his own game-changing book: *The Omnivore's Dilemma*.

As Carson and Pollan prove, the act of writing, of communicating, can have enormous impact environmentally. I am firmly of the conviction that now, more than ever, we are in need of talented environmental writers. Successfully communicating our current environmental condition, the skill that Carson and Pollan mastered, is sorely needed today. It also provides an answer to the question of "Environmentally, what can I do to help?" In short, follow Rachel Carson's example.

So, how about the flipside of our literary coin: how can the act of carefully reading help save the planet? For quite some time (thousands of years, in fact) human beings have been considering their relationship to our planet. However, in the era of modern environmentalism, this project took on new meaning and urgency, as a number of thinkers—quite a few of whom are anthologized in this book—wanted to better understand our present environmental situation and how we found ourselves in it.

While Carson and Pollan directly made studies of our environmental predicament, the writers reprinted in the pages of this book study texts, both the writings that were long ago handed down to us and those that are being generated today, in order to better understand the relationship that our species has to our planet. To understand how, it will be useful to compare environmental literary criticism to a more well-known form of textual analysis: feminist criticism.

As Cheryll Glotfelty noted fifteen years ago in the Introduction (which is included in its entirety in this book) to her very influential *The Ecocriticism Reader*, "[j]ust as feminist criticism examines language and literature from a gender-conscious perspective," environmental critics explore how nature and the natural world are imagined through literary texts. Such literary representations are, incidentally, not only generated by particular cultures, they play a significant role in generating those cultures.

Thus, if we wish to understand our contemporary attitudes and beliefs, our literary history is an excellent place to start.

Jane Austen's novel *Pride and Prejudice* provides a useful feminist example. If you have read the book, or even just seen one of the film adaptations, you know the essential problem that the Bennett family faces. In spite of the fact that the family has five children, none of them will be allowed to inherit the family estate. Why not? Because they are all women. In this patriarchal culture, the family inheritance has been structured to only allow it to pass from man to man. In many respects, this fact was ignored or downplayed by generations of critical readers. However, as feminist criticism came on the scene in the 1960s and 1970s, a new generation of critics began looking very carefully at literature in order to understand how patriarchy and misogyny have been functioning for centuries.

Literature of all sorts, not just important works of art like *Pride and Prejudice*, are useful in this regard, as they record both how people lived, as well as perspectives on this life. Read between the lines: Jane Austen has quite a bit to say about patriarchy.

Environmental literary critics, also known as ecocritics, a contraction for "ecological critics," or more precisely, "ecological literary or cultural critics," (sometimes also called "green" critics, especially in Britain), similarly look to a range of texts in order to understand how we have traditionally understood our relationship to the planet.

How does this work in practice? A few years ago, a particularly astute student observed to me that *Silent Spring* would not have been possible without Henry David Thoreau and the British Romantic poets (who preceded Carson by more than a century). In order to make such an apt observation, one needs to be an ecocritic.

For *Silent Spring* to succeed at urging us to undertake steps to preserve the environment, we first, clearly, need to care about the environment. But, at the risk of asking a seemingly obvious question, why do we care about the environment? Isn't it just natural that we do? In fact, this attitude is arguably not natural at all, but was constructed, in part, by artists and writers.

As England was, in many respects, the first technologically modern country on the planet (having played a major role in inaugurating the so-called Industrial Revolution), a range of writers responded by celebrating what was quickly receding across the British Isles: areas still relatively untouched by modernity and industrialization. I have in mind here poets like Blake, Shelley, and Wordsworth. An American equivalent, although a later one, would, of course, be Thoreau. These writers passionately and repeatedly argued that wild places, like forests and mountains, were sublime and precious, worth preserving at nearly any cost.

In order to understand the significance of what these writers did, it is important to realize that forest and mountains were not always thought of this way. For example, in medieval England, forests were generally imagined as dark and foreboding places, the home of wild animals and criminals, where people like Robin Hood were to be found. Of course, Robin Hood was, at least in modern versions of the story, a good criminal, but his story emerges from an era when forests were indeed dangerous places, inhabited by very dangerous people outside the reach of law. Moreover, as England had not yet eradicated its wolf population (something that it would do before the emergence of the Renaissance), there were also wolves in the forests, which routinely killed people, often children venturing into forests. Consequently, if we had lived in medieval England, our view of forests would be very different than it is today.

Instead of seeing them as beautiful and inviting, we would have likely thought them frightening and dangerous, justifiably a source of great anxiety.

Similarly, if we had lived in medieval and Renaissance England, mountains would have also likely seemed problematic. For example, when the writer John Evelyn encountered the Alps while traveling in the second half of the seventeenth century, he described them as strange and frightening. Evelyn's view was pretty typical of his time.

What a change this is from the way that similar mountains would be described by John Muir just two centuries later! Observing Mt Whitney, the highest mountain in the contiguous United States and the closet thing that we have to the Alps, Muir notes that "Thousands of tired, nerve-shaken, over-civilized people are beginning to find out that going to the mountains is going home; that wildness is necessity; that mountain parks and reservations are useful not only as fountains of timber and irrigating rivers, but as fountains of life."[1]

This is an increasingly accurate account of how mountains were being seen by the end of the nineteenth century. Muir's observation, incidentally, offers a provocative explanation for the change in perspective. With the growth of industrialization and the loss of wild places across the continent, "over-civilized people" (as Muir calls them) were no longer seeing mountains as foreboding and dangerous, but instead as a sort of antidote for industrial modernity, the last enclave of nature.

It is clear that, between the Renaissance and the second half of the nineteenth century, as a response to the growth of technological modernity and industrialization, mountains, forests and nature in general were increasingly not being seen as dangerous and foreboding, but instead as inviting and renewing.

Flash forward a hundred years to 1962, when Rachel Carson's *Silent Spring* first appeared, and we find the influence of Romantic writers alive, well, and incredibility pervasive. You need not have ever read either Thoreau or Wordsworth to have felt their influence in 1962 (or even today), as their writing and the love of nature it fostered influence us all in thousands of ways. A clear indication of this fact is that John Muir's words just seem right to us: "that wildness is necessity; that mountain parks and reservations are useful not only as fountains of timber and irrigating rivers, but as fountains of life."

It is provocative, and maybe even a little shocking, to realize that what we see when we look at a forest or mountain is, to some extent, culturally constructed. In this case, constructed over a century ago.

Consequently, as my student argued, *Silent Spring* would, in some sense, not have been possible without Romantic writers teaching us (even now, 200 years later) the importance of preserving and caring for nature. Speaking to an audience that she knew valued nature, Rachel Carson was thus able to passionately argue for its preservation. Had we never come to value nature to the degree encouraged by the Romantic poets, Carson's message may well have had far less of an impact.

Why do I believe it to be the case that our perception has changed dramatically over the centuries? Thanks for this insight must go to ecocritics who argued that the perception of forests and mountains (what we sometimes broadly refer to as "nature") is, to a large degree, historically and culturally dependent.

Let's pause for a moment on that. In response to the idea that forests and mountains are inherently beautiful, the suggestion here is that there is little inherent in this view. Indeed, this view, at least in its present incarnation, is relatively new, having been constructed in the past few centuries. Incidentally, lest you think that the work of writers is done in this regard (as the Romantics and generations of writers after them have done a pretty good job of celebrating the worth and wonder of forests and mountains), it is the case that a variety of new and experimental environmental poetry is now being written.

For example, in many respects, *Silent Spring* was revolutionary because it drew attention to environmental devastation. (Obviously, this is a 180-degree turn from the Romantic poets, who often drew attention to and celebrated pristine nature.) In the closing quarter of the twentieth century, a variety of poets, either directly or indirectly influenced by Rachel Carson and the emerging modern environmental movement, began to direct themselves to built environments, such as suburbs and cities, actual sites of environmental devastation, and dangerous environmental practices, like the wholesale use of insecticides. In addition, they are increasingly now drawing attention to climate change and our present global environment situation. Such works can often be jarring, but that is the point, as they want to draw attention to the worsening condition of the earth. In the twenty-first century a new generation of poets is attempting, in this and other ways, to change the way we think about our relationship to the planet. We can only hope that they will be as influential as their forebears.

In the pages to come, we will see the birth and maturation of ecocriticism as displayed by quite a few of the major voices in the field, including those who provided major interventions. While the work that has appeared in the twenty-first century is often very different from, and sometimes even sharply at odds with, earlier studies, the thinkers anthologized here all share a commitment in better understanding the relationship that our species has to our planet.

Note

1   John Muir, *Our National Parks* (Houghton, Mifflin; 1901), 1.

PART I

First-Wave Ecocriticism

First-Wave Introduction

FOR AS LONG AS human beings have been writing, and reflecting on what others have written, we have been considering the relationship that we have with our environment. This began long before Plato and shows no sign of stopping anytime soon. Indeed, because the idea of "nature" has been given so much thought, it is, as an early ecocritic (Raymond Williams, who is anthologized below) noted, perhaps the most difficult of all ideas to understand.

In spite of the fact that nature is such an old and difficult concept, in the 1960s and 1970s a number of literary and cultural critics, including Lynn White, Jr., Leo Marx, Carolyn Merchant, and Williams (all of whom are reprinted below), began considering what literature can tell us about our relationship to the natural world, as well as our current environmental crisis. In many respects, these were the first modern environmental critics. Perhaps not surprisingly, the term "ecocriticism" was coined in the 1970s.

As to the works that they considered, although authors such as Thoreau and Wordsworth may first come to mind in this context, literary responses to environmental concerns are as old as the issues themselves. Deforestation, air pollution, endangered species, wetland loss, animal rights, and rampant consumerism have all been appearing as controversial issues in Western literature for hundreds, and in some cases, thousands of years. For example, *The Epic of Gilgamesh*, which is nearly 5000 years old, is a fascinating text to consider in this context, as it explores how a culture came to grips with the fact that it needed to deforest vast tracts of land in order to thrive.

Similarly, in the essays below, Marx, Williams, and Merchant offer, respectively, early ecocritical readings of Shakespeare, the early modern poet Ben Jonson, and Francis Bacon, the so-called founder of modern science. However, the most controversial early ecocritic is likely Lynn White, Jr., who in 1967 provided us with a fascinating reading of the opening chapters of the Bible, reprinted in its entirety below. White boldly and unabashedly declared that "Christianity is the most anthropocentric religion that the world has seen." In addition to containing an enormously influential ecocritical reevaluation (which has been challenged as being overly simplistic) of Christianity, this statement also makes an important assumption: that anthropocentricism, which is an ethic that makes human interests central, is problematic.

Following White and others (such as Aldo Leopold), many ecocritics have found the notion of putting human concerns above those of other species worrisome. In response to such anthropocentricism, they offered "ecocentrism" (closely related to "biocentrism"), which does not privilege the interests of any one species, such as human beings, over any other in the biosphere. Not surprisingly, many of these early ecocritics found "wilderness" particularly appealing (as did nature writers such as Thoreau), as these places were imagined as being untouched by human concerns.

Following on this thinking, the 1980s saw the enormous influence of the deep ecology movement, which called for a radical revaluation of the relationship that human beings have to the environment, especially particular places on the globe that we inhabit, in part through a staunch rejection of anthropocentricism. Although the term "deep ecology" was coined by the Norwegian philosopher Arne Naess, some of its tenets can be found in contemporary writers of the time like the poet Gary Snyder. Both Naess and Snyder are anthologized here. Inspired by White and others, this group saw anthropocentricism as a hallmark of a shallow form of ecology that they vehemently rejected. Moreover, Snyder and others argued, following White, that alternative spiritual traditions, like Buddhism, were more environmentally benign than Christianity. Other thinkers, like Paul Shepard, added to the deep ecology platform by suggesting that human beings once had a far more environmentally sound relationship to the earth, now lost.

Although all of the above writers can be broadly thought of as ecocritics, with the exception of Marx and Williams, none of them were trained literary critics. Both White and Merchant, for example, were historians. However, in the in the 1990s, experienced and well-regarded literary critics, most notably Jonathan Bate and Lawrence Buell, began to consider the intersection of literature and the environment.

With the growth of technological modernity, which began in the 16th and 17th centuries, came increased interest in the implications of technology, industrialization, urbanization, and other environmentally important topics. Because these issues began appearing regularly in 19th and 20th century literature, in the 1990s ecocritics began paying a good deal of attention to these relatively recent texts. For example, Bate was interested in Wordsworth, Buell in Thoreau. Following Wordsworth and Thoreau, both Bate and Buell were primarily interested in wilderness and other rural locales, which their texts celebrated. As we shall see in Part II of this Reader, in the 21st century, a new generation of ecocritics would come to question this focus. Even in the 1990s, William Cronon, who is reprinted here along with Bate and Buell, urged that our perceptions of wilderness, which are in some sense inherited from Wordsworth, Thoreau, and other early environmentalists, should not be taken at face value.

While Bate, Buell, and others helped establish ecocriticism in universities as a respected form of literary analysis, *The Ecocriticism Reader* introduced the field to a range of individuals, both in and out of the academy. Coeditor Cheryll Glotfelty's Introduction is included below.

Because *The Ecocriticism Reader* was so effective at introducing the field, many people were not aware of the fact that ecocriticism was already beginning to undergo radical transformations at the time of its publication. This "second wave" of ecocriticism is the subject of Part II of this Reader.

Chapter 1

Leo Marx

SHAKESPEARE'S AMERICAN FABLE

If any man shall accuse these reports of partiall falshood, supposing them to be but Utopian, and legendarie fables, because he cannot conceive, that plentie and famine, a temperate climate, and distempered bodies, felicities, and miseries can be reconciled together, let him now reade with judgement, but let him not judge before he hath read.

A True Declaration of the estate of the Colonie
in Virginia. . . . London. 1610

SOME OF THE CONNECTIONS between *The Tempest* and America are well known. We know, for one thing, that Shakespeare wrote the play three or possibly four years after the first permanent colony had been established at Jamestown in 1607. At the time all of England was in a state of excitement about events across the Atlantic. Of course, the play is not in any literal sense about America; although Shakespeare is nowhere explicit about the location of the "uninhabited island," so far as he allows us to guess it lies somewhere in the Mediterranean off the coast of Africa. For the dramatist's purpose it might be anywhere. Nevertheless, it is almost certain that Shakespeare had in mind the reports of a recent voyage to the New World. In 1609 the *Sea Adventure,* one of a fleet of ships headed for Virginia, was caught in a violent storm and separated from the rest. Eventually it ran aground in the Bermudas and all aboard got safely to shore. Several people wrote accounts of the episode, and unmistakable echoes of at least two of them may be heard in *The Tempest,* particularly in the storm scene. At one point, moreover, Ariel refers to having fetched dew from the "still-vex'd Bermoothes." Though all of these facts are well known and reasonably well established, they do not in themselves suggest a particularly significant relation between the play and America. They indicate only that Shakespeare was aware of what his countrymen were doing in the Western hemisphere.[1]

But when, in addition to the external facts, we consider the action of *The Tempest,* a more illuminating connection with America comes into view. The play, after all, focuses upon a highly civilized European who finds himself living in a prehistoric wilderness. Prospero's situation is in many ways the typical situation of voyagers in newly discovered lands. I am thinking of the remote setting, the strong sense of place and its hold on the mind, the hero's struggle with raw nature on the one hand and the corruption within his own civilization on the other, and, finally, his impulse to effect a general reconciliation between the forces of civilization and nature. Of course, this is by no means a uniquely American situation. The conflict between art and nature is a universal theme, and it has been a special concern of writers working in the pastoral tradition from the time of Theocritus and Virgil. Besides, the subject has a long foreground in Shakespeare's own work – witness *A Midsummer Night's Dream, As You Like It,* and *The Winter's Tale.* Nevertheless, the theme is one of which American experience affords a singularly vivid instance: an unspoiled landscape suddenly invaded by advance parties of a dynamic, literate, and purposeful civilization. It would be difficult to imagine a more dramatic coming together of civilization and nature. In fact, Shakespeare's theme is inherent in the contradictory images of the American landscape that we find in Elizabethan travel reports, including those which he seems to have read before writing *The Tempest.*

1

Most Elizabethan ideas of America were invested in visual images of a virgin land. What most fascinated Englishmen was the absence of anything like European society; here was a landscape untouched by history – nature unmixed with art. The new continent looked, or so they thought, the way the world might have been supposed to look before the beginning of civilization. Of course the Indians also were a source of fascination. But their simple ways merely confirmed the identification of the New World with primal nature. They fit perfectly into the picture of America as a mere landscape, remote and unspoiled, and a possible setting for a pastoral retreat. But this does not mean that Shakespeare's contemporaries agreed about the character or the promise of the new land. Quite the contrary. Europeans never had agreed about the nature of nature; nor did they now agree about America. The old conflict in their deepest feelings about the physical universe was imparted to descriptions of the terrain. Elizabethan travel reports embody sharply contrasting images of the American landscape.

At one extreme, among the more popular conceptions, we find the picture of America as paradise regained. According to his account of a voyage to Virginia in 1584, Captain Arthur Barlowe was not yet in sight of the coast when he got a vivid impression that a lovely garden lay ahead. We "found shole water," he writes, "wher we smelt so sweet, and so strong a smel, as if we had bene in the midst of some delicate garden abounding with all kinde of odoriferous flowers. . . ." Barlowe, captain of a bark dispatched by Sir Walter Raleigh, goes on to describe Virginia in what was to become a cardinal image of America: an immense garden of "incredible abundance." The idea of America as a garden is the controlling metaphor of his entire report. He describes the place where the men first put ashore as

> . . . so full of grapes, as the very beating and surge of the Sea overflowed them, of which we found such plentie, as well there as in all places else, both on the sand and on the greene soile of the hils . . . that I thinke in all the world the like abundance is not to be found: and my selfe having scene those parts of Europe that most abound, find such difference as were incredible to be written.

Every detail reinforces the master image: Virginia is a land of plenty; the soil is "the most plentifull, sweete, fruitfull, and wholsome of all the worlde"; the virgin forest is not at all like the "barren and fruitles" woods of eastern Europe, but is full of the "highest and reddest Cedars of the world." One day Barlowe watches an Indian catching fish so rapidly that in half an hour he fills his canoe to the sinking point. Here Virginia stands not only for abundance, but for the general superiority of a simple, primitive style of life. Geography controls culture: the natives are "most gentle, loving and faithfull, voide of all guile and treason, and such as live after the maner of the golden age."[2]

The familiar picture of America as a site for a new golden age was a commonplace of Elizabethan travel literature, and there are many reasons for its popularity. For one thing, of course, the device made for effective propaganda in support of colonization. Projects like those of Raleigh required political backing, capital, and colonists. Even in the sixteenth century the American countryside was the object of something like a calculated real estate promotion. Besides, fashionable tendencies in the arts helped to popularize the image of a new earthly paradise. During the Renaissance, when landscape painting emerged as a separate genre, painters discovered – or rather, as Kenneth Clark puts it, rediscovered – the garden. The ancient image of an enchanted garden gave the first serious painters of landscape their most workable organizing motif. To think about landscape at all in this period, therefore, was to call forth a vision of benign and ordered nature. And a similar concern makes itself felt in Elizabethan literature. Pastoral poetry in English has never in any other period enjoyed the vogue it had then. The exploration of North America coincided with the publication of Spenser's Virgilian poem, *The Shepheards Calendar* (1579) and Sidney's *Arcadia* (1590), to name only two of the more famous Elizabethan pastorals. It is impossible to separate the taste for pastoral and the excitement, felt throughout Europe, about the New World. We think of the well-known golden age passage in *Don Quixote* and Michael Drayton's *Poems Lyrick and Pastoral*, both of which appeared about 1605. Drayton's volume included "To the Virginian Voyage," with its obvious debt to Captain Barlowe's report. He praises "VIRGINIA / Earth's only paradise," where

> . . . Nature hath in store
> Fowl, venison, and fish,
>   And the fruitfull'st soil,
>   Without your toil,
> Three harvests more,
> All greater than your wish.
>
> To whom the golden age
> Still Nature's laws doth give,
>   Nor other cares that tend
>   But them to defend
> From winter's rage,
> That long there doth not live.

As in Barlowe's report, the new land smells as sweet to the approaching voyager as the most fragrant garden:

> When as the luscious smell
> Of that delicious land,
>   Above the sea's that flow's,
>   The clear wind throws,
> Your hearts to swell
> Approaching the dear strand.

The age was fascinated by the idea that the New World was or might become Arcadia, and we hardly need to itemize the similarities between the "gentle, loving, and faithfull" Indians of Virginia and the shepherds of pastoral. In Elizabethan writing the distinction between primitive and pastoral styles of life is often blurred, and devices first used by Theocritus and Virgil appear in many descriptions of the new continent.[3]

Although fashionable, the image of America as a garden was no mere rhetorical commonplace. It expressed one of the deepest and most persistent of human motives. When Elizabethan voyagers used this device they were drawing upon utopian aspirations that Europeans always had cherished, and that had given rise, long before the discovery of America, to a whole series of idealized, imaginary worlds. Besides the golden age and Arcadia, we are reminded of Elysium, Atlantis, and enchanted gardens, Eden and Tirnanogue and the fragrant bower where the Hesperides stood watch over the golden apples. Centuries of longing and revery had been invested in the conception. What is more, the association of America with idyllic places was destined to outlive Elizabethan fashions by at least two and a half centuries. It was not until late in the nineteenth century that this way of thinking about the New World lost its grip upon the imagination of Europe and America. As for the ancillary notion of the new continent as a land of plenty, that, as we all know, is now stronger than ever. Today some historians stress what the sixteenth-century voyager called "incredible abundance" as perhaps the most important single distinguishing characteristic of American life. In our time, to be sure, the idea is less closely associated with the landscape than with science and technology.[4]

Elizabethans, however, did not always fancy that they were seeing Arcadia when they gazed at the coast of North America. Given a less inviting terrain, a bad voyage, a violent storm, hostile Indians, or, most important, different presuppositions about the universe, America might be made to seem the very opposite of a bountiful garden. Travelers then resorted to another conventional metaphor of landscape depiction. In 1609, for example, when William Strachey's vessel reached the New World, it was caught, as he puts it, in "a dreadfull storme and hideous . . . which swelling, and roaring as it were by fits, . . . at length did beate all light from heaven; which like an hell of darkenesse turned blacke upon us. . . ." After the ship was beached, Strachey and his company realized that they were on one of the "dangerous and dreaded . . . Ilands of the Bermuda." His report is one that Shakespeare probably was thinking about when he wrote *The Tempest*. In this "hideous wilderness" image of landscape, the New World is a place of hellish darkness; it arouses the fear of malevolent forces in the cosmos, and of the cannibalistic and bestial traits of man. It is associated with the wild men of medieval legend.[5]

No doubt the best-known example of this reaction appears in William Bradford's account of an event that occurred shortly after the Bermuda wreck. When the *May-flower* stood off Cape Cod in September 1620, Bradford (as he later recalled) looked across the water at what seemed to him a "hidious and desolate wilderness, full of wild beasts and willd men." Between the pilgrims and their new home, he saw only "deangerous shoulds and roring breakers." So far from seeming an earthly paradise, the landscape struck Bradford as menacing and repellent.

> Nether could they, as it were, goe up to the tope of Pigsah, to vew from this willdernes a more goodly cuntrie to feed their hops; for which way soever they turnd their eys (save upward to the heavens) they could have litle solace or content in respecte of any outward objects. For summer being done, all things stand upon them with a wetherbeaten face; and the whole countrie, full of woods and thickets, represented a wild and savage hiew. If they looked behind them, their was the mighty ocean which they had passed, and was now as a maine barr and goulfe to separate them from all the civili parts of the world.

This grim sight provoked one of the first of what has been an interminable series of melancholy inventories of the desirable – not to say indispensable – items of civilization absent from the raw continent. His people, said Bradford, had "no friends to wellcome them, nor inns to entertaine or refresh their weatherbeaten bodys, no houses or much less townes to repaire too, to seeke for succoure." Instead of abundance and joy, Bradford saw deprivation and suffering in American nature.[6]

Here, then, is a conception of the New World that is radically opposed to the garden. On the spectrum of Elizabethan images of America the hideous wilderness appears at one end and the garden at the other. The two views are traditionally associated with quite different ideas of man's basic relation to his environment. We might call them ecological images. Each is a kind of root metaphor, a poetic idea displaying the essence of a system of value. Ralph Waldo Emerson had some such concept in mind when he observed, in *English Traits,* that the views of nature held by any people seem to "determine all their institutions." In other words, each image embodies a quite distinct notion of America's destiny – a distinct social ideal.[7]

To depict the new land as a lovely garden is to celebrate an ideal of immediate, joyous fulfillment. It must be admitted, however, that the word "immediate" conceals a crucial ambiguity. How immediate? we may well ask. At times the garden is used to represent the sufficiency of nature in its original state. Then it conveys an impulse-centered, anarchic, or primitivistic view of life. But elsewhere the garden stands for a state of cultivation, hence a less exalted estimate of nature's beneficence. Although important, the line between the two is not sharp. Both the wild and the cultivated versions of the garden image embody something of that timeless impulse to cut loose from the constraints of a complex society. In Elizabethan travel literature the image typically carries a certain sense of revulsion – quickened no doubt by the discovery of new lands – against the deprivation and suffering that had for so long been accepted as an unavoidable basis for civilization. To depict America as a garden is to express aspirations still considered utopian – aspirations, that is, toward abundance, leisure, freedom, and a greater harmony of existence.

To describe America as a hideous wilderness, however, is to envisage it as another field for the exercise of power. This violent image expresses a need to mobilize energy, postpone immediate pleasures, and rehearse the perils and purposes of the community. Life in a garden is relaxed, quiet, and sweet, like the life of Virgil's Tityrus, but survival in a howling desert demands action, the unceasing manipulation and mastery of the forces of nature, including, of course, human nature. Colonies established in the desert require aggressive, intellectual, controlled, and well-disciplined people. It is hardly surprising that the New England Puritans favored the hideous wilderness image of the American landscape.[8]

What is most revealing about these contrasting ideas of landscape is not, needless to say, their relative accuracy in picturing the actual topography. They are not representational images. America was neither Eden nor a howling desert. These are poetic metaphors, imaginative constructions which heighten meaning far beyond the limits of fact. And yet, like all effective metaphors, each had a basis in fact. In a sense, America was *both* Eden and a howling desert; the actual conditions of life in the New World did lend plausibility to both images. The infinite resources of the virgin land really did make credible, in minds long habituated to the notion of unavoidable scarcity, the ancient dream of an abundant and harmonious life for all. Yet, at the same time, the savages, the limitless spaces, and the violent climate of the country did threaten to engulf the new civilization. In the reports of voyagers there was evidence to support either view, and during the age of Elizabeth many Englishmen seized upon one or the other as representing the truth about America and her prospects.

But there were others who recognized the contradiction and attempted to understand or at least to express it. Sylvester Jourdain, who wrote a report on the Bermuda wreck of 1609, observes that the islands were widely considered "a most prodigious and inchanted place, affoording nothing but gusts, stormes, and foule weather; which made every Navigator and Mariner to avoide them . . . as they would shunne the Devili himselfe. . . ." It was all the more surprising, therefore, when the castaways discovered that the climate was "so temperate and the Country so aboundantly fruitful of all fit necessaries" that they were able to live in comfort for nine months. Experience soon led them to reconsider the legendary horror of the place. Jourdain (one of the writers with whom Shakespeare apparently was familiar) finally puts it this way: "whereas it [Bermuda] hath beene, and is still accounted, the most dangerous infortunate, and most forlorne place of the world, it is in truth the richest, healthfullest, and pleasing land, (the quantity and bignesse thereof considered) and meerely naturall, as ever man set foote upon."[9]

William Strachey, in his report, also confronts the ambiguity of nature in the New World. As already mentioned, he had been impressed by the legendary hideousness of the islands:

> . . . they be so terrible to all that ever touched on them, and such tempests, thunders, and other fearefull objects are seene and heard about them, that they be called commonly, The Devils Ilands, and are feared and avoyded of all sea travellers alive, above any other place in the world.

Then in the very next sentence Strachey acknowledges the contrary evidence: "Yet it pleased our mercifull God, to make even this hideous and hated place, both the place of our safetie, and meanes of our deliverance." By invoking Providence he can admit the attractions of the islands without revising the standard opinion of Bermuda as a hideous wilderness. There were a number of devices for coping with these contradictory ideas about America. One writer, anxious to correct the dismal reports about life at Jamestown during the early years, attacks the problem head on. Having begun with a stock and no doubt transparently propagandistic celebration of Virginia's abundance, and aware at the same time that the actual calamities were well known, he interjects the direct appeal to the reader's credulity that I quote at the head of this chapter. For him the problem is to persuade readers to accept an image of America in which "felicities and miseries can be reconciled together. . . ."[10]

But if some Elizabethan travelers discovered that the stock images of America embraced a contradiction, few had the wit to see what mysteries it veiled. Few recognized that a most striking fact about the New World was its baffling hospitality to radically opposed interpretations. If America seemed to promise everything that men always had wanted, it also threatened to obliterate much of what they already had achieved. The paradox was to be a cardinal subject of our national literature, and beginning in the nineteenth century our best writers were able to develop the theme in all its complexity. Not that the conflict was in any sense peculiar to American experience. It had always been at the heart of pastoral; but the discovery of the New World invested it with new relevance, with fresh symbols.

Notes

1   For a general survey, see Robert Ralston Cawley, *The Voyagers and Elizabethan Drama*, Boston, 1938; and the same author's "Shakespeare's Use of the Voyagers in *The Tempest*," *PMLA*, XLI (1926), 688–726; more recently Frank Kermode has reviewed the evidence in the revised Arden Edition of *The Tempest*, London, 1954, pp. xxv–xxxiv; Ariel: I, ii, 229. I am following the Arden text.

2   "The first voyage made to the coasts of America . . ." in Richard Hakluyt, *The Principle Navigations Voyages Traffiques and Discoveries of the English Nation*, Glasgow, 1904, 12 vols., VIII, 297–310.

3   Kenneth Clark, *Landscape into Art*, Edinburgh, 1956, Ch. I.

4   My discussion of utopianism draws upon George Kateb, *Utopia and Its Enemies*, New York, 1963; David Potter, *People of Plenty: Economic Abundance and the American Character*, Chicago, 1954.

5   Strachey, "A true reportory of the wracke, and redemption of Sir Thomas Gates Knight; upon, and from the Ilands of the Bermudas . . .," *Hakluytus Posthumus or Purchas His Pilgrimes,* ed. Samuel Purchas, Glasgow, 1906, 20 vols., XIX, 6, 12; Cawley, *The Voyagers,* p. 347ff, and Richard Bernheimer, *Wild Men in the Middle Ages: A Study in Art, Sentiment, and Demonology,* Cambridge, Mass., 1942.

6   *History of Plymouth Plantation, 1606–1646,* ed. William T. Davis, New York, 1908, pp. 94–96.

7   The concept of "root metaphor" is developed by Stephen C. Pepper in *World Hypotheses, A Study in Evidence,* Berkeley, 1942; Emerson, *Complete Works,* 11 vols., Boston, 1885, V, 52.

8   For the way American conditions nurtured the utilitarian germ at the center of Puritan thought, see Perry Miller, *The New England Mind: The Seventeenth Century,* New York, 1939, especially pp. 393ff; Miller's views are extended by Alan Heimert, "Puritanism, the Wilderness, and the Frontier," *NEQ,* XXVI (1953), 361–82; Robert K. Merton has demonstrated the connections between English Puritanism and the development of technologically advanced capitalism in his "Science, Technology, and Society in Seventeenth-Century England," *Osiris,* Bruges, 1938, IV, II.

9   *A Discovery of the Barmudas,* ed. Joseph Quincy Adams, Scholars' Facsimiles and Reprints, New York, 1940, pp. 8ff, first published in 1610.

10   "A true reportory," Purchas, XIX, 13; anon., "A True Declaration of the estate of the Colonie in Virginia, with a confutation of such scandalous reports as have tended to the disgrace of so worthy an enterprise . . ., London, 1610," *Tracts and Other Papers,* ed. Peter Force, Washington, 1844, 4 vols.; III, 14.

Chapter 2

Carolyn Merchant

NATURE AS FEMALE

THE WORLD WE HAVE lost was organic. From the obscure origins of our species, human beings have lived in daily, immediate, organic relation with the natural order for their sustenance. In 1500, the daily interaction with nature was still structured for most Europeans, as it was for other peoples, by close-knit, cooperative, organic communities.

Thus it is not surprising that for sixteenth-century Europeans the root metaphor binding together the self, society, and the cosmos was that of an organism. As a projection of the way people experienced daily life, organismic theory emphasized interdependence among the parts of the human body, subordination of individual to communal purposes in family, community, and state, and vital life permeating the cosmos to the lowliest stone.

The idea of nature as a living organism had philosophical antecedents in ancient systems of thought, variations of which formed the prevailing ideological framework of the sixteenth century. The organismic metaphor, however, was immensely flexible and adaptable to varying contexts, depending on which of its presuppositions was emphasized. A spectrum of philosophical and political possibilities existed, all of which could be subsumed under the general rubric of *organic*.

NATURE AS NURTURE: CONTROLLING IMAGERY.   Central to the organic theory was the identification of nature, especially the earth, with a nurturing mother: a kindly beneficent female who provided for the needs of mankind in an ordered, planned universe. But another opposing image of nature as female was also prevalent: wild and uncontrollable nature that could render violence, storms, droughts, and general chaos. Both were identified with the female sex and were projections of human perceptions onto the external world. The metaphor of the earth as a nurturing mother was gradually to vanish as a dominant image as the Scientific Revolution proceeded to mechanize and to rationalize the world view. The second image, nature as disorder, called forth an important modern idea, that of power over nature. Two new ideas, those of mechanism and of the domination and mastery of nature, became core concepts of the modern world. An organically oriented mentality in which female principles played an important role was undermined and replaced by a mechanically oriented mentality that either eliminated or used female principles in an exploitative manner. As

Western culture became increasingly mechanized in the 1600s, the female earth and virgin earth spirit were subdued by the machine.[1]

The change in controlling imagery was directly related to changes in human attitudes and behavior toward the earth. Whereas the nurturing earth image can be viewed as a cultural constraint restricting the types of socially and morally sanctioned human actions allowable with respect to the earth, the new images of mastery and domination functioned as cultural sanctions for the denudation of nature. Society needed these new images as it continued the processes of commercialism and industrialization, which depended on activities directly altering the earth—mining, drainage, deforestation, and assarting (grubbing up stumps to clear fields). The new activities utilized new technologies—lift and force pumps, cranes, windmills, geared wheels, flap valves, chains, pistons, treadmills, under- and overshot watermills, fulling mills, flywheels, bellows, excavators, bucket chains, rollers, geared and wheeled bridges, cranks, elaborate block and tackle systems, worm, spur, crown, and lantern gears, cams and eccentrics, ratchets, wrenches, presses, and screws in magnificent variation and combination.

These technological and commercial changes did not take place quickly; they developed gradually over the ancient and medieval eras, as did the accompanying environmental deterioration. Slowly over many centuries early Mediterranean and Greek civilization had mined and quarried the mountainsides, altered the forested landscape, and overgrazed the hills. Nevertheless, technologies were low level, people considered themselves parts of a finite cosmos, and animism and fertility cults that treated nature as sacred were numerous. Roman civilization was more pragmatic, secular, and commercial and its environmental impact more intense. Yet Roman writers such as Ovid, Seneca, Pliny, and the Stoic philosophers openly deplored mining as an abuse of their mother, the earth. With the disintegration of feudalism and the expansion of Europeans into new worlds and markets, commercial society began to have an accelerated impact on the natural environment. By the sixteenth and seventeenth centuries, the tension between technological development in the world of action and the controlling organic images in the world of the mind had become too great. The old structures were incompatible with the new activities.

Both the nurturing and domination metaphors had existed in philosophy, religion, and literature. The idea of dominion over the earth existed in Greek philosophy and Christian religion; that of the nurturing earth, in Greek and other pagan philosophies. But, as the economy became modernized and the Scientific Revolution proceeded, the dominion metaphor spread beyond the religious sphere and assumed ascendancy in the social and political spheres as well. These two competing images and their normative associations can be found in sixteenth-century literature, art, philosophy, and science.

The image of the earth as a living organism and nurturing mother had served as a cultural constraint restricting the actions of human beings. One does not readily slay a mother, dig into her entrails for gold or mutilate her body, although commercial mining would soon require that. As long as the earth was considered to be alive and sensitive, it could be considered a breach of human ethical behavior to carry out destructive acts against it. For most traditional cultures, minerals and metals ripened in the uterus of the Earth Mother, mines were compared to her vagina, and metallurgy was the human hastening of the birth of the living metal in the artificial womb of the furnace—an abortion of the metal's natural growth cycle before its time. Miners offered propitiation to the deities of the soil and subterranean world, performed ceremonial sacrifices, and observed strict cleanliness, sexual abstinence, and fasting before violating the sacredness of the living earth by sinking a mine. Smiths assumed an awesome responsibility in precipitating the metal's birth through smelting, fusing, and beating it with hammer and anvil; they were often accorded the status of shaman in tribal rituals and their tools were thought to hold special powers.

The Renaissance image of the nurturing earth still carried with it subtle ethical controls and restraints. Such imagery found in a culture's literature can play a normative role within the culture. Controlling images operate as ethical restraints or as ethical sanctions—as subtle "oughts" or "ought-nots." Thus as the descriptive metaphors and images of nature change, a behavioral restraint can be changed into a sanction. Such a change in the image and description of nature was occurring during the course of the Scientific Revolution.

It is important to recognize the normative import of descriptive statements about nature. Contemporary philosophers of language have critically reassessed the earlier positivist distinction between the "is" of science and the "ought" of society, arguing that descriptions and norms are not opposed to one another by linguistic separation into separate "is" and "ought" statements, but are contained within each other. Descriptive statements about the world can presuppose the normative; they are then ethic-laden. A statement's normative function lies in the use itself as description. The norms may be tacit assumptions hidden within the descriptions in such a way as to act as invisible restraints or moral ought-nots. The writer or culture may not be conscious of the ethical import yet may act in accordance with its dictates. The hidden norms may become conscious or explicit when an alternative or contradiction presents itself. Because language contains a culture within itself, when language changes, a culture is also changing in important ways. By examining changes in descriptions of nature, we can then perceive something of the changes in cultural values. To be aware of the interconnectedness of descriptive and normative statements is to be able to evaluate changes in the latter by observing changes in the former.[2]

Not only did the image of nature as a nurturing mother contain ethical implications but the organic framework itself, as a conceptual system, also carried with it an associated value system. Contemporary philosophers have argued that a given normative theory is linked with certain conceptual frameworks and not with others. The framework contains within itself certain dimensions of structural and normative variation, while denying others belonging to an alternative or rival framework.

We cannot accept a framework of explanation and yet reject its associated value judgments, because the connections to the values associated with the structure are not fortuitous. New commercial and technological innovations, however, can upset and undermine an established conceptual structure. New human and social needs can threaten associated normative constraints, thereby demanding new ones.

While the organic framework was for many centuries sufficiently integrative to override commercial development and technological innovation, the acceleration of such changes throughout western Europe during the sixteenth and seventeenth centuries began to undermine the organic unity of the cosmos and society. Because the needs and purposes of society as a whole were changing with the commercial revolution, the values associated with the organic view of nature were no longer applicable; hence the plausibility of the conceptual framework itself was slowly, but continuously, being threatened.

In order to make this interpretation of cultural change convincing, it will be advantageous to examine the variations of the organic framework, focusing on its associated female imagery and pointing out the values linked to each of the variants. It will then be possible to show how, in the context of commercial and technological change, the elements of the organic framework—its assumptions and values about nature—could be either absorbed into the emerging mechanical framework or rejected as irrelevant.

The Renaissance view of nature and society was based on the organic analogy between the human body, or microcosm, and the larger world, or macrocosm. Within this larger framework, however, a number of variants on the organic theme were possible. The primary view of nature was the idea that a designed hierarchical order existed in the cosmos and society corresponding to the organic integration of the parts of the body—a projection of the human being onto the cosmos. The term nature comprehended both the innate character and disposition of people and animals and the inherent creative power operating within material objects and phenomena. A second image was based on nature as an active unity of opposites in a dialectical tension. A third was the Arcadian image of nature as benevolent, peaceful, and rustic, deriving from Arcadia, the pastoral interior of the Greek Peloponnesus. Each of these interpretations had different social implications: the first image could be used as a justification for maintaining the existing social order, the second for changing society toward a new ideal, the third for escaping from the emerging problems of urban life. Drawing on the work of literary critics and historians of science and art, we can construct a spectrum of images of nature and delineate their associated value systems.

LITERARY IMAGES.   The Chaucerian and typically Elizabethan view of nature was that of a kindly and caring motherly provider, a manifestation of the God who had imprinted a designed, planned order on the world.[3] This order imposed ethical norms of behavior on the human being, the central feature of which was behavioral self-restraint in conformity with the pattern of the natural order. Each organic creature was responsible for maintaining its own place and expressing itself within the natural order and was a necessary part of the whole, but was not the whole itself. The Elizabethan first had to understand his or her own place dictated by the cosmic and social order and then to act in accordance with the traditional reason and restraint that would maintain the balance and harmony of the whole. This reverence for nature's law was expressed by Richard Hooker (1593): "See we not plainly that obedience of creatures unto the law of nature is the stay of the whole world." Nature operated "without capacity or knowledge," solely on the basis of "her dexterity and skill," as the instrument of God's expression in the mundane world. Whatever was known of God was taught by nature, "God being the author of Nature, her voice is but his instrument. By her from him we receive whatsoever in sort we learn."[4] Here nature is God's involuntary agent, a benevolent teacher of the hidden pattern and values God employed in creating the visible cosmos (*natura naturata,* the natural creation). A somewhat less orthodox view saw her as a creative force *(natura naturans)*—a soul with a will to generate mundane forms.

In Shakespeare's tragedy *King Lear,* the king, as human nature, represented Renaissance man, whose worldly existence was part of a larger patterned whole and of the contemporary hierarchical social order. His human nature symbolized the medieval-Renaissance cosmos whose patterns must not be violated. Lear's nature was a composite structure of the qualities of benevolence, comfort, and generosity, dictating honor and charity in his own ethical behavior as father of the household and reverence for his authority and wisdom on the part of his daughters.

Lear's daughter Cordelia represented utopian nature, or nature as the ideal unity of the opposites, a second image of nature within the larger spectrum of the organic framework. She was strength and gentleness hewn as one: "passion and order, innocence and maturity, defenselessness and strength, daughter and mother, maid and wife."[5] She represented simplicity in unity and the balance of the contraries. She was the mature integration of society and of nature as ideally reflected in the human being. She stood for unity, wholeness, and virtue—the utopian expression of human nature. Cordelia's nature was the human symbol of the new Jerusalem of the millenarian movements of the Middle Ages, the utopias of the Renaissance, and the religious sects of the subsequent civil war period in England, which attempted to improve society. The dialectical image of nature, here symbolized by a woman, represented the impetus to move society forward toward a new ideal.

Pastoral poetry and art prevalent in the Renaissance presented another image of nature as female—an escape backward into the motherly benevolence of the past. Here nature was a refuge from the ills and anxieties of urban life through a return to an unblemished Golden

Age. Depicted as a garden, a rural landscape, or a peaceful fertile scene, nature was a calm, kindly female, giving of her bounty. Against an idyllic backdrop, sheep grazed contently, birds sang melodies, and trees bore fruit. Wild animals, thorns, snakes, and vultures were nowhere to be found. Human beings meditated on the beauties of nature far removed from the violence of the city.[6]

The pastoral tradition had its roots in nostalgia for the Homeric Golden Age, for the uncorrupted Garden of Eden, and escape from the ills of the city. It echoed the poetic tradition of Virgil (70–19 B.C.) and Juvenal (A.D. 60–140). Virgil wrote of spending old age "amid familiar streams and holy springs";[7] Juvenal yearned for the rural town in which

> Springs bubbling up from the grass, no need
>   for windlass or bucket,
> Plenty to water your flowers, if they need
>   it without any trouble.[8]

The Arcadia theme, eulogized in the pastoral poetry of Philip Sidney (1554–86; *Arcadia,* 1590) and Edmund Spenser (1552–99; *The Shepheard's Calendar,* 1579), appeared in many poetic and artistic settings in which nature was idealized as a benevolent nurturer, mother, and provider. The sixteenth-century French painting "St. Genevieve with Her Flock" depicts the virgin surrounded by a flock of sheep within a protective stone circle on a hillside of trees and blooming flowers, well outside the city in the background. Here the female image of nature and the virgin, symbol of the earth spirit, are fused with the circular symbolism of order and protective encasement. In Lucas Cranach's painting "The Nymph of the Spring" (1518), the female earth nymph rests in a bed of flowers while doves, symbols of peace, feed near the edge of a trickling stream and deer water on its farther bank. The "Birth of Venus" (1482) and the "Primavera" (1477–78) of Sandro Botticelli portray the virgin in conjunction with the earth mother, who is covered with a gown and wreath of flowers, both symbols of female fertility. In the seventeenth century, Nicolas Poussin and other landscape painters illustrated the transitory nature of the Arcadian experience by sometimes inserting a death's head into their works of art.

But while the pastoral tradition symbolized nature as a benevolent female, it contained the implication that nature when plowed and cultivated could be used as a commodity and manipulated as a resource. Nature, tamed and subdued, could be transformed into a garden to provide both material and spiritual food to enhance the comfort and soothe the anxieties of men distraught by the demands of the urban world and the stresses of the marketplace. It depended on a masculine perception of nature as a mother and bride whose primary function was to comfort, nurture, and provide for the well-being of the male. In pastoral imagery, both nature and women are subordinate and essentially passive. They nurture but do not control or exhibit disruptive passion. The pastoral mode, although it viewed nature as benevolent, was a model created as an antidote to the pressures of urbanization and mechanization. It represented a fulfillment of human needs for nurture, but by conceiving of nature as passive, it nevertheless allowed for the possibility of its use and manipulation. Unlike the dialectical image of nature as the active unity of opposites in tension, the Arcadian image rendered nature passive and manageable.

PHILOSOPHICAL FRAMEWORKS.   In his *Timaeus,* Plato endowed the whole world with life and likened it to an animal. The deity "framed one visible animal comprehending within itself all other animals of a kindred nature." Its shape was round, since it had no need for eyes, ears, or appendages. Its soul was female, "in origin and excellence prior to and older than the body," and made "to be ruler and mistress, of whom the body was to be the subject." The soul permeated the corporeal body of the universe, enveloping it and "turning herself within herself." The earth "which is our nurse" was placed at the immovable center of the cosmos.[9]

For Plato, this female world soul was the source of motion in the universe, the bridge between the unchanging eternal forms and the changing, sensible, temporal lower world of nature. The Neoplatonism of Plotinus (A.D. 204–70), which synthesized Christian philosophy with Platonism, divided the female soul into two components. The higher portion fashioned souls from the divine ideas; the lower portion, *natura,* generated the phenomenal world. The twelfth-century Christian Cathedral School of Chartres, which interpreted the Bible in conjunction with the *Timaeus,* personified Natura as a goddess and limited the power attributed to her in pagan philosophies by emphasizing her subservience to God. Nature was compared to a midwife who translated Ideas into material things; the Ideas were likened to a father, the matter to a mother, and the generated species to a child. In Platonic and Neoplatonic symbolism, therefore, both nature and matter were feminine, while the Ideas were masculine. But nature, as God's agent, in her role as creator and producer of the material world, was superior to human artists both in creativity and in ease of production. She was more powerful than humans, but still subordinate to God.[10]

An allegory (1160) by Alain of Lille, of the School of Chartres, portrays Natura, God's powerful but humble servant, as stricken with grief at the failure of man (in contrast to other species) to obey her laws. Owing to faulty supervision by Venus, human beings engage in adulterous sensual love. In aggressively penetrating the secrets of heaven, they tear Natura's undergarments, exposing her to the view of the vulgar. She complains that "by the unlawful assaults of man alone the garments of my modesty suffer disgrace and division."

Natura was a replica of the cosmos. Set in her crown as jewels were the signs of the zodiac and the planets; decorating her robe, mantle, tunic, and undergarments were birds, water creatures, earth animals, herbs, and trees; on her shoes were flowers. Her torn tunic, indicative of the need to protect nature's secrets from misuse, exemplifies the rhetorical role of imagery. The specific moral of Alain's allegory is that nature has no power to enforce her own laws. After the disobedience that resulted in the fall of Adam and Eve, unity in the created world can only be maintained by moral choices; human reason must control human lust.[11]

Renaissance Neoplatonism illustrates the image of the macrocosm enlivened by the female soul. The Neoplatonic alchemist Robert Fludd (1574–1637) pictured the world soul as a woman connected by her right hand to God, represented by the Hebrew tetragrammaton—the four consonants JHVH—transmitted by a golden chain to the terrestrial world below. Natura was also pictured as the mother goddess Isis, her flowing hair drawn through a sphere representing the world, her mantle decorated at the top by stars and the bottom by flowers and her womb by a half-moon whose rays fertilize the earth. On opposite ears are the sun and moon, representing the male and female principles in the natural world. In her left hand she holds a pail, symbol of the flooding Nile, which irrigated the earth, and with her right she shakes the sistrum, a rattle representing the unceasing constant motion and internal vigor of nature.

The ancient philosophy of Aristotle, recovered in the twelfth century, was also based on the organic theory of the primacy of internal growth and development within nature. In his *Metaphysics,* Aristotle defined nature (*physis*) as "the source of movement of natural objects, being present in them either potentially or in complete reality."[12] Each individual object could be explained by specifying four "causes": material (the matter out of which it was made), formal (its shape or the arrangement of its parts), efficient (the moving force), and final (the purpose or ultimate end for which the object existed). In natural objects as opposed to artificially created products, the material and efficient causes were unified such that the material substratum had its principle of motion or change within it. The material of a tree or a child caused its growth, whereas a table had to be produced by a builder. Motion, like growth, was the internal development of the potential toward the final form or actual existence of an individual being—a girl becomes a woman, a chicken develops into a hen. In nature the end toward which an object developed was its form or shape; in artificial products, such as a house, the form was distinct from its purpose as a dwelling.

Aristotle differed from the Presocratics, who defined nature in terms of a material substratum such as water (Thales, ca. 585 B.C.), air (Anaximenes, ca. 525 B.C.), fire (Heraclitus, ca. 478 B.C.), but he concurred with them in stressing the primacy of growth, change, and process in the natural world. He opposed Plato's dualism between imperfect appearances and pure perfect forms by asserting that the form existed in the individual object rather than as a separate transcendent level of reality.

Aristotelian philosophy, while unifying matter and form in each individual being, associated activity with maleness and passivity with femaleness. Form reigned superior over dead, passive matter. Socially, Aristotle found the basis for male rule over the household in the analogy that, as the soul ruled the body, so reason and deliberation, characteristic of men, should rule the appetites supposedly predominant in women.

Aristotle's biological theory viewed the female of the species as an incomplete or mutilated male, since the coldness of the female body would not allow the menstrual blood to perfect itself as semen. In the generation of offspring, the female contributed the matter or passive principle. This was the material on which the active male principle, the semen, worked in creating the embryo. The male was the real cause of the offspring. "The female, as female, is passive, and the male, as male, is active, and the principle of movement comes from him." Power and motion were contributed solely by the semen. The male supplied none of the matter from which the embryo developed: "Nor does he emit anything of such nature as to exist within that which is generated, as part of the material embryo, but that he only makes a living creature by the power which resides in the semen."[13]

The female supplied the nutriment—the catamenia, or menstrual blood—on which the qualities of the male could operate. The combination of semen with menstrual blood was like the curdling of cheese, just as rennet acts by coagulating milk. The male contributed the movement necessary for the embryo to develop, as well as the form it would take.

Both the efficient and formal causes were derived from the male principle and were the active cause of the offspring. Nature in her creative work used the semen as a tool just as the carpenter, through motion, imparted shape and form to the wood on which he worked. Since no material was ever transferred from the body of the carpenter to the wood, by analogy the male did not contribute any matter, but rather the force and power of the generation.

The Aristotelian theory of generation appeared at the basis of some alchemical theories. To change base metals to gold or silver, or to create the philosopher's stone—a substance thought to effect such a change—the qualities or form of the lowly metal must be removed, leaving the passive primary matter. The new more noble form, the active male principle, was then introduced and unified with the base female matter to produce the new metal.

Aristotelian ideas about human generation were also projected onto the cosmos. In the sixteenth century, the marriage and impregnation of the female earth by the higher celestial masculine heavens was a stock description of biological generation in nature. The movements of the celestial heavens produced semen, which fell in the form of dew and rain on the receptive female earth. A famous passage in *On the Revolutions of the Celestial Spheres* (1543) by Nicolaus Copernicus (1473–1543), reviver of the heliocentric hypothesis, draws on the marriage of the masculine heavens with the female earth: "Meanwhile, the earth conceives by the sun and becomes pregnant with annual offspring."[14] Such basic attitudes toward male-female roles in biological generation where the female and the earth are both passive receptors could easily become sanctions for exploitation as the organic context was transformed by the rise of commercial capitalism.

A radical alternative to the hierarchical view that the female was inferior appeared in the monistic form of ancient gnosticism, based (like Shakespeare's Cordelia) on the unity of the opposites and the equality of male-female principles. The transmission of gnostic ideas of androgyny provided an alternative view of generation and carried with it more positive implications and attitudes toward nature as female in the Renaissance. But these ideas lay outside the mainstream of Western Christian culture. Gnostic texts available in the Renaissance had been preserved through extensive quotation in the polemical writings of the early church fathers who attempted to refute the doctrine.

The gnostic tradition was a body of texts (written in the first three centuries A.D.) condemned as a heretical form of early Christianity. Centered in hellenistic Alexandria, it synthesized Christianity with the spiritual teachings of Babylonia and Persia to the east, and Greece and Rome to the west. Gnosticism (stemming from *knowledge*) maintained an original unity of male-female opposites in a transcendent God, but a dualism between God and the mundane world, between good and evil, between spirit and matter. By emanation God produced a female generative principle, which created angels and then the visible world; the light of God mingled with matter in the lower world. The religious goal of gnosticism was other-worldly salvation through knowledge. In contrast to orthodox Christians, some sects worshipped the serpent for inducing Eve to taste the fruit of knowledge, the beginning of gnosis on earth. The coiled serpent biting its own tail symbolized the unity of the opposites good and bad, and the cosmic metamorphic cycles.

Some of the early gnostic Christians who described God as androgynous prayed to both the father and the mother and interpreted the account of the creation in the first chapter of Genesis to mean that a male-female God created men and women in its image. In these interpretations God was a dyad of opposites existing in harmony in one being. The divine mother was named Wisdom, or *Sophia,* a Greek translation of the Hebrew *hokhmah.* Wisdom was the creative power, "self-generating, self-discovering its own mother, its own father, its own sister, its own son: father, mother, unity, root of all things."[15] Her wisdom was bestowed on men and women. Human nature, like God, consisted of a unity of equal male-female principles. Evidence for the appeal of gnostic androgyny to women is indicated by their attraction to these heretical groups during the period A.D. 150–200, when Christianity was struggling to gain its stature as a world religion. Here they could play important roles from which they had been excluded by orthodox churches, including healer, evangelist, priest, prophet, and teacher.

Gnostic philosophy, and its assignment of equal importance to male and female principles in generation, permeated many alchemical treatises. The gnostic trinity—father, mother, and son—first appeared in a work of the third or fourth century, *Chrysopeia* ("Gold-Making"), attributed to Cleopatra. The *Emerald Tablet* of Hermes Trismegistus (a mythical alchemist to whom was attributed the gnostic *Corpus Hermeticum,* A.D. 100–300) emphasized the equality of the two great male and female principles in nature, the sun and moon: "The sun is its father, the moon is its mother. Wind is carried in its belly, the earth is its nurse."[16] In the gnostic tradition in alchemy many of the earliest alchemical treatises were either written by or attributed to women: Isis; Mary the Jewess, identified with Moses' sister Miriam; Cleopatra; and Theosobia, sister of Zosimus, an alchemist of the fourth century A.D.

> Noticeable also is the importance given to women by the Hermetic [alchemist].
> In Majer's etching the virgin is, like her ancestor Eve, the instigator. And a
> woman is the alchemist's symbol of nature. He follows her tracks, which lead
> to perfection. It may be recalled that Magdalene and Sophia are the most

important and active figures in the *Pistis Sophia* and that the earthly incarnation of the heavenly mother is the main feature in the dogma of Simon Magus. Flamel's transmutation took place when his wife was present; and in the *Liber Mutus,* an alchemical tract, it is recommended that before starting the operation the alchemist and his wife should kneel and pray before the oven. The union of the soul and spirit, of the male and female essence, has its counterpart in heaven: the sun is the father and the moon, the mother.[17]

In gnostic texts available in the sixteenth century, the Mother Sophia, or eightness, created the king or father, who in turn generated the seven heavens.[18] The mother produced four terrestrial elements after the pattern of the higher celestial elements. In some gnostic interpretations, the archetypal Adam was created androgynous and composed of eight parts.

For Paracelsus (1490–1541), the eight gnostic matrices were all mothers. Moreover, in contrast to Aristotle, he assigned equality to the male and female principles in sexual generation:

> When the seed is received in the womb, nature combines the seed of the man and the seed of the woman. Of the two seeds, the better and stronger will form the other, according to its nature. The seed from the man's brain and that from the woman's brain together make only one brain; but the child's brain is formed according to the one which is the stronger of the two, and it becomes like this seed but never completely like it.[19]

For some Paracelsians, the eight parts of the gnostic Adam were divided into four celestial fathers and four terrestial elements or mothers. The fathers provided astral semina that fertilized the female elemental matrices, which, activated by the central fire of the earth, rose up to receive the astral semina. For some alchemists, the philosopher's stone embodied the unity of the contraries resulting from the conjunction of the four mothers and the four fathers.

Scholar Ralph Cudworth noted in 1678 that the pagans "call God male and female together" and that "the Orphic theology calls the first principle hermaphroditic, or male and female together; thereby denoting that essence that is generative or productive of all things."[20]

In alchemy, permeated by male-female dualism, the hermaphrodite Mercurius symbolized the androgynous unity of the opposites. The unification of male and female principles, represented by the alchemical marriage of the sun and the moon and by the union of the male mineral agent mercury and the female *materia prima* (prime matter), resulted in the male-female hermaphrodite. The tree symbolized the vegetative nurturing principle; the snake, the animated life-giving principle. The heat of the alchemical oven represented the male element; the egg-shaped retort, the female womb.[21]

Thomas Vaughan (1622–66), alchemist and mystic, described the sun and the moon as two equal peers, the consummation of their marriage as a total unity resulting in the nurturing of their seed in the womb of the earth:

> There is in every star and in this elemental world a certain principle which is the "bride of the sun." These two in their coition do emit semen, which seed is carried in the womb of nature. But the ejection of it is performed invisibly and in a sacred silence, for this is the conjugal mystery of heaven and earth, their act of generation, a thing done in private between particular males and females; but how much more think you between the two universal natures. Know therefore

that it is impossible for you to extract or receive any seed from the sun without this feminine principle which is the wife of the sun. . . . Know then for certain that the magician's sun and moon are two universal peers, male and female, a king and queen regents, always young and never old. These two are adequate to the whole world and coextended through the whole universe. The one is not without the other, God having united them in His work of creation in a solemn, sacramental union. It will then be a hard and difficult enterprise to rob the, husband of his wife, to part those asunder who God has put together, for they sleep both in the same bed, and he that discovers the one must needs see the other.[22]

What fate did these differing images of nature meet as the Scientific Revolution began to mechanize the world view? Both pastoral art and Aristotelian philosophy saw the female sex as passive and receptive. Pastoral imagery could easily be incorporated into a mechanized industrialized world as an escape from the frustrations of the marketplace. The pastoral had been an antidote to the ills of urbanization in ancient times, and it continued to play that role in the commercial revolution. It became particularly significant as an image dictating the transformation and cultivation of the wilderness in American culture. Explorers of the new world, who described the scenery as a lovely garden fragrant with flowers, brightened by the sounds of marvelous new and beautiful birds, provided an impetus for settlement across the Atlantic. The cultivation of a bountiful mother earth helped to hasten the disruption and exploitation of new and "virgin" lands.

The Aristotelian and Platonic conception of the passivity of matter could also be incorporated into the new mechanical philosophy in the form of inert "dead" atoms, constituents of a new machinelike world in which change came about through external forces, a scheme that readily sanctioned the manipulation of nature. The Neoplatonic female world soul, the internal source of activity in nature, would disappear, to be replaced by a carefully contrived mechanism of subtle particles in motion.

The idea of the androgynous equality of male-female principles would eventually become more clearly articulated as the principle of the dialectic, either as the unity of opposites in idealism or as the struggle of the opposites in dialectical materialism. I will have occasion to note its progress in several social and philosophical contexts as the struggle for equality, against social hierarchy, continued.

THE GEOCOSM: THE EARTH AS A NURTURING MOTHER.   Not only was nature in a generalized sense seen as female, but also the earth, or geocosm, was universally viewed as a nurturing mother, sensitive, alive, and responsive to human action. The changes in imagery and attitudes relating to the earth were of enormous significance as the mechanization of nature proceeded. The nurturing earth would lose its function as a normative restraint as it changed to an inanimate dead physical system.

The macrocosm theory, as we have seen, likened the cosmos to the human body, soul, and spirit with male and female reproductive components. Similarly, the geocosm theory compared the earth to the living human body, with breath, blood, sweat, and elimination systems.

For the Stoics, who flourished in Athens during the third century B.C., after the death of Aristotle, and in Rome through the first century A.D., the world itself was an intelligent organism; God and matter were synonymous. Matter was dynamic, composed of two forces: expansion and condensation—the former directed outward, the latter inward. The tension between them was the inherent force generating all substances, properties, and living forms in the cosmos and the geocosm.

Zeno of Citium (ca. 304 B.C.) and M. Tullius Cicero (106–43 B.C.) held that the world reasons, has sensation, and generates living rational beings: "The world is a living and wise being, since it produces living and wise beings."[23] Every part of the universe and the earth was created for the benefit and support of another part. The earth generated and gave stability to plants, plants supported animals, and animals in turn served human beings; conversely, human skill helped to preserve these organisms. The universe itself was created for the sake of rational beings—gods and men—but God's foresight insured the safety and preservation of all things. Humankind was given hands to transform the earth's resources and was given dominion over them: timber was to be used for houses and ships, soil for crops, iron for plows, and gold and silver for ornaments. Each part and imperfection existed for the sake and ultimate perfection of the whole.

The living character of the world organism meant not only that the stars and planets were alive, but that the earth too was pervaded by a force giving life and motion to the living beings on it. Lucius Seneca (4 B.C.–A.D. 65), a Roman Stoic, stated that the earth's breath nourished both the growths on its surface and the heavenly bodies above by its daily exhalations:

> How could she nourish all the different roots that sink into the soil in one place and another, had she not an abundant supply of the breath of life? . . . all these [heavenly bodies] draw their nourishment from materials of earth . . . and are sustained . . . by nothing else than the breath of the earth. . . . Now the earth would be unable to nourish so many bodies . . . unless it were full of breath, which it exhales from every part of it day and night.[24]

The earth's springs were akin to the human blood system; its other various fluids were likened to the mucus, saliva, sweat, and other forms of lubrication in the human body, the earth being organized ". . . much after the plan of our bodies, in which there are both veins and arteries, the former blood vessels, the latter air vessels. . . . So exactly alike is the resemblance to our bodies in nature's formation of the earth, that our ancestors have spoken of veins [springs] of water." Just as the human body contained blood, marrow, mucus, saliva, tears, and lubricating fluids, so in the earth there were various fluids. Liquids that turned hard became metals, such as gold and silver; other fluids turned into stones, bitumens, and veins of sulfur. Like the human body, the earth gave forth sweat: "There is often a gathering of thin, scattered moisture like dew, which from many points flows into one spot. The dowsers call it *sweat*, because a kind of drop is either squeezed out by the pressure of the ground or raised by the heat."

Leonardo da Vinci (1452–1519) enlarged the Greek analogy between the waters of the earth and the ebb and flow of human blood through the veins and heart:

> The water runs from the rivers to the sea and from the sea to the rivers, always making the same circuit. The water is thrust from the utmost depth of the sea to the high summits of the mountains, where, finding the veins cut, it precipitates itself and returns to the sea below, mounts once more by the branching veins and then falls back, thus going and coming between high and low, sometimes inside, sometimes outside. It acts like the blood of animals which is always moving, starting from the sea of the heart and mounting to the summit of the head.[25]

The earth's venous system was filled with metals and minerals. Its veins, veinlets, seams, and canals coursed through the entire earth, particularly in the mountains. Its humors flowed from the veinlets into the larger veins. The earth, like the human, even had its own elimination system. The tendency for both to break wind caused earthquakes in the case of the former and another type of quake in the latter:

> The material cause of earthquakes . . . is no doubt great abundance of wind, or store of gross and dry vapors, and spirits, fast shut up, and as a man would say, emprisoned in the caves, and dungeons of the earth; which wind, or vapors, seeking to be set at liberty, and to get them home to their natural lodgings, in a great fume, violently rush out, and as it were, break prison, which forcible eruption, and strong breath, causeth an earthquake.[26]

Its bowels were full of channels, fire chambers, glory holes, and fissures through which fire and heat were emitted, some in the form of fiery volcanic exhalations, others as hot water springs. The most commonly used analogy, however, was between the female's reproductive and nurturing capacity and the mother earth's ability to give birth to stones and metals within its womb through its marriage with the sun.

In his *De Rerum Natura* of 1565, the Italian philosopher Bernardino Telesio referred to the marriage of the two great male and female powers: "We can see that the sky and the earth are not merely large parts of the world universe, but are of primary—even principal rank. . . . They are like mother and father to all the others."[27] The earth and the sun served as mother and father to the whole of creation: all things are "made of earth by the sun and that in the constitution of all things the earth and the sun enter respectively as mother and father." According to Giordano Bruno (1548–1600), every human being was "a citizen and servant of the world, a child of Father Sun and Mother Earth."[28]

A widely held alchemical belief was the growth of the baser metals into gold in womb-like matrices in the earth. The appearance of silver in lead ores or gold in silvery assays was evidence that this transformation was under way. Just as the child grew in the warmth of the female womb, so the growth of metals was fostered through the agency of heat, some places within the earth's crust being hotter and therefore hastening the maturation process. "Given to gold, silver, and the other metals [was] the vegetative power whereby they could also reproduce themselves. For, since it was impossible for God to make anything that was not perfect, he gave to all created things, with their being, the power of multiplication."[29] The sun acting on the earth nurtured not only the plants and animals but also "the metals, the broken sulfuric, bituminous, or nitrogenous rocks; . . . as well as the plants and animals—if these are not made of earth by the sun, one cannot imagine of what else or by what other agent they could be made."[30]

Several theories accounted for the growth of metals and minerals. In the Aristotelian theory, the earth gave off exhalations under the influence of the sun's warmth. From the dry exhalations grew stones, from the wet metals, both being formed within the earth or on its surface. Sixteenth-century theories held that minerals grew from a combination of celestial influences, primarily the sun, and a formative power within the earth.[31]

In the liquid seed theory, the earth was a matrix or mother to the seeds of stones and minerals. The seeds of minerals and metals fermented water, transforming it into a mineral juice and then into the metal itself. Stones were generated from their own seminal principles or seeds, thereby preserving their species. Suitable nooks and crannies within the earth formed matrices or wombs for the nurturing and development of the infant seed. Neither the air nor the bodies of plants and animals were suitable mothers; only the rocks on the edges of ore veins, and special crannies in the earth's crust could act as matrices. Jerome Cardan (1550) and Bernard Palissy (1580) believed that metals reproduced by liquid seeds deposited by water; others set forth the thesis that mineral juices were formed into metals by degrees, expanding and taking on new matter until they grew into visible metals.[32]

A third theory, the lapidifying (stone-forming) juice theory, hypothesized a fluid or juice that circulated through the earth's body in the veins, and cracks, and pores beneath its surface just as blood ebbed and flowed within the human body. This *succus lapidescens,* combined with the principles of heat and cold, was the origin of stones and minerals. The mineral or stony matter was held in solution by the liquid *succus* until it evaporated out by the action of heat or deposited its matter through the action of cold.[33]

The earth's womb was the matrix or mother not only of metals but also of all living things. Paracelsus compared the earth to a female whose womb nurtured all life.

> Woman is like the earth and all the elements and in this sense she may be considered a matrix; she is the tree which grows in the earth and the child is like the fruit born of the tree. . . . Woman is the image of the tree. Just as the earth, its fruits, and the elements are created for the sake of the tree and in order to sustain it, so the members of woman, all her qualities, and her whole nature exist for the sake of her matrix, her womb . . . .
>
> And yet woman in her own way is also a field of the earth and not at all different from it. She replaces it, so to speak; she is the field and the garden mold in which the child is sown and planted.[34]

The earth in the Paracelsian philosophy was the mother or matrix giving birth to plants, animals, and men.

The image of the earth as a nurse, which had appeared in the ancient world in Plato's *Timeaus* and the *Emerald Tablet* of Hermes Trismegistus, was a popular Renaissance metaphor. According to sixteenth-century alchemist Basil Valentine, all things grew in the womb of the earth, which was alive, and vital, and the nurse of all life:

> The quickening power of the earth produces all things that grow forth from it, and he who says that the earth has no life makes a statement flatly contradicted by facts. What is dead cannot produce life and growth, seeing that it is devoid of the quickening spirit. . . . This spirit is the life and soul that dwell in the earth, and are nourished by heavenly and sidereal influences. . . . This spirit is itself fed by the stars and is thereby rendered capable of imparting nutriment to all things that grow and of nursing them as a mother does her child while it is yet in the womb. . . . If the earth were deserted by this spirit it would be dead . . . .[35]

Cambridge Platonist Henry More (1614–87) referred to the sixteenth-century doctrine of the earth as a nurse and the possibility of its going dry and becoming sterile:

> For though we should admit, with Cardan and other naturalists, that the earth at first brought forth all manner of animals as well as plants, and that they might be fastened by the navel to their common mother the earth, as they are now to the female in the womb; yet we see she is grown sterile and barren, and her births of animals are now very inconsiderable. Wherefore what can it be but a providence, that while she did bear she sent out male and female, that when her own prolific virtue was wasted, yet she might be a dry nurse, or an officious grandmother, to thousands of generations?[36]

In general, the Renaissance view was that all things were permeated by life, there being no adequate method by which to designate the inanimate from the animate. It was difficult to differentiate between living and nonliving things, because of the resemblance in structures. Like plants and animals, minerals and gems were filled with small pores, tublets, cavities, and streaks, through which they seemed to nourish themselves. Crystalline salts were compared to plant forms, but criteria by which to differentiate the living from the nonliving could not successfully be formulated. This was due not only to the vitalistic framework of the period but to striking similarities between them. Minerals were thought to possess a lesser degree of the vegetative soul, because they had the capacity for medicinal action and often took the form of various parts of plants. By virtue of the vegetative soul, minerals and stones grew in the human body, in animal bodies, within trees, in the air and water, and on the earth's surface in the open country.[37]

Popular Renaissance literature was filled with hundreds of images associating nature, matter, and the earth with the female sex. The earth was alive and considered to be a beneficent, receptive, nurturing female. For most writers there was a mingling of traditions based on ancient sources. In general, the pervasive animism of nature created a relationship of immediacy with the human being. An I-thou relationship in which nature was considered to be a person-writ-large was sufficiently prevalent that the ancient tendency to treat it as another human still existed. Such vitalistic imagery was thus so widely accepted by the Renaissance mind that it could effectively function as a restraining ethic.

In much the same way, the cultural belief-systems of many American-Indian tribes had for centuries subtly guided group behavior toward nature. Smohalla of the Columbia Basin Tribes voiced the Indian objections to European attitudes in the mid-1800s:

> You ask me to plow the ground! Shall I take a knife and tear my mother's breast? Then when I die she will not take me to her bosom to rest.
>
> You ask me to dig for stone! Shall I dig under her skin for her bones? Then when I die I cannot enter her body to be born again.
>
> You ask me to cut grass and make hay and sell it, and be rich like white men! But how dare I cut off my mother's hair?[38]

In the 1960s, the Native-American became a symbol in the ecology movement's search for alternatives to Western exploitative attitudes. The Indian animistic belief-system and reverence for the earth as a mother were contrasted with the Judeo-Christian heritage of dominion over nature and with capitalist practices resulting in the "tragedy of the commons" (exploitation of resources available for any person's or nation's use). But as will be seen, European culture was more complex and varied than this judgment allows. It ignores the Renaissance philosophy of the nurturing earth as well as those philosophies and social movements resistant to mainstream economic change.

NORMATIVE CONSTRAINTS AGAINST THE MINING OF MOTHER EARTH.   If sixteenth-century descriptive statements and imagery can function as an ethical constraint and if the earth was widely viewed as a nurturing mother, did such imagery actually function as a norm against improper use of the earth? Evidence that this was indeed the case can be drawn from theories of the origins of metals and the debates about mining prevalent during the sixteenth century.

The ancient Greek philosophers Anaxagoras (500–428 B.C.), Theophrastus (370–278 B.C.), and Dionysius of Periegetes (fl. A.D. 86–96) believed that metals were plants growing beneath the earth's surface and that veins of gold were like the roots and branches of trees. Metals were believed merely to be a lower form of life than vegetables and animals, reproducing themselves through small metallic seeds.

A popular Renaissance belief held about mining was the metaphor of the golden tree. The earth deep within its bowels produced and gave form to the metals, which then rose as mist up through the trunk, branches, and twigs of a great tree whose roots originated at the earth's center. The large branches contained the great veins of minerals, the smaller the metallic ores. Miners had

> . . . found by experience that the vein of gold is a living tree and that by all ways that it spreadeth and springeth from the root by the soft pores and passages of the earth putting forth branches even unto the uppermost part of the earth and ceaseth not until it discover itself unto the open air: at which time it showeth forth certain beautiful colors instead of flowers, round stones of golden earth instead of fruits and thin plates instead of leaves.[39]

Once the veins of ore were mined, it was believed that new ore grew again within a few years. Diamond mines in the East Indies were filled with new diamonds; sulfur mines were soon replenished. Iron ore continued to grow in the mines of Elba off the coast of Italy; the iron ore fields of Saga in Germany refilled within ten years. Silver twigs resembling plants grew in the shafts of abandoned mines in the Joachim Valley. In his *Art of Metals* (1640), Albaro Barba, director of the Potosi mines in the Spanish West Indies, wrote, "All of us know that in the rich hill at Potosi the stones, which divers years we have left behind us, thinking there was not plate enough in them to make it worth our labor, we now bring home and find abundant plate in them, which can be attributed to nothing but the perpetual generation of silver."[40] The image of Mother Earth and her generative role in the production of metals continued to be significant well into the eighteenth century.

What ethical ideas were held by ancient and early modern writers on the extraction of the metals from the bowels of the living earth? The Roman compiler Pliny (A.D. 23–79), in his *Natural History,* had specifically warned against mining the depths of Mother Earth, speculating that earthquakes were an expression of her indignation at being violated in this manner:

> We trace out all the veins of the earth, and yet . . . are astonished that it should occasionally cleave asunder or tremble: as though, forsooth, these signs could be any other than expressions of the indignation felt by our sacred parent! We penetrate into her entrails, and seek for treasures . . . as though each spot we tread upon were not sufficiently bounteous and fertile for us![41]

He went on to argue that the earth had concealed from view that which she did not wish to be disturbed, that her resources might not be exhausted by human avarice:

> For it is upon her surface, in fact, that she has presented us with these substances, equally with the cereals, bounteous and ever ready, as she is, in supplying us with all things for our benefit! It is what is concealed from our view, what is sunk far beneath her surface, objects, in fact, of no rapid formation, that urge us to our ruin, that send us to the very depths of hell. . . . when will be the end of thus exhausting the earth, and to what point will avarice finally penetrate!

Here, then, is a striking example of the restraining force of the beneficent mother image— the living earth in her wisdom has ordained against the mining of metals by concealing them in the depths of her womb. In addition the mining of gold contributed to human corruption and avarice. "The worst crime against mankind [was] committed by him who was the first to put a ring upon his fingers." In the age of barter, people were happy, but since then "man has learned how to challenge both nature and art to become the incitements to vice!"

While mining gold led to avarice, extracting iron was the source of human cruelty in the form of war, murder, and robbery. Its use should be limited to agriculture and those activities that contributed to the "honors of more civilized life":

> For by the aid of iron we lay open the ground, we plant trees, we prepare our vineyard trees, and we force our vines each year to resume their youthful state, by cutting away their decayed branches. It is by the aid of iron that we construct houses, cleave rocks, and perform so many other useful offices of life. But it is with iron also that wars, murders, and robberies are effected, . . . not only hand to hand, but . . . by the aid of missiles and winged weapons, now launched from engines, now hurled by the human arm, and now furnished with feathery wings. Let us therefore acquit nature of a charge that here belongs to man himself.

In past history, Pliny stated, there had been instances in which laws were passed to prohibit the retention of weapons and to ensure that iron was used solely for innocent purposes, such as the cultivation of fields.

In the *Metamorphoses* (A.D. 7), the Roman poet Ovid wrote of the violence done to the earth during the age of iron. In the preceding Golden Age, "people were unaggressive, and unanxious."

> And Earth, untroubled,
> Unharried by hoe or plowshare, brought forth all
> That men had need for, and those men were happy,
> Gathering berries from the mountain sides,
> Cherries, or black caps, and the edible acorns.
> Spring was forever, with a west wind blowing
> Softly across the flowers no man had planted,
> And Earth, unplowed, brought forth rich grain; the field,
> Unfallowed, whitened with wheat, and there were rivers
> Of milk, and rivers of honey, and golden nectar
> Dripped from the dark-green oak-trees.[42]

During the Iron Age, evil was let loose in the form of trickery, slyness, plotting, swindling, and violence, as men dug into the earth's entrails for iron and gold:

> The rich earth
> Was asked for more; they dug into her vitals,
> Pried out the wealth a kinder lord had hidden
> In stygian shadow, all that precious metal,
> The root of evil. They found the guilt of iron,
> And gold, more guilty still. And War came forth.

The violation of Mother Earth resulted in new forms of monsters, born of the blood of her slaughter:

> Jove struck them down
> With thunderbolts, and the bulk of those huge bodies
> Lay on the earth, and bled, and Mother Earth,
> Made pregnant by that blood, brought forth new bodies,
> And gave them, to recall her older offspring,

>The forms of men. And this new stock was also
>Contemptuous of gods, and murder-hungry
>And violent. You would know they were sons of blood.

Seneca also deplored the activity of mining, although, unlike Pliny and Ovid, he did not consider it a new vice, but one that had been handed down from ancient times. "What necessity caused man, whose head points to the stars, to stoop, below, burying him in mines and plunging him in the very bowels of innermost earth to root up gold?" Not only did mining remove the earth's treasures, but it created "a sight to make [the] hair stand on end—huge rivers and vast reservoirs of sluggish waters." The defiling of the earth's waters was even then a noteworthy consequence of the quest for metals.[43]

These ancient strictures against mining were still operative during the early years of the commercial revolution when mining activities, which had lapsed after the fall of Rome, were once again revived. Ultimately, such constraints would have to be defeated by proponents of the new mercantilist philosophy.[44]

An allegorical tale, reputedly sent to Paul Schneevogel, a professor at Leipzig about 1490–95, expressed opposition to mining encroachments into the farmlands of Lichtenstat in Saxony, Germany, an area where the new mining activities were developing rapidly. Reminiscent of Alain of Lille's *Natura* and her torn gown and illustrative of the force of the ancient strictures against mining is the following allegorical vision of an old hermit of Lichtenstat. Mother Earth, dressed in a tattered green robe and seated on the right hand of Jupiter, is represented in a court case by "glib-tongued Mercury" who charges a miner with matricide. Testimony is presented by several of nature's deities:

>Bacchus complained that his vines were uprooted and fed to the flames and his most sacred places desecrated. Ceres stated that her fields were devastated; Pluto that the blows of the miners resound like thunder through the depths of the earth, so that he could hardly reside in his own kingdom; the Naiad, that the subterranean waters were diverted and her fountains dried up; Charon that the volume of the underground, waters had been so diminshed that he was unable to float his boat on Acheron and carry the souls across to Pluto's realm, and the Fauns protested that the charcoal burners had destroyed whole forests to obtain fuel to smelt the miner's ores.[45]

In his defense, the miner argued that the earth was not a real mother, but a wicked stepmother who hides and conceals the metals in her inner parts instead of making them available for human use.

The final judgment, handed down by Fortune, stated that if men deign "to mine and dig in mountains, to tend the fields, to engage in trade, to injure the earth, to throw away knowledge, to disturb Pluto and finally to search for veins of metal in the sources of rivers, their bodies ought to be swallowed up by the earth, suffocated by its vapors . . . intoxicated by wine, . . . afflicted with hunger and remain ignorant of what is best. These and many other dangers are proper of men. Farewell."

In the old hermit's tale, we have a fascinating example of the relationship between images and values. The older view of nature as a kindly mother is challenged by the growing interests of the mining industry in Saxony, Bohemia, and the Harz Mountains, regions of newly found prosperity. The miner, representing these newer commercial activities, transforms the image of the nurturing mother into that of a stepmother who wickedly conceals her bounty from the deserving and needy children. In the seventeenth century, the image will be seen to undergo yet another transformation, as natural philosopher Francis Bacon

(1561–1626) sets forth the need for prying into nature's nooks and crannies in searching out her secrets for human improvement.

Henry Cornelius Agrippa's polemic *The Vanity of Arts and Sciences* (1530) reiterated some of the moral strictures against mining found in the ancient treatises, quoting the passage from Ovid portraying miners digging into the bowels of the earth in order to extract gold and iron. "These men," he declared, "have made the very ground more hurtful and pestiferous, by how much they are more rash and venturous than they that hazard themselves in the deep to dive for pearls." Mining thus despoiled the earth's surface, infecting it, as it were, with an epidemic disease. Of all cultures that have mined for metals, "only the Scythians . . . condemned the use of gold and silver, resolving to keep themselves eternally free from public avarice. There was an ancient law among the Romans against the superfluity of gold. And indeed, it were to be wished that men would aspire with the same eagerness to heaven, that they descend into the bowels of the earth, allured with that vein of riches that are so far from making a man happy, that they repent too often of their time and labor so ill bestowed."[46]

If mining were to be freed of such strictures and sanctioned as a commercial activity, the ancient arguments would have to be refuted. This task was taken up by Georg Agricola (1494–1555), who wrote the first "modern" treatise on mining. His *De Re Metallica* ("On Metals," 1556) marshalled the arguments of the detractors of mining in order to refute them and thereby promote the activity itself.

According to Agricola, people who argued against the mining of the earth for metals did so on the basis that nature herself did not wish to be discovered what she herself had concealed:

> The earth does not conceal and remove from our eyes those things which are useful and necessary to mankind, but, on the contrary, like a beneficent and kindly mother she yields in large abundance from her bounty and brings into the light of day the herbs, vegetables, grains, and fruits, and trees. The minerals, on the other hand, she buries far beneath in the depth of the ground, therefore they should not be sought.[47]

This argument, taken directly from Pliny, reveals the normative force of the image of the earth as a nurturing mother.

A second argument of the detractors, reminiscent of Seneca and Agrippa, and based on Renaissance "ecological" concerns was the disruption of the natural environment and the pollutive effects of mining.

> But, besides this, the strongest argument of the detractors [of mining] is that the fields are devastated by mining operations, for which reason formerly Italians were warned by law that no one should dig the earth for metals and so injure their very fertile fields, their vineyards, and their olive groves. Also they argue that the woods and groves are cut down, for there is need of wood for timbers, machines, and the smelting of metals. And when the woods and groves are felled, then are exterminated the beasts and birds, many of which furnish a pleasant and agreeable food for man. Further, when the ores are washed, the water which has been used poisons the brooks and streams, and either destroys the fish or drives them away. Therefore the inhabitants of these regions, on account of the devastation of their fields, woods, groves, brooks, and rivers, find great difficulty in procuring the necessaries of life, and by reason of the destruction of the timber they are forced to greater expense in erecting buildings. Thus it is said, it is clear to all that there is greater detriment from mining than the value of the metals which the mining produces.

Agricola may have been alluding to laws passed by the Florentines between 1420 and 1485, preventing people from dumping lime into rivers upstream from the city for the purpose of "poisoning or catching fish," as it caused severe problems for those living downstream. The laws were enacted both to preserve the trout, "a truly noble and impressive fish" and to provide Florence with "a copious and abundant supply of such fish." But these laws passed to safeguard the waters of the Arno and the areas of the Castino and Pistoian Apennines were not obeyed, and complaints mounted· that "the rivers are empty of fish, and the fish are worse." By 1477, new laws protected the entire domain around Florence, includingthe Arno, Sieve, and Serchio rivers and their tributaries, from the diverting and damming of rivers and the poisoning of fish with lime, nutshells, or the reputedly toxic Aaron's Rod plant.[48]

Such ecological consciousness, however, suffered because of the failure of law enforcement, as well as because of the continuing progress of mining activities. Agricola, in his response to the detractors of mining, pointed out the congruences in the need to catch fish and to construct metal tools for the well-being of the human race. His effort can be interpreted as an attempt to liberate the activity of mining from the constraints imposed by the organic framework and the nurturing earth image, so that new values could sanction and hasten its development and progress.

To the argument that, because the metals lie in the earth "enclosed and hidden from sight [and] should not be taken out," Agricola countered with the example of catching fish, which lie concealed in the depths of the waters.[49] "Nature has given the earth . . . to man that he might cultivate it and draw out of its caverns metals and other mineral products," without which the earth could not be cultivated, fish caught, sheep sheared, animals slaughtered, or food cooked. Without the metals, men would "return to the acorns and fruits and berries of the forest. They would feed upon the herbs and roots which they plucked up with their nails. They would dig out caves in which to lie down at night, a . . . condition . . . utterly unworthy of humanity, with its splendid and glorious natural endowment."

To the argument that the woods were cut down and the price of timber therefore raised, Agricola responded that most mines occurred in unproductive, gloomy areas. Where the trees were removed from more productive sites, fertile fields could be created, the profits from which would reimburse the local inhabitants for their losses in timber supplies. Where the birds and animals had been destroyed by mining operations, the profits could be used to purchase "birds without number" and "edible beasts and fish elsewhere" and refurbish the area.

The vices associated with the metals—anger, cruelty, discord, passion for power, avarice, and lust—should be attributed instead to human conduct: "It is not the metals which are to be blamed, but the evil passions of men which become inflamed and ignited; or it is due to the blind and impious desires of their minds." Agricola's arguments are a conscious attempt to separate the older normative constraints from the image of the metals themselves so that new values can then surround them.

Edmund Spenser's treatment of Mother Earth in the *Faerie Queen* (1595) was representative of the concurrent conflict of attitudes about mining the earth. Spenser entered fully into the sixteenth-century debates about the wisdom of mining, the two greatest sins against the earth being, according to him, avarice and lust. The arguments associating mining with avarice had appeared in the ancient texts of Pliny, Ovid, and Seneca, while during Spenser's lifetime the sermons of Johannes Mathesius, entitled *Bergpostilla, oder Sarepta* (1578), inveighed against the moral consequences of human greed for the wealth created by mining for metals.[50]

In Spenser's poem, Guyon presents the arguments against mining taken from Ovid and Agricola, while the description of Mammon's forge is drawn from the illustrations to the *De Re Metallica*. Gold and silver pollute the spirit and debase human values just as the mining operation itself pollutes the "purest streams" of the earth's womb:

> Then gan a cursed hand the quiet wombe
> Of his great Grandmother with Steele to wound,
> And the hid treasures in her sacred tombe
> With Sacrilege to dig. Therein he found
> Fountaines of gold and silver to abound,
> Of which the matter of his huge desire
> And pompous pride eftsoones he did compound.[51]

The earth in Spenser's poem is passive and docile, allowing all manner of assault, violence, ill-treatment, rape by lust, and despoilment by greed. No longer a nurturer, she indiscriminately, as in Ovid's verse, supplies flesh to all life and lacking in judgment brings forth monsters and evil creatures. Her offspring fall and bite her in their own death throes. The new mining activities have altered the earth from a bountiful mother to a passive receptor of human rape.

John Milton's *Paradise Lost* (1667) continues the Ovidian image, as Mammon leads "bands of pioners with Spade and Pickaxe" in the wounding of the living female earth:

> . . . By him first
> Men also, and by his suggestion taught,
> Ransack'd the Center, and with impious hands
> Rifl'd the bowels of thir mother Earth
> For Treasures better hid. Soon had his crew
> Op'nd into the Hill a spacious wound
> And dig'd out ribs of Gold.[52]

Not only did mining encourage the moral sin of avarice, it was compared by Spenser to the second great sin, human lust. Digging into the matrices and pockets of earth for metals was like mining the female flesh for pleasure. The sixteenth- and seventeenth-century imagination perceived a direct correlation between mining and digging into the nooks and crannies of a woman's body. Both mining and sex represent for Spenser the return to animality and earthly slime. In the *Faerie Queen*, lust is the basest of all human sins. The spilling of human blood, in the rush to rape the earth of her gold, taints and muddies the once fertile fields.

The sonnets of the poet and divine John Donne (1573–1631) also played up the popular identity of mining with human lust. The poem "Love's Alchemie" begins with the sexual image, "Some that have deeper digged loves Myne than I,/say where his centrique happiness doth lie."[53] The Platonic lover, searching for the ideal or "centrique" experience of love, begins by digging for it within the female flesh, an act as debasing to the human being as the mining of metals is to the female earth. Happiness is not to be obtained by avarice for gold and silver, nor can the alchemical elixir be produced from base metals. Nor does ideal love result from an ascent up the hierarchical ladder from base sexual love to the love of poetry, music, and art to the highest Platonic love of the good, virtue, and God.

The same equation appears in Elegie XVIII, "Love's Progress":

> Search every spheare
> And firmament, our Cupid is not there:
> He's an infernal god and under ground,
> With Pluto dwells, where gold and fire abound:
> Men to such Gods, their sacrificing Coles,
> Did not in Altars lay, but pits and holes.
> Although we see Celestial bodies move

> Above the earth, the earth we Till and love:
> So we her ayres contemplate, words and heart
> And virtues; but we love the Centrique part.[54]

Lust and love of the body do not lead to the celestial love of higher ideals; rather, physical love is associated with the pits and holes of the female body, just as the love of gold depends on the mining of Pluto's caverns within the female earth, "the earth we till and love." Love of the sexual "centrique" part of the female will not lead to the aery spiritual love of virtue. The fatal association of monetary revenue with human avarice, lust, and the female mine is driven home again in the last lines of the poem:

> Rich Nature hath in women wisely made
> Two purses, and their mouths aversely laid:
> They then, which to the lower tribute owe,
> That way which that Exchequer looks, must go.

Avarice and greed after money corrupted the soul, just as lust after female flesh corrupted the body.

The comparison of the female mine with the new American sources of gold, silver, and precious metals appears again in Elegie XIX, "Going to Bed." Here, however, Donne turns the image upside down and uses it to extoll the virtues of the mistress:

> License my roaving hands, and let them go,
> Before, behind, between, above, below.
> O my America! my new-found-land,
> My kingdome, safelist when with one man man'd
> My Myne of precious stones, My Emperie,
> How blest am I in this discovering thee!

In these lines, the comparison functions as a sanction—the search for precious gems and metals, like the sexual exploration of nature or the female, can benefit a kingdom or a man.

Moral restraints were thus clearly affiliated with the Renaissance image of the female earth and were strengthened by associations with greed, avarice, and lust. But the analogies were double-edged. If the new values connected with mining were positive, and mining was viewed as a means to improve the human condition, as they were by Agricola, and later by Bacon, then the comparison could be turned upside down. Sanctioning mining sanctioned the rape or commercial exploration of the earth—a clear illustration of how constraints can change to sanctions through the demise of frameworks and their associated values as the needs, wants, and purposes of society change: The organic framework, in which the Mother Earth image was a moral restraint against mining, was literally undermined by the new commercial activity.

Notes

1   On the tensions between technology and the pastoral ideal in American culture, see Leo Marx, *The Machine in the Garden* (New York: Oxford University Press, 1964). On the domination of nature as female, see Annette Kolodny, *The Lay of the Land* (Chapel Hill: University of North Carolina Press, 1975); Rosemary Radford Ruether, "Women, Ecology, and the Domination of Nature," *The Ecumenist* 14 (1975): 1–5; William Leiss, *The Domination of Nature* (New York: Braziller, 1972). On the roots of the ecological crisis, see Donald Hughes, *Ecology in Ancient Civilizations* (Albuquerque: University

of New Mexico Press, 1976); Lynn White, Jr., *Medieval Technology and Social Change* (New York: Oxford University Press, 1966); and L. White, Jr., "Historical Roots of Our Ecologic Crisis," in White, Jr. *Machina ex Deo* (Cambridge, Mass.: M. I. T. Press, 1968), pp. 75–94; Reijer Hooykaas, *Religion and the Rise of Modern Science* (Grand Rapids, Mich.: Eerdmans, 1972); Christopher Derrick, *The Delicate Creation: Towards a Theology of the Environment* (Old Greenwich, Conn.: Devin-Adair, 1972). On traditional rituals in the mining of ores and in metallurgy, see Mircea Eliade, *The Forge and the Crucible*, trans. Stephan Corrin (New York: Harper & Row, 1962), pp. 42, 53–70, 74, 79–96. On the divergence between attitudes and practices toward the environment, see Yi-Fu Tuan, "Our Treatment of the Environment in Ideal and Actuality," *American Scientist* (May-June 1970): 246–49.

2   Stanley Cavell, "Must We Mean What We Say?" in Colin Lyas, ed., *Philosophy and Linguistics* (London: Macmillan, 1971), pp. 131–65; see esp. 148, 165. On frameworks and values see Charles Taylor, "Neutrality in Political Science," in Alan Ryan, ed., *The Philosophy of Social Explanation* (London: Oxford University Press, 1973) pp. 139–70, see esp. pp. 144–46, 154–55.

3   On the Elizabethan view of nature and Shakespeare's *King Lear*, see John Danby, *Shakespeare's Doctrine of Nature: A Study of King Lear* (London: Faber and Faber, 1949), pp. 20–21, 26, 28, 133, 126.

4   Richard Hooker, *Of the Laws of Ecclesiastical Polity*, ed. W. Speed Hill (Cambridge, Mass.: Harvard University Press, 1977, first published, 1594): Bk. I, Chap. 3.3, p. 66, Chap. 3.4, p. 68; Chap. 8, pp. 3–5. Danby, pp. 24–27. Eustace M. W. Tillyard, *The Elizabethan World Picture* (New York: Random House Vintage, 1959 [?]), p. 46.

5   Danby, p. 133. The interpretation of Cordelia is Danby's.

6   The discussion of the pastoral tradition draws on Joseph W. Meeker, *The Comedy of Survival: Studies in Literary Ecology* (New York: Scribner's, 1972), pp, 81–89, and L. Marx, *The Machine in the Garden*, pp. 26, 28–29, 36–43. Also relevant are Walter W. Greg, *Pastoral Poetry and Pastoral Drama* (London: Bullen, 1906); William Empson, *Some Versions of the Pastoral* (London: Chatto & Windus, 1950); Michael Putnam, *Virgil's Pastoral Art: Studies in the Eclogues* (Princeton, N.J.: Princeton University Press, 1970); Bruno Snell, "Arcadia: The Discovery of a Spiritual Landscape," in *The Discovery of the Mind: The Greek Origins of European Thought*, trans. T. G. Rosenmeyer (Oxford: Blackwell, 1953); Hallett Smith, "Pastoral Poetry," *Elizabethan Poetry: A Study in Conventions, Meanings, and Expression* (Cambridge, Mass.: Harvard University Press, 1952); Erwin Panofsky, "Et in Arcadia Ego: Poussin and the Elegaic Tradition," in *Meaning in the Visual Arts: Papers in and on Art History* (Garden City, N.Y.: Doubleday, 1957).

7   Quoted in Meeker, p. 82.

8   Quoted in Meeker, pp. 82–83.

9   Plato, *The Timaeus* (written ca. 360 B.C.), in *The Dialogues of Plato*, trans. Benjamin Jowett (New York: Random House, 1937), vol. 2, pp. 14, 16, 17, 18, 21. For a commentary, see Francis MacDonald Cornford, *Plato's Cosmology* (New York: Liberal Arts Press, 1937). On Plato's views on women, see Anne Dickason, "Anatomy and Destiny: The Role of Biology in Plato's Views of Women," *The Philosophical Forum* 5 (1973–74): 45–53.

10   Bernard Silvestris, *De Mundi Universitate* (written ca. 1136), ed. Carl Sigmund Barach and Johann Wrobel (Innsbruck: Wagner, 1876); B. Silvestris, *Cosmographia*, trans. Winthrop Wetherbee (New York: Columbia University Press, 1973), pp. 65–127; George D. Economou, *The Goddess Natura in Medieval Literature* (Cambridge, Mass.: Harvard University Press, 1972), pp. 54, 63.

11   Alain of Lille, *De Planctu Naturae* (written ca. 1202), in Thomas Wright, ed., *The Anglo-Latin Satirical Poets and Epigrammatists* (Wiesbaden: Kraus Reprint, 1964), vol. 2, pp. 441, 467; Economou, pp. 73, 76, 77, 82. English translation: Alain of Lille, *The Complaint of Nature*, trans. Douglas Moffat (New York: Henry Holt, 1908), see esp. pp. 3, 4, 11, 15, 41, 44. "I marvel," then I said, "wherefore certain parts of thy tunic, which should be like the connection of marriage, suffer division in that part of their texture where the fancies of art give the image of man." "Now from what we have touched on previously," she answered, "thou canst deduce what the figured gap and rent mystically show. For since, as we have said before, many men have taken arms against their mother in evil and violence, they thereupon, in fixing between them and her a vast gulf of dissension, lay on me the hands of outrage, and themselves tear apart my garments piece by piece, and, as far as in them lies, force me, stripped of dress, whom they ought to clothe with reverential honor, to come to shame like a harlot. This tunic, then, is made with this rent, since by the unlawful assaults of man alone the garments of my modesty suffer disgrace and division" [p. 41].

12   Aristotle, *Metaphysics* (written ca. 335–322 B.C.), in Richard McKeon, ed., *The Basic Works of Aristotle* (New York: Random House, 1971), p. 755, line 1015^a5; see also *Physics*, in *Basic Works*, p. 237, line 193^a28; pp. 240–41, lines 194^b16–195^a14.

13   Aristotle, *De Generatione Animalium* (written ca. 335–322 B.C.), trans. Arthur Platt (Oxford, England: Clarendon Press, 1910), Bk. I, Chap. 19, lines 729^b13, 730^a1–3. See also lines 739^b21–27, 727^b31,

730^{a}15, 730^{b}10–25. For a discussion, see Maryanne Cline Horowitz, "Aristotle and Woman," *Journal of the History of Biology* 9, no. 2 (Fall 1976): 183–213; Joseph Needham, *A History of Embryology* (Cambridge, England: The University Press, 1934); Anthony Preus, "Science and Philosophy in Aristotle's Generation of Animals," *Journal of the History of Biology* 3 (Spring 1970): 1–52. Arthur William Meyer, *The Rise of Embryology* (Stanford, Cal.: Stanford University Press, 1939), Chap. 2, pp. 17–27. Caroline Whitbeck, "Theories of Sex Difference," *The Philosophical Forum* 5 (Fall-Winter 1973–74): 54–80, esp. 55–57.

14   Nicolaus Copernicus, *On the Revolutions of the Heavenly Spheres,* trans. A. M. Duncan (New York: Barnes & Noble, 1976; first Latin ed. 1543), Bk. I, Chap. 10, p. 50. See also Frank Sherwood Taylor, *The Alchemists* (New York: Schumann. 1949), Chap. 2; Walter Pagel and Maryanne Winder, "The Higher Elements and Prime Matter in Renaissance Naturalism and in Paracelsus," *Ambix* 21 (1974): 93–127 (see p. 95).

15   Elaine Pagels, "What Became of God the Mother? Conflicting Images of God in Early Christianity," *Signs* 2, no. 2 (Winter 1976): 297. See also pp. 293–303 for a discussion of women and gnosticism. The discussion of gnosticism draws on Hans Jonas, *The Gnostic Religion* (Boston: Beacon Press, 1958), Chaps. 2–4, 7, 8, and Kurt Seligmann, *Magic, Supernaturalism, and Religion* (New York: Pantheon Books, 1948), pp. 60–66.

16   Quoted in Seligmann, p. 85. See also p. 80.

17   *Ibid.,* pp. 128–29.

18   The following discussion of gnosticism draws on Walter Pagel and Maryanne Winder, "The Eightness of Adam and Related Gnostic Ideas in the Paracelsian Corpus," *Ambix* 16 (1969): 119–39; Pagel and Winder, "The Higher Elements," pp. 94, 96–97, and Walter Pagel, "Das Rätsel der Acht Mütter im Paracelsischen Corpus," *Sudhoff's Archiv für Geschichte der Medizin* 59 (1975): 254–66.

19   Theophrastus Paracelsus, *Selected Writings,* ed. J. Jacobi (Princeton, N.J.: Princeton University Press, 1951), p. 27. On the gnostic sources of Paracelsus' philosophy, see Walter Pagel, "Paracelsus and the Neoplatonic and Gnostic Tradition," *Ambix* 8 (1960): 125–66; W. Pagel, "Paracelsus, Traditionalism and Medieval Sources," in Lloyd G. Stevenson and Robert D. Multhauf, eds., *Medicine, Science, and Culture* (Baltimore, Md.: Johns Hopkins Press, 1968), pp. 57–75; W. Pagel, *Paracelsus* (New York: Karger, 1958), pp. 204–17. Paracelsus' attitude toward women, however, remains ambiguous; for example, "How can one be an enemy of woman—whatever she may be? The world is peopled with her fruits, and that is why God lets her live so long, however loathsome she may be" (Jacobi, ed., p. 26); "He who contemplates woman should see in her the material womb of man; she is man's world, from which he is born" (*Ibid.*).

20   Ralph Cudworth, *The True Intellectual System of the Universe* (New York: Gould and Newman, 1838; first published 1678), vol. 1, p. 404.

21   Carl G. Jung, *Alchemical Studies* in Herbert Read and others, eds., *Collected Works* (Princeton, N.J.: Princeton University Press, 1953), vol. 13, pp. 211–44; F.S. Taylor, Chap. 11; K. Seligmann, p. 98.

22   Thomas Vaughan, "Anima Magica Abscondita," in Arthur E. Waite, ed., *The Works of Thomas Vaughan* (London: Theosophical Publishing House, 1919; first published 1650), p. 94.

23   M. Tullius Cicero, *Of the Nature of the Gods,* ed. T. Francklin (London, 1775), Bk. II, Chap. 8, p. 96. See also Chaps. 53, 60.

24   Lucius Seneca, *Physical Science in the Time of Nero; Being a Translation of the Quaestiones Naturales of Seneca,* (written ca. A.D. 65), trans. John Clarke (London: Macmillan, 1910). Quotations in order are taken from Bk. VI, Chap. 16, pp. 244–45; Bk. III, Chap. 15, pp. 126, 127. On the Stoic conception of nature see Eduard Zeller, *The Stoics, Epicureans, and Sceptics* (London: Longmans Green, 1870), pp. 134–94.

25   Translated and quoted in F. M. Cornford, *Plato's Cosmology,* p. 330.

26   Gabriel Harvey, *Pleasant and Pithy Familiar Discourse of the Earthquake in Aprill Last,* quoted in Walter M. Kendrick, "Earth of Flesh, Flesh of Earth: Mother Earth in the *Faerie Queen,*" *Renaissance Quarterly* 27 (1974): 548–53, see p. 544. On the earth's veins and bowels, see Georg Agricola, *De Re Metallica,* 1556, trans. Herbert C. Hoover and Lou H. Hoover (New York: Dover, 1950; first published, 1556); p. 1. See also excerpts of Agricola, *De Ortu et Causis Subterraneorum* (first published 1546), in Kirtley F. Mather, ed., *Source Book in Geology* (New York: McGraw-Hill, 1939), p. 7; Athanasius Kircher, *Mundus Subterraneous* (Amsterdam, 1678) in Mather, ed., pp. 17–19.

27   Bernardino Telesio, *De Rerum Natura Iuxta Propria Principia* (Naples, 1587; first published, 1565). Excerpts translated in Arturo B. Fallico and Herman Shapiro, eds. and trans., *Renaissance Philosophy* (New York: Modern Library, 1967), vol. 1, pp. 308–9.

28   Giordano Bruno, *The Expulsion of the Triumphant Beast* (first published 1584), trans. and ed. Arthur D. Imerti (New Brunswick, N. J.: Rutgers University Press, 1964), p. 72.

29   Marco Antonio della Frata et Montalbano, *Pratica Minerale Trattrato* (Bologna, 1678), p. 2; as quoted in Frank Dawson Adams, *The Birth and Development of the Geological Sciences* (New York: Dover, 1938), p. 306.

30   Telesio, in Fallico and Shapiro, p. 309.

31   Aristotle, *Meteorologica* (written, ca. 335–322 B.C.), trans. E. W. Webster, in W. D. Ross, ed., *The Works of Aristotle Translated into English* (Oxford, England: Clarendon Press, 1923), vol. 3, line 339a. See Adams, p. 84; examples cited include Konrad von Megenberg, *Das Buch der Natur* (Augsberg: J. Bämler, 1475); Gregorius Reisch, *Margarita Philosophica* (Strasbourg, 1504); Hieronymus Savonarola, *Compendium Totius Philosophiae tam Naturalis quam Moralis* (Venice, 1542): Giorgio Camillo Maffei, *Scala Naturale* (Venice, 1563); Andreas Baccius, *De Gemmis et Lapidibus Pretiosis* (Frankfurt, 1603); Leonardus Camillus, *Speculum Lapidum* (Venice, 1502), Bk. I.

32   Adams, pp. 84–90, 290, 292; examples cited include Thomas Sherley, *A Philosophical Essay Declaring the Probable Causes Whence Stones Are Produced in the Greater World* (London: 1672), pp. 23–128; M.J.C. Schwiegger, *De Ortu Papidum*, dissertation, University of Wittenburg, 1665; Jerome Cardan, *De Subtilitate* (Nuremberg, 1550); Bernard Palissy, *Discours Admirables de la Nature des Eau et Founteines tant Naturelles qu'Artificelles, des Metaus, des Sels et Salines* (Paris, 1580), pp. 122, 134; John Webster, *Metallographa, or An History of Metals* (London, 1671), p. 70; Robert Boyle, *The Skeptical Chemist* (London: Everyman's Library, 1967), pp. 194, 202; Edward Jorden, *A Discourse of Natural Bathes and Mineral Waters* (London, 1669), p. 51.

33   Adams, pp. 90–94; examples include Agricola, *De Ortu et Causis Subterraneorum;* Giorgio Baglivi, *De Vegetatione Lapidum in Opera Omnia* (London, 1714), p. 497.

34   Paracelsus, ed. Jacobi, p. 25; Pagel, "Das Rätsel der Acht Mütter," p. 255; Paracelsus, in Karl Sudhoff and Wilhelm Mattiessen, eds., *Sämtliche Werke* (Munich: Barth, 1922–33), Abt. I, vol. 13, p. 88.

35   Basil Valentine, "The Fifth Key," from *The Practica, with Twelve Keys, and an Appendix Thereto Concerning the Great Stone of the Ancient Sages,* reprinted in *The Hermetic Museum Restored and Enlarged . . .* (Frankfurt, 1678), trans. Arthur Edward Waite (New York: Samuel Weiser, 1974; first published 1893), vol. I, p. 333.

36   Henry More, "An Antidote Against Atheism" (first published 1653) in *A Collection of Several Philosophical Writings of Dr. Henry More* (London, 1712), p. 65.

37   Adams, pp. 94, 102–36; Cardan, *De Subtilitate,* Bk. VII; D. C. Goodman, "The Saltish Seed: Crystals and Life in the Seventeenth Century," *Abstracts of Papers Presented to the XVth International Congress of the History of Science* (Edinburgh, 1977), p. 167.

38   Smohalla (Columbia Basin Tribes), voicing fundamental cause of all great periods of Indian unrest (mid-1800s), quoted in Alfonso Ortiz and Margaret Ortiz, eds., *To Carry Forth the Vine* (New York: Columbia University Press, 1978). On Indian, animistic, and Western belief systems, see Calvin Martin, *Keepers of the Game* (Berkeley and Los Angeles: University of California Press, 1978); Henri Frankfurt and H. A. Frankfurt, *The Intellectual Adventure of Ancient Man* (Chicago: University of Chicago Press, 1977); Lynn White, Jr., "Historical Roots of Our Ecologic Crisis" (cited in note 1); Garrett Hardin, "The Tragedy of the Commons," *Science* 162 (1968): 1243–48.

39   Peter Martyr, *The History of Truayle in the West and East Indies and other countryes lying either way toward the fruitful and ryche Molucceas, gathered in part and done into Englyshe by Richard Eden, Newly set in order augmented and finished by Richard Willes Third Decade* (London, 1577), quoted in Adams, p. 287. This viewpoint also appeared in Johann Rudolf Glauber's *Operis Mineralis* (Amsterdam, 1652), Pt. II and in the 18th century in Johann Joachim Becker (1635–82), *Natur Kündigung der Metallen* (Frankfurt, 1705) and Emmanuel König, *Regnum Minerale* (Basel, 1703). Discussed in Adams, pp, 286–89, 293.

40   Albaro Alonzo Barba, *The Art of Metals,* trans. Earl of Sandwich (London, 1669; first published 1640), p. 49; as quoted in Adams, p. 294. R. Boyle, *The Skeptical Chemist* (p. 191), concurred in the belief that stones grew from the roofs of caves, and that water could be transformed into minerals. This occurrence "is very notable because from thence we deduce that earth, by a metallic plastik principle latent in it, may be in process of time changed into a metal."

41   Pliny, *Natural History* (written ca. A.D. 23–79), trans. J. Bostock and H. T. Riley (London: Bohn, 1858), vol. 6, Bk. 33, Chap. 1, pp. 68–69. Subsequent quotations are from pp. 69, 71, 70 and 205–6.

42   Publius Ovid, *Metamorphoses* (written A.D. 7), trans. Rolfe Humphries (Bloomington: Indiana University Press, 1955), Bk. I, p. 6, line 100. Subsequent quotations are from lines 101–11, 137–43, 155–62. See also Kendrick, "Earth of Flesh," p. 539.

43   Seneca, *Natural Questions,* trans. John Clarke, Bk. V, Chap. 15, pp. 207–8.

44   See Erik Erikson on the conflict of values in the mining regions surrounding the "transition from the agrarian preoccupation with mud, soil, and fertility to the miner's preoccupation with rock, dirt, and the chances of a haul; and beyond this, the mercantile aim of amassing metal and money, shiny and

yet 'dirty' and all subject to a new adventurous and boundless avarice which the church tried to crush with all her might—and at the same time to monoplize." E. Erikson, *Young Man Luther* (New York: Norton, 1958), pp. 53–61. On the revival of mining in the fifteenth century after a long lapse from the fall of Rome through the Middle Ages, see William Barclay Parsons, *Engineers and Engineering in the Renaissance* (Cambridge, Mass: M.I.T. Press, 1968), pp. 177–200.

45   Adams, pp. 172–73. Niavis [Dr. Paul Schneevogel], *Judicum Jovis* (Leipzig: Kachelhofen, n.d.).

46   Henry Cornelius Agrippa, *De Incertitude et Vanitale Omnium Scientiarum et Artum* (Antwerp, 1530). English translation: *The Vanity of Arts and Sciences* (London, 1694), pp. 81, 82.

47   Georg Agricola, *De Re Metallica,* pp. 6–7, 8.

48   Richard Trexler, "Measures Against Water Pollution in Fifteenth-Century Florence," *Viator* 5 (1974): 455–67, see pp. 463, 466–67. Other articles on attempts to deal with water pollution in medieval Europe include Lynn Thorndike, "Sanitation, Baths, and Street Cleaning in the Middle Ages and Renaissance," *Speculum* 3 (1928): 192–203, and Ernest Sabine, "City Cleaning in Medieval London," *Speculum* 12 (January 1937): 19–43.

49   Agricola, *De Re Metallica,* Hoover trans., quotations on pp. 12, 13, 14, 12, 17, 16.

50   Johannes Mathesius, *Bergpostilla, oder Sarepta, darinn von allerley Bergkwerck und Metallen, was ir ey enschaft und natur* (Nürnberg, 1578).

51   Quoted in Kendrick, "Earth of Flesh," p. 538. Edmund Spenser, *The Faerie Queen,* ed. John Upton, 2 vols. (London, 1758; first published 1590/5), Bk. II, Canto 7, verse 17. On Spenser's participation in the sixteenth-century debates on mining, his use of Agricola, and the description of Mammon's forge, see Kendrick, pp. 537–41. *Faerie Queen,* vol. 1, Bk. II, Canto VII, verse 15: "At the well-head the purest streames arise;/But mucky filth his braunching armes annoyes,/And with uncomely weedes the gentle wave accloyes." Mammon's forge is described in vol. I, Bk. II, Canto VII, verses 35–36. On Spenser's association of lust with mining see Kendrick, pp. 544–45.

52   John Milton, *Paradise Lost* (first published 1667), ed. Scott Elledge (New York: Norton, 1975), Bk. I, lines 684–90.

53   John Donne, *Poems of John Donne,* ed. Herbert Grierson (London: Oxford University Press; 1957), p. 35. For an analysis of "Love's Alchemie," see Clay Hunt, *Donne's Poetry* (New Haven, Conn.: Yale University Press, 1954), pp. 33–41.

54   Donne, *Poems,* Elegie XVIII, "Love's Progress," p. 104, lines 27–36, lines 91–94; Elegie XIX, p. 107, lines 25–30.

Chapter 3

Raymond Williams

THE COUNTRY AND THE CITY

A Problem of Perspective

THE INITIAL PROBLEM IS one of perspective. A few years ago I was sent a book for review: a country book, in a familiar idiom, that I would normally have enjoyed reading. But there in front of the experience was a formula:

> A way of life that has come down to us from the days of Virgil has suddenly ended.

In detail, certainly, this was curious. From Virgil? Here? A way of country life?

But in outline, of course, the position was familiar. As it is put in a memorable sentence, in the same book:

> A whole culture that had preserved its continuity from earliest times had now received its quietus.

It had happened, it seemed, in the last fifty years: say since the First World War. But this raised a problem. I remembered a sentence in a critically influential book: Leavis and Thompson's *Culture and Environment*, published in 1932. The 'organic community' of 'Old England' had disappeared; 'the change is very recent indeed'. This view was primarily based on the books of George Sturt, which appeared between 1907 and 1923. In *Change in the Village*, published in 1911, Sturt wrote of the rural England 'that is dying out now'. Just back, we can see, over the last hill.

But then what seemed like an escalator began to move. Sturt traced this ending to two periods: enclosure after 1861 and residential settlement after 1900. Yet this at once takes us into the period of Thomas Hardy's novels, written between 1871 and 1896 and referring back to rural England since the 1830s. And had not critics insisted that it was here, in Hardy, that we found the record of the great climacteric change in rural life: the disturbance and destruction of what one writer has called the 'timeless rhythm of agriculture and the seasons'? And that was also the period of Richard Jefferies, looking back from the 1870s to the 'old

Hodge', and saying that there had been more change in rural England in the previous half-century—that is, since the 1820s—than in any previous time. And wasn't George Eliot, in *Mill on the Floss* (1860) and in *Felix Holt* (1866), looking back, similarly, to the old rural England of the 1820s and early 1830s?

But now the escalator was moving without pause. For the 1820s and 1830s were the last years of Cobbett, directly in touch with the rural England of his time but looking back to the happier country, the old England of his boyhood, during the 1770s and 1780s. Thomas Bewick, in his *Memoir,* written during the 1820s, was recalling the happier village of his own boyhood, in the 1770s. The decisive change, both men argued, had happened during their lifetimes. John Clare, in 1809, was also looking back—

> Oh, happy Eden of those golden years

—to what seems, on internal evidence, to be the 1790s, though he wrote also, in another retrospect on a vanishing rural order, of the 'far-fled pasture, long evanish'd scene'.

Yet still the escalator moved. For the years of Cobbett's and of Bewick's boyhood were the years of Crabbe's *The Village* (1783)

> No longer truth, though shown in verse, disdain,
> But own the Village Life a life of pain

and of Goldsmith's *The Deserted Village* (1769)

> E'en now, methinks, as pondering here I stand
> I see the rural virtues leave the land.

And by ordinary arithmetic, in the memory of Sweet Auburn—

> loveliest village of the plain,
> Where health and plenty cheer'd the labouring swain,
> Where smiling spring its earliest visit paid,
> And parting summer's lingering blooms delay'd;
> Dear lovely bowers of innocence and ease,
> Seats of my youth, when every sport could please

—back we would go again, over the next hill, to the 1750s.

It is clear, of course, as this journey in time is taken, that something more than ordinary arithmetic and something more, evidently, than ordinary history, is in question. Against sentimental and intellectualised accounts of an unlocalised 'Old England', we need, evidently, the sharpest scepticism. But some at least of these witnesses were writing from direct experience. What we have to inquire into is not, in these cases, historical error, but historical perspective. Indeed the fact of what I have called the escalator may be an important clue to the real history, but only when we begin to see the regularity of its pattern.

It is worth, perhaps, getting on the escalator again, since all we have done so far is to move 'Old England' and its timeless agricultural rhythms back from the early twentieth century to the middle of the eighteenth century. When we remember 'our mature, settled eighteenth century', we may not, after all, have made very much difference to the ordinary accounts. Shall we then go back to Philip Massinger, in the early 1620s, in *The City Madam* and *A New Way to Pay Old Debts*? Here the new commercialism is breaking the old landed settlement and its virtues. Here is the enclosing and engrossing Sir Giles Overreach. Here is the corruption of an older rural civilisation:

> Your father was
> An honest country farmer, goodman Humble,
> By his neighbours ne'er called Master. Did your pride
> Descend from him?

We can't say, but we can go on back to Bastard's *Chrestoleros,* in 1598, where the same complaints are being made, or, if we are asked to assume that the disturbance occurred at the turn of the century, to Thomas More's *Utopia,* in 1516, where another old order is being destroyed:

> For looke in what partes of the realme doth growe the fynest and therfore dearest woll, there noblemen and gentlemen, yea and certeyn abbottes, holy men no doubt, not contenting them selfes with the yearely revenues and profytes, that were wont to grow to theyr forefathers and predecessours of their landes, nor beynge content that they live in rest and pleasure nothinge profiting, yea much noyinge the weale publique, leave no ground for tillage, thei inclose all into pastures; thei throw doune houses; they plucke downe townes, and leave nothing standynge, but only the churche to be made a shepehouse. And as though you lost no small quantity of grounds by forestes, chases, laundes and parkes, those good holy men turne all dwellinge places and all glebeland into desolation and wildernes.

Except that then, of course, we find ourselves referred back to the settled Middle Ages, an organic society if ever there was one. To the 1370S, for example, when Langland's Piers Plowman sees the dissatisfaction of the labourers, who will not eat yesterday's vegetables but must have fresh meat, who blame God and curse the King, but who used not to complain when Hunger made the Statutes. Must we go beyond the Black Death to the beginning of the Game Laws, or to the time of Magna Carta, when Innocent III writes:

> the serf serves; terrified with threats, wearied by corvees, afflicted with blows, despoiled of his possessions?

Or shall we find the timeless rhythm in Domesday, when four men out of five are villeins, bordars, cotters or slaves? Or in a free Saxon world before what was later seen as the Norman rape and yoke? In a Celtic world, before the Saxons came up the rivers? In an Iberian world, before the Celts came, with their gilded barbarism? Where indeed shall we go, before the escalator stops?

One answer, of course, is Eden, and we shall have to look at that well-remembered garden again. But first we must get off the escalator, and consider its general movement.

Is it anything more than a well-known habit of using the past, the 'good old days', as a stick to beat the present? It is clearly something of that, but there are still difficulties. The apparent resting places, the successive Old Englands to which we are confidently referred but which then start to move and recede, have some actual significance, when they are looked at in their own terms. Of course we notice their location in the childhoods of their authors, and this must be relevant. Nostalgia, it can be said, is universal and persistent; only other men's nostalgias offend. A memory of childhood can be said, persuasively, to have some permanent significance. But again, what seemed a single escalator, a perpetual recession into history, turns out, on reflection, to be a more complicated movement: Old England, settlement, the rural virtues—all these, in fact, mean different things at different times, and quite different values are being brought to question. We shall need precise analysis of each kind of retrospect, as it comes. We shall see successive stages of the criticism which the retrospect supports: religious, humanist, political, cultural. Each of these stages is worth examination in itself. And then, within each of these questions, but returning us finally to a formidable and central question, there is a different consideration.

The witnesses we have summoned raise questions of historical fact and perspective, but they raise questions, also, of literary fact and perspective. The things they are saying are not all in the same mode. They range, as facts, from a speech in a play and a passage in a novel to an argument in an essay and a note in a journal. When the facts are poems, they are also, and perhaps crucially, poems of different kinds. We can only analyse these important structures of feeling if we make, from the beginning, these critical discriminations. And then the first problem of definition, a persistent problem of form, is the question of pastoral, of what is known as pastoral.

References

The Pattern under the Plough; G. Ewart Evans; London, 1966; 17.

Culture and Environment; F. R. Leavis and Denys Thompson; London, 1933; 87.

Change in the Village; George Sturt (George Bourne); London, 1912; 7.

Helpstone; John Clare; in *Poems*, ed. J. W. Tibble; 2 vols.; London, 1935.

The Village; George Crabbe; in *Poetical Works of George Crabbe*; ed. A. J. and R. M. Carlyle; Oxford, 1914.

The Deserted Village; Oliver Goldsmith; in *Complete Poetical Works*; ed. A. Dobson; Oxford, 1906.

The City Madam; Philip Massinger; Act IV, sc iv.

Utopia; ed. J. H. Lupton; Oxford, 1895; 39–40.

Selected Letters of Innocent III; ed. Cheney and Semple; Edinburgh, 1953.

Chapter 4

Lynn White, Jr.[1]

THE HISTORICAL ROOTS OF OUR ECOLOGIC CRISIS

ACONVERSATION WITH ALDOUS HUXLEY not infrequently put one at the receiving end of an unforgettable monologue. About a year before his lamented death he was discoursing on a favorite topic: Man's unnatural treatment of nature and its sad results. To illustrate his point he told how, during the previous summer, he had returned to a little valley in England where he had spent many happy months as a child. Once it had been composed of delightful grassy glades; now it was becoming overgrown with unsightly brush because the rabbits that formerly kept such growth under control had largely succumbed to a disease, myxomatosis, that was deliberately introduced by the local farmers to reduce the rabbits' destruction of crops. Being something of a Philistine, I could be silent no longer, even in the interests of great rhetoric. I interrupted to point out that the rabbit itself had been brought as a domestic animal to England in 1176, presumably to improve the protein diet of the peasantry.

All forms of life modify their contexts. The most spectacular and benign instance is doubtless the coral polyp. By serving its own ends, it has created a vast undersea world favorable to thousands of other kinds of animals and plants. Ever since man became a numerous species he has affected his environment notably. The hypothesis that his fire-drive method of hunting created the world's great grasslands and helped to exterminate the monster mammals of the Pleistocene from much of the globe is plausible, if not proved. For 6 millennia at least, the banks of the lower Nile have been a human artifact rather than the swampy African jungle which nature, apart from man, would have made it. The Aswan Dam, flooding 5000 square miles, is only the latest stage in a long process. In many regions terracing or irrigation, over-grazing, the cutting of forests by Romans to build ships to fight Carthaginians or by Crusaders to solve the logistics problems of their expeditions, have profoundly changed some ecologies. Observation that the French landscape falls into two basic types, the open fields of the north and the *bocage* of the south and west, inspired Marc Bloch to undertake his classic study of medieval agricultural methods. Quite unintentionally, changes in human ways often affect nonhuman nature. It has been noted, for example, that the advent of the automobile eliminated huge flocks of sparrows that once fed on the horse manure littering every street.

The history of ecologic change is still so rudimentary that we know little about what really happened, or what the results were. The extinction of the European aurochs as late as

1627 would seem to have been a simple case of overenthusiastic hunting. On more intricate matters it often is impossible to find solid information. For a thousand years or more the Frisians and Hollanders have been pushing back the North Sea, and the process is culminating in our own time in the reclamation of the Zuider Zee. What, if any, species of animals, birds, fish, shore life, or plants have died out in the process? In their epic combat with Neptune have the Netherlanders overlooked ecological values in such a way that the quality of human life in the Netherlands has suffered? I cannot discover that the questions have ever been asked, much less answered.

People, then, have often been a dynamic element in their own environment, but in the present state of historical scholarship we usually do not know exactly when, where, or with what effects man-induced changes came. As we enter the last third of the 20th century, however, concern for the problem of ecologic backlash is mounting feverishly. Natural science, conceived as the effort to understand the nature of things, had flourished in several eras and among several peoples. Similarly there had been an age-old accumulation of techno-logical skills, sometimes growing rapidly, sometimes slowly. But it was not until about four generations ago that Western Europe and North America arranged a marriage between science and technology, a union of the theoretical and the empirical approaches to our natural environment. The emergence in widespread practice of the Baconian creed that scientific knowledge means technological power over nature can scarcely be dated before about 1850, save in the chemical industries, where it is anticipated in the 18th century. Its acceptance as a normal pattern of action may mark the greatest event in human history since the invention of agriculture, and perhaps in nonhuman terrestrial history as well.

Almost at once the new situation forced the crystallization of the novel concept of ecology; indeed, the word *ecology* first appeared in the English language in 1873. Today, less than a century later, the impact of our race upon the environment has so increased in force that it has changed in essence. When the first cannons were fired, in the early 14th century, they affected ecology by sending workers scrambling to the forests and mountains for more potash, sulfur, iron ore, and charcoal, with some resulting erosion and deforestation. Hydrogen bombs are of a different order; a war fought with them might alter the genetics of all life on this planet. By 1285 London had a smog problem arising from the burning of soft coal, but our present combustion of fossil fuels threatens to change the chemistry of the globe's atmosphere as a whole, with consequences which we are only beginning to guess. With the population explosion, the carcinoma of planless urbanism, the now geological deposits of sewage and garbage, surely no creature other than man has ever managed to foul its nest in such short order.

There are many calls to action, but specific proposals, however worthy as individual items, seem too partial, palliative, negative: ban the bomb, tear down the billboards, give the Hindus contraceptives and tell them to eat their sacred cows. The simplest solution to any suspect change is, of course, to stop it, or, better yet, to revert to a romanticized past: make those ugly gasoline stations look like Anne Hathaway's cottage or (in the Far West) like ghost-town saloons. The "wilderness area" mentality invariably advocates deep-freezing an ecology, whether San Gimignano or the High Sierra, as it was before the first Kleenex was dropped. But neither atavism nor prettification will cope with the ecologic crisis of our time.

What shall we do? No one yet knows. Unless we think about fundamentals, our specific measures may produce new backlashes more serious than those they are designed to remedy.

As a beginning we should try to clarify our thinking by looking, in some historical depth, at the presuppositions that underlie modern technology and science. Science was tradition-ally aristocratic, speculative, intellectual in intent; technology was lower-class, empirical, action-oriented. The quite sudden fusion of these two, towards the middle of the 19th century, is surely related to the slightly prior and contemporary democratic revolutions which, by reducing social barriers, tended to assert a functional unity of brain and hand. Our ecologic crisis is the product of an emerging, entirely novel, democratic culture. The issue is whether a democratized world can survive its own implications. Presumably we cannot unless we rethink our axioms.

The Western Traditions of Technology and Science

One thing is so certain that it seems stupid to verbalize it: both modern technology and modern science are distinctively *Occidental*. Our technology has absorbed elements from all over the world, notably from China; yet everywhere today, whether in Japan or in Nigeria, successful technology is Western. Our science is the heir to all the sciences of the past, especially perhaps to the work of the great Islamic scientists of the Middle Ages, who so often outdid the ancient Greeks in skill and perspicacity: al-Rāzi in medicine, for example; or ibnal-Haytham in optics; or Omar Khay-yám in mathematics. Indeed, not a few works of such geniuses seem to have vanished in the original Arabic and to survive only in medieval Latin translations that helped to lay the foundations for later Western developments. Today, around the globe, all significant science is Western in style and method, whatever the pigmentation or language of the scientists.

A second pair of facts is less well recognized because they result from quite recent historical scholarship. The leadership of the West, both in technology and in science, is far older than the so-called Scientific Revolution of the 17th century or the so-called Industrial Revolution of the 18th century. These terms are in fact outmoded and obscure the true nature of what they try to describe—significant stages in two long and separate developments. By A.D. 1000 at the latest—and perhaps, feebly, as much as 200 years earlier—the West began to apply water power to industrial processes other than milling grain. This was followed in the late 12th century by the harnessing of wind power. From simple beginnings, but with remarkable consistency of style, the West rapidly expanded its skills in the development of power machinery, labor-saving devices, and automation. Those who doubt should contemplate that most monumental achievement in the history of automation: the weight-driven mechanical clock, which appeared in two forms in the early 14th century. Not in craftsmanship but in basic technological capacity, the Latin West of the later Middle Ages far outstripped its elaborate, sophisticated, and esthetically magnificent sister cultures, Byzantium and Islam. In 1444 a great Greek ecclesiastic, Bessarion, who had gone to Italy, wrote a letter to a prince in Greece. He is amazed by the superiority of Western ships, arms, textiles, glass. But above all he is astonished by the spectacle of water-wheels sawing timbers and pumping the bellows of blast furnaces. Clearly, he had seen nothing of the sort in the Near East.

By the end of the 15th century the technological superiority of Europe was such that its small, mutually hostile nations could spill out over all the rest of the world, conquering, looting, and colonizing. The symbol of this technological superiority is the fact that Portugal, one of the weakest states of the Occident, was able to become, and to remain for a century, mistress of the East Indies. And we must remember that the technology of Vasco da Gama and Albuquerque was built by pure empiricism, drawing remarkably little support or inspiration from science.

In the present-day vernacular understanding, modern science is supposed to have begun in 1543, when both Copernicus and Vesalius published their great works. It is no derogation of their accomplishments, however, to point out that such structures as the *Fabrica* and the *De revolutionibus* do not appear overnight. The distinctive Western tradition of science, in fact, began in the late 11th century with a massive movement of translation of Arabic and Greek scientific works into Latin. A few notable books—Theophrastus, for example—escaped the West's avid new appetite for science, but within less than 200 years effectively the entire corpus of Greek and Muslim science was available in Latin, and was being eagerly read and criticized in the new European universities. Out of criticism arose new observation, speculation, and increasing distrust of ancient authorities. By the late 13th century Europe had seized global scientific leadership from the faltering hands of Islam. It would be as absurd to deny the profound originality of Newton, Galileo, or Copernicus as to deny that of the 14th century scholastic scientists like Buridan or Oresme on whose work they built. Before the 11th century, science scarcely existed in the Latin West, even in Roman times. From the 11th century onward, the scientific sector of Occidental culture has increased in a steady crescendo.

Since both our technological and our scientific movements got their start, acquired their character, and achieved world dominance in the Middle Ages, it would seem that we cannot understand their nature or their present impact upon ecology without examining fundamental medieval assumptions and developments.

Medieval View of Man and Nature

Until recently, agriculture has been the chief occupation even in "advanced" societies; hence, any change in methods of tillage has much importance. Early plows, drawn by two oxen, did not normally turn the sod but merely scratched it. Thus, cross-plowing was needed and fields tended to be squarish. In the fairly light soils and semiarid climates of the Near East and Mediterranean, this worked well. But such a plow was inappropriate to the wet climate and often sticky soils of northern Europe. By the latter part of the 7th century after Christ, however, following obscure beginnings, certain northern peasants were using an entirely new kind of plow, equipped with a vertical knife to cut the line of the furrow, a horizontal share to slice under the sod, and a moldboard to turn it over. The friction of this plow with the soil was so great that it normally required not two but eight oxen. It attacked the land with such violence that cross-plowing was not needed, and fields tended to be shaped in long strips.

In the days of the scratch-plow, fields were distributed generally in units capable of supporting a single family. Subsistence farming was the presupposition. But no peasant owned eight oxen: to use the new and more efficient plow, peasants pooled their oxen to form large plow-teams, originally receiving (it would appear) plowed strips in proportion to their contribution. Thus, distribution of land was based no longer on the needs of a family but, rather, on the capacity of a power machine to till the earth. Man's relation to the soil was profoundly changed. Formerly man had been part of nature; now he was the exploiter of nature. Nowhere else in the world did farmers develop any analogous agricultural implement. Is it coincidence that modern technology, with its ruthlessness toward nature, has so largely been produced by descendants of these peasants of northern Europe?

This same exploitive attitude appears slightly before A.D. 830 in Western illustrated calendars. In older calendars the months were shown as passive personifications. The new Frankish calendars, which set the style for the Middle Ages, are very different: they show men coercing the world around them—plowing, harvesting, chopping trees, butchering pigs. Man and nature are two things, and man is master.

These novelties seem to be in harmony with larger intellectual patterns. What people do about their ecology depends on what they think about themselves in relation to things around them. Human ecology is deeply conditioned by beliefs about our nature and destiny—that is, by religion. To Western eyes this is very evident in, say, India or Ceylon. It is equally true of ourselves and of our medieval ancestors.

The victory of Christianity over paganism was the greatest psychic revolution in the history of our culture. It has become fashionable today to say that, for better or worse, we live in "the post-Christian age." Certainly the forms of our thinking and language have largely ceased to be Christian, but to my eye the substance often remains amazingly akin to that of the past. Our daily habits of action, for example, are dominated by an implicit faith in perpetual progress which was unknown either to Greco-Roman antiquity or to the Orient. It is rooted in, and is indefensible apart from, Judeo-Christian teleology. The fact that Communists share it merely helps to show what can be demonstrated on many other grounds: that Marxism, like Islam, is a Judeo-Christian heresy. We continue today to live, as we have lived for about 1700 years, very largely in a context of Christian axioms.

What did Christianity tell people about their relations with the environment?

While many of the world's mythologies provide stories of creation, Greco-Roman mythology was singularly incoherent in this respect. Like Aristotle, the intellectuals of the ancient West denied that the visible world had had a beginning. Indeed, the idea of a beginning was impossible in the framework of their cyclical notion of time. In sharp contrast, Christianity inherited from Judaism not only a concept of time as nonrepetitive and linear but also a striking story of creation. By gradual stages a loving and all-powerful God had created light and darkness, the heavenly bodies, the earth and all its plants, animals, birds, and fishes. Finally, God had created Adam and, as an afterthought, Eve to keep man from being lonely. Man named all the animals, thus establishing his dominance over them. God planned all of this explicitly for man's benefit and rule: no item in the physical creation had any purpose save to serve man's purposes. And, although man's body is made of clay, he is not simply part of nature: he is made in God's image.

Especially in its Western form, Christianity is the most anthropocentric religion the world has seen. As early as the 2nd century both Tertullian and Saint Irenaeus of Lyons were insisting that when God shaped Adam he was foreshadowing the image of the incarnate Christ, the Second Adam. Man shares, in great measure, God's transcendence of nature. Christianity, in absolute contrast to ancient paganism and Asia's religions (except, perhaps, Zoroastrianism), not only established a dualism of man and nature but also insisted that it is God's will that man exploit nature for his proper ends.

At the level of the common people this worked out in an interesting way. In Antiquity every tree, every spring, every stream, every hill had its own *genius loci,* its guardian spirit. These spirits were accessible to men, but were very unlike men; centaurs, fauns, and mermaids show their ambivalence. Before one cut a tree, mined a mountain, or dammed a brook, it was important to placate the spirit in charge of that particular situation, and to keep it placated. By destroying pagan animism, Christianity made it possible to exploit nature in a mood of indifference to the feelings of natural objects.

It is often said that for animism the Church substituted the cult of saints. True; but the cult of saints is functionally quite different from animism. The saint is not *in* natural objects; he may have special shrines, but his citizenship is in heaven. Moreover, a saint is entirely a man; he can be approached in human terms. In addition to saints, Christianity of course also had angels and demons inherited from Judaism and perhaps, at one remove, from Zoroastrianism. But these were all as mobile as the saints themselves. The spirits *in* natural objects, which formerly had protected nature from man, evaporated. Man's effective monopoly on spirit in this world was confirmed, and the old inhibitions to the exploitation of nature crumbled.

When one speaks in such sweeping terms, a note of caution is in order. Christianity is a complex faith, and its consequences differ in differing contexts. What I have said may well apply to the medieval West, where in fact technology made spectacular advances. But the Greek East, a highly civilized realm of equal Christian devotion, seems to have produced no marked technological innovation after the late 7th century, when Greek fire was invented. The key to the contrast may perhaps be found in a difference in the tonality of piety and thought which students of comparative theology find between the Greek and the Latin Churches. The Greeks believed that sin was intellectual blindness, and that salvation was found in illumination, orthodoxy—that is, clear thinking. The Latins, on the other hand, felt that sin was moral evil, and that salvation was to be found in right conduct. Eastern theology has been intellectualist. Western theology has been voluntarist. The Greek saint contemplates; the Western saint acts. The implications of Christianity for the conquest of nature would emerge more easily in the Western atmosphere.

The Christian dogma of creation, which is found in the first clause of all the Creeds, has another meaning for our comprehension of today's ecologic crisis. By revelation, God had given man the Bible, the Book of Scripture. But since God had made nature, nature also must reveal the divine mentality. The religious study of nature for the better understanding of God was known as natural theology. In the early Church, and always in the Greek East, nature was conceived primarily as a symbolic system through which God speaks to men: the ant is a sermon to sluggards; rising flames are the symbol of the soul's aspiration. This view of nature was essentially artistic rather than scientific. While Byzantium preserved and copied great numbers of ancient Greek scientific texts, science as we conceive it could scarcely flourish in such an ambience.

However, in the Latin West by the early 13th century natural theology was following a very different bent. It was ceasing to be the decoding of the physical symbols of God's communication with man and was becoming the effort to understand God's mind by discovering how his creation operates. The rainbow was no longer simply a symbol of hope first sent to Noah after the Deluge: Robert Grosseteste, Friar Roger Bacon, and Theodoric of Freiberg produced startlingly sophisticated work on the optics of the rainbow, but they did it as a venture in religious understanding. From the 13th century onward, up to and including Leibnitz and Newton, every major scientist, in effect, explained his motivations in religious terms. Indeed, if Galileo had not been so expert an amateur theologian he would have got into far less trouble: the professionals resented his intrusion. And Newton seems to have regarded himself more as a theologian than as a scientist. It was not until the late 18th century that the hypothesis of God became unnecessary to many scientists.

It is often hard for the historian to judge, when men explain why they are doing what they want to do, whether they are offering real reasons or merely culturally acceptable reasons. The consistency with which scientists during the long formative centuries of Western science said that the task and the reward of the scientist was "to think God's thoughts after him" leads one to believe that this was their real motivation. If so, then modern Western science was cast in a matrix of Christian theology. The dynamism of religious devotion, shaped by the Judeo-Christian dogma of creation, gave it impetus.

An Alternative Christian View

We would seem to be headed toward conclusions unpalatable to many Christians. Since both *science* and *technology* are blessed words in our contemporary vocabulary, some may be happy at the notions, first, that, viewed historically, modern science is an extrapolation of natural theology and, second, that modern technology is at least partly to be explained as an Occidental, voluntarist realization of the Christian dogma of man's transcendence of, and rightful mastery over, nature. But, as we now recognize, somewhat over a century ago science and technology—hitherto quite separate activities—joined to give mankind powers which, to judge by many of the ecologic effects, are out of control. If so, Christianity bears a huge burden of guilt.

I personally doubt that disastrous ecologic backlash can be avoided simply by applying to our problems more science and more technology. Our science and technology have grown out of Christian attitudes toward man's relation to nature which are almost universally held not only by Christians and neo-Christians but also by those who fondly regard themselves as post-Christians. Despite Copernicus, all the cosmos rotates around our little globe. Despite Darwin, we are *not*, in our hearts, part of the natural process. We are superior to nature, contemptuous of it, willing to use it for our slightest whim. The newly elected Governor of California, like myself a churchman but less troubled than I, spoke for the Christian tradition when he said (as is alleged), "when you've seen one redwood tree, you've seen them all." To a Christian a tree can be no more than a physical fact. The whole concept of the sacred grove is alien to Christianity and to the ethos of the West. For nearly 2 millennia Christian missionaries have been chopping down sacred groves, which are idolatrous because they assume spirit in nature.

What we do about ecology depends on our ideas of the man-nature relationship. More science and more technology are not going to get us out of the present ecologic crisis until we find a new religion, or rethink our old one. The beatniks, who are the basic revolutionaries of our time, show a sound instinct in their affinity for Zen Buddhism, which conceives of the man-nature relationship as very nearly the mirror image of the Christian view. Zen, however, is as deeply conditioned by Asian history as Christianity is by the experience of the West, and I am dubious of its viability among us.

Possibly we should ponder the greatest radical in Christian history since Christ: Saint Francis of Assisi. The prime miracle of Saint Francis is the fact that he did not end at the stake, as many of his left-wing followers did. He was so clearly heretical that a General of the Franciscan Order, Saint Bonaventure, a great and perceptive Christian, tried to suppress the early accounts of Franciscanism. The key to an understanding of Francis is his belief in the virtue of humility—not merely for the individual but for man as a species. Francis tried to depose man from his monarchy over creation and set up a democracy of all God's creatures. With him the ant is no longer simply a homily for the lazy, flames a sign of the thrust of the soul toward union with God; now they are Brother Ant and Sister Fire, praising the Creator in their own ways as Brother Man does in his.

Later commentators have said that Francis preached to the birds as a rebuke to men who would not listen. The records do not read so: he urged the little birds to praise God, and in spiritual ecstasy they flapped their wings and chirped rejoicing. Legends of saints, especially the Irish saints, had long told of their dealings with animals but always, I believe, to show their human dominance over creatures. With Francis it is different. The land around Gubbio in the Apennines was being ravaged by a fierce wolf. Saint Francis, says the legend, talked to the wolf and persuaded him of the error of his ways. The wolf repented, died in the odor of sanctity, and was buried in consecrated ground.

What Sir Steven Ruciman calls "the Franciscan doctrine of the animal soul" was quickly stamped out. Quite possibly it was in part inspired, consciously or unconsciously, by the belief in reincarnation held by the Cathar heretics who at that time teemed in Italy and southern France, and who presumably had got it originally from India. It is significant that at just the same moment, about 1200, traces of metempsychosis are found also in western Judaism, in the Provençal *Cabbala*. But Francis held neither to transmigration of souls nor to pantheism. His view of nature and of man rested on a unique sort of pan-psychism of all things animate and inanimate, designed for the glorification of then-transcendent Creator, who, in the ultimate gesture of cosmic humility, assumed flesh, lay helpless in a manger, and hung dying on a scaffold.

I am not suggesting that many contemporary Americans who are concerned about our ecologic crisis will be either able or willing to counsel with wolves or exhort birds. However, the present increasing disruption of the global environment is the product of a dynamic technology and science which were originating in the Western medieval world against which Saint Francis was rebelling in so original a way. Their growth cannot be understood historically apart from distinctive attitudes toward nature which are deeply grounded in Christian dogma. The fact that most people do not think of these attitudes as Christian is irrelevant. No new set of basic values has been accepted in our society to displace those of Christianity. Hence we shall continue to have a worsening ecologic crisis until we reject the Christian axiom that nature has no reason for existence save to serve man.

The greatest spiritual revolutionary in Western history, Saint Francis, proposed what he thought was an alternative Christian view of nature and man's relation to it: he tried to substitute the idea of the equality of all creatures, including man, for the idea of man's limitless rule of creation. He failed. Both our present science and our present technology are so tinctured with orthodox Christian arrogance toward nature that no solution for our ecologic crisis can be expected from them alone. Since the roots of our trouble are so largely religious, the remedy must also be essentially religious, whether we call it that or not We must rethink and refeel our nature and destiny. The profoundly religious, but heretical, sense of the primitive Franciscans for the spiritual autonomy of all parts of nature may point a direction. I propose Francis as a patron saint for ecologists.

Notes

1   The author is professor of history at the University of California, Los Angeles. This is the text of a lecture delivered 26 December 1966 at the Washington meeting of the AAAS.

Chapter 5

Arne Naess[1]

THE DEEP ECOLOGICAL MOVEMENT: SOME PHILOSOPHICAL ASPECTS

1. Deep Ecology on the Defensive

INCREASING PRESSURES FOR GROWTH have placed the vast majority of ecologists and other environmental professionals into a defensive position. Let me illustrate.

The field ecologist K, who both professionally and personally vigorously advocated deep ecological principles in the late sixties, encountered considerable resistance. Colleagues in the university said he should keep to his science and not meddle in philosophical and political matters. He should resist the temptation to become a prominent "popularizer" through exposure in the mass media. Nevertheless, he continued and influenced thousands (including myself). He became a recognized professional 'expert' in assessing the damage done when bears killed or maimed sheep or other domestic animals in Norway. According to the law, their owners are to be paid damages. Licensed hunters can get permission to shoot a bear if its misdeeds become considerable.[2] Growth pressures required consolidating the sheep industry, and sheepowners became fewer, richer, and more prone to live in towns. Due to wage increases, they could not afford to hire shepherds to watch the flock, so the sheep were left alone even more than before. And growth now required placing sheep on what were traditionally "bear territories." In spite of this invasion, bear populations grew, and troubles multiplied.

What was K's reaction? Setting limits to human encroachments on bear territory? Direct application of his deep ecology perspective? Quite the contrary. He adopted a shallow wild-life management perspective which defended the sheepowners: more money in compensation for losses, quicker compensation, and immediate hiring of hunters to reduce the bear population. Other deep ecologists noted with concern the change of his public "image;" had K really abandoned his former value priorities? Privately he insisted: No. But, in public, he was silent.

The reason for K's unexpected actions was not difficult to find: the force of economic growth was so strong that the laws protecting bears would be changed in a direction highly unfavorable to the bears if the sheepowners were not soon pacified by accepting some of their demands. And some of their demands seemed reasonable. After all, it did cost a lot of money to hire and equip rescuers to locate a flock of sheep which had been harassed by a bear and, further, to prove the bear's guilt. And the bureaucratic procedures involved were time consuming. In short, K had not changed his basic value priorities at all. Rather, he had adopted a purely defensive compromise. He stopped promoting his deep ecological philosophy publicly in order to retain credibility and standing among opponents of his principles.

And what is true of K is true of thousands more. These people often hold responsible positions in society, where they might strengthen responsible environmental policy, but, given the exponential forces of growth, their publications are limited to narrowly professional and specialized concerns. Their writings are surely competent, but lack a deeper and more comprehensive perspective (although I admit that there are some brilliant exceptions). If professional ecologists persist in voicing their value priorities, their jobs are often in peril, or they tend to lose influence and status among those who are in charge of general policies. Privately, they may admit the necessity for deep and far-reaching changes, but they remain silent in public. As a result, their positive impact on the public has largely vanished. Deeply concerned people feel abandoned by the 'experts'.

In ecological debate many participants know a lot about particular conservation policies in particular places, and many others have strong opinions regarding fundamental philosophical questions of environmental ethics, but only a few have both qualities. When they are silent, the loss is formidable.

Let me illustrate again. A family of four decides to acquire four chairs for a small room, newly added to the home. They buy the chairs and all have peace of mind. But then one of them gets an urge to put ten more chairs into the room. Two of the family who are technically talented and eager to satisfy any "need," use their time to solve the sophisticated physical and mathematical problems involved. They ask the fourth member to work overtime to get the money to purchase the ten chairs. But she answers that the chairs are unnecessary for a life rich in intrinsic values and simple in means. She begins to argue for her view, but the two technocrats insist that first she should work through all the alternative solutions to the 10-Chair problem. At last she wonderfully simplifies the argument. If the ten chairs are not a desired end, it is pointless to discuss the means by which this might be achieved. The technically talented find other outlets for their surplus energy, for there are always enough legitimate problems to work on.

The complicated question of how industrial societies can increase energy production with the least undesirable consequences is of the same kind: a waste of time if the increase is pointless in relation to ultimate ends. When thousands of experts hired by government and other big institutions devote their time to this complicated problem, it is difficult for the public to learn that many of them judge the problem pointless and irrelevant. What is relevant, according to them, are the problems of how to stabilize and eventually decrease consumption without loss of life quality.

2. A Call to Speak Out

What I advocate and argue for is this: even those who completely subsume ecological policies under the narrow ends of human health and well-being cannot attain their more modest aims, at least not fully and easily, without being joined by supporters of deep ecology. They need what these people have to contribute, as this will work for them more often than it works against them. Those in charge of environmental policies, even if they are resource-oriented (and growth tolerating?) decision makers, will increasingly welcome if only for tactical and not fundamental reasons, what deep ecologists have to say. Even though the more radical ethic may seem nonsensical or untenable to them, they know that its advocates are doing in practice conservation work that sooner or later must be done. They concur with the practice, although they operate from diverging theories. If I am right, the time is ripe for professional deep ecologists to break their silence and freely express their deepest concerns. A bolder advocacy of deep ecology by those who are working within the shallow, resource-oriented 'environmental' sphere is the best strategy for regaining some of the strength of this movement among the general public, and thereby to contribute, however modestly, toward a turning of the tide.

What do I mean by saying that even the more modest aims of shallow environmentalism have a need for deep ecology? We can see this by considering the World Conservation Strategy prepared by the International Union for Conservation of Nature and Natural Resources (IUCN) with the advice, cooperation and financial assistance of the United Nations Environmental Programme (UNEP) and the World Wildlife Fund (WWF). The argument in this important publication is through and through homocentric in the sense that all its recommendations are justified in terms of their effects upon human health and well-being. Even the recomended environmental ethic, with its attendant environmental education campaign, has humans in harmony with nature for human good. "A new ethic, embracing plants and animals as well as people, is required for human societies to live in harmony with the natural world on which they depend for survival and well-being."[3] Such an ethic would surely be more effective if it were acted upon by people who believe in its validity, rather than by those who merely believe in its usefulness. This, I think, will come to be understood more and more by those in charge of educational policies. Quite simply, it is indecent for a teacher to proclaim an ethic only for tactical reasons. Further, this point applies to all aspects of world conservation strategy. Conservation strategy will be more eagerly implemented by persons who love what they are conserving, and who are convinced that what they love is intrinsically lovable. Such lovers will not want to hide their attitudes and values, but rather will increasingly give voice to them in public. They have a genuine ethics of conservation, not merely a tactically useful instrument for social and political ends.

In short, environmental education campaigns can fortunately combine anthropocentric arguments with a practical land and sea ethic based either on a deeper and more fundamental naturalistic philosophical or religious perspective, and on a set of norms resting on intrinsic values. But the inherent strength of this overall position will be lost if those who work professionally on environmental problems do not give public testimony to these fundamental norms.

This article is hortatory, in the positive etymological sense of that word. I seek "to urge, incite, instigate, encourage, cheer" (Latin: hortari). This may seem unacademic in a philosophical journal, but I consider it justifiable because of an intimate relationship between hortatory sentences and basic philosophical views which I will formulate in Section 8 below.

3. What is Deep Ecology?

The term 'deep ecological movement' has so far been used without trying to define it. One should not expect much from definitions of movements. Think of terms like 'conservatism,' 'liberalism,' or 'feminist movement.' And there is no need that supporters should adhere to exactly the same definition. In what follows, a set of principles, or key terms and phrases, agreed upon by George Sessions and myself, are tentatively proposed as basic to deep ecology.[4]

(1)   The well-being and flourishing of human and non-human Life on Earth have value in themselves (synonyms: intrinsic value, inherent value). These values are independent of the usefulness of the non-human world for human purposes.

(2)   Richness and diversity of life forms contribute to the realization of these values and are also values in themselves.

(3)   Humans have no right to reduce this richness and diversity except to satisfy vital needs.

(4)   The flourishing of human life and cultures is compatible with a substantial decrease of the human population. The flourishing of non-human life requires such a decrease.

(5)   Present human interference with the non-human world is excessive, and the situation is rapidly worsening.

(6)   Policies must therefore be changed. These policies affect basic economic, technological, and ideological structures. The resulting state of affairs will be deeply different from the present.

(7)   The ideological change is mainly that of appreciating life quality (dwelling in situations of inherent value) rather than adhering to an increasingly higher standard of living. There will be a profound awareness of the difference between big and great.

(8)   Those who subscribe to the foregoing points have an obligation directly or indirectly to try to implement the necessary changes.

Comments on the Basic Principles:

Re (1):

This formulation refers to the biosphere, or more accurately to the ecosphere as a whole. This includes individuals, species, populations, habitat, as well as human and nonhuman cultures. From our current knowledge of all-pervasive intimate relationships, this implies a fundamental deep concern and respect. Ecological processes on the planet should, on the whole, remain intact. "The world environment should remain 'natural'" (Gary Snyder).

The term "life" is used here in a more comprehensive non-technical way to refer also to what biologists classify as "non-living": rivers (watersheds), landscapes, ecosystems. For supporters of deep ecology, slogans such as "let the river live" illustrate this broader usage so common in most cultures.

Inherent value, as used in (1), is common in deep ecology literature ("The presence of inherent value in a natural object is independent of any awareness, interest, or appreciation of it by any conscious being.")[5]

Re (2):

More technically, this is a formulation concerning diversity and complexity. From an ecological standpoint, complexity and symbiosis are conditions for maximizing diversity. So-called simple, lower, or primitive species of plants and animals contribute essentially to richness and diversity of life. They have value in themselves and are not merely steps toward the so-called higher or rational life forms. The second principle presupposes that life itself, as a process over evolutionary time, implies an increase of diversity and richness. The refusal to acknowledge that some life forms have greater or lesser intrinsic value than others (see points 1 and 2) runs counter to the formulations of some ecological philosophers and New Age writers.

Complexity, as referred to here, is different from complication. Urban life may be more complicated than life in a natural setting without being more complex in the sense of multifaceted quality.

Re (3):

The term "vital need" is left deliberately vague to allow for considerable latitude in judgment. Differences in climate and related factors, together with differences in the structures of societies as they now exist, need to be considered. (For some Eskimos, snowmobiles are necessary today to satisfy vital needs, not to tourists).

Re (4):

People in the materially richest countries cannot be expected to reduce their excessive interference with the non-human world to a moderate level overnight. The stabilization and reduction of the human population will take time. Interim strategies need to be developed. But this in no way excuses the present complacency. The extreme seriousness of our current situation must first be realized. But the longer we wait the more drastic will be the measures needed. Until deep changes are made, substantial decreases in richness and diversity are liable to occur: the rate of extinction of species will be ten to one hundred times greater than any other period of earth history.

Re (5):

This formulation is mild. For a realistic assessment of the situation, see the unabbreviated version of the I.U.C.N.'s World Conservation Strategy. There are other works to be highly recommended, such as Gerald Barney's *Global 2000 Report to the President of the United States*.

The slogan of "noninterference" does not imply that humans should not modify some ecosystems as do other species. Humans have modified the earth and will probably continue to do so. At issue is the nature and extent of such interference.

The fight to preserve and extend areas of wilderness or near-wilderness should continue and should focus on the general ecological functions of these areas (one such function: large wilderness areas are required in the biosphere to allow for continued evolutionary speciation of animals and plants). Most present designated wilderness areas and game preserves are not large enough to allow for such speciation.

Re (6):

Economic growth as conceived and implemented today by the industrial states is incompatible with (1) – (5). There is only a faint resemblance between ideal sustainable forms of economic growth and present policies of the industrial societies. And "sustainable" still means "sustainable in relation to humans."

Present ideology tends to value things because they are scarce and because they have a commodity value. There is prestige in vast consumption and waste (to mention only several relevant factors).

Whereas "self-determination," "local community," and "think globally, act locally," will remain key terms in the ecology of human societies, nevertheless the implementation of deep changes requires increasingly global action, action across borders.

Governments in Third World countries are mostly uninterested in deep ecological issues. When the governments of industrial societies try to promote ecological measures through Third World governments, then practically nothing is accomplished (e.g., with problems of desertification). Given this situation, support for global action through non-governmental international organizations becomes increasingly important. Many of these organizations are able to act globally "from grassroots to grassroots" thus avoiding negative governmental interference.

Cultural diversity today requires advanced technology, that is, techniques that advance the basic goals of each culture. So-called soft, intermediate, and alternative technologies are steps in this direction.

Re (7):

Some economists criticize the term 'quality of life' because it is supposed to be vague. But on closer inspection, what they consider to be vague is actually the non-quantitative nature of the term. One cannot quantify adequately what is important for the quality of life as discussed here, and there is no need to do so.

Re (8):

There is ample room for different opinions about priorities: what should be done first, what next? What is most urgent? What is clearly necessary as opposed to what is highly desirable but not absolutely pressing?

The above formulations may be useful for many supporters of the deep ecology movement. But others will certainly feel they are imperfect, even misleading. If they need to formulate in a few words what is basic in deep ecology, they will propose an alternative set of sentences. I shall of course be glad to refer to them as alternatives. There ought to be a measure of diversity in what is considered basic and common.

Should we call the movement 'the deep ecological movement'?[6] There are at least six other designations which cover most of the same issues: "Ecological Resistance", used by John Rodman in important discussions; "The New Natural Philosophy" coined by Joseph Meeker; "Eco-philosophy," used by Sigmund Kvaloy and others to emphasize (1) a highly critical assessment of industrial growth societies from a general ecological point of view and (2) the ecology of the human species; "Green Philosophy and Politics," while the term "green" is often used in Europe, in the United States "green" has a misleading association with the rather "blue" Green Revolution; "Sustainable Earth Ethics," as used by G. Tyler Miller; and "Ecosophy", eco-wisdom, which is my own favorite term. Others could also be mentioned.

Why use the adjective "deep"? This question will be easier to answer after the contrast is made between shallow and deep ecological concerns.

What I am talking about is not a philosophy in any academic sense, nor is it institutionalized as a religion or an ideology. Various persons come together in campaigns and direct actions. They form a circle of friends supporting the same kind of lifestyle, which others term "simple," but they themselves think is rich and many sided. They agree on a vast array of political issues, although they may otherwise support different political parties. As in all social movements, slogans and rhetoric are indispensible for ingroup coherence. They react together against the same threats in a predominately nonviolent way. Perhaps the most influential participants are artists and writers who do not articulate their insights in terms of professional philosophy, but do express themselves in art or poetry. For these reasons, I use the term 'movement' rather than 'philosophy.'

4. Deep versus Shallow Ecology

A number of key terms and slogans from the environmental debate will clarify the contrast between the shallow and deep ecology movements.

A. *Pollution*

Shallow approach: Technology seeks to purify the air and water and to spread pollution more evenly. Laws limit permissible pollution. Polluting industries are preferably exported to developing countries.

Deep approach: Pollution is evaluated from a biospheric point of view,[7] not centering on its effects on human health, but on life as a whole, including life conditions of every species and system. The shallow reaction to acid rain is to avoid action by demands of more research, demands to find species of trees tolerating high acidity etc., whereas the deep approach concentrates on what is going on in the total ecosystem and asks for high priority fight against the economy and technology responsible for acid rain.

The priority is to fight deep causes of pollution, not merely the superficial, short range effects. The third and fourth worlds cannot afford to pay the total cost of the war against pollution in their regions, and consequently they require the assistance of the first and second worlds. Exporting pollution is not only a crime against humanity, but also against life.

B. *Resources*

Shallow approach: The emphasis is upon resources for humans, especially for the present generation in affluent societies. On this view, the resources of the earth belong to those who have the technology to exploit them. There is confidence that resources will not be depleted because, as they get rarer, a high market price will conserve them, and substitutes will be found through technological progress. Further, animals, plants, and natural objects are valuable only as resources for humans. If no human use is known, they can be destroyed with indifference.

Deep approach: The concern here is with resources and habitat for all life forms for their own sake. No natural object is conceived of solely as a resource. This then leads to a critical evaluation of human modes of production and consumption. It is asked: to what extent does an increase here favor ultimate values in human life? To what extent does it satisfy vital needs, locally and globally? How can economic, legal, and educational institutions be changed to counteract destructive increases? How can resource use serve the quality of life rather than the economic standard of living as generally promoted in consumerism? There is an emphasis here on an ecosystem approach rather than just the consideration of isolated life forms or local situations. There is a long-range maximal perspective of time and place.

C. *Population*

Shallow approach: The threat of (human) overpopulation is seen mainly as a problem for developing countries. One condones or even cheers population increases in one's own country for shortsighted economic, military, or other reasons; an increase in the number of humans is considered a value in itself or as economically profitable. The issue of "optimum population for humans" is discussed without reference to the question of the "optimum population" of other life forms. The destruction of wild habitats caused by an increasing human population is accepted as an inevitable evil. Drastic decreases of wild life forms tend to be accepted as long as species are not driven to extinction. Animal social relations are ignored. The long term substantial reduction of the global human population is not seen as a desired goal. One has a right to defend one's own borders against "illegal aliens," no matter what the population pressures elsewhere.

Deep approach: It is recognized that excessive pressures on planetary life conditions stem from the human population explosion. The pressure stemming from industrial societies is a major factor, and population reduction must have a high priority in those societies, as well as in developing countries. Estimates of an optimal human population vary. Some quantitative estimates are 100 million, 500 million, and 1000 million, but it is recognized that there must be a long range, humane reduction through mild but tenacious political and economic measures. This will make possible, as a result of increased habitat, population growth for thousands of species which are now constrained by human pressures.

D. Cultural diversity and appropriate technology

Shallow approach: Industrialization of the kind manifested in the West is held to be the goal for developing countries. The universal adoption of Western technology is compatible with mild cultural diversity and the conservation of good (from the Western point of view) elements in present nonindustrial societies. There is a low estimate of deep cultural differences which deviate significantly from Western standards.

Deep approach: Cultural diversity is an analogue on the human level to the biological richness and diversity of life forms. We should give high priority to cultural anthropology in education in industrial societies. We should limit the impact of Western technology upon presently existing nonindustrial countries and defend the fourth world against foreign domination. Political and economic policies should favor subcultures within industrialized societies. Local, soft technologies will allow a basic cultural assessment of any technical innovations, freely criticizing socalled advanced technology and concepts of "progress."

E. Land and sea ethics

Shallow approach: Landscapes, ecosystems, rivers, and other wholes of nature are cut into fragments, disregarding larger units and gestalts. These fragments are regarded as the properties and resources of individuals, organizations, or states. Conservation is argued in terms of "multiple use" and "cost/benefit analysis." Social costs and long term ecological costs are not included. Wildlife management conserves nature for "future generations of humans." The erosion of soils or of ground water quality is noted as a human loss, but a strong belief in future technological progress makes deep changes seem unnecessary.

Deep approach: Earth does not belong to humans. The Norwegian landscapes, rivers, fauna and flora, and the surrounding sea are not the property of Norwegians. Humans only inhabit the lands, using resources to satisfy vital needs. If their nonvital needs conflict with the vital needs of nonhumans, humans might yield. The destruction now going on will not be cured by a technological fix. Current arrogant notions in industrial (and other) societies must be resisted.

F. Education and scientific enterprise

Shallow approach: The degradation of the environment and resource depletion necessitates the further training of experts who can advise on how to combine economic growth with maintaining a healthy environment We are likely to need highly manipulative technology when global economic growth makes further degradation inevitable. The scientific enterprise must continue giving priority to the "hard" sciences. This necessitates high educational standards with intense competition in relevant "tough" areas of learning.

Deep approach: Education should concentrate on increased sensitivity to nonconsumptive goods and on such consumables as we have enough of for all, provided sane ecological policies are adopted. Education will therefore counteract the excessive valuation of things with a price tag. There should be a shift from concentration upon "hard" to "soft" sciences, stressing local and the global culture. The eductional objective of the World Conservation Strategy, "building support for conservation," should be accorded priority within the deeper framework of respect for the biosphere.

In the future, there will be no shallow movement, if shallow policies are increasingly adopted by governments and, thus, need no support by a special social movement.

5. But why a "Deep" Ecology?

The decisive difference concerns willingness to question and to appreciate the importance of questioning every economic and political policy in public. The questioning is "deep" and public. It asks "why" more insistently and consistently, taking nothing for granted. Deep ecology can readily admit the practical effectiveness of homocentric arguments. "It is essential for conservation to be seen as central to human interests and aspirations. At the same time, people-from heads of state to the members of rural communities-will most readily be brought to demand conservation if they themselves recognize the contribution of conservation to the achievement of their needs, as perceived by them, and the solution of their problems, as perceived by them."[8] Since most policies serving the biosphere also serve humanity in the long run, they may, at least initially, be accepted on the basis of narrow "homocentric" arguments.

But such a tactical approach has significant limitations. There are three dangers: some policies based on successful homocentric arguments turn out to violate or compromise unduly the objectives of deeper argumentation; the strong motivation to fight for decisive change and the willingness to serve a great cause is weakened; and the complicated arguments in human-centered conservation documents such as the World Conservation Strategy go beyond the time and ability of many people to assimilate and understand and also tend to provoke interminable technical disagreements among experts. Special interest groups with narrow short-term exploitative objectives which run counter to saner ecopolicies often exploit these disagreements and thereby stall the debate and steps toward effective action. When arguing from deep ecological premises, most of the complicated proposed technological fixes need not be discussed at all. The relative merits of alternative technology proposals in industrial societies concerned with how to increase energy production are pointless if our vital needs have already been met. The focus on vital issues activates mental energy and strengthens motivation. The shallow environmental approach, on the other hand, tends to make the human population more passive and disinterested in environmental issues.

The deep ecological movement tries to clarify the fundamental presuppositions underlying our economic approach in terms of value priorities, philosophy, and religion. In the shallow movement, argument comes to a halt long before this. The deep ecology movement is therefore "the ecology movement which questions deeper."

The terms 'egalitarianism,' 'homocentrism,' 'anthropocentrism,' and 'human chauvinism' are often used to characterize points of view on the shallow-deep ecology spectrum. But these terms usually function as slogans which are open to misinterpretation. They can imply that man is in some respects only a "plain citizen" (Aldo Leopold) of the planet on a par with all other species, but they are sometimes interpreted as denying that humans have any "extraordinary" traits, or that in situations involving vital interests, humans have no overriding obligations towards their own kind. They have!

In any social movement, rhetoric has an essential function in keeping members fighting together under the same banner. Rhetorical formulations also serve to provoke interest among the outsiders. Of the better known slogans, one might mention "Nature knows best," "Small is beautiful," and "All things hang together." But clearly all things in the universe do not hang together at the levels of quantum physics or relativity theory. The slogan only expresses a doctrine of global, not cosmic, relevance.

Only a minority of deep ecologists are academic philosophers, such as myself. While deep ecology need not be a finished philosophical system, this does not mean that its philosophers should not try to be as clear as possible. So a discussion of deep ecology as a derivational system may be of value.

6. Deep Ecology illustrated as a Derivational System

Underlying the eight tenets or principles presented in section three, there are still more basic positions and norms which reside in philosophical systems and various world religions. Schematically we may represent the total views implied in the movement by streams of derivation from the most fundamental norms and descriptive assumptions to particular decisions in actual life situations.

This pyramidal model has some features in common with hypothetico-deductive systems. The main difference, however, is that some sentences at the top (= deepest) level are normative, and are preferably expressed by imperatives. This makes it possible to arrive at imperatives at the lowest derivational level, the crucial level in terms of decisions. Thus, there are oughts in our premises, as well as in our conclusions. We do not move from an is to an ought.

Just as in a hypothetico-deductive system in physics, where only the two upper levels of the pyramid are thought of as forming physics as a system, so also in normative systems, only the upper levels are considered to be part of the total system. The sentences in the lowest part are changing from day to day as life situations change.

The above derivational structure of a total view must not be taken too seriously. It is not meant in any restrictive way to characterize creative thinking within the deep ecological movement. That thinking moves freely in any direction. But some of us with a professional background in science and analytical philosophy find it helpful.[9]

Answers to ultimate questions, i.e., the highest normative principles and basic assumptions about the world, occur in the upper part of the derivational pyramid. The first three basic principles of deep ecology (see section 3 above) belong to the upper level of the pyramid because they assert, in a general way, life in its diversity as a value in itself, thus forming a norm against undue human interference. The next four (4–7) tenets belong to the middle region because they are more local, they view what is going on at the present. This involves factual claims and projections about the consequences of present policies in industrial and nonindustrial countries. An application of the last tenet (8) is at the lowest derivational level because it imposes an obligation to take part in actions to change policies. Such an obligation must be derivable from principles higher up in the pyramid.

There are few propositions at the top of the pyramid, a great variety at the middle level, and innumerable recommendations at the bottom.

7. Multiple Roots of the Deep Ecology Principles

The deep ecological movement seriously questions the presuppositions of shallow argumentation. Even what counts as a rational decision is challenged, because "rational" is always defined in relation to specific aims and goals. If a decision is rational in relation to the lower level aims and goals of our pyramid but not in relation to the highest level, then the decision should not be judged to be rational. If an environmentally oriented policy decision is not linked to intrinsic values, its rationality is yet undetermined. The deep movement connects rationality with a set of philosophical and religious foundations. One cannot expect the ultimate premises to constitute rational conclusions. There are no "deeper" premises available.

The deep ecological questioning reveals the fundamental normative orientations. Shallow argumentation stops before reaching fundamentals or jumps from the ultimate to the particular, that is, from level 1 to level 4.

It is not only normative claims that are at stake. Most (perhaps all) norms presuppose ideas about how the world functions. Typically the vast majority of propositions needed in normative systems are descriptive. This holds of all levels.

Notice, however, that it does not follow that supporters of deep ecology must have, on ultimate issues, identical beliefs. They do have common attitudes about intrinsic values in nature, but these can, in turn (at a still deeper level), be derived from different, mutually incompatible sets of ultimate beliefs.

Thus, while a specific decision may be judged as rational from within the derivational system (if there is such) of shallow ecology, it might be judged irrational from within the derivational system of deep ecology. What is rational within the deep ecology derivational pyramid does not require unanimity in ontology and fundamental ethics. Deep ecology as a conviction, with its subsequently derived practical recommendations, can follow from several more comprehensive worldviews.

Those engaged in the deep movement have so far revealed their philosophical or religious homes mainly to be in Christianity, Buddhism, Taoism, or philosophy. The top level of the derivational pyramid can therefore be made up of normative and descriptive principles which belong to forms of Christianity, Buddhism, Taoism, and various philosophical creeds.

Since the late seventies, numerous Christians in Europe and America, some of them teachers of theology, have taken part actively in the deep ecological movement. Their interpretations of the Bible and their theological positions in general have been reformed from what was, until recently, a dominating crudely anthropocentric emphasis within Christianity.

There is an intimate relation between some forms of Buddhism and the deep ecological movement. The history of Buddhist thought and practice, especially the principles of non-violence, non-injury and reverence for life, sometimes makes it easier for Buddhists to understand and appreciate that movement than it is for Christians, despite a (sometimes overlooked) blessedness which Jesus recommended in peace-making. I mention taoism chiefly because there is some basis for calling John Muir a Taoist.[10]

Ecosophies are not religions in the classical sense, but are general philosophies inspired by ecology. In the next section I will further introduce Ecosophy T.

The adherents of different religions and philosophies disagree and may not even ulti-mately understand each other at the foundational levels of conviction and experience. But they can have important derived views in common, and these, though themselves derived, are nevertheless deep enough to form what I wish to call the upper level of the deep ecology derivational pyramid.

Some have worried that the mixture of religion and environmentalism could prove a source of dogmatism, intolerance, and "mysticism" (in the sense of obscurantism). So far, there is no evidence that this is happening. Nature mysticism has little to do with obscu-rantism.[11]

8. Ecosophy T

The main theoretical complaint against shallow ecology is not that it is based on a well-articulated but incorrect philosophical or religious foundation. It is, rather, that there is a lack of depth-or complete absence-of guiding philosophical or religious foundations.

In his excellent book on how to "live in the environment," G. Tyler Miller writes:

> The American attitude (and presumably that of most industrialized nations) toward nature can be expressed as eight basic beliefs [four of which are repro-duced here].

> 1.   Humans are the source of all value.
> 2.   Nature exists only for our use.
> 3.   Our primary purpose is to produce and consume. Success is based on material wealth.
> 4.   Production and consumption must rise endlessly because we have a right to an ever increasing material level of living.

But he adds an important reservation:

> Although most of us probably would not accept all of these statements, we act individually, corporately, and governmentally as if we did-and this is what counts.[12]

When they are so baldly exposed, we might find that very few persons would actually subscribe to what Miller characterizes as "the American attitude." Nevertheless, as Miller notices, most modern people (and not only Americans!) behave as if they believed such a creed. There is no articulated philosophical or religious view from which "the American attitude" is carefully justified.

[T]he shallow movement has not offered examples of total views comprising the four levels. I am tempted to say that there will be no examples. Serious attempts to find a deep justification of the way life on the planet is treated today (including the threats of using nuclear "weapons") are doomed to failure. What I say is meant as a challenge: is there a philosopher somewhere who would like to try?

My main purpose in announcing that I feel at home in "Ecosophy T" is didactic and dialectic. I hope to get others to announce their philosophy. If they say they have none, I maintain that they have, but perhaps don't know their own views, or are too modest or inhib-ited to proclaim what they believe. Following Socrates I want to provoke questioning until others know where they stand on basic matters of life and death. This is done using ecological issues, and also by using Ecosophy ? as a foil. But Socrates pretended in debate that he knew nothing. My posture seems to be the opposite. I may seem to know everything and to derive it magically from a small set of hypotheses about the world. But both interpretations are misleading! Socrates did not consistently claim to know nothing, nor do I in my Ecosophy ? pretend to have all that comprehensive a knowledge. He claimed to know, for instance, about the fallibility of humans claims to know.

So, here is Ecosophy T!

Its fundamental norm is 'Self-realization!' But I do not use this expression in any narrow, individualistic sense. I want to give it an expanded meaning based on the distinction between Self and self conceived in certain Eastern traditions of âtman, comprising all the life forms, and selves (jivas) as usually interpreted in social and personal life. Using five words: maximum (long range, universal) Self realization![13] If I had to give up the term fearing its inevitable misunderstanding, I would use the term 'symbiosis'. "Maximize Self-realization!" could be interpreted in the direction of colossal egotrips. But "Maximize symbiosis!" could be interpreted in the opposite direction, that of the elimination of individuality in favor of collectivity.

Viewed systematically, not individually, maximum Self-realization implies maximizing the manifestations of life. So I next derive the second term, "Maximize (long range, universal) diversity!" A corollary is that the higher the levels of Self-realization which are attained by a person, the more any further increase depends upon the Self-realization of others. Increased self-identification is increased identification with others. "Altruism" is a natural consequence of this identification.

This leads to an hypothesis about an inescapable increase of identification with other beings when one's own self-realization increases. We increasingly see ourselves in others, and others in ourselves. The self is extended and deepened as a natural process of the realization of its potentialities in others.

Universalizing, we can derive the norm, "Self-realization for every being!" From "Diversity!" and a hypothesis that maximum diversity implies a maximum of symbiosis, is derived the norm "Maximum symbiosis!" Further, we work for life conditions such that there is a minimum of coercion in the life of others. And so on![14]

A philosophy as a world view inevitably has implications in practical situations. Ecosophy T therefore without apology moves on to concrete questions of life style. These will obviously show great variation because of differences in hypotheses about the world in which each of us living, and in the 'factual' statements about the concrete situation in which we make a decision. I shall limit myself to a couple of areas where my "style" of thinking and behaving seem somewhat strange to friends and others who know a little about my philosophy. Firstly, a somewhat extreme appreciation of diversity; positive appreciation of the existence of styles and behaviors which I personally detest or find nonsensical (but not clearly incompatible with symbiosis); enthusiasm for "the mere" diversity of species or varieties within a genus of plants or animals; support, as the head of a department of philosophy, of doctrinal theses completely at odds with my own inclinations, with only the requirement that the authors are able to understand fairly adequately some basic features of the kind of philosophy I myself feel at home with; combination of seemingly incompatible interests and behaviors, which makes for an increase of subcultures within industial states and might to some extent help future cultural diversity. So much about "diversity!"

Secondly, I have a somewhat extreme appreciation of what Kant calls beautiful actions (good actions based on inclination), in contrast to dutiful ones. The choice of the formulation 'Self-realization!' is in part motivated by the belief that maturity in humans can be measured along a scale from selfishness to Selfishness, that is, broadening and deepening the self, rather than measures of dutiful altruism. I see joyful sharing and caring as a natural process (which, I regret, is somewhat retarded in myself).

Thirdly, I believe that many-sided, high level Self-realization is more easily reached through a "spartan" life-style than through the material standard of average citizens of industrial states.

The simple formulations of the deep ecology platform and Ecosophy T are not meant primarily to be used among philosophers, but in dialogues with "the experts." When I wrote to them personally, asking whether they accept the 8 points of the platform, many answered positively in relation to most or all points. And this includes top people in ministries of oil and energy! But it is still an open question to what extent they are willing to let their written answers be widely published. It is also an open question to what extent they try to influence their colleagues who use only shallow argumentation. The main conclusion is moderately encouraging: there is a philosophy of the man/nature relationship widely accepted among established experts responsible for environmental decisions which requires a pervasive, substantial change of present policies-in favor of our "living" planet, and not only for short-sighted human interests.

Notes

1   The MS has been edited by Professor George Sessions in 1984.
2   For more about interspecific community relationships, see Arne Naess, "Self-realization in Mixed Communities of Humans, Bears, Sheep, and Wolves," *Inquiry* 22 (1979): 321–41.
3   Quotation from Section 13, "building support for conservation."
4   I cannot here do justice to the many authors who have contributed to the understanding of the emerging deep ecology movement. Only two will be mentioned. The newsletters written by George Sessions, Dept. of Philosophy, Sierra College, Rocklin, CA, are indispensable. There are six letters, April 76, May 79, April 81, May 82, May 83, May 84, about 140 pages in all. The significant contributions by poets and artists are fully recognized. Most of the materials are summarized by Sessions in "Shallow and Deep Ecology: A Review of the Philosophical Literature," in an excellent collection of articles, *Ecological Consciousness*, eds. R.C. Schultz and J.D. Hughes (Washington: University Press of America, 1981). Bill Devall provides a short survey, in part historical, in his potent article, "The Deep Ecology Movement," *Natural Resources Journal* 20 (1980). See also Devall and Sessions, *Deep Ecology: Living As If Nature Mattered* (Layton, Utah: Peregrine Smith Press, 1984).
5   Tom Regan, "The Nature and Possibility of an Environmental Ethics," *Environmental Ethics* 3 (1981): 19–34, citation on p. 30.
6   I proposed the name 'Deep, Long-Range Ecology Movement' in a lecture at the 3rd World Future Research conference, Bucharest, September 1972. A summary of that lecture: "The Shallow and the Deep, Long-Range Ecology Movement" was published in *Inquiry* 16 (1973): 95–100. Within the deep ecology movement it is fairly common to use the term 'deep ecologist', whereas 'shallow ecologist', I am glad to say, is rather uncommon. Both terms may be considered arrogant and slightly misleading. I prefer to use the awkward, but more egalitarian expression 'supporter of the deep (or shallow) ecology movement', avoiding personification. Also, it is common to call deep ecology consistently anti-anthropocentric. This has led to misconceptions, see my "A Defence of the Deep Ecology Movement," *Environmeatal Ethics* 5 (1983).
7   The technical term 'biospheric' should perhaps be avoided because it favors the scientifically fruitful distinction between biosphere and ecosphere. I use the term 'life' in a broad sense common in everyday speech, and may therefore speak of landscapes and larger systems of the ecosphere as "living"—ultimately speaking of the life of the planet. The biospheric point of view referred to in the text is not a narrower point of view than the ecospheric because bios is used in a broad sense.
8   *World Conservation Strategy*, section 13, concluding paragraph.
9   Many authors take some steps towards derivational structures, offering mild systematizations. The chapter on "environmental ethics and hope" in G. Tyler Miller, *Living in the Environment*, 3rd ed. (Belmont: Wadsworth, 1983) is a valuable start, but the derivational relations are unclear. The logic and semantics of simple models of normative systems is briefly discussed in my "Notes on the Methodology of Normative Systems," *Methodology and Science* 10 (1977): 64–79. For defense of the thesis that as soon as persons assert anything at all we assume a total view, implicit with ontology, methodology, epistemology and ethics, see my "Reflections about Total Views," *Philosophy and*

Phenomenological Research 25 (1964–65): 16–29. The best and wittiest warning against taking system-atizations too seriously is to be found in Soren Kierkegaard, *Concluding Unscientific Postscript.*

10   Trusting Bill Devall, one may say that "Muir is now understood as the first Taoist of American ecology." Devall, "John Muir as. Deep Ecologist," *Environmental Review* 6 (1982); see also Michael Cohen, *The Pathless Way: John Muir and American Wilderness,* (Madison: Univ. of Wisconsin Press, 1984).

11   For empirical studies of attitudes of "Wilderness-users," see the survey by Chris. R. Kent (16438 Clymer St., Granada Hills, CA 91344) in his thesis "The Experiential Process of Nature Mysticism . . .," Humboldt State Univ., 1981.

12   *Living in the Environment,* 489.

13   The term *âtman* is not taken in its absolutistic senses, not as a permanent indestructible "soul." This makes it consistent with those Buddhist denials (the *avâtman* doctrine) that the *âtman* is to be taken in absolutist senses. Within the Christian tradition some theologians distinguish "ego" and "true self" in ways similar to these distinctions in Eastern religion. See the ecophilosophical interpretation of the gospel of Luke in Stephen Verney's *Onto the New Age,* (Glasgow: Collins 1976) 33–41.

14   For criticism and defence of this fundamental norm, and my answer, see *In Sceptical Wonder, Essays in Honor of Arne Naess,* (Oslo: University Press, 1982). My main exposition of Ecosophy T was originally offered in the Norwegian work *Okologi, samfunn og livsstil,* (Oslo: University Press, 5th ed, 1976). Even there, the exposition is sketchy.

Chapter 6

Paul Shepard

ECOLOGY AND MAN: A VIEWPOINT

Ecology is sometimes characterized as the study of a natural "web of life." It would follow that man is somewhere in the web or that he in fact manipulates its strands, exemplifying what Thomas Huxley called "man's place in nature." But the image of a web is too meager and simple for the reality. A web is flat and finished and has the mortal frailty of the individual spider. Although elastic, it has insufficient depth. However solid to the touch of the spider, for us it fails to denote the *eikos*—the habitation—and to suggest the enduring integration of the primitive Greek domicile with its sacred hearth, bonding the earth to all aspects of society.

Ecology deals with organisms in an environment and with the processes that link organism and place. But ecology as such cannot be studied, only organisms, earth, air, and sea can be studied. It is not a discipline: there is no body of thought and technique which frames an ecology of man.[1] It must be therefore a scope or a way of seeing. Such a *perspective* on the human situation is very old and has been part of philosophy and art for thousands of years. It badly needs attention and revival.

Man is in the world and his ecology is the nature of that *inness*. He is in the world as in a room, and in transience, as in the belly of a tiger or in love. What does he do there in nature? What does nature do there *in him*? What is the nature of the transaction? Biology tells us that the transaction is always circular, always a mutual feedback. Human ecology cannot be limited strictly to biological concepts, but it cannot ignore them. It cannot even transcend them. It emerges from biological reality and grows from the fact of interconnection as a general principle of life. It must take a long view of human life and nature as they form a mesh or pattern going beyond historical time and beyond the conceptual bounds of other humane studies. As a natural history of what it means to be human, ecology might proceed the same way one would define a stomach, for example, by attention to its nervous and circulatory connections as well as its entrance, exit, and muscular walls.

Many educated people today believe that only what is unique to the individual is important or creative, and turn away from talk of populations and species as they would from talk of the masses. I once knew a director of a wealthy conservation foundation who had misgivings about the approach of ecology to urgent environmental problems in America because its concepts of communities and systems seemed to discount the individual.

Communities to him suggested only followers, gray masses without the tradition of the individual. He looked instead—or in reaction—to the profit motive and capitalistic formulas, in terms of efficiency, investment, and production. It seemed to me that he had missed a singular opportunity. He had shied from the very aspect of the world now beginning to interest industry, business, and technology as the biological basis of their—and our—affluence, and which his foundation could have shown to be the ultimate basis of all economics.

Individual man *has* his particular integrity, to be sure. Oak trees, even mountains, have selves or integrities too (a poor word for my meaning, but it will have to do). To our knowledge, those other forms are not troubled by seeing themselves in more than one way, as man is. In one aspect the self is an arrangement of organs, feelings, and thoughts—a "me"—surrounded by a hard body boundary: skin, clothes, and insular habits. This idea needs no defense. It is conferred on us by the whole history of our civilization. Its virtue is verified by our affluence. The alternative is a self as a center of organization, constantly drawing on and influencing the surroundings, whose skin and behavior are soft zones contacting the world instead of excluding it. Both views are real and their reciprocity significant. We need them both to have a healthy social and human maturity.

The second view—that of relatedness of the self—has been given short shrift. Attitudes toward ourselves do not change easily. The conventional image of a man, like that of the heraldic lion, is iconographic; its outlines are stylized to fit the fixed curves of our vision. We are hidden from ourselves by habits of perception. Because we learn to talk at the same time we learn to think, our language, for example, encourages us to see ourselves—or a plant or animal—as an isolated sack, a thing, a contained self. Ecological thinking, on the other hand, requires a kind of vision across boundaries. The epidermis of the skin is ecologically like a pond surface or a forest soil, not a shell so much as a delicate interpenetration. It reveals the self enabled and extended rather than threatened as part of the landscape and the ecosystem, because the beauty and complexity of nature are continuous with ourselves.

And so ecology as applied to man faces the task of renewing a balanced view where now there is man-centeredness, even pathology of isolation and fear. It implies that we must find room in "our" world for all plants and animals, even for their otherness and their opposition. It further implies exploration and openness across an inner boundary—an ego boundary—and appreciative understanding of the animal in ourselves which our heritage of Platonism, Christian morbidity, duality, and mechanism have long held repellant and degrading. The older counter-currents—relics of pagan myth, the universal application of Christian compassion, philosophical naturalism, nature romanticism and pantheism—have been swept away, leaving only odd bits of wreckage. Now we find ourselves in a deteriorating environment which breeds aggressiveness and hostility toward ourselves and our world.

How simple our relationship to nature would be if we only had to choose between protecting our natural home and destroying it. Most of our efforts to provide for the natural in our philosophy have failed—run aground on their own determination to work out a peace at arm's length. Our harsh reaction against the peaceable kingdom of sentimental romanticism was evoked partly by the tone of its dulcet facade but also by the disillusion to which it led. Natural dependence and contingency suggest togetherness and emotional surrender to mass behavior and other lowest common denominators. The environmentalists matching culture and geography provoke outrage for their over-simple theories of cause and effect, against the sciences which sponsor them and even against a natural world in which the theories may or may not be true. Our historical disappointment in the nature of nature has created a cold climate for ecologists who assert once again that we are limited and obligated. Somehow they must manage in spite of the chill to reach the centers of humanism and technology, to convey there a sense of our place in a universal vascular system without depriving us of our self-esteem and confidence.

Their message is not, after all, all bad news. Our natural affiliations define and illumine freedom instead of denying it. They demonstrate it better than any dialectic. Being more enduring than we individuals, ecological patterns—spatial distributions, symbioses, the streams of energy and matter and communication—create among individuals the tensions and polarities so different from dichotomy and separateness. The responses, or what theologians call "the sensibilities" of creatures (including ourselves) to such arrangements grow in part from a healthy union of the two kinds of self already mentioned, one emphasizing integrity, the other relatedness. But it goes beyond that to something better known to 12th century Europeans or Paleolithic hunters than to ourselves. If nature is not a prison and earth a shoddy way-station, we must find the faith and force to affirm its metabolism as our own— or rather, our own as part of it. To do so means nothing less than a shift in our whole frame of reference and our attitude towards life itself, a wider perception of the landscape as a creative, harmonious being where relationships of things are as real as the things. Without losing our sense of a great human destiny and without intellectual surrender, we must affirm that the world is a being, a part of our own body.[2]

Such a being may be called an ecosystem or simply a forest or landscape. Its members are engaged in a kind of choreography of materials and energy and information, the creation of order and organization. (Analogy to corporate organization here is misleading, for the distinction between social (one species) and ecological (many species) is fundamental). The pond is an example. Its ecology includes all events: the conversion of sunlight to food and the food-chains within and around it, man drinking, bathing, fishing, plowing the slopes of the watershed, drawing a picture of it, and formulating theories about the world based on what he sees in the pond. He and all the other organisms at and in the pond act upon one another, engage the earth and atmosphere, and are linked to other ponds by a network of connections like the threads of protoplasm connecting cells in living tissues.

The elegance of such systems and delicacy of equilibrium are the outcome of a long evolution of interdependence. Even society, mind and culture are parts of that evolution. There is an essential relationship between them and the natural habitat: that is, between the emergence of higher primates and flowering plants, pollinating insects, seeds, humus, and arboreal life. It is unlikely that a manlike creature could arise by any other means than a long arboreal sojourn following and followed by a time of terrestriality. The fruit's complex construction and the mammalian brain are twin offspring of the maturing earth, impossible, even meaningless, without the deepening soil and the mutual development of savannas and their faunas in the last geological epoch. Internal complexity, as the mind of a primate, is an extension of natural complexity, measured by the variety of plants and animals and the variety of nerve cells—organic extensions of each other.

The exuberance of kinds as the setting in which a good mind could evolve (to deal with a complex world) was not only a past condition. Man did not arrive in the world as though disembarking from a train in the city. He continues to arrive, somewhat like the birth of art, a train in Roger Fry's definition, passing through many stations, none of which is wholly left behind. This idea of natural complexity as a counterpart to human intricacy is central to an ecology of man. The creation of order, of which man is an example, is realized also in the number of species and habitats, an abundance of landscapes lush and poor. Even deserts and tundras increase the planetary opulence. Curiously, only man and possibly a few birds can appreciate this opulence, being the world's travelers. Reduction of this variegation would, by extension then, be an amputation of man. To convert all "wastes"—all deserts, estuaries, tundras, ice-fields, marshes, steppes and moors—into cultivated fields and cities would impoverish rather than enrich life esthetically as well as ecologically. By esthetically, I do not mean that weasel term connoting the pleasure of baubles. We have diverted ourselves with litterbug campaigns and greenbelts in the name of esthetics while the fabric of our very environment is unravelling. In the name of conservation, too, such things are done, so that conservation becomes ambiguous. Nature is a fundamental "resource" to be sustained for our own well-being. But it loses in the translation into usable energy and commodities. Ecology may testify as often against our uses of the world, even against conservation techniques of control and management for sustained yield, as it does for them. Although ecology may be treated as a science, its greater and overriding wisdom is universal.

That wisdom can be approached mathematically, chemically, or it can be danced or told as a myth. It has been embodied in widely scattered economically different cultures. It is manifest, for example, among pre-Classical Greeks, in Navajo religion and social orientation, in Romantic poetry of the 18th and 19th centuries, in Chinese landscape painting of the 11th century, in current Whiteheadian philosophy, in Zen Buddhism, in the world view of the cult of the Cretan Great Mother, in the ceremonials of Bushman hunters, and in the medieval Christian metaphysics of light. What is common among all of them is a deep sense of engagement with the landscape, with profound connections to surroundings and to natural processes central to all life.

It is difficult in our language even to describe that sense. English becomes imprecise or mystical—and therefore suspicious—as it struggles with "process" thought. Its noun and verb organization shapes a divided world of static doers separate from the doing. It belongs to an idiom of social hierarchy in which all nature is made to mimic man. The living world is perceived in that idiom as an upright ladder, a "great chain of being," an image which seems at first ecological but is basically rigid, linear, condescending, lacking humility and love of otherness.

We are all familiar from childhood with its classifications of everything on a scale from the lowest to the highest: inanimate matter/vegetative life/lower animals/higher animals/men/angels/gods. It ranks animals themselves in categories of increasing good: the vicious and lowly parasites, pathogens and predators/the filthy decay and scavenging organisms/indifferent wild or merely useless forms/good tame creatures/and virtuous beasts domesticated for human service. It shadows the great man-centered political scheme upon the world, derived from the ordered ascendency from parishioners to clerics to bishops to cardinals to popes, or in a secular form from criminals to proletarians to aldermen to mayors to senators to presidents.

And so is nature pigeonholed. The sardonic phrase, "the place of nature in man's world," offers, tongue-in-cheek, a clever footing for confronting a world made in man's image and conforming to words. It satirizes the prevailing philosophy of anti-nature and human omniscience. It is possible because of an attitude which—like ecology—has ancient roots, but whose modern form was shaped when Aquinas reconciled Aristotelian homocentrism with Judeo-Christian dogma. In a later setting of machine technology, puritanical capitalism, and an urban ethos it carves its own version of reality into the landscape like a schoolboy initialing a tree. For such a philosophy nothing in nature has inherent merit. As one professor recently put it, "The only reason anything is done on this earth is for people. Did the rivers, winds, animals, rocks, or dust ever consider my wishes or needs? Surely, we do all our acts in an earthly environment, but I have never had a tree, valley, mountain, or flower thank me for preserving it."[3] This view carries great force, epitomized in history by Bacon, Descartes, Hegel, Hobbes, and Marx.

Some other post-Renaissance thinkers are wrongly accused of undermining our assurance of natural order. The theories of the heliocentric solar system, of biological evolution, and of the unconscious mind are held to have deprived the universe of the beneficence and purpose to which man was a special heir and to have evoked feelings of separation, of antipathy towards a meaningless existence in a neutral cosmos. Modern despair, the arts of anxiety, the politics of pathological individualism and predatory socialism were not, however, the results of Copernicus, Darwin and Freud. If man was not the center of the universe, was not created by a single stroke of Providence, and is not ruled solely by rational intelligence, it does not follow therefore that nature is defective where we thought it perfect. The astronomer, biologist and psychiatrist each achieved for mankind corrections in sensibility. Each showed the interpenetration of human life and the universe to be richer and more mysterious than had been thought.

Darwin's theory of evolution has been crucial to ecology. Indeed, it might have helped rather than aggravated the growing sense of human alienation had its interpreters emphasized predation and competition less (and, for this reason, one is tempted to add, had Thomas Huxley, Herbert Spencer, Samuel Butler and G. B. Shaw had less to say about it). Its bases of universal kinship and common bonds of function, experience and value among organisms were obscured by pre-existing ideas of animal depravity. Evolutionary theory was exploited to justify the worst in men and was misused in defense of social and economic injustice. Nor was it better used by humanitarians. They opposed the degradation of men in the service of industrial progress, the slaughter of American Indians, and child labor, because each treated men "like animals." That is to say, men were not animals, and the temper of social reform was to find good only in attributes separating men from animals. Kindness both towards and among animals was still a rare idea in the 19th century, so that using men as animals could mean only cruelty.

Since Thomas Huxley's day the non-animal forces have developed a more subtle dictum to the effect that, "Man may be an animal, but he is more than an animal, too!" The *more* is really what is important. This appealing aphorism is a kind of anesthetic. The truth is that we are ignorant of what it is like or what it means to be any other kind of creature than we are. If we are unable to truly define the animal's experience of life or "being an animal" how can we isolate our animal part?

The rejection of animality is a rejection of nature as a whole. As a teacher, I see students develop in their humanities studies a proper distrust of science and technology. What concerns me is that the stigma spreads to the natural world itself. C. P. Snow's "Two Cultures," setting the sciences against the humanities, can be misunderstood as placing nature against art. The idea that the current destruction of people and environment is scientific and would be corrected by more communication with the arts neglects the hatred for this world carried by our whole culture. Yet science as it is now taught does not promote a respect for nature. Western civilization breeds no more ecology in Western science than in Western philosophy. Snow's two cultures cannot explain the antithesis that splits the world, nor is the division ideological, economic or political in the strict sense. The antidote he proposes is roughly equivalent to a liberal education, the traditional prescription for making broad and well-rounded men. Unfortunately, there is little even in the liberal education of ecology-and-man. Nature is usually synonymous with either natural resources or scenery, the great stereotypes in the minds of middle class, college-educated Americans.

One might suppose that the study of biology would mitigate the humanistic—largely literary—confusion between materialism and a concern for nature. But biology made the mistake at the end of the 17th century of adopting a *modus operandi* or life style from physics, in which the question why was not to be asked, only the question how. Biology succumbed to its own image as an esoteric prologue to technics and encouraged the whole society to mistrust naturalists. When scholars realized what the sciences were about it is not surprising that they threw out the babies with the bathwater: the information content and naturalistic lore with the rest of it. This is the setting in which academia and intellectual America undertook the single-minded pursuit of human uniqueness, and uncovered a great mass of pseudo distinctions such as language, tradition, culture, love, consciousness, history and awe of the supernatural. Only men were found to be capable of escape from predictability, determinism, environmental control, instincts and other mechanisms which "imprison" other life. Even biologists, such as Julian Huxley, announced that the purpose of the world was to produce man, whose social evolution excused him forever from biological evolution. Such a view incorporated three important presumptions: that nature is a power structure shaped after human political hierarchies; that man has a monopoly of immortal souls; and omnipotence will come through technology. It seems to me that all of these foster a failure of responsible behavior in what Paul Sears calls "the living landscape" except within the limits of immediate self-interest.

What ecology must communicate to the humanities—indeed, as a humanity—is that such an image of the world and the society so conceived are incomplete. There is overwhelming evidence of likeness, from molecular to mental, between men and animals. But the dispersal of this information is not necessarily a solution. The Two Culture idea that the problem is an information bottleneck is only partly true; advances in biochemistry, genetics, ethology, paleoanthropology, comparative physiology and psychobiology are not self-evidently unifying. They need a unifying principle not found in any of them, a wisdom in the sense that Walter B. Cannon used the word in his book *Wisdom of the Body*,[4] about the community of self-regulating systems within the organism. If the ecological extension of that perspective is correct, societies and ecosystems as well as cells have a physiology, and insight into it is built into organisms, including man. What was intuitively apparent last year—whether aesthetically or romantically—is a find of this year's inductive analysis. It seems apparent to me that there is an ecological instinct which probes deeper and more comprehensively than science, and which anticipates every scientific confirmation of the natural history of man.

It is not surprising, therefore, to find substantial ecological insight in art. Of course there is nothing wrong with a poem or dance which is ecologically neutral; its merit may have nothing to do with the transaction of man and nature. It is my impression, however, that students of the arts no longer feel that the subject of a work of art—what it "represents"—is without importance, as was said about 40 years ago. But there are poems and dances as there are prayers and laws attending to ecology. Some are more than mere comments on it. Such creations become part of all life. Essays on nature are an element of a functional or feedback system influencing men's reactions to their environment, messages projected by men to themselves through some act of design, the manipulation of paints or written words. They are natural objects, like bird nests. The essay is as real a part of the community—in both the one-species sociological and many-species ecological senses—as are the songs of choirs or crickets. An essay is an Orphic sound, words that make knowing possible, for it was Orpheus as Adam who named and thus made intelligible all creatures.

What is the conflict of Two Cultures if it is not between science and art or between national ideologies? The distinction rather divides science and art within themselves. An example within science was the controversy over the atmospheric testing of nuclear bombs and the effect of radioactive fallout from the explosions. Opposing views were widely published and personified when Linus Pauling, a biochemist, and Edward Teller, a physicist, disagreed. Teller, one of the "fathers" of the bomb, pictured the fallout as a small factor in a world-wide struggle, the possible damage to life in tiny fractions of a percent, and even noted that evolutionary progress comes from mutations. Pauling, an expert on the hereditary material, knowing that most mutations are detrimental, argued that a large absolute number of people might be injured, as well as other life in the world's biosphere.

The humanness of ecology is that the dilemma of our emerging world ecological crises (over-population, environmental pollution, etc.) is at least in part a matter of values and ideas. It does not divide men as much by their trades as by the complex of personality and experience shaping their feelings towards other people and the world at large. I have mentioned the disillusion generated by the collapse of unsound nature philosophies. The anti-nature position today is often associated with the focusing of general fears and hostilities on the natural world. It can be seen in the behavior of control-obsessed engineers, corporation people selling consumption itself, academic superhumanists and media professionals fixated on political and economic crisis; neurotics working out psychic problems in the realm of power over men or nature, artistic symbol-manipulators disgusted by anything organic. It includes many normal, earnest people who are unconsciously defending themselves or their families against a vaguely threatening universe. The dangerous eruption of humanity in a deteriorating environment does not show itself as such in the daily experience of most people, but is felt as general tension and anxiety. We feel the pressure of events not as direct causes but more like omens. A kind of madness arises from the prevailing nature-conquering, nature-hating and self- and world-denial. Although in many ways most Americans live comfortable, satiated lives, there is a nameless frustration born of an increasing nullity. The aseptic home and society are progressively cut off from direct organic sources of health and increasingly isolated from the means of altering the course of events. Success, where its price is the misuse of landscapes, the deterioration of air and water and the loss of wild things, becomes a pointless glut, experience one-sided, time on our hands an unlocalized ache.

The unrest can be exploited to perpetuate itself. One familiar prescription for our sick society and its loss of environmental equilibrium is an increase in the intangible Good Things: more Culture, more Security and more Escape from pressures and tempo. The "search for identity" is not only a social but an ecological problem having to do with a sense of place and time in the context of all life. The pain of that search can be cleverly manipulated to keep the *status quo* by urging that what we need is only improved forms and more energetic expressions of what now occupy us: engrossment with ideological struggle and military power, with productivity and consumption as public and private goals, with commerce and urban growth, with amusements, with fixation on one's navel, with those tokens of escape or success already belabored by so many idealists and social critics so ineffectually.

To come back to those Good Things: the need for culture, security and escape are just near enough to the truth to take us in. But the real cultural deficiency is the absence of a true *cultus* with its significant ceremony, relevant mythical cosmos, and artifacts. The real failure in security is the disappearance from our personal lives of the small human group as the functional unit of society and the web of other creatures, domestic and wild, which are part of our humanity. As for escape, the idea of simple remission and avoidance fails to provide for the value of solitude, to integrate leisure and natural encounter. Instead of these, what are foisted on the puzzled and troubled soul as Culture, Security and Escape are more art museums, more psychiatry, and more automobiles.

The ideological status of ecology is that of a resistance movement. Its Rachel Carsons and Aldo Leopolds are subversive (as Sears recently called ecology itself[5]). They challenge the public or private right to pollute the environment, to systematically destroy predatory animals, to spread chemical pesticides indiscriminately, to meddle chemically with food and water, to appropriate without hindrance space and surface for technological and military ends; they oppose the uninhibited growth of human populations, some forms of "aid" to "underdeveloped" peoples, the needless addition of radioactivity to the landscape, the extinction of species of plants and animals, the domestication of all wild places, large-scale manipulation of the atmosphere or the sea, and most other purely engineering solutions to problems of and intrusions into the organic world.

If naturalists seem always to be *against* something it is because they feel a responsibility to share their understanding, and their opposition constitutes a defense of the natural systems to which man is committed as an organic being. Sometimes naturalists propose projects too, but the project approach is itself partly the fault, the need for projects a consequence of linear, compartmental thinking, of machine-like units to be controlled and manipulated. If the ecological crisis were merely a matter of alternative techniques, the issue would belong among the technicians and developers (where most schools and departments of conservation have put it).

Truly ecological thinking need not be incompatible with our place and time. It does have an element of humility which is foreign to our thought, which moves us to silent wonder and glad affirmation. But it offers an essential factor, like a necessary vitamin, to all our engineering and social planning, to our poetry and our understanding. There is only one ecology, not a human ecology on one hand and another for the subhuman. No one school or theory or project or agency controls it. For us it means seeing the world mosaic from the human vantage without being man-fanatic. We must use it to confront the great philosophical problems of man—transience, meaning, and limitation—without fear. Affirmation of its own organic essence will be the ultimate test of the human mind.

Notes

1   There is a branch of sociology called Human Ecology, but it is mostly about urban geography.
2   See Alan Watts, "The World is Your Body," in *The Book on the Taboo Against Knowing Who You Are.* New York: Pantheon Books, 1966.
3   Clare A. Gunn in *Landscape Architecture*, July 1966, p. 260.
4   New York: W. W. Norton, 1932.
5   Paul B. Sears, "Ecology—a subversive subject," *BioScience*, 14(7):11, July 1964.

Chapter 7

Gary Snyder

THE PLACE, THE REGION, AND THE COMMONS

"When you find your place where you are, practice occurs."

DŌGEN [1985]

The World Is Places

WE EXPERIENCE SLUMS, prairies, and wetlands all equally as "places." Like a mirror, a place can hold anything, on any scale. I want to talk about place as an experience and propose a model of what it meant to "live in place" for most of human time, presenting it initially in terms of the steps that a child takes growing into a natural community. (We have the terms *enculturation* and *acculturation*, but nothing to describe the process of becoming placed or re-placed.) In doing so we might get one more angle on what a "civilization of wildness" might require.

For most Americans, to reflect on "home place" would be an unfamiliar exercise. Few today can announce themselves as someone *from* somewhere. Almost nobody spends a lifetime in the same valley, working alongside the people they knew as children. Native people everywhere (the very term means "someone born there") and Old World farmers and city people share this experience of living in place. Still—and this is very important to remember—being inhabitory, being place-based, has never meant that one didn't travel from time to time, going on trading ventures or taking livestock to summer grazing. Such working wanderers have always known they had a home-base on earth, and could prove it at any campfire or party by singing their own songs.

The heart of a place is the home, and the heart of the home is the firepit, the hearth. All tentative explorations go outward from there, and it is back to the fireside that elders return. You grow up speaking a home language, a local vernacular. Your own household may have some specifics of phrase, of pronunciation, that are different from the *domus*, the *jia* or *ie* or *kum*, down the lane. You hear histories of the people who are your neighbors and tales involving rocks, streams, mountains, and trees that are all within your sight. The myths of world-creation tell you how *that mountain* was created and how *that peninsula* came to be there. As you grow bolder you explore your world outward from the firepit (which is the center of each universe) in little trips. The childhood landscape is learned on foot, and a map is inscribed in the mind—trails and pathways and groves—the mean dog, the cranky old man's house, the pasture with a bull in it—going out wider and farther. All of us carry within us a picture of the terrain that was learned roughly between the ages of six and nine. (It could as easily be an urban neighborhood as some rural scene.) You can almost totally recall the place you walked, played, biked, swam. Revisualizing that place with its smells and textures, walking through it again in your imagination, has a grounding and settling effect. As a contemporary thought we might also wonder how it is for those whose childhood landscape was being ripped up by bulldozers, or whose family moving about made it all a blur. I have a friend who still gets emotional when he recalls how the avocado orchards of his southern California youth landscape were transformed into hillside after hillside of suburbs.

Our place is part of what we are. Yet even a "place" has a kind of fluidity: it passes through space and time—"ceremonial time" in John Hanson Mitchell's phrase. A place will have been grasslands, then conifers, then beech and elm. It will have been half riverbed, it will have been scratched and plowed by ice. And then it will be cultivated, paved, sprayed, dammed, graded, built up. But each is only for a while, and that will be just another set of lines on the palimpsest. The whole earth is a great tablet holding the multiple overlaid new and ancient traces of the swirl of forces. Each place is its own place, forever (eventually) wild. A place on earth is a mosaic within larger mosaics—the land is all small places, all precise tiny realms replicating larger and smaller patterns. Children start out learning place by learning those little realms around the house, the settlement, and outward.

One's sense of the scale of a place expands as one learns the *region*. The young hear further stories and go for explorations which are also subsistence forays—firewood gathering, fishing, to fairs or to market. The outlines of the larger region become part of their awareness. (Thoreau says in "Walking" that an area twenty miles in diameter will be enough to occupy a lifetime of close exploration on foot—you will never exhaust its details.)

The total size of the region a group calls home depends on the land type. Every group is territorial, each moves within a given zone, even nomads stay within boundaries. A people living in a desert or grassland with great visible spaces that invite you to step forward and walk as far as you can see will range across tens of thousands of square miles. A deep old-growth forest may rarely be traveled at all. Foragers in gallery forests and grasslands will regularly move broadly, whereas people in a deep-soiled valley ideal for gardens might not go far beyond the top of the nearest ridge. The regional boundaries were roughly drawn by climate, which is what sets the plant-type zones—plus soil type and landforms. Desert wastes, mountain ridges, or big rivers set a broad edge to a region. We walk across or wade through the larger and smaller boundaries. Like children first learning our homeland we can stand at the edge of a big river, or on the crest of a major ridge, and observe that the other side is a different soil, a change of plants and animals, a new shape of barn roof, maybe less or more rain. The lines between natural regions are never simple or clear, but vary according to such criteria as biota, watersheds, landforms, elevation. (See Jim Dodge, 1981.) Still, we all know—at some point—that we are no longer in the Midwest, say, but in the West. Regions seen according to natural criteria are sometimes called bioregions.

(In pre-conquest America people covered great distances. It is said that the Mojave of the lower Colorado felt that everyone at least once in their lives should make foot journeys to the Hopi mesas to the east, the Gulf of California to the south, and to the Pacific.)

Every region has its wilderness. There is the fire in the kitchen, and there is the place less traveled. In most settled regions there used to be some combination of prime agricultural land, orchard and vine land, rough pasturage, woodlot, forest, and desert or mountain "waste." The de facto wilderness was the extreme backcountry part of all that. The parts less visited are "where the bears are." The wilderness is within walking distance—it may be three days or it may be ten. It is at the far high rough end, or the deep forest and swamp end, of the territory where most of you all live and work. People will go there for mountain herbs, for the trapline, or for solitude. They live between the poles of home and their own wild places.

Recollecting that we once lived in places is part of our contemporary self-rediscovery. It grounds what it means to be "human" (etymologically something like "earthling"). I have a friend who feels sometimes that the world is hostile to human life—he says it chills us and kills us. But how could we *be* were it not for this planet that provided our very shape? Two conditions—gravity and a livable temperature range between freezing and boiling—have given us fluids and flesh. The trees we climb and the ground we walk on have given us five fingers and toes. The "place" (from the root *plat*, broad, spreading, flat) gave us far-seeing eyes, the streams and breezes gave us versatile tongues and whorly ears. The land gave us a stride, and the lake a dive. The amazement gave us our kind of mind. We should be thankful for that, and take nature's stricter lessons with some grace.

Understanding the Commons

I stood with my climbing partner on the summit of Glacier Peak looking all ways round, ridge after ridge and peak after peak, as far as we could see. To the west across Puget Sound were the farther peaks of the Olympic Mountains. He said: "You mean there's a senator for all this?" As in the Great Basin, crossing desert after desert, range after range, it is easy to think there are vast spaces on earth yet unadministered, perhaps forgotten, or unknown (the endless sweep of spruce forest in Alaska and Canada)—but it is all mapped and placed in some domain. In North America there is a lot that is in public domain, which has its problems, but at least they are problems we are all enfranchised to work on. David Foreman, founder of the Earth First! movement, recently stated his radical provenance. Not out of Social Justice, Left Politics, or Feminism did I come—says David—but from the Public Lands Conservation movement—the solid stodgy movement that goes back to the thirties and before. Yet these land and wildlife issues were what politicized John Muir, John Wesley Powell, and Aldo Leopold—the abuses of public land.

American public lands are the twentieth-century incarnation of a much older institution known across Eurasia—in English called the "commons"—which was the ancient mode of both protecting and managing the wilds of the self-governing regions. It worked well enough until the age of market economies, colonialism, and imperialism. Let me give you a kind of model of how the commons worked.

Between the extremes of deep wilderness and the private plots of the farmstead lies a territory which is not suitable for crops. In earlier times it was used jointly by the members of a given tribe or village. This area, embracing both the wild and the semi-wild, is of critical importance. It is necessary for the health of the wilderness because it adds big habitat, overflow territory, and room for wildlife to fly and run. It is essential even to an agricultural village economy because its natural diversity provides the many necessities and amenities that the privately held plots cannot. It enriches the agrarian diet with game and fish. The shared land supplies firewood, poles and stone for building, clay for the kiln, herbs, dye plants, and much else, just as in a foraging economy. It is especially important as seasonal or fulltime open range for cattle, horses, goats, pigs, and sheep.

In the abstract the sharing of a natural area might be thought of as a matter of access to "common pool resources" with no limits or controls on individual exploitation. The fact is that such sharing developed over millennia and always within territorial and social contexts. In the peasant societies of both Asia and Europe there were customary forms that gave direction to the joint use of land. They did not grant free access to outsiders, and there were controls over entry and use by member households. The commons has been defined as "the undivided land belonging to the members of a local community as a whole." This definition fails to make the point that the commons is both specific land *and* the traditional community institution that determines the carrying capacity for its various subunits and defines the rights and obligations of those who use it, with penalties for lapses. Because it is traditional and *local*, it is not identical with today's "public domain," which is land held and managed by a central government. Under a national state such management may be destructive (as it is becoming in Canada and the United States) or benign (I have no good examples)—but in no case is it locally managed. One of the ideas in the current debate on how to reform our public lands is that of returning them to regional control.

An example of traditional management: what would keep one household from bringing in more and more stock and tempting everyone toward overgrazing? In earlier England and in some contemporary Swiss villages (Netting, 1976), the commoner could only turn out to common range as many head of cattle as he could feed over the winter in his own corrals. This meant that no one was allowed to increase his herd from outside with a cattle drive just for summer grazing. (This was known in Norman legal language as the rule of *levancy and couchancy*: you could only run the stock that you actually had "standing and sleeping" within winter quarters.)

The commons is the contract a people make with their local natural system. The word has an instructive history: it is formed of *ko*, "together," with (Greek) *moin*, "held in common." But the Indo-European root *mei* means basically to "move, to go, to change." This had an archaic special meaning of "exchange of goods and services within a society as regulated by custom or law." I think it might well refer back to the principle of gift economies: "the gift must always move." The root comes into Latin as *munus*, "service performed for the community" and hence "municipality."

There is a well-documented history of the commons in relation to the village economies of Europe and England. In England from the time of the Norman Conquest the enfeoffed knights and overlords began to gain control over the many local commons. Legislation (the Statute of Merton, 1235) came to their support. From the fifteenth century on the landlord class, working with urban mercantile guilds and government offices, increasingly fenced off village-held land and turned it over to private interests. The enclosure movement was backed by the big wool corporations who found profit from sheep to be much greater than that from farming. The wool business, with its exports to the Continent, was an early agribusiness that had a destructive effect on the soils and dislodged peasants. The arguments for enclosure in England—efficiency, higher production—ignored social and ecological effects and served to cripple the sustainable agriculture of some districts. The enclosure movement was stepped up again in the eighteenth century: between 1709 and 1869 almost five million acres were transferred to private ownership, one acre in every seven. After 1869 there was a sudden reversal of sentiment called the "open space movement" which ultimately halted enclosures and managed to preserve, via a spectacular lawsuit against the lords of fourteen manors, the Epping Forest.

Karl Polanyi (1975) says that the enclosures of the eighteenth century created a population of rural homeless who were forced in their desperation to become the world's first industrial working class. The enclosures were tragic both for the human community and for natural ecosystems. The fact that England now has the least forest and wildlife of all the nations of Europe has much to do with the enclosures. The takeover of commons land on the European plain also began about five hundred years ago, but one-third of Europe is still not privatized. A survival of commons practices in Swedish law allows anyone to enter private farmland to pick berries or mushrooms, to cross on foot, and to camp out of sight of the house. Most of the former commons land is now under the administration of government land agencies.

A commons model can still be seen in Japan, where there are farm villages tucked in shoestring valleys, rice growing in the *tanbo* on the bottoms, and the vegetable plots and horticulture located on the slightly higher ground. The forested hills rising high above the valleys are the commons—in Japanese called *iriai*, "joint entry." The boundary between one village and the next is often the very crests of the ridges. On the slopes of Mt. Hiei in Kyoto prefecture, north of the remote Tendai Buddhist training temples of Yokkawa, I came on men and women of Ohara village bundling up slender brush-cuttings for firewood. They were within the village land. In the innermost mountains of Japan there are forests that are beyond the reach of the use of any village. In early feudal times they were still occupied by remnant hunting peoples, perhaps Japanese-Ainu mixed-blood survivors. Later some of these wildlands were appropriated by the government and declared "Imperial Forests." Bears became extinct in England by the thirteenth century, but they are still found throughout the more remote Japanese mountains, even occasionally just north of Kyoto.

In China the management of mountain lands was left largely to the village councils—all the central government wanted was taxes. Taxes were collected in kind, and local specialties were highly prized. The demands of the capital drew down Kingfisher feathers, Musk Deer glands, Rhinoceros hides, and other exotic products of the mountains and streams, as well as rice, timber, and silk. The village councils may have resisted overexploitation of their resources, but when the edge of spreading deforestation reached their zone (the fourteenth century seems to be a turning point for the forests of heartland China), village land management crumbled. Historically, the seizure of the commons—east or west—by either the central government or entrepreneurs from the central economy has resulted in degradation of wild lands and agricultural soils. There is sometimes good reason to kill the Golden Goose: the quick profits can be reinvested elsewhere at a higher return.

In the United States, as fast as the Euro-American invaders forcefully displaced the native inhabitants from their own sorts of traditional commons, the land was opened to the new settlers. In the arid West, however, much land was never even homesteaded, let alone patented. The native people who had known and loved the white deserts and blue mountains were now scattered or enclosed on reservations, and the new inhabitants (miners and a few ranchers) had neither the values nor the knowledge to take care of the land. An enormous area was de facto public domain, and the Forest Service, the Park Service, and the Bureau of Land Management were formed to manage it. (The same sorts of land in Canada and Australia are called "Crown Lands," a reflection of the history of English rulers trying to wrest the commons from the people.)

In the contemporary American West the people who talk about a "sagebrush rebellion" might sound as though they were working for a return of commons land to local control. The truth is the sagebrush rebels have a lot yet to learn about the place—they are still relative newcomers, and their motives are not stewardship but development. Some westerners are beginning to think in long-range terms, and these don't argue for privatization but for better range management and more wilderness preservation.

The environmental history of Europe and Asia seems to indicate that the best management of commons land was that which was locally based. The ancient severe and often irreversible deforestation of the Mediterranean Basin was an extreme case of the misuse of the commons by the forces that had taken its management away from regional villages (Thirgood, 1981). The situation in America in the nineteenth and early twentieth centuries was the reverse. The truly local people, the Native Americans, were decimated and demoralized, and the new population was composed of adventurers and entrepreneurs. Without some federal presence the poachers, cattle grazers, and timber barons would have had a field day. Since about 1960 the situation has turned again: the agencies that were once charged with conservation are increasingly perceived as accomplices of the extractive industries, and local people—who are beginning to be actually local—seek help from environmental organizations and join in defense of the public lands.

Destruction extends worldwide and "encloses" local commons, local peoples. The village and tribal people who live in the tropical forests are literally bulldozed out of their homes by international logging interests in league with national governments. A well-worn fiction used in dispossessing inhabitory people is the declaration that the commonly owned tribal forests are either (1) private property or (2) public domain. When the commons are closed and the villagers must buy energy, lumber, and medicine at the company store, they are pauperized. This is one effect of what Ivan Illich calls "the 500-year war against subsistence."

So what about the so-called tragedy of the commons? This theory, as now popularly understood, seems to state that when there are open access rights to a resource, say pasturage, everyone will seek to maximize his take, and overgrazing will inevitably ensue. What Garrett Hardin and his associates are talking about should be called "the dilemma of common-pool resources." This is the problem of overexploitation of "unowned" resources by individuals or corporations that are caught in the bind of "If I don't do it the other guy will" (Hardin and Baden, 1977). Oceanic fisheries, global water cycles, the air, soil fertility—all fall into this class. When Hardin et al. try to apply their model to the historic commons it doesn't work, because they fail to note that the commons was a social institution which, historically, was never without rules and did not allow unlimited access (Cox, 1985).

In Asia and parts of Europe, villages that in some cases date back to neolithic times still oversee the commons with some sort of council. Each commons is an entity with limits, and the effects of overuse will be clear to those who depend on it. There are three possible contemporary fates for common pool resources. One is privatization, one is administration by government authority, and the third is that—when possible—they become part of a true commons, of reasonable size, managed by local inhabitory people. The third choice may no longer be possible as stated here. Locally based community or tribal (as in Alaska) land-holding corporations or cooperatives seem to be surviving here and there. But operating as it seems they must in the world marketplace, they are wrestling with how to balance tradition and sustainability against financial success. The Sealaska Corporation of the Tlingit people of southeast Alaska has been severely criticized (even from within) for some of the old-growth logging it let happen.

We need to make a world-scale "Natural Contract" with the oceans, the air, the birds in the sky. The challenge is to bring the whole victimized world of "common pool resources" into the Mind of the Commons. As it stands now, any resource on earth that is not nailed down will be seen as fair game to the timber buyers or petroleum geologists from Osaka, Rotterdam, or Boston. The pressures of growing populations and the powers of entrenched (but fragile, confused, and essentially leaderless) economic systems warp the likelihood of any of us seeing clearly. Our perception of how entrenched they are may also be something of a delusion.

Sometimes it seems unlikely that a society as a whole can make wise choices. Yet there is no choice but to call for the "recovery of the commons"—and this in a modern world which doesn't quite realize what it has lost. Take back, like the night, that which is shared by all of us, that which is our larger being. There will be no "tragedy of the commons" greater than this: if we do not recover the commons—regain personal, local, community, and peoples' direct involvement in sharing (in *being*) the web of the wild world—that world will keep slipping away. Eventually our complicated industrial capitalist/socialist mixes will bring down much of the living system that supports us. And, it is clear, the loss of a local commons heralds the end of self-sufficiency and signals the doom of the vernacular culture of the region. This is still happening in the far corners of the world.

The commons is a curious and elegant social institution within which human beings once lived free political lives while weaving through natural systems. The commons is a level of organization of human society that includes the nonhuman. The level above the local commons is the bioregion. Understanding the commons and its role within the larger regional culture is one more step toward integrating ecology with economy.

References

Cox, Susan Jane Buck. "No Tragedy in the Commons." *Environmental Ethics*, Spring 1985.

Dodge, Jim. "Living by Life." *CoEvolutions Quarterly*, Winter 1981.

Dōgen, *Moon in a Dewdrop: Writings of Zen Master Dōgen*. Tanahashi, Kazuaki (trans.). San Francisco: North Point, 1985.

Hardin, Garrett, and John Baden. *Managing the Commons*. San Francisco: W. H. Freeman, 1977.

Illich, Ivan. *Shadow Work*. London: Marion Boyars, 1981.

Mitchell, John H. *Ceremonial Time*. New York: Doubleday, 1984.

Muir, John. "Wild Wool." In *Wilderness Essays*. Salt Lake City: Peregrine Smith, 1984.

Netting, R. "What Alpine Peasants Have in Common: Observations on Communal Tenure in a Swiss Village." *Human Ecology*, 1976.

Polanyi, Karl. *The Great Transformation*. New York: Octagon Books, 1975.

Thirgood, J. V. *Man and the Mediterranean Forest: A History of Resource Depletion*. New York: Academic Press, 1981.

Thoreau, Henry David. "Wild Apples." In *The Natural History Essays*. Salt Lake City: Peregrine Smith, 1984.

Chapter 8

Jonathan Bate

THE ECONOMY OF NATURE

T HE WORD 'ECOLOGY' (*OEKOLOGIE*) was coined in 1866 by the German zoologist Ernst Haeckel and defined more fully by the same scientist in 1870:

> By ecology we mean the body of knowledge concerning the economy of nature
> – the investigation of the total relations of the animal both to its inorganic and to
> its organic environment; including above all, its friendly and inimical relations
> with those animals and plants with which it comes directly or indirectly into
> contact – in a word, ecology is the study of all those complex interrelations
> referred to by Darwin as the conditions of the struggle for existence.[1]

Ecology, then, is a holistic science, concerned in the largest sense with the relationship between living beings and their environment. The living beings with which Haeckel was concerned were animals and plants; as an academic discipline ecology began, and in many quarters it has remained, as one of the non-human sciences. The first person to have applied the term to man's relationship with the environment seems – appropriately enough for what has become an alternative, radical ideology – to have been a woman.[2] Ellen Swallow (*nomen est omen?*) was a campaigner for clean air and water and better urban living conditions in the increasingly industrialized eastern United States of the late nineteenth century. She was, to quote a recent historian of science, 'a crusader for establishing a scientific basis for bettering human life',[3] and as part of her campaign she appropriated Haeckel's word: 'For this knowledge of right living we have sought a new name. . . . as theology is the science of religious life, and biology the science of life, . . . so let Oekology be hence the worthiest of the applied sciences which teaches the principles on which to found healthy . . . and happy life.'[4] The first appearance of Haeckel's word in the popular press was in a reference to Ellen Swallow's theories in the *Boston Globe* of November 1892. From an early stage, then, the term served to denominate both a biological science and an environmental attitude.

As constituted by its earliest academic practitioners, ecology was a science built upon the Darwinian concept of evolution by natural selection according to adaptability to environment. Indeed, the book in which Haeckel coined the word was called *Generelle Morphologie der Organismen: Allgemeine Grundzüge der organischen Formen-wissenschaft, mechanisch begründet durch die von Charles Darwin reformirte Descendenz-Theorie* ('General morphology of organisms: universal characteristics of the science of organic forms, established mechanically through the theory of descent reformed by Charles Darwin'); Haeckel's chief inspiration was the argument in *The Origin of Species* concerning the 'web of complex relations' by which all animals and plants are bound to each other, remote as they may be from one another in the scale of nature. But ecology had other roots besides Darwin, as is clear from Haeckel's use in his definition of the term 'the economy of nature'. This venerable phrase takes us back into a long tradition of natural religion; coined by Sir Kenelm Digby in 1658, its most famous occurrence was as the title of Linnaeus' 1749 essay, 'Specimen academicum de Oeconomia Naturae', known to English readers as 'The Oeconomy of Nature' from Benjamin Stillingfleet's translation in *Miscellaneous Tracts relating to Natural History, Husbandry, and Physick* (1759). 'By the Oeconomy of Nature,' Linnaeus wrote, 'we understand the all-wise disposition of the Creator in relation to natural things, by which they are fitted to produce general ends, and reciprocal uses.'[5] To classify organisms in the Linnaean fashion is to reveal nature's complex, divinely inspired order. The economy of nature is to be found throughout Enlightenment natural philosophy, whether in the biology of Linnaeus or the geology of Hutton. The latter's 'Theory of the Earth' was 'a view of that system of mineral oeconomy, in which may be perceived every mark of order and design, of provident wisdom and benevolence'; it sought to demonstrate that 'there is a system in nature' and that in the long perspective of geological time nature's economy is benign – 'with such wisdom has nature ordered things in the oeconomy of this world, that the destruction of one continent is not brought about without the renovation of the earth in the production of another'.[6] We are in that realm of physico-theology associated with the line from John Ray's *The Wisdom of God manifested in the Works of the Creation* (1691) to William Paley's *Natural Theology* (1802).

Even freethinkers who denied the divine source shared the belief that nature has its economy and its economic laws. Thus *The Botanic Garden* (1789–91) of Erasmus Darwin – whom Coleridge called 'the everything, except the Christian'[7] – was at once an assault on the theological premises of such works as Hutton's 'Theory of the Earth' and a popularization of Linnaeus. The aim of the poem, Darwin said in his Advertisement, was 'to inlist Imagination under the banner of Science' and 'to induce the ingenious to cultivate the knowledge of Botany, by introducing them to the vestibule of that delightful science, and recommending to their attention the immortal works of the celebrated Swedish Naturalist, LINNEUS'. In good Linnaean fashion, part one of Erasmus Darwin's work was actually entitled *The Economy of Vegetation*, though the poem itself is concerned more with creation than taxonomy. One of its principal emphases is the vital role that vegetation plays in the overall economy of nature – a footnote describes the process of photosynthesis whereby the exposure of plants to sunlight creates 'vital air or oxygene gas' which 'rises into the atmosphere and replenishes it with the food of life'.[8] Darwin's subsequent work, *Zoonomia* (1794–96), continued in a vein of theological scepticism combined with a firm belief that nature operated according to a systematic economy. *Zoonomia* is one of a number of late eighteenth-century texts expounding the laws of organic life on evolutionary principles; it was by combining these principles with those of another economic system, Thomas Malthus's theory of the struggle for existence in human population, that Charles Darwin, Erasmus's grandson, was able to develop his theory of evolution by natural selection.

Fundamental to all these developments was the practice of field observation. The eye that is fixed on the natural world sees the economy at work:

> The most insignificant insects and reptiles are of much more consequence, and
> have much more influence in the oeconomy of nature, than the incurious are
> aware of; and are mighty in their effect, from their minuteness, which renders

them less an object of attention; and from their numbers and fecundity. Earth-worms, though in appearance a small and despicable link in the chain of nature, yet, if lost, would make a lamentable chasm.[9]

This is Gilbert White in Selborne, from where it is a short step to those key Romantic texts, Coleridge's notebooks and the journals of Dorothy Wordsworth and Henry David Thoreau. For all his resistance to pantheism, Coleridge was a scrupulous, deeply inquiring observer of the natural world; the very subtlety of his own intelligence attuned him to the economy of nature: 'The finest edge, into which the meditative mind of a Contemplator was ever ground, is but the back of the Blade in comparison with the Subtlety of Nature.'[10] As will be shown in the next chapter, Ruskin attributed his own capacity to see the landscape and the sky to Wordsworth's example; if he had known Dorothy's journals, he would have discovered that Wordsworth's eye for the detailed observation of nature was opened by his sister. And as for Thoreau, the whole project of his writing might be summed up as an attempt to develop a human economy that is responsive and responsible in its relationship with the economy of nature. By a symbolically appropriate palaeographic error the invention of the word 'ecology' was for a time actually attributed to Thoreau: the editors of his *Correspondence*, published in 1958, misread 'geology' and had him speaking in 1858, eight years prior to Haeckel, of 'Botany, Ecology, etc.' (the error crept into the 1972 Supplement of the *Oxford English Dictionary*).

Thoreau would occupy the central place in a study of the Romantic ecology in the United States. There are major distinctions to be made between American and British ecological attitudes, not least because of differences of size and space – Wordsworth's mighty Helvellyn would be but a foothill in the Rockies. The British tradition I am tracing is much concerned with *localness*, with small enclosed vales; the American environmental tradition is far more preoccupied with vastness and with threatened wilderness (John Muir's High Sierra), as de Tocqueville recognized:

> It is this consciousness of destruction, this *arrière-pensée* of quick and inevitable change that gives, we feel, so peculiar a character and such a touching beauty to the solitudes of America. One sees them with melancholy pleasure; one is in some sort of a hurry to admire them. Thoughts of the savage, natural grandeur that is going to come to an end, become mingled with splendid anticipations of the triumphant march of civilisation. One feels proud to be a man, and at the same time one experiences I cannot say what bitter regret at the power that God has granted us over nature. One's soul is shaken by contradictory thoughts and feelings, but all the impressions it receives are great and leave a deep mark.[11]

Where the Wordsworths and Thoreau stand apart from the Darwins and Haeckel is in their emphasis on a symbiosis between the economy of nature and the activities of humankind. Erasmus Darwin wrote footnotes about photosynthesis, while Wordsworth wrote poems about how flowers may vitalize the human spirit. Once late eighteenth-century scientists had shown that plants are literally 'the food of life', since without photosynthesis there would be no oxygen in the atmosphere and therefore no life, Romantic poets could argue that plants are also food for the spirit. Scientists made it their business to describe the intricate economy of nature; Romantics made it theirs to teach human beings how to live as part of it. They foreshadowed Ellen Swallow in the move from theoretical description to an applied science of healthy and happy living. The 'Romantic ecology' reverences the green earth because it recognizes that neither physically nor psychologically can we live without green things; it proclaims that there is 'one life' within us and abroad, that the earth is a single vast ecosystem which we destabilize at our peril. In sharp contrast to the so-called 'Romantic Ideology', the Romantic ecology has nothing to do with flight from the material world, from history and society – it is in fact an attempt to enable mankind the better to live in the material world by entering into harmony with the environment.

In book eight of *The Excursion*, Wordsworth's Wanderer discourses on 'changes in the Country from the manufacturing spirit'. He sees manufacturing towns expanding in a vast sprawl; 'He sees the barren wilderness erased,/Or disappearing'; 'With you I grieve,' he cries,

> when on the darker side
> Of this great change I look; and there behold
> Such outrage done to nature as compels
> The indignant power to justify herself;
> Yea, to avenge her violated rights,
> For England's bane.[12]

Man ought to be 'earth's thoughtful lord' (164), but he has abnegated his responsibilities in the name of material gain. The dark Satanic mills are the temples of a new religion of capital:

> Men, maidens, youths,
> Mother and little children, boys and girls,
> Enter, and each the wonted task resumes
> Within this temple, where is offered up
> To Gain, the master-idol of the realm,
> Perpetual sacrifice.

> (*Excursion*, viii. 180–85)

The people are no longer to be seen 'Breathing fresh air, and treading the green earth' (280); no longer is there a 'green margin of the public way' (372), a common space that belongs to all the people. Of the erasure of supposedly barren waste land, Wordsworth implicitly says with William Cobbett, ' "Wastes indeed!" Give a dog an ill-name. Was Horton Heath a waste? Was it a "waste" when a hundred perhaps of healthy boys and girls were playing there of a Sunday instead of creeping about covered with filth in the alleys of a town?'[13]

According to Wordsworth's impassioned vision, the child's vitality is destroyed and his unity with nature is lost when he is put to work in a cotton mill:

> His raiment, whiten'd o'er with cotton-flakes
> Or locks of wool, announces whence he comes.
> Creeping his gait and cowering, his lip pale,
> His respiration quick and audible . . .
> The limbs increase; but liberty of mind
> Is gone for ever; and this organic frame,
> So joyful in its motions, is become
> Dull, to the joy of her own motions dead;
> And even the touch, so exquisitely poured
> Through the whole body, with a languid will
> Performs its functions; rarely competent
> To impress a vivid feeling on the mind
> Of what there is delightful in the breeze,

> The gentle visitations of the sun,
> Or lapse of liquid element – by hand,
> Or foot, or lip, in summer's warmth – perceived.
>
> (*Excursion*, viii. 309–12. 321–32)

In the world of Richard Arkwright's water-powered spinning frame, the 'organic frame' is dulled and oppressed. Imprisoned in the factory, enslaved to wage labour, the child has lost that primal 'liberty' which is embodied in the mind's joyful responsiveness to breeze and sun and water. The Wanderer does not omit to speak of the favourable effects of industry, but his main concern is to produce graphic images of the deprivation and dehumanization that are the price of 'progress'. In this, he is voicing the concerns that Ellen Swallow later brought together under the banner of ecology.

By the mid-1830s *The Excursion* had been printed four times and sold more copies than any other volume of Wordsworth's poetry.[14] In 1835, however, it was another work which became the first of Wordsworth's productions to reach a fifth edition. It was his steadiest seller, going through five further editions between 1842 and 1859. It was without question the most widely read work of the most admired English poet of the first half of the nineteenth century. Different editions have different titles, but the work became commonly known as *A Guide to the Lakes*. It was, to quote Mary Moorman, 'more constantly in demand than any of his poetry'.[15] Matthew Arnold's story about meeting a cleric who admired the *Guide* and asked if its author had written anything else is not entirely frivolous.

'New historicist' literary critics have taught us that poems are not free-floating aesthetic objects, that, like all texts, they have a social materiality, they carry ideological freight. But, paradoxically, most such critics working on the Romantic period have gone on privileging poetry by devoting the best of their own work to readings of such canonical texts as 'Tintern Abbey', *The Prelude*, 'To Autumn', and *Don Juan*. To think for a moment of Wordsworth as pre-eminently not the author of 'Tintern Abbey' and *The Prelude* but the compiler of the *Guide to the Lakes* will thus be not only to recover an important nineteenth-century view of him, but also to begin to move away from narrow canonicity. If we are to historicize Romanticism, we must bring the *Guide* from the periphery to the centre. The neglect of it is quite extraordinary. Jerome McGann's sense that there have been too many readings of Romanticism in terms of idealist aesthetic theory is supported by the fact that what has interested critics most about the *Guide* has been its relation to those now well-worn categories, the sublime, the beautiful, and the picturesque.[16] A far more novel – and historically revealing – approach to the *Guide* will be to undertake the kind of textual morphology at which McGann himself excels.

The *Guide* was first written in the form of an introduction and accompanying text for the Rev. Joseph Wilkinson's *Select Views in Cumberland, Westmoreland, and Lancashire*, published in monthly parts in 1810 (and reissued, without Wordsworth's knowledge, with coloured versions of the engravings, in 1821). It first appeared under Wordsworth's name in *The River Duddon, A Series of Sonnets: Vaudracour & Julia: and Other Poems. To which is annexed, A Topographical Description of the Country of the Lakes, in the North of England* in 1820. This edition carried the explanatory advertisement:

> This Essay, which was first published several years ago as an Introduction to some Views of the Lakes, by the Rev. Joseph Wilkinson, (an expensive work, and necessarily of limited circulation,) is now, with emendations and additions, attached to these volumes; from a consciousness of its having been written in the same spirit which dictated several of the poems, and from a belief that it will tend materially to illustrate them.

It first appeared independently as *A Description of the Scenery of the Lakes in The North of England* in 1822, in an edition of 500 copies which was exhausted immediately and reprinted with some revisions the following year in an edition of 1,000. The 1822 edition included a new account of an excursion up Scafell Pike and the 1823 added an account of an excursion to Ullswater – both were based closely and without acknowledgement on unpublished material by Dorothy Wordsworth. The *Guide* appeared in 1835 under the auspices of a Kendal publisher (previous editions having been published in London), with the title *A Guide Through the District of the Lakes in the North of England, with a Description of the Scenery, etc. For the Use of Tourists and Residents. Fifth Edition, with considerable additions.* In this edition, the 'Directions and Information for the Tourist' became a separate prefatory division, set apart from the main body of the *Guide*, which by this time had three principal sections, 'View of the country as formed by nature', 'Aspect of the country, as affected by its inhabitants', and 'Changes, and rules of taste for preventing their bad effects'. Wordsworth began this edition by saying that his purpose was 'to furnish a Guide or Companion for the *Minds* of Persons of taste, and feeling for Landscape, who might be inclined to explore the District of the Lakes with that degree of attention to which its beauty may fairly lay claim', but that he would begin by getting out of the way 'the humble and tedious Task of supplying the Tourist with directions'.[17]

Then in 1842 it became part of *A Complete Guide to the Lakes, Comprising Minute Directions for the Tourist, With Mr Wordsworth's Description of the Scenery of the Country, etc. And Three Letters on the Geology of the Lake District, by the Rev. Professor Sedgwick, Edited by the Publisher* (i.e. John Hudson of Kendal). Wordsworth explained in a letter to Adam Sedgwick, the first Woodwardian Professor of Geology in the University of Cambridge, that in the tourist market his guide was being outsold by others which attended more to the needs of 'the *Body* of the Tourist', that he had tried to remedy this defect but found the work troublesome and '*infra dig.*', and that he had therefore turned the '*guide matter*' over to the publisher Hudson, who had undertaken to interweave it with further matter compiled by himself but to leave 'all that related to *mind*' entire and separate from the rest. In addition, Thomas Gough of Kendal would 'promote the Botany' (he furnished a table listing the woods and fells where some 250 species of plant could be found); with Sedgwick's geological contribution, 'a Book would be produced answering every purpose that could be desired'.[18] This was the version which went through five editions in seventeen years; Sedgwick added a fourth letter on geology to the 1846 edition and an extremely important fifth one to that of 1853. There was a consonance between poet and scientist: for Sedgwick, as for Wordsworth, the mountains 'give back to us, as the earth's touch did of old to the giant's body, new spirits and enduring strength.'[19] The allusion is to the story of Antaeus, a myth about the need to keep in touch with the earth.

A text that began as accompaniment to the productions of a clergyman cashing in on the vogue for the picturesque eventually became accompanied by the productions of a clergyman who was one of the crucial figures in the history of the science of geology. The textual morphology of the *Guide* is a fascinating index of the shift from the age of Gilpin and Farington to that of Lyell and Darwin. Sedgwick actually used the opportunity provided by Wordsworth to contribute to that highly significant nineteenth-century genre, the self-consciously popularizing work on geology:

> I wish to address more general readers – any intelligent traveller whose senses are open to the beauties of the country around him, and who is ready to speculate on such matters of interest as it offers to him. I will therefore endeavour to avoid technical language as far as I am able, and I do not profess to teach, in a few pages, the geology of a most complicated country (for that would be an idle

attempt); but rather to open the mind to the nature of the subject, and to point out the right way towards a comprehension of some of its general truths.[20]

It is no exaggeration to say that the name and nature of the Silurian and Cambrian systems gained currency outside scientific circles chiefly because of Sedgwick's letters in the *Guide*. And in the case of the 1853 edition, the *Guide* was used by Sedgwick for the statement of his case in his great dispute with Sir Roderick Murchison over the latter's fallacious extension of his Silurian system into 20,000 feet of strata which did not belong to it.

In addition to its picturesque and geological functions, the *Guide* served as a complement to one of Wordsworth's most favourably received poetic productions, the *Duddon* volume,[21] and as a pocket companion for tourists. In the latter of these manifestations it belonged in a genre going back to the works of the eighteenth-century travellers who formed the new taste for the wildness of the Lakes, John Brown, Thomas Gray, and Thomas West. Wordsworth's book is, however, unlike earlier guides in two key respects. First, it is, as the textual history shows, a multi-purpose text: it invites all kinds of appropriation, all kinds of use – it aims to answer 'every purpose that could be desired'. It is not *merely* for the tourist; as is clear from Wordsworth's disparaging remarks about the tediousness of the '*guide matter*', it uses the popular guidebook format to put Wordsworth's own concerns across to the public. If the text is intended to answer every purpose that could be desired, it may certainly answer my desired purpose, for it to stand as exemplar of the Romantic ecology – especially as Wordsworth's own concerns in those parts of the *Guide* which pertain to the mind were, as we shall see, fundamentally ecological. This is in fact the second respect in which it is unlike other guides: where West and his followers all wrote exclusively for *visitors* to the Lakes, Wordsworth aimed to show what it meant to *dwell* there. It is symptomatic that in writing of the rootedness of Lakeland cottages Wordsworth included some lines of verse from the unpublished manuscript of *Home at Grasmere*, a poem which [. . .] was cardinal to his sense of himself as a dweller in Westmorland. Where earlier guide writers adopted the picturesque tourist's point of view and rarely descended from their stations, Wordsworth's approach was holistic: he moved from nature to the natives, exploring the relationship between land and inhabitant; then in his third section he considered the evolving and increasingly disruptive influence of man on his environment. Sedgwick's contribution rendered the text more holistic still, in that the letters on geology supplemented the Wordsworthian analysis of the surfaces of nature and the interaction between man and nature with an account of the depths of nature, of the fossil record which revealed 'countless ages before man's being' and taught 'of laws as unchangeable as the oracles of nature – of harmonies then in preparation' (1853 edn, p. 219). By the time we reach this text we have come a long way from Thomas West and his attempt to make a visit to the Lakes comparable to the composition of a landscape painting. The geologist's hammer has replaced the Claude glass.

I have laboured the point about the different textual manifestations of the *Guide* because they throw into question the proposition that Romantic discourse attempts to seal itself hermetically off from materiality. The history of this central Romantic text constitutes a successive series of engagements with highly varied and highly material discourses such as tourism and geology. The Romantic Ideology is supposed to purvey a myth of individual inspiration, of the isolated and privileged poet, yet this text is a composite production, shaped and reshaped according to the needs of the market, a pooling of the resources of figures as varied as Wilkinson, Wordsworth, Dorothy, Hudson, Sedgwick, and Gough. At certain moments, the very notion of this text having an individual author becomes unstable: for instance, the text in the first edition repeatedly refers to as 'mine' the accompanying drawings that were not by the author of the text. Furthermore, the extrinsic materiality of the book is matched by the intrinsic materiality of certain key passages in the text. For Marilyn Butler, the later Wordsworth 'ceases to see others as social phenomena; they are objects for contemplation, images of apparent alienation which the poet's imagination translates into private emblems of his troubled communion with nature.'[22] In the *Guide*, however, people are seen firmly in relation to their material environment. Among Wordsworth's chief concerns are the management of trees and the architecture of rural buildings. What are these, if not 'social phenomena'? Critics like Butler and McGann are too limited in their view of society: modern ecological politics teaches us that to consider society only in terms of production, income, and ownership is insufficient. What is done to the land is as important as who owns it. Equal distribution of the means of agricultural production is not much use if the land is poisoned.

Section First of the *Guide*, 'View of the country as formed by nature', begins with Wordsworth taking the reader to an imaginary station on a cloud midway between Great Gable and Scafell, from where the eight valleys of the Lake District may be seen stretched out like spokes from the nave of a wheel. By substituting an imaginary station for an actual one, Wordsworth differentiates his *Guide* from those intended only for the bodies of tourists; with the image of the wheel, he introduces the idea of a unified place with a common centre. The remainder of Section First develops this sense of the unity of the country as formed by nature. Mountains, vales, and lakes all work together; even the humble tarn makes a necessary contribution to the whole: 'In the economy of Nature these are useful, as auxiliars to Lakes; for if the whole quantity of water which falls upon the mountains in time of storm were poured down upon the plains without intervention . . . the habitable grounds would be much more subject than they are to inundation' (p. 39). Thomas West never seemed to notice tarns, presumably because he did not deem them either picturesque or sublime. Where other guides concerned themselves with how the more majestic lakes contributed to the charm of a scene, Wordsworth's was interested in the function performed within the ecosystem by the smaller and higher bodies of still water.

In Section Second, the native inhabitants of the district are seen to share in this natural unity. 'The economy of Nature' and the human economy are brought together as the hand of man is 'incorporated with and subservient to the powers and processes of Nature' (p. 61). Man works in partnership with his environment. Thus Lakeland cottages may be said rather 'to have grown than to have been erected; – to have risen, by an instinct of their own, out of the native rock'; the buildings 'in their very form call to mind the processes of Nature' and thus 'appear to be received into the bosom of the living principle of things' (pp. 62–63). Not even the places dedicated to Christian worship violate the *religio loci*. A consequence of such integration with nature is an integrated social structure: until recently there has been 'a perfect Republic of Shepherds and Agriculturists, among whom the plough of each man was confined to the maintenance of his own family, or to the occasional accommodation of his neighbour' (p. 67). There was no nobleman, knight, or squire; the ruling power was nature, not some human overlord. It is here that Wordsworth speaks [. . .] of the district of the Lakes as an 'almost visionary mountain republic' (p. 68).

But all this has changed as a result of influx and innovation, the subject of Section Third. New residents who are not rooted in the land have brought dissonant new building styles; worse, in accordance with the 'craving for prospect', their new houses have been built on obtrusive sites where they do not 'harmonize with the forms of Nature'. The rage for picturesque 'improvement' has resulted in the alteration of the contours of the principal island on Windermere lake: 'Could not the margin of this noble island be given back to Nature?' asks Wordsworth, very much in the tone of a modern conservationist (p. 72). Worst of all is the introduction of larch plantations. Wordsworth makes a powerful distinction between the way in which nature forms woods and forests, a gradual and selective process shaped by conditions of soil, exposure to wind, and so on, and the environmentally and aesthetically harmful practices of artificial planting.

The new proprietors and tourists will not go away; the function of the *Guide* is to educate them to care for the delicate ecosystem, as we would now call it, of the Lakes. 'In this wish,' Wordsworth concludes Section Third, 'the author will be joined by persons of pure taste throughout the whole island, who, by their visits (often repeated) to the Lakes in the North of England, testify that they deem the district a sort of national property, in which every man has a right and interest who has an eye to perceive and a heart to enjoy' (p. 92). In that phrase 'a sort of national property' may be seen the origins of the National Trust and the Lake District National Park. The key figure in this history was the Wordsworthian-Ruskinian, Canon Hardwicke Rawnsley. In 1883, taking his cue from a battle in which Wordsworth had fought in the 1840s, he launched a campaign against a Bill for the extension of the railway into the heart of the Lakes. He established a Lake District Defence Society and fought not only against the railway but for the establishment of public footpath rights. He gained support from the social reformer Octavia Hill, to whom he had been introduced by Ruskin, and Robert Hunter of the Commons Preservation Society, a group in the vanguard of the open space movement which was agitating for the preservation of green land in and around London. In 1895 Rawnsley, Hill, and Hunter had 'The National Trust for Places of Historic Interest and Natural Beauty' registered as a charity.[23] The whole concept of a place of 'Natural Beauty' was bound up with Romanticism and the Lake District – the trigger for the public meeting at which the formation of the Trust was first discussed had been the news that a number of sites in the Lakes, including the Falls of Lodore immortalized by Southey and Wordsworth, were up for sale. Among the Trust's first acquisitions were Brandelhow Park and Grange Fell on Derwentwater, Gowbarrow Park – site of the daffodils – on Ullswater, Queen Adelaide's Hill on Windermere, and Burrows Field near Ambleside. In its annual report of 1904 the Trust picked up on Wordsworth's idea of 'a sort of national property' and advocated the creation of a National Park in the heart of the Lake District, though it was not until the National Parks and Access to the Countryside Act of 1949 that this was actually established.

The 1949 Act drew together conservation, planning, and access. It was based on the recommendations of a committee set up in 1947 under Sir Arthur Hobhouse; that committee had accepted the definition of a National Park propounded in the Dower Report of 1945:

> an extensive area of beautiful and relatively wild country in which for the
> nation's benefit and by appropriate national decision and action, (a) the charac-
> teristic landscape beauty is strictly preserved, (b) access and facilities for public
> open air enjoyment are amply provided, (c) wildlife and buildings and places of
> architectural and historic interest are suitably protected, while (d) established
> farming use is effectively maintained.[24]

Each element of this definition may be traced back to the values of Wordsworth's *Guide:* the maintaining of the place for the benefit of the whole nation; the conception of landscape beauty, with a particular emphasis on wild (sublime) country; the belief in the importance of the open air; the respect for buildings that have a history in the place; and the recognition that traditional agricultural practices are integral to the identity of the place. Wordsworth would have been pleased that shepherds still work on the hills of Westmorland and Cumberland, since, in contrast to the American model, the English and Welsh National Parks do not consist of enclosed areas owned by the government; the land in them remains privately owned – a considerable amount of it by the National Trust, which remains a private charity – and may be used for commercial activities such as farming and forestry. Conservation is sought by means of planning rather than possession.

All who walk in the National Parks are legatees of Wordsworth, his sister and his friends, who derived so much of their spiritual nourishment from walking and looking in the way that is suggested by such entries in Dorothy's journals as the following:

> William had slept very ill – he was tired and had a bad headache. We walked around the two lakes. Grasmere was very soft and Rydale was extremely beautiful from the pasture side. Nab Scar was just topped by a cloud which cutting it off as high as it could be cut off made the mountain look uncommonly lofty. We sate down a long time in different places.[25]

Wordsworth and Coleridge were walking poets every bit as much as they were poets of the imagination. Imagine Alexander Pope composing poetry: we see him sitting in a patron's house or a coffee-house. Imagine Wordsworth or Coleridge composing: we see them in the open air, as Hazlitt did—

> Coleridge has told me that he himself liked to compose in walking over uneven ground, or breaking through the straggling branches of a copse-wood; whereas Wordsworth always wrote (if he could) walking up and down a straight gravel walk, or in some spot where the continuity of his verse met with no collateral interruption.[26]

Hazlitt is interested in the distinction between Wordsworth's steadiness and Coleridge's variety, but the observation reveals the importance of walking – walking above all in the vicinity of their homes in the Quantocks and then the Lake District – for both poets' work. The National Parks, with their openness to walkers, sustain the spirit of the Wordsworth who, according to De Quincey, had by the 1830s 'traversed a distance of 175 to 180,000 English miles' on foot, 'a mode of exertion which, to him, stood in the stead of wine, spirits, and all other stimulants whatsoever to the animal spirits; to which he has been indebted for a life of unclouded happiness, and we for much of what is most excellent in his writings'.[27]

Whenever Canon Rawnsley made the case for the preservation of the Lake District, he cited the example of Wordsworth. The dedication to one of his books is characteristic: 'to my friend and fellow-labourer William Henry Hills, who has done more than any man in the district, to keep our English lakeland, undisfigured, and "secure from rash assault", for the health, rest, and inspiration of the people'.[28] Here the quotation from Wordsworth's 'Sonnet on the projected Kendal and Windermere Railway' is a fixed point of reference. For Rawnsley, there is no contradiction between opposing the extension of the railway into the Lakes and the idea that the Lakes belong to 'the people'. Like Wordsworth, it was to the *rash* assault that he objected. This is an important point, because Wordsworth's concern for the preservation of the Lakes has often been put down to a selfish desire to keep away artisan day trippers from Manchester. But in his 1844 letters to the *Morning Post* concerning the projected Kendal and Windermere Railway, Wordsworth's principal objection was to large-scale organized Sunday outings:

> Packing off men after this fashion, for holiday entertainment, is, in fact, treating them like children. They go at the will of their master, and must return at the same, or they will be dealt with as transgressors. . . . Let [the Master-manufacturers] consent to a Ten Hours' Bill, with little or, if possible, no

diminution of wages, and the necessaries of life being more easily procured, the mind will develope itself accordingly, and each individual would be more at liberty to make at his own cost excursions in any direction which might be most inviting to him. There would then be no need for their masters sending them in droves scores of miles from their homes and families to the borders of Windermere, or anywhere else.[29]

It is precisely this problem of *mass* tourism that threatens the Lake District today, though ironically the rash assault comes from cars and coaches, not the railway. Changing historical conditions bring different methods of putting ideals into practice: in the nineteenth century the railway represented a threat and there was a need for the protective demarcation of 'Areas of Outstanding Natural Beauty', whereas now the railway is back in environmental favour and the Green Party advocates the abolition of the National Park system on the grounds that the whole country should be subject to the stringent planning regulations that apply in the Parks.

Between Wordsworth and Rawnsley there was John Ruskin himself, another admirer of the Westmorland cottage's adaptation to its environment, another protestor against extension of the railway into the Lakes. He is an absolutely key figure in my story, for it was through him more than anyone else that the Wordsworthian ecology entered into a broader – and indeed an explicitly political – nineteenth-century environmental tradition. As Wordsworth in his letters on the projected Kendal and Windermere Railway set the environmental effects of railway excursions in the context of factory conditions and the need for shorter working hours, so Ruskin recognized that there is an intimate connection between the conditions in which we work and the way in which we live with nature.[30]

In the *Guide* Wordsworth lamented the decline of cottage industry. He explained that until recently the estatesmen of the Lakes had relied on two sources of income, their flocks and the home manufacture by their women and children of the produce of their flocks. 'But, by the invention and universal application of machinery, this second resource has been cut off' (p. 90). The whole balance of the economy of the district was thus upset. In the 1880s, however, the 'Ruskin Linen Industry' was established under the auspices of Marion Twelves and Albert Fleming, disciples of *Fors Clavigera*; this initiative led to the revival of the cottage economy in several villages. It was Ruskin's involvement with schemes such as this that Rawnsley had in mind when, at the unveiling of the Ruskin memorial on Friar's Crag above Derwentwater, he spoke of

> the worker's friend, the man who more than others of his time so believed in the possibilities of a happier life for the working men, that he set himself against traditions and the ordinary accepted theories of capital and labour . . . and taught that all good work might be worship, and was meant for joy, and that no good work was possible until a man had ceased to be a hand, a mere machine, a cog in an iron wheel, and had been allowed to bring his mind and soul to the task, under conditions that admitted of happiness and health.[31]

This instance of Ruskin's involvement with artisan production in the Lakes suggests a new reading of the relationship between Romanticism, hand-loom weaving, and nature. The argument of the *Guide* is not that nature can provide comfort and draw attention away from bad harvests and the decline of cottage industry, but that the economy of nature and the cottage economy depend on one another. Labour is harmonized with nature. The securing of the place and the restoring of its local small-scale industries are twin goals for which Wordsworth and Ruskin worked.

The traditional view of the Romantic return to nature is that it is a form of escapism. Wordsworth escapes to the Lake District to get away from the harsh political realities of the Terror; the Victorian Romantics escape into a world of medievalism to get away from laissez-faire capitalism and grimy factories. Freud thought that we need nature for the same reason that we need mental phantasy. He drew the analogy in the twenty-third of his *Introductory Lectures on Psycho-Analysis*:

> The creation of the mental domain of phantasy has a complete counterpart in the establishment of 'reservations' and 'nature-parks' in places where the inroads of agriculture, traffic, or industry threaten to change the original face of the earth rapidly into something unrecognizable. The 'reservation' is to maintain the old condition of things which has been regretfully sacrificed to necessity everywhere else; there everything may grow and spread as it pleases, including what is useless and even what is harmful. The mental realm of phantasy is also such a reservation reclaimed from the encroaches of the reality-principle.[32]

But is it productive to oppose our need for nature to the reality-principle? A more useful approach may be that of Hazlitt in his *Round Table* essay 'On the Love of the Country'. Hazlitt claims that no one has ever explained the true source of our attachment to natural objects or of the soothing emotions which the country infuses in us. People have talked of beauty, of freedom from care, of silence and tranquillity, of the healthiness and simplicity of life in the country as opposed to that in the city. But none of these explanations comes to the underlying principle. Hazlitt then cites a passage in Rousseau's *Confessions* where Jean-Jacques describes how he moved into a certain room and was immediately particularly endeared to it because he could see 'a little spot of green' from his window and this was the first time since his childhood that he had had such an object constantly before him. Natural objects, Hazlitt says, are always associated with *recollection*:

> It is because natural objects have been associated with the sports of our childhood, with air and exercise, with our feelings in solitude, when the mind takes the strongest hold of things, and clings with the fondest interest to whatever strikes its attention; with change of place, the pursuit of new scenes, and thoughts of distant friends: it is because they have surrounded us in almost all situations, in joy and in sorrow, in pleasure and in pain; because they have been one chief source and nourishment of our feelings, and a part of our being, that we love them as we do ourselves.[33]

Our mental processes in the face of nature work according to the principle of the association of ideas, but what is distinctive about this attachment is 'the transferable nature of our feelings with respect to physical objects' (iv. 19). Loving one person doesn't make you love another person, but loving one tree makes you love all trees. You are affected by a sunset or a spring day not because of its inherent beauty but because it brings with it all the thoughts and feelings you've had in the face of previous sunsets and previous spring days. 'Thus Nature is a kind of universal home, and every object it presents to us an old acquaintance with unaltered looks' (iv. 20). All this is very Wordsworthian, and it is symptomatic that at the centre of Hazlitt's essay there are quotations from the Immortality Ode and 'Tintern Abbey':

> To me the meanest flower that blows can give
> Thoughts that do often lie too deep for tears.
>
> ['Ode']

and

> Nature never did betray
> The heart that lov'd her; 'tis her privilege,
> Through all the years of this our life, to lead
> From joy to joy.

['Tintern Abbey']

Ideologically speaking, the problem with this view of nature is that it depends on individual feeling, on consciousness, on the leisure to enjoy sunsets and spring days. But Hazlitt's essay is marked by a strong democratic instinct: nature is a home for *all* – even those who do not own property – and the feelings it arouses are ones that 'all can enter into'. It was William Morris's dream that one day 'This land we have loved in our love and our leisure' might be available to those who live in grim 'grey homes'.[34] And in this context it is worth considering a letter sent by a factory-worker together with his contribution to the National Trust's appeal to acquire land round Derwentwater, launched on the occasion of Ruskin's death in 1900: 'I am a working man and cannot afford more than 2s., but I once saw Derwentwater and can never forget it. I will do what I can to get my mates to help.'[35] If Hazlitt's argument is right, this man loved Derwentwater out of something more intrinsic to his identity than a desire to get away from smoke and work. Besides, there is the example of John Clare, whose writing suggests that he gained his identity through his bond with his native landscape and lost it in madness when he was displaced from that land. Nature may matter to a farm-labourer as well as to someone who looks at it over a five-barred gate. Furthermore, the link in Clare's poetry between nature and both the recovery of lost childhood and the possibility of some kind of endurance provides strong support for the argument of Hazlitt's essay. In his poem 'The Eternity of Nature' Clare contrasts the permanence of the daisy with the transience of the individual human's life and even of the posthumous life afforded to the poet. Sublimity and durability are founded in the minutiae of nature: the poem is built on the idea of, to reiterate Hazlitt's phrase, 'the transferable nature of our feelings with respect to physical objects'. It asserts that the daisy plucked by the future child is in some senses the same as the daisy we see now:

> Leaves from eternity are simple things
> To the world's gaze – whereto a spirit clings
> Sublime and lasting – trampled underfoot
> The daisy lives and strikes its little root
> Into the lap of time – centurys may come
> And pass away into the silent tomb
> And still the child hid in the womb of time
> Shall smile and pluck them when this simple rhyme
> Shall be forgotten like a churchyard-stone
> Or lingering lie unnoticed and alone
> When eighteen hundred years our common date
> Grows many thousands in their marching state
> Aye still the child with pleasure in his eye
> Shall cry 'The daisy!' – a familiar cry–
> And run to pluck it.[36]

When he started to write poetry, Clare knew nothing of the industrial revolution and had never been to London. His work demonstrates that the Romantic concept of integration with nature is not only a reaction against urbanization and that it should not be dismissed as some kind of surplus-value or discarded among the baggage of bourgeois ideology. England's greatest communist knew that it was more than this. Like Hazlitt, he saw that nature is a universal home:

> when we can get beyond that smoky world, there, out in the country we may still see the works of our fathers yet alive amidst the very nature they were wrought into, and of which they are so completely a part: for there indeed if anywhere, in the English country, in the days when people cared about such things, was there a full sympathy between the works of man and the land they were made for: – the land . . . is neither prison nor palace, but a decent home.[37]

That is from William Morris's first public lecture, on 'The Decorative Arts'. Morris can be reclaimed as a father not only of the British Labour Party but also of the green movement.[38] E. P. Thompson's 1955 biography argued that Morris had to shed his Romanticism before he could grow into his socialism. But the ideals of his Romanticism formed the foundation of his socialism; the utopian communism of *News from Nowhere* would not have been possible without the Romantic poetry of *The Earthly Paradise*. If we trace the 'Romantic Ideology' forward into Morris and the prose-poet Ruskin, it becomes something far removed from German idealist aesthetics. It becomes an ideology that is concerned, for instance, with architectural style and town-planning. In chapter seven of *News from Nowhere* the houses of Piccadilly stand in carefully cultivated gardens which run over with flowers and fruit trees. Morris's vision continues:

> We came presently into a large open space, sloping somewhat towards the south, the sunny site of which had been taken advantage of for planting an orchard, mainly, as I could see, of apricot trees, in the midst of which was a pretty gay little structure of wood, painted and gilded, that looked like a refreshment stall. . . . A strange sensation came over me; I shut my eyes to keep out the sight of the sun glittering on this fair abode of gardens, and for a moment there passed before them a phantasmagoria of another day. A great space surrounded by tall ugly houses, with an ugly church, at the corner and a nondescript ugly cupolaed building at my back; the roadway thronged with a sweltering and excited crowd, dominated by omnibuses crowded with spectators. In the midst a paved befountained square, populated only by a few men dressed in blue, and a good many singularly ugly bronze images (one on top of a tall column).[39]

Here the Romantic imagination is being used not to transcend nature but to reconstruct Trafalgar Square on ecological principles.

Whatever our class, nature can do something for us. Alan Liu writes that 'nature is the name under which we use the nonhuman to validate the human, to interpose a mediation able to make humanity more easy with itself'.[40] This seems to me to describe accurately what nature does for Wordsworth, for Hazlitt, for Clare, for Morris, for the factory-labourer who contributed to the Derwentwater appeal. However, Liu links this statement to the claim that *'There is no nature'*, in other words that 'nature' is nothing more than an anthropomorphic construct created by Wordsworth and the rest for their own purposes. The polemical desire to reject any casual recourse to 'nature' as panacea for social ills has the unfortunate consequence of occluding any consideration of the whole question of human society's stewardship of 'the features and products of the earth itself, as contrasted with those of human civilization' (*OED*'s thirteenth sense of the word). 'Nature' is a term that needs to be contested, not rejected. It is profoundly unhelpful to say '*There is no nature*' at a time when our most urgent need is to address and redress the consequences of human civilization's insatiable desire to consume the products of the earth. We are confronted for the first time in history with the possibility of there being no part of the earth left untouched by man. 'Human civilization' has always been in the business of altering the land, whether through deforestation or urbanization or mining or enclosure or even the artificial reimposition of 'nature' through landscaping in the manner of William Kent and Capability Brown. But until now there have always been domains into which 'human civilization' does not extend; there has always been a 'state of nature'. Enclosure and landscape gardening have had no effect on the higher fellsides and tarns of Westmorland. Chernobyl, however, has. There is a difference not merely in degree but in kind between local changes to the surface configuration of the land and the profound transformations of the economy of nature that take place when the land is rendered radioactive or the ozone layer is depleted. When there have been a few more accidents at nuclear power stations, when there are no more rainforests, and when every wilderness has been ravaged for its mineral resources, then let us say '*There is no nature*'.

Furthermore, even if we continue to think anthropomorphically, it is essential to modify the idea that we use nature to validate ourselves, 'to make humanity more easy with itself'. For if 'the nonhuman' is to do something for us, we must do something for it – not least give it space, allow it to continue to exist. Rousseau recognized that we need the conception of a state of nature in order to have a critical understanding of the nature of civilization. Hazlitt's argument about nature as a universal home depends on its endurance, its constancy. A tree helps us to live because it is the same as the trees we saw in our childhood. If we destroy all the trees, we will irremediably disrupt not only the economy of nature but also our own social and psychological economy.

Such images of reciprocity are alien to classical Marxist discourse. Marx characterized the relationship between man and nature in terms of dialectical opposition rather than unity. Man is defined as different from the animals by virtue of his mastery of nature, his 'working-over of inorganic nature'.[41] Nature is the raw material for production; it is approached in terms of its use-value. The whole concept of society having an economic base with a legal and political superstructure fails to address the fact that the economy of human society may in the end be dependent on something larger, the economy of nature. Friedrich Engels is more amenable to ecological reading than Marx – while alert to the poverty of agricultural labourers, he emphasized the benefits of 'fresh country air' and 'healthful work in garden or field'[42] – but the industrial pollution of Eastern Europe remains as a monument to the absence of ecological thinking in Marxist *praxis*.[43] Where capitalism has its Three Mile Island, Marxist-Leninism has its Chernobyl. Even the passage of Freud which I have quoted seems to take for granted the priority which capitalists and Marxists share: the nature-reserve and the park are associated with the old condition of things which must be sacrificed to the 'necessity' of economic progress. Note that phrase about everything being left alone in the nature-reserve 'including what is useless and even what is harmful': Freud is being wholly anthropocentric – he means useless and harmful to man, but much that is useless and even harmful within the human economy will be useful and beneficial within the economy of nature. This is Gilbert White's point about earth-worms.

Marxist criticism claims to bring texts down from the idealist stratosphere into the material world. But a materialism which follows Marx's tenth thesis on Feuerbach in taking the standpoint of human society inevitably finds itself falling in with high capitalism's privileging of the wealth of nations over the wealth of nature. Until quite recently the Romantics were valued precisely because they set themselves against the ideology of capital and offered an alternative, holistic vision – because, we may say, they were the first ecologists. Ellen

Swallow defined ecology as an applied science that will teach the principles on which to found healthy and happy life. John Ruskin proposed the 'strange political economy' that 'the question for the nation is not how much labour it employs, but how much life it produces. . . . THERE IS NO WEALTH BUT LIFE. Life, including all its powers of love, of joy, and of admiration.'[44] Such passages as this from *Unto This Last* are the nineteenth century's most vigorous riposte to the Benthamism which claimed that it is from material well-being that man derives the main part of his pleasure. Ruskin's conception of love, joy, and admiration was learnt from Wordsworth: in the fiftieth letter of *Fors Clavigera* he said that he took Wordsworth's single line, 'We live by admiration, hope, and love' (*Excursion*, iv. 763), as his literal guide in all education. Furthermore, Ruskin's magnificent critique of the theory of divided labour – 'It is not, truly speaking, the labor that is divided, but the men: – Divided into mere segments of men – broken into small fragments and crumbs of life'[45] – may be traced back to Wordsworth. As Leslie Stephen perceived,

> The division of labour, celebrated with such enthusiasm by Adam Smith, tends to crush all real life out of its victims. The soul of the political economist may rejoice when he sees a human being devoting his whole faculties to the performance of one subsidiary operation in the manufacture of a pin. . . . This is the evil which is constantly before Wordsworth's eyes, as it has certainly not become less prominent since his time. The danger of crushing the individual is a serious one according to his view. . . . Men must be taught what is the really valuable part of their natures, and what is the purest happiness to be extracted from life. . . . Many powerful thinkers have illustrated Wordsworth's doctrine more elaborately, but nobody has gone more decisively to the root of the matter.[46]

The powerful thinker whom Stephen has in mind here is undoubtedly Ruskin: the emphasis on 'life' follows *Unto This Last* and the allusion to pin manufacture is drawn from 'The Nature of Gothic'. These Ruskinian texts, not Marx's *Capital*, were the inspirational force behind the socialism of Morris and others; English socialism is at root more 'green' than it is 'Marxist'. As Morris wrote in 'How I became a Socialist', 'I had never so much as opened Adam Smith, or heard of Ricardo, or of Karl Marx. . . . how deadly dull the world would have been twenty years ago but for Ruskin! It was through him that I learned to give form to my discontent.'[47] Morris found foreshadowings of his critique of the prevailing theory of labour and capital in one other Victorian sage, Thomas Carlyle, but the latter's vituperations in such texts as *Past and Present* are not built on the Wordsworthian ecology which Morris shared with Ruskin.

The exemplary English ecologist is the Ruskin who undermined the very premises of nineteenth-century capitalist and Marxist theory with his claim that the fundamental material basis of political economy was not money, labour, and production but 'Pure Air, Water, and Earth'. In the fourth essay of *Unto This Last*, Ruskin gave credit to John Stuart Mill for departing from the conventions of political economy by admitting that there was value in nature. He was thinking in particular of a passage in the *Principles of Political Economy* in which Mill wrote in Wordsworthian fashion of the importance of solitude – solitude in the presence of natural beauty and grandeur – for the health of both individual and society, and then went on to express concern about the destruction to the environment that was being caused by economic progress:

> Nor is there much satisfaction in contemplating the world with nothing left to the spontaneous activity of nature; with every rood of land brought into cultivation, which is capable of growing food for human beings; every flowery waste or

natural pasture ploughed up, all quadrupeds or birds which are not domesticated for man's use exterminated as his rivals for food, every hedgerow or superfluous tree rooted out, and scarcely a place left where a wild shrub or flower could grow without being eradicated as a weed in the name of improved agriculture.[48]

Having cited Mill, Ruskin made his own case. He argued that a maximum of woodland was needed in order to keep the air pure, that the growth of industrial manufacturing was not the answer to the problems of world poverty, and that the quality of human life is not dependent on economic growth alone. It was here that he wrote the words which form the epigraph to my book.

Some years later, in the fifth letter of *Fors Clavigera* Ruskin wrote once again of the dangers of pollution and of the importance of trees for their effect on the atmosphere. He perceived the relationship between deforestation and drought. His prescience is remarkable; his rousing rhetoric demands a long quotation:

> The first three [principles of political economy], I said, are Pure Air, Water, and Earth.
>
> Heaven gives you the main elements of these. You can destroy them at your pleasure, or increase, almost without limit, the available quantities of them.
>
> You can vitiate the air by your manner of life, and of death, to any extent. You might easily vitiate it so as to bring such a pestilence on the globe as would end all of you. . . . everywhere, and all day long, you are vitiating it with foul chemical exhalations; and the horrible nests, which you call towns, are little more than laboratories for the distillation into heaven of venomous smokes and smells, mixed with effluvia from decaying animal matter, and infectious miasmata from purulent disease.
>
> On the other hand, your power of purifying the air, by dealing properly and swiftly with all substances in corruption; by absolutely forbidding noxious manufactures; and by planting in all soils the trees which cleanse and invigorate earth and atmosphere, – is literally infinite. You might make every breath of air you draw, food.
>
> Secondly, your power over the rain and river-waters of the earth is infinite. You can bring rain where you will, by planting wisely and tending carefully; – drought where you will, by ravage of woods and neglect of the soil. You might have the rivers of England as pure as the crystal of the rock; – beautiful in falls, in lakes, in living pools; – so full of fish that you might take them out with your hands instead of nets. Or you may do always as you have done now, turn every river of England into a common sewer, so that you cannot so much as baptize an English baby but with filth, unless you hold its face out in the rain; and even *that* falls dirty.[49]

The contrast between the beauty of falls, lakes, and living pools, and the smokes and smells, the exhalations and effluvia, the murky waters, of manufacturing industry places Ruskin in the tradition of book eight of *The Excursion*, where Wordsworth writes of 'that brook converting as it runs / Into an instrument of deadly bane' (viii. 257–58). There are aspects of late Ruskin which we will want to reject – the moral opprobriousness; the obsessive, near-paranoid tone; the element of feudalism in the alternative vision proposed – but then all readings, all uses, of literary texts are selective. Though the ecologies of Wordsworth, of Ruskin and of Morris, of Ellen Swallow, are by no means identical to our own, are very much of the nineteenth century, the core of their thinking, so much of which is summed up in the fifth letter of *Fors*, is familiar and is modern. They are the fathers and mothers of our environmental tradition.

To close this chapter with the question of pure water and air. As has been noted, one version of the *Guide to the Lakes* was published with the *River Duddon* sonnet cycle, which ends with the river flowing out from Cumbria into the Irish Sea; today, if we ascend Coniston Old Man, the mountain beneath which Ruskin lived in the years when he was writing *Fors*, the most prominent sight on the coast is the Sellafield nuclear reprocessing plant, with its abysmal record for dumping contaminated waste. 'Still glides the Stream, and shall for ever glide,' wrote Wordsworth of the Duddon in his concluding sonnet; but now it is not only water that glides inexorably into the sea off Wordsworth's coast. As for the air, let us go back into the stratosphere for a moment, not in metaphor but in meteorology. The young Ruskin [. . .] learnt from Wordsworth how to look at clouds; the old Ruskin looked at the clouds and became convinced that the weather was undergoing radical change. Writing from Brantwood by Coniston on 13 August 1879, he attributed the air quality – 'one loathsome mass of sultry and foul fog, like smoke' – to the exhalations from 'Manchester devil's darkness'.[50] The central argument of his extraordinary late work *The Storm-Cloud of the Nineteenth Century* was that the signs of the sky were signs of the times: 'Blanched Sun, – blighted grass, – blinded man'.[51] A preposterous idea: how could human 'progress' alter the configuration of weather across the globe? People said Ruskin was mad.

Notes

1   Translated and quoted in Robert P. McIntosh, *The Background of Ecology: Concept and Theory* (Cambridge, 1985), pp. 7–8.

2   For an attempt to link ecological consciousness and feminism, see Carolyn Merchant, *The Death of Nature: Women, Ecology, and the Scientific Revolution* (San Francisco, 1980; repr. London, 1982).

3   *Background of Ecology*, p. 20.

4   Quoted, Robert Clarke, *Ellen Swallow: The Woman who Founded Ecology* (Chicago, 1973), p. 120.

5   Quoted, Donald Worster, *Nature's Economy: The Roots of Ecology* (San Francisco, 1977), pp. 37–38.

6   James Hutton, 'Theory of the Earth; or an Investigation of the Laws observable in the Composition, Dissolution, and Restoration of Land upon the Globe', *Transactions of the Royal Society of Edinburgh*, 1 (1788), pt 2, 209–304 (pp. 287, 304, 294).

7   To Josiah Wade, 27 Jan. 1796, *Collected Letters of Samuel Taylor Coleridge*, ed. E. L. Griggs, 6 vols (Oxford, 1956–71), i. 177. In the same letter Coleridge remarks on Darwin's atheistic rejection of Hutton.

8   *The Economy of Nature* (London, 1791), canto iv, line 34, note. Though not named as such until the 1890s, photosynthesis was first studied in the 1770s.

9   Gilbert White, *The Natural History of Selborne* (1789), Letter XXXV, 20 May 1777.

10   MS Egerton 2801, f. 58 (watermark 1827), in *Inquiring Spirit: A Coleridge Reader*, ed. Kathleen Coburn (1951; repr. New York, 1968), p. 223.

11   Alexis de Tocqueville, 'A Fortnight in the Wilds', in *Journey to America*, trans. George Lawrence, ed. J. P. Mayer (London, 1959), p. 372. For Thoreau's Romantic ecology, see the discussion in Worster, *Nature's Economy*.

12   *Excursion*, viii. 129–30, 151–56, quoted from the text in vol. 5 of *Wordsworth's Poetical Works*, ed. Ernest de Sélincourt and Helen Darbishire, 5 vols (Oxford, 1940–49); the text as orginally published in 1814 had the additional line 'Through strong temptation of those gainful arts' between 'there behold' and 'Such outrage'.

13   Quoted, W. G. Hoskins and L. D. Stamp, *The Common Lands of England and Wales* (London, 1963), p. 61.

14   See W. J. B. Owen, 'Costs, Sales, and Profits of Longman's Editions of Wordsworth', *The Library*, 5th series, 12 (1957), 93–107.

15   Moorman, *William Wordsworth, A Biography: The Later Years 1803–1850* (Oxford, 1965), p. 384n.

16   See, for example, J. R. Nabholtz, 'Wordsworth's *Guide to the Lakes* and the Picturesque Tradition', *Modern Philology*, 61 (1964), 288–97; W. J. B. Owen, 'Wordsworth's Aesthetics of Landscape',

Wordsworth Circle, 7 (1976), 70–82; and, most recently, Theresa M. Kelley, *Wordsworth's Revisionary Aesthetics* (Cambridge, 1988), chap. 2.

17   *Wordsworth's Guide to the Lakes. The Fifth Edition (1835)*, ed. Ernest de Sélincourt (Oxford, 1906, repr. 1977), p. 1. Subsequent quotations will be from this, the most readily available edition, but for textual apparatus see vol. 2 of *The Prose Works of William Wordsworth*, ed. W. J. B. Owen and J. W. Smyser, 3 vols (Oxford, 1974).

18   Wordsworth to Adam Sedgwick, late March 1842, in *Letters of William Wordsworth: A New Selection*, ed. Alan G. Hill (Oxford, 1984), p. 303. On Wordsworth's friendship with Sedgwick, see further Marilyn Gaull, "From Wordsworth to Darwin: 'On to the Fields of Praise'", *Wordsworth Circle*, 10 (1979), 33–48. For an important account of the influence of geological theory, and in particular catastrophism, on the language of the early Wordsworth, notably in the French Revolution section of *The Prelude*, see Alan Bewell, *Wordsworth and the Enlightenment* (New Haven, 1989), part 4. Bewell is one of the few critics to recognize the importance of environmental discourse for a reading of Wordsworth; he is especially useful on the eighteenth-century inheritance, in particular Montesquieu's belief that climate and soil exercise a formative influence on politics.

19   'Geology of the Lake District', in Hudson's *Complete Guide to the Lakes*, quoted from 4th edn (1853), p. 219.

20   'Geology of the Lake District', Letter 1, *Complete Guide*, p. 170.

21   Reviewing the *Duddon* volume, the *British Review* praised the 'Topographical Description of the Country of the Lakes' as both a valuable illustration of the poems and high in its own 'absolute merit' (vol. 16, Sept. 1820, p. 38).

22   Butler, *Romantics, Rebels and Reactionaries* (Oxford, 1981), p. 67.

23   For the early history of the Trust, see John Gaze, *Figures in a Landscape* (London, 1988).

24   Dower Report on National Parks in England and Wales (Cmnd 6628), quoted in *The Discovery of the Lake District*, Victoria and Albert Museum exhibition catalogue (London, 1984), p. 164.

25   31 Jan. 1802, in *Journals of Dorothy Wordsworth*, 2nd edn by Mary Moorman (Oxford, 1971), p. 82.

26   'My First Acquaintance with Poets', in *The Complete Works of William Hazlitt*, ed. P. P. Howe, 21 vols (London, 1930–34), xvii. 119.

27   Essay on Wordsworth in *Tait's Edinburgh Magazine* (1839), in De Quincey, *Recollections of the Lakes and the Lake Poets*, ed. David Wright (Harmondsworth and New York, 1970), p. 135.

28   Rawnsley, *Literary Associations of the English Lakes*, 2 vols (Glasgow, 1894, repr. 1901), dedication page.

29   Appendix 2 of de Sélincourt's edn of the *Guide*, pp. 158–59. See further, Stephen Prickett's discussion of Wordsworth's two railway sonnets in 'Macaulay's Vision of 1930: Wordsworth and the Battle for the Wilderness', *Essays and Studies*, 39 (1986), 104–17.

30   Ruskin's importance for this tradition is still insufficiently recognized, though Bernard Richards makes a good beginning in his essay 'Ruskin and Conservation', *The Texas Quarterly*, 21 (1978), 65–73.

31   Rawnsley, *Ruskin and the English Lakes* (Glasgow, 1901), pp. 212–13. See also chap. 5, 'Ruskin and the Home Art Industries in the Lake District'.

32   Freud, *Introductory Lectures*, trans. Joan Riviere (London, 1922), pp. 311–12. Quoted as a chapter epigraph in Keith Thomas's invaluable *Man and the Natural World: Changing Attitudes in England 1500–1800* (London, 1983).

33   *Complete Works of Hazlitt*, iv. 18. Hazlitt's argument is not quite as original as he claims: it is in some respects foreshadowed by Johnson in *Rambler*, 36, 21 July 1750.

34   See Morris's poem 'The Message of the March Wind', in his *The Pilgrims of Hope* (1885).

35   Quoted, B. L. Thompson, *The Lake District and the National Trust* (Kendal, 1946), pp. 42–43.

36   John Clare, *Selected Poetry*, ed. Geoffrey Summerfield (London, 1990), p. 158. Grevel Lindop quotes part of this passage in support of a similar point to mine in 'The Language of Nature and the Language of Poetry: The 1988 Pete Laver Lecture', *Wordsworth Circle*, 20 (1989), 2–9 (p. 3).

37   William Morris, *News from Nowhere and Selected Writings and Designs*, ed. Asa Briggs (Harmondsworth, 1984), p. 96.

38   For the relationship between socialism and green politics in the late nineteenth century, see Peter C. Gould's excellent study, *Early Green Politics: Back to Nature, Back to the Land, and Socialism in Britain 1880–1900* (Brighton and New York, 1988). For a recognition of Morris's centrality to any conception of 'green socialism', see Raymond Williams, 'Socialism and Ecology', in his *Resources of Hope*, ed. Robin Gable (London, 1989), 210–26.

39   Morris, *News from Nowhere, and Selected Writings*, ed. Briggs, p. 217.

40   *Wordsworth: The Sense of History* (Stanford, 1989), p. 38.

41   *Karl Marx: Selected Writings*, ed. David McLellan (Oxford, 1977), p. 82.

42   *The Condition of the Working Class in England* (1845; English edn, 1892, repr. St Albans, 1969), p. 38.

43   See, however, Howard L. Parsons's attempt to construct a 'socialist Ecology' in the introduction to his *Marx and Engels on Ecology* (Westport, Conn., 1977).

44   *Unto This Last: Four Essays on the First Principles of Political Economy* (1862), essay IV, 'Ad Valorem', in *The Complete Works of John Ruskin*, Library Edition, ed. E. T. Cook and Alexander Wedderburn, 39 vols (London, 1903–12), xvii. 104–5. Library Edition cited hereafter as *LE*.

45   'The Nature of Gothic', para. xvi, in *The Stones of Venice*, vol. ii (*LE* x. 196).

46   Leslie Stephen, 'Wordsworth's Ethics', in *Hours in a Library*, new edn, 3 vols (London, 1909), ii. 275–76. The reference to Adam Smith is supported by a footnote referring to Wordsworth's 'how dire a thing/Is worshipped in that idol proudly named/"The Wealth of Nations" ' (1850 *Prelude*, xiii. 77–79).

47   *News from Nowhere and Selected Writings*, pp. 34–35.

48   *Principles of Political Economy*, book iv, chap. 6, para. 2, in vol. 3 of *Collected Works of John Stuart Mill*, gen. ed. J. M. Robson (Toronto, 1965), p. 756.

49   *Fors Clavigera*, Letter V, 1 May 1871 (*LE* xxvii. 91–92).

50   *The Storm-Cloud of the Nineteenth Century* (1884), Lecture 1 (*LE* xxxiv. 37).

51   *Storm-Cloud, LE* xxxiv. 40.

Chapter 9

Lawrence Buell

REPRESENTING THE ENVIRONMENT

The profound kinship of language with the world was thus dissolved . . . Things and words were to be separated from one another . . . Discourse was still to have the task of speaking that which is, but it was no longer to be anything more than what it said.
—Michel Foucault, *The Order of Things*

That everything we say is false because everything we say falls short of being everything that could be said is an adolescent sort of error.
—Hilary Putnam, *Realism with a Human Face*

I think of two landscapes—one outside the self, the other within. The external landscape is the one we see—not only the line and color of the land and its shading at different times of the day, but also its plants and animals in season, its weather, its geology, the record of its climate and evolution . . . One learns a landscape finally not by knowing the name or identity of everything in it, but by perceiving the relationships in it—like that between the sparrow and the twig . . .

The second landscape I think of is an interior one, a kind of projection within a person of a part of the exterior landscape . . . the speculations, intuitions, and formal ideas we refer to as "mind" are a set of relationships in the interior landscape with purpose and order . . . The interior landscape responds to the character and subtlety of an exterior landscape; the shape of the individual is affected by land as it is by genes.
—Barry Lopez, "Landscape and Narrative"

IDEOLOGY [. . .] is after all only one of several filters through which literature sifts the environments it purports to represent. These filters begin with the human sensory apparatus itself, which responds much more sensitively for example at the level of sight than of smell and even at the visual level is highly selective: we perceive discrete objects better than objects in relation, and large objects much better than the average life-form (about the size of a small insect).[1] For these reasons our reconstructions of environment cannot be other than skewed and partial. Even if this were not so, even if human perception could perfectly register environmental stimuli, literature could not. Even when it professes the contrary, art removes itself from nature. Physical texts derive from dead plants. Even "imagistic" symbols like certain Chinese characters or visual configurations pronounced onomatopoeically are signs far more abstract than animal tracks on snow. Writing and reading are acts usually performed indoors, unachievable without long shifts of attention away from the natural environment. There is a crotchety justice to a late Victorian complaint about natural history essays: "Who would give a tinker's dam for a description of a sunset that *he* hadn't seen? Damn it, it's like kissing a pretty girl by proxy."[2]

Yet from another point of view the emphasis on disjunction between text and world seems overblown. To most lay readers, nothing seems more obvious than the proposition that literature of a descriptive cast, be it "fictional" or "nonfictional," portrays "reality," even if imperfectly. John Stuart Mill, who found solace in Wordsworth's compelling rendition of physical nature, would have been astonished by the stinginess of the modern argument that Wordsworth reckoned nature as at best a convenience and at worst an impediment to the imagination. Most amateur Thoreauvians would find equally strange the claim that in Thoreau's *Journal* "when the mind sees nature what it sees is its difference from nature," a million-word paper trail of unfulfilled desire.[3] In contemporary literary theory, however, the capacity of literary writers to render a faithful mimesis of the object world is reckoned indifferent at best, and their interest in doing so is thought to be a secondary concern.[4]

One basis for this divergence between commonsensical and specialized wisdom may be that the modern understanding of how environmental representation works has been derived from the study of the fictive genres rather than nonfiction. The consequence of this is suggested by the common omnibus term used for designating the sphere of the nonhuman environment in literary works: setting. It deprecates what it denotes, implying that the physical environment serves for artistic purposes merely as backdrop, ancillary to the main event. The most ambitious monograph on place in literature criticizes Thomas Hardy's evocation of Egdon heath (which "almost puts his work into the kind of place-saturated fiction which is expressly devoted to the assault upon a mountain") and commends by contrast the Parisian chapters of Henry James's *Ambassadors* as containing "the barest minimum of detail and the maximum of personal reflection on these details."[5] In "good" writing, then, it would seem that the biota has only a bit part. If we map literary history from this angle of vision, we reinforce the impression that attentive representation of environmental detail is of minor importance even in writing where the environment figures importantly as an issue. In American literature, the main canonical forms of environmental writing are the wilderness romance and the lyric meditation on the luminous natural image or scene. Cooper's *Deerslayer*, Faulkner's "Bear," Bryant's poem "To the Fringed Gentian," Whitman's "Out of the Cradle," Robert Frost's "Design"—of such is the core of these traditions comprised. It is easy to persuade oneself on the basis of the average critical discussion of these works that the literary naturescape exists for its formal or symbolic or ideological properties rather than as a place of literal reference or as an object of retrieval or contemplation for its own sake. It is unthinkable that Bryant could have sought to immerse himself in the natural history of the gentian, or Frost in observing spiders. And so professors of literature, whatever their behavior in ordinary life, easily become antienvironmentalists in their professional practice.

Yet the explanation cannot simply be that literature specialists mostly study novels and poems, for during the past two decades we have ranged freely across the human sciences, subjecting ethnography and phenomonology and even scientific monographs to literary analysis almost as readily as sonnets and short stories. Today, as Carolyn Porter has said, "we confront a virtually horizonless discursive field in which . . . the traditional boundaries between the literary and the extraliterary have faded."[6] No doubt we have derived our critical skepticism or disdain for the notion that literature does or can represent physical reality from the idea of writing as construct, whether this idea takes the form of the old-fashioned formalist theory of the literary work as artifact or the contemporary theory of writing as discourse. Thus, during the very half-century since Aldo Leopold, as environmental writing in America has unprecedentedly thriven, literary theory has been making the idea of a literature devoted to recuperating the factical environment seem quaintly untheoretical. All major strains of contemporary literary theory have marginalized literature's referential dimension by privileging structure, text(uality), ideology, or some other conceptual matrix that defines the space discourse occupies apart from factical "reality," as the epigraph from Foucault imagines having been done once and for all during the classical era. New critical formalism did so by insisting that the artifact was its own world, a heterocosm. Structualism and poststructualism broke down the barrier between literary and nonliterary, not however to rejoin literary discourse to the world but to conflate all verbal artifacts within a more spacious domain of textuality. Quarreling with this unworldliness, Marxist and Marxoid (for example, Foucaultian) models of analysis during the 1980s combined with poststructualism in Anglo-America to generate the so-called new historicism, which set text within context. But it did so in terms of the text's status as a species of cultural production or ideological work. In this type of formulation, literature's appropriation of the world in the service of some social allegiance or commitment seemed to render merely epiphenomenal the responsiveness of literature to the natural world either in its self-existence as an assemblage or plenum or in the form of a gestalt that can impress itself on the mind or text in the fundamental and binding way that the epigraph from Lopez envisages. It seems that literature is simply not thought to have the power to do this, that such power it might have is thought to have been overridden by the power of imagination, textuality, and culture over the malleable, plastic world that it bends to its will. Whitman, in "Song of Myself," may insist that "I lean and loafe at my ease observing a spear of summer grass," but there is no grass, no summer, no loafer (despite the title-page illustration done from a photograph of Whitman himself). No, there is only an image, a symbol, a projection, a persona, a vestige or democratic deformation of aristocratic pastoral (compare Thomas Gray's "disporting on the margent green"), a contortion of heptameter.

The historicist movement that succeeded poststructuralism as the dominant theoretical paradigm of literary studies during the 1980s attached greater importance than its formalist and structuralist predecessors to art's mimetic function and might thus seem to be more environment-responsive. Yet it turns out to interpose obstacles no less daunting to making the case for representation in the affirmative sense. The recent dismantling of nineteenth-century realism is instructive here.[7] Within a decade it has become almost hackneyed to point out that so-called realism, far from being a transparent rendering, is a highly stylized ideological or psychohistorical artifact that we have sloppily agreed to call realistic. The powerful rereading by art historian Michael Fried of the high point of realism in American painting, Thomas Eakins's *Gross Clinic*, is a striking example of the new orthodoxy in formation. Although Fried by no means denies the painting's graphic fidelity to documentary detail (the wincing observers, the blood on the scalpel, the almost violent dominance of the surgeon over the patient and the operating room), he argues that the painting is much more fundamentally shaped by intertextual and psycho-biographical forces. The referent, the text-clinic correspondence itself, seems almost epiphenomenal.[8]

Ironically, during the same period that "realism" has been deconstructed, historians and social scientists have often drawn on realistic fiction for evidentiary support. One cultural geographer, for example, praises John Steinbeck's *Grapes of Wrath* as providing "focus for instruction in migration, settlement forms, economic systems, cultural dualism, agricultural land use patterns, transportation technology and social change," as well as "a window on geographic phenomena broadly ranging from mental maps to economic infrastructures."[9]

And why not? I am not the first to wonder whether the discrediting of realism as an attempted transparency has gone too far. George Levine, for one, urges that "the dominant distaste for anything that smacks of the empirical" within the human sciences "needs to be overcome, just as the scientists' tendency to dismiss theory and antirealism must be." Levine contends that "the discriminations that have been obliterated between objectivity and subjectivity, scientific and literary discourse, history and fiction, are in effect, still operative" and that they "need to be recuperated, if modified."[10] His statement about differences in representational mode between disciplines I would apply to the literary field itself. There is a mimetic difference hard to specify but uncontroversial to posit between the Chicago of Theodore Dreiser's *Sister Carrie* and the places of Italo Calvino's *Invisible Cities*, a difference also between Calvino's cities and the cities of Marco Polo's original *Travels*. There is a difference between the relatively "uncomposed" western photographs of Timothy O'Sullivan and nineteenth-century landscape photographs of a more "luminist" persuasion like those by Thomas Moran.[11] In the theory—or countermyth—of representation that I develop in this chapter, these differences are not just symptoms of Dreiser's petit-bourgeois romance of commodities or Calvino's avant-gardist critique (or perhaps reflection) of the more abstract commodifications of contemporary globalized capitalism.[12] My account of the reality of these fictional realities does not deny that they can profitably be so read but focuses on the recuperation of natural objects and the relation between outer and inner landscapes as primary projects.

Notes

1   See for example Yi-fu Tuan, "Common Traits in Perception: The Senses," in *Topophilia: A Study of Environmental Perception, Attitudes, and Values* (1974; rpt., with new preface, New York: Columbia University Press, 1990), pp. 5–12; E. V. Walter, *Placeways: A Theory of the Human Environment.* (Chapel Hill: University of North Carolina Press, 1988), pp. 132–45 and passim; and Hans Jonas's classic essay "The Nobility of Sight" (1953), in *The Phenomenon of Life: Toward a Philosophical Biology* (1966; rpt. Chicago: University of Chicago Press, 1982), which points out that "since the days of Greek philosophy sight has been hailed as the most excellent of the senses" (p. 135).

2   Samuel A. Jones to A. W. Hosmer, 16 April 1903, in *Toward the Making of Thoreau's Modern Reputation*, ed. Fritz Oehlschlaeger and George Hendrick (Urbana: University of Illinois Press, 1979), p. 387.

3   Sharon Cameron, *Writing Nature: Henry Thoreau's Journal* (New York: Oxford University Press, 1985), p. 44. In "A Crisis in My Mental History," Mill explains why reading Wordsworth helped him get through his breakdown: "In the first place, these poems addressed themselves powerfully to one of the strongest of my pleasurable susceptibilities, the love of rural objects and natural scenery" (John Stuart Mill, *Autobiography* [New York: Columbia University Press, 1924], p. 103). See also Jonathan Bate, *Romantic Ecology: Wordsworth and the Romantic Tradition* (London: Routledge, 1991), pp. 14ff., for thoughtful reflections on the current unfashionableness of Mill's response and the need to take it more seriously.

4   For a sophisticated anatomy of contemporary debates about the viability and politics of representation from a perspective professedly neither for nor against mimesis, see Christopher Prendergast, *The Order of Mimesis: Balzac, Stendhal, Nerval, Flaubert* (Cambridge, Eng.: Cambridge University Press, 1986), a study deeply informed by poststructuralist and antecedent literary and philosophical theory. To make an elegant story extremely short, Prendergast finds more problems with "a wholesale rejection of the idea of mimesis" than with retention of some version of mimesis, although all versions seem problematic (pp. 252–53). For my purposes, the utility of his discussion is limited by his concentration on fiction and his understanding of mimesis as a textualized internalization of social norms; but I have found his intricately lucid presentation most enlightening.

5   Leonard Lutwack, *The Role of Place in Literature* (Syracuse: Syracuse University Press, 1984), p. 24. At the outset, Lutwack declares that "a concern for time rather than place is the mark of civilization . . . the maturation of an individual is a process of growing away from nature" (p. 4).

6   Carolyn Porter, "History and Literature: 'After the New Historicism,' " *New Literary History*, 21 (1990): 257.

7   This deconstructive process effectively began with *American Realism: New Essays*, ed. Eric Sundquist (Baltimore: Johns Hopkins University Press, 1982). Among subsequent books, perhaps the most

pertinent here are two by contributors to that collection: Amy Kaplan, *The Social Construction of American Realism* (Chicago: University of Chicago Press, 1988), and Michael Davitt Bell, *The Problem of American Realism: Studies in the Cultural History of a Literary Idea* (Chicago: University of Chicago Press, 1993). The confident tone of Kaplan's opening statement indicates how quickly the revisionary reading has taken hold: "from an objective reflection of contemporary social life, realism has become a fictional conceit, or deceit, packaging and naturalizing an official version of the ordinary" (p. 1). A third contributor's study, Philip Fisher's *Hard Facts: Setting and Form in the American Novel* (New York: Oxford University Press, 1985), gives much more attention to the quality of thingness as such in realist representation (see "The Life History of Objects: The Naturalist Novel and the City," pp. 128–78), though his major concern is the symbolic properties of things as psychograms, sociological gestalts, commodity forms, etc. At least as influential as any Americanist work in the reinterpretation of realism, however, have been more general Marxist and Marxoid treatises like Fredric Jameson's *The Political Unconscious: Narrative as a Socially Symbolic Act* (Ithaca: Cornell University Press, 1981).

8   Michael Fried, *Realism, Writing, Disfiguration* (Chicago: University of Chicago Press, 1987). Fried finds realism a "blandly normalizing bias" that confuses cause with effect and by limiting intention "to an initial choice of subject and point of view plus a general will to realism . . . implies a prejudicial conception of the realistic project as merely photographic" (pp. 64, 10–11). If this "exact transcription" model of realism were the best that a theory of realism's realism could manage, then one could understand Fried's displeasure.

9   Christopher Salter, "John Steinbeck's *The Grapes of Wrath* as a Primer for Cultural Geography," in *Humanistic Geography and Literature: Essays on Experience of Place*, ed. Douglas C. D. Pocock (London: Croom Helm, 1981), pp. 156–57. Salter and William J. Lloyd's coauthored *Landscape in Literature* (Washington: Association of American Geographers, 1977) reflects on the limits of realist assumptions while defending their viability within limits. I by no means wish to suggest that all cultural geographers are empirical mimeticists. The contemporary interest in "reading" place as text has also drawn geographers to poststructuralist and Marxist theory; see, for example, J. Duncan and N. Duncan, "(Re)reading the Landscape," *Society and Space*, 6 (1988): 117–26; and especially Edward W. Soja, *Postmodern Geographies: The Reassertion of Space in Critical Social Theory* (London: Verso, 1989). The broader point is that a number of contemporary humanistic geographers have turned to literary sources to tell them things about landscape that "scientific" geography seems not to register. In approaching literature as a supplementary resource, geographers are never so naive as to take it to be a distortion-free mirror of the object-world, nor are they unanimous in their methodologies of reading. As a group, however, their work emphasizes the ways in which literature seeks to engage and reveal actual landscapes. For further illustration of the range of perspectives brought to bear in this body of scholarship, see "Focus: Literary Landscapes—Geography and Literature," ed. L. Anders Sandberg and John S. Marsh, *The Canadian Geographer*, 32 (1988): 266–76.

10   George Levine, "Scientific Realism and Literary Representation," *Raritan*, 10, no. 4 (Spring 1991): 23, 21. See also Levine's editorial introduction to the symposium *Realism and Representation: Essays on the Problem of Realism in Relation to Science, Literature, and Culture* (Madison: University of Wisconsin Press, 1993), which is helpful for bibliography as well as commentary. (As Levine notes, however, "strong" realism is scantly represented in the collection.) In humanistic fields outside literature, some of the recent work of Hilary Putnam is pertinent, especially *The Many Faces of Realism* (LaSalle, Ill.: Open Court Press, 1987) and the papers collected as *Realism with a Human Face*, ed. James Conant (Cambridge: Harvard University Press, 1990). What to me is most interesting about Putnam's project is his attempt to establish a ground for realism that frees it from having to meet standards of "scientific" objectivity.

11   O'Sullivan's photographs, remarks Barbara Novak, "seem to arise without the intervention of ideas about 'art,' from a one-to-one encounter of camera and nature. The artist's control, though convention-free, is of course present, but often in the most informal way, as if the photographs were taking themselves" ("Landscape Permuted: From Painting to Photography," in *Photography in Print Writings from 1816 to the Present*, ed. Vicki Goldberg [New York: Simon and Schuster, 1981], p. 176).

12   I wish to dodge the vexed question of whether surrealism and avant-gardism generally are hegemonic or insurgent. My inclination, as on the subject of pastoral's ideological valence, is to say: either or both.

Chapter 10

William Cronon

THE TROUBLE WITH WILDERNESS; OR, GETTING BACK TO THE WRONG NATURE

The time has come to rethink wilderness

THIS WILL SEEM A HERETICAL claim to many environmentalists, since the idea of wilderness has for decades been a fundamental tenet—indeed, a passion—of the environmental movement, especially in the United States. For many Americans wilderness stands as the last remaining place where civilization, that all too human disease, has not fully infected the earth. It is an island in the polluted sea of urban-industrial modernity, the one place we can turn for escape from our own too-muchness. Seen in this way, wilderness presents itself as the best antidote to our human selves, a refuge we must somehow recover if we hope to save the planet. As Henry David Thoreau once famously declared, "In Wildness is the preservation of the World."[1]

But is it? The more one knows of its peculiar history, the more one realizes that wilderness is not quite what it seems. Far from being the one place on earth that stands apart from humanity, it is quite profoundly a human creation—indeed, the creation of very particular human cultures at very particular moments in human history. It is not a pristine sanctuary where the last remnant of an untouched, endangered, but still transcendent nature can for at least a little while longer be encountered without the contaminating taint of civilization. Instead, it is a product of that civilization, and could hardly be contaminated by the very stuff of which it is made. Wilderness hides its unnaturalness behind a mask that is all the more beguiling because it seems so natural. As we gaze into the mirror it holds up for us, we too easily imagine that what we behold is Nature when in fact we see the reflection of our own unexamined longings and desires. For this reason, we mistake ourselves when we suppose that wilderness can be the solution to our culture's problematic relationships with the nonhuman world, for wilderness is itself no small part of the problem.

To assert the unnaturalness of so natural a place will no doubt seem absurd or even perverse to many readers, so let me hasten to add that the nonhuman world we encounter in wilderness is far from being merely our own invention. I celebrate with others who love wilderness the beauty and power of the things it contains. Each of us who has spent time there can conjure images and sensations that seem all the more hauntingly real for having engraved themselves so indelibly on our memories. Such memories may be uniquely our own, but they are also familiar enough to be instantly recognizable to others. Remember this? The torrents of mist shoot out from the base of a great waterfall in the depths of a Sierra canyon, the tiny droplets cooling your face as you listen to the roar of the water and gaze up toward the sky through a rainbow that hovers just out of reach. Remember this too: looking out across a desert canyon in the evening air, the only sound a lone raven calling in the distance, the rock walls dropping away into a chasm so deep that its bottom all but vanishes as you squint into the amber light of the setting sun. And this: the moment beside the trail as you sit on a sandstone ledge, your boots damp with the morning dew while you take in the rich smell of the pines, and the small red fox—or maybe for you it was a raccoon or a coyote or a deer—that suddenly ambles across your path, stopping for a long moment to gaze in your direction with cautious indifference before continuing on its way. Remember the feelings of such moments, and you will know as well as I do that you were in the presence of something irreducibly nonhuman, something profoundly Other than yourself. Wilderness is made of that too.

And yet: what brought each of us to the places where such memories became possible is entirely a cultural invention. Go back 250 years in American and European history, and you do not find nearly so many people wandering around remote corners of the planet looking for what today we would call "the wilderness experience." As late as the eighteenth century, the most common usage of the word "wilderness" in the English language referred to landscapes that generally carried adjectives far different from the ones they attract today. To be a wilderness then was to be "deserted," "savage," "desolate," "barren"—in short, a "waste," the word's nearest synonym. Its connotations were anything but positive, and the emotion one was most likely to feel in its presence was "bewilderment"—or terror.[2]

Many of the word's strongest associations then were biblical, for it is used over and over again in the King James Version to refer to places on the margins of civilization where it is all too easy to lose oneself in moral confusion and despair. The wilderness was where Moses had wandered with his people for forty years, and where they had nearly abandoned their God to worship a golden idol.[3] "For Pharoah will say of the Children of Israel," we read in Exodus, "They are entangled in the land, the wilderness hath shut them in."[4] The wilderness was where Christ had struggled with the devil and endured his temptations: "And immediately the Spirit driveth him into the wilderness. And he was there in the wilderness for forty days tempted of Satan; and was with the wild beasts; and the angels ministered unto him."[5] The "delicious Paradise" of John Milton's Eden was surrounded by "a steep wilderness, whose hairy sides/Access denied" to all who sought entry.[6] When Adam and Eve were driven from that garden, the world they entered was a wilderness that only their labor and pain could redeem. Wilderness, in short, was a place to which one came only against one's will, and always in fear and trembling. Whatever value it might have arose solely from the possibility that it might be "reclaimed" and turned toward human ends—planted as a garden, say, or a city upon a hill.[7] In its raw state, it had little or nothing to offer civilized men and women.

But by the end of the nineteenth century, all this had changed. The wastelands that had once seemed worthless had for some people come to seem almost beyond price. That Thoreau in 1862 could declare wildness to be the preservation of the world suggests the sea change that was going on. Wilderness had once been the antithesis of all that was orderly and good—it had been the darkness, one might say, on the far side of the garden wall—and yet now it was frequently likened to Eden itself. When John Muir arrived in the Sierra Nevada in 1869, he would declare, "No description of Heaven that I have ever heard or read of seems half so fine."[8] He was hardly alone in expressing such emotions. One by one, various corners of the American map came to be designated as sites whose wild beauty was so spectacular that a growing number of citizens had to visit and see them for themselves. Niagara Falls was the first to undergo this transformation, but it was soon followed by the Catskills, the Adirondacks, Yosemite, Yellowstone, and others. Yosemite was deeded by the U.S. government to the state of California in 1864 as the nation's first wildland park, and Yellowstone became the first true national park in 1872.[9]

By the first decade of the twentieth century, in the single most famous episode in American conservation history, a national debate had exploded over whether the city of San Francisco should be permitted to augment its water supply by damming the Tuolumne River in Hetch Hetchy valley, well within the boundaries of Yosemite National Park. The dam was eventually built, but what today seems no less significant is that so many people fought to prevent its completion. Even as the fight was being lost, Hetch Hetchy became the battle cry of an emerging movement to preserve wilderness. Fifty years earlier, such opposition would have been unthinkable. Few would have questioned the merits of "reclaiming" a wasteland like this in order to put it to human use. Now the defenders of Hetch Hetchy attracted wide-spread national attention by portraying such an act not as improvement or progress but as desecration and vandalism. Lest one doubt that the old biblical metaphors had been turned completely on their heads, listen to John Muir attack the dam's defenders. "Their arguments," he wrote, "are curiously like those of the devil, devised for the destruction of the first garden—so much of the very best Eden fruit going to waste; so much of the best Tuolumne water and Tuolumne scenery going to waste."[10] For Muir and the growing number of Americans who shared his views, Satan's home had become God's own temple.

The sources of this rather astonishing transformation were many, but for the purposes of this essay they can be gathered under two broad headings: the sublime and the frontier. Of the two, the sublime is the older and more pervasive cultural construct, being one of the most important expressions of that broad transatlantic movement we today label as romanticism; the frontier is more peculiarly American, though it too had its European antecedents and parallels. The two converged to remake wilderness in their own image, freighting it with moral values and cultural symbols that it carries to this day. Indeed, it is not too much to say that the modern environmental movement is itself a grandchild of romanticism and post-frontier ideology, which is why it is no accident that so much environmentalist discourse takes its bearings from the wilderness these intellectual movements helped create. Although wilderness may today seem to be just one environmental concern among many, it in fact serves as the foundation for a long list of other such concerns that on their face seem quite remote from it. That is why its influence is so pervasive and, potentially, so insidious.

To gain such remarkable influence, the concept of wilderness had to become loaded with some of the deepest core values of the culture that created and idealized it: it had to become sacred. This possibility had been present in wilderness even in the days when it had been a place of spiritual danger and moral temptation. If Satan was there, then so was Christ, who had found angels as well as wild beasts during His sojourn in the desert. In the wilderness the boundaries between human and nonhuman, between natural and supernatural, had always seemed less certain than elsewhere. This was why the early Christian saints and mystics had often emulated Christ's desert retreat as they sought to experience for themselves the visions and spiritual testing He had endured. One might meet devils and run the risk of losing one's soul in such a place, but one might also meet God. For some that possibility was worth almost any price.

By the eighteenth century this sense of the wilderness as a landscape where the supernatural lay just beneath the surface was expressed in the doctrine of the *sublime*, a word whose modern usage has been so watered down by commercial hype and tourist advertising that it retains only a dim echo of its former power.[11] In the theories of Edmund Burke, Immanuel Kant, William Gilpin, and others, sublime landscapes were those rare places on earth where one had more chance than elsewhere to glimpse the face of God.[12] Romantics had a clear notion of where one could be most sure of having this experience. Although God might, of course, choose to show Himself anywhere, He would most often be found in those vast, powerful landscapes where one could not help feeling insignificant and being reminded of one's own mortality. Where were these sublime places? The eighteenth-century catalog of their locations feels very familiar, for we still see and value landscapes as it taught us to do. God was on the mountaintop, in the chasm, in the waterfall, in the thundercloud, in the rainbow, in the sunset. One has only to think of the sites that Americans chose for their first national parks— Yellowstone, Yosemite, Grand Canyon, Rainier, Zion—to realize that virtually all of them fit one or more of these categories. Less sublime landscapes simply did not appear worthy of such protection; not until the 1940s, for instance, would the first swamp be honored, in Everglades National Park, and to this day there is no national park in the grasslands.[13]

Among the best proofs that one had entered a sublime landscape was the emotion it evoked. For the early romantic writers and artists who first began to celebrate it, the sublime was far from being a pleasurable experience. The classic description is that of William Wordsworth as he recounted climbing the Alps and crossing the Simplon Pass in his autobiographical poem *The Prelude*. There, surrounded by crags and waterfalls, the poet felt himself literally to be in the presence of the divine—and experienced an emotion remarkably close to terror:

> The immeasurable height
> Of woods decaying, never to be decayed,
> The stationary blasts of waterfalls,
> And in the narrow rent at every turn
> Winds thwarting winds, bewildered and forlorn,
> The torrents shooting from the clear blue sky,
> The rocks that muttered close upon our ears,
> Black drizzling crags that spake by the way-side
> As if a voice were in them, the sick sight
> And giddy prospect of *the* raving stream,
> The unfettered clouds and region of the Heavens,
> Tumult and peace, the darkness and the light—
> Were all like workings of one mind, the features
> Of the same face, blossoms upon one tree;
> Characters of the great Apocalypse,
> The types and symbols of Eternity,
> Of first, and last, and midst, and without end.[14]

This was no casual stroll in the mountains, no simple sojourn in the gentle lap of nonhuman nature. What Wordsworth described was nothing less than a religious experience, akin to that of the Old Testament prophets as they conversed with their wrathful God. The symbols he detected in this wilderness landscape were more supernatural than natural, and they inspired more awe and dismay than joy or pleasure. No mere mortal was meant to linger long in such a place, so it was with considerable relief that Wordsworth and his companion made their way back down from the peaks to the sheltering valleys.

Lest you suspect that this view of the sublime was limited to timid Europeans who lacked the American know-how for feeling at home in the wilderness, remember Henry David Thoreau's 1846 climb of Mount Katahdin, in Maine. Although Thoreau is regarded by many today as one of the great American celebrators of wilderness, his emotions about Katahdin were no less ambivalent than Wordsworth's about the Alps.

> It was vast, Titanic, and such as man never inhabits. Some part of the beholder,
> even some vital part, seems to escape through the loose grating of his ribs as he

ascends. He is more lone than you can imagine. . . . Vast, Titanic, inhuman Nature has got him at disadvantage, caught him alone, and pilfers him of some of his divine faculty. She does not smile on him as in the plains. She seems to say sternly, why came ye here before your time? This ground is not prepared for you. Is it not enough that I smile in the valleys? I have never made this soil for thy feet, this air for thy breathing, these rocks for thy neighbors. I cannot pity nor fondle thee here, but forever relentlessly drive thee hence to where I *am* kind. Why seek me where I have not called thee, and then complain because you find me but a stepmother?[15]

This is surely not the way a modern backpacker or nature lover would describe Maine's most famous mountain, but that is because Thoreau's description owes as much to Wordsworth and other romantic contemporaries as to the rocks and clouds of Katahdin itself. His words took the physical mountain on which he stood and transmuted it into an icon of the sublime: a symbol of God's presence on earth. The power and the glory of that icon were such that only a prophet might gaze on it for long. In effect, romantics like Thoreau joined Moses and the children of Israel in Exodus when "they looked toward the wilderness, and behold, the glory of the Lord appeared in the cloud."[16]

But even as it came to embody the awesome power of the sublime, wilderness was also being tamed—not just by those who were building settlements in its midst but also by those who most celebrated its inhuman beauty. By the second half of the nineteenth century, the terrible awe that Wordsworth and Thoreau regarded as the appropriately pious stance to adopt in the presence of their mountaintop God was giving way to a much more comfortable, almost sentimental demeanor. As more and more tourists sought out the wilderness as a spectacle to be looked at and enjoyed for its great beauty, the sublime in effect became domesticated. The wilderness was still sacred, but the religious sentiments it evoked were more those of a pleasant parish church than those of a grand cathedral or a harsh desert retreat. The writer who best captures this late romantic sense of a domesticated sublime is undoubtedly John Muir, whose descriptions of Yosemite and the Sierra Nevada reflect none of the anxiety or terror one finds in earlier writers. Here he is, for instance, sketching on North Dome in Yosemite Valley:

> No pain here, no dull empty hours, no fear of the past, no fear of the future. These blessed mountains are so compactly filled with God's beauty, no petty personal hope or experience has room to be. Drinking this champagne water is pure pleasure, so is breathing the living air, and every movement of limbs is pleasure, while the body seems to feel beauty when exposed to it as it feels the campfire or sunshine, entering not by the eyes alone, but equally through all one's flesh like radiant heat, making a passionate ecstatic pleasure glow not explainable.

The emotions Muir describes in Yosemite could hardly be more different from Thoreau's on Katahdin or Wordsworth's on the Simplon Pass. Yet all three men are participating in the same cultural tradition and contributing to the same myth: the mountain as cathedral. The three may differ in the way they choose to express their piety—Wordsworth favoring an awe-filled bewilderment, Thoreau a stern loneliness, Muir a welcome ecstasy—but they agree completely about the church in which they prefer to worship. Muir's closing words on North Dome diverge from his older contemporaries only in mood, not in their ultimate content:

> Perched like a fly on this Yosemite dome, I gaze and sketch and bask, oftentimes settling down into dumb admiration without definite hope of ever learning

much, yet with the longing, unresting effort that lies at the door of hope, humbly prostrate before the vast display of God's power, and eager to offer self-denial and renunciation with eternal toil to learn any lesson in the divine manuscript.[17]

Muir's "divine manuscript" and Wordsworth's "Characters of the great Apocalypse" were in fact pages from the same holy book. The sublime wilderness had ceased to be a place of satanic temptation and become instead a sacred temple, much as it continues to be for those who love it today.

But the romantic sublime was not the only cultural movement that helped transform wilderness into a sacred American icon during the nineteenth century. No less important was the powerful romantic attraction of primitivism, dating back at least to Rousseau—the belief that the best antidote to the ills of an overly refined and civilized modern world was a return to simpler, more primitive living. In the United States, this was embodied most strikingly in the national myth of the frontier. The historian Frederick Jackson Turner wrote in 1893 the classic academic statement of this myth, but it had been part of American cultural traditions for well over a century. As Turner described the process, easterners and European immigrants, in moving to the wild unsettled lands of the frontier, shed the trappings of civilization, rediscovered their primitive racial energies, reinvented direct democratic institutions, and thereby reinfused themselves with a vigor, an independence, and a creativity that were the source of American democracy and national character. Seen in this way, wild country became a place not just of religious redemption but of national renewal, the quintessential location for experiencing what it meant to be an American.

One of Turner's most provocative claims was that by the 1890s the frontier was passing away. Never again would "such gifts of free land offer themselves" to the American people. "The frontier has gone," he declared, "and with its going has closed the first period of American history."[18] Built into the frontier myth from its very beginning was the notion that this crucible of American identity was temporary and would pass away. Those who have celebrated the frontier have almost always looked backward as they did so, mourning an older, simpler, truer world that is about to disappear forever. That world and all of its attractions, Turner said, depended on free land—on wilderness. Thus, in the myth of the vanishing frontier lay the seeds of wilderness preservation in the United States, for if wild land had been so crucial in the making of the nation, then surely one must save its last remnants as monuments to the American past—and as an insurance policy to protect its future. It is no accident that the movement to set aside national parks and wilderness areas began to gain real momentum at precisely the time that laments about the passing frontier reached their peak. To protect wilderness was in a very real sense to protect the nation's most sacred myth of origin.

Among the core elements of the frontier myth was the powerful sense among certain groups of Americans that wilderness was the last bastion of rugged individualism. Turner tended to stress communitarian themes when writing frontier history, asserting that Americans in primitive conditions had been forced to band together with their neighbors to form communities and democratic institutions. For other writers, however, frontier democracy for communities was less compelling than frontier freedom for individuals.[19] By fleeing to the outer margins of settled land and society—so the story ran—an individual could escape the confining strictures of civilized life. The mood among writers who celebrated frontier individualism was almost always nostalgic; they lamented not just a lost way of life but the passing of the heroic men who had embodied that life. Thus Owen Wister in the introduction to his classic 1902 novel *The Virginian* could write of "a vanished world" in which "the horseman, the cow-puncher, the last romantic figure upon our soil" rode only "in his historic yesterday" and would "never come again." For Wister, the cowboy was a man who gave his word and kept it ("Wall Street would have found him behind the times"), who did not talk lewdly to women ("Newport would have thought him old-fashioned"), who worked and played hard, and whose "ungoverned hours did not unman him."[20] Theodore Roosevelt wrote with much the same nostalgic fervor about the "fine, manly qualities" of the "wild rough-rider of the plains." No one could be more heroically masculine, thought Roosevelt, or more at home in the western wilderness:

> There he passes his days, there he does his life-work, there, when he meets death, he faces it as he has faced many other evils, with quiet, uncomplaining fortitude. Brave, hospitable, hardy, and adventurous, he is the grim pioneer of our race; he prepares the way for the civilization from before whose face he must himself disappear. Hard and dangerous though his existence is, it has yet a wild attraction that strongly draws to it his bold, free spirit.[21]

This nostalgia for a passing frontier way of life inevitably implied ambivalence, if not downright hostility, toward modernity and all that it represented. If one saw the wild lands of the frontier as freer, truer, and more natural than other, more modern places, then one was also inclined to see the cities and factories of urban-industrial civilization as confining, false, and artificial. Owen Wister looked at the post-frontier "transition" that had followed "the horseman of the plains," and did not like what he saw: "a shapeless state, a condition of men and manners as unlovely as is that moment in the year when winter is gone and spring not come, and the face of Nature is ugly."[22] In the eyes of writers who shared Wister's distaste for modernity, civilization contaminated its inhabitants and absorbed them into the faceless, collective, contemptible life of the crowd. For all of its troubles and dangers, and despite the fact that it must pass away, the frontier had been a better place. If civilization was to be redeemed, it would be by men like the Virginian who could retain their frontier virtues even as they made the transition to post-frontier life.

The mythic frontier individualist was almost always masculine in gender: here, in the wilderness, a man could be a real man, the rugged individual he was meant to be before civilization sapped his energy and threatened his masculinity. Wister's contemptuous remarks about Wall Street and Newport suggest what he and many others of his generation believed— that the comforts and seductions of civilized life were especially insidious for men, who all too easily became emasculated by the femininizing tendencies of civilization. More often than not, men who felt this way came, like Wister and Roosevelt, from elite class backgrounds. The curious result was that frontier nostalgia became an important vehicle for expressing a peculiarly bourgeois form of antimodernism. The very men who most benefited from urban-industrial capitalism were among those who believed they must escape its debilitating effects. If the frontier was passing, then men who had the means to do so should preserve for themselves some remnant of its wild landscape so that they might enjoy the regeneration and renewal that came from sleeping under the stars, participating in blood sports, and living off the land. The frontier might be gone, but the frontier experience could still be had if only wilderness were preserved.

Thus the decades following the Civil War saw more and more of the nation's wealthiest citizens seeking out wilderness for themselves. The elite passion for wild land took many forms: enormous estates in the Adirondacks and elsewhere (disingenuously called "camps" despite their many servants and amenities), cattle ranches for would-be rough riders on the Great Plains, guided big-game hunting trips in the Rockies, and luxurious resort hotels wherever railroads pushed their way into sublime landscapes. Wilderness suddenly emerged as the landscape of choice for elite tourists, who brought with them strikingly urban ideas of the countryside through which they traveled. For them, wild land was not a site for productive labor and not a permanent home; rather, it was a place of recreation. One went to the wilderness not as a producer but as a consumer, hiring guides and other backcountry residents who could serve as romantic surrogates for the rough riders and hunters of the frontier if one was willing to overlook their new status as employees and servants of the rich.

In just this way, wilderness came to embody the national frontier myth, standing for the wild freedom of America's past and seeming to represent a highly attractive natural alternative to the ugly artificiality of modern civilization. The irony, of course, was that in the process wilderness came to reflect the very civilization its devotees sought to escape. Ever since the nineteenth century, celebrating wilderness has been an activity mainly for well-to-do city folks. Country people generally know far too much about working the land to regard *un*worked land as their ideal. In contrast, elite urban tourists and wealthy sportsmen projected their leisure-time frontier fantasies onto the American landscape and so created wilderness in their own image.

There were other ironies as well. The movement to set aside national parks and wilderness areas followed hard on the heels of the final Indian wars, in which the prior human inhabitants of these areas were rounded up and moved onto reservations. The myth of the wilderness as "virgin," uninhabited land had always been especially cruel when seen from the perspective of the Indians who had once called that land home. Now they were forced to move elsewhere, with the result that tourists could safely enjoy the illusion that they were seeing their nation in its pristine, original state, in the new morning of God's own creation.[23] Among the things that most marked the new national parks as reflecting a post-frontier consciousness was the relative absence of human violence within their boundaries. The actual frontier had often been a place of conflict, in which invaders and invaded fought for control of land and resources. Once set aside within the fixed and carefully policed boundaries of the modern bureaucratic state, the wilderness lost its savage image and became safe: a place more of reverie than of revulsion or fear. Meanwhile, its original inhabitants were kept out by dint of force, their earlier uses of the land redefined as inappropriate or even illegal. To this day, for instance, the Blackfeet continue to be accused of "poaching" on the lands of Glacier National Park that originally belonged to them and that were ceded by treaty only with the proviso that they be permitted to hunt there.[24]

The removal of Indians to create an "uninhabited wilderness"—uninhabited as never before in the human history of the place—reminds us just how invented, just how constructed, the American wilderness really is. To return to my opening argument: there is nothing natural about the concept of wilderness. It is entirely a creation of the culture that holds it dear, a product of the very history it seeks to deny. Indeed, one of the most striking proofs of the cultural invention of wilderness is its thoroughgoing erasure of the history from which it sprang. In virtually all of its manifestations, wilderness represents a flight from history. Seen as the original garden, it is a place outside of time, from which human beings had to be ejected before the fallen world of history could properly begin. Seen as the frontier, it is a savage world at the dawn of civilization, whose transformation represents the very beginning of the national historical epic. Seen as the bold landscape of frontier heroism, it is the place of youth and childhood, into which men escape by abandoning their pasts and entering a world of freedom where the constraints of civilization fade into memory. Seen as the sacred sublime, it is the home of a God who transcends history by standing as the One who remains untouched and unchanged by time's arrow. No matter what the angle from which we regard it, wilderness offers us the illusion that we can escape the cares and troubles of the world in which our past has ensnared us.[25]

This escape from history is one reason why the language we use to talk about wilderness is often permeated with spiritual and religious values that reflect human ideals far more than the material world of physical nature. Wilderness fulfills the old romantic project of secularizing Judeo-Christian values so as to make a new cathedral not in some petty human building but in God's own creation, Nature itself. Many environmentalists who reject traditional notions of the Godhead and who regard themselves as agnostics or even atheists nonetheless express feelings tantamount to religious awe when in the presence of wilderness—a fact that testifies to the success of the romantic project. Those who have no difficulty seeing God as the expression of our human dreams and desires nonetheless have trouble recognizing that in a secular age Nature can offer precisely the same sort of mirror.

Thus it is that wilderness serves as the unexamined foundation on which so many of the quasi-religious values of modern environmentalism rest. The critique of modernity that is one of environmentalism's most important contributions to the moral and political discourse of our time more often than not appeals, explicitly or implicitly, to wilderness as the standard against which to measure the failings of our human world. Wilderness is the natural, Unfallen antithesis of an unnatural civilization that has lost its soul. It is a place of freedom in which we can recover the true selves we have lost to the corrupting influences of our artificial lives. Most of all, it is the ultimate landscape of authenticity. Combining the sacred grandeur of the sublime with the primitive simplicity of the frontier, it is the place where we can see the world as it really is, and so know ourselves as we really are—or ought to be.

But the trouble with wilderness is that it quietly expresses and reproduces the very values its devotees seek to reject. The flight from history that is very nearly the core of wilderness represents the false hope of an escape from responsibility, the illusion that we can somehow wipe clean the slate of our past and return to the tabula rasa that supposedly existed before we began to leave our marks on the world. The dream of an unworked natural land-scape is very much the fantasy of people who have never themselves had to work the land to make a living—urban folk for whom food comes from a supermarket or a restaurant instead of a field, and for whom the wooden houses in which they live and work apparently have no meaningful connection to the forests in which trees grow and die. Only people whose rela-tion to the land was already alienated could hold up wilderness as a model for human life in nature, for the romantic ideology of wilderness leaves precisely nowhere for human beings actually to make their living from the land.

This, then, is the central paradox: wilderness embodies a dualistic vision in which the human is entirely outside the natural. If we allow ourselves to believe that nature, to be true, must also be wild, then our very presence in nature represents its fall. The place where we are is the place where nature is not. If this is so—if by definition wilderness leaves no place for human beings, save perhaps as contemplative sojourners enjoying their leisurely reverie in God's natural cathedral—then also by definition it can offer no solution to the environmental and other problems that confront us. To the extent that we celebrate wilderness as the measure with which we judge civilization, we reproduce the dualism that sets humanity and nature at opposite poles. We thereby leave ourselves little hope of discovering what an ethical, sustainable, *honorable* human place in nature might actually look like.

Worse: to the extent that we live in an urban-industrial civilization but at the same time pretend to ourselves that our *real* home is in the wilderness, to just that extent we give ourselves permission to evade responsibility for the lives we actually lead. We inhabit civili-zation while holding some part of ourselves—what we imagine to be the most precious part—aloof from its entanglements. We work our nine-to-five jobs in its institutions, we eat its food, we drive its cars (not least to reach the wilderness), we benefit from the intricate and all too invisible networks with which it shelters us, all the while pretending that these things are not an essential part of who we are. By imagining that our true home is in the wilderness, we forgive ourselves the homes we actually inhabit. In its flight from history, in its siren song of escape, in its reproduction of the dangerous dualism that sets human beings outside of nature—in all of these ways, wilderness poses a serious threat to responsible environmentalism at the end of the twentieth century.

By now I hope it is clear that my criticism in this essay is not directed at wild nature per se, or even at efforts to set aside large tracts of wild land, but rather at the specific habits of thinking that flow from this complex cultural construction called wilderness. It is not the things we label as wilderness that are the problem—for nonhuman nature and large tracts of the natural world *do* deserve protection—but rather what we ourselves mean when we use that label. Lest one doubt how pervasive these habits of thought actually are in contemporary environmentalism, let me list some of the places where wilderness serves as the ideological underpinning for environmental concerns that might otherwise seem quite remote from it. Defenders of biological diversity, for instance, although sometimes appealing to more utilitarian concerns, often point to "untouched" ecosystems as the best and richest repositories of the undiscovered species we must certainly try to protect. Although at first blush an apparently more "scientific" concept than wilderness, biological diversity in fact invokes many of the same sacred values, which is why organizations like the Nature Conservancy have been so quick to employ it as an alternative to the seemingly fuzzier and more problematic concept of wilderness. There is a paradox here, of course. To the extent that biological diversity (indeed, even wilderness itself) is likely to survive in the future only by the most vigilant and self-conscious management of the ecosystems that sustain it, the ideology of wilderness is potentially in direct conflict with the very thing it encourages us to protect.[26]

The most striking instances of this have revolved around "endangered species," which serve as vulnerable symbols of biological diversity while at the same time standing as surrogates for wilderness itself. The terms of the Endangered Species Act in the United States have often meant that those hoping to defend pristine wilderness have had to rely on a single endangered species like the spotted owl to gain legal standing for their case—thereby making the full power of sacred land inhere in a single numinous organism whose habitat then becomes the object of intense debate about appropriate management and use.[27] The ease with which anti-environmental forces like the wise-use movement have attacked such single-species preservation efforts suggests the vulnerability of strategies like these.

Perhaps partly because our own conflicts over such places and organisms have become so messy, the convergence of wilderness values with concerns about biological diversity and endangered species has helped produce a deep fascination for remote ecosystems, where it is easier to imagine that nature might somehow be "left alone" to flourish by its own pristine devices. The classic example is the tropical rain forest, which since the 1970s has become the most powerful modern icon of unfallen, sacred land—a veritable Garden of Eden—for many Americans and Europeans. And yet protecting the rain forest in the eyes of First World environmentalists all too often means protecting it from the people who live there. Those who seek to preserve such "wilderness" from the activities of native peoples run the risk of reproducing the same tragedy—being forceably removed from an ancient home—that befell American Indians. Third World countries face massive environmental problems and deep social conflicts, but these are not likely to be solved by a cultural myth that encourages us to "preserve" peopleless landscapes that have not existed in such places for millennia. At its worst, as environmentalists are beginning to realize, exporting American notions of wilderness in this way can become an unthinking and self-defeating form of cultural imperialism.[28]

Perhaps the most suggestive example of the way that wilderness thinking can underpin other environmental concerns has emerged in the recent debate about "global change." In 1989 the journalist Bill McKibben published a book entitled *The End of Nature*, in which he argued that the prospect of global climate change as a result of unintentional human manipulation of the atmosphere means that nature as we once knew it no longer exists.[29] Whereas earlier generations inhabited a natural world that remained more or less unaffected by their actions, our own generation is uniquely different. We and our children will henceforth live in a biosphere completely altered by our own activity, a planet in which the human and the natural can no longer be distinguished, because the one has overwhelmed the other. In McKibben's view, nature has died, and we are responsible for killing it. "The planet," he declares, "is utterly different now."[30]

But such a perspective is possible only if we accept the wilderness premise that nature, to be natural, must also be pristine—remote from humanity and untouched by our common past. In fact, everything we know about environmental history suggests that people have been manipulating the natural world on various scales for as long as we have a record of their passing. Moreover, we have unassailable evidence that many of the environmental changes we now face also occurred quite apart from human intervention at one time or another in the earth's past.[31] The point is not that our current problems are trivial, or that our devastating effects on the earth's ecosystems should be accepted as inevitable or "natural." It is rather that we seem unlikely to make much progress in solving these problems if we hold up to ourselves as the mirror of nature a wilderness we ourselves cannot inhabit.

To do so is merely to take to a logical extreme the paradox that was built into wilderness from the beginning: if nature dies because we enter it, then the only way to save nature is to kill ourselves. The absurdity of this proposition flows from the underlying dualism it expresses. Not only does it ascribe greater power to humanity than we in fact possess—physical and biological nature will surely survive in some form or another long after we ourselves have gone the way of all flesh—but in the end it offers us little more than a self-defeating counsel of despair. The tautology gives us no way out: if wild nature is the only thing worth saving, and if our mere presence destroys it, then the sole solution to our own unnaturalness, the only way to protect sacred wilderness from profane humanity, would seem to be suicide. It is not a proposition that seems likely to produce very positive or practical results.

And yet radical environmentalists and deep ecologists all too frequently come close to accepting this premise as a first principle. When they express, for instance, the popular notion that our environmental problems began with the invention of agriculture, they push the human fall from natural grace so far back into the past that all of civilized history becomes a tale of ecological declension. Earth First! founder Dave Foreman captures the familiar parable succinctly when he writes,

> Before agriculture was midwifed in the Middle East, humans were in the wilderness. We had no concept of "wilderness" because everything was wilderness and *we were a part of it*. But with irrigation ditches, crop surpluses, and permanent villages, we became *apart from* the natural world. . . . Between the wilderness that created us and the civilization created by us grew an ever-widening rift.[32]

In this view the farm becomes the first and most important battlefield in the long war against wild nature, and all else follows in its wake. From such a starting place, it is hard not to reach the conclusion that the only way human beings can hope to live naturally on earth is to follow the hunter-gatherers back into a wilderness Eden and abandon virtually everything that civilization has given us. It may indeed turn out that civilization will end in ecological collapse or nuclear disaster, whereupon one might expect to find any human survivors returning to a way of life closer to that celebrated by Foreman and his followers. For most of us, though, such a debacle would be cause for regret, a sign that humanity had failed to fulfill its own promise and failed to honor its own highest values—including those of the deep ecologists.

In offering wilderness as the ultimate hunter-gatherer alternative to civilization, Foreman reproduces an extreme but still easily recognizable version of the myth of frontier primitivism. When he writes of his fellow Earth Firsters that "we believe we must return to being animal, to glorying in our sweat, hormones, tears, and blood" and that "we struggle against the modern compulsion to become dull, passionless androids," he is following in the footsteps of Owen Wister.[33] Although his arguments give primacy to defending biodiversity and the autonomy of wild nature, his prose becomes most passionate when he speaks of preserving "the wilderness experience." His own ideal "Big Outside" bears an uncanny resemblance to that of the frontier myth: wide open spaces and virgin land with no trails, no signs, no facilities, no maps, no guides, no rescues, no modern equipment. Tellingly, it is a land where hardy travelers can support themselves by hunting with "primitive weapons (bow and arrow, atlatl, knife, sharp rock)."[34] Foreman claims that "the primary value of wilderness is not as a proving ground for young Huck Finns and Annie Oakleys," but his heart is with Huck and Annie all the same. He admits that "preserving a quality wilderness experience for the human visitor, letting her or him flex Paleolithic muscles or seek visions, remains a tremendously important secondary purpose."[35] Just so does Teddy Roosevelt's rough rider live on in the greener garb of a new age.

However much one may be attracted to such a vision, it entails problematic consequences. For one, it makes wilderness the locus for an epic struggle between malign civilization and benign nature, compared with which all other social, political, and moral concerns seem trivial. Foreman writes, "The preservation of wildness and native diversity is *the* most important issue. Issues directly affecting only humans pale in comparison."[36] Presumably so do any environmental problems whose victims are mainly people, for such problems usually surface in landscapes that have already "fallen" and are no longer wild. This would seem to exclude from the radical environmentalist agenda problems of occupational health and safety in industrial settings, problems of toxic waste exposure on "unnatural" urban and agricultural sites, problems of poor children poisoned by lead exposure in the inner city, problems of famine and poverty and human suffering in the "overpopulated" places of the earth—problems, in short, of environmental justice. If we set too high a stock on wilderness, too many other corners of the earth become less than natural and too many other people become less than human, thereby giving us permission not to care much about their suffering or their fate.

It is no accident that these supposedly inconsequential environmental problems affect mainly poor people, for the long affiliation between wilderness and wealth means that the only poor people who count when wilderness is *the* issue are hunter-gatherers, who presumably do not consider themselves to be poor in the first place. The dualism at the heart of wilderness encourages its advocates to conceive of its protection as a crude conflict between the "human" and the "nonhuman"—or, more often, between those who value the nonhuman and those who do not. This in turn tempts one to ignore crucial differences *among* humans and the complex cultural and historical reasons why different peoples may feel very differently about the meaning of wilderness.

Why, for instance, is the "wilderness experience" so often conceived as a form of recreation best enjoyed by those whose class privileges give them the time and resources to leave their jobs behind and "get away from it all"? Why does the protection of wilderness so often seem to pit urban recreationists against rural people who actually earn their living from the land (excepting those who sell goods and services to the tourists themselves)? Why in the debates about pristine natural areas are "primitive" peoples idealized, even sentimentalized, until the moment they do something unprimitive, modern, and unnatural, and thereby fall from environmental grace? What are the consequences of a wilderness ideology that devalues productive labor and the very concrete knowledge that comes from working the land with one's own hands?[37] All of these questions imply conflicts among different groups of people, conflicts that are obscured behind the deceptive clarity of "human" vs. "nonhuman." If in answering these knotty questions we resort to so simplistic an opposition, we are almost certain to ignore the very subtleties and complexities we need to understand.

But the most troubling cultural baggage that accompanies the celebration of wilderness has less to do with remote rain forests and peoples than with the ways we think about ourselves—we American environmentalists who quite rightly worry about the future of the earth and the threats we pose to the natural world. Idealizing a distant wilderness too often means not idealizing the environment in which we actually live, the landscape that for better or worse we call home. Most of our most serious environmental problems start right here, at home, and if we are to solve those problems, we need an environmental ethic that will tell us as much about *using* nature as about *not* using it. The wilderness dualism tends to cast any use as *ab*-use, and thereby denies us a middle ground in which responsible use and non-use might attain some kind of balanced, sustainable relationship. My own belief is that only by exploring this middle ground will we learn ways of imagining a better world for all of us: humans and nonhumans, rich people and poor, women and men, First Worlders and Third Worlders, white folks and people of color, consumers and producers—a world better for humanity in all of its diversity and for all the rest of nature too. The middle ground is where we actually live. It is where we—all of us, in our different places and ways—make our homes.

That is why, when I think of all the times I myself have comes closest to experiencing what I might call the sacred in nature, I often find myself remembering wild places closer to home. I think, for instance, of a small pond near my house where water bubbles up from limestone springs to feed a series of pools that rarely freeze in winter and so play home to waterfowl that stay here for the protective warmth even in the coldest of winter days, gliding silently through steaming mists as the snow falls from the gray February skies. I think of a November evening long ago when I found myself on a Wisconsin hilltop in rain and dense fog, only to have the setting sun break through the clouds to cast an otherworldly golden light on the misty farms and woodlands below, a scene so unexpected and joyous that I lingered past dusk so as not to miss any part of the gift that had come my way. And I think perhaps most especially of the blown-out, bankrupt farm in the sand country of central Wisconsin where Aldo Leopold and his family tried one of the first American experiments in ecological restoration, turning ravaged and infertile soil into carefully tended ground where the human and nonhuman could exist side by side in relative harmony. What I celebrate about such places is not *just* their wildness, though that certainly is among their most important qualities; what I celebrate even more is that they remind us of the wildness in our own backyards, of the nature that is all around us if only we have eyes to see it.

Indeed, my principal objection to wilderness is that it may teach us to be dismissive or even contemptuous of such humble places and experiences. Without our quite realizing it, wilderness tends to privilege some parts of nature at the expense of others. Most of us, I suspect, still follow the conventions of the romantic sublime in finding the mountaintop more glorious than the plains, the ancient forest nobler than the grasslands, the mighty canyon more inspiring than the humble marsh. Even John Muir, in arguing against those who sought to dam his beloved Hetch Hetchy valley in the Sierra Nevada, argued for alternative dam sites in gentler valleys of the foothills—a preference that had nothing to do with nature and everything with the cultural traditions of the sublime.[38] Just as problematically, our frontier traditions have encouraged Americans to define "true" wilderness as requiring very large tracts of roadless land—what Dave Foreman calls "The Big Outside." Leaving aside the legitimate empirical question in conservation biology of how large a tract of land must be before a given species can reproduce on it, the emphasis on big wilderness reflects a romantic frontier belief that one hasn't really gotten away from civilization unless one can go for days at a time without encountering another human being. By teaching us to fetishize sublime places and wide open country, these peculiarly American ways of thinking about wilderness encourage us to adopt too high a standard for what counts as "natural." If it isn't hundreds of square miles big, it if doesn't give us God's-eye views or grand vistas, if it doesn't permit us the illusion that we are alone on the planet, then it really isn't natural. It's too small, too plain, or too crowded to be *authentically* wild.

In critiquing wilderness as I have done in this essay, I'm forced to confront my own deep ambivalence about its meaning for modern environmentalism. On the one hand, one of my own most important environmental ethics is that people should always be conscious that they are part of the natural world, inextricably tied to the ecological systems that sustain their lives. Any way of looking at nature that encourages us to believe we are separate from nature—as wilderness tends to do—is likely to reinforce environmentally irresponsible behavior. On the other hand, I also think it no less crucial for us to recognize and honor nonhuman nature as a world we did not create, a world with its own independent, nonhuman reasons for being as it is. The autonomy of nonhuman nature seems to me an indispensable corrective to human arrogance. Any way of looking at nature that helps us remember—as wilderness also tends to do—that the interests of people are not necessarily identical to those of every other creature or of the earth itself is likely to foster *responsible* behavior. To the extent that wilderness has served as an important vehicle for articulating deep moral values regarding our obligations and responsibilities to the nonhuman world, I would not want to jettison the contributions it has made to our culture's ways of thinking about nature.

If the core problem of wilderness is that it distances us too much from the very things it teaches us to value, then the question we must ask is what it can tell us about *home*, the place where we actually live. How can we take the positive values we associate with wilderness and bring them closer to home? I think the answer to this question will come by broadening our sense of the otherness that wilderness seeks to define and protect. In reminding us of the world we did not make, wilderness can teach profound feelings of humility and respect as we confront our fellow beings and the earth itself. Feelings like these argue for the importance of self-awareness and self-criticism as we exercise our own ability to transform the world around us, helping us set responsible limits to human mastery—which without such limits too easily becomes human hubris. Wilderness is the place where, symbolically at least, we try to withhold our power to dominate.

Wallace Stegner once wrote of

> the special human mark, the special record of human passage, that distinguishes man from all other species. It is rare enough among men, impossible to any other form of life. *It is simply the deliberate and chosen refusal to make any marks at all.* . . . We are the most dangerous species of life on the planet, and every other species, even the earth itself, has cause to fear our power to exterminate. But we are also the only species which, when it chooses to do so, will go to great effort to save what it might destroy.[39]

The myth of wilderness, which Stegner knowingly reproduces in these remarks, is that we can somehow leave nature untouched by our passage. By now it should be clear that this for the most part is an illusion. But Stegner's deeper message then becomes all the more compelling. If living in history means that we cannot help leaving marks on a fallen world, then the dilemma we face is to decide what kinds of marks we wish to leave. It is just here that our cultural traditions of wilderness remain so important. In the broadest sense, wilderness teaches us to ask whether the Other must always bend to our will, and, if not, under what circumstances it should be allowed to flourish without our intervention. This is surely a question worth asking about everything we do, and not just about the natural world.

When we visit a wilderness area, we find ourselves surrounded by plants and animals and physical landscapes whose otherness compels our attention. In forcing us to acknowledge that they are not of our making, that they have little or no need of our continued existence, they recall for us a creation far greater than our own. In the wilderness, we need no reminder that a tree has its own reasons for being, quite apart from us. The same is less true in the gardens we plant and tend ourselves: there it is far easier to forget the otherness of the tree.[40] Indeed, one could almost measure wilderness by the extent to which our recognition of its otherness requires a conscious, willed act on our part. The romantic legacy means that wilderness is more a state of mind than a fact of nature, and the state of mind that today most defines wilderness is *wonder*. The striking power of the wild is that wonder in the face of it requires no act of will, but forces itself upon us—as an expression of the nonhuman world experienced through the lens of our cultural history—as proof that ours is not the only presence in the universe.

Wilderness gets us into trouble only if we imagine that this experience of wonder and otherness is limited to the remote corners of the planet, or that it somehow depends on pristine landscapes we ourselves do not inhabit. Nothing could be more misleading. The tree in the garden is in reality no less other, no less worthy of our wonder and respect, than the tree in an ancient forest that has never known an ax or saw—even though the tree in the forest reflects a more intricate web of ecological relationships. The tree in the garden could easily have sprung from the same seed as the tree in the forest, and we can claim only its location and perhaps its form as our own. Both trees stand apart from us; both share our common world. The special power of the tree in the wilderness is to remind us of this fact. It can teach us to recognize the wildness we did not see in the tree we planted in our own backyard. By seeing the otherness in that which is most unfamiliar, we can learn to see it too in that which at first seemed merely ordinary. If wilderness can do this—if it can help us perceive and respect a nature we had forgotten to recognize as natural—then it will become part of the solution to our environmental dilemmas rather than part of the problem.

This will only happen, however, if we abandon the dualism that sees the tree in the garden as artificial—completely fallen and unnatural—and the tree in the wilderness as natural—completely pristine and wild. Both trees in some ultimate sense are wild; both in a practical sense now depend on our management and care. We are responsible for both, even though we can claim credit for neither. Our challenge is to stop thinking of such things according to a set of bipolar moral scales in which the human and the nonhuman, the unnatural and the natural, the fallen and the unfallen, serve as our conceptual map for understanding and valuing the world. Instead, we need to embrace the full continuum of a natural landscape that is also cultural, in which the city, the suburb, the pastoral, and the wild each has its proper place, which we permit ourselves to celebrate without needlessly denigrating the others. We need to honor the Other within and the Other next door as much as we do the exotic Other that lives far away—a lesson that applies as much to people as it does to (other) natural things. In particular, we need to discover a common middle ground in which all of these things, from the city to the wilderness, can somehow be encompassed in the word "home." Home, after all, is the place where finally we make our living. It is the place for which we take responsibility, the place we try to sustain so we can pass on what is best in it (and in ourselves) to our children.[41]

The task of making a home in nature is what Wendell Berry has called "the forever unfinished lifework of our species." "The only thing we have to preserve nature with," he writes, "is culture; the only thing we have to preserve wildness with is domesticity."[42] Calling a place home inevitable means that we will *use* the nature we find in it, for there can be no escape from manipulating and working and even killing some parts of nature to make our home. But if we acknowledge the autonomy and otherness of the things and creatures around us—an autonomy our culture has taught us to label with the word "wild"—then we will at least think carefully about the uses to which we put them, and even ask if we should use them at all. Just so can we still join Thoreau in declaring that "in Wildness is the preservation of the World," for *wildness* (as opposed to wilderness) can be found anywhere: in the seemingly tame fields and woodlots of Massachusetts, in the cracks of a Manhattan sidewalk, even in the cells of our own bodies. As Gary Snyder has wisely said, "A person with a clear heart and open mind can experience the wilderness anywhere on earth. It is a quality of one's own consciousness. The planet is a wild place and always will be."[43] To think ourselves capable of causing "the end of nature" is an act of great hubris, for it means forgetting the wildness that dwells everywhere within and around us.

Learning to honor the wild—learning to remember and acknowledge the autonomy of the other—means striving for critical self-consciousness in all of our actions. It means that deep reflection and respect must accompany each act of use, and means too that we must always consider the possibility of non-use. It means looking at the part of nature we intend to turn toward our own ends and asking whether we can use it again and again and again— sustainably—without its being diminished in the process. It means never imagining that we can flee into a mythical wilderness to escape history and the obligation to take responsibility for our own actions that history inescapably entails. Most of all, it means practicing remembrance and gratitude, for thanksgiving is the simplest and most basic of ways for us to recollect the nature, the culture, and the history that have come together to make the world as we know it. If wildness can stop being (just) out there and start being (also) in here, if it can start being as humane as it is natural, then perhaps we can get on with the unending task of struggling to live rightly in the world—not just in the garden, not just in the wilderness, but in the home that encompasses them both.

Notes

1   Henry David Thoreau, "Walking," *The Works of Thoreau*, ed. Henry S. Canby (Boston: Houghton Mifflin, 1937), 672.

2   *Oxford English Dictionary*, s.v. "wilderness"; see also Roderick Nash, *Wilderness and the American Mind*, 3rd ed. (New Haven: Yale Univ. Press, 1982), 1–22; and Max Oelschlaeger, *The Idea of Wilderness: From Prehistory to the Age of Ecology* (New Haven: Yale Univ. Press, 1991).

3   Exodus 32:1–35, KJV.

4   Exodus 14:3, KJV.

5   Mark 1:12–13, KJV; see also Matthew 4:1–11; Luke 4:1–13.

6   John Milton, "Paradise Lost," *John Milton: Complete Poems and Major Prose*, ed. Merritt Y. Hughes (New York: Odyssey Press, 1957), 280–81, lines 131–42.

7   I have discussed this theme at length in "Landscapes of Abundance and Scarcity," in Clyde Milner et al., eds., *Oxford History of the American West* (New York: Oxford Univ. Press, 1994), 603–37. The classic work on the Puritan "city on a hill" in colonial New England is Perry Miller, *Errand into the Wilderness* (Cambridge: Harvard Univ. Press, 1956).

8   John Muir, *My First Summer in the Sierra* (1911), reprinted in *John Muir: The Eight Wilderness Discovery Books* (London: Diadem; Seattle: Mountaineers, 1992), 211.

9   Alfred Runte, *National Parks: The American Experience*, 2nd ed. (Lincoln: Univ. of Nebraska Press, 1987).

10   John Muir, *The Yosemite* (1912), reprinted in *John Muir: Eight Wilderness Discovery Books*, 715.

11   Scholarly work on the sublime is extensive. Among the most important studies are Samuel Monk, *The Sublime: A Study of Critical Theories in XVIII-Century England* (New York: Modern Language Association, 1935); Basil Willey, *The Eighteenth-Century Background: Studies on the Idea of Nature in the Thought of the Period* (London: Chattus and Windus, 1949); Marjorie Hope Nicolson, *Mountain Gloom and Mountain Glory: The Development of the Aesthetics of the Infinite* (Ithaca: Cornell Univ. Press, 1959); Thomas Weiskel, *The Romantic Sublime: Studies in the Structure and Psychology of Transcendence* (Baltimore: Johns Hopkins Univ. Press, 1976); Barbara Novak, *Nature and Culture: American Landscape Painting, 1825–1875* (New York: Oxford Univ. Press, 1980).

12   The classic works are Immanuel Kant, *Observations on the Feeling of the Beautiful and Sublime* (1764), trans. John T. Goldthwait (Berkeley: Univ. of California Press, 1960); Edmund Burke, *A Philosophical Enquiry into the Origin of Our Ideas of the Sublime and Beautiful*, ed. James T. Boulton (1958; Notre Dame: Univ. of Notre Dame Press, 1968); William Gilpin, *Three Essays: On Picturesque Beauty; on Picturesque Travel; and on Sketching Landscape* (London, 1803).

13   See Ann Vileisis, "From Wastelands to Wetlands" (unpublished senior essay, Yale Univ., 1989); Runte, *National Parks*.

14   William Wordsworth, "The Prelude," bk. 6, in Thomas Hutchinson, ed., *The Poetical Works of Wordsworth* (London: Oxford Univ. Press, 1936), 536.

15   Henry David Thoreau, *The Maine Woods* (1864), in *Henry David Thoreau* (New York: Library of America, 1985), 640–41.

16   Exodus 16:10, KJV.

17   John Muir, *My first Summer in the Sierra*, 238. Part of the difference between these descriptions may reflect the landscapes the three authors were describing. [. . .] Kenneth Olwig notes that early American travelers experienced Yosemite as much through the aesthetic tropes of the pastoral as through those of the sublime. The ease with which Muir celebrated the gentle divinity of the Sierra Nevada had much to do with the pastoral qualities of the landscape he described.

18   Frederick Jackson Turner, *The Frontier in American History* (New York: Henry Holt, 1920), 37–38.

19   Richard Slotkin has made this observation the linchpin of his comparison between Turner and Theodore Roosevelt. See Slotkin, *Gunfighter Nation: The Myth of the Frontier in Twentieth-Century America* (New York: Atheneum, 1992), 29–62.

20   Owen Wister, *The Virginian: A Horseman of the Plains* (New York: Macmillan, 1902), viii–ix.

21   Theodore Roosevelt, *Ranch Life and the Hunting Trail* (1888; New York: Century, 1899), 100.

22   Wister, *Virginian*, x.

23   On the many problems with this view, see William M. Denevan, "The Pristine Myth: The Landscape of the Americas in 1492," *Annals of the Association of American Geographers* 82 (1992): 369–85.

24   Louis Warren, "The Hunter's Game: Poachers, Conservationists, and Twentieth-Century America," (Ph.D. diss., Yale University, 1994).

25   Wilderness also lies at the foundation of the Clementsian ecological concept of the climax. See Michael Barbour's essay in this [chapter's original] volume, as well as my introduction.

26   On the many paradoxes of having to manage wilderness into order to maintain the appearance of an unmanaged landscape, see John C. Hendee et al., *Wilderness Management*, USDA Forest Service Miscellaneous Publication No. 1365 (Washington, D.C.: Government Printing Office, 1978).

27   See James Proctor's essay in this [chapter's original] volume.

28   See Candace Slater's essay in this [chapter's original] volume. This argument has been powerfully made by Ramachandra Guha, "Radical American Environmentalism: A Third World Critique," *Environmental Ethics* 11 (1989): 71–83.

29   Bill McKibben, *The End of Nature* (New York: Random House, 1989).

30   Ibid., 49.

31   Even comparable extinction rates have occurred before, though we surely would not want to emulate the Cretaceous-Tertiary boundary extinctions as a model for responsible manipulation of the biosphere!

32   Dave Foreman, *Confessions of an Eco-Warrior* (New York: Harmony Books, 1991), 69 (italics in original). For a sampling of other writings by followers of deep ecology and/or Earth First!, see Michael Tobias, ed., *Deep Ecology* (San Diego: Avant Books, 1984); Bill Devall and George Sessions, *Deep Ecology: Living as if Nature Mattered* (Salt Lake City: Gibbs Smith, 1985); Michael Tobias, *After Eden: History, Ecology, and Conscience* (San Diego: Avant Books, 1985); Dave Foreman and Bill Haywood, eds., *Ecodefense: A Field Guide to Monkey Wrenching*, 2nd ed. (Tucson: Ned Ludd Books, 1987); Bill Devall, *Simple in Means, Rich in Ends: Practicing Deep Ecology* (Salt Lake City: Gibbs Smith, 1988); Steve Chase, ed., *Defending the Earth: A Dialogue between Murray Bookchin & Dave Foreman* (Boston: South End Press, 1991); John Davis, ed., *The Earth First! Reader: Ten Years of Radical Environmentalism* (Salt Lake City: Gibbs Smith, 1991); Bill Devall, *Living Richly in an Age of Limits: Using Deep Ecology for an Abundant Life* (Salt Lake City: Gibbs Smith, 1993); Michael E. Zimmerman et al., eds., *Environmental Philosophy: From Animal Rights to Radical Ecology* (Englewood Cliffs, N.J.: Prentice-Hall, 1993). A useful survey of the different factions of radical environmentalism can be found in Carolyn Merchant, *Radical Ecology: The Search for a Livable World* (New York: Routledge, 1992). For a very interesting critique of this literature (first published in the anarchist newspaper *Fifth Estate*), see George Bradford, *How Deep Is Deep Ecology?* (Ojai, Calif.: Times Change Press, 1989).

33   Foreman, *Confessions of an Eco-Warrior*, 34.

34   Ibid., 65. See also Dave Foreman and Howie Wolke, *The Big Outside: A Descriptive Inventory of the Big Wilderness Areas of the U.S.* (Tucson: Ned Ludd Books, 1989).

35   Foreman, *Confessions of an Eco-Warrior*, 63.

36   Ibid., 27.

37   See Richard White's essay in this [chapter's original] volume, and compare its analysis of environmental knowledge through work with Jennifer Price's analysis of environmental knowledge through consumption. It is not much of an exaggeration to say that the wilderness experience is essentially consumerist in its impulses.

38   Cf. Muir, *Yosemite, in John Muir: Eight Wilderness Discovery Books*, 714.

39   Wallace Stegner, ed., *This Is Dinosaur: Echo Park Country and Its Magic Rivers* (New York: Knopf, 1955), 17 (italics in original).

40   Katherine Hayles helped me see the importance of this argument.

41   Analogous arguments can be found in John Brinckerhoff Jackson, "Beyond Wilderness," *A Sense of Place, a Sense of Time* (New Haven: Yale Univ. Press, 1994), 71–91, and in the wonderful collection of essays by Michael Pollan, *Second Nature: A Gardener's Education* (New York: Atlantic Monthly Press, 1991).

42   Wendell Berry, *Home Economics* (San Francisco: North Point, 1987), 138, 143.

43   Gary Snyder, quoted in *New York Times*, "Week in Review," Sept. 18, 1994, 6.

Chapter 11

Cheryll Glotfelty

LITERARY STUDIES IN AN AGE OF ENVIRONMENTAL CRISIS

LITERARY STUDIES IN OUR POSTMODERN age exist in a state of constant flux. Every few years, it seems, the profession of English must "redraw the boundaries" to "remap" the rapidly changing contours of the field. One recent, authoritative guide to contemporary literary studies contains a full twenty-one essays on different methodological or theoretical approaches to criticism. Its introduction observes:

> Literary studies in English are in a period of rapid and sometimes disorienting change. . . . Just as none of the critical approaches that antedate this period, from psychological and Marxist criticism to reader-response theory and cultural criticism, has remained stable, so none of the historical fields and subfields that constitute English and American literary studies has been left untouched by revisionist energies. . . . [The essays in this volume] disclose some of those places where scholarship has responded to contemporary pressures.[1]

Curiously enough, in this putatively comprehensive volume on the state of the profession, there is no essay on an ecological approach to literature. Although scholarship claims to have "responded to contemporary pressures," it has apparently ignored the most pressing contemporary issue of all, namely, the global environmental crisis. The absence of any sign of an environmental perspective in contemporary literary studies would seem to suggest that despite its "revisionist energies," scholarship remains *academic* in the sense of "scholarly to the point of being unaware of the outside world" (*American Heritage Dictionary*).

If your knowledge of the outside world were limited to what you could infer from the major publications of the literary profession, you would quickly discern that race, class, and gender were the hot topics of the late twentieth century, but you would never suspect that the earth's life support systems were under stress. Indeed, you might never know that there was an earth at all. In contrast, if you were to scan the newspaper headlines of the same period, you would learn of oil spills, lead and asbestos poisoning, toxic waste contamination, extinction of species at an unprecedented rate, battles over public land use, protests over nuclear waste dumps, a growing hole in the ozone layer, predictions of global warming, acid rain, loss of topsoil, destruction of the tropical rain forest, controversy over the Spotted Owl in the Pacific Northwest, a wildfire in Yellowstone Park, medical syringes washing onto the shores of Atlantic beaches, boycotts on tuna, overtapped aquifers in the West, illegal dumping in the East, a nuclear reactor disaster in Chernobyl, new auto emissions standards, famines, droughts, floods, hurricanes, a United Nations special conference on environment and development, a U.S. president declaring the 1990s "the decade of the environment," and a world population that topped five billion. Browsing through periodicals, you would discover that in 1989 *Time* magazine's person of the year award went to "The Endangered Earth."

In view of the discrepancy between current events and the preoccupations of the literary profession, the claim that literary scholarship has responded to contemporary pressures becomes difficult to defend. Until very recently there has been no sign that the institution of literary studies has even been aware of the environmental crisis. For instance, there have been no journals, no jargon, no jobs, no professional societies or discussion groups, and no conferences on literature and the environment. While related humanities disciplines, like history, philosophy, law, sociology, and religion have been "greening" since the 1970s, literary studies have apparently remained untinted by environmental concerns. And while social movements, like the civil rights and women's liberation movements of the sixties and seventies, have transformed literary studies, it would appear that the environmental movement of the same era has had little impact.

But appearances can be deceiving. In actual fact, as the publication dates for some of the essays in this anthology substantiate, individual literary and cultural scholars have been developing ecologically informed criticism and theory since the seventies; however, unlike their disciplinary cousins mentioned previously, they did not organize themselves into an identifiable group; hence, their various efforts were not recognized as belonging to a distinct critical school or movement. Individual studies appeared in a wide variety of places and were categorized under a miscellany of subject headings, such as American Studies, regionalism, pastoralism, the frontier, human ecology, science and literature, nature in literature, landscape in literature, or the names of the authors treated. One indication of the disunity of the early efforts is that these critics rarely cited one another's work; they didn't know that it existed. In a sense, each critic was inventing an environmental approach to literature in isolation. Each was a single voice howling in the wilderness. As a consequence, ecocriticism did not become a presence in the major institutions of power in the profession, such as the Modern Language Association (MLA). Graduate students interested in environmental approaches to literature felt like misfits, having no community of scholars to join and finding no job announcements in their area of expertise.

Birth of Environmental Literary Studies

Finally, in the mid-eighties, as scholars began to undertake collaborative projects, the field of environmental literary studies was planted, and in the early nineties it grew. In 1985 Frederick O. Waage edited *Teaching Environmental Literature: Materials, Methods, Resources*, which included course descriptions from nineteen different scholars and sought to foster "a greater presence of environmental concern and awareness in literary disciplines."[2] In 1989 Alicia Nitecki founded *The American Nature Writing Newsletter*, whose purpose was to publish brief essays, book reviews, classroom notes, and information pertaining to the study of writing on nature and the environment. Others have been responsible for special environmental issues of established literary journals.[3] Some universities began to include literature courses in their environmental studies curricula, a few inaugurated new institutes or programs in nature and culture, and some English departments began to offer a minor in environmental literature. In 1990 the University of Nevada, Reno, created the first academic position in Literature and the Environment.

Also during these years several special sessions on nature writing or environmental literature began to appear on the programs of annual literary conferences, perhaps most notably the 1991 MLA special session organized by Harold Fromm, entitled "Ecocriticism: The Greening of Literary Studies," and the 1992 American Literature Association symposium chaired by Glen Love, entitled "American Nature Writing: New Contexts, New Approaches." In 1992, at the annual meeting of the Western Literature Association, a new Association for the Study of Literature and Environment (ASLE) was formed, with Scott Slovic elected first president. ASLE's mission: "to promote the exchange of ideas and information pertaining to literature that considers the relationship between human beings and the natural world" and to encourage "new nature writing, traditional and innovative scholarly approaches to environmental literature, and interdisciplinary environmental research." In its first year, ASLE's membership swelled to more than 300; in its second year that number doubled, and the group created an electronic-mail computer network to facilitate communication among members; in its third year, 1995, ASLE's membership had topped 750 and the group hosted its first conference, in Fort Collins, Colorado. In 1993 Patrick Murphy established a new journal, *ISLE: Interdisciplinary Studies in Literature and Environment*, to "provide a forum for critical studies of the literary and performing arts proceeding from or addressing environmental considerations. These would include ecological theory, environmentalism, conceptions of nature and their depictions, the human/nature dichotomy and related concerns."[4]

By 1993 then, ecological literary study had emerged as a recognizable critical school. The formerly disconnected scattering of lone scholars had joined forces with younger scholars and graduate students to become a strong interest group with aspirations to change the profession. The origin of ecocriticism as a critical approach thus predates its recent consolidation by more than twenty years.

Definition of Ecocriticism

What then *is* ecocriticism? Simply put, ecocriticism is the study of the relationship between literature and the physical environment. Just as feminist criticism examines language and literature from a gender-conscious perspective, and Marxist criticism brings an awareness of modes of production and economic class to its reading of texts, ecocriticism takes an earth-centered approach to literary studies.

Ecocritics and theorists ask questions like the following: How is nature represented in this sonnet? What role does the physical setting play in the plot of this novel? Are the values expressed in this play consistent with ecological wisdom? How do our metaphors of the land influence the way we treat it? How can we characterize nature writing as a genre? In addition to race, class, and gender, should *place* become a new critical category? Do men write about nature differently than women do? In what ways has literacy itself affected humankind's relationship to the natural world? How has the concept of wilderness changed over time? In what ways and to what effect is the environmental crisis seeping into contemporary literature and popular culture? What view of nature informs U.S. Government reports, corporate advertising, and televised nature documentaries, and to what rhetorical effect? What bearing might the science of ecology have on literary studies? How is science itself open to literary analysis? What cross-fertilization is possible between literary studies and environmental discourse in related disciplines such as history, philosophy, psychology, art history, and ethics?

Despite the broad scope of inquiry and disparate levels of sophistication, all ecological criticism shares the fundamental premise that human culture is connected to the physical world, affecting it and affected by it. Ecocriticism takes as its subject the interconnections between nature and culture, specifically the cultural artifacts of language and literature. As a critical stance, it has one foot in literature and the other on land; as a theoretical discourse, it negotiates between the human and the nonhuman.

Ecocriticism can be further characterized by distinguishing it from other critical approaches. Literary theory, in general, examines the relations between writers, texts, and the world. In most literary theory "the world" is synonymous with society—the social sphere. Ecocriticism expands the notion of "the world" to include the entire ecosphere. If we agree with Barry Commoner's first law of ecology, "Everything is connected to everything else," we must conclude that literature does not float above the material world in some aesthetic ether, but, rather, plays a part in an immensely complex global system, in which energy, matter, *and ideas* interact.

But the taxonomic name of this green branch of literary study is still being negotiated. In *The Comedy of Survival: Studies in Literary Ecology* (1972) Joseph W. Meeker introduced the term *literary ecology* to refer to "the study of biological themes and relationships which appear in literary works. It is simultaneously an attempt to discover what roles have been played by literature in the ecology of the human species."[5] The term *ecocriticism* was possibly first coined in 1978 by William Rueckert in his essay "Literature and Ecology: An Experiment in Ecocriticism" [. . .]. By ecocriticism Rueckert meant "the application of ecology and ecological concepts to the study of literature." Rueckert's definition, concerned specifically with the science of ecology, is thus more restrictive than the one proposed in this [i.e. Glotfelty's] anthology, which includes all possible relations between literature and the physical world.[6] Other terms currently in circulation include *ecopoetics, environmental literary criticism*, and *green cultural studies*.

Many critics write environmentally conscious criticism without needing or wanting a specific name for it. Others argue that a name is important. It was precisely because the early studies lacked a common subject heading that they were dispersed so widely, failed to build on one another, and became both difficult to access and negligible in their impact on the profession, Some scholars like the term *ecocriticism* because it is short and can easily be made into other forms like *ecocritical* and *ecocritic*. Additionally, they favor *eco-* over *enviro-* because, analogous to the science of ecology, ecocriticism studies relationships between things, in this case, between human culture and the physical world. Furthermore, in its connotations, *enviro-* is anthropocentric and dualistic, implying that we humans are at the center, surrounded by everything that is not us, the environment. *Eco-*, in contrast, implies interdependent communities, integrated systems, and strong connections among constituent parts. Ultimately, of course, usage will dictate which term or whether any term is adopted. But think of how convenient it would be to sit down at a computerized database and have a single term to enter for your subject search. . . .

The Humanities and the Environmental Crisis

Regardless of what name it goes by, most ecocritical work shares a common motivation: the troubling awareness that we have reached the age of environmental limits, a time when the consequences of human actions are damaging the planet's basic life support systems. We are there. Either we change our ways or we face global catastrophe, destroying much beauty and exterminating countless fellow species in our headlong race to apocalypse. Many of us in colleges and universities worldwide find ourselves in a dilemma. Our temperaments and talents have deposited us in literature departments, but, as environmental problems compound, work as usual seems unconscionably frivolous. If we're not part of the solution, we're part of the problem.

How then can we contribute to environmental restoration, not just in our spare time, but from within our capacity as professors of literature?[7] The answer lies in recognizing that current environmental problems are largely of our own making, are, in other words, a by-product of culture. As historian Donald Worster explains,

> We are facing a global crisis today, not because of how ecosystems function but rather because of how our ethical systems function. Getting through the crisis requires understanding our impact on nature as precisely as possible, but even more, it requires understanding those ethical systems and using that understanding to reform them. Historians, along with literary scholars, anthropologists, and philosophers, cannot do the reforming, of course, but they can help with the understanding.[8]

Answering the call to understanding, scholars throughout the humanities are finding ways to add an environmental dimension to their respective disciplines. Worster and other historians are writing environmental histories, studying the reciprocal relationships between humans and land, considering nature not just as the stage upon which the human story is acted out, but as an actor in the drama. They trace the connections among environmental conditions, economic modes of production, and cultural ideas through time.

Anthropologists have long been interested in the connection between culture and geography. Their work on primal cultures in particular may help the rest of us not only to respect such people's right to survive, but also to think about the value systems and rituals that have helped these cultures live sustainably.

Psychology has long ignored nature in its theories of the human mind. A handful of contemporary psychologists, however, are exploring the linkages between environmental conditions and mental health, some regarding the modern estrangement from nature as the basis of our social and psychological ills.

In philosophy, various subfields like environmental ethics, deep ecology, ecofeminism, and social ecology have emerged in an effort to understand and critique the root causes of environmental degradation and to formulate an alternative view of existence that will provide an ethical and conceptual foundation for right relations with the earth.

Theologians, too, are recognizing that, as one book is subtitled, "The Environment Is a Religious Issue." While some Judeo-Christian theologians attempt to elucidate biblical precedents for good stewardship of the earth, others re-envision God as immanent in creation and view the earth itself as sacred. Still other theologians turn to ancient Earth Goddess worship, Eastern religious traditions, and Native American teachings, belief systems that contain much wisdom about nature and spirituality.[9]

Literary scholars specialize in questions of value, meaning, tradition, point of view, and language, and it is in these areas that they are making a substantial contribution to environmental thinking. Believing that the environmental crisis has been exacerbated by our fragmented, compartmentalized, and overly specialized way of knowing the world, humanities scholars are increasingly making an effort to educate themselves in the sciences and to adopt interdisciplinary approaches.

Survey of Ecocriticism in America

Many kinds of studies huddle under the spreading tree of ecological literary criticism, for literature and the environment is a big topic, and should remain that way. Several years ago, when I was attempting to devise a branding system that would make sense of this mixed herd,

Wallace Stegner—novelist, historian, and literary critic—offered some wise counsel, saying that if he were doing it, he would be inclined to let the topic remain "large and loose and suggestive and open, simply literature and the environment and all the ways they interact and have interacted, without trying to codify and systematize. Systems are like wet rawhide," he warned; "when they dry they strangle what they bind."[10] Suggestive and open is exactly what ecocriticism ought to be, but in order to avoid confusion in the following brief survey of ecocritical work to date, I am going to do some codifying. Let us hereby agree that the system is not to be binding. Nonetheless, Elaine Showalter's model of the three developmental stages of feminist criticism provides a useful scheme for describing three analogous phases in ecocriticism.[11]

The first stage in feminist criticism, the "images of women" stage, is concerned with representations, concentrating on how women are portrayed in canonical literature. These studies contribute to the vital process of consciousness raising by exposing sexist stereotypes—witches, bitches, broads, and spinsters—and by locating absences, questioning the purported universality and even the aesthetic value of literature that distorts or ignores altogether the experience of half of the human race. Analogous efforts in ecocriticism study how nature is represented in literature. Again, consciousness raising results when stereotypes are identified—Eden, Arcadia, virgin land, miasmal swamp, savage wilderness—and when absences are noticed: where *is* the natural world in this text? But nature per se is not the only focus of ecocritical studies of representation. Other topics include the frontier, animals, cities, specific geographical regions, rivers, mountains, deserts, Indians, technology, garbage, and the body.

Showalter's second stage in feminist criticism, the women's literary tradition stage, likewise serves the important function of consciousness raising as it rediscovers, reissues, and reconsiders literature by women. In ecocriticism, similar efforts are being made to recuperate the hitherto neglected genre of nature writing, a tradition of nature-oriented nonfiction that originates in England with Gilbert White's *A Natural History of Selbourne* (1789) and extends to America through Henry Thoreau, John Burroughs, John Muir, Mary Austin, Aldo Leopold, Rachel Carson, Edward Abbey, Annie Dillard, Barry Lopez, Terry Tempest Williams, and many others. Nature writing boasts a rich past, a vibrant present, and a promising future, and ecocritics draw from any number of existing critical theories—psychoanalytic, new critical, feminist, Bakhtinian, deconstructive—in the interests of understanding and promoting this body of literature. As evidence that nature writing is gaining ground in the literary marketplace, witness the staggering number of anthologies that have been published in recent years.[12] In an increasingly urban society, nature writing plays a vital role in teaching us to value the natural world.

Another effort to promulgate environmentally enlightened works examines mainstream genres, identifying fiction and poetry writers whose work manifests ecological awareness. Figures like Willa Cather, Robinson Jeffers, W. S. Merwin, Adrienne Rich, Wallace Stegner, Gary Snyder, Mary Oliver, Ursula Le Guin, and Alice Walker have received much attention, as have Native American authors, but the horizon of possibilities remains suggestively open. Corresponding to the feminist interest in the lives of women authors, ecocritics have studied the environmental conditions of an author's life—the influence of place on the imagination—demonstrating that where an author grew up, traveled, and wrote is pertinent to an understanding of his or her work. Some critics find it worthwhile to visit the places an author lived and wrote about, literally retracing the footsteps of John Muir in the Sierra, for example, to experience his mountain raptures personally, or paddling down the Merrimac River to apprehend better the physical context of Thoreau's meandering prose.

The third stage that Showalter identifies in feminist criticism is the theoretical phase, which is far reaching and complex, drawing on a wide range of theories to raise fundamental questions about the symbolic construction of gender and sexuality within literary discourse. Analogous work in ecocriticism includes examining the symbolic construction of species. How has literary discourse defined the human? Such a critique questions the dualisms prevalent in Western thought, dualisms that separate meaning from matter, sever mind from body, divide men from women, and wrench humanity from nature. A related endeavor is being carried out under the hybrid label "ecofeminism," a theoretical discourse whose theme is the link between the oppression of women and the domination of nature. Yet another theoretical project attempts to develop an ecological poetics, taking the science of ecology, with its concept of the ecosystem and its emphasis on interconnections and energy flow, as a metaphor for the way poetry functions in society. Ecocritics are also considering the philosophy currently known as deep ecology, exploring the implications that its radical critique of anthropocentrism might have for literary study.

The Future of Ecocriticism

An ecologically focused criticism is a worthy enterprise primarily because it directs our attention to matters about which we need to be thinking. Consciousness raising is its most important task. For how can we solve environmental problems unless we start thinking about them?

I noted above that ecocritics have aspirations to change the profession. Perhaps I should have written that I have such aspirations for ecocriticism. I would like to see ecocriticism become a chapter of the next book that redraws the boundaries of literary studies. I would like to see a position in every literature department for a specialist in literature and the environment. I would like to see candidates running on a green platform elected to the highest offices in our professional organizations. We have witnessed the feminist and multi-ethnic critical movements radically transform the profession, the job market, and the canon. And because they have transformed the profession, they are helping to transform the world.

A strong voice in the profession will enable ecocritics to be influential in mandating important changes in the canon, the curriculum, and university policy. We will see books like Aldo Leopold's *A Sand County Almanac* and Edward Abbey's *Desert Solitaire* become standard texts for courses in American literature. Students taking literature and composition courses will be encouraged to think seriously about the relationship of humans to nature, about the ethical and aesthetic dilemmas posed by the environmental crisis, and about how language and literature transmit values with profound ecological implications. Colleges and universities of the twenty-first century will require that all students complete at least one interdisciplinary course in environmental studies. Institutions of higher learning will one day do business on recycled-content paper—some institutions already do.

In the future we can expect to see ecocritical scholarship becoming ever more interdisciplinary, multicultural, and international. The interdisciplinary work is well underway and could be further facilitated by inviting experts from a wide range of disciplines to be guest speakers at literary conferences and by hosting more interdisciplinary conferences on environmental topics. Ecocriticism has been predominantly a white movement. It will become a multi-ethnic movement when stronger connections are made between the environment and issues of social justice, and when a diversity of voices are encouraged to contribute to the discussion. This volume focuses on ecocritical work in the United States. The next collection may well be an international one, for environmental problems are now global in scale and their solutions will require worldwide collaboration.[13]

In 1985, Loren Acton, a Montana ranch boy turned solar astronomer, flew on the Challenger Eight space shuttle as payload specialist. His observations may serve to remind us of the global context of ecocritical work:

Looking outward to the blackness of space, sprinkled with the glory of a universe of lights, I saw majesty—but no welcome. Below was a welcoming planet. There, contained in the thin, moving, incredibly fragile shell of the biosphere is everything that is dear to you, all the human drama and comedy. That's where life is; that's where all the good stuff is.[14]

Essays in this Collection

This book is intended to serve as a port of entry to the field of ecocriticism. As ecocriticism gains visibility and influence within the profession, increasing numbers of people have been asking the question, "What *is* ecocriticism?" Many others who are developing an interest in ecocriticism want to know what to read to learn more about this approach to literary studies. Professors who are familiar with ecocriticism and its history nevertheless have had difficulty teaching the subject because until now there has been no general introductory text.

Together, the essays in this anthology provide an answer to the question, "What is ecocriticism?" These essays will help people new to this field to gain a sense of its history and scope, and to become acquainted with its leading scholars. These are the essays with which anyone wishing to undertake ecocritical scholarship ought to be familiar. In addition, this anthology of seminal and representative essays will facilitate teaching; no longer will professors have to rely on the dog-eared photocopies that have been circulating in the ecocritical underground, nor will they need to worry about violating copyright laws.

This sourcebook, consisting of both reprinted and original essays, looks backward to origins and forward to trends. Many of the seminal works of ecocriticism—works of the 1970s by Joseph Meeker, William Rueckert, and Neil Evernden, for example—received little notice when first published, and have since become difficult to obtain. One of the purposes of this anthology is to make available those early gems, thereby acknowledging the roots of modern ecocriticism and giving credit where credit is due. Another purpose of the anthology is to present exemplary recent essays, fairly general in nature, representing a wide range of contemporary ecocritical approaches.

In selecting essays for this volume, then, we have sought to include not only the classics but pieces on the cutting edge. In our coverage of theory, we have avoided essays choked with technical jargon in favor of accessible pieces written in lucid prose. In addition, we have chosen what we consider to be works of brilliance, those pieces that open doors of understanding, that switch on a light bulb in the mind, that help the reader to see the world in a new way. In our coverage of criticism, we have avoided essays that treat a single author or a single work in favor of general essays, discussing a variety of texts and representing a range of critical approaches. While some of the critical essays are argumentative, others are instructional in nature, designed to introduce the reader to a body of literature (such as Native American literature), a genre (such as American nature writing), or a critical approach (such as Bakhtinian dialogics). In short, we sincerely believe that every selection herein is a "must read" essay.

The book is divided into three sections, reflecting the three major phases of ecocritical work. We begin with theory in order to raise some fundamental questions about the relationship between nature and culture and to provide a theoretical foundation upon which to build the subsequent discussions of literary works. The second section studies representations of nature in fiction and drama, including reflections on the ecological significance of literary modes and narrative structures, from Paleolithic hunting stories to postmodern mystery novels. The final section focuses on environmental literature in America, encompassing both Native American stories and the Thoreauvian nature-writing tradition.

Notes

1 Stephen Greenblatt and Giles Gunn, eds., *Redrawing the Boundaries: The Transformation of English and American Literary Studies* (New York: MLA, 1992) 1–3.

2 Frederick O. Waage, ed., *Teaching Environmental Literature: Materials, Methods, Resources* (New York: MLA, 1985) viii.

3 Special environmental issues of humanities journals include *Antaeus* 57 (Autumn 1986), ed. Daniel Halpern, reprint, as *On Nature* (San Francisco: North Point Press, 1987); *Studies in the Humanities* 15.2 (December 1988), "Feminism, Ecology and the Future of the Humanities," ed. Patrick Murphy; *Witness* 3.4 (Winter 1989), "New Nature Writing," ed. Thomas J. Lyon; *Hypatia* 6.1 (Spring 1991), "Ecological Feminism," ed. Karen J. Warren; *North Dakota Quarterly* 59.2 (Spring 1991), "Nature Writers/Writing," ed. Sherman Paul and Don Scheese; CEA *Critic* 54.1 (Fall 1991), "The Literature of Nature," ed. Betsy Hilbert; *West Virginia University Philological Papers* 37 (1991), "Special Issue Devoted to the Relationship Between Man and the Environment," ed. Armand E. Singer; *Weber Studies* 9.1 (Winter 1992.), "A Meditation on the Environment," ed. Neila C. Seshachari; *Praxis* 4 (1993), "Denatured Environments," ed. Tom Crochunis and Michael Ross; *Georgia Review* 47.1 (Spring 1993), "Focus on Nature Writing," ed. Stanley W. Lindberg and Douglas Carlson; *Indiana Review* 16.1 (Spring 1993), a special issue devoted to writing on nature and the environment, ed. Dorian Gossy; *Ohio Review* 49 (1993), "Art and Nature: Essays by Contemporary Writers," ed. Wayne Dodd; *Theater* 25.1 (Spring/Summer 1994), special section on "Theater and Ecology," ed. Una Chaudhuri; *Weber Studies* 11.3 (Fall 1994), special wilderness issue, ed. Neila C. Seshachari and Scott Slovic.

4 Information on *The American Nature Writing Newsletter*, the Association for the Study of Literature and Environment (ASLE), and *ISLE* can be found in the Periodicals and Professional Organizations section at the back of this [i.e. Glotfelty's] book.

5 Joseph W. Meeker, *The Comedy of Survival: Studies in Literary Ecology* (New York: Scribner's, 1972) 9. A chapter of Meeker's seminal work is reprinted in this [i.e. Glotfelty's] anthology.

6 Wendell V. Harris in "Toward an Ecological Criticism: Contextual versus Unconditioned Literary Theory" (*College English* 48.2 [February 1986]: 116–31) draws upon Saussure's distinction between *langue* and *parole*, defining "ecological" theories (he includes speech-act theory, the sociology of knowledge, argumentation theory, and discourse analysis) as those that investigate the individual *parole* and the interactive contexts—the "interpretive ecologies" (129)—that make communication possible.

  Marilyn M. Cooper in "The Ecology of Writing" (*College English* 48.4 [April 1986]: 364–75) proposes an "ecological model of writing, whose fundamental tenet is that writing is an activity through which a person is continually engaged with a variety of socially constituted systems" (367).

  Harris and Cooper use the science of ecology (specifically its concepts of webs, habitat, and community) as an explanatory metaphor to develop a model of human communication, but they do not explore how this human activity interacts with the physical world, and so their studies are not ecocritical as I am proposing that the term be used.

7 Although this book focuses on scholarship, it is through teaching that professors may ultimately make the greatest impact in the world. For ideas on teaching, see Waage, *Teaching Environmental Literature;* CEA *Critic* 54.1 (Fall 1991), which includes a section entitled "Practicum," 43–77; Cheryll Glotfelty, "Teaching Green: Ideas, Sample Syllabi, and Resources," and William Howarth, "Literature of Place, Environmental Writers," both in *ISLE* 1.1 (Spring 1993): 151–78; Cheryll Glotfelty, "Western, Yes, But Is It Literature? Teaching Ronald Lanner's *The Pinon Pine*," *Western American Literature* 27.4 (February 1993): 303–10. The Association for the Study of Literature and Environment (ASLE) maintains a syllabus exchange available to its members. For a provocative discussion of the role of higher education in general, see David W. Orr, *Ecological Literacy: Education and the Transition to a Postmodern World* (Albany: State University of New York Press, 1992).

8 Donald Worster, *The Wealth of Nature: Environmental History and the Ecological Imagination* (New York: Oxford University Press, 1993) 27.

9 I do not presume to have full command of the range of environmental work in these and other related fields, but I can direct the reader to some good introductory books and key journals.

  In environmental history, see the journal *Environmental History Review*. In addition, see Donald Worster, ed., *The Ends of the Earth: Perspectives on Modern Environmental History* (New York: Cambridge University Press, 1988); Worster, *The Wealth of Nature;* Richard White, "American Environmental History: The Development of a New Historical Field," *Pacific Historical Review* 54.3 (August 1985): 297–335; "A Round Table: Environmental History," *Journal of American History* 76.4 (March 1990), which includes a lead essay by Donald Worster and responding statements by Alfred W. Crosby, Richard White, Carolyn Merchant, William Cronon, and Stephen J. Pyne.

In anthropology, see Marvin Harris, *Cannibals and Kings: The Origins of Cultures* (New York: Vintage, 1991); Mark Nathan Cohen, *Health and the Rise of Civilization* (New Haven: Yale University Press, 1989).

In psychology, see Irwin Altman and Joachim F. Wohlwill, eds., *Behavior and the Natural Environment* (New York: Plenum Press, 1983); Rachel Kaplan and Stephen Kaplan, *The Experience of Nature: A Psychological Perspective* (New York: Cambridge University Press, 1989); Theodore Roszak, *The Voice of the Earth* (New York: Simon and Schuster, 1992); Morris Berman, *Coming to Our Senses: Body and Spirti in the Hidden History of the West* (New York: Bantam, 1989); Paul Shepard, *Nature and Madness* (San Francisco: Sierra Club, 1982); Theodore Roszak, Mary E. Gomes, and Allen D. Kanner, eds., *Ecopsychology: Restoring the Earth, Healing the Mind* (San Francisco: Sierra Club, 1995).

In philosophy, see the journal *Environmental Ethics*. An excellent introductory anthology is Michael E. Zimmerman et al., eds., *Environmental Philosophy: From Animal Rights to Radical Ecology* (Englewood Cliffs, N.J.: Prentice Hall, 1993). Also good are Carolyn Merchant, *Radical Ecology: The Search for a Livable World* (New York: Routledge, 1992); Max Oelschlaeger, ed., *The Wilderness Condition: Essays on Environment and Civilization* (Washington, D.C.: Island Press, 1992).

In theology, a fine introduction to the current environmental thinking of a variety of the world's major religions is Steven C. Rockefeller and John C. Elder, eds., *Spirit and Nature: Why the Environment Is a Religious Issue* (Boston: Beacon, 1992). See also Charles Birch et al., eds., *Liberating Life: Contemporary Approaches to Ecological Theology* (Maryknoll, N.Y.: Orbis Books, 1990); Eugene C. Hargrove, ed., *Religion and Environmental Crisis* (Athens: University of Georgia Press, 1986).

10   Wallace Stegner, letter to the author, 28 May 1989.

11   See Elaine Showalter, "Introduction: The Feminist Critical Revolution," *The New Feminist Criticism: Essays on Women, Literature, and Theory*, ed. Elaine Showalter (New York: Pantheon, 1985) 3–17. I first presented these ideas in a conference paper: Cheryll Burgess [Glotfelty], "Toward an Ecological Literary Criticism," annual conference of the Western Literature Association, Coeur d'Alene, Idaho, October 1989.

12   The following are only some of the most recent nature writing and nature poetry anthologies:

Adkins, Jan, ed. *Ragged Mountain Portable Wilderness Anthology*. Camden, Maine: International Marine Publishing, 1993.

Anderson, Lorraine, ed. *Sisters of the Earth: Women's Prose and Poetry about Nature*. New York: Vintage, 1991.

Begiebing, Robert J., and Owen Grumbling, eds. *The Literature of Nature: The British and American Traditions*. Medford, N.J.: Plexus, 1990.

Finch, Robert, and John Elder, eds. *The Norton Book of Nature Writing*. New York: Norton, 1990.

Halpern, Daniel, ed. *On Nature*. San Francisco: North Point Press, 1987.

Knowles, Karen, ed. *Celebrating the Land: Women's Nature Writings, 1850–1991*. Flagstaff, Ariz.: Northland, 1992.

Lyon, Thomas J., ed. *This Incomperable Lande: A Book of American Nature Writing*. Boston: Houghton Mifflin, 1989.

Lyon, Thomas J., and Peter Stine, eds. *On Nature's Terms: Contemporary Voices*. College Station: Texas A&M University Press, 1992.

Merrill, Christopher, ed. *The Forgotten Language: Contemporary Poets and Nature*. Salt Lake City: Gibbs M. Smith, 1991.

Morgan, Sarah, and Dennis Okerstrom, eds. *The Endangered Earth: Readings for Writers*. Boston: Allyn and Bacon, 1992.

Murray, John A., ed. *American Nature Writing 1994*. San Francisco: Sierra Club, 1994.

—. *Nature's New Voices*. Golden, Colo.: Fulcrum, 1992.

Pack, Robert, and Jay Parini, eds. *Poems for a Small Planet: Contemporary American Nature Poetry*. Hanover: University Press of New England, 1993.

Ronald, Ann, ed. *Words for the Wild: The Sierra Club Trailside Reader*. San Francisco: Sierra Club, 1987.

Sauer, Peter, ed. *Finding Home: Writing on Nature and Culture from Orion Magazine*. Boston: Beacon, 1992.

Slovic, Scott H., and Terrell F. Dixon, eds. *Being in the World: An Environmental Reader for Writers*. New York: Macmillan, 1993.

Swann, Brian, and Peter Borrelli, eds. *Poetry from the Amicus Journal*. Palo Alto, Calif.: Tioga, 1990.

Walker, Melissa. *Reading the Environment*. New York: Norton, 1994.

Wild, Peter, ed. *The Desert Reader*. Salt Lake City: University of Utah Press, 1991.

13   For a promising first step in international collaboration, see *The Culture of Nature: Approaches to the Study of Literature and Environment*, ed. Scott Slovic and Ken-ichi Noda (Kyoto: Minerva Press, 1995).

14   This quote, and many others from astronauts and cosmonauts around the world, is printed in *The Home Planet*, ed. Kevin W. Kelley (New York: Addison-Wesley, 1988) 21. I am proud to say that Loren Acton is my father.

Works Cited

Greenblatt, Stephen, and Giles Gunn, eds. *Redrawing the Boundaries: The Transformation of English and American Literary Studies*. New York: MLA, 1992.

Kelley, Kevin W., ed. *The Home Planet*. New York: Addison-Wesley, 1988.

Meeker, Joseph. *The Comedy of Survival: Studies in Literary Ecology*. New York: Scribner's, 1972.

Rueckert, William. "Literature and Ecology: An Experiment in Ecocriticism." *Iowa Review* 9.1 (Winter 1978): 71–86.

Showalter, Elaine, ed. *The New Feminist Criticism: Essays on Women, Literature, and Theory*. New York: Pantheon, 1985.

Waage, Frederick O., ed. *Teaching Environmental Literature: Materials, Methods, Resources*. New York: MLA, 1985.

Worster, Donald. *The Wealth of Nature: Environmental History and the Ecological Imagination*. New York: Oxford University Press, 1993.

PART II

Second-Wave Ecocriticism

Second-Wave Introduction

LAWRENCE BUELL MADE POPULAR the useful distinction between first- and second-wave ecocritical approaches in his 2005 book, *The Future of Environmental Criticism*. Buell distinguished between older (generally speaking, twentieth-century) environmental criticism, which was often preoccupied with nature writing, wilderness, and texts such as Thoreau's *Walden*, and twenty-first-century work that is generally more concerned with a variety of landscapes (including places like cities) and timely environmental issues.

Second-wave environmental critics, careful not to overly romanticize wilderness (as did some of their predecessors), are more likely to direct themselves to sites of environmental devastation and texts that do the same, such as Rachel Carson's *Silent Spring*. Consequently, writers such as Thoreau and Wordsworth, who were the darlings of first-wave environmental criticism, have generally received less attention from the second wave. While some first-wave environmental critics might cringe at the thought, a study of the celebration of flowers and mountains in Romantic poetry may be of far less interest to the second wave than an assessment of A.R. Ammons's book-length poem *Garbage*.

One of the important advantages of this shift in focus is that, because environmental criticism is now directed to present environmental issues rather than an improbable pastoral past (i.e. some sort of imagined pristine "wilderness"), it is poised to have real cultural and political relevance in the twenty-first century.

Second-wave environmental critics can still take up some of the same interests as their predecessors, though they are generally very aware of the implications of doing so. For example, a second-wave ecocritic might note that Rachel Carson intentionally (especially in the pastoral opening of *Silent Spring*) romanticized nature as a rhetorical strategy designed to enlist readers to combat threats to the environment. This approach is very different than first-wave environmental criticism, as a second-wave ecocritic would generally not be led by Carson into making a fetish of nature (as sometimes happened in the first wave); rather, exploring how such romanticizing takes place, such an approach would draw attention to the manner by which this rhetorical strategy influenced the first wave of environmental critics — who were in many cases blind to the influence.

While the shift to second-wave ecocritical approaches is obviously important, it needs to be noted that current ecocritics owe a debt of thanks to the first wave of work in the field. Had an interest in ecocritical approaches not been fostered in the closing decades of the twentieth century, which, in practical terms, resulted in courses and other programing in a range of universities, second-wave ecocriticism would not have had a foundation on which to build.

Second-wave ecocritics have taken up a range of issues. One of the first was environmental justice ("EJ"). Starting in the 1980s, a number of individuals, such as Robert D. Bullard, began to draw attention to the fact that issues like race, class, gender, and sexual preference need to be taken up by ecocritics, who had sometimes been oblivious to them. In his *Dumping in Dixie: Race, Class and Environmental Quality*, Bullard made clear that poor communities, especially poor black communities in the southern U.S., suffered more damage from air and water pollution, for example, as their communities were more often home to industrial operations and toxic dumps. In addition to Bullard's consideration of race and EJ, Stacy Alaimo's exploration of the intersection between feminist concerns and EJ and Catriona Mortimer-Sandilands's important essay on "Queer Ecologies" are anthologized here, as is the Introduction to the watershed collection *The Environmental Justice Reader*.

Following some of the writers that they considered, first-wave ecocritics were often preoccupied with the local and place. For example, because Thoreau was particularly attentive to the area surrounding Walden Pond, ecocritics studying him consequently propounded an environmental ethics centered on the importance of such places. However, now that our environmental problems are truly global in scale and understood as interconnected by our atmosphere and oceans, second-wave ecocritics like Ursula K. Heise and Anna Lowenhaupt Tsing (both anthologized here) urge us to reconsider issues of scale. Similarly and related to the above concerns with EJ, Graham Huggan and Rob Nixon took up "Environmentalism and Postcolonialism" (which is the title of Nixon's essay included here).

Other second-wave ecocritics, like Bruno Latour, Timothy Morton, Dana Phillips, and Kate Soper (all represented in this book), have approached environmental issues from a decidedly theoretical position. Such work can sometimes be surprising, as it may not deal with environmental issues as directly we might expect. For example, the Association for the Study of Literature and Environment (ASLE) named Robert N. Watson's *Back to Nature* as the "best book of ecocriticism" published in 2005–6, in spite of the fact that this book is not primarily referencing the environmental resonances that emerged with its title phrase in the 1960s and 70s; rather, in this book, "back to nature" signals something like "back to reality" or, to be more precise in the phenomenological sense Watson intends, it means "back to 'the things themselves.' " The thesis of *Back to Nature* is that in the Renaissance there emerged an anxiety over whether poets and artists could succeed at representing between the boards of a book "the things themselves" we encounter in the environment. Consequently, this is a highly theoretical work that does not significantly touch on important environmental issues emerging at the time, such as air pollution, deforestation, endangered species, wetland loss, and so forth. Nonetheless, *Back to Nature* is in fact an important ecocritical work, as it fascinatingly explores how late Renaissance writers squarely dealt with the issue of how to represent the environment.

Watson's work signals another recent interest. Because our environmental crisis has been brewing for thousands of years, second-wave environmental critics need not just work with relatively recent primary texts (which many first-wave critics did, as modern environmental attitudes were often thought of as having emerged in the past two centuries or so). For example, because the first commission to study London's now famous air-pollution problem was convened nearly a century before the poet Geoffrey Chaucer penned his *Canterbury Tales*, environmental critics working with medieval and Renaissance texts are ideally positioned to explore the birth of our attitudes toward urban air pollution. Consequently, the literature of nearly any period can be of interest to second-wave ecocritics as a way of helping us understand the emergence of our present environmental crisis. In addition to Watson, there are essays here by Alfred Siewers considering medieval texts, Gabriel Egan taking up Shakespeare, and Beth Tobin discussing the literature of the 18th century.

In 1903, W.E.B. Du Bois presciently suggested that "the problem of the Twentieth Century is the problem of the color-line." With a nod to Du Bois, Lawrence Buell opened his 2005 book on *The Future of Environmental Criticism* by suggesting that, although issues of race are still very much with us, our emerging global environmental crisis will be the greatest problem of the coming century. As Buell is, sadly, very likely correct, environmental criticism will be crucially important in the twenty-first century, and will no doubt experience many "waves" of interest. It seems likely that future ecocriticism will move in the direction second-wave critics are now charting, rather than looking back in a sentimental way to overly romanticized accounts of the environment. Similarly, ecocritical approaches that do not take into account issues of environmental justice (or more accurately, injustice) will no doubt seem simplistic and perhaps even worrisome. In addition, critics such as Robert Watson will likely continue to theoretically explore the nature of the art that deals with nature. Moreover, as Watson makes clear on the first page of the Introduction to his *Back to Nature* (anthologized here), "ecocriticism seems to be booming in its test markets (British Romanticism and the literature of the American West) and now seems ready to push its way back to the Renaissance," as well as into all other periods of literary study.

Because of the environmental justice movement, ecocriticism greatly benefited from the work of literary critics exploring issues like gender, class, race, and colonialism. Ecocritics are now returning (and will very likely in the future continue to return) the favor by showing how an environmental approach can enrich critical work in the fields, such a colonial studies, from which environmental justice borrowed. In this sense, ecocriticism will, like the methodological approaches that preceded it, both remain a discrete field of literary study and inform other approaches. Consequently, many critical studies may have a "green" tint to them without being primarily works of ecocriticism.

Chapter 12

Joni Adamson, Mei Mei Evans, and Rachel Stein

ENVIRONMENTAL JUSTICE POLITICS, POETICS, AND PEDAGOGY

IN THE FALL OF 1999, delegations of environmental activists, trade unionists, Buddhist monks, indigenous peoples, and "raging grannies," representing many countries of the world, converged in Seattle, Washington, to protest the World Trade Organization's support of multinational corporate objectives and trade agreements that contribute to the building of a global economy where control over local environments, communities, cultures, education, and health care is no longer in the hands of the people but in the hands of big business. The Seattle protests, and more recently, those in Toronto, Canada, and Genoa, Italy, dramatically recall struggles of the past several decades by such activists as rubber tappers in the Amazon protecting their traditional rain forest homelands, villagers of the Chipko movement in northern India fighting against deforestation, and Ogoni dissidents detained by the military government of Nigeria for their opposition to large-scale oil drilling in fields where they once cultivated yams and cassava. The last quarter of the twentieth century also saw the emergence of similar struggles in the United States: Navajo sheepherders fighting the encroachment of the world's largest open-pit coal mine into sacred lands, women in South Central Los Angeles opposing the siting of a hazardous waste burning facility in their neighborhood, residents of a Memphis, Tennessee, neighborhood calling on the Environmental Protection Agency and the U.S. military to contain and remove toxic substances escaping into the air, water, and soil from an arms storage facility near their homes, and members of several American Indian tribes in the Northwest advocating the removal of dams that threaten their salmon-based cultures.

Each of these specifically located struggles may be said to have contributed to what we today recognize as a global environmental justice movement. This book, inspired by the activists, artists, teachers, and scholars who are working to make social and environmental justice a reality, seeks to examine the issues, events, cultural productions, and educational initiatives emerging from the environmental justice movement worldwide. We define environmental justice as the right of all people to share equally in the benefits bestowed by a healthy environment. We define the environment, in turn, as the places in which we live, work, play, and worship. Environmental justice initiatives specifically attempt to redress the disproportionate incidence of environmental contamination in communities of the poor and/or communities of color, to secure for those affected the right to live un-threatened by the risks posed by environmental degradation and contamination, and to afford equal access to natural resources that sustain life and culture. As members of marginalized communities have mobilized around issues of environmental degradation affecting their families, communities, and work sites, they have illuminated the crucial intersections between ecological and social justice concerns.

In the last several decades, environmental justice movements around the world have grown out of convergences between civil rights movements, antiwar and antinuclear movements, women's movements, and grassroots organizing around environmental issues. One defining moment in the history of the U.S. environmental justice movement was the publication in 1987 of a report sponsored by the United Church of Christ Commission for Racial Justice (UCC-CRJ). The report, a compilation of the results of a national study, found race to be the leading factor in the location of commercial hazardous waste facilities and determined that poor and people of color communities suffer a disproportionate health risk: 60 percent of African American and Latino communities and over 50 percent of Asian/Pacific Islanders and Native Americans live in areas with one or more uncontrolled toxic waste sites. Following publication of the report, the Reverend Benjamin Chavis, then executive director of the UCC-CRJ, coined the term "environmental racism," which he defined as "racial discrimination in environmental policy-making and the enforcement of regulations and laws, the deliberate targeting of people of color communities for toxic waste facilities, the official sanctioning of the life-threatening presence of poisons and pollutants in our communities, and history of excluding people of color from leadership in the environmental movement."[1]

Another watershed moment in the history of the movement, this time international in scope, occurred in 1991, when over three hundred community leaders from the United States, Canada, Central and South America, and the Marshall Islands convened the First National People of Color Environmental Leadership Summit in Washington, D.C. The purpose of the meeting was to bring together leaders from people of color communities worldwide who could shape the contours of a multiracial movement for environmental change founded on the political ideology of working from the grassroots. Delegates took a stand against environmental racism and drew up seventeen "Principles of Environmental Justice" outlining a broad and deep political commitment to pursue environmental justice and "to secure our political, economic, and cultural liberation that has been denied for over 500 years of colonization and oppression."[2]

Environmental justice movements call attention to the ways disparate distribution of wealth and power often leads to correlative social upheaval and the unequal distribution of environmental degradation and/or toxicity. For example, in Chiapas, Mexico, members of the Zapatista National Liberation Army commanded the world's attention when they took over four sizable towns on January 1, 1994, the day the North American Free Trade Agreement (NAFTA) went into effect, and later insisted that Mexico's government bring indigenous peoples into all deliberations affecting their cultural, economic, and environmental futures. Indeed, by calling into question global institutions such as NAFTA, which favor large multinational agribusiness at the expense of small subsistence farmers, the Zapatistas brought the urgency of the issues at the center of the environmental justice movement into international prominence and demonstrated that disgruntled groups of women, farmers, indigenous peoples, or urban city dwellers have the power to confront large governments, corporations, and even global steamrollers such as NAFTA or the World Trade Organization. These groups have also mandated awareness within the mainstream environmental movement to issues of race, class, and gender, among others, as well as within social justice movements to the foundational importance of ecological integrity to a community's sense of well-being.

Although the worldwide environmental justice movement is still relatively young, there is already a vast literature on the subject by scholars in the fields of social science, environmental science, and philosophy. This writing documents the efforts of local groups to organize, mobilize, and empower themselves to take charge of their own lives, communities, and environments. Many of the essays in this volume build upon landmark texts in the movement authored by such scholar/activists as Robert Bullard, Pratap Chatterje, Ward Churchill, Giovanna Di Chiro, Winona LaDuke, Mathias Finger, Laura Pulido, Wolfgang Sachs, Vandana Shiva, and Jace Weaver. Contributors extend the literature by analyzing the connections between different incidents of environmental degradation and economic exploitation while at the same time emphasizing the local, regional, and cultural complexities of the struggles taking place at those sites.

This volume also points to the growing number of expressive writers and artists representing environmental justice struggles in their works. Novelists, essayists, playwrights, and poets as diverse as Jimmy Santiago Baca, Octavia Butler, Ana Castillo, Mahasweta Devi, Linda Hogan, Winona LaDuke, Barbara Neely, Simon Ortiz, Adrienne Rich, Marilynne Robinson, Ken Saro-Wiwa, Leslie Marmon Silko, Helen Maria Viramontes, Gerald Vizenor, Alice Walker, and Karen Tei Yamashita, among others, write about the environmental hazards faced by communities of color and economically and politically disenfranchised communities. They have created a literature that depicts the social, material, and spiritual devastation that results when, for example, hydroelectric projects destroy tribal lands and water, when poisonous and radioactive materials originating at local factories, mines, garbage incinerators, and agricultural areas threaten human health and life, or when traditional agro-pastoral farmers are unable to compete with corporate agribusiness executives. Other nontraditional literary forms and cultural production including testimonies, oral histories, manifestoes, and street theater are also being used to draw our attention to and enhance our understanding of the experience of living with the effects of environmental racism. Grassroots groups are producing poster graphics, sculpture, murals, and public greening projects. Regional environmental justice issues appear in media arts such as video and film, in Internet web art and computer-generated graphics, and in academic and community scholarship, including lectures, essays, radio programs, field trips, and community flyers.

As Robert Figueroa explains [. . .], environmental justice is such a contemporary area of concern that those who enter into discussion of this issue have the opportunity to "engage the subject matter while the origin of many terms, meanings, concepts and associated action . . . is in its earliest developmental stages" [. . .]. In the environmental justice courses he teaches, Figueroa encourages students "to feel that they are a part of the community of scholars and activists working to clarify these issues by developing ways of articulating the problems and solutions." Like Figueroa, the editors of this volume have as their goal the creation of a text that will encourage teachers, students, and community members to see themselves as part of the global community working to clarify and promote the issues surrounding the environmental justice movement. The book takes a multivocal approach: our collection of activist testimonies, interviews, political analyses, curricular accounts, and literary comparisons emphasizes the dialogic nature of political resolution for environmental social experiences of environmental injustices. Contributors point out the paths that U.S. and international environmental justice movements are taking, articulate the problems and solutions that environmental justice initiatives address, and envision the potentiality of future collaborations between artists, activists, scholars, teachers, and students working toward environmental justice.

The Environmental Justice Reader: Politics, Poetics, and Pedagogy expands the field of environmental justice studies by offering new case studies, including cultural analysis of environmental justice arts, and by providing pedagogical essays that encourage teachers to incorporate these issues and texts into their classrooms. By means of section headings, "Politics," "Poetics," and "Pedagogy," we assert that both teaching and making art are intrinsically political acts. Both require a skillful examination, negotiation, and transformation of the tensions that sometimes manifest in more overtly "political" responses. As illustrated by the roundtable discussion between Simon Ortiz, Teresa Leal, Devon Peña, and Terrell Dixon that opens this book, the separation of these impulses has too often been artificial and unnecessary, and our text is an attempt to join political, poetic, and pedagogical acts of resistance back together.

Politics

In her essay for the Politics section of this book, Valerie Kuletz suggests that, too often, researchers and scholars have been content to simply present a "postmortem of an already disastrous situation." She argues, instead, for a "proactive scholarship" that points out patterns of environmentally destructive and socially unjust activity and that also identifies resistance movements working for community and environmental survival [. . .]. Such proactive scholarship points us toward solutions and encourages action rather than hand-wringing, which is exactly the intent of the essays included in the book's first section. The essays assembled in "Politics" expand the limited focus of mainstream environmental movements, explain the interrelationships of environmental problems and social concerns, and explore particular environmental justice struggles that have emerged in the United States and other regions of the world, such as Mexico, Africa, and the Pacific Islands. The essays add new critical perspectives to the existing body of environmental justice scholarship, describe the wide range of issues that may be grouped together under this heading, and examine the different strategies adopted by community groups faced with environmental injustices.

The Politics section opens with a cluster of first-person testimonies in which citizen-activists Doris Bradshaw, Sterling Gologergen, Edgar Mouton, Alberto Saldamando, and Paul Smith speak directly of the grassroots movements that have formed in their regions to address the environmental toxicity endangering their communities and call attention to other environmental threats to their cultural survival as well. Their voices give urgency to the analyses contained in the essays that follow.

Next follow two essays discussing Hispano and Native American environmental justice issues in the southwestern region of the United States. Joni Adamson's "Throwing Rocks at the Sun: An Interview with Teresa Leal" examines the lifelong efforts of one woman to name, fight against, and find solutions to the interrelated problems that threaten women, workers, and the environment in the border region between the United States and Mexico. Devon Peña's "Endangered Landscapes and Disappearing Peoples? Identity, Place, and Community in Ecological Politics" describes the interrelationship of cultural and ecological preservation evidenced within the struggle of traditional Hispano acequia farmers to maintain collective land and water rights in the face of development, logging, and mining interests that threaten both traditional agriculture and culture.

The southeastern United States, an area notorious for toxic waste dumping and expo-sure within communities of color, gave rise to some of the earliest environmental justice movements in the 1980s. Andrea Simpson's "Who Hears Their Cry? African American Women and the Fight for Environmental Justice in Memphis, Tennessee" focuses upon the difficulties that activist Doris Bradshaw faces as her organization, The Tennessee Concerned Citizens Committee, fights toxic waste sites in a working-class African American commu-nity. In particular, Simpson discusses the obstacle of confronting scientific experts who deny residents' claims of environmentally caused illnesses. In a similar vein, but very different locale, Nelta Edwards's "Radiation, Tobacco, and Illness in Point Hope, Alaska: Approaches to the 'Facts' in Contaminated Communities" describes the Atomic Energy Commission's experimentation with radioactive materials near Point Hope, Alaska, in the 1950s and the current efforts of Inupiat people living in that area to link their high incidence of cancer to radiation exposure, despite the negation of scientists. The situation leads Edwards to conclude that environmental justice movements must find ways to argue their claims beyond the limits of the current scientific framework. Examining related issues of nuclear colonialism in the Pacific region, Valerie Kuletz's 'The Movement for Environmental Justice in the Pacific Islands" traces the Nuclear Free and Independent Pacific Movement, which has emerged in resistance to decades of nuclear testing, and new plans for storage of nuclear and toxic waste in this extensive region.

Poetics

As Julie Sze suggests in her essay, the environmental justice movement is not only a political movement concerned with public policy, but also "a cultural movement interested in issues of ideology and representation." By calling attention to the importance of cultural productions that offer us insider perspectives on the environmental justice struggles so crucial to building political solidarity, the middle section's examination of environmental justice poetics breaks new ground. This section also functions as a conduit between the sections on politics and pedagogy in its exploration of the many expressive arts used to transform toxic landscapes, to voice community experiences of environmental racism, and to imaginatively convey the issues at stake in environmental justice struggles. The section opens with several essays that explain how environmental justice literature radically expands both the mainstream nature-writing canon and environmental justice discourse. T. V. Reed's "Toward an Environmental Justice Ecocriticism" exposes the limitations of mainstream ecocritics' valorization of wilderness-based, white-authored nature writing, and advocates a more inclusive, class- and race-conscious ecocriticism that articulates the complex human relationships to environment expressed in culturally diverse literature, such as poetry by June Jordan and Adrienne Rich. In "From Environmental Justice Literature to the Literature of Environmental Justice," Julie Sze explains how cultural productions, such as Karen Tei Yamashita's novel *Tropic of Orange*, use metaphors and imagery in ways that expand the social-science orientation of much environmental justice discourse and imaginatively reframe issues of environmental racism.

Contributors to this section argue for an expansion of the canon of environmental literature by focusing upon texts that incorporate racial, ethnic, class, and sexual differences, and that emphasize intersections between social oppressions and environmental issues. Mei Mei Evans's " 'Nature' and Environmental Justice" argues that hegemonic U.S. conceptions of racial, gender, and sexual identity have excluded women, people of color, and gays and lesbians from natural space. She reads texts that contest dominant cultural assumptions regarding who may enter "nature" in order to experience its transformative effects. The next two essays examine gendered representations of injustice, illness, and activism. Rachel Stein's "Activism as Affirmation: Gender and Environmental Justice in Linda Hogan's *Solar Storms* and Barbara Neely's *Blanche Cleans Up*" focuses upon women's fictional accounts of actual environmental justice struggles. Their portrayals of the hydroelectric project that destroyed Cree and Inuit homelands in Canada and of lead poisoning of African American children in Boston emphasize how these environmental injustices invade families, put children at risk, and radicalize women to take direct political action against the threats to their communities. In "Some Live More Downstream than Others: Cancer, Gender, and Environmental Justice," Jim Tarter writes as both a literary scholar and as a cancer survivor who has lost family members to this disease. Tarter focuses upon cancer as an environmental injustice in which class and gender are significant risk factors, and his reading of Carson's *Silent Spring* and Steingraber's *Living Downstream: An Ecologist Looks at Cancer and the Environment* analyzes their authorial positions as cancer survivors, scientists, and activists. In a very different neocolonial political context, Susan Comfort's "Struggle in Ogoniland: Ken Saro-Wiwa and the Cultural Politics of Environmental Justice" examines the complex authorial positioning of Saro-Wiwa, whose journalism and fiction tirelessly advocated for the Ogoni communities that have been devastated by oil mining, enclosure, and civil war.

A number of the essays in this collection focus on rural struggles over water and land rights affecting communities of color in varied regions of the United States and Canada. Tom Lynch's 'Toward a Symbiosis of Ecology and Justice: Water and Land Conflicts in Frank Waters, John Nichols, and Jimmy Santiago Baca" focuses on writers who portray Hispano struggles to maintain the water and land rights to sustain traditional cultures and agricultures in the Sangre de Cristo watershed. Similarly, in "Saving the Salmon, Saving the People: Environmental Justice and Columbia River Tribal Literatures," Janis Johnson focuses on the efforts of Northwest Indian tribes and environmental groups to remove dams on the Snake River in order to restore the salmon runs so crucial to tribal economies, religions, and identities.

The Poetics section concludes with an essay that focuses upon the transformative power inherent in varied forms of activist art produced within those communities affected by environmental injustice. As Giovanna Di Chiro observes in her interview with Baltimore-area artist/activists Cinder Hypki and Bryant "Spoon" Smith, "Sustaining the 'Urban Forest' and Creating Landscapes of Hope," community-based environmental art projects confront the following fundamental questions: What counts as "green"? Where is the "environment" located? What are we trying to "sustain" and for whom? Di Chiro argues that the artistic images produced by grassroots groups contest the paralyzing stereotypes of inner-city dwellers as, at best, unconcerned and unproductive, and, at worst, menacing and destructive.

Pedagogy

In the final section, four college professors discuss their strategies for teaching undergraduate environmental justice courses in a range of disciplines and institutions. Soenke Zehle writes that environmental justice education must "translate the mantra of ecology (all is connected) into a web of concrete relations that includes not only ecological but cultural, economic, and political processes." The essays in this section share strategies for this process of translation and raise wide-ranging theoretical questions about the ways in which educational institutions are implicated in environmental racism. They describe the value of expanded programs of environmental studies that encompass environmental justice and transnational environmental issues, and they explain approaches for introducing environmental justice materials into a variety of disciplines, such as environmental studies, philosophy, literature, and women's studies, within a range of college settings.

The first two essays articulate overarching approaches and concepts of environmental justice that might be applicable to a variety of programs and curricula. Robert Figueroa, who teaches interdisciplinary philosophy courses on environmental justice at Colgate University, explains in "Teaching for Transformation: Lessons from Environmental Justice" that the study of environmental justice requires students to understand interconnections between theory and practice. He recommends service-learning projects and case studies that expose students to environmental justice as a social movement. In "Notes on Cross-Border

Environmental Justice Education," Soenke Zehle discusses key concepts, such as ecological democracy, subaltern environmentalism, colonialism and commodities, eco-internationalism, and media ecology, that serve as the framework for the interdisciplinary, transnational environmental justice courses that he teaches at SUNY-Binghamton. The last two essays explain pedagogical strategies and curricular materials useful for bringing environmental justice curriculum to different student bodies. In "Changing the Nature of Environmental Studies: Teaching Environmental Justice to 'Mainstream' Students," Steve Chase describes the successful efforts of graduate students to lobby for courses on environmental justice within the Environmental Studies program at Antioch New England, and he discusses his own pedagogical strategies for generating enthusiasm for this subject among predominantly white, middle-class students who may not at first appreciate its relevance. In "Teaching Literature of Environmental Justice in an Advanced Gender Studies Course," Jia-Yi Cheng-Levine describes the course she offered at the University of Houston's racially diverse downtown campus, in which she emphasized the interrelated effects of colonization and multinational capitalism upon women and the environment. Her curriculum blends study of literary texts, such as those discussed in the Poetics section of this collection, with secondary studies of environmental justice theory and movements.

Conclusion

With the exception of the roundtable discussion that follows this introduction [in *The Environmental Justice Reader* (to which the remainder of this Conclusion refers)], all of the essays included in this volume are previously unpublished. Their interdisciplinary nature is readily apparent from the varying source documentation one finds from essay to essay. Taken as a whole, this collection moves environmental justice studies in new directions, beyond an exclusive focus on documenting environmental racism. Many of the essays explore intersections between race and other aspects of social identity that are pertinent to achieving justice, such as class, gender, family and community relations, sexuality, cultural and ethnic traditions, transnational economics, and geographic location. The studies highlight the complexity and urgency of environmental justice issues and urge us to expand our perspectives as we articulate the full range of social concerns at stake, and work toward truly just solutions.

This volume also expands our understanding of the wide range of environmental issues that impact communities of color and poor communities. Communities are not only struggling to alleviate various sorts of health-threatening toxic exposures, they are also fighting to maintain access to the natural resources that sustain cultural identities and traditional lifeways in the face of transnational corporate development based on attitudes toward the natural world that are often completely at odds with their own. While environmental justice has often been thought to be an urban issue, a number of essays focus upon rural concerns and struggles over land and water rights. Although our text is primarily based in the United States of America, several contributors also widen the focus of environmental justice studies by analyzing the complex threats posed to communities of color around the world by transnational neocolonial forces.

Furthermore, our text includes the arts and teaching as important aspects of environmental justice work. Essays detail the way that writers and artists voice community concerns and visions, articulate the complexities of righting environmental injustices, and invite outsiders to imaginatively enter embattled communities to experience the issues from within. Art is also a tool employed by activists and community members for community building. As Bryant Smith and Cinder Hypki explain in their interview with Giovanna Di Chiro, people must have visions of possibility in order to shape and guide our struggles for justice and imagine alternatives to current tragedies and blight.

In the roundtable discussion that follows this introduction, Devon Peña touches on a theme that we, as editors, see emerging throughout this book: that as a result of grassroots activism and cultural production focused on environmental and economic justice issues, people are moving beyond the simple critique of environmental racism and the awareness of how globalism is destroying the planet and are now actively recovering and promoting the sustainable alternatives to environmental destruction found in diverse ethnic, tribal, and pastoral cultures. He observes that all over the world, place-based activists and community shareholders refuse to despair over the "end of nature"; instead they experiment with locally controlled, self-managed, community-owned, worker-cooperative-type organizations that are almost entirely unrecognized by the general population. Like many of the other activist, academic, literary, pedagogical voices in this volume, Peña urges us to move beyond a politics of negativism and find a pathway to ecological sustainability and social justice. Perhaps Teresa Leal, cochair of the Southwest Network for Environmental and Economic Justice, best expresses the call for all to work for solutions to our environmental and social problems in her interview in this volume when she says that we all must "throw rocks at the sun." Leal explains that environmental justice workers understand the enormity of the challenge; they know that their fight against giant multinational corporations or local developers or industrial plants may be daunting and that their efforts to stem the destruction of the world's cultures and environments sometimes seems an impossible goal. However, according to Leal, we must continue to keep our eyes on the prize and to aim for the sun because "change comes only when a few brave hearts dare to throw the first rock."

We, as editors, hand you this book as a testament to the brave hearts who have dared to throw the first rocks. We invite you to join with the many worldwide who are working for environmental justice. As huge and hopeless as the task may at first appear, each of us has something to contribute. Let us aim our volleys at the sun.

Notes

1   Chavis is quoted in Giovanna Di Chiro, "Nature as Community: The Convergence of Environment and Social Justice," in *Uncommon Ground: Rethinking the Human Place in Nature*, ed. William Cronon (New York: Norton, 1996), 304.

2   Ibid., 306. All seventeen Principles of Environmental Justice are reprinted in this article.

Chapter 13

Stacy Alaimo and Susan Hekman

EMERGING MODELS OF MATERIALITY IN FEMINIST THEORY

THE PURPOSE OF THIS anthology [i.e. *Material Feminisms*, the volume in which this chapter was originally published (to which all additional references of this kind in this chapter refer)] is to bring the material, specifically the materiality of the human body and the natural world, into the forefront of feminist theory and practice. This is no small matter indeed, and we expect this collection to spark intense debate. Materiality, particularly that of bodies and natures, has long been an extraordinarily volatile site for feminist theory—so volatile, in fact, that the guiding rule of procedure for most contemporary feminisms requires that one distance oneself as much as possible from the tainted realm of materiality by taking refuge within culture, discourse, and language. Our thesis is that feminist theory is at an impasse caused by the contemporary linguistic turn in feminist thought. With the advent of postmodernism and poststructuralism, many feminists have turned their attention to social constructionist models. They have focused on the role of language in the constitution of social reality, demonstrating that discursive practices constitute the social position of women. They have engaged in productive and wide-ranging analyses and deconstructions of the concepts that define and derogate women.

The turn to the linguistic and discursive has been enormously productive for feminism. It has fostered complex analyses of the interconnections between power, knowledge, subjectivity, and language. It has allowed feminists to understand gender from a new and fruitful perspective. For example, it has allowed feminists to understand how gender has been articulated with other volatile markings, such as class, race, and sexuality, within cultural systems of difference that function like a language (à la Ferdinand de Saussure). The rigorous deconstructions of Jacques Derrida and Luce Irigaray (especially within *Speculum of the Other Woman*) have exposed the pernicious logic that casts woman as subordinated, inferior, a mirror of the same, or all but invisible. At the forefront of this turn to the linguistic is the influence of postmodern thought in feminist theory. The strength of postmodern feminism is to reveal that since its inception, Western thought has been structured by a series of gendered dichotomies. Postmodern feminists have argued that the male/female dichotomy informs all the dichotomies that ground Western thought: culture/nature, mind/body, subject/object, rational/emotional, and countless others. Postmodern feminists have further argued that it is imperative not to move from one side of the dichotomy to the other, to reverse the privileging of concepts, but to deconstruct the dichotomy itself, to move to an understanding that does not rest on oppositions.

Feminist theory and practice have been significantly enriched by these postmodern insights. Postmodern analysis has revealed the liability of defining and fixing the identity of "woman" in any location or of attempting to assert the superiority of the feminine over the masculine. Indeed, within queer theory, especially, the "feminine" and the "masculine" have been productively unmoored, contested, and redeployed. But it is now apparent that the move to the linguistic, particularly in its postmodern variant, has serious liabilities as well as advantages. In short, postmodernism has not fulfilled its promise as a theoretical grounding for feminism. Although postmoderns claim to reject all dichotomies, there is one dichotomy that they appear to embrace almost without question: language/reality. Perhaps due to its centrality in modernist thought, postmoderns are very uncomfortable with the concept of the real or the material. Whereas the epistemology of modernism is grounded in objective access to a real/natural world, postmodernists argue that the real/material is entirely constituted by language; what we call the real is a product of language and has its reality only in language. In their zeal to reject the modernist grounding in the material, postmoderns have turned to the discursive pole as the exclusive source of the constitution of nature, society, and reality. Far from deconstructing the dichotomies of language/reality or culture/nature, they have rejected one side and embraced the other. Even though many social constructionist theories grant the existence of material reality, that reality is often posited as a realm entirely separate from that of language, discourse, and culture. This presumption of separation has meant, in practice, that feminist theory and cultural studies have focused almost entirely on the textual, linguistic, and discursive.

Defenders of postmodernism would argue that this is a misreading of the postmodern position or even that we cannot identify a single postmodern position in any case. Theorists such as Gilles Deleuze and Michel Foucault do, in fact, accommodate the material in their work. Their use of the material, furthermore, has been reflected in the work of other theorists. William Connolly, for example, employs the materiality of Deleuze in his *Neuropolitics* (2002). And feminist theorists such as Claire Colebrook and Ladelle McWhorter have drawn upon Deleuze and Foucault to enable them to engage with materiality in significant and revealing ways. Nonetheless, the material force of the work of Deleuze, and especially of Foucault, is often overlooked because of the exclusive focus on the discursive. Furthermore, the tendency to focus on the discursive at the expense of the material has been particularly evident in feminist versions of postmodernism. Judith Butler, perhaps the most notable feminist postmodern, is frequently criticized for her "loss" of the material, specifically the materiality of the body. The feminist debate over her *Gender Trouble* (1990) and *Bodies That Matter* (1993) is evidence, in the eyes of many feminists, that postmodern feminism has retreated from the material.[1]

This retreat from materiality has had serious consequences for feminist theory and practice. Defining materiality, the body, and nature as products of discourse has skewed discussions of these topics. Ironically, although there has been a tremendous outpouring of scholarship on "the body" in the last twenty years, nearly all of the work in this area has been confined to the analysis of discourses *about* the body. While no one would deny the ongoing importance of discursive critique and rearticulation for feminist scholarship and feminist politics, the discursive realm is nearly always constituted so as to foreclose attention to lived, material bodies and evolving corporeal practices. An emerging group of feminist theorists of the body are arguing, however, that we need a way to talk about the materiality of the body as itself an active, sometimes recalcitrant, force. Women *have* bodies; these bodies have pain as well as pleasure. They also have diseases that are subject to medical interventions that may or may not cure those bodies. We need a way to talk about these bodies and the materiality they inhabit. Focusing exclusively on representations, ideology, and discourse excludes lived experience, corporeal practice, and biological substance from consideration. It makes it nearly impossible for feminism to engage with medicine or science in innovative, productive, or affirmative ways—the only path available is the well-worn path of critique. Moreover, bracketing or negating materiality can actually inhibit the development of a robust understanding of discursive production itself, since various aspects of materiality contribute to the development and transformation of discourses. Note Donna Haraway's formulation in this volume of the "material-discursive," which refuses to separate the two.

Environmental feminists have long insisted that feminism needs to take the materiality of the more-than-human world seriously. The mainstream of feminist theory, however, has, more often than not, relegated ecofeminism to the backwoods, fearing that any alliance between feminism and environmentalism could only be founded upon a naïve, romantic account of reality.[2] As Stacy Alaimo argues in *Undomesticated Ground: Recasting Nature as Feminist Space* (2000), predominant feminist theories, from Simone de Beauvoir to Gayle Rubin and Monique Wittig, have pursued a "flight from nature," relentlessly disentangling "woman" from the supposed ground of essentialism, reductionism, and stasis. The problem with this approach, however, is that the more feminist theories distance themselves from "nature," the more that very "nature" is implicitly or explicitly reconfirmed as the treacherous quicksand of misogyny. Clearly, feminists who are also environmentalists cannot be content with theories that replicate the very nature/culture dualism that has been so injurious—not only to nonhuman nature but to various women, Third World peoples, indigenous peoples, people of color, and other marked groups. Rather than perpetuate the nature/culture dualism, which imagines nature to be the inert ground for the exploits of Man, we must reconceptualize nature itself. Nature can no longer be imagined as a pliable resource for industrial production or social construction. Nature is agentic—it acts, and those actions have consequences for both the human and nonhuman world. We need ways of understanding the agency, significance, and ongoing transformative power of the world—ways that account for myriad "intra-actions" (in Karen Barad's terms) between phenomena that are material, discursive, human, more-than-human, corporeal, and technological. Since the denigration of nature and the disregard for materiality cannot be entirely disaggregated, material feminism demands profound—even startling—reconceptualizations of nature.

One of the most significant areas of discontent within feminism is feminist science studies. Initially, feminist critiques of science focused on the androcentrism of science—the masculine constructions, perspectives, and epistemologies that structure scientific practice. Following the social studies of science, feminists argued that scientific concepts constitute the reality they study, that science, like all other human activities, is a social construction. Despite the persuasiveness of this position, however, questions began to arise about the viability of this approach. Feminist and other critics of science began to explore alternative approaches that bring the material back into science without losing the insights of social constructionism. The "new empiricism" of feminist science critics like Sandra Harding, Helen Longino, Lorraine Code, and Lynne Hankinson Nelson represents attempts to retain an empirical, material element without abandoning social construction.

Significant as this work has been, recent work in science studies promises to "make matter matter" in more significant ways. Theorists such as Bruno Latour and Andrew Pickering have begun to develop innovative theories that combine social construction with an understanding of the ontology and agency of the material world. Instead of focusing on the epistemology of scientific concepts, they have turned the focus to ontology and materiality. Feminist science critics Donna Haraway and Karen Barad have developed theories that define

the human, nonhuman, technological, and natural as agents that jointly construct the parameters of our common world. They have demonstrated that this interaction has wide-ranging
implications for the place of women and others in that world. Elizabeth A. Wilson also insists
on the ongoing, mutual, co-constitution of mind and matter. Her book *Psychosomatic: Feminism
and the Neurological Body* (2004) refuses to merely critique neuroscience from a cultural
perspective, but instead brings detailed accounts of the neurological body to bear on
feminist thought.

Our intent in this anthology is to address the dis-ease in contemporary feminist
theory and practice that has resulted from the loss of the material. But our intervention in
this debate is a very specific one. Many within the feminist community have railed against
the loss of the material. Many have argued that we must develop theories that bring the
material back into feminist theory and practice; however, few have been successful in
developing these theories. Our intention in compiling this anthology has been to seek out
those few. We have sought theorists who do not simply lament the loss of the material but,
rather, attempt to formulate approaches that address this problem. The essays we have
collected here are seeking to define what Bruno Latour calls a "new settlement," a new way
of understanding the relationship between discourse and matter that does not privilege
the former to the exclusion of the latter. Karen Barad has argued that we must "construct
a ballast" against the tendency in feminism to define theory as unconstrained play. This
collection is intended to be a key element of that construction.

We have brought together thinkers who are attempting to move beyond discursive
construction and grapple with materiality. A central element of that attempt, however, is to
build on rather than abandon the lessons learned in the linguistic turn. The new settlement
we are seeking is not a return to modernism. Rather, it accomplishes what the postmoderns
failed to do: a deconstruction of the material/discursive dichotomy that retains both elements
without privileging either. The theorists assembled here have been working to revise the
paradigms of poststructuralism, postmodernism, and cultural studies in ways that can more
productively account for the agency, semiotic force, and dynamics of bodies and natures. The
most daunting aspect of such projects is to radically rethink materiality, the very "stuff" of
bodies and natures. The innovative work of these theorists and many others constitutes what
we are calling the "material turn" in feminist theory, a wave of feminist theory that is taking
matter seriously.[3]

The material turn in feminist theory opens up many fundamental questions about
ontology, epistemology, ethics, and politics, questions that are explored in the essays in this
volume. "Material feminists" want to know how we can define the "real" in science and how
we can describe nonhuman agency in a scientific context. The theories emerging from feminists who explore this perspective are redefining our understanding of the relationships
among the natural, the human, and the nonhuman. They are developing theories in which
nature is more than a passive social construction but is, rather, an agentic force that interacts
with and changes the other elements in the mix, including the human. For these theorists,
nature "punches back" at humans and the machines they construct to explore it in ways that
we cannot predict. Feminist theorists of the body want definitions of human corporeality that
can account for how the discursive and the material interact in the constitution of bodies.
They explore the question of nonhuman and post-human nature and its relationship to the
human. One of the central topics in this approach is the question of agency, particularly the
agency of bodies and natures. Material feminists explore the interaction of culture, history,
discourse, technology, biology, and the "environment," without privileging any one of these
elements.

Material feminism opens up new ethical and political vistas as well. Redefining the
human and nonhuman has ethical implications: discourses have material consequences

that require ethical responses. Ethics must be centered not only on those discourses but on the material consequences as well. Material feminism suggests an approach to ethics that displaces the impasse of cultural relativism. Cultural relativism entails that all ethical positions are equal, that we cannot make any cross-cultural judgments. This impasse has stymied feminists who want to reveal the abuses against women in other cultures. A material ethics entails, on the contrary, that we can compare the very real material consequences of ethical positions and draw conclusions from those comparisons. We can, for example, argue that the material consequences of one ethics is more conducive to human and nonhuman flourishing than that of another. Furthermore, material ethics allows us to shift the focus from ethical principles to ethical practices. Practices are, by nature, embodied, situated actions. Ethical practices, which unfold in time and take place in particular contexts, invite the recognition of and response to expected as well as unexpected material phenomena. Particular ethical practices, situated both temporally and physically, may also allow for an openness to the needs, the significance, and the liveliness of the more-than-human world. Ethical practices—as opposed to ethical principles—do not seek to extend themselves over and above material realities, but instead emerge from them, taking into account multiple material consequences. Although a focus on ethical practices is not foundational in the modernist sense, it allows us to compare the material effects of those practices in a way disallowed by a strictly discursive approach.

Material feminism also requires a new political dimension. Political decisions are scripted onto material bodies; these scripts have consequences that demand a political response on the part of those whose bodies are scripted. Karen Barad's (1998) discussion of the political consequences of the invention and use of the sonogram to study the unborn fetus is an excellent example of the politics entailed by material feminism. The use of the sonogram on female pregnant bodies has political repercussions for all women in our society, redefining both "life" and "rights" in a political context. Barad's work also illustrates another aspect of material feminism: the interface between the scientific, technological, political, and human. It is impossible to neatly separate these elements; they are "mangled" together (in Andrew Pickering's terms) in the mix of political and social practice, and this mangle has material, political, and ethical dimensions.

Material feminism also transforms environmental politics, which is, of course, intimately related to environmental science. Indeed, the "truth" of scientific statements about the environment affects the direction of political decisions. Defining all scientific statements as equally valid social constructions does not provide environmentalists with a means of arguing for their positions. Current "debates" about global warming in which political conservatives attempt to discredit a veritable avalanche of scientific data from around the globe stand as a case in point. Clearly, environmental politics demands a renewed understanding that science can disclose indispensable knowledge about nonhuman creatures, ecosystems, and other natural forces. Unlike modernist or even postmodernist accounts that "background," in Val Plumwood's terms, the natural world—imagining it as a mere resource for technological progress or social construction—material feminism must insist that nature be considered a noteworthy actor within the realm of politics as well as science. Catriona Sandilands, in *The Good-Natured Feminist: Ecofeminism and the Quest for Democracy*, proposes, for example, a radical democratic project that would make space for nature in politics, not as a "positive, human-constructed presence, but as an enigmatic, active Other" (1999, 181). Sandilands recasts the political landscape in order to imagine ongoing democratic conversations in which nonhuman nature can participate in nondiscursive ways.

Moreover, thinking through the co-constitutive materiality of human corporeality and nonhuman natures offers possibilities for transforming environmentalism itself. Rather than centering environmental politics on a wilderness model, which severs human from nature and undergirds anti-environmentalist formulations that pit, say, spotted owls against loggers, beginning with the co-extensive materiality of humans and nonhumans offers multiple possibilities for forging new environmental paths. Environmental justice movements, for example, locate "the environment" not in some distant place, but within homes, schools, workplaces, and neighborhoods. These movements reveal that lower-class peoples, indigenous peoples, and people of color carry a disproportionate toxic load. Tracing the traffic in toxins involves scientific/economic/political/ethical analyses of realms and interest groups heretofore imagined separately, for example, those of health, medicine, occupational safety, disability rights, and environmental justice, as well as "traditional" environmentalisms devoted to the welfare of wild creatures. The same material substance, in this case, a particular toxin such as mercury or dioxin, may affect the workers who produce it, the neighborhood in which it is produced, the domesticated and wild animals that ingest it, and the humans who ingest the animals who have ingested it. Beginning with material substances rather than already constituted social groups may, in fact, allow for the formation of unexpected political coalitions and alliances.

The emerging theories of materiality developed in material feminisms are crucial for every aspect of feminist thought: science studies, environmental feminisms, corporeal feminisms, queer theory, disability studies, theories of race and ethnicity, environmental justice, (post-) Marxist feminism, globalization studies, and cultural studies. The essays in this anthology are a first step toward not just articulating these theories but integrating them into what amounts to a new paradigm for feminist thought. It is our thesis that this paradigm is currently emerging and that it is a necessary and exhilarating move for contemporary feminism. While this volume brings together some of the most thought-provoking and innovative theorists of the new "material feminism," no single volume can hope to represent every point of emergence; thus, this volume should be read in dialogue with the work of Luce Irigaray, Rosi Braidotti, Myra J. Hird, Susan Wendell, Ladelle McWhorter, Val Plumwood, Susan Squier, Lynda Birke, Mette Bryld, Nina Lykke, Gloria Anzaldúa, and others. We hope that this collection will encourage readers to forge their own connections between the essays included here and the work of other feminist scholars who insist upon the meaning, force, and value of materiality.

The essays in the first part of the book, "Material Theory," outline the broad parameters of the issues confronting material feminisms. Elizabeth Grosz takes on an issue that has been taboo in feminist accounts of science—Darwin's evolutionary theory—and argues that it can be useful to feminism. Grosz argues that feminists need a complex and subtle account of what biology is and how biology facilitates and makes possible cultural existence. To achieve this goal, she asserts, feminists should incorporate the most influential biological theory of the nineteenth century—Darwin's theory of evolution. Grosz identifies aspects of Darwin's thought that can be used to develop a feminist approach to biology. Her argument offers a kind of template for how the "new" feminist critiques of science should operate. Nothing is out-of-bounds; all possibilities are considered. And most importantly, the materiality of the subject of science is paramount.

The subject of Claire Colebrook's essay is what she calls the "new vitalism." Although she rejects the conservative vitalism of thinkers such as Bergson, Colebrook asserts that a radical feminist materialism must be grounded in a redefined vitalism. Colebrook discusses the work of Elizabeth Grosz along with that of Marx, Hegel, Bergson, Judith Butler, Michel Foucault, and Gilles Deleuze, analyzing the philosophical and political reverberations of their conceptions of matter. Each analysis yields important insights into the redefinition of matter. Regarding Marx, Colebrook argues that the Marxist concept of dialectical materialism counters the depoliticizing of history by emphasizing bodily needs. Her rereading of feminist critiques of matter leads her to reform matter as "positive difference." Her bold formulations take the matter of corporeality seriously by refusing to posit the substance of the body as a mere blank slate for cultural constructions. Indeed, Colebrook emphasizes the extent to which matter can itself alter those systems. She concludes with an image of feminist art criticism and a feminist politics that "frees matter from the human through the human."

Susan Hekman's essay presents an argument for the movement from epistemology to ontology in contemporary feminist thought. Arguing that the focus on epistemology has had detrimental effects, Hekman asserts that we should embrace an ontological perspective that brings the material back into the forefront of feminism. Hekman's key argument is that we should replace a view of language as constituting reality to one that defines this relationship in terms of disclosure. If we define language as disclosing reality, she argues, we can retain a notion of the materiality of the world without abandoning the insights of social construction. Hekman uses this perspective to develop what she calls a social ontology of the subject, an approach that defines identity as both material and social.

Many of the authors in this collection rely on the work of Karen Barad to ground their approaches. Her essay included here makes it clear why her theory is so central to this emerging perspective. Barad's goal is to articulate "how matter comes to matter" and to define what she calls "posthumanist performativity." Her concept incorporates the material and the discursive, the human and the nonhuman, the natural and the cultural, while challenging these dichotomies and the givenness of the categories. Barad identifies her position as "agential realism," a position she derives from the work of Niels Bohr. Far from rejecting poststructuralist insights about language, Barad incorporates these insights while at the same time revealing where theorists such as Foucault and Butler fall short. Barad's powerful and influential theory reveals the unique strengths of the "material feminism" we are advocating.

The second part of the book, "Material World," addresses the principal subject of science: nature. The "nature" of science, however, is entangled with the nature of philosophy, politics, literature, and popular culture. The multiple, overdetermined, and potent notions of nature have hardly been neutral when it comes to race, gender, or sexuality. Feminists have long had to combat the "nature" of misogyny—the very bedrock of essentialism, biological determinism, homophobia, and racism. Thus, the longstanding, pernicious associations between "woman" and "nature" in Western culture—associations that are rarely advantageous to either woman or nature—have made "nature" a treacherous terrain for feminism. Yet as several of us have argued, distancing feminism from.the category of nature only serves to calcify nature as a solid ground for heterosexist infrastructure. Whereas most postmodern and poststructuralist feminisms have sought to disentangle "woman" from "nature"— for significant reasons, to be sure—material feminism seeks a thorough redefinition and transvaluation of nature. Nature, as understood by material feminism, is rarely a blank, silent resource for the exploits of culture. Nor is it the repository of sexism, racism, and homophobia. Instead, it is an active, signifying force; an agent in its own terms; a realm of multiple, inter- and intra-active cultures. This sort of nature—a nature that is, expressly, *not* the mirror image of culture—is emerging from the overlapping fields of material feminism, environmental feminism, environmental philosophy, and green cultural studies.

Donna Haraway's work, which has been essential for the development of all of the aforementioned fields, offers comprehensive and compelling transformations of the category of nature. The nature-culture divide is unthinkable within Haraway's conceptual universe, a universe that is replete with "material-semiotic actors" and such rich and revealing figures as the cyborg, the trickster coyote, and the Onco Mouse. Her essay in this volume takes on the question of what "nature" means in the complex practices of contemporary society. The stories with which she begins the essay illustrate that our understanding of nature must be able to incorporate historically located people, other organisms, and technological artifacts.

"Nature" must encompass demarcation and continuity among actors that are both human and nonhuman, organic and inorganic. The practice of "otherworldly conversations"—in which various nonhuman entities participate as subjects rather than objects—provides one model for ethical relations that respect difference and allow for mutual transformation.

In "Viscous Porosity: Witnessing Katrina," Nancy Tuana brings together the key themes of this collection. First, she articulates the theoretical basis that inspires *Material Feminisms*: what she calls the interactionist ontology of viscous porosity. This theoretical position rematerializes the social and takes seriously the agency of the natural. It attends to the process of becoming in which unity is dynamic and always interactive, and agency is diffusely enacted in complex networks of relations. Second, she provides a brilliant illustration of how viscous porosity works by "witnessing" Katrina. Her analysis includes levees, the Army Corp of Engineers, global warming, the hurricane, the local politics of New Orleans, shell middens, the federal government, racial politics, and the poor and disabled populations of New Orleans. In a compelling argument, Tuana illustrates how the "dance of agency" brings all these elements together in the phenomenon we call "Katrina" and how their interaction destroys our neat divisions between human and nonhuman, biological and cultural. Tuana's essay graphically articulates the theoretical and practical implications of the perspective we are developing.

Vicki Kirby offers an intrepid argument for reconceptualizing the nature of nature by considering the possibility that what we have been calling culture "was really nature all along." Indeed, understanding nature via the values and terms of contemporary (cultural) criticism, such as articulation, reinvention, and the cacophony of multiple signifying agents, allows Kirby to dislodge the assumption that all naturalizing arguments are inherently conservative. Once nature is no longer presumed to be the realm of prescriptive, immutable, and retrogressive truths, feminism can carefully reconsider whether the heretofore negative conflation of "woman" and "nature" may actually offer possibilities for discussing the question of origins.

Both Stacy Alaimo and Catriona Mortimer-Sandilands situate human bodies within specific environmental contexts, reading human processes and events as inseparable from specific biophysical relations and interconnections. Alaimo's essay argues that imagining human corporeality as trans-corporeality, in which the human opens out into a more-than-human world, underlines the extent to which the corporeal substance of the human is ultimately inseparable from "the environment." The space-time of trans-corporeality is a site of both pleasure and danger—the pleasures of desire, surprise, and lively emergence, as well as the dangers of pain, toxicity, and death. Alaimo focuses, however, on toxic bodies, arguing that although they are not something to celebrate, toxic bodies may help lead feminist theory out of the false dilemma of having to choose between a romanticized valorization of bodies and natures or an anti-essentialist flight from the grounds of our being. As a particularly vivid example of trans-corporeal space, toxic bodies insist that environmentalism, human health, and social justice cannot be severed, since they are all continually emergent from zones of intra-activity (in Barad's terms) that are as biological as they are political, as material as they are social. Alaimo promotes trans-corporeal feminisms that encourage us to imagine ourselves in constant interchange with the "environment" and, paradoxically, perhaps, to imagine an "epistemological space" that allows for both the unpredictable becomings of other creatures and the limits of human knowledge.

Catriona Mortimer-Sandilands begins her essay, "Landscape, Memory, and Forgetting: Thinking through (My Mother's) Body and Place," by analyzing recent debates in environmental phenomenology that highlight the "relations between body, mind, and landscape." She departs from most environmental phenomenology by insisting upon the "particular techno-historical relationships between human bodies and others." Her wide-ranging essay weaves together environmental philosophy, an analysis of Jane Urquhart's novel *A Map of Glass*, scientific accounts of Alzheimer's disease, and a personal, poetic account of her mother's life with Alzheimer's. She argues, against David Abram, that we have not, in fact, "lost all traces of the environmental physicality of our memories." And she urges us to consider how we can "cultivate an awareness of and respect for this process through our environmental philosophies and activisms."

The final group of essays, "Material Bodies," focuses on the question of how feminist theory can rethink the materiality of human corporeality. Although there has been a veritable explosion of scholarship within feminist theory and feminist cultural studies about "the body," the overwhelming majority of that work analyzes discourses and representations—exclusively. This textual universe sometimes seems worlds apart from lived materiality and the often obdurate substance and unexpected agencies of corporeality. However, material feminisms that take the physicality of the human body into account are emerging.

Tobin Siebers's discussion of disability takes on one of the pillars of poststructuralist thought: the rejection of experience. Siebers questions the poststructuralist banishing of experience, asking whether this strategy is radical or reactionary. Relying on the emerging realist theory of identity, Siebers argues that social identities are both constructed and real. He concludes that the experience of disabled people embodies identities that may contain legitimate claims to knowledge and that this knowledge, once verified, is a valuable weapon against the oppression of minority people.

The question of identity and identity politics is also the focus of Michael Hames-García's essay Examining the contradictions between social and biological conceptions of race, Hames-García argues that what is needed now is creative experimentation with racial identities rather than their abandonment. Against the critics of identity politics, Hames-García develops the thesis that racial identities can be useful, productive, and transformative; their progressive political potential can benefit from a substantive account of their material reality. Turning to Castells's theory of "project identities," Hames-García concludes that we need creative racial identity projects more than we need philosophical arguments against race.

Suzanne Bost turns her attention to bodies as they appear in the recent autobiographical writings of Chicana feminists. Bost's intervention is to use disability studies to examine the shifting matter of bodies in the work of Gloria Anzaldúa and Cherríe Moraga. Exploring a territory previously defined exclusively in terms of race and sex, Bost reveals how these authors' accounts of pain, illness, and disability uncover new dimensions in Chicana feminism. Using the "permeable and migratory politics of disability," she argues that the disabled subjects in the works of Anzuldúa and Moraga speak to the aims of Chicana feminism better than identity politics.

Elizabeth A. Wilson questions the way feminist critiques of psychopharmaceuticals emphasize the social rather than the biological. These accounts, in both academic and popular feminist writing, criticize the medical and pharmaceutical establishments—as well as the wider culture—for tranquilizing women's (social) discontent. Wilson takes a very different approach to the question of psychopharmaceuticals. By focusing directly on the specific biological effects of the SSRI and SNRI antidepressants, Wilson constructs innovative feminist positions that confound traditional understandings of mind and body. Most remarkably, perhaps, she suggests that it is possible to understand the psychoanalytic process of "transference" occurring at a microbiological level. If the "talking cure" can be understood as organic, as biological as well as mental, then our most basic understandings of "mind" and "matter" need be radically rewritten. Wilson's essay demonstrates how an unflinching engagement with biological specificities can allow feminist science studies to productively challenge established feminist positions.

Susan Bordo's piece, "Cassie's Hair," provides a fitting conclusion to the volume. Like Tuana's analysis of Katrina, Bordo provides an example of how the biological and the social interact. Bordo contrasts abstract conceptions of "difference" with the sense of difference that develops from specific practices that bring one into contact with materiality—in this case, the materiality of her biracial daughter's hair. Feminism has long held that even intimate, familial relations can be infused with political forces, but Bordo's essay suggests that the physicality of bodies can itself beckon us toward more complex understandings of how the personal, the political, *and* the material are braided together.

One of the most exciting aspects of this particular volume is that it reveals the remarkable intersections between scholars working in separate areas. In so doing, it encourages fruitful conversations between the fields of corporeal feminism, environmental feminism, and feminist science studies. The reader may notice, for example, that most of the essays in this volume address not only the topic of the part in which they appear, but the topics of the other two parts as well. Categories and organizational schemes are always provisional, to be sure, but perhaps the overlap and emerging dialogue between the essays is also a result of the topic itself, for attending to materiality erases the commonsensical boundaries between human and nature, body and environment, mind and matter. In short, taking matter seriously entails nothing less than a thorough rethinking of the fundamental categories of Western culture. In the process, these categories may become nearly unrecognizable. Thus, it is our hope that this volume will offer a substantial response to Teresa de Lauretis's recent call in *Critical Inquiry* to "break the piggy bank of saved conceptual schemata and reinstall uncertainty in all theoretical applications, starting with the primacy of the 'cultural' and its many 'turns' " (2004, 368). Such uncertainty requires risk, to be sure, as the specter of essentialism continues to haunt feminism. We think the risks are worth taking, however, since the emerging body of thought we are calling "material feminism" promises bold, provocative, and potent reconceptualizations of the material terrains of our shared worlds.

Notes

1   More evidence of discontent can be found in recent critiques of feminist anti-essentialism. Many have argued that at this point the denouncement of essentialism has become a rigid orthodoxy, more prohibitive and policing than productive. The debates over essentialism are almost always, at some level, debates about the nature and force of materiality.

2   It is ironic that feminist poststructuralism and postmodernism tend to distance themselves from the category of nature if, as Verena Andermatt Conley contends, "the driving force of poststructuralist thought is indissolubly linked to ecology" (1997, 7). By demonstrating how ecology influenced poststructuralist thinkers, Conley radically revised predominant understandings of these theories.

3   Other important discussions of the "new materialism" include Susan Squier and Melissa M. Littlefield (2004) and Myra J. Hird (2004a, 2004b), The "new materialism" overlaps with what we term "material feminism." See also the special issue of *Feminist Theory* (5.2, 2004) edited by Squier and Littlefield that focuses on the "new materialism" within science studies. "Material feminisms" and "new materialism" also overlap with what Iris van der Tuin (2006) terms "Third Wave Materialism." It is important to distinguish what we are calling "material feminism"—which is emerging primarily from corporeal feminism, environmental feminism, and science studies—from "materialist" feminism, which emerges from, or is synonymous with, Marxist feminism. Even as many of the theorists of what we are calling "material feminism" have been influenced by Marxist theory, post-Marxism, and cultural studies, their definition of "materiality" is not, or is not exclusively, Marxist. For more on "materialist" feminism, see the work of Christine Delphy, Michele Barrett, Annette Kuhn, Ann Marie Wolpe, and Rosemary Hennessy. Gerald Landry and Donna MacLean distinguish "materialist feminism" from Marxist feminism by noting that the latter "holds class contradictions and class analysis to be central," whereas the former also focuses on "race, sexuality, imperialism and colonialism, and anthropocentrism" (1993, 229). Teresa Ebert, in *Ludic Feminism and After: Postmodernism, Desire, and Labor in Late Capitalism*, critiques poststructuralist and postmodern

feminisms, arguing that their "ludic matterism" perceives materiality as "sign/textuality or as the matter of the body," thus displacing the Marxist conception of matter as "the praxis of labor and the contradictions and class conflicts in which it is always involved" (1996, 34, 35). Even as labor and class remain essential concepts for feminist analysis and critique, they cannot encompass the materiality of human corporeality or, certainly, of nonhuman nature.

References

Alaimo, Stacy. 2000. *Undomesticated Ground: Recasting Nature as Feminist Space*. Ithaca, N.Y.: Cornell University Press.

Barad, Karen. 1998. "Getting Real: Technoscientific Practices and the Materialization of Reality." *differences: A Journal of Feminist Cultural Studies* 10.2: 87–128.

Butler, Judith. 1993. *Bodies That Matter: On the Discursive Limits of "Sex."* New York: Routledge.

———. 1990. *Gender Trouble: Feminism and the Subversion of Identity*. New York: Routledge.

Conley, Verena Andermatt. 1997. *Ecopolitics: The Environment in Poststructuralist Thought*. New York: Routledge.

De Lauretis, Teresa. 2004. "Statement Due." *Critical Inquiry* 30.2: 365–68.

Ebert, Teresa. 1996. *Ludic Feminism and After: Postmodernism, Desire, and Labor in Late Capitalism*. Ann Arbor: University of Michigan Press.

Hird, Myra J. 2004a. "Feminist Matters: New Materialist Considerations of Sexual Difference." *Feminist Theory* 5.2: 223–32.

———. 2004b. *Sex, Gender and Science*. New York: Palgrave.

Irigaray, Luce. 1985. *Speculum of the Other Woman*. Trans. Gillian Gill. Ithaca, NY.: Cornell University Press.

Landry, Donna, and Gerald MacLean. 1993. *Materialist Feminisms*. Cambridge: Blackwell.

Sandilands, Catriona. 1999. *The Good-Natured Feminist: Ecofeminism and the Quest for Democracy*. Minneapolis: University of Minnesota Press.

Squier, Susan, and Melissa M. Littlefield. 2004. "Feminist Theory and/of Science." *Feminist Theory* 5.2 (special issue): 123–26.

Van der Tuin, Iris. 2006. "Third Wave Materialism." Paper presented at the Society for the Study of Science, Literature, and the Arts in Amsterdam.

Wilson, Elizabeth A. 2004. *Psychosomatic: Feminism and the Neurological Body*. Durham, N.C.: Duke University Press.

Chapter 14

Robert D. Bullard

RACE, CLASS, AND THE POLITICS
OF PLACE

THE SOUTHERN UNITED STATES, with its unique history and its plantation-economy legacy, presents an excellent opportunity for exploring the environment-development dialectic, residence-production conflict, and residual impact of the de facto industrial policy (i.e., "any job is better than no job") on the region's ecology. The South during the 1950s and 1960s was the center of social upheavals and the civil rights movement. The 1970s and early 1980s catapulted the region into the national limelight again, but for different reasons. The South in this latter period was undergoing a number of dramatic demographic, economic, and ecological changes. It had become a major growth center.

Growth in the region during the 1970s was stimulated by a number of factors. They included (1) a climate pleasant enough to attract workers from other regions and the "underemployed" workforce already in the region, (2) weak labor unions and strong right-to-work laws, (3) cheap labor and cheap land, (4) attractive areas for new industries, i.e., electronics, federal defense, and aerospace contracting, (5) aggressive self-promotion and booster campaigns, and (6) lenient environmental regulations.[1] Beginning in the mid-1970s, the South was transformed from a "net exporter of people to a powerful human magnet."[2] The region had a number of factors it promoted as important for a "good business climate," including "low business taxes, a good infrastructure of municipal services, vigorous law enforcement, an eager and docile labor force, and a minimum of business regulations."[3]

The rise of the South intensified land-use conflicts revolving around "use value" (neighborhood interests) and "exchange value" (business interests). Government and business elites became primary players in affecting land-use decisions and growth potentialities. The "growth machine," thus, sometimes pitted neighborhood interests against the interests of industrial expansion. However, economic boosters could usually count on their promise of jobs as an efficient strategy of neutralizing local opposition to growth projects. Harvey Molotch emphasized the importance of jobs as a selling point in growth machine politics:

> Perhaps the key ideological prop for the growth machine, especially in terms of sustaining support from the working-class majority, is the claim that growth "makes jobs." This claim is aggressively promulgated by developers, builders,

and chambers of commerce; it becomes part of the statesman talk of editorialists and political officials. Such people do not speak of growth as useful to profits— rather, they speak of it as necessary for making jobs.[4]

Competition intensified as communities attempted to expand their work force and lure new industries away from other locations. There was a "clear preference for clean industries that require highly skilled workers over dirty industries that use unskilled workers."[5] Many communities could not afford to be choosy. Those communities that failed to penetrate the clean industry market were left with a choice of dirty industry or no industry at all. These disparities typify the changing industrial pattern in the South.

Before moving to the next section, we need to delineate the boundaries of the South. We have chosen to use the U.S. Bureau of the Census South Region, sixteen states and the District of Columbia, as the study area. The South has the largest population of any region in the country. More than 75.4 million inhabitants, nearly one-third of the nation's population, lived in the South in 1980.[6] All of the southern states experienced a net in-migration during the 1970s. The South, during the 1970s and 1980s, also grew at a faster rate than the nation as a whole—a factor that had important economic, political, and ecological implications.

The South also has the largest concentration of blacks in the country. In 1980, more than 14 million blacks lived in the region. Blacks were nearly one-fifth of the region's population. In the 1970s the region's black population increased by nearly 18 percent. In 1980, six of the southern states had black populations that exceeded 20 percent (35.2 percent of the population in Mississippi, 30.4 percent in South Carolina, 29.4 percent in Louisiana, 26.8 percent in Georgia, 25.6 percent in Alabama, and 22.4 percent in North Carolina).

Consequences of Uneven Development

The South has gone to great lengths to shed its image as a socially and economically "backward" region. However, slick public relations and image management campaigns have not been able to hide decades of neglect and underdevelopment. Many of the old problems remain, while new problems were created as a direct result of the new growth. Migrants to urban areas and incumbent residents who had marginal skills generally found themselves in the growing unemployment lines.[7] Individuals who do not have the requisite education often become part of the region's expanding underclass.

The South's new prosperity was mainly confined to metropolitan areas. Growth in the urban South heightened status differences between rich and poor and between blacks and whites. Poverty coexisted amid affluence. Poverty, however, represented a source of cheap labor. The large pool of docile and nonunionized labor was part of the so-called "good business climate."[8]

William Falk and Thomas Lyson described the uneven economic development and plight of rural southerners in their book *High Tech, Low Tech, No Tech*. The authors wrote:

> Not all citizens have benefited from the upturn in the southern economy. In fact, many may not have benefited at all. Blacks, women, and people living in rural areas have, in varying degrees, received little or none of the job opportunities and economic affluence that has washed over the region. The quality of life and opportunity for improvement for these "people left behind" have remained essentially unchanged over the last fifty years.[9]

Development disparities are heightened by business policies that direct jobs away from minority communities through the systematic avoidance of urban ghettos and rural blackbelt counties. The blackbelt represents geopolitical power (or the potential for empowerment). It also represents the epitome of American apartheid with its rigid segregation practices, second-class status for blacks, and staunch white resistance to black majority rule. Falk and Lyson studied 147 southern blackbelt counties (a band of counties with 40 percent or more black population extending from North Carolina to Louisiana) and discovered these areas lagging far behind other counties in the region, partly because of the concentration of unskilled, poorly educated workers. The authors summed up their findings by writing:

> If the SMSA counties are seen as the "pride of the South," the Black Belt can be viewed as the "Sunbelt's stepchild." The industrial growth and development that has washed over the region has left the 147 Black Belt counties with a residue of slow growth and stagnant and declining industries. . . . High tech industries have virtually ignored the Black Belt. . . . In short, by any yardstick of industrial development, the Black Belt remains mired in the backwater of the southern economy.[10]

The persistent problem of uneven development and economic disparities caused many writers to challenge the existence of a "New" South. Chet Fuller, a black journalist, traveled across the region in the late 1970s and discovered that "the much touted progress of some southern cities is more illusion than reality."[11] The region was portrayed as booming with industrial growth and expanding employment opportunities that were once closed to the black masses. The New South was promoted as a changed land where blacks could now share in the American Dream. Fuller argued that "power has not changed hands in the South, not from white hands to black hands."[12] What is "new" about an area where blacks are systematically denied access to jobs, housing, and other residential amenities?

Black communities still suffer from institutionalized discrimination. Discriminatory practices occur at various levels of government and affect the location of polling places, municipal landfills, and toxic-waste dumps. Discrimination, thus, involves a "process of defending one group's privilege gained at the expense of another."[13] Black communities and their inhabitants must defend themselves against hostile external forces that shape land-use decisions and environmental policies.

Why focus on the South? The South has always been home for a significant share of the black population. More than 90 percent of black Americans lived in the southern states at the turn of the [twentieth] century. A little more than one-half (53 percent) of all blacks were living in the region in 1980, the same percentage as in 1970.[14] In an effort to improve their lives, millions of rural blacks migrated from the South to other regions of the nation. From the mid-1940s to the late 1960s, nearly 4.5 million more blacks left the South than migrated to it. Beginning in the mid-1970s, however, the number of blacks moving into the South exceeded the number departing for other regions of the country. For the period 1975–80, over 415,000 blacks moved into the South, while 220,000 left the region (or a net inmigration of 195,000 blacks), thereby reversing the longstanding black exodus. More than 411,000 blacks migrated to the South during the 1980–85 period while 324,000 moved out of the region, a net in-migration of 87,000 blacks.[15]

As industry and jobs relocated to the region, job seekers followed. More than 17 million new jobs were added in the South between 1960 and 1985, compared to 11 million jobs added in the West, and a combined total of 13 million jobs added in the Midwest and Northeast.[16] The challenges that the South must face rest with how its resources—housing, jobs, public services, political representation, etc.—are shared with blacks who historically have not gotten their fair share of the region's amenities. The major reason for this discrepancy has been the location preferences of businesses. Industries that relocated to the South generally built new factories where they could find surplus white labor and "avoided places with a high ratio of poor and unskilled blacks."[17] The plight of millions of blacks has been exacerbated by the combination of economic recession (and depression-like conditions in many black communities), federal budget cuts, growing tension among individuals competing for limited jobs and other scarce resources, and the federal retreat on enforcement of civil rights and antidiscrimination laws.[18]

The social climate of the South was changed dramatically by the civil rights movement. Some gains were also made in the political arena. Most of these gains were made after the passage of the Voting Rights Act of 1965. There were 1,469 black elected officials in 1970, 4,912 in 1980, and 5,654 in 1984.[19] The number of black officeholders increased to 6,681 in 1987. There were twenty-three blacks in the U.S. Congress in 1989. This number represented only 5.3 percent of the 435 members of the U.S. House of Representatives. There were no blacks in the U.S. Senate.

Only four blacks from the Deep South were serving in Congress (Harold Ford of Memphis, Mickey Leland of Houston, John Lewis of Atlanta, and Michael Espy of Yazoo City, Mississippi) in 1989. Espy and Lewis were first elected in 1986. Espy became the first black elected to Congress from Mississippi since Reconstruction. Although some 53 percent of the nation's blacks live in the South, 62 percent of the black elected officials were found in the region.[20] In spite of the progress that has been made since the civil rights movement of the 1960s and 1970s, blacks remain underrepresented as political officeholders.[21] They are also underrepresented in policy-making boards and commissions, including industrial and environmental regulatory bodies. The interests of all-white industrial boards, zoning commissions, and governmental regulatory bodies may run counter to those of the black community. Until these policy-setting institutions are made more inclusive, we are likely to find an intensification of locational conflicts and charges of racial discrimination.

Notes

1   U.S. Department of Housing and Urban Development, *Report of the President's Commission for a National Agenda for the Eighties* (Washington, D.C.: U.S. Government Printing Office, 1980), pp. 165–69; John D. Kasarda, "Implications of Contemporary Distribution Trends for National Urban Policy," *Social Science Quarterly* 61 (December 1980): 373–400.

2   John D. Kasarda, Michael D. Irwin, and Holly L. Hughes, "The South Is Still Rising," *American Demographics* 8 (June 1986): 34.

3   G. William Domhoff, "The Growth Machine and the Power Elite: A Challenge to Pluralists and Marxists Alike," in Robert J. Waste, ed., *Community Power: Directions for Future Research* (Newbury Park, Calif.: Sage, 1986), p. 58.

4   Harvey L. Molotch, "The City as a Growth Machine: Toward a Political Economy of Place," *American Journal of Sociology* 82 (September 1976): 320.

5   Domhoff, "The Growth Machine and the Power Elite," p. 61.

6   U.S. Bureau of the Census, *State and Metropolitan Area Data Book 1982* (Washington, DC.: U.S. Government Printing Office, 1982), p. xxx.

7   Robert D. Bullard, "Blacks and the New South: Challenges of the Eighties," *Journal of Intergroup Relations* 15 (Summer 1987): 25.

8   David C. Perry and Alfred J. Watkins, eds., *The Rise of the Sunbelt Cities* (Beverly Hills: Sage, 1977), p. 77; Robert D Bullard, ed., *In Search of the New South: The Black Urban Experience in the 1970s and 1980s* (Tuscaloosa: University of Alabama Press, 1989), Chapter 1.

9   William W. Falk and Thomas A. Lyson, *High Tech, Low Tech, No Tech: Recent Industrial and Occupational Change in the South* (Albany: State University of New York Press, 1988), pp. 2–3.

10   Ibid., p. 55.

11   Chet Fuller, "I Hear Them Call It the New South," *Black Enterprise* 12 (November 1981): 41.

12   Ibid., pp. 41–44.

13   Joe R. Feagin and Clairece Booher Feagin, *Discrimination American Style: Institutional Racism and Sexism* (Malabar, Fla.: Robert E. Krueger Publishing, 1986), p. 9.

14   William C. Matney and Dwight L. Johnson, *America's Black Population: A Statistical View 1970–1982* (Washington, D.C.: U.S. Government Printing Office, 1983), p. 1.

15   Ibid., p. 2; Isaac Robinson, "Blacks Move Back to the South," *American Demographics* 9 (June 1986): 40–43.

16   Kasarda et al., "The South Is Still Rising," p. 32.

17   Gurney Breckenfeld, "Refilling the Metropolitan Doughnut," in David C. Perry and Alfred J. Watkins, eds., *The Rise of the Sunbelt Cities* (Beverly Hills: Sage, 1977), p. 238.

18   See Robert D. Bullard, *Invisible Houston: The Black Experience in Boom and Bust* (College Station: Texas A & M University Press, 1987), pp. 2–13; William J. Wilson, *The Truly Disadvantaged: The Inner City, the Underclass, and Public Policy* (Chicago: University of Chicago Press, 1987), pp. 180–81; John D. Kasarda, "Caught in the Web of Change," *Society* 21 (1983): 41–47; William J. Wilson, "The Black Underclass," *Wilson Quarterly* (Spring 1984): pp. 88–99; David Beers and Diana Hembree, "The New Atlanta: A Tale of Two Cities," *Nation* 244 (March 1987): 347, 357–60; Margaret Edds, *Free at Last: What Really Happened When Civil Rights Came to Southern Politics* (Bethesda: Adler and Adler, 1987), pp. 51–76; Bradley R. Rice, "Atlanta: If Dixie Were Atlanta," in Richard M. Bernard and Bradley R. Rice, eds., *Sunbelt Cities: Politics and Growth Since World War II* (Austin: University of Texas Press, 1984), pp. 31–57; Art Harris, "Too Busy to Hate," *Esquire* 103 (June 1985): 129–33; Charles Jaret, "Black Migration and Socioeconomic Inequality in Atlanta and the Urban South," *Humboldt Journal of Social Relations* 14 (Summer 1987): 62–105; Nathan McCall, "Atlanta: City of the Next Generation," *Black Enterprise* 17 (May 1987): 56–58.

19   Joint Center for Political Studies, *Black Elected Officials: A National Roster* (New York: UNIPUB, 1984), p. 61.

20   Michael Preston, Lenneal J. Henderson, Jr., and Paul Puryear, eds., *The New Black Politics: The Search for Political Power* (New York: Longman, 1987), p. vii.

21   Chandler Davidson, ed., *Minority Vote Dilution* (Washington, D.C.: Howard University Press, 1984), 1–26.

Chapter 15

Catriona Mortimer-Sandilands and Bruce Erickson

A GENEALOGY OF QUEER ECOLOGIES

Introduction: Queering Ecology on Brokeback Mountain

IN A NOW-FAMOUS scene from Ang Lee's Academy Award winning film *Brokeback Mountain*,[1] characters Ennis Del Mar and Jack Twist have had a bit too much whiskey to drink around the fire at their camp in the Big Horn Mountains of eastern South Dakota and Wyoming, where they are employed by Joe Aguirre in the summer of 1963 to herd and protect his sheep for the grazing season. In the middle of the scene, Ennis drunkenly insists on sleeping outside the tent by the dying fire, but in the middle of the night Jack calls him into the tent and Ennis staggers in. As a brilliant full moon surfs on top of the clouds, Jack reaches over and pulls a sleeping Ennis's arm around him; Ennis wakes and jolts himself away roughly but Jack pursues him and holds onto his jacket. A long second transpires as Jack looks into Ennis's eyes and Ennis meets his gaze, understanding. They have fast, fierce sex, and with no time for so much as a postcoital cigarette, the scene abruptly changes to the next morning, Ennis crawling out of the tent with a visible hangover, cocking his rifle, leaving the campsite without conversation. His next words to Jack are later that day. Rifle still in hand, he sits down beside him and says: "That was a one-shot thing we had going on there." Jack responds: "It's nobody's business but ours." Ennis insists: "You know I ain't queer." Jack agrees: "Me, neither." But that evening, in a warmly lit tent interior, they kiss tenderly and visibly relax into each other's bodies: they may not be queer, but a rose by any other name apparently smells as sweet.

Although a lot more happens in *Brokeback Mountain* that is worthy of comment, notably the contrast between the heterosexual relationships both men develop and the deeply romantic and eventually tragic "high-altitude fucking," to quote Jack, in which the couple engages periodically for the next twenty years, we begin this collection of writings on queer ecologies with that scene because it displays quite dramatically three important junctures at which lgbtq (lesbian/gay/bisexual/transgender/queer) and environmental politics (both defined broadly) intersect.[2] First, Jack and Ennis's shared refusal to name themselves as "queer" is part of an ongoing narrative strategy by which the film distances both men from the taint of urban, effeminate—what Judith Halberstam has called "metronormative"—articulations of gay male identity (2005, 36). Jack and Ennis are cowboys; they know about guns and horses; they eat baked beans and drink whiskey from the bottle rather than having cassoulet with cabernet sauvignon. When Ennis says that he is "not queer," we understand that he means he is not *that* kind of queer: genteel, sensitive, feminine, "gay" in any sense of the word. He is an ordinary white, working-class, masculine-male ranch hand who just happens to have passionate sex and fall in love with an almost equally butch rodeo king.[3] There is nothing queer about it; indeed, their masculine identities are repeatedly confirmed in both this scene and the film as a whole, and the sex unfolds almost *naturally* as part of a deepening, homosocial intimacy that would be as welcome in a camp full of Boy Scouts as it would in a group of urban gay men: indeed, possibly *more* welcome.

Although the politics are not simple and the movie is much commented upon,[4] the point we emphasize is that the presentation of Ennis and Jack in this rural-masculine manner has the effect of "naturalizing" their relationship insofar as their attraction and love can be read as entirely separate and distinct from what have, throughout much of the twentieth century, been presented as "unnatural" or "degenerate" sexualities. We will return to this issue presently; what we stress here is that, for a popular audience, sympathy for and identification with Ennis and Jack's tragic romance is based on the story's effective disarticulation of same-sex love and desire from gay identity, the former of which is presented as natural—masculine, rural, virile—in opposition to the latter's spectral invocation of historical and ongoing discourses of *perversion*. These discourses, as we will suggest below, are an important point of conversation between queer and ecological politics because they reveal the powerful ways in which understandings of nature inform discourses of sexuality, and also the ways in which understandings of sex inform discourses of nature; they are linked, in fact, through a strongly evolutionary narrative that pits the perverse, the polluted and the degenerate against the fit, the healthy, and the natural.

The second queer ecological connection going on in *Brokeback Mountain* is that it is not at all accidental that our sex scene takes place on Brokeback Mountain. Although, as we discover later in the film, even this remote space is not immune to the possibility of heteronormative surveillance, it is clear that, up in the mountains, Jack and Ennis are free to explore their sexual relationship in a way that is simply not possible in the small Wyoming town from which they set out. Wilderness is, in this film, portrayed as a vast field of homoerotic possibility; the two rugged men romp and tumble freely, watched, for the most part, only by rugged mountains. Their desire is both constituted and consummated in a lush hanging river valley surrounded by trees and dramatic, snow-striped peaks; wilderness becomes a "safe" place for outlaw sex, and although there is, later in the film, one sexual encounter between Jack and Ennis in a seedy motel, their ongoing relationship is almost completely located in this one, remote spot.

Clearly, there are relationships between Jack and Ennis's virility and the virility of the wild landscape; the one's masculinity confirms the other's, and both are also affected by their explicit contrast to the claustrophobic and emasculating spaces of domesticity represented by Jack's and Ennis's wives and children.[5] But there is also an interesting subversion of dominant discourses that attach wilderness spaces to performances of *heterosexual* masculinity. As we will discuss below, at least since the early twentieth century, wild spaces have been understood and organized in a way that presents nature—and its personal domination in the guise of hunting, fishing, climbing, and other outdoor activities—as a site for the enactment of a specific heteromasculinity. Particularly in the late nineteenth century, a period that also saw the beginnings of the wilderness preservation and conservation movements, the vast changes that were taking place in North American cities—immigration, urban expansion, industrialization, women's increasing economic independence, and the transformation of the economy from entrepreneurial to corporate capitalism, to name a few factors—created a huge amount of social anxiety, particularly for elite white men. Where once such men could be reasonably confident of their dominance, their power was now called quite radically into question, and outdoor pursuits came to serve as a new space for elite enactments of white male superiority. Again, to cut a long story short, white men came to assert their increasingly heterosexual identities in the wilderness explicitly against the urban specter of the queer, the immigrant, and the communist, a legion of feminized men who were clearly not of the same manly caliber as the likes of Theodore Roosevelt.[6] This second connection between queer and ecology is thus about the fact that different kinds of nature *spaces* have also come to be overlain with sexual meanings; wilderness areas are highly heterosexualized—increasingly so with the postwar rise of family camping—and urban nature spaces are organized by specific sexual ideals and practices, both in the dominant view and in the many resistances that have taken place to that view.

The third and final connection that is made between queer and ecological politics in that *Brokeback Mountain* scene actually concerns the sheep. Specifically, the presence of the sheep and the resulting fact that Jack and Ennis are *shepherds*, locates the film in a long history of pastoral depictions of nature and landscape and, indeed, an equally long history of pastoral representations of male same-sex eroticism. Beginning with ancient Greek "lyric poetry [such as Theocritus's *Idylls*] depicting the life of shepherds or herdsmen" (Shuttleton 2000, 127), the pastoral tradition emphasizes rural simplicity and, indeed, paints the rustic life of the shepherd in the pasture as a sort of Arcadian, golden age of leisure and erotic play. In ancient Greece and Rome, much of that erotic play was between men, and despite subsequent "homophobic Christian and humanist ethical prescriptions . . . [that] have repeatedly sought to erase or veil pastoral's queer libidinal economies to produce hetero-normative Arcadias" (127), gay scholars and authors (and others) have used this homoerotic literary and artistic tradition to imagine a queer history, a queer space, and indeed a queer nature: the idealized, bucolic "natu-ralness" of pastoral homoeroticism calls into question the idea that heterosexuality is the only "natural" sex around. Clearly, the portrayal of Jack and Ennis exploring their sexual relation-ship on a pasture in the mountains, surrounded by sheep and with little else to do (although this pastoral is interrupted by both homophobes and coyotes), ties their story, and the land-scape of Brokeback Mountain, to a historical, homoerotic Arcadia,[7] and possibly also to a tradition of representation that resists the normative pairing of nature with *hetero*sexuality.

So there's a lot going on in *Brokeback Mountain* that indicates an ongoing historical, polit-ical, spatial, and literary relationship between sex and nature. (Who would have guessed that two "not-queer" white guys fucking among the sheep would be so interesting?) As the film shows us clearly, ideas and practices of nature, including both bodies and landscapes, are located in particular productions of sexuality, and sex is, both historically and in the present, located in particular formations of nature. The critical analysis of these locations and co-productions is what we mean by "queer ecology": there is an ongoing relationship between sex and nature that exists institutionally, discursively, scientifically, spatially, politically, poetically, and ethically, and it is our task to interrogate that relationship in order to arrive at a more nuanced and effective sexual and environmental understanding. Specifically, the task of a queer ecology is to probe the intersections of sex and nature with an eye to developing a sexual politics that more clearly includes considerations of the natural world and its biosocial constitution, and an environmental politics that demonstrates an understanding of the ways in which sexual relations organize and influence both the material world of nature and our perceptions, experiences, and constitutions of that world. Queer, then, is both noun and verb in this project: ours is an ecology that may begin in the experiences and perceptions of non-heterosexual individuals and communities, but is even more importantly one that calls into question heteronormativity itself as part of its advocacy around issues of nature and environment—and vice versa.

Hence this book. The thirteen authors gathered together in the pages of *Queer Ecologies* have all asked important questions at interrelated conjunctures of sex and nature, oriented to probing and challenging the biopolitical knots through which both historical and current relations of sexualities and environments meet and inform one another. Ranging from an analysis of "queer animals" as subjects of environmental and other popular fascination, to a political interrogation of colonial discourses organizing sex (especially sex between men) as an ecological threat, to histories of lesbian and gay creations of natural space, to a consideration of Ellen Meloy's erotic, hybrid nature writing as a specifically ecological future for queer desire, the essays in this collection take up diverse challenges and possibilities posed by the powerful collision of sex and nature. Collectively, we ask: What does it mean that ideas, spaces, and practices designated as "nature" are often so vigorously defended against queers in a society in which that very nature is increasingly degraded and exploited? What do queer interrogations of science, politics, and desire then offer to environmental understanding? And how might a clearer attention to issues of nature and environment—as discourse, as space, as ideal, as practice, as relationship, as potential—inform and enrich queer theory, lgbtq politics, and research into sexuality and society?

In light of the rich range of issues and perspectives included in the following chapters, the role of this introduction is not to cover the same territory in advance. Instead, and beginning with the triad of intersections between histories of sexuality and nature apparent in *Brokeback Mountain*, what we would like to offer is a sort of lightly sketched genealogy of the implicit question posed in the pairing of "queer" with "ecology": What are some of the ways in which the terms have been related, and what kinds of intersection might be specified by their juxtaposition? Specifically, and although there are certainly other ways of conceiving of the histories of this convergence (in particular, we are overlooking a substantial literature on gender and technology that has significantly influenced many of the queer natures appearing in these pages, and also acknowledge the decided Anglo-American-centrism of our introductory account),[8] we suggest that there have been three major areas in which issues of sexuality and nature have been caught up in the same question; these three strands of intersection are what bring us to this collection, even as the essays within it depart from that triad in significant ways. In this introductory essay, then, we will do three things to help narrate the coming-into-being of the project in which we are engaged. First, we will consider some of the historical connections that have been made between discourses of sexuality and nature, focused on the naturalization of particular sexual behaviors in the midst of the rise of evolutionary and sexological thought in the early twentieth century, and also on more recent scientific and critical work on animal sexual relations and environmental change as a sort of evolutionary/ecological practice of "putting sex into discourse." Second, we will explore some ways in which historical and contemporary formations of natural space have been organized by changing understandings and agendas related to sexuality, and in particular, how nature-spaces were and are often designed to regulate sexual activity but with mixed results, including gay, lesbian, and other appropriations of landscapes for a wide variety of queer purposes. Finally, we will document some of the ways queer-identified scholars and others have envisioned a nascent ecology in a variety of literary, philosophical, and pedagogical projects that insist on highlighting, subverting, and transforming heteronormative nature relations. Spanning a wide range of disciplines and locations, these knots of inquiry are key traditions of queer ecological conversation upon which this collection rests.

Notes

1   Early versions of parts of this introduction previously appeared in Mortimer-Sandilands (2005). *Brokeback Mountain* won the 2006 Academy Awards for Best Director, Best Adapted Screenplay, and Best Score. The film is based on the short story "Brokeback Mountain" by E. Annie Proulx in *Close Range* (1999).

2   There are various versions of this abbreviation in current usage—glbt, lgbttq, etc. We have, in this volume, retained each author's individual choice.

3   Although we do not have space to explore this point here, Jack is actually a bit more "gay" than Ennis, and this characterization is quite important. Jack allows himself to dream of the two men sharing a life and a future together; Ennis cannot or will not. Jack eventually pursues other men; Ennis does not. Jack is killed, possibly as a result of homophobic violence; Ennis is not. At the end of the day, the film does not leave much space open for positive expressions of gay identification, let alone same-sex relationships. And as Kathleen Chamberlain and Victoria Somogyi (2006) point out, while the opening of the film in 1963 could be read as an accurate portrayal of the absence of public representations of gay male community at the time, the fact that the film also ends, in the mid-1980s, with no change to that absence erases the entire history of the post-Stonewall emergence of gay men and lesbians into public life and unwittingly reinforces the story in which rural places are only and always dangerous places for queers.

4   For a selection of critical perspectives on the film, see the Fall 2006 issue of *Intertexts* (Lubbock) and the Spring 2007 issue of *Film Quarterly*.

5   There are ways in which both Jack and Ennis are *imperfectly* virile in the heteromasculine mode, especially in their class positions, which leave Jack married to a woman who approves of his death and Ennis living in a trailer afraid to talk to his daughter. We consider also that their unsuitability for heterosexuality effectively de-naturalizes it: their "natural" masculinity is expressed together in the wilderness and institutionalized heterosexuality is clearly an effeminized and unnatural space in which both men suffocate (and Jack dies). There are many notes of misogyny, here, that are also apparent in other instances of the gay pastoral.

6   Roosevelt haunts *Brokeback Mountain:* he went to nearly the same region that Ennis is from to remake himself in light of accusations that he was effeminate.

7   Although there are clear differences between Wyoming and Arcadia, both physically and economically.

8   Donna Haraway's work (e.g., 1991) is an important place from which to consider the potential of feminist science and technology studies to "queer" nature Literatures on non-Western sexualities and their relations to non-Western creations of nature clearly reveal other kinds of queer ecologies in addition to resistances to the Anglo-American ones on which we generally rely here; see Pflugfelder (1999).

References

Chamberlain, Kathleen, and Victoria Somogyi. 2006. "You Know I Ain't Queer": *Brokeback Mountain* as the Not-Gay Cowboy Movie. *Intertexts* (Lubbock) 10.2: 129–44, 195–96.

Haraway, Donna. 1991. *Simians, Cyborgs and Women*. New York: Routledge.

Lee, Ang, dir. 2006. Motion picture. *Brokeback Mountain*. Paramount Pictures.

Mortimer-Sandilands, Catriona. 2005. Unnatural Passions? Toward a Queer Ecology. *Invisible Culture* 9. http://www.rochester.edu/in_visible_culture/Issue_9/title9.html.

Pflugfelder, Gregory M. 1999. *Cartographies of Desire: Male-Male Sexuality in Japanese Discourse, 1600–1950*. Berkeley and Los Angeles: University of California Press.

Proulx, E. Annie. 1999. *Close Range: Wyoming Stories*. New York: Charles Scribner.

Shuttleton, David. 2000. The Queer Politics of Gay Pastoral. In *De-Centring Sexualities: Politics and Representation Beyond the Metropolis*, ed. Richard Phillips, Diane Watt, and David Shuttleton, 125–46. London: Routledge.

Chapter 16

Ursula K. Heise

THE HITCHHIKER'S GUIDE
TO ECOCRITICISM

The Emergence of Ecocriticism

THE FIRST FEW FRAMES of the Belgian comic-strip artist Raymond Macherot's work "Les Croquillards" (1957) provide a shorthand for some of the issues that concern environmentally oriented criticism, one of the most recent fields of research to have emerged from the rapidly diversifying matrix of literary and cultural studies in the 1990s. A heron is prompted to a lyrical reflection on the change of seasons by a leaf that gently floats down to the surface of his pond[1]: "Ah! the poetry of autumn . . . dying leaves, wind, departing birds. . . ." This last thought jolts him back to reality: "But—I'm a migratory bird myself! . . . Good grief! What've I been thinking?" And off he takes on his voyage south, only to be hailed by the protagonists, the field rats Chlorophylle and Minimum (the latter under the spell of a bad cold), who hitch a ride to Africa with him. "Are you traveling on business?" he asks his newfound passengers. "No, for our health," they answer.

The scene unfolds around two conceptual turns relevant to eco-criticism. The speaking animal, a staple of comic strips, is credited with an aesthetic perception of nature that relies on the long Western tradition of associating beauty with ephemerality: autumn's appeal arises from its proximity to death, decay, and departure, a beauty the wind will carry away in an instant. But ironically this Romantic valuation of nature separates the heron from his innate attunement to its rhythms: the falling leaf makes him sink into autumnal reverie and forget to seek out warmer latitudes. As soon as he takes flight, however, Macherot once again twists the idea of seasonal migration by turning the heron into a sort of jetliner on bird wings transporting what might be business or leisure travelers. What is (or should be) natural for the bird is not so for the rats, whose illness hints at another type of failure to adapt to seasonal rhythms. On one hand, this comic strip humorously raises the question whether an aesthetic appreciation of nature brings one closer to it or alienates one from it; on the other, it highlights the tension between bonds to nature that are established by innate instinct, those that arise through aesthetic valuation, and those that are mediated by modern-day travel. The heron's flight remains comically suspended between the vocabularies of nature, art, and international business. In what ways do highly evolved and self-aware beings relate to nature? What roles do language, literature, and art play in this relation? How have modernization and globalization processes transformed it? Is it possible to return to more ecologically attuned ways of inhabiting nature, and what would be the cultural prerequisites for such a change?

This is a sample of issues that are often raised in ecocriticism, a rapidly growing field in literary studies. The story of its institutional formation has been told in detail and from several perspectives (Cohen 9–14; Garrard 3–15; Glotfelty, "Introduction" xvii–xviii, xxii–xxiv; Love 1–5; Branch and Slovic xiv–xvii)[2]: scattered projects and publications involving the connection between literature and the environment in the 1980s led to the founding of ASLE, the Association for the Study of Literature and the Environment, during a convention of the Western Literature Association in 1992. In 1993 the journal *ISLE: Interdisciplinary Studies in Literature and Environment* was established, and in 1995 ASLE started holding biennial conferences. Seminal texts and anthologies such as Lawrence Buell's *The Environmental Imagination* (1995), Kate Soper's *What Is Nature?* (1995), and Cheryll Glotfelty and Harold Fromm's *Ecocriticism Reader* (1996) followed, as well as special journal issues (Murphy, *Ecology; Ecocriticism*). At the same time, newly minted ecocritics began to trace the origins of their intellectual concerns back to such seminal works in American and British literary studies as Henry Nash Smith's *Virgin Land* (1950), Leo Marx's *The Machine in the Garden* (1964), Roderick Nash's *Wilderness and the American Mind* (1967), Raymond Williams's *The Country and the City* (1973), Joseph Meeker's *The Comedy of Survival* (1974), and Annette Kolodny's *The Lay of the Land* (1975). ASLE membership grew rapidly, topping a thousand in the early years of the new century, and offspring organizations in Australia–New Zealand, Korea, Japan, India, and the United Kingdom were founded, as was, most recently, the independent European Association for the Study of Literature, Culture and Environment (EASLCE).

Given the steadily increasing urgency of environmental problems for ever more closely interconnected societies around the globe, the explosion of articles and books in the field may not strike one as particularly surprising. But what is remarkable about this burst of academic interest is that it took place at such a late date; most of the important social movements of the 1960s and 1970s left their marks on literary criticism long before environmentalism did, even though environmentalism succeeded in establishing a lasting presence in the political sphere. Why this delay?

The main reason lies no doubt in the development of literary theory between the late 1960s and the early 1990s. Under the influence of mostly French philosophies of language, literary critics during this period took a fresh look at questions of representation, textuality, narrative, identity, subjectivity, and historical discourse from a fundamentally skeptical perspective that emphasized the multiple disjunctures between forms of representation and the realities they purported to refer to. In this intellectual context, the notion of nature tended to be approached as a sociocultural construct that had historically often served to legitimize the ideological claims of specific social groups. From Roland Barthes's call in 1957 "always to strip down Nature, its 'laws' and its 'limits,' so as to expose History there, and finally to posit Nature as itself historical" (*Mythologies* 175; trans. mine) to Graeme Turner's claim in 1990 that "Cultural Studies defines itself in part . . . through its ability to explode the category of 'the natural' " (qtd. in Hochman 10), the bulk of cultural criticism was premised on an overarching project of denaturalization. This perspective obviously did not encourage connections with a social movement aiming to reground human cultures in natural systems and whose primary pragmatic goal was to rescue a sense of the reality of environmental degradation from the obfuscations of political discourse.

By the early 1990s, however, the theoretical panorama in literary studies had changed considerably. New historicism had shaded into American cultural studies, which styled itself antitheoretical as much as theoretical, signaling not so much the advent of a new paradigm as the transition of the discipline into a field of diverse specialties and methodologies no longer ruled by any dominant framework. Ecocriticism found its place among this expanding matrix of coexisting projects, which in part explains the theoretical diversity it has attained in a mere dozen years. But this diversity also results from its relation to the sociopolitical forces that spawned it. Unlike feminism or postcolonialism, ecocriticism did not evolve gradually as the academic wing of an influential political movement. It emerged when environmentalism had already turned into a vast field of converging and conflicting projects and given rise to two other humanistic subdisciplines, environmental philosophy and history. This diversity resonates in the different names by which the field has been identified: *ecocriticism* has imposed itself as a convenient shorthand for what some critics prefer to call *environmental criticism, literary-environmental studies, literary ecology, literary environmentalism*, or *green cultural studies* (see Buell, *Future* 11–12).

Changes in the perceived cultural relevance of biology also helped to open up the conceptual space for ecocriticism. Sociobiological approaches that had been rejected in the 1970s reentered debate in the 1990s as genetic research and biotechnologies began to shed new light on old questions about innate and acquired behavior. While many of these questions have remained intensely controversial among scientists and humanities scholars and while many ecocritics are highly critical of sociobiology and evolutionary psychology, there can be no doubt that the 1990s offered a climate very different from that of earlier decades for investigating the relation between nature and culture. This is not to say that the early 1990s marked an altogether welcoming moment for the articulation of an environmentalist perspective on culture. The so-called science wars, brewing since the 1980s, came to a head with Paul Gross and Norman Levitt's polemical repudiation of constructivist approaches to science in their book *Higher Superstition* (1994). The physicist Alan Sokal's faux-poststructuralist essay on quantum mechanics in the journal *Social Text* in 1996 took the confrontation between scientists and their critics to a new level of ferocity as well as public awareness. Ecocriticism, with its triple allegiance to the scientific study of nature, the scholarly analysis of cultural representations, and the political struggle for more sustainable ways of inhabiting the natural world, was born in the shadow of this controversy. Even though the grounds of the debate have shifted since then, the underlying issues of realism and representation that informed the science wars continue to pose challenges for ecocritical theory.

Because of the diversity of political and cross-disciplinary influences that went into its making, ecocriticism is not an easy field to summarize. Even if ecocritics, perhaps more than other academic scholars, still long for a sense of community and shared holistic ideals, the reality is that they diverge widely in their views. Recent vigorous critiques and ripostes are healthy signs of a rapidly expanding field. Somewhat like cultural studies, ecocriticism coheres more by virtue of a common political project than on the basis of shared theoretical and methodological assumptions, and the details of how this project should translate into the study of culture are continually subject to challenge and revision. For this reason, ecocriticism has also become a field whose complexities by now require the book-length introductions that have appeared over the last two years: Greg Garrard's *Ecocriticism* (2004), Buell's *The Future of Environmental Criticism* (2005), and, shorter and sketchier, Walter Rojas Pérez's *La ecocrítica hoy* (2004).

Environmentalism and the Critique of Modernity

Like feminism and critical race studies, eco-criticism started with a critical reconceptualization of modernist notions of human psychological identity and political subject-hood. The ecocritical attempt to think beyond conceptual dichotomies that modernity, the Enlightenment, and science were thought to have imposed on Western culture—the separation of subject and object, body and environment, nature and culture—articulated itself, as it did in other fields, through the combination of analytic modes of academic discourse with more experientially based forms of writing that Scott Slovic has called "narrative scholarship" ("Ecocriticism"). But ecocriticism in its first stage differed sharply from other forms of "postmodern" thought in that it sought to redefine the human subject not so much in relation to the human others that subjecthood had traditionally excluded as in relation to the nonhuman world. Environmentalism and ecocriticism aim their critique of modernity at its presumption to know the natural world scientifically, to manipulate it technologically and exploit it economically, and thereby ultimately to create a human sphere apart from it in a historical process that is usually labeled "progress." This domination strips nature of any value other than as a material resource and commodity and leads to a gradual destruction that may in the end deprive humanity of its basis for subsistence. Such domination empties human life of the significance it had derived from living in and with nature and alienates individuals and communities from their rootedness in place.

Projected alternatives to this kind of modernity extend from deep ecology to social ecology. Deep ecology foregrounds the value of nature in and of itself, the equal rights of other species, and the importance of small communities. Social ecology, by contrast, tends to value nature primarily in its human uses and has affinities with political philosophies ranging from anarchism and socialism to feminism. Deep ecology, associated often with a valuation of wild and rural spaces, self-sufficiency, a sense of place, and local knowledge and sometimes with an alternative spirituality, played an important part in the early stages of ecocriticism. Especially for Americanists, this philosophy resonated with writers from Thoreau (in a certain reading of his work) to Wendell Berry, Edward Abbey, and Gary Snyder. From the late 1990s on, however, the field gradually moved to the more social-ecological positions that dominate ecocriticism today (Buell, *Future* 97–98).

This shift was prompted in part by the sheer numerical expansion of the field, which led scholars from a wide variety of intellectual backgrounds to bring their interests to bear on environmental issues. In part it also emerged under the pressure of explicit challenges to the field: like other areas of cultural theory, ecocriticism saw its initial assumptions questioned for what they had socially excluded, historically erased, and textually forgotten (or refused) to account for.[3] The historicization of the wilderness concept by the environmental historian William Cronon is undoubtedly one of the most important critiques. Unlike ecological movements in other parts of the world, Cronon argues, environmentalism in the United States tends to hold up an ideal of landscapes untouched by human beings as the standard against which actual landscapes are measured. But this standard is problematic in its relation to past and future. It conceals the fact that the apparently transhistorical ideal of *wilderness* only acquired connotations of the sublime and sacred in the nineteenth century and that the cultural valuation of pristine and uninhabited areas led to the displacement of native inhabitants and in some cases to the creation of official parks. Far from being nature in its original state, such wildernesses were the product of cultural processes. The wilderness concept makes it difficult for a political program to conceptualize desirable forms of human inhabitation, relying as it does on the categorical separation of human beings from nature.

For ecocritics, who had often referred to statements such as Thoreau's "In wildness is the preservation of the world" as touchstones, Cronon's critique prompted a reexamination of established environmental authors as well as a broadening of the canon. Greater attention to women's and Native American literature shifted the emphasis to more communal engagements with a natural world conceived as always intertwined with human existence.[4] But greater inclusiveness also brought more challenges, since not all minority literatures proved as easy to assimilate into ecocritical concerns as Native American texts, many of whose authors had long been active in the environmental movement. African American literature, for example, as Michael Bennett and others have shown, is difficult to address with standard ecocritical vocabulary, since African American authors tend to associate rural life and sometimes even wild places with memories of slavery and persecution rather than with peaceful refuge (see Wallace and Armbruster). "[O]f what use is ecocriticism if the culture under consideration has a different relationship with pastoral space and wilderness than the ideal kinship that most nature writers and ecocritics assume and seek?" Bennett asks, and he emphasizes that "even the most inviting physical environment cannot be considered separately from the sociopolitical structures that shape its uses and abuses" (195, 201).

Critiques such as these led to increased emphasis on urban spaces (Bennett and Teague; Dixon; MacDonald) as well as on issues of social inequality that environmental problems often overlap. From the turn of the millennium, environmental-justice criticism increasingly influenced the field by drawing attention to social and racial inequalities in both access to natural resources and exposure to technological and ecological risk (Martínez-Alier; Adamson, Evans, and Stein). "Aesthetic appreciation of nature has not only been a class-coded activity, but the insulation of the middle and upper classes from the most brutal effects of industrialization has played a crucial role in environmental devastation," T. V. Reed argues in his call for an ecocriticism that fuses concerns for natural preservation with those for distributive justice (151). Along with the emergence of a fully post-structuralist ecocriticism (about which more later on), this critical agenda has opened up the full gamut of concepts and methods from cultural studies for environmental criticism.

The shift to a more in-depth engagement with the sociopolitical framing of environmental issues has also fundamentally, if not always explicitly, altered the way in which most ecocritics view the relation between modernity and nature. In earlier types of environmental scholarship, nature tended to be envisioned as a victim of modernization but also as its opposite and alternative; nature is now more often viewed as inextricably entwined with modernity—both as a concept and in the material shape in which we experience it today. More than that, environmentalists and ecocritics have begun to see how their search for a more authentic relation to nature is itself a product of modernization. The geographer David Harvey points out that

> the problem of authenticity is itself peculiarly modern. Only as modern industrialization separates us from the process of production and we encounter the environment as a finished commodity does it emerge. . . . The final victory of modernity . . . is not the disappearance of the non-modern world, but its artificial preservation and reconstruction. . . . The search for an authentic sense of community and of an authentic relation to nature among many radical and ecological movements is the cutting edge of exactly such a sensibility.
>
> (301–02)

Understanding itself in this way, as both derived from and resistant to modernity, may also help ecocriticism develop modes of critique of the modern that are less dependent than they have been so far on recourse to premodern forms of inhabitation and culture.

Scientific Intersections

Ecocriticism's engagement with modernization has been partly shaped by environmentalists' ambivalence toward scientific inquiry (see Heise). On one hand, science is viewed as a root cause of environmental deterioration, both in that it has cast nature as an object to be analyzed and manipulated and in that it has provided the means of exploiting nature more radically than was possible by premodern means. On the other hand, environmentalists are aware that the social legitimation of environmental politics and their own insights into the state of nature centrally depend on science. In ecocriticism, this ambivalence has translated into divergent perceptions of how the sciences should inform cultural inquiry.

At one end of the spectrum, a small number of ecocritics, such as Joseph Carroll and Glen Love, would like to make the life sciences in general and evolutionary theory in particular the foundation of literary study, following E. O. Wilson's idea of "consilience." Starting from the idea that culture is based on the human "adapted mind"—that is, "a biologically constrained set of cognitive and motivational characteristics" (Carroll vii)—this group seeks to explain cultural phenomena in terms of what they accomplish for human adaptation and survival. Many scholars in the humanities almost instinctively recoil in horror from such a sociobiological agenda, associating it with social Darwinism or Nietzschean ideology and the legitimations they have historically provided for various forms of political hegemony. But, in fairness, Darwinian theory should not simply be conflated with such ideological appropriations: Carroll categorically dismisses social Darwinism as a value-laden misinterpretation of evolutionary theory (xiv).

The more crucial question is what contribution an adaptationist approach, with its concept of human nature as a "universal, species-typical array of behavioral and cognitive characteristics" (vii), might be able to make to a discipline that has recently invested most of its theoretical capital in historical and cultural diversity. One answer is that there is no compelling reason why cultural inquiry has to focus on cultural differences rather than similarities. Fair enough—literary criticism certainly used to be more interested in universals than it has been in the last three decades. If the adaptationist approach can produce an analysis of cultural and literary universals that is descriptive rather than normative and that does not rely on the values of one particular culture dressed up as human nature (as was usually done in earlier attempts to define universals), it deserves to be heard as part of a full theory of culture. Obviously, an important part of such an analysis would have to be a careful examination of the terms used to describe the object of study: words such as *literature, aesthetics, narrative*, and *culture* itself have complex cultural histories and cannot be taken for granted in a biologically based approach.

What is less clear is how such an adaptationist understanding might inflect the vast areas of literary study that are concerned with historically and culturally specific phenomena. Human anatomy and physiology have not changed substantially over the last few thousand years, whereas cultural forms have varied enormously over the same time period. While a biological perspective might provide a general background, it seems at present unlikely to transform the study of such variations in the near future. In this sense, literary Darwinism offers not so much a competing theoretical approach as the outline of a different research area (culture, in its most abstract and universally human dimensions and evolutionary functions) that only partially overlaps with what most cultural scholars focus on today (cultures, in their historically and locally specific dimensions and social functions).

Most ecocritical work is shaped by science in a more indirect but no less important way. Ecology, for many environmentalists a countermodel against "normal" analytic science, has opened the way for a holistic understanding of how natural systems work as vast interconnected webs that, if left to themselves, tend toward stability, harmony, and self-regeneration. A fully mature ecosystem, the climax community of classical ecology, consists of a set of animals and plants ideally adapted to their environment. With such a standard in mind, science can be easily associated with a set of ideal values and a code of ethics: "Ecology . . . seemed to be a science that dealt with harmony, a harmony found in nature, offering a model for a more organic, cooperative human community" (Worster 363). Understood in this way, science can help determine what kinds of human interventions into the natural world are acceptable and what types of cultures are to be considered superior or inferior, and it can help ecocriticism evaluate texts that engage with nature. A powerful image behind an important social movement, the idea of holistic, self-regenerating ecosystems has catalyzed political, legal, and cultural changes that have unquestionably benefited the environment and human welfare (340–87).

But by the time ecocriticism emerged in the 1990s, this idea had already been exposed as no longer in accord with the state of knowledge in ecological science. Even by the 1960s, ecology had become a more analytic, empirical, and mathematical field than it was at its emergence in the late nineteenth century. Holistic notions of universal connectedness, stability, and harmony had lost much of their credibility among ecological scientists, for the most part engaged in specialized research (372–79). As environmental historians realized, ecology no longer offered a general foundation for "morality and causality": "Historians thought ecology was the rock upon which they could build environmental history; it turned out to be a swamp" (White 1113, 1114). The biologist Daniel Botkin's popular scientific book *Discordant Harmonies* (1990) brought such insights to a broader public by presenting a different and more complex image of ecosystems as dynamic, perpetually changing, and often far from stable or balanced: "We have tended to view nature as a Kodachrome still-life, much like a tourist-guide illustration . . . but nature is a moving picture show" (6).

This idea is taken up in the first book-length critique of ecocriticism, Dana Phillips's *The Truth of Ecology* (2003), which lambasts environmental scholars for adhering to an obsolete notion of ecological science and for transferring ecological terms to literary study by means of mere metaphor (42–82). Phillips is certainly right in cautioning ecocritics against undue metaphorization, moralization, or spiritualization of scientific concepts and in calling for more up-to-date scientific literacy—a literacy that, one should mention, would minimally require some training in quantitative methods that does not to date form part of cultural scholars' education. Yet a comprehensive alternative model for linking ecology and ecocriticism does not emerge from his analysis. Perhaps, given the varied and controversial nature of current connections between the humanities and sciences, such a model would be a rather tall order. Nevertheless, because of the importance of ecological science for environmentally oriented criticism, Garrard is surely right that defining their relation more clearly is one of the key challenges for ecocritical scholarship (178).

Those ecocritics who situate their work at the poststructuralist end of the spectrum would go one step further than Phillips by not only criticizing particular ideas about the environment wrongly believed to derive from science but also exposing the concept of the environment itself as a cultural construct. In his study of antebellum American literature, for example, David Mazel emphasizes that his analysis

> is not . . . about some myth *of* the environment, as if the environment were an ontologically stable, foundational entity we have a myth *about*. Rather, the environment is *itself* a myth, a "grand fable," a complex fiction, a widely shared, occasionally contested, and literally ubiquitous narrative. . . . [T]his study treats the environment as a discursive construction, something whose "reality" derives from the ways we write, speak, and think about it.
>
> (xii)

Mazel examines how early America's self-definition as "Nature's Nation" generates environmental discourses that end up bolstering conservative social agendas despite their professed progressive politics (xii). This resolutely constructivist and politically oriented argument is quite familiar from new historicism and cultural studies. To the extent that a scientific view of nature forms part of the analysis at all, it is to study science's role in the emergence of a socioculturally grounded conception of the environment. Most ecocritics have been reluctant to go as far as Mazel in reducing nature to a discursive reality, but he illustrates one extreme of the theoretical spectrum: while literary Darwinists subordinate cultural phenomena to scientific explanation, ecopoststructuralists subordinate material reality and its scientific explanation to cultural analysis. Ecocritical inquiry, most of which adopts a more dialectical perspective on the relation between culture and science, plays itself out in the tension between these two extremes.[5]

Realisms: Perception and Representation

This tension between realist and constructivist approaches crucially involves questions about how our perception of the environment is culturally shaped and how that perception is mediated through language and literature. One strand of ecocriticism critical of modernist thought has tended to privilege philosophies and modes of writing that seek to transcend divisions between culture and nature, subject and object, and body and environment. The European phenomenological tradition has provided some of the most powerful impulses for thinking beyond such dichotomies. The German philosopher Martin Heidegger's notion of "dwelling" as part of human essence and as a form of existence that allows other forms of being to manifest themselves (160–64) has been interpreted as proto-environmentalist by some. The French phenomenologist Maurice Merleau-Ponty's emphasis on bodily experience, and especially the erotic metaphor that undergirds the "embrace of the flesh of the world," spelled out in his *Le visible et l'invisible*, (188–95, 302–04), has been taken up by some ecocritics as a way of envisioning the physical interrelatedness of body and habitat. The Norwegian philosopher Arne Naess's "deep ecology," finally, itself influenced by Heidegger, portrays environmentalism as the realization of a self that encompasses both the individual and the cosmos (171–76).

The influence of these phenomenological approaches makes itself felt in numerous literary works and critical analyses that focus on the importance of a "sense of place," on "dwelling," "reinhabitation" (Snyder), or an "erotics of place" (T. Williams). Sometimes this cognitive, affective, and ethical attachment to place is envisioned in terms of epiphanic fusions with the environment: Edward Abbey describes in *Desert Solitaire* how after a prolonged solitary stay in the wilderness, he began to perceive a leaf when he looked at his hand (251); Snyder's "Second Shaman Song" and one of Aldo Leopold's sketches feature similar experiences of total immersion.[6] This emphasis on interrelatedness had led some ecocritics to revise assumptions of conventional rhetoric—for example, the pathetic fallacy, which "is a fallacy only to the ego clencher," as Neil Evernden puts it: "There is no such thing as an individual, only . . . individual as a component of place, defined by place" (101, 103). Since metaphor is a particularly easy way of establishing such connections between mind, body, and place, it is not surprising that ecocriticism has engaged poetry more than other schools of criticism have in recent decades.[7]

The interest in modes of thought and language that reduce or nullify the distance between the experiencing body and experienced environment has been productive for ecocriticism and set it apart from other theoretical approaches. Yet the difficulties of such a perspective are also quite obvious. In the pursuit of physical connectedness between body and environment, language and texts might initially function as mediating tools but can in the end be little more than obstacles—as they are for Macherot's lyrically minded waterfowl (see also Phillips 11–20). Physical closeness also usually refers to the individual's encounter with nature, but some feminist and indigenous perspectives understand this encounter as a fundamentally communal one. Phenomenological approaches tend not to offer clear models for mediated and collective experiences of nature; neither do they provide the means for explaining how the authenticity of natural encounters is itself culturally shaped. To the extent that this postulation of authenticity relies on the assumption that all modern subjects are alienated from nature, it is difficult to describe the particular forms of alienation suffered by socially disenfranchised groups.

This is not to say that attention to the real differences that class, gender, and race make in the experience of nature does not come with its own set of representational problems. As Buell has convincingly shown, many instances of "toxic discourse"—accounts of pollution, health threats, and the displacement of native inhabitants—that at first sight look realistic rely in fact on tropes and genres with long traditions in American literary history (*Writing* 35–54). The rhetorical power of such accounts derives precisely from their reliance on such traditions. To give one well-known example, Rachel Carson's influential indictment of pesticide overuse in *Silent Spring* (1962) skillfully uses tropes of the pastoral, biblical apocalypse, nuclear fear (in her comparisons of chemical contamination with radioactive fallout), and 1950s anti-Communism ("a grim specter has crept upon us almost unnoticed" [3]; Killingsworth and Palmer 27–32). Problems of textuality and literariness therefore surface at both ends of the ecocritical spectrum, in phenomenologically informed explorations of the encounter between body and environment as well as in politically oriented approaches to the disjunctions between body, community, and nature that result from environmental pollution and social oppression.

Poststructuralists circumvent such difficulties by presenting nature as a purely discursive construction. But like feminists and race theorists who emphasized the cultural rather than biological grounding of their objects of study, these critics must face the objection that such a view plays into the enemy's hand by obfuscating the material reality of environmental degradation. This problem may be a minor one for academic cultural theory, which surely stands to be enriched by the poststructuralist approach, as Mazel argues (xv), but it is serious for green politics. In the end, it seems likely that strong constructivist positions will be less convincing to ecocritics, many of whom are also green activists, than weak constructivist ones that analyze cultural constructions of nature with a view toward the constraints that the real environment imposes on them (see Hayles; Soper 151–55). This would also seem the most promising theoretical ground from which to pursue the analysis of environmental literature in its relation to cultural and rhetorical traditions, on one hand, and social as well as scientific realities, on the other.

Thinking Globally

Along with its theoretical diversity and interdisciplinarity, the rapid expansion of its analytic canon is one of the most striking features of ecocriticism. British Romanticism and twentieth-century American literature initially proved the most fertile fields of inquiry, as two cultural moments with a decisive influence on current conceptions of nature. Jonathan Bate's *Romantic Ecology* (1991) and *Song of the Earth* (2000) as well as Karl Kroeber's *Ecological Literary Criticism* (1994) blazed the environmental trail in studies of Romanticism; Slovic's *Seeking Awareness in American Nature Writing* (1992) and Buell's *Environmental Imagination* foregrounded the importance of nature writing for the American literary canon. Slovic's and Buell's efforts were accompanied by a multitude of other studies of American literature, often with a focus on nonfiction and nature poetry by such writers as Thoreau, Emerson, John Muir, Mary Austin, Robinson Jeffers, Edward Abbey, Gary Snyder, Wendell Berry, Annie Dillard, and Barry Lopez. A second wave of publications placed greater emphasis on women writers, from Willa Cather and Adrienne Rich to Terry Tempest Williams and Karen Tei Yamashita, and on Native American literature, from Leslie Marmon Silko to Simon Ortiz, Linda Hogan, and Joy Harjo. This shift in themes and authors was accompanied by a broadening of the generic horizon. Science fiction came into view as a genre with important environmental dimensions, as did film and computer games. At the same time, ecocritics have developed analyses of cultural institutions and practices outside the arts, from landscape architecture and green consumerism to various forms of tourism and the national park system.

Critics such as Patrick Murphy and Slovic have also made sustained efforts to spread ecocritical analysis to the study of other cultures and languages, though their success has been limited. Ecocriticism has achieved fairly good coverage of Australian, British, Canadian, and United States literatures, but eco-critical work on languages other than English is still scarce,[8] and some of it is not well connected to scholarship in English. Murphy's monumental anthology *Literature of Nature: An International Source-book* (1998) represents a first heroic effort to put ecocriticism on a truly comparatist and global basis. Yet its coverage remains uneven, not only because there are more essays on anglophone than on other literatures but also because essays on some countries cover several hundred years (India), others only one literary period (Taiwan), and yet others a single author (Brazil). The surprising selectiveness of the bibliographies in some of these essays is symptomatic of broader international disjunctures.[9] Works on British or American environmental literature tend to refer to one another but not to work like Jorge Marcone's and Candace Slater's on Latin American texts or Axel Goodbody's and Heather Sullivan's on German literature, even though much of this work is available in English. Critical anthologies are usually not received by anglophone ecocritics when their focus of study lies outside English-based literatures.[10] Ecocriticism is a good deal more international than cultural studies was initially, but its geographic scope is not evident in most of the published work. Obviously, part of the problem is linguistic: monolingualism is currently one of ecocriticism's most serious intellectual limitations. The environmentalist ambition is to think globally, but doing so in terms of a single language is inconceivable— even and especially when that language is a hegemonic one.

Precisely because ecocritical work encompasses many literatures and cultures, it would also stand to gain from a closer engagement with theories of globalization (Garrard 178).[11] To date, environmental-justice ecocriticism is the only branch of the field that has addressed globalization issues in any depth. To put it somewhat simplistically, this type of ecocriticism rejects economic globalization, which it understands to be dominated by transnational corporations, but welcomes cultural border crossings and alliances, especially when they are initiated by the disenfranchised in the current economic world order. The interdependencies of these two forms of globalization, however, deserve closer theoretical scrutiny. Ecological issues are situated at a complex intersection of politics, economy, technology, and culture; envisioning them in their global implications requires an engagement with a variety of theoretical approaches to globalization, especially, for ecocritics, those that focus on its cultural dimensions. With such a theoretical framework to link together the pieces of its international and interdisciplinary mosaic, ecocriticism promises to become one of the most intellectually exciting and politically urgent ventures in current literary and cultural studies.

Notes

1   URSULA K. HEISE, associate professor of English and comparative literature at Stanford University, is the author of *Chronoschisms: Time, Narrative, and Postmodernism* (Cambridge UP, 1997). She is finishing a book manuscript entitled "Sense of Place and Sense of Planet: The Environmental Imagination of the Global."

2   See also the useful typology of ecocriticism in Reed 148–49.
3   See Cohen for a more chronological account of these challenges.
4   Space constraint makes it impossible for me to give a detailed account of the role of ecofeminism here, whose intellectual trajectory and complexity deserve an essay of their own.
5   As Levin sums it up, "Much recent [ecocritical] work can be divided into two competing critical camps: realists, who advocate a return to nature as a means of healing our modern/postmodern alienation, and social constructionists, who see that nature as a discursive strategy and adopt a more skeptical stance with regard to its alleged healing properties. . . . [T]he dialectical critics from the two different camps appear to have more in common with each other than the more and less sophisticated representatives of the same camp" (175).
6   On Snyder, see Buell, *Environmental Imagination* 166–67; on Leopold, see Berthold-Bond 23–24.
7   Admittedly, the emphasis has been on fairly conventional forms of poetry from Romanticism to the present. More recently, however, experimental poetry has come into focus, from the founding of the journal *Ecopoetics*, in 2001, to Cooperman's work on Olson, Hart's on Eigner, and Fletcher's on Ashbery (175–224).
8   Research by Americanists outside the United States includes work by Hollm; Mayer; and Suberchicot. In her 2004 presidential address to the American Studies Association, Shelley Fisher Fishkin foregrounded the importance of more sustained attention to such research in American studies at large (35–40).
9   Even in single national traditions, some of the omissions are surprising: the essay on Brazil does not refer to Soares's critical anthology *Ecologia e literatura* (1991), and none of the four pieces on Japan in Murphy's anthology mentions Colligan-Taylor's *The Emergence of Environmental Literature in Japan* (1990).
10   For example, Larsen, Nøjgaard, and Petersen's *Nature: Literature and Its Otherness* (1997).
11   Guha's critique of American environmentalism and Guha and Martínez-Alier's *Varieties of Environmentalism* provide good starting points for such an inquiry.

Works Cited

Abbey, Edward. *Desert Solitaire: A Season in the Wilderness*. New York: Ballantine, 1968.

Adamson, Joni, Mei Mei Evans, and Rachel Stein, eds. *The Environmental Justice Reader: Politics, Poetics, and Pedagogy*. Tucson: U of Arizona P, 2002.

Armbruster, Karla, and Kathleen R. Wallace, eds. *Beyond Nature Writing: Exploring the Boundaries of Ecocriticism*. Charlottesville: U of Virginia P, 2001.

Barthes, Roland. *Mythologies*. Paris: Seuil, 1957.

Bate, Jonathan. *Romantic Ecology: Wordsworth and the Environmental Tradition*. London: Routledge, 1991.

———. *The Song of the Earth*. London: Picador, 2000.

Bennett, Michael. "Anti-pastoralism, Frederick Douglass, and the Nature of Slavery." Armbruster and Wallace 195–210.

Bennett, Michael, and David W. Teague, eds. *The Nature of Cities: Ecocriticism and Urban Environments*. Tucson: U of Arizona P, 1999.

Berthold-Bond, Daniel. "The Ethics of 'Place': Reflections on Bioregionalism." *Environmental Ethics* 22 (2000): 5–24.

Botkin, Daniel B. *Discordant Harmonies: A New Ecology for the Twenty-First Century*. New York: Oxford UP, 1990.

Branch, Michael P., and Scott Slovic, eds. *The ISLE Reader: Ecocriticism, 1993–2003*. Athens: U of Georgia P, 2003.

Buell, Lawrence. *The Environmental Imagination: Thoreau, Nature Writing, and the Formation of American Culture*. Cambridge: Harvard UP, 1995.

———. *The Future of Environmental Criticism: Environmental Crisis and Literary Imagination*. Oxford: Blackwell, 2005.

———. *Writing for an Endangered World: Literature, Culture, and Environment in the U.S. and Beyond*. Cambridge: Harvard UP, 2001.

Carroll, Joseph. *Literary Darwinism: Evolution, Human Nature, and Literature*. New York: Routledge, 2004.

Carson, Rachel. *Silent Spring*. Boston: Houghton, 1962.

Cohen, Michael P. "Blues in the Green: Ecocriticism under Critique." *Environmental History* 9 (2004): 9–36.

Colligan-Taylor, Karen. *The Emergence of Environmental Literature in Japan*. New York: Garland, 1990.

Cooperman, Matthew. "Charles Olson: Archaeologist of Morning, Ecologist of Evening." Tallmadge and Harrington 208–28.

Cronon, William. "The Trouble with Wilderness; or, Getting Back to the Wrong Nature." *Uncommon Ground: Rethinking the Human Place in Nature*. Ed. Cronon. New York: Norton, 1995. 69–90.

Dixon, Terrell, ed. *City Wilds: Essays and Stories about Urban Nature*. Athens: U of Georgia P, 2002.

Ecocriticism. Spec. issue of *New Literary History* 30.3 (1999): 505–716.

Evernden, Neil. "Beyond Ecology: Self, Place, and the Pathetic Fallacy." Glotfelty and Fromm 92–104.

Fishkin, Shelley Fisher. "Crossroads of Cultures: The Transnational Turn in American Studies." *American Quarterly* 57 (2005): 17–57.

Fletcher, Angus. *A New Theory for American Poetry: Democracy, the Environment, and the Future of Imagination*. Cambridge: Harvard UP, 2004.

Garrard, Greg. *Ecocriticism*. London: Routledge, 2004.

Glotfelty, Cheryll. "Introduction: Literary Studies in an Age of Environmental Crisis." Glotfelty and Fromm xv–xxxvii.

Glotfelty, Cheryll, and Harold Fromm, eds. *The Ecocriticism Reader: Landmarks in Literary Ecology*. Athens: U of Georgia P, 1996.

Goodbody, Axel. "Deutsche Ökolyrik: Comparative Observations on the Emergence and Expression of Environmental Consciousness in West and East German Poetry." *German Literature at a Time of Change, 1989–1990: German Unity and German Identity in Literary Perspective*. Ed. Arthur Williams, Stuart Parkes, and Roland Smith. Bern: Lang, 1991. 373–400.

———. " 'Es stirbt das Land an seinen Zwecken': Writers, the Environment and the Green Movement in the GDR." *German Life and Letters* 47 (1994): 325–36.

Gross, Paul R., and Norman Levitt. *Higher Superstition: The Academic Left and Its Quarrels with Science*. Baltimore: Johns Hopkins UP, 1994.

Guha, Ramachandra. "Radical American Environmentalism and Wilderness Preservation: A Third World Critique." *Environmental Ethics* 11 (1989): 71–84.

Guha, Ramachandra, and Joan Martínez-Alier. *Varieties of Environmentalism: Essays North and South*. London: Earthscan, 1997.

Hart, George. "Postmodernist Nature/Poetry: The Example of Larry Eigner." Tallmadge and Harrington 315–32.

Harvey, David. *Justice, Nature and the Geography of Difference*. Oxford: Blackwell, 1996.

Hayles, N. Katherine. "Constrained Constructivism: Locating Scientific Inquiry in the Theater of Representation." *Realism and Representation: Essays on the Problem of Realism in Relation to Science, Literature, and Culture*. Ed. George Levine. Madison: U of Wisconsin P, 1993. 27–43.

Heidegger, Martin. "Bauen Wohnen Denken." *Vorträge und Aufsätze*. Ed. Friedrich-Wilhelm von Herrmann. Frankfurt am Main: Klostermann, 2000. 145–64.

Heise, Ursula K. "Science and Ecocriticism." *American Book Review* 18 (1997): 4–6.

Hochman, Jhan. *Green Cultural Studies: Nature in Film, Novel, and Theory*. Moscow: U of Idaho P, 1998.

Hollm, Jan. *Die angloamerikanische Ökotopie: Literarische Entwürfe einer grünen Welt*. Frankfurt am Main: Lang, 1998.

Killingsworth, M. Jimmie, and Jacqueline S. Palmer. "Millennial Ecology: The Apocalyptic Narrative from Silent Spring to Global Warming." *Green Culture: Environmental Rhetoric in Contemporary America*. Ed. Carl G. Herndl and Stuart C. Brown. Madison: U of Wisconsin P, 1996. 21–45.

Kolodny, Annette. *The Lay of the Land: Metaphor as History and Experience in American Life and Letters*. Chapel Hill: U of North Carolina P, 1975.

Kroeber, Karl. *Ecological Literary Criticism: Romantic Imagining and the Biology of Mind*. New York: Columbia UP, 1994.

Larsen, Svend Eric, Morten Nøjgaard, and Annelise Ballegard Petersen, eds. *Nature: Literature and Its Otherness / La littérature et son autre*. Odense, Den.: Odense UP, 1997.

Levin, Jonathan. "Beyond Nature? Recent Work in Ecocriticism." *Contemporary Literature* 43 (2002): 171–86.

Love, Glen A. *Practical Ecocriticism: Literature, Biology, and the Environment*. Charlottesville: U of Virginia P, 2003.

MacDonald, Scott. "Ten+ (Alternative) Films about American Cities." Branch and Slovic 217–39.

Macherot, Raymond. "Les croquillards." *Chlorophylle à Coquefredouille*. N.p.: Le Lombard, 1998. 7–52.

Marcone, Jorge. "De retorno a lo natural: *La serpiente de oro*, la 'novela de la selva' y la crítica ecológica." *Hispania* 81 (1998): 299–308.

———. "Jungle Fever: Primitivism in Environmentalism: Rómulo Gallegos's *Canaima* and the Romance of the Jungle." *Primitivism and Identity in Latin America: Essays on Art, Literature, and Culture*. Ed. Erik Camayd-Freixas and José Eduardo González. Tucson: U of Arizona P, 2000. 157–72.

Martínez-Alier, Joan. " 'Environmental Justice' (Local and Global)." *The Cultures of Globalization*. Ed. Fredric Jameson and Masao Miyoshi. Durham: Duke UP, 1998. 312–26.

Marx, Leo. *The Machine in the Garden: Technology and the Pastoral Ideal in America*. New York: Oxford UP, 1964.

Mayer, Sylvia. *Naturethik und Neuengland-Regionalliteratur: Harriet Beecher Stowe, Rose Terry Cooke, Sarah Orne Jewett, Mary E. Wilkins Freeman*. Heidelberg: Winter, 2004.

Mazel, David. *American Literary Environmentalism*. Athens: U of Georgia P, 2000.

Meeker, Joseph. *The Comedy of Survival: Literary Ecology and a Play Ethic*. 3rd ed. Tucson: U of Arizona P, 1997.

Merleau-Ponty, Maurice. *Le visible et l'invisible: Suivi de notes de travail*. Ed. Claude Lefort. Paris: Gallimard, 1964.

Murphy, Patrick D., ed. *Ecology in Latin American and Caribbean Literature*. Spec. issue of *Hispanic Journal* 19.2 (1998): 199–342.

———, ed. *Literature of Nature: An International Sourcebook*. Chicago: Fitzroy Dearborn, 1998.

Naess, Arne. *Ecology, Community and Lifestyle: Outline of an Ecosophy*. Trans. David Rothenberg. Cambridge: Cambridge UP, 1989.

Nash, Roderick. *Wilderness and the American Mind*. New Haven: Yale UP, 1967.

Phillips, Dana. *The Truth of Ecology: Nature, Culture, and Literature in America*. Oxford: Oxford UP, 2003.

Reed, T. V. "Toward an Environmental Justice Ecocriticism." Adamson, Evans, and Stein 145–62.

Rojas Pérez, Walter. *La ecocrítica hoy*. San José, Costa Rica: Aire Moderno, 2004.

Slater, Candace. *Entangled Edens: Visions of the Amazon*. Berkeley: U of California P, 2002.

Slovic, Scott. "Ecocriticism: Storytelling, Values, Communication, Contact." *ASLE Related Conferences and Abstracts*. 7 Dec. 2005 <http://www.asle.umn.edu/conf/other_conf/wla/1994/slovic.html>.

——. *Seeking Awareness in American Nature Writing: Henry Thoreau, Annie Dillard, Edward Abbey, Wendell Berry, Barry Lopez*. Salt Lake City: U of Utah P, 1992.

Smith, Henry Nash. *Virgin Land: The American West as Symbol and Myth*. Cambridge: Harvard UP, 1950.

Snyder, Gary. "Reinhabitation." *A Place in Space: Ethics, Aesthetics, and Watersheds*. Washington: Counterpoint, 1995. 183–91.

Soares, Angélica. *Ecologia e literatura*. Rio de Janeiro: Tempo Brazileiro, 1992.

Sokal, Alan D. "Transgressing the Boundaries: Toward a Transformative Hermeneutics of Quantum Gravity." *Social Text* 46–47 (1996): 217–52.

Soper, Kate. *What Is Nature? Culture, Politics and the Non-human*. Oxford: Blackwell, 1995.

Suberchicot, Alain. *Littérature américaine et écologie*. Paris: Harmattan, 2002.

Sullivan, Heather I. "Organic and Inorganic Bodies in the Age of Goethe: An Ecocritical Reading of Ludwig Tieck's 'Rune Mountain' and the Earth Sciences." *ISLE* 10.2 (2003): 21–46.

Tallmadge, John, and Henry Harrington, eds. *Reading under the Sign of Nature: New Essays in Ecocriticism*. Salt Lake City: U of Utah P, 2000.

Wallace, Kathleen R., and Karla Armbruster. "The Novels of Toni Morrison: 'Wild Wilderness Where There Was None.' " Armbruster and Wallace 211–30.

White, Richard. "Environmental History, Ecology, and Meaning." *Journal of American History* 76 (1990): 1111–16.

Williams, Raymond. *The Country and the City*. New York: Oxford UP, 1973.

Williams, Terry Tempest. "Yellowstone: The Erotics of Place." *An Unspoken Hunger: Stories from the Field*. New York: Pantheon, 1994. 81–87.

Wilson, Edward O. *Consilience: The Unity of Knowledge*. New York: Knopf, 1998.

Worster, Donald. *Nature's Economy: A History of Ecological Ideas*. 2nd ed. Cambridge: Cambridge UP, 1994.

Chapter 17

Graham Huggan and Helen Tiffin

"INTRODUCTION" TO *POSTCOLONIAL ECOCRITICISM: LITERATURE, ANIMALS, ENVIRONMENT*

IN APRIL 2000, THE AMERICAN magazine *Time* published a commemorative Earth Day issue. Featuring a beaming Bill Clinton in Botswana and, more sinisterly, a series of double-page spreads advertising Ford Motor Company's commitment to the environment, the magazine duly joined the millennial rallying cry to save the planet, issued on behalf of a country that has done far less than one might reasonably expect to protect the global environment but far more than it could possibly have hoped to 'reinvent the imperial tradition for the twenty-first century' (Lazarus 2006: 20) – a country that has actively and aggressively contributed to what many now acknowledge to be the chronic endangerment of the contemporary late-capitalist world.

In a very different vein, the same year also saw a re-issue of *The Unquiet Woods*, the Indian historian Ramachandra Guha's classic account of the Chipko movement – a 1970s peasant revolt against commercial forestry practices in the Northern Indian Himalayan region which is often considered to be a paradigmatic example of those grassroots, often Third World-based, resistance movements that are sometimes bracketed under the capacious heading: the 'environmentalism of the poor' (Guha and Martinez-Alier 1997). Taking its cue from one of the movement's populist leaders, Sunderlal Bahaguna, Guha's book suggests that 'the ecological crisis in Himalaya is not an isolated event [but] has its roots in the [modern] materialistic civilization [that] makes man the butcher of Earth' (Bahaguna, quoted in Guha 2000: 179). For all that, Guha's aim is not to show how modernity *per se* has contributed to ecological destruction in twentieth-century India – still less to suggest that peasant movements like Chipko are doomed remnants of a superseded pre-modern era – but rather to outline some of the ways in which state-planned industrialisation in postcolonial India, even while it claims to practise one version or other of sustainable development, has only succeeded in 'pauperizing millions of people in the agrarian sector and diminishing the stock of plant, water and soil resources at a terrifying rate' (196).

Is there any way of reconciling the Northern environmentalisms of the rich (always potentially vainglorious and hypocritical) and the Southern environmentalisms of the poor (often genuinely heroic and authentic)? Is there any way of narrowing the ecological gap between coloniser and colonised, each of them locked into their seemingly incommensurable worlds? The opposing terms seem at once necessary and overblown, starkly distinct yet hopelessly entangled.[1] After all, in their different ways, *Time* magazine and Guha's book are *both* arguing the need to bring postcolonial and ecological issues together as a means of challenging continuing imperialist modes of social and environmental dominance; while both are suggesting, at the same time, that allegedly egalitarian terms like 'postcolonial' and 'ecological' are eminently co-optable for a variety of often far-from-egalitarian (national) state interests and (transnational) corporate-capitalist concerns.

How are we to read the burgeoning alliance between postcolonial and environmental studies, the increasing convergence of postcolonialism and ecocriticism, in such conflicted, even contradictory, contexts? In one sense, the case for 'green postcolonialism' (Huggan and Tiffin 2007) or 'postcolonial ecocriticism' (Cilano and DeLoughrey 2007) is painfully obvious.[2] As Pablo Mukherjee (2006) puts it:

> Surely, any field purporting to theorise the global conditions of colonialism and imperialism (let us call it postcolonial studies) cannot but consider the complex interplay of environmental categories such as water, land, energy, habitat, migration with political or cultural categories such as state, society, conflict, literature, theatre, visual arts. Equally, any field purporting to attach interpretative importance to environment (let us call it eco/environmental studies) must be able to trace the social, historical and material co-ordinates of categories such as forests, rivers, bio-regions and species.
>
> (144)

In another sense, however, the coming together of postcolonial and eco/environmental studies is hedged about with seemingly insurmountable problems. For one thing, the two fields are notoriously difficult to define, not least by their own practitioners; and they are not necessarily united even in their most basic interpretative methods or fundamental ideological concerns. Internal divisions – e.g. those between broadly Marxist and post-structuralist positions within postcolonial studies, or those between environmental and animal-rights activism within eco/environmental studies – are constitutive of both fields, but these may easily be glossed over in broad-based attempts to find similarities, e.g. the commitment to social and environmental justice, or differences, e.g. what Cilano and DeLoughrey (2007) call the 'unproblematized division between people (on the postcolonial side) and nature (on the ecocritical one)' (75). Large-scale distinctions based on the initially attractive view that postcolonial studies and eco/environmental studies offer mutual correctives to each other turn out on closer inspection to be perilous. The easy assertion, for instance, that the postcolonial field is inherently anthropocentric (human-centred) overlooks a long history of ecological concern in postcolonial criticism; while any number of examples could be mustered to fend off the counter-charge that eco/environmental studies privileges a white male western subject, or that it fails to factor cultural difference into supposedly universal environmental and bioethical debates. Even more subtle discriminations such as Nixon's or Buell's may not hold up to closer critical scrutiny, while Murphy's well-intentioned calls for diversity and inclusivity are insufficiently grounded, disguising the Anglo-American biases that make their own critical pluralism possible – a common critique of ecocriticism (which is perhaps more inclusive than some of its detractors imagine) that holds, too, for postcolonial criticism (which is perhaps less inclusive than some of its advocates attest).

One way out of this morass is to insist that the proper subject of postcolonialism is colonialism, and to look accordingly for the colonial/imperial underpinnings of environmental practices in both 'colonising' and 'colonised' societies of the present and the past. Here, postcolonial ecocritics have frequently followed the lead of the influential British environmental historians Alfred Crosby and Richard Grove, whose work reveals the historical embeddedness of ecology in the European imperial enterprise, without necessarily endorsing the Eurocentrism lurking behind these two authors' own critical attitudes (Tiffin 2007). A further irony is that the flexibility of Crosby's term *ecological imperialism* – which ranges in implication and intensity from the violent appropriation of indigenous land to the ill-considered introduction of non-domestic livestock and European agricultural practices – has tended to come at the cost of its historical specificity, either blurring the boundaries between very different forms of environmentalism or, in a move arguably characteristic of postcolonial criticism, collapsing imperialism into an all-purpose concept-metaphor that fails to distinguish between general ideologies of domination and specific socio-historical effects.

One characteristically broad understanding of ecological imperialism is that of the Australian ecofeminist Val Plumwood (2001), who links her philosophical attack on the dualistic thinking that continues to structure human attitudes to the environment to the masculinist, 'reason-centred culture' that once helped secure and sustain European imperial dominance, but now proves ruinous in the face of mass extinction and the fast-approaching 'biophysical limits of the planet' (5). Any *historical* analysis of practices and patterns of ecological imperialism, Plumwood insists, must return to this *philosophical* basis, acknowledging those forms of instrumental reason that view nature and the animal 'other' as being either external to human needs, and thus effectively dispensable, or as being in permanent service to them, and thus an endlessly replenishable resource (4–5).

Another form of ecological imperialism goes under the more contemporary-sounding term *biocolonisation*, used by a variety of environmental and bioscientific scholars to cover the broadly biopolitical implications of current western technological experiments and trends (Kimball 1996; Shiva 1997). Examples here range from biopiracy – e.g. the corporate raiding of indigenous natural-cultural property and embodied knowledge – to western-patented genetic modification (the 'Green Revolution') and other recent instances of biotechnological suprematism and 'planetary management' (Ross 1991) in which the allegedly world-saving potential of science is seconded for self-serving western needs and political ends.

A third form of ecological imperialism is *environmental racism*, defined by the American environmental philosopher Deane Curtin as 'the connection, in theory and practice, of race and the environment so that the oppression of one is connected to, and supported by, the oppression of the other' (2005: 145). Environmental racism has both positive and negative components, accruing just as easily to those considered romantically to be in harmony with nature, e.g. the familiar trope of the 'ecological Indian' (Krech 2000), as to those accused of damaging their environment on the basis of cultural attributes directly or indirectly associated with their race. Environmental racism is perhaps best understood as a sociological phenomenon, exemplified in the environmentally discriminatory treatment of socially marginalised or economically disadvantaged peoples, and in the transference of ecological problems from their 'home' source to a 'foreign' outlet (whether *discursively*, e.g. through the more or less wholly imagined perception of other people's 'dirty habits', or *materially*, e.g. through the actual re-routing of First World commercial waste). Above all else, though, environmental racism is an extreme form of what Plumwood calls 'hegemonic centrism' – the self-privileging view that she sees as underlying racism, sexism and colonialism alike, all of which support and reconfirm each other, and all of which have historically been conscripted for the purposes of exploiting nature while 'minimising non-human claims to [a shared] earth' (2001: 4).

Racism and speciesism

For Plumwood, these claims extend both to environmental and animal actors, since what she calls 'our [collective] failure to situate dominant forms of human society ecologically [has been] matched by our failure to situare non-humans ethically, as the plight of non-human species continues to worsen' (2001: 2). 'Hegemonic centrism' thus accounts not only for environmental *racism*, but also for those forms of institutionalised *speciesism* that continue to be used to rationalise the exploitation of animal (and animalised human) 'others' in the name of a 'human- and reason-centred culture that is at least a couple of millennia old' (2001: 8). As Plumwood argues, the western definition of humanity depended – and still depends – on the presence of the 'not-human': the uncivilised, the animal and animalistic. European justi-fication for invasion and colonisation proceeded from this basis, understanding non-European lands and the people and animals that inhabited them as 'spaces', 'unused, underused or empty' (2003: 53). The very ideology of colonisation is thus one where anthropocentrism and Eurocentrism are inseparable, with the anthropocentrism underlying Eurocentrism being used to justify those forms of European colonialism that see 'indigenous cultures as "primitive", less rational, and closer to children, animals and nature' (2003: 53).

Within many cultures – and not just western ones – anthropocentrism has long been naturalised. The absolute prioritisation of one's own species' interests over those of the silenced majority is still regarded as being 'only natural'. Ironically, it is precisely through such appeals to nature that other animals and the environment are often excluded from the privileged ranks of the human, rendering them available for exploitation. As Cary Wolfe, citing Jacques Derrida, puts it:

> [T]he humanist concept of subjectivity is inseparable from the discourse and institution of a speciesism which relies on the tacit acceptance that the full tran-scendence to the human requires the sacrifice of the animal and the animalistic, which in turn makes possible a symbolic economy in which we can engage in a 'non-criminal putting to death', as Derrida phrases it, not only of animals but of humans as well by marking them as animal.
>
> (1998: 39)

The effectiveness of this discourse of species is that 'when applied to social others of whatever sort', it relies upon 'the taking for granted of the institution of speciesism; that is, upon the ethical acceptability of the systematic, institutionalised killing of non-human others' (39). In other words, in assuming a natural prioritisation of humans and human interests over those of other species on earth, we are both generating and repeating the racist ideologies of impe-rialism on a planetary scale. In working towards a genuinely post-imperial, environmentally based conception of community, then, a re-imagining and reconfiguration of the human place in nature necessitates an interrogation of the category of the human itself and of the ways in which the construction of ourselves *against* nature – with the hierarchisation of life forms that construction implies – has been and remains complicit in colonialist and racist exploitation from the time of imperial conquest to the present day.

Postcolonial studies has come to understand environmental issues not only as central to the projects of European conquest and global domination, but also as inherent in the ideolo-gies of imperialism and racism on which those projects historically – and persistently – depend. Not only were other people often regarded as part of nature – and thus treated instrumentally as animals – but also they were forced or co-opted over time into western views of the environment, thereby rendering cultural and environmental restitution difficult if not impossible to achieve. Once invasion and settlement had been accomplished, or at least once administrative structures had been set up, the environmental impacts of western atti-tudes to human being-in-the-world were facilitated or reinforced by the deliberate (or acci-dental) transport of animals, plants and peoples throughout the European empires, instigating widespread ecosystem change under conspicuously unequal power regimes.[3]

Despite the recent advances of eco/environmental criticism, English studies in general, and postcolonial studies more particularly, have yet to resituate the species boundary and environmental concerns at the centre of their enquiries; yet the need to examine these interfaces between nature and culture, animal and human, is urgent and never more pertinent than it is today. After all, postcolonialism's concerns with conquest, colonisation, racism and sexism, along with its investments in theories of indigeneity and diaspora and the relations between native and invader societies and cultures, are also the central concerns of animal and environmental studies. Moreover, as the American environmental historian Donald Worster acknowledges, it is in the myriad relationships between material practices and ideas – especially in cross-cultural contexts – that day-to-day planetary life is lived and futures are governed: practices and ideas that are inseparable from issues of *representation* – as will be made clear throughout this book.

In his historical studies *The Columbian Exchange* (1973) and *Ecological Imperialism* (1986), Alfred Crosby considers the ways in which both materials and ideas were exchanged between Old World and New in a number of anything but even contexts. In the colonies of occupation, these radical inequalities or exchanges seemed most evident – or at least initially – in the military and political arenas, while in the settler colonies it was the results of *environmental* imperialism that were often most immediately clear. Different conceptions of being-in-the-world had indeed long been exchanged by individuals or groups under colonialist circumstances: eastern religions had intrigued Europeans for several centuries, while the oral cultures of the Pacific Islands and Africa had provoked interest and admiration in many westerners as well. But in Australia, North America, New Zealand and South Africa, genuine curiosity about and respect for indigenous cultures, philosophies and religions was rare, and even the most well-intentioned of missionaries, settlers and administrators tended to conceive of themselves as conferring (or imposing) the gifts of civilisation upon the benighted heathen with little or no interest in receiving his or her philosophical gifts in return.

Settlers arrived with crops, flocks and herds, and cleared land, exterminating local ecosystems, while human, animal and plant specimens taken to Europe from these 'new' worlds were, by contrast, few and often inert in form. (Interestingly enough, no human, animal or plant, whether wild or domesticated, transported from the colonies to Europe was in a position to wreak comparable havoc on European ecosystems.) Moreover, they did not arrive as part of traditional agricultural or pastoral practices or with the authority of the normative; instead, they were isolated exotics:

> Indians paraded before royal courts; like turkeys and parrots in cages were the innocent signifiers of an otherness that was [. . .] exotic, that is, non-systematic, carrying no meaning other than that imposed by the culture to which they were exhibited.
>
> (Wasserman 1984: 132)

European imports to the newly settled colonies – humans, animals, plants – were regarded on the other hand as necessary and 'natural' impositions on, or substitutes for, the local bush or wilderness; and even if these invading species were initially difficult to establish or acclimatise, they soon prospered in lands where their control predators were absent. The genuinely natural ways of indigenous ecosystems were irretrievably undone as 'wild' lands were cleared for farming or opened up to pastoralism.

Skewed as they were in favour of the colonising culture, such exchanges were nevertheless often more complex in practice than this apparently simple pattern of invasion, land-clearing and destruction might lead us to suppose. As Worster (1985) suggests, material and ideological impositions are often disturbed by the complexities of the local elements they seek to displace and by the inappropriate, contradictory ideas and practices they catalyse; and thus it was that European/western human and environmental relations, once transported to the colonies, underwent pressures that were sometimes transformative in their turn. Inefficacious as they might frequently have seemed, the indigenous peoples, as well as animals and plants, of the colonies also altered – albeit to a limited extent – European/western conceptions and practices. More usually, however, ideas of animal treatment and land use initially formed in Europe predisposed colonial administrators and settlers to a facile belief in the apparently limitless resources of the settler colonies. Such places, after all, were apparently untamed, unowned and, above all, *unused;* and, accordingly, settlers set about rendering them productive and profitable through imported methods rather than by accommodating them to local circumstances.

As Virginia Anderson shows in her scrupulously researched 2004 study *Creatures of Empire: How Domestic Animals Transformed Early America*, such invasions of animals and plants were by no means systematic; nor did the animals and plants themselves (or, for that matter, practices of animal husbandry and cultivation) in the new environments of the early North American colonies remain unchanged. Anderson focuses on three settlement areas from New England to the Chesapeake, and on the settler-invaders' importation of domestic cattle and their effects on the environment; on Native American (Indian) attitudes, practices and livelihoods; on relationships between the settlers and various Indian cultures; and to some extent on animals, both domestic and wild, themselves.

Although concerned exclusively with early settlement in America, Anderson's study necessarily raises the issue of the part played by animals in human histories. In its discussion of conflicts and, more rarely, co-operation between settlers and Indians over land and livestock, *Creatures of Empire* interrogates animal categories many westerners tend to take as givens: wild and tame; game and produce; animals and ownership; and, ultimately, relations between and definitions of humans and animals themselves. For example, as Anderson argues, cattle, horses, pigs and goats – all of which had been transported across the Atlantic with great difficulty – were generally seen by colonists as serving two viral purposes. The first was to provide food and labour, but the second was to provide a model of civilised living for the indigenous population. The domestication of animals – the discipline required by animal husbandry – was seen to exert civilising (Christianising) influences on the native populations. Meanwhile, as the colonists became increasingly familiar with Indian living conditions, they regarded such domesticating practices as a key to curing Indian 'laziness'.

In pre-invasion Australia, the nature of the environment had dictated nomadism as the only way of life for both people and animals, bur native North American groups needed to be only partially nomadic. Indian cultural groups occupied particular territories, and there were semi-permanent settlements where the women cultivated corn, although hunting forest animals provided the Indians with their vital sustainable base. This general dependence on hunting allowed the American colonists to exaggerate 'the extent of native mobility in order to undermine Indians' territorial claims' (Anderson 2004: 191). And, as in Australia and South Africa, the growing numbers of colonists regarded the lands they occupied as theirs by right, while the alleged nomadism of the Indians suggested to them that there was no native interest in land ownership. The same attitudes were applied to animals. The transported stock 'naturally' belonged to the settlers, while native animals, the very basis of Indian existence, were 'naturally' considered fair game. Not surprisingly, then, livestock and game increasingly became the subjects of human conflict.

Anderson shows however that, as encroaching white settlement forced such issues, there were early attempts at compromise and adaptation on both sides. 'Nursing separate grievances, Indians and colonists struggled to resolve the seemingly intractable problems that livestock created' (191). Such attempts at resolution 'partook as much of diplomacy as of law' and proceeded in an 'unsystematic and ad hoc fashion', with both Indians and colonists 'groping their way towards expedients that helped to reduce friction, if not to eliminate its root cause' (191). But as settler numbers increased and more and more forest was cleared to pasture livestock, native animal habitats (and thus animal numbers) were drastically reduced. More and more cattle went semi-wild and strayed into Indian areas, and the informal agreements necessarily became less effective for both parties.

The English colonists had 'invariably judged the Indians' obvious "failure" to domesticate New World beasts as evidence of their backwardness' (32). But with 'ample protein readily available through hunting, [the] Indians [of New England and the Chesapeake] had no incentive to domesticate animals for food, even if likely candidates had been present' (33). Until the increasing disappearance of game forced them into stock husbandry in the service of the settlers, they had no reason to adopt this so-called 'civilised' mode. Moreover, the colonists' distinction between 'domesticated' and 'wild' was obviously quite unfamiliar to Native Americans. Various Indian groups had formed 'loose associations with wild dogs for purposes of hunting' (36), while Indian women often encouraged hawks to help protect their corn crops; but the absence of the European distinction in Indian culture formed much of the basis of the conflict and misunderstanding. Indians did not own living animals in the same way as the colonists, and to the Indians these were strange new wild creatures whose powers had yet to be assessed and understood (39).

Yet *both* cultures hunted (wild) animals and, as Anderson argues, this might have provided some commonality. Both tracked animals in order to kill them, and both had rituals associated with the practice; they shared an enthusiasm for the chase, for the male camaraderie that hunting afforded together with the peculiar male satisfaction of killing. Both regarded hunting as useful practice for warfare. But the rock on which potential similarities foundered was the very different views held by Indians and colonists about human relations with their animal prey:

> Aware of the power of animal spirits, native hunters treated their prey with respect and performed rituals defined by reciprocity. Although not quite a relationship of equals, the connection between Indians and prey was not essentially hierarchical. But notions of domination and subordination were central to the English, who believed that the act of hunting epitomized the divinely sanctioned ascendancy of humankind over animals.
>
> (58)

This was a fundamental difference, and English attitudes to the social and cultural roles of hunting also eroded potential commonality. Because Indian women were the agriculturalists, Indian men were perceived as lazy, energised only by the hunt. In English eyes, hunting was a pastime, an upper-class social ritual, not a survival necessity. And, ironically, it was this upper-class model that came most readily to mind:

> Had colonists perceived a parallel between native hunters and lower-ranking Englishmen who trapped game in order to put meat on the table, they might have acquired some understanding of a vital part of Indian culture. By likening Indian men to gentlemen of leisure, however, colonists indulged moral judgements that had little to do with social and economic conditions in native villages.
>
> (62)

Once such an assumption had been made, it became part of a persisting stereotype, encouraging the view that Indians 'who wasted time with hunting and also failed to domesticate animals obviously needed to learn how to exploit properly the abundant fauna the Lord had placed in the New World for the benefit of humans' (62).

If, as Crosby and, to a lesser degree, Anderson argue, the triumph of Anglo-European settlers over North American (and subsequently South African and Australian) indigenous populations was effected over the ensuing centuries through environmental – and hence cultural – derangement on a vast scale, such destructive changes were premised on *ontological* and *epistemological* differences between European and Indian ideas of human and animal being-in-the-world. The ultimate irony of this hegemonic triumph is that in the twenty-first century the West is increasingly attempting to re-think and re-capture practices gener-ated through the very respect for animals and nature that the early settlers so righteously scorned.

Aesthetics, advocacy, activism

As Lawrence Buell has aptly remarked, 'criticism worthy of its name arises from commit-ments deeper than professionalism' (2005: 97), and in the genesis and subsequent practice of the relatively new fields of postcolonial and eco/environmental studies, such commitment has usually been both evident and energising. Postcolonial critiques of European imperialism and colonialism, as well as studies of their post-independence legacies, have from the outset been informed by ethical and political concerns, while the burgeoning area of environmental analysis and critique, particularly though by no means exclusively in the humanities, has in large part emerged out of genuine alarm at the future of the planetary environment and its inhabitants. Such concerns come in the wake of taken-for-granted human domination where anthropocentrism and western imperialism are intrinsically interwoven. Consequently, both postcolonial critique and eco/environmental studies have been, and remain, 'deeply polem-ical' (Buell 2005: 97) while maintaining their commitment to a rigorous scholarship – one which, however, finds itself increasingly compromised by a global capitalism that has not always been challenged to the same degree as the imperial behaviours it instantiates and inspires.

A similar caveat applies to the crossover field of postcolonial ecocriticism, which also involves an 'aesthetics committed to politics' (Cilano and DeLoughrey 2007: 84), with its historical understandings of the socio-political origins of environmental issues overriding the apolitical tendencies of earlier forms of ecocriticism that often seemed either to follow an escapist pastoral impulse or to favour an aesthetic appreciation of nature for its own sake (Heise 2006; Levin 2002). Not that ecocriticism required a sudden influx of postcoloni-alists to reform it, having long since gone through its own social-ecological – if not explicitly postcolonial – turn.[4] Indeed, it seems necessary to point out that the convergence of postcolonial and eco/environmenral studies over the last decade or so is neither intellectually unbidden nor historically unanticipated; rather, it has given greater visibility, in the first case, to the ecological dimensions of earlier postcolonial analyses and, in the second, to the increasingly global outreach of a US-based ecocriticism that had always been aware of its own 'eco-parochialist' tendencies, and that had often shared postcolonial-ism's distrust for national self-congratulation and unmarked racial politics (as Robert Young among others points out, non-western ecofeminism significantly pre-dates the emergence of North American ecocriticism, showing the way for western practitioners' ongoing self-examination of their own motives and laying the basis for their own internal gendered/racialised critiques).

What the postcolonial/ecocritical alliance brings out, above all, is the need for a broadly materialist understanding of the changing relationship between people, animals and environ-ment – one that requires attention, in turn, to the cultural politics of representation as well as to those more specific 'processes of mediation [. . .] that can be recuperated for anti-colonial critique' (Cilano and DeLoughrey 2007: 79). This suggests (1) the continuing centrality of the imagination and, more specifically, imaginative *literature* to the task of post-colonial ecocriticism and (2) the mediating function of social and environmental *advocacy*, which might turn imaginative literature into a catalyst for social action and exploratory literary analysis into a full-fledged form of engaged cultural critique.

While Cheryll Glotfelty's definition of ecocriticism as 'a study of the relationship between literature and the physical environment' (Glotfelty and Fromm 1996: xviii) remains influential, the primary role of literary analysis in ecocriticism is increasingly disputed; and, as Glotfelty herself admits, its mandate is now usually accepted as extending to the fields of environmental philosophy and bioethics, where, 'as a theoretical discourse, [it] negotiates between the human and the nonhuman worlds' (xix).[5] Equally disputed is ecocriticism's relationship with the biological and environmental sciences, especially ecology, which some ecocritics are legitimately accused of invoking more in hope than understanding, and from which leading concepts (holistic systems, interdependence, energy transfer, etc.) continue to be drawn – less literally than metaphorically – as wishful means of explaining 'the way in which literature functions in the world' (O'Brien 2007: 182). Ecology, it might be argued, rends to function more as *aesthetics* than as *methodology* in eco/environmental criticism, providing the literary-minded critic with a storehouse of individual and collective metaphors through which the socially transformative workings of the 'environmental imagination' (Buell 1995) can be mobilised and performed.

As the American ecocritic Lawrence Buell, from whose work the term is drawn, suggests, the environmental imagination engages a set of aesthetic preferences for ecocriticism which is not necessarily restricted to environmental realism or nature writing, but is especially attentive to those forms of fictional and non-fictional writing that highlight nature and natural elements (landscape, flora and fauna, etc.) as self-standing agents, rather than support structures for human action, in the world (Buell 1995; also Armbruster and Wallace 2001). While it would be a mistake to see ecocriticism as being more concerned with inhabiting the world than with changing it – as being fundamentally more interested in phenomenological than political processes – it is clearly the case that *postcolonial* ecocriticism tips the balance towards the latter, and that its own aesthetic choices reflect this (although postcolonial criticism, like eco/environmental criticism, still needs to be understood as a particular *way of reading*, rather than a specific corpus of literary and other cultural texts). This way of reading is as much affective as analytical – not that the two terms are mutually exclusive – and morally attuned to the continuing abuses of authority that operate in humanity's name. Literary analysis, in this last sense, works towards confirming an environmental ethic that sees 'environmental justice, social justice, and economic justice [not as dissonant competitors] but as parts of the same whole' (Curtin 2005: 7).

What all of this suggests is that postcolonial ecocriticism – like several other modes of ecocriticism – performs an *advocacy* function both in relation to the real world(s) it inhabits and to the imaginary spaces it opens up for contemplation of how the real world might be transformed. The word 'advocacy' needs to be treated carefully here, for as Elaine Raglon and Marian Scholtmeijer among others argue, it is by no means always the case that either postcolonial or environmental literature overtly (or even covertly) advocates for a particular human constituency, species, place or ecosystem (Raglon and Scholtmeijer 2007: 123). Nor, even when it does, are the forms of advocacy it promotes necessarily compatible; for example, *environmental* literature may well appeal to broader ecological systems and processes that *animal* literature rejects in favour of more specific human-animal interactions, while *postcolonial* literature is more likely to show the conflicts that arise when different forms of advocacy are brought together, e.g. by examining the social, cultural and political factors at play in the eviction of local (indigenous) people from nature reserves and wildlife parks (Elder, Wolch and Emel 1998; Raglon and Scholtmeijer 2007).

If postcolonial ecocriticism draws out the advocacy function that is often embedded within postcolonial, animal and environmental literature, it tends to do so with an eye on that literature's specific aesthetic properties, without succumbing to an instrumental view of literature as 'self-consciously directed and shaped by [a desired outcome] and a coherent set of ideas' (Raglon and Scholtmeijer 2007: 123). After all, postcolonial and eco/environmental writing, even if it is directed towards specific goals (e.g. the desire to protect wilderness, or to promote the rights of abused animals and/or peoples), is always likely to transcend its categorisation as 'protest literature', while not even in its most direct forms is it a transparent document of exploitation or a propagandistic blueprint for the liberation of the oppressed. Accordingly, postcolonial ecocriticism preserves the aesthetic function of the literary text while drawing attention to its social and political usefulness, its capacity to set out symbolic guidelines for the material transformation of the world (Huggan and Tiffin 2007). To that extent, it can be seen as an interventionist or even activist enterprise, along the lines of Robert Young's shorthand definition of postcolonialism as 'a politics and philosophy of activism that contests the disparity [between western and non-western cultures/peoples], and so continues in a new way the anti-colonial struggles of the past' (4).

For Young, activism has as much to do with the need for epistemic decolonisation – what the Kenyan writer Ngũgĩ wa Thiong'o calls the 'decolonisation of the mind' – as with more directly physical forms of social struggle, and with theorising the ideas of a political practice that is 'morally committed to transforming the conditions of exploitation and poverty in which large sections of the world's population live out their daily lives' (Young 2003: 6). This view, strongly inflected by Marxism, finds its equivalent in the eco-materialist stance of literary/cultural critics like Pablo Mukherjee, whose work looks at the ways in which contemporary postcolonial crises are inextricably connected with ecological crises, or environmental philosophers like Deane Curtin, whose self-given task is to sketch out the lineaments of a libertarian environmental ethic for a postcolonial world (Mukherjee 2006; Curtin 2005). For both Mukherjee and Curtin, as for Young, critical intervention can itself be considered to be a form of activism, and the critique of colonialism proves to be indistinguishable from an attack on the global-capitalist system that continues to support colonialism in the present, much as it sustained it in the past. This suggests, in turn, that postcolonial ecocriticism is broadly *eco-socialist* in inspiration, and is less likely to be sympathetic to positions like that of Jonathan Bate, who envisions the transference from a 'red' to a 'green' politics and who, while committed to social change, remains careful to distinguish between a phenomenological ecopoetics and an instrumental ecopolitics in a broad-based attempt to account for what it might mean to dwell authentically and responsibly on earth.[6]

However, to call all postcolonial ecocriticism 'eco-socialist' runs the risk of being both rhetorically inaccurate and politically programmatic, and it might be better to see it from a range of not necessarily compatible methodological, ideological and, not least, *cultural* perspectives – as will turn out to be the case in this book. Here, the recent work of scholars like Anthony Vital proves particularly useful. In his excellent 2008 essay 'Toward an African Ecocriticism', Vital suggests that the best way to reconcile postcolonial criticism and eco/environmental criticism might be to take into account 'the complex interplay of social history with the natural world, and how language both shapes and reveals such interactions' (90). It is not enough, however, to acknowledge that all understandings of the world are delivered through language, but necessary to qualify 'this assumption with the recognition that different languages [. . .] permit varieties of understanding' that are both historically determined and socially/culturally formed (90). The task of postcolonial criticism, in this context, is to explore 'how different cultural understandings of society and nature' – understandings necessarily inflected by ongoing experiences of colonialism, sexism and racism – 'have been deployed in specific historical moments by writers in the making of their art' (90). These sentiments are very much of a piece with the approach adopted in this book, which, also in the spirit of Vital's essay, perceives 'a new kind of concern for the environment emerging in the post-colonial era, one attuned to histories of unequal development and varieties of discrimination' (90); and, one might add, to the historical interaction between ideologies of empire and ideologies of genre. The book is interested, in this last sense, in how particular genres and modes – pastoral, for instance, or the beast fable – have been transformed in different cultural and historical contexts, and in how postcolonial writers from a variety of regions have adapted environmental discourses, which have often been shaped in western (European) interests, to their own immediate ends. The book is equally concerned with demonstrating the knowledge of *non*-western (non-European) societies and cultures, which has always been part of the postcolonial critical project (Young 2003: 4–7), and is a task to which ecocriticism – both in spite and because of its Euro-American origins – is increasingly committed at a time when 'the environmentalist ambition is to think globally, but doing so in terms of a single language is inconceivable – even and especially when that language is a hegemonic one' (Heise 2006: 513). In reaching out across languages and cultures, postcolonial ecocriticism is paradoxically driven – as is this book – by the impossibility of its own utopian ambitions: to make exploitation and discrimination of all kinds, both human and nonhuman, visible in the world; and, in so doing, to help make them obsolete.

Writing wrongs

Since the 1990s, ecological issues have engaged a number of humanities scholars who regard them as not marginal but foundational to their disciplines. For researchers in geography, anthropology, philosophy and politics, for instance, animal and environmental considerations are increasingly seen as the necessary *basis* for human studies. But whereas in previous decades, literary studies had often taken the lead in mapping major humanities field shifts – the turn to critical theory ushered in by English's marriage with philosophy in the late 1960s or the rise of post-colonial studies in the 1980s and 90s, for instance – the literary has lagged behind in this most recent of revolutions. One obvious reason has been that literature, with its traditional emphasis on plot, character and psychological states, has been seen perforce as being focused on individuals or groups of humans, or at least anthropomorphised animals, even in genres such as traditional pastoral or romantic elegy where human interaction with, and apparent concern for, the natural world come to the fore. The emphasis of pastoral has generally been on the impact of the environment on the human rather than the other way around. And while literature has certainly dealt with the fates and even the psychologies of animals, these have – at least until recently – been highly anthropomorphised, acting more often than not as a staple of fiction for children rather than adult readers. For western writers, at least, it has been more difficult to anthropomorphise the environment which, far from having its own providential fortunes and narrative trajectories, has been regarded as a mere backdrop against which human lives are played out. And even when writers have given some attention to the natural (extra-human) environment, critics have generally downplayed its significance in their own considerations of the work. Similarly, potential emphasis on the importance of animal subjects – the death of a pet, disease in a sheep flock – tends to focus attention on the *human* reactions to such loss or losses.

Since the 1990s, however, there has been evidence in both literature and literary criticism of the centralising of ecological issues in literary studies, leading to some radical experiments in genre practice, point of view/interpretative focus, and other potentially innovating aspects of literary form. Not that these about-turns are likely to strike us as being entirely unfamiliar. After all, during the latter half of the twentieth century apparently peripheral issues and marginal literatures had come to assume an increasingly important place in both public and scholarly reading practices while exercising significant – and persistent – re-interpretative pressure on European canonical works. Yet all such critical/stylistic revolutions, displacing as they do the earlier paradigms, are given to producing *aporia* in their turn; and among these, as we argue in this book, are the formative roles played by the environment and animals in shaping human lives. To understand why this lag has occurred in both English studies and postcolonial studies in particular, we need to consider the hegemonic role of English literature and literary studies in colonial education systems, together with the ways in which, through colonial institutions and practices, western ideologies suborned and supplanted other ways of (human) being-in-the-world (Ashcroft, Griffiths and Tiffin 1989; Viswanathan 1990). For colonialist interpretation necessarily resulted in the destruction or erosion of alternative apprehensions of animals and environment, blocking understanding of those crucial interactions between the human and the 'extra-human' (Plumwood 2001) that form the substance of this book.

If the conjunction of postcolonialism and ecocriticism has begun to prove mutually illuminating in terms of, say, colonial genesis and continuing human inequalities and environmental abuses, the two areas have often been in conflict. While there are numerous instances of individual ecocritics questioning the promotion of conservationist ideals over those of human development where, as is often the case, the two are in competition, ecocriticism has tended as a whole to prioritise extra-human concerns over the interests of disadvantaged human groups, while post-colonialism has been routinely, and at times unthinkingly, anthropocentric (Huggan 2004; Nixon 2005). Meanwhile, whereas ecocriticism, at least in part, has developed out of literary studies in response to changes in per-ception of the extra-human and its place in literature, animal studies (except where it is regarded as a sub-branch of ecocriticism) has developed independently through disciplines such as philosophy, zoology and religion. Not surprisingly, then, zoocriticism – as we might term its practice in literary studies – is concerned not just with animal *representation* but also with animal *rights*, and this different genesis and trajectory from that of ecocriticism necessarily informs its intersection with the postcolonial. And just as ecocriticism and animal studies have developed rather differently, the two fields' conjunctions with post-colonialism to this point have also proceeded unevenly. Since Alfred Crosby's pioneering demonstration of the significance of environmental factors (under which he includes non human animals) in imperial conquest and subsequent colonisation, a number of studies of the intersections between the fields of ecocriticism and postcolonialism have been produced (Cilano and DeLoughrey 2007; Huggan 2004; Nixon 2005; O'Brien 2001). By contrast, zoocriticism, understood here in the context of intersections between animal studies and postcolonialism, is still in its infancy (see, however, Armstrong 2008, an early but instantly seminal work). As it is emerging, post-colonial zoocriticism shares with post-colonial ecocriticism the exploration of conflicted areas and problems: wildlife protection and conservation on land needed for poor human communities; human communities evicted from their homeland to make way for game parks to benefit wealthy tourists; and, contained within these and other examples, a deep concern for rights (Raglon and Scholtmeijer 2007). Yet further conflicts and concerns inevitably arise within the field of zoocriticism, many of them attached to the philosophical limitations of rights discourses themselves. Should animals, for example, have equal rights with humans; and if so, under which circumstances? With whose rights should we begin, and with whose rights – with what possible philosophical understanding and/or legal notion of rights – can we end? (Mitchell, in Wolfe 2003: ix–xiv). In postcolonial texts, where vilification of designated 'others' was and is frequently metaphorised as a question of civilisation versus savagery, human versus animal, whose wrongs are eventually to be righted, and – given human/animal similarities or the inextricable link between racism and speciesism – whose equalities are to be acknowledged and inequalities fought against; and in whose *name*, not just what *form*?

It thus bears reminding that, in bringing these apparently independent fields together, we are concerned not just with competing interests in terms of rights, but also with those broader categories – including the category of 'rights' itself – that such interests necessarily call into question. One thing seems certain: if the wrongs of colonialism – its legacies of continuing human inequalities, for instance – are to be addressed, still less redressed, then the very category of the *human*, in relation to animals and environment, must also be brought under scrutiny. After all, traditional western constitutions of the human as the 'not-animal' (and, by implication, the 'not-savage') have had major, and often catastrophic, repercussions not just for animals themselves but for all those the West now considers human but were formerly designated, represented and treated as animal. The persistence of such openly discriminatory categorisations invites an endless repetition of the wrongs of the past (Wolfe 2003). This book seeks accordingly to raise questions of rights and wrongs – both in the past and in the present – through the focal area of *representation*, primarily though not exclusively literary representation, since it is representation in all its forms which produces 'that mental type of encounter in which perceptions, ideologies, ethics, laws and myths' have become part of our 'dialogue with nature' (Worster 1994). But at the same time, we recognise that the very idea of rights, especially the granting or extending of rights to others of all kinds, may itself be regarded as in essence anthropocentric, since it is only the dominant (human) group that is in the position to do so; we are thus interested in the philosophical possibility of the wrongness of rights while remaining committed to the moral imperative of righting wrongs as well.[7]

As might be expected, the book seeks neither to offer solutions to these complex questions nor to resolve the intellectual and moral challenges they raise, but rather to examine a pressing situation in which postcolonial writing, theory and practice finds itself increasingly confronted by a variety of broadly extra-human concerns. Given the relatively uneven development of ecocriticism and zoocriticism, differing approaches to their intersections with the postcolonial have necessarily been adopted here, and although we fully recognise that these fields frequently overlap, we have chosen nonetheless to divide the book into two largely self-sustaining parts.

The first part of the book, which is divided into two sections, focuses on the intersection of postcolonial and environmental issues as these have emerged across the historical faultlines of literary genre. In the first section, we argue that one of the central tasks of postcolonial ecocriticism to date has been to contest western ideologies of development, but without necessarily dismissing the idea of 'development' itself as a mere tool of the technocratic West. We duly enquire into the relative successes of postcolonial authors, at least some of whom self-consciously double as social and environmental activists, in pursuing anti- or counter-developmental methods in their literary work. Beginning with a consideration of probably the two most visible postcolonial writer-activists in the field, Arundhati Roy and Ken Saro-Wiwa, we then go on to look at a wide range of anti- and/or counter-developmental strategies in literary works by writers from the Caribbean and, especially, Pacific Islands regions, including Jamaica Kincaid, Epeli Hau'ofa, Witi Ihimaera and Patricia Grace. While we suggest that all of these writers are against the kind of developmentalism that panders to global-corporate interests, the works in question fall short of arguing that globalisation, and the potentially destructive forms of social/environmental development it fosters, can simply be bypassed. Rather, the battle is not so much against development itself as an intrinsically harmful activity or process as against the flagrant social and environmental abuses that continue to be perpetrated in its name. Hence the broadly *counter*-developmental, rather than explicitly *anti*-developmental, thrust of much of the material studied in the section, which is committed to recognising the existence of alternative social and environmental knowledges that are neither acknowledged nor necessarily understood by development experts in the West.

In bringing to light these alternative knowledges and knowledge-systems, the first section emphasises postcolonised communities' sense of their own cultural identities and entitlements, which often represent the ontological basis for their territorial claims to belong. Claims and counter-claims of entitlement and belonging – which are often at heart ontological rather than specifically juridical questions – form the basis for the material we go on to study in the second section, which, like the first, shows both the political and aesthetic implications of postcolonial literature's continuing pursuit of social and environmental justice in an unevenly developed world. The literary mode on which this section focuses is *pastoral*, used by a variety of postcolonial writers, particularly from so-called 'settler societies' (here: Australia, Canada and South Africa), to explore the tensions between contradictory forms of social and political allegiance through which the juridical pressures of entitlement clash with the ontological insistence to belong. These tensions are historically – and necessarily – complex. Pastoral, we suggest, is about the legitimation of highly codified relations between socially differentiated people – relations mediated by, but also mystified by, supposedly universal cultural attitudes to land. We seek to contribute to the demystification of these and other like-minded attitudes by charting the political implications and imperatives of pastoral across a range of work by the Australian poets Judith Wright and Oodgeroo Noonuccal and the South African novelists Nadine Gordimer and J.M. Coetzee. A further sub-section looks at the rather different, if no less conflicted, history of pastoral representation in the Caribbean via the work of the Trinidad-born writer V.S. Naipaul, which – going against the grain of Naipaul criticism – is held to champion post-pastoral forms of communal existence that implicitly support the interconnectedness of land and labour in pursuit of a socially responsible life. We then end with an extended coda on the (literal) staging of conflicts of entitlement and belonging, mostly within a cross-cultural indigenous performance context in which the stage becomes a contested space where different spatial fantasies and histories are accumulated, and the land is revealed both as speaking subject and as disputed object of discursive management and material control.

The second part of the book shifts from a broadly *ecocritical* to a more narrowly *zoocritical* focus. It is divided into three sections, each of which adopts a slightly different emphasis, but all of which are effectively co-dependent, with primary texts floating from one section to another and a strongly anti-anthropocentric argument driving the whole. The first section considers the impact and legacies of colonialist asset stripping, colonial discourse, and Christian missionising. It initially uses Joseph Conrad's turn-of-the-century novella *Heart of Darkness* to consider what is omitted in his celebrated critique of Belgian colonialism, and to assess some of the ways in which a canonical colonial text has been influential in both Europe and its former colonies (including those of Africa) in disseminating an authoritative version of Africa to the west. Chinua Achebe's critique of Conrad's racism is discussed with reference to the ways in which African characters in Conrad's text are excised through their lack of speech and purely metaphoric function; Barbara Gowdy's novel *The White Bone* is then considered in response to both. We also discuss the benefits and dangers of anthropomorphic representation and language in humans and animals; some brief reflec-tions on J.M. Coetzee's fictional treatise *The Lives of Animals* then bring the section to a close.

In the second section of Part II, we consider the role of Christianity – particularly the Bible – in colonisation, as well as responses to a Christian interpellation that marginalises women and animals. The symbolic Christian sacrament has links to pre-Christian cannibal rituals, and this leads us into a discussion of the role of cannibalism, both in practice and as metaphor, as foundational in the imperial 'othering' of animals and humans. Daniel Defoe's *Robinson Crusoe* is the canonical text that forms the basis of this discussion, and considerations of conquest and commerce are raised again here in different contexts. Carnivory (meat-eating) also comes under scrutiny in postcolonial re-writings of the wrongs embedded in imperial and/or anthropocentric attitudes to animals and humans. Texts to be considered include Timothy Findley's *Not Wanted on the Voyage*, Thomas King's *Green Grass, Running Water*, Yann Martel's *Life of Pi*, Samuel Selvon's *Moses Ascending*, and J.M. Coetzee's *Elizabeth Costello*.

The third and final section considers questions of animal and human agency, cross-species contact including sexuality, and clashes between human and animal interests in post-colonised contexts. Texts here include Amitav Ghosh's *The Hungry Tide*, Peter Goldsworthy's *Wish*, Marian Engel's *Bear*, and Zakes Mda's *The Whale Caller*. Drawing on the work of Jacques Derrida, we also consider a number of postcolonial texts that envision more equitable relations between animals and humans, and humans and other humans, including Robyn Williams' *2007* and J.M. Coetzee's *Elizabeth Costello*. As in other sections in Part II, the overall thrust of the argument is that the *righting* of imperialist wrongs necessarily involves our *writing* of the wrongs that have been done — and are still being done — to animals, and demands our critical engagement with the ways in which both continuing problems of abuse and their potential amelioration are represented in British colonial and Anglophone post-colonial texts.

The book then closes with a postscript that brings its central arguments fully up to date in the context of what is now increasingly asserted to be a 'post-natural' or even a 'post-human' world. For some critics, the relentless manipulation of nature foreshadows the inevitable death of nature (Merchant 1980); for others, nature now extends to other, scientifically manufactured forms (Haraway 1997). Whether contemporary technoscience is to be seen as a neo-colonialist enterprise is moot, as is the view that it has ushered in a new era of the posthuman. Meanwhile, critical attacks on humanism's continuing ideological insufficiencies point to its intellectual rationale for the imperial civilising mission and for other authoritarian regimes and systems which, both consciously and unconsciously, have abused humanity in humanity's name. Whether the human is to be renewed, even as humanism is discarded, must remain an open question in a postcolonial context: one which — for better or worse — has often expressly articulated both the centrality of human experience and a variety of humanist concerns. But as our brief concluding discussions of the work of Zadie Smith and Margaret Atwood suggest, human liberation will never be fully achieved without challenging the historical conditions under which human societies have constructed themselves in hierarchical relation to other societies, *both* human *and* nonhuman, and without imagining new ways in which these societies, understood as being ecologically connected, can be creatively transformed.

Notes

1   Binaries of this type continue to plague both postcolonial and environmental studies, prompting critics such as Guha [. . .] to speak exasperatedly of a 'cowboys-and-Indians' approach to contemporary social-environmental conflicts. However, as Guha is also ready to acknowledge, there *is* a viable distinction to be made between what he and Juan Martinez-Alier (1997) call 'full-stomach' and 'empty-belly' environmentalisms — the latter sometimes being a matter of mere survival — under conditions of conspicuously uneven development in the global-capitalist world. Marxist critics like Neil Lazarus make a similar point about the 'new imperialism', which stifles conflict even as it repeat-

edly provokes it, and which requires concerted opposition from postcolonial critics who have para-doxically 'failed to recognise the unremitting actuality and indeed . . . intensification of imperialist social relations in the times and spaces of the postcolonial world' (2006: 12). Lazarus overstates the case, but his point still stands that it is quite possible – indeed, vitally necessary – to speak *both* of entangled allegiances in the contemporary capitalist world order *and* of continuing struggles that pit obvious exploiters against the obviously exploited, the visible oppressor against the equally visible oppressed.

2   Although the terms 'green postcolonialism' or, more commonly used, 'post-colonial ecocriticism' are often used interchangeably, the different combination of noun and qualifying adjective implies that it is postcolonialism, in the first case, and ecocriticism, in the second, that is being rendered subject to revisionist critique. 'Postcolonial ecocriticism' will be used in this book [i.e. *Postcolonial Ecocriticism: Literature, Animals, Environment*, the volume in which this chapter was originally published (to which all additional references of this kind in this chapter refer)] from here on as a way not just of opening out the postcolonial dimensions of ecocriticism, but also of suggesting that the critical study of environmental literature may play its part in the undoing of the epistemological hierarchies and boundaries – nowhere more apparent than under historical and/or contemporary conditions of colo-nialism – that have set humans against other animals, and both against an externalised natural world. What actually counts as 'environmental literature' is moot, and is further complicated by the inclu-sion of animals, the formalised study of which has not always been in keeping with the tenets of ecocriticism as an analytical mode (for a more inclusive approach, see Garrard 2004; also Tiffin *et al.* 2007). For a critique of the insufficiencies of ecocriticism *vis-à-vis* animals, see section two of this Introduction and, especially, Part II of this volume; for a further consideration of environmental modes and genres, see section three of the Introduction and Part I.

3   Such primary transformations frequently laid the foundations for today's international trade patterns, whose inequalities in design and implementation are euphemised as a new, positive 'globalisation'. On the complex connections between imperialism and globalisation – and on globalisation as in effect a form of 'new imperialism' – see Brennan *et al.* (2004) and Harvey (2005); see also endnote 7 below.

4   See, for example, Buell (1995), who, while conceding that there is 'continuing stress and disputation within the [environmental] movement as well as resistance from opposing interests', argues that its primary task has increasingly become to raise public consciousness of interlinked social and environ-mental issues that require immediate action and change (97–98). For a useful thumbnail sketch of shifting emphases both within global environmental movements and the still largely academic, western-based discipline of ecocriticism, see also Heise 2006.

5   While the interdisciplinary remit of postcolonial ecocriticism is increasingly recognised (see, for example, Cilano and DeLoughrey 2007), the position of literature and literary studies within this disciplinary mix is uncertain – as in other branches of contemporary ecocriticism. To some extent, this book observes the conventional distinction between *ecocriticism* as a literature-centred, if not literature-exclusive, approach that highlights cultural representational strategies and *green cultural studies* as a cluster of more conspicuously cross-disciplinary critical initiatives in which the category of 'nature' is looked upon with suspicion and the category of 'culture' is treated inclusively, with a particular view to the analysis of popular forms (Head 1998; O'Brien 2007). According to these terms, the book is more an exercise in ecocriticism than green cultural studies, though – as subse-quent sections illustrate – it is as committed to *animal* as to *environmental* issues, which is by no means always the case in ecocriticism, and which (among other reasons) leads it to adopt a methodologically hybrid, internally inconsistent approach.

6   For a more detailed analysis of Bate's distinction between ecopoetics and ecopolitics, articulated most clearly in his 2000 study *The Song of the Earth* [London: Picador]. For useful summaries of ecocriticism's phenomenological legacy, see also Garrard 2004 (esp. Chapter 6), Heise, and Levin.

7   See, for example, the important work of the American critic Joseph Slaughter, whose 2008 book *Human Rights, Inc.* begins by pointing out the apparent paradox that we are currently living in an Age of Human Rights and an Age of Human Rights Abuse. Slaughter attributes this paradox to what he calls the 'discursive victory of human rights' in the contemporary era (2). Human rights, he says, have triumph[ed] in their apparent banality, but this progress narrative tends to disregard the fact that human rights violations – like the international law designed to prevent them – have become 'increas-ingly systematic, corporate and institutional', with some violations being committed in the 'Orwellian name of human rights themselves' (2). Taking its cue from Slaughter, this book opens out three problem areas for the discourse of rights: universalism, anthropocentrism and globalisation. In the first category, we might say, following Slaughter, that just because (human) rights supposedly have universal application doesn't make them universally legible: there is a considerable gap between what

people *should* know about rights – including their own rights – and what they *actually* know. In the second, the prosecution of human rights is contingent on the general acceptance of the category 'human', but as our book hopefully makes clear, this category can no longer be taken for granted in what is emerging increasingly (if by no means incontestably) as a 'posthuman' world. And finally in the third, the contradictions built into (human) rights discourses tend to be confirmed by current conditions of globalisation: while it is true that the increasing inter-connectedness of modern life allows for the possibility of global systems of adjudication and governance, even the utopian goal of global citizenship, it also provides a rationale fot uneven development and the human rights abuses that stem from it. Similarly, the globalist mantra of interconnectedness isn't necessarily an ecological mantra, often being driven by neo-liberal rather than egalitarian principles, or by neo-liberal principles that use egalitarian principles to their own ends.

References

Anderson, Virginia De John (2004) *Creatures of Empire: How Domestic Animals Transformed Early America*, New York: Oxford University Press.

Armbruster, Karla and Kathleen R. Wallace (eds) (2001) *Beyond Nature Writing: Expanding the Boundaries of Ecocriticism*, Charlottesville: University of Virginia Press.

Ashcroft, Bill, Gareth Griffiths and Helen Tiffin (1989) *The Empire Writes Back: Theory and Practice in Post-Colonial Literatures*, London: Routledge.

Brennan, Timothy (2004), 'From Development to Globalization: Postcolonial Studies and Globalization Theory', in Neil Lazarus (ed.) *The Cambridge Companion to Postcolonial Literary Studies*, Cambridge: Cambridge University Press, 120–38.

Buell, Lawrence (2005) *The Future of Environmental Criticism: Environmental Crisis and Literary Imagination*, Oxford: Blackwell.

—— (1995) *The Environmental Imagination: Thoreau, Nature Writing, and the Formation of American Culture*, Cambridge, MA: Harvard University Press.

Cilano, Cara and Elizabeth DeLoughrey (2007) 'Against Authenticity: Global Knowledges and Postcolonial Ecocriticism', *Interdisciplinary Studies in Literature and Environment* 14, 1, 71–86.

Crosby, Alfred W. (1986) *Ecological Imperialism: The Biological Expansion of Europe, 900–1900*, Cambridge: Cambridge University Press.

—— (1973) *The Columbian Exchange: Biological and Cultural Consequences of 1492*, Connecticut: Greenwood Press.

Curtin, Deane (2005) *Environmental Ethics for a Postcolonial World*, Lanham, MD: Rowman & Littlefield.

Elder, Glen, Jennifer Wolch and Jody Emel (1998) 'Le Pratique Sauvage: Race, Place and the Human–Animal Divide', in Jennifer Wolch and Jody Emel (eds) *Animal Geographies: Place, Politics and Identity in the Nature-Culture Borderlands*, London: Verso, 72–90.

Garrard, Greg (2004) *Ecocriticism*, London: Routledge.

Glotfelty, Cheryll and Harold Fromm (eds) (1996) *The Ecocriticism Reader: Landmarks in Literary Ecology*, Athens: University of Georgia Press.

Guha, Ramachandra (2000) *The Unquiet Woods: Ecological Change and Peasant Resistance in the Himalayas*, Berkeley: University of California Press.

Guha, Ramachandra and Juan Martinez-Alier (1997) *Varieties of Environmentalism: Essays North and South*, London: Earthscan.

Haraway, Donna (1997) *Modest Witness @ Second Millennium: FemaleMan Meets Onco-Mouse: Feminism and Technoscience*, New York: Routledge.

Harvey, David (2005) *The New Imperialism* (2nd edn), New York: Oxford University Press.

Heise, Ursula (2006) 'The Hitchhiker's Guide to Ecocriticism', *PMLA* 121, 2, 503–16.

Huggan, Graham (2004) '"Greening" Postcolonialism: Ecocritical Perspectives', *Modern Fiction Studies* 50, 3, 701–33.

Huggan, Graham and Helen Tiffin (eds) (2007) 'Green Postcolonialism', special issue of *Interventions* 9, 1.

Kimball, Andrew (1996) 'Biocolonization', in J. Mander and E. Goldsmith (eds) *The Case Against the Global Economy*, San Francisco; Sierra Club Books.

Krech, Shepard III (2000) *The Ecological Indian: Myth and History*, New York: Norton.

Lazarus, Neil (2006) 'Postcolonial Studies after the Invasion of Iraq', *New Formations* 59, 10–22.

Merchant, Carolyn (1980) *The Death of Nature: Women, Ecology, and the Scientific Revolution*, London: HarperCollins.

Mukherjee, Pablo (2006) 'Surfing the Second Waves: Amitav Ghosh's Tide Country', *New Formations* 59, 144–57.

Nixon, Rob (2005) 'Environmentalism and Postcolonialism', in Ania Loomba, Suvir Kaul, Matti Bunzl, Antoinette Burton and Jed Esty (eds) *Postcolonial Studies and Beyond*, Durham, NC: Duke University Press, 233–51.

O'Brien, Susie (2007) '"Back to the World": Reading Ecocriticism in a Postcolonial Context', in H. Tiffin (ed.) *Five Emus to the King of Siam: Environment and Empire*, Amsterdam: Rodopi, 177–99.

—— (2001) 'Articulating a World of Difference: Ecocriticism, Postcolonialism and Globalization', *Canadian Literature* 170/171, 140–58.

Plumwood, Val (2003) 'Decolonizing Relationships with Nature', in William H. Adams and Martin Mulligan (eds) *Decolonizing Nature: Strategies for Conservation in a Post-Colonial Era*, London: Earthscan, 51–78.

—— (2001) *Environmental Culture: The Ecological Crisis of Reason*, London: Routledge.

Raglon, Rebecca and Marian Scholtmeijer (2007) '"Animals are not Believers in Ecology": Mapping Critical Differences between Environmental and Animal Advocacy Literatures', *Interdisciplinary Studies in Literature and Environment* 14, 2, 123–39.

Shiva, Vandana (1997) *Biopiracy: the Plunder of Nature and Knowledge*, New York: South End Press.

Tiffin, Helen (ed.) (2007) *Five Emus to the King of Siam: Environment and Empire*, Amsterdam: Rodopi.

Viswanathan, Gauri (1990) *Masks of Conquest: Literary Studies and British Rule in India*, London: Faber & Faber.

Vital, Anthony (2008) 'Toward an African Ecocriticism: Postcolonialism, Ecology and Life & Times of Michael K', *Research in African Literatures* 39, 1, 87–106.

Wasserman, Renata (1984), 'Re-inventing the New World: Cooper and Alencar', *Comparative Literature* 36, 2, 130–45.

Wolfe, Cary (ed.) (2003) *Zoontologies: The Question of the Animal*, Minneapolis: University of Minnesota Press.

—— (1998) 'Old Orders for New: Ecology, Animal Rights, and the Poverty of Humanism', *Diacritics* 28, 2, 21–40.

Worster, Donald (1994) [1977] *Nature's Economy: A History of Ecological Ideas* (2nd edn), Cambridge: Cambridge University Press.

—— (1985) [1977] *Nature's Economy: A History of Ecological Ideas*, Cambridge: Cambridge University Press.

Young, Robert (2003) *Postcolonialism: A Very Short Introduction*, Oxford: Oxford University Press.

Chapter 18

Rob Nixon

ENVIRONMENTALISM AND POSTCOLONIALISM

WHAT WOULD IT MEAN to bring environmentalism into dialogue with postcolonialism? These are currently two of the most dynamic areas in literary studies, yet their relationship continues to be one of reciprocal indifference or mistrust. A broad silence characterizes most environmentalists' stance toward postcolonial literature and theory, while postcolonial critics typically remain no less silent on the subject of environmental literature. What circumstances have shaped this mutual reluctance? And what kinds of intellectual initiatives might best advance an overdue dialogue?

Let me begin with the events that set my thinking on these issues in motion. In October 1995, the *New York Times* Sunday magazine featured an essay by Jay Parini entitled "The Greening of the Humanities."[1] Parini described the rise to prominence of environmentalism in the humanities, especially in literature departments. At the end of the essay, he named twenty-five writers and critics whose work was central to this environmental studies boom. Something struck me as odd about the list, something that passed unmentioned in the article: all twenty-five writers and critics were American.

This unselfconscious parochialism was disturbing, not least because at that time I was active in the campaign to release Ken Saro-Wiwa, the Ogoni author held prisoner without trial for his environmental and human rights activism in Nigeria.[2] Two weeks after Parini's article appeared, the Abacha regime executed Saro-Wiwa, making him Africa's most visible environmental martyr. Here was a writer—a novelist, poet, memoirist, and essayist—who had died fighting the ruination of his Ogoni people's farmland and fishing waters by European and American oil conglomerates in cahoots with a despotic African regime. Yet, clearly, Saro-Wiwa's writings were unlikely to find a home in the kind of environmental literary lineage outlined by Parini. The more ecocriticism I read, the more this impression was confirmed. I encountered some illuminating books by Lawrence Buell, Cheryll Glotfelty, Harold Fromm, Daniel Payne, Scott Slovic, and many others.[3] Yet these authors tended to canonize the same self-selecting genealogy of American writers: Ralph Waldo Emerson, Henry David Thoreau, John Muir, Aldo Leopold, Edward Abbey, Annie Dillard, Terry Tempest Williams, Wendell Berry, and Gary Snyder.[4] All are writers of influence and accomplishment, yet all are drawn from within the boundaries of a single nation. Environmental literary anthologies, college course Web sites, and special journal issues on ecocriticism revealed similar patterns of predominance. Accumulatively, I realized that literary environmentalism was developing de facto as an off-shoot of American studies.

The resulting national self-enclosure seemed peculiar: one might surely have expected environmentalism to be more, not less, transnational than other fields of literary inquiry. It was unfortunate that a writer like Saro-Wiwa, who had long protested what he termed "ecological genocide," could find no place in the environmental canon.[5] Was this because he was an African? Was it because his work revealed no special debt to Thoreau, to the wilderness tradition, or to Jeffersonian agrarianism? Instead, the fraught relations between ethnicity, pollution, and human rights animated Saro-Wiwa's writings. As did the equally fraught relations between local, national, and global politics. It was futile, he recognized, to try to understand or protest the despoiling of his people's water, land, and health within a purely national framework. For Ogoniland's environmental ruin resulted from collaborative plunder by those he dubbed Nigeria's "internal colonialists" and by the unanswerable, transnational power of Shell and Chevron.[6]

Saro-Wiwa's canonical invisibility in the United States seemed all the more telling given the role that America played in his emergence as an environmental writer. The United States buys half of Nigeria's oil and Chevron has emerged as a significant Ogoniland polluter.[7] More affirmatively, it was on a trip to Colorado that Saro-Wiwa witnessed a successful environmental campaign to stop corporate logging.[8] This experience contributed to his decision to mobilize international opinion by voicing his people's claims not just in the language of human rights but in environmental terms as well. Yet it was clear from the prevailing ecocritical perspective in literary studies that someone like Saro-Wiwa—whose environmentalism was at once profoundly local and profoundly international—would be bracketed as an African, the kind of writer best left to the postcolonialists.

I became aware, however, of a second irony: that postcolonial literary critics have, in turn, shown scant interest in environmental concerns, regarding them implicitly as, at best, irrelevant and elitist, at worst as sullied by "green imperialism."[9] Saro-Wiwa's distinctive attempt to fuse environmental and minority rights was unlikely to achieve much of a hearing in either camp.

These, then, were the circumstances that got me thinking about the mutually constitutive silences that have developed between environmental and postcolonial literary studies. Broadly speaking, there are four main schisms between the dominant concerns of postcolonialists and ecocritics. First, postcolonialists have tended to foreground hybridity and cross-culturation. Ecocritics, on the other hand, have historically been drawn more to discourses of purity: virgin wilderness and the preservation of "uncorrupted" last great places.[10] Second, postcolonial writing and criticism largely concern themselves with displacement, while environmental literary studies has tended to give priority to the literature of place. Third, and relatedly, post-colonial studies has tended to favor the cosmopolitan and the transnational. Postcolonialists are typically critical of nationalism, whereas the canons of environmental literature and criticism have developed within a national (and often nationalistic) American framework. Fourth, postcolonialism has devoted considerable attention to excavating or reimagining the marginalized past: history from below and border histories, often along transnational axes of migrant memory. By contrast, within much environmental literature and criticism, something different happens to history. It is often repressed or subordinated to the pursuit of timeless, solitary moments of communion with nature. There is a durable tradition within American natural history writing of erasing the history of colonized peoples through the myth of the empty lands. Postcolonialist critics are wary of the role that this strain of environmental writing (especially wilderness writing) has played in burying the very histories that they themselves have sought to unearth.

Postcolonial critics understandably feel discomfort with preservationist discourses of purity, given the role such discourses have played historically in the racially unequal distribution of post-Enlightenment human rights. In the context of a romantic primordialism, the colonized, especially women, have been repeatedly naturalized as objects of heritage to be owned, preserved, or patronized rather than as the subjects of their own land and legacies. Once cultures have been discursively assimilated to nature (not least through the settler tradition of viewing the United States as "nature's nation"), they have been left more vulnerable to dispossession—whether in the name of virgin wilderness preservation or the creation of nuclear test zones.[11]

Autobiographical divergences have doubtlessly sharpened intellectual differences between postcolonial writers and ecocritics over the politics of purity, place, nation, and history. The preeminent critics associated with postcolonialism—Kwame Anthony Appiah, Homi K. Bhabha, Edward Said, Sara Suleri, Gayatri Chakravorty Spivak, and Gauri Viswanathan, among others—have lived across national boundaries in ways that have given a personal edge to their intellectual investment in questions of dislocation, cultural syncretism, and transnationalism. Conversely, the most prominent environmental writers and critics are mono-nationals with a deep-rooted experiential and imaginative commitment to a particular American locale: Vermont for John Elder, the Sierra Nevada for Gary Snyder, Appalachian Kentucky for Wendell Berry, Utah in Terry Tempest Williams's case.

This tension between a postcolonial preoccupation with displacement and an ecocritical preoccupation with an ethics of place needs to be further situated in terms of cosmopolitanism, on the one hand, and bioregionalism, on the other.[12] Bioregionalism, in Parini's words, entails a responsiveness to "one's local part of the earth whose boundaries are determined by a location's natural characteristics rather than arbitrary administrative boundaries."[13] Gary Snyder and ecocritics like John Elder and David Orr are all vocal advocates of a bioregional ethic. Orr connects ecological destruction to the way people can graduate from college "with obligations to no place in particular. Their knowledge is mostly abstract, equally applicable in New York or San Francisco."[14] Similarly, Elder argues that "the traditional model in education has been cosmopolitanism. I've come to prefer a concentric and bioregional approach to learning. . . . It makes sense—educationally—to begin with local writing; then you expand, adding layers of knowledge."[15]

There is much to be said for this approach: it can help instill in us an awareness of our impact on our immediate environment, help ground our sense of environmental responsibility. However, from a postcolonial perspective, a bioregional ethic poses certain problems. For the concentric rings of the bioregionalists more often open out into transcendentalism than into transnationalism. All too frequently, we are left with an environmental vision that remains inside a spiritualized and naturalized national frame.

Much of the American imaginative and critical literature associated with bioregionalism tends toward a style of spiritual geography premised on what I call spatial amnesia. Within a bioregional center-periphery model, the specificity and moral imperative of the local typically opens out not into the specificities of the international but into transcendental abstraction. In this way, a prodigious amount of American environmental writing and criticism makes expansive gestures while remaining amnesiac toward non-American geographies that vanish over the intellectual skyline.

The environmentalist advocacy of an ethics of place has, all too often, morphed into hostility toward displaced people. Edward Abbey's rants against Mexican immigrants, Mary Austin's anti-Semitism, and the Sierra Club's disastrous referendum on zero immigration all evidence a xenophobic strain running through ethics-of-place environmentalism.[16] With the Sierra Club in mind, Richard Rodriguez has noted how the weeping Amerindian in the public service commercial first became an environmental talisman and then, in a grim historical irony, was invoked against the immigrant descendants of indigenous populations heading north from Mexico and Central America.[17]

An exclusionary ethics of place can easily lapse into jingoistic transcendentalism, as in an essay that the Montana author, Rick Bass, wrote in defense of southern Utah's Red Rock country. "The unprotected wilderness of the West," Bass declared

> is one of our greatest strengths as a country. Another is our imagination, our tendency to think rather than to accept—to challenge, to ask why and what if, to create rather than to destroy. This questioning is a kind of wildness, a kind of strength, that many have said is peculiarly American. Why place that strength in jeopardy? To lose Utah's wilderness would be to strip westerners and all Americans of a raw and vital piece of our soul, our identity, and our ability to imagine. . . . The print of a deer or lion in the sand, in untouched country, as you sleep—it is these things that allow you, allow us, to continue being American, rather than something else, anything else, everything else.[18]

In trying to rally Americans to a worthy preservationist cause, Bass may be resorting here to what Spivak calls "strategic essentialism."[19] After all, it is the American people's representatives who will determine the fate of Red Rock country. But such essentialism, strategic or otherwise, comes at a cost, for Bass aggrandizes and naturalizes the American national character in ways politically perturbing. How do we square his intimation that creative questioning is "peculiarly American" with Americans' widespread, unquestioning ignorance of the disastrous consequences (not least environmental consequences) of US foreign policy? Bass's position is predicated on, among other things, a failure of geographical imagination—a kind of superpower parochialism.

If your frame is Red Rock country, the United States may seem quintessentially a nation of questioners who seek "to create rather than to destroy." But from the vantage point of the 1 million Vietnamese still suffering the health consequences of Agent Orange, or from the perspective of vulnerable microminorities in Nigeria, Ecuador, or West Papua, places where American extraction industry giants like Chevron, Texaco, and Freeport McMoran run rampant, a reluctance to destroy may not seem as definitive an American value. We should temper Bass's blinkered econationalism with Aldo Leopold's sobering reminder of what else it means, in environmental terms, to be an American: "When I go birding in my Ford, I am devastating an oil field, and re-electing an imperialist to get me rubber."[20]

Bass's exaltation of the American soul as pure imagination—a higher soul in search of "untouched country"—has, moreover, a dubious settler lineage. It is precisely such thinking that has impeded the American environmental movement's efforts to diversify its support base. From the perspective of North America's First Peoples, the white soul dream of "untouched country" has meant cultural erasure and dispossession. It contributed, classically, to the Ahwahneechee's eviction from Yosemite as part of Yosemite's reinvention as pure wilderness.[21]

For people relegated to the unnatural margins of nature's nation—like gay minority writers Rodriguez and Melvin Dixon—the wilderness experience can look ominously purified (as opposed to pure). In his ironically titled essay "True West," Rodriguez describes how, setting off on a hike, he hears, three minutes beyond the trailhead, rustling in the bushes. Instead of experiencing transcendental uplift, he fears ambush by "Snow White and the seven militias."[22] And in *Ride Out the Wilderness*, poet-critic Dixon has chronicled how African Americans have associated wilderness with the travail of exile: it is more a place of eviction and historical hauntings than of redemptive silences.[23]

Our intellectual challenge, then, is how to draw on the strengths of bioregionalism without succumbing to ecoparochialism. Here one might heed the call by the British natural historian Richard Mabey for a less brittle, less exclusionary environmental ethics. As Mabey writes, "the challenge, in a world where the differences between native and stranger are fading, is to discover veins of local character which are distinctive without being insular and withdrawn."[24] Yet in response to the blurring of the distinction between native and stranger we have frequently witnessed a defensive tendency to naturalize rootedness and stigmatize as alien people who look or talk differently. Precisely this kind of defensiveness prompted, in a British context, Paul Gilroy to question the racial implications of Raymond Williams's ethics of place.

Williams (whose *The Country and the City* stands as a compendious precursor to ecocriticism) championed what he called "rooted settlements" or "natural communities." These were communities in which "lived, worked and placeable social identities" provided anchorage against the dislocating effects of global capitalism and the abstractions of national identity.[25] However, Williams's advocacy of "natural communities" was accompanied, on occasion, by a suspicion not just of capitalism's dislocating effects but of dislocated people themselves, as when Williams expressed sympathy for local resistance, in rural British communities, to "the most recent immigrations of more visibly different peoples."[26] It proved insufficient, Williams argued, to say that these newcomers "are as British as you are." Because that was to invoke "a merely legal definition of what it is to be British. . . . Any effective awareness of social identity depends on actual and sustained social relationships. To reduce social identity to formal definitions . . . is to collude with the alienated superficialities of 'the nation.' "[27] Writing from a more cosmopolitan, postcolonial perspective, Gilroy voiced alarm at such sentiments. He pointed out that Williams's vision of natural community meant that minority immigrants and their British-born descendants would find themselves typecast as innately foreign and treated as second-class citizens.[28] How many generations, one might ask, does it take to get upgraded to "natural"?

The terms of this exchange are directly pertinent to the project, still in its infancy, of giving environmental literary studies an international dimension.[29] Gilroy's unease with the implications of Williams's remarks dramatizes the need for us to recuperate, imaginatively and politically, experiences of hybridity, displacement, and transnational memory for any viable spatial ethic. Postcolonialism can help diversify our thinking beyond the dominant paradigms of wilderness and Jeffersonian agrarianism in ways that render ecocriticism more accommodating of what I call a transnational ethics of place.

Such an ethics can help us, for example, rethink the pastoral in terms of colonial and postcolonial transnationalism. As an imaginative tradition, English pastoral has long been both nationally definitive and fraught with anxiety. At the heart of English pastoral lies the idea of the nation as garden idyll into which neither labor nor violence intrudes.[30] To stand as a self-contained national heritage landscape, English pastoral has depended on the screening out of colonial spaces and histories, much as the American wilderness ideal has entailed an amnesiac relationship toward the Amerindian wars of dispossession.[31]

But what happens when memories of colonial space intrude on pastoralism, disturbing its pretensions to national self-definition and self-containment? The result is a kind of writing that I call postcolonial pastoral, writing that refracts an idealized nature through memories of environmental and cultural degradation in the colonies. Postcolonial pastoral can be loosely viewed as a kind of environmental double consciousness.

We can see this double consciousness at work in V. S. Naipaul's autobiographical novel *The Enigma of Arrival*, which draws on his life on a manorial estate in Wiltshire—Thomas Hardy country, the heartland of English pastoral.[32] Naipaul self-consciously appends himself, in this novel, to the imaginative lineage of English pastoral by invoking William Constable,

John Ruskin, Oliver Goldsmith, Thomas Gray, William Wordsworth, William Cobbett, Richard Jeffries, and Hardy. In the process, Naipaul engages the centuries-long English tradition of *hortus conclusus*, the enclosed garden.

However, Naipaul's perspective is that of an uprooted immigrant whose vision of England can never be nationally self-enclosed. In other words, his experience of pastoral cannot be contained by the historical and spatial amnesias demanded by an all-English frame. Instead, through the double consciousness of postcolonial pastoral, Naipaul experiences the *hortus conclusus* as indissociable from transnational, colonial environments and memories. The counterpoint to the Wiltshire manor garden that he inhabits is the Trinidadian sugar plantation to which his grandparents were indentured from India. Thus Naipaul views his environment through the double prism of postcolonial pastoral: behind the wealth and tranquility of an English idyll, he remembers the painful, dystopian shadow garden of the transatlantic plantation that helped make that idyll possible.

The most exhilarating recent exploration of transnational shadow gardens has come from the Caribbean historian Richard Drayton. In *Nature's Government*—on the surface, a history of the Royal Botanical Gardens at Kew—Drayton examines, in his words, "how the natural sciences became included in an ideology of 'Improvement' which ordered enclosure at home and expansion abroad."[33] Kew, for Drayton, constitutes not a self-enclosed English space, but part of an extraordinary·web of imperial gardens stretching from St. Vincent to South Africa, Ceylon, Australia, and beyond, gardens that became implicated in global developments not just in botanical knowledge but also in economic power, political policy, and imperial administration. Drayton's book provides some answers to a question that Jamaica Kincaid has posed repeatedly in literary form. Kincaid, the *New Yorker's* former gardening columnist (and the only anticolonial gardening columnist the magazine will likely ever have), is equally impassioned about lupines and colonial history. At the heart of much of her nonfiction stands this blunt question: "What is the relationship between gardening and conquest?"[34]

Kincaid herself exemplifies that relationship. The British transported her violated ancestors to Antigua. But colonial ships also carried to Antigua the alien plants and animals that have since spread across the island. Kincaid's interest in Antigua's environmental viability thus becomes inseparable from her obsession with her ancestral memories of displacement. From where she stands, the separation of botany from the history of slavery seems profoundly unnatural. That much becomes apparent in "The Flowers of Empire," an essay in which Kincaid recounts how, in a moment of botanical rapture, colonial history ambushed her:

> One day I was walking through the glasshouse area of Kew Gardens in London when I came upon the most beautiful hollyhock I had ever seen. Hollyhocks are among my favorite flowers, but I had never seen one quite like this. It had the characteristic large, flared petal, and it was a most beautiful yellow, a clear yellow, as if it—the color yellow—were just born, delicate, just at the beginning of its history as "yellow." It was on looking at the label on which was written its identification that my whole being was sent awhirl. It was not a hollyhock at all but gossypium, the common cotton. Cotton all by itself exists in perfection, with malice toward none. But it played a tormented, malevolent role in the bondage of my ancestors.[35]

Here, as in Naipaul's *Enigma of Arrival*, Kincaid's passion for nature is complicated by her postcolonial double consciousness.

One can read Kincaid's writings against John Elder's insistence that bio-regionalism constitutes a more responsible pedagogical model than cosmopolitanism. For Kincaid confounds such oppositions. *A Small Place*, her non-fictional book about Antigua and tourism, could be read as bioregional in approach: it takes, as its starting point, the natural boundaries of this tiny island. Yet the small place where Kincaid stands, the place where knowledge must begin, is inextricably local *and* transnational.[36] Place is displacement, for British colonists killed off the indigenous inhabitants and replaced them with transported slaves. In the process, the colonists turned what was a well-wooded island into a desert, clearing the forests to grow slave crops—sugar and cotton.[37] As a result of this slave-era environmental degradation, the island has lost its ability to retain water and, to this day, is forced to import it.

This colonial-induced drought has deepened Antigua's economic reliance on tourism. So, ironically, a place scarred by a long history of coercive labor and violence has been reinvented as an Edenic retreat where Europeans and North Americans can experience nature as pure—a paradise beyond reach of work and time. We can thus read *A Small Place* as Kincaid's effort to return this Eden to a transnational ethics of place. In this way, Kincaid allows us to see Antigua, like Naipaul's Trinidad, as a shadow island, a corrective to the spatial amnesia of a self-contained, regenerative English pastoral of the kind evident in, for example, the conclusion to E. M. Forster's *Howard's End*.[38]

"Alien Soil," Kincaid's essay on English and colonial nature, captures the paradox of her position. In England, she is on alien soil; in Antigua, an island where none of the people and few of the plants are native, the soil constitutes the historic ground of her alienation. In Kincaid's words: "I come from a people with a wretched historical relationship to growing things."[39] However, despite that relationship, Kincaid retains a huge passion for botany and gardening—a passion that she recognizes as part of her English inheritance through conquest. Yet she turns that inheritance against itself by insisting that her botanical enthusiasms be refracted through the prism of colonial history.

This is well-illustrated by her response to an entry in the *Oxford Companion of Gardens* on George Clifford, the eighteenth-century Anglo-Dutch banker who built a gargantuan glasshouse filled with plants collected from around the world. That glasshouse proved indispensable to Linnaeus when "Adam-like [he] invented modern plant nomenclature."[40] Kincaid observes how

> the plants in [Clifford's] glasshouse could only have come to him through—and I quote from *Oxford Companion to Gardens*—"the influence of the world trade being developed by maritime powers such as the Netherlands and Great Britain." This being way of expressing an extraordinary history event—"trade being developed," leaving out the nature of the trade being developed: trade in people and the things that they possessed, plants, animals, and so on—never ceases to amaze me.
>
> I do not mind the glasshouse; I do not mind the botanical garden. This is not so grand a gesture on my part. It is mostly an admission of defeat—to mind would be completely futile; I cannot do anything about it anyway. I only mind the absence of this acknowledgment: that perhaps every good thing that stands before us comes at a great cost to someone else.[41]

Kincaid's pained reflections here echo Walter Benjamin's insistence that "there is no document of civilization which is not at the same time a document of barbarism."[42]

Ecological literary critics have been slow to absorb the kinds of provocative transnational thinking that has gathered strength in other disciplines central to the greening of the humanities, disciplines like history, geography, and anthropology.[43] Postcolonial literary critics, by contrast, have tended to shy away from environmental issues as if they were soft, Western, bourgeois concerns. But the notion that environmental politics are a luxury politics for the world's wealthy is clearly untenable. As Gayatri Spivak, one of the few postcolonial literary scholars to even allude to environmental issues, has argued, "the local in the South directly engages global greed."[44]

Any postcolonialist dismissal of environmentalism as marginal to "real" politics is belied by the current proliferation of indigenous environmental movements across the global South. Saro-Wiwa was not some isolated epic hero: his actions were indicative of a myriad non-Western environmental campaigns locally motivated, locally led, and internationally inflected. We are witnessing, on the environmental front, something similar to the mutation of feminism, which was often dismissed, twenty or thirty years ago, as white, privileged, and irrelevant to the needs of third world women. We have seen what counts as feminism radically changed by the rise of local social movements that have decentered and diversified the agenda of women's rights in ethnic, geographic, religious, sexuality, and class terms. In recent years, we have witnessed a similar decentering in environmentalism, one that has begun to shift the terms of the decisive debates away from issues like purity preservation and Jeffersonian-style agrarianism.

As William Beinart and Peter Coates have argued, "all human activity alters the composition of the natural world which in itself is never static. A critique which regards all change as decay begs the very legitimacy of human survival."[45] Non-Western environmental movements are typically alert to the interdependence of human survival and environmental change in situations where the illusion of a static purity cannot be sustained, far less exalted as an ideal. Such movements are also typically aware of how easily foreign forces—transnational corporations, the World Bank, or NGOs, often in cahoots with authoritarian regimes—can destroy the delicate, always mutable, mesh between cultural traditions, social justice, and ecosystems.

In Ecuador, one such locally led campaign, Acción Ecológica, mobilized the nation's Confederation of Indigenous Nationalities against Texaco, whose ransacking of the environment echoed the plunder, ten thousand miles away, that generated Nigeria's Movement of the Survival of the Ogoni People.[46] In India, the corporatizing of biodiversity has proved a major rallying point: 200,000 Indian farmers descended on Delhi in the so-called Seed Satyagraha to protest transnational efforts to wrest control over the reproduction and distribution of seeds from traditional farmers.

Wangari Maathai, Kenya's first woman professor, has been imprisoned and tortured for helping instigate mass tree plantings to protest rampant deforestation. In 1998, when Kenya's kleptocratic government began expropriating and selling off the publicly held Karura Forest to developers of luxury housing, students at the University of Nairobi and Kenyatta University launched another dissident tree planting. The government's brutal response produced campus riots that closed down both universities in defense of what student leader Wycliffe Mwebi called the "moral right to defend the environment against a corrupt land grab."[47]

If it is no longer viable to view environmentalism as a Western luxury, how are we best to integrate environmental issues into our approach to postcolonial literature and vice versa? Among many possible productive starting places, one could turn to the current wave of interest in Black Atlantic studies and seek to give it an environmental dimension. Black Atlanticism stands as one of the most energizing paradigms to have emerged in literary and cultural studies during the past decade. Yet the questions it raises—about transnational identities, the triangular trade in people and commodities, the multiple passages of modernity—remain cordoned off from environmental considerations. The literary possibilities are alluring: not just in Kincaid's oeuvre but also in the work of writers like Derek Walcott (starting with his assertion, "the sea is history"), Aimé Césaire, Wilson Harris, Michelle Cliff, and Patrick Chamoiseau, among others.[48]

By integrating approaches from environmental and Black Atlantic studies, we might help bridge the divide between the ecocritical study of America's minority literatures (a recent growth area) and the ecocritical study of post-colonial literatures, which remains extremely rudimentary. The recent influential anthology, *Literature and the Environment* evidences the problems with this divide.[49] In one important regard, this makes for an encouraging volume: it is the first environmental anthology to include a significant spread of minority writers, many of them foregrounding issues that the environmental justice movement has prioritized. By acknowledging what Langston Hughes, bell hooks, Louis Owens, Clarissa Pinkola Estes, and Marilou Awiakta (among others) add to environmental debate and testimony, the anthology marks a shift away from the American ecocritical obsession with wilderness writing and the literature of Jeffersonian agrarianism. Several of the essays address indigenous land rights, community displacement, and toxicity, often in the context of urban or poor rural experience. Encouragingly, these are some of the American concerns that most readily connect with the environmental priorities that predominate in postcolonial writing. It is here that one recognizes the richest possibilities for a more transnational rapprochement.

However, in helping redefine the field, *Literature and the Environment* (despite its expansive title) restricts itself to an almost all-American cast. Of the 104 contributions, only one is non-American: a maverick Wordsworth poem. So while applauding this diversification of environmental literature, we should be careful not to confuse American multiculturalism with international diversity, or assume that the latter flows automatically from the former. The urgent need for a more global inclusiveness remains unaddressed.

The geographical distribution of interest in Lawrence Buell's otherwise brilliant recent study, *Writing for an Endangered World: Literature, Culture, and Environment in the U.S. and Beyond*, raises some similar issues.[50] Buell's earlier, and justly influential, study *The Environmental Imagination* centered on American nature writing and was composed in the shadow of Thoreau. Buell's sequel, however, takes a more generous, creative view of what counts as environmental literature, opening up questions of toxicity, biodegradation, urban experience, and "engineered environments."[51] This enables Buell to engage, through detailed readings, a series of American minority writers: Gwendolyn Brooks, John Edgar Wideman, Richard Wright, and Linda Hogan, among them.[52]

However, the expanded American diversity of Buell's later work is not matched by an attentiveness to diversity elsewhere. The limitations of trying to generate a global vision from an American-centered account of environmental writing becomes evident in Buell's solitary reading of a postcolonial text, Mahasweta Devi's "Pterodactyl, Puran Sahay, and Pirtha," a Bengali short story translated into English by Gayatri Spivak.[53]

After praising "Pterodactyl" as a trenchant fiction of environmental justice, Buell remarks that the novella's "sometimes esoteric cultural particularism . . . may seem to make it an odd detour from the U.S.-focused texts I have mainly been discussing."[54] The image of a "detour" and the reference to Devi's "esoteric cultural particularism" foreground the intellectual challenge for ecocritics of moving beyond a center-periphery model. The unsettling implication is that somehow American texts transcend "cultural particularism," are always already universalized in ways that postcolonial ones are not.

In terms of bridging possibilities, Buell's work on toxic discourse represents the most promising recent theoretical initiative.[55] The prospects it opens up for comparative international readings are almost inexhaustible. Rebecca Solnit, for instance, has brilliantly evoked the resistance to nuclear testing in Nevada by Western Shoshone battling for their land rights in collaboration with environmental protestors. Yet instead of placing Solnit's *Savage Dreams* within the standard Americanist ecocanon, it could be repositioned in an international context that would engage, comparatively, the land claims and toxic history of Australia's Aboriginal downwinders, as recounted in *Yami: The Autobiography of Yami Lester*.[56] Solnit and Lester, in turn, could be read productively alongside Arundhati Roy's *The Cost of Living*, Marilynne Robinson's *Mother Country*, and Scott Malcomson's *Tuturani*, which explore, respectively, the lethal repercussions of nuclear testing and nuclear pollution in South Asia, Britain, and the Marshall Islands and Bikini Atoll.[57]

Much of the new work to be done is comparative: the Australian Aboriginal environmentalist Fabienne Bayet's reflections on indigenous traditions of nonproprietary land possession bear fruitful comparison, for example, with Leslie Marmon Silko's account of Pueblo land values.[58] However, for the work ahead, we cannot rely only on American terms of comparison. How, for example, would our assumptions about what constitutes environmental literature have to change if we generated eco-inflected rereadings of classic African novels like Bessie Head's *Where Rain Clouds Gather*, Chinua Achebe's *Things Fall Apart*, Cheikh H. Kane's *Ambiguous Adventure*, J. M. Coetzee's *Life and Times of Michael K*, and Ngugi wa Thiong'o's *A Grain of Wheat?*[59]

International oil literature offers us, pedagogically, an unusually rich resource. We can draw on it both to diversify the environmental literary canon and dramatize for students the connections between questions of transnational environmental justice and their local consumer choices.[60] Oil literature allows us to connect writers as various as Upton Sinclair (on the California oil boom), the Nigerians Saro-Wiwa, J. P. Clark, and Tayo Olafioye, the great Jordanian-born novelist Abdelrahman Munif, and Joe Kane (on Texaco in Ecuador).[61]

But we need to go beyond simply diversifying the canon; we need to re-imagine the prevailing paradigms. That much is evident from the enormous difficulty Saro-Wiwa had in gaining an audience in the United States and Europe. When he first appealed to Greenpeace representatives, they said they did not work in Africa—it was off their environmental map.[62] Wherever he went, Saro-Wiwa was treated as an unfathomable anomaly—an African writer claiming to be an environmentalist? And claiming, moreover, that his people's human rights were being violated by environmental ethnocide? Part of Saro-Wiwa's problem in gaining a hearing for the Ogoni was not just economic and political—it was imaginative as well.

Saro-Wiwa campaigned for environmental justice. But he also campaigned, in effect, against a center-periphery paradigm. He had to contend not just with environmental racism but with prejudicial failures of geographical imagining. In American intellectual and media terms, a region like Ogoniland is almost completely unimaginable.[63] Yet the writings of Saro-Wiwa, like those of Arundhati Roy, allow us to engage (in ways that the self-perpetuating national lineage of Thoreau, Muir, Abbey, Snyder, and the others does not) environmental politics through conflicts between subnational microminorities, autocratic nation-states, and transnational macro-economic powers.[64]

In trying to diversify our thinking, we need to ensure that we do not end up asking an environmental variant of Saul Bellow's dismissive question: "Where is the Zulu Tolstoy?" If we go scouting the equatorial forests for the Timorese Thoreau (or his Cameroonian cousin), we will return alone. Nor can we content ourselves with the current move toward nominal international variety—an Ishimure Michiko or Wordsworth text decorating the American ecocanon much as Virginia Woolf or Jane Austen once graced otherwise all-male courses and, later, a nominal Toni Morrison or Alice Walker was used to "diversify" white courses on women's writing.[65]

To reject an add-on solution to the challenges of diversity is to refuse a vision of environmentalism as invented at the center and exported to (or imposed on) the periphery.[66] Such center-periphery thinking constitutes both a source of postcolonialists' pervasive indifference to environmentalism and, conversely, a source of the debilitating strain of superpower parochialism that lingers among many American ecocritics and writers. Just as subaltern studies embarked on a project of provincializing the West, so, too, we need to provincialize American environmentalism if we are to regenerate and diversify the field.

Ours is an age in which the combined wealth of the world's 550 billionaires exceeds that of the 3 billion humans who constitute the planet's poorest 50 percent. Five hundred corporations command 70 percent of world trade. In an era of giga-mergers and nanosecond transnationalisms, we cannot persist with the kind of isolationist thinking that has, in different ways, impeded both postcolonial and ecocritical responses to globalization.[67] The isolation of postcolonial literary studies from environmental concerns has limited the field's intellectual reach. Likewise, ecocriticism's predominantly American studies frame has proven inadequate, not least because we cannot afford to stop seeing the broader connections. Invisibility has its costs, as Arundhati Roy reminds us: globalization, she observes, is "like a light which shines brighter and brighter on a few people and the rest are in darkness, wiped out. They simply can't be seen. Once you get used to not seeing something, then, slowly, it's no longer possible to see it."[68] In the classroom, in our writing, and in the media, we need to widen that beam.

The dialogue I have sought to outline can help us rethink oppositions between bioregionalism and cosmopolitanism, between transcendentalism and transnationalism, between an ethics of place and the experience of displacement. Through such a rapprochement, we can begin to think, simultaneously, for example, about nature-induced states of transport and the vast, brutal history of humans forcibly transported. In the process, we can aspire to a more historically answerable and geographically expansive sense of what constitutes our environment and which literary works we entrust to voice its parameters. This is an ambitious but crucial task, not least because, for the foreseeable future, literature departments are likely to remain influential players in the greening of the humanities.

Notes

1   Jay Parini, "The Greening of the Humanities," *New York Times* Sunday magazine, October 23, 1995, 52–53.
2   Rob Nixon, "The Oil Weapon," *New York Times*, November 17, 1995. For a fuller discussion of the issues at stake, see Nixon, "Pipedreams."
3   Buell, *The Environmental Imagination*; Glotfelty and Fromm, *The Ecocritical Reader*; Payne, *Voices in the Wilderness*; and Slovic, *Seeking Awareness in American Nature Writing*. Buell does stress the need to give international dimension to environmental literary studies, but in design and emphasis, *The Environmental Imagination* remains within an Americanist paradigm.
4   For a classic instance of these limitations, see Oelschlaeger's *The Idea of Wilderness*.
5   Saro-Wiwa, *Nigeria*, 71.
6   Saro-Wiwa, *A Month and A Day*, 7.
7   Ibid., 80.
8   Ibid., 79.
9   For an influential postcolonial challenge to the American wilderness obsession, see Guha, "Radical American Environmentalism and Wilderness Preservation."
10   For an invaluable critique of the wilderness tradition of "purity," see Cronon, "The Trouble with Wilderness."
11   See J. M. Coetzee's terse assessment that "it is certainly true that the politics of expansion has uses for the rhetoric of the sublime." Coetzee, *White Writing*, 62.
12   For an excellent discussion of the dangers of an excessive preoccupation with displacement, see Kumar, *Passport Photos*, 13–14. See also, Ian Buruma, "The Romance of Exile," *New Republic*, February 12, 2001, 23–30.
13   Parini, "The Greening of the Humanities," 53.
14   Quoted in ibid., 53.
15   Quoted in ibid., 53.
16   On Abbey's anti-immigrant environmentalism, which became more prominent in his later years, see Scarce, *Eco-warriors*, 92. For Austin's anti-Semitism, see Athanasiou, *Divided Planet*, 297.
17   Rodriguez, *Days of Obligation*, 5.
18   Rick Bass, "A Landscape of Possibility," *Outside*, December 1995, 100–101.
19   Spivak, *The Post-colonial Critic*, 72.
20   Aldo Leopold, "Game and Wildlife Conservation," in Leopold, *Game Management*, 23.
21   For a brilliant account of this process, see Solnit, *Savage Dreams*, 215–385.

22 Rodriguez, "True West," 331.

23 Dixon, *Ride Out the Wilderness*.

24 Mabey, *Landlocked*, 71.

25 Williams, *Towards 2000*, 195. For a related perspective on community and place, see Williams, "Homespun Philosophy," *New Statesman and Society*, June 19, 1992, 8–9. See also his *The Country and the City*.

26 Williams, *Towards 2000*, 195.

27 Ibid., 195.

28 Gilroy, *"There Ain't No Black in the Union Jack,"* 49–50. Stuart Hall questions Williams's prioritizing of rooted settlements in similar terms. See Hall, "Our Mongrel Selves," *New Statesman and Society*, June 19, 1992, 6–7.

29 To date, the most useful resource on environmental writing beyond the United States is Murphy's *Literature of Nature*. Scott Slovic has sought to counter the complaint "that environmental literature is an exclusively Americanist preserve" by pointing to, among other things, the rise in international submissions to the premier journal in the field, *ISLE: Interdisciplinary Studies in Literature and Environment*. Yet the subjects and authors of environmental literary criticism remain overwhelmingly American. The internationalizing of ecocriticism, moreover, should not simply involve additive diversification in a center-periphery fashion. As I have argued above, we need to address the way ecocriticism's dominant models and intellectual priorities remain skewed by their American genesis, not least, by their failure to engage the rich traditions of postcolonial literature and thought. See Slovic, "Forum on Literatures of the Environment," 1102.

30 Williams's *The Country and the City* remains the most wide-ranging account of the English pastoral tradition.

31 For the most eloquent and economical account of the relationship between wilderness thinking and Amerindian dispossession in the United States, see Cronon, "The Trouble with Wilderness," 95–96. Solnit's *Savage Dreams* is also quite brilliant in this regard.

32 Naipaul, *The Enigma of Arrival*.

33 Drayton, *Nature's Government*, xvi.

34 Kincaid, *My Garden*, 132.

35 Ibid., 139.

36 Kincaid, *A Small Place*.

37 Ibid., 16.

38 Forster, *Howard's End*.

39 Kincaid, "Alien Soil," in Kidder, ed., *The Best American Essays*, 211.

40 Kincaid, *My Garden*, 143.

41 Ibid., 137.

42 Walter Benjamin, "Theses on the Philosophy of History," in Benjamin, *Illuminations*, 256.

43 One thinks here of innovative works like Grove, *Green Imperialism*; Griffiths and Robin, *Ecology and Empire*; Arnold and Guha, *Nature, Culture, Imperialism*; and Beinart and Coates, *Environment and History*.

44 Spivak, "Attention: Postcolonialism!" 166.

45 Beinart and Coates, *Environment and History*, 3. This book offers a fine comparative history of national parks in the United States and South Africa.

46 See Kane, *Savages*; Sawyer, "The Politics of Petroleum"; and Selverston, *The 1990 Indigenous Uprising in Ecuador*.

47 Quoted in ibid., 18.

48 For the rich possibilities to be found in this kind of intellectual rapprochement, see the Canadian critic Casteel's, "New World Pastoral."

49 Anderson, Slovic, and O'Grady, *Literature and the Environment*. Of the 104 essays and poems included by the editors, 26 are by African American, Amerindian, Latina/o, or Asian American writers. This marks a significant advance over the more typical spectrum of Glotfelty and Fromm's influential *Ecocriticism Reader*, which found room for only two "minority" essays out of twenty-six.

50 Buell, *Writing for an Endangered World*.

51 Ibid., 24.

52 The broader scheme of the second book also encourages Buell to discuss some urban European writers, notably Charles Dickens, Virginia Woolf, and James Joyce.

53 Mahasweta Devi, "Pterodactyl, Puran Sahay, and Pirtha," in Devi, *Imaginary Maps*, 95–96.

54 Buell, *Writing for an Endangered World*, 230.

55 ibid., 30–54.

56 Lester, *Yami*.

57 Roy, *The Cost of Living*; Robinson, *Mother Country*; and Malcomson, *Tuturani*.

58   See Bayet, "Overturning the Doctrine"; and Silko, *"Yellow Woman" and "A Beauty of the Spirit."*
59   Head, *Where Rain Clouds Gather*; Achebe, *Things Fall Apart*; Kane, *Ambiguous Adventure*; Coetzee, *Life and Times of Michael K.*; and Thiong'o, *Grain of Wheat*. Are there ways, for example, to link Ngugi's account of a resistant Gikuyu culture of the forest during the anticolonial struggle with student efforts, in the 1990s, to safeguard Kenyan forests from neocolonial rapacity? For a preliminary foray into connections of this sort, see Slaymaker, "Echoing the Other(s)."
60   Rob Nixon, "The Hidden Lives of Oil," *Chronicle of Higher Education*, April 5, 2002, B7–B9.
61   Sinclair, *Oil!*; Clark, *All for Oil*; and Olafioye, *A Carnival of Looters*; Kane, *Savages*. The finest, and certainly the most teachable, of Munif's novels is *Cities of Salt*.
62   See Saro-Wiwa, *A Month and a Day*, 88.
63   Ogoniland belongs to the tropical belt that runs through the Amazon, West and Central Africa, Indonesia, and Papua and New Guinea, a zone that possesses the world's most diverse, ethnically fractured populations (four hundred ethnicities in Nigeria, several thousand in New Guinea), as well as unusually rich natural resources—oil, precious minerals, and timber. It is in this strip that American, European, and Japanese extraction-industry multinationals operate (frequently supported by dictatorial regimes) with maximum violence and impunity.
64   Pedagogically, an excellent place to start would be to read Saro-Wiwa's prison diary, *A Month and a Day* alongside both Wole Soyinka's prefigurative early play *The Swamp Dwellers* and recent work by Nigerian environmental philosopher Kolawole Owolabi, for instance, *Because of Our Future*. For a resonant comparison, one could turn to Joe Kane's account in *Savages* of another contest between an equatorial microminority (Ecuador's Huarorani Indians) and a petroleum multinational (Texaco).
65   The two contemporary ecocritics who seem most alive to the need to internationalize the field are Jonathan Bate and Patrick D. Murphy. Bate's *The Song of the Earth* places English romantic poetry center stage, but includes ecocritical readings of several contemporary British and American poets, as well as the West Indian poet Edward Kamau Brathwaite and the Australian writer Les Murray. Murphy's analyses, while predominantly American, are more geographically expansive than most. He includes a fine chapter on Ishimure Michiko and another entitled "Worldly Diversity." Murphy's title, *Further Afield in the Study of Nature-Oriented Literature*, however, suggests (like Buell's "detour") the tenacity of ecocriticism's center-periphery model.
66   For an excellent theoretical account of the conceptual limitations that result from a center-periphery model, see Timothy Mitchell, "The Stage of Modernity," in Mitchell, *Questions of Modernity*, 1–34. Mitchell's critique focuses on Western-centered genealogies of modernity, but many of his insights can be applied adaptively to ecocriticism.
67   Clearly, a narrowing of the divides between these two powerful intellectual currents only marks a beginning. In search of a truly international, interdisciplinary response, we would need to move beyond postcolonialism's Anglo- and Francophone emphases toward more fully global imaginings. But a postcolonial-environmental rapprochement would represent an invaluable start.
68   Roy quoted in Madeleine Bunting, "Dam Buster," *Guardian* (London), July 28, 2001.

References

Achebe, Chinua. *Things Fall Apart*. New York: Knopf, 1994.

Anderson, Lorraine, Scott Slovic, and John O'Grady, eds. *Literature and the Environment: A Reader on Nature and Culture*. New York: Longman, 1999.

Arnold, David, and Ramachandra Guha, eds. *Nature, Culture, Imperialism: Essays of the Environmental History of South Asia*. Delhi: Oxford University Press, 1995.

Athanasiou, Tom. *Divided Planet: The Ecology of Rich and Poor*. Boston: Little, Brown, 1996.

Bate, Jonathan. *The Song of the Earth*. Cambridge, MA: Harvard University Press, 2000.

Bayet, Fabienne. "Overturning the Doctrine: Indigenous People and Wilderness—Being Aboriginal in the Environmental Movement." In *The Great New Wilderness Debate*, ed. J. Baird Callicott and Michael P. Nelson, 314–24. Athens: University of Georgia Press, 1998.

Beinart, William, and Peter Coates. *Environment and History: The Taming of Nature in the USA and South Africa*. London: Routledge, 1995.

Benjamin, Walter. *Illuminations*. Ed. Hannah Arendt. Trans. Harry Zohn. New York: Harcourt, Brace, and World, 1968.

Buell, Lawrence. *The Environmental Imagination: Thoreau, Nature Writing, and the Formation of American Culture*. Cambridge, MA: Harvard University Press, 1996.

———. *Writing for an Endangered World: Literature, Culture, and Environment in the U.S. and Beyond*. Cambridge, MA: Harvard University Press, 2001.

Casteel, Sarah Phillips. "New World Pastoral: The Caribbean Garden and Emplacement in Gisele Pineau and Shani Mootoo." *Interventions* 5, no. 1 (2003): 12–28.

Clark, J. P. *All for Oil*. Lagos: Malthouse Press, 2000.

Coetzee, J. M. *Life and Times of Michael K*. New York: Penguin, 1995.

———. *White Writing: On the Culture of Letters in South Africa*. New Haven, CT: Yale University Press, 1988.

Cronon, William. "The Trouble with Wilderness; Or, Getting Back to the Wrong Nature." In *Uncommon Ground: Rethinking the Human Place in Nature*, ed. Cronon, 69–90. New York: Norton, 1996.

Dixon, Melvin. *Ride Out the Wilderness: Geography and Identity in Afro-American Literature*. Urbana: University of Illinois Press, 1987.

Drayton, Richard. *Nature's Government: Science, Imperial Britain, and the "Improvement" of the World*. New Haven, CT: Yale University Press, 2000.

Forster, E. M. *Howard's End*. 1910. New York: Penguin, 1975.

Gilroy, Paul. *"There Ain't No Black in the Union Jack"*: The Cultural Politics of Race and Nation. London: Hutchinson, 1987.

Glotfelty, Cheryll, and Harold Fromm, eds. *The Ecocritical Reader: Landmarks in Literary Ecology*. Athens: University of Georgia Press, 1996.

Griffiths, Tom, and Libby Robin. *Ecology and Empire: Environmental History of Settler Societies*. Seattle: University of Washington Press, 1997.

Grove, Richard. *Green Imperialism: Colonial Expansion, Tropical Island Edens, and the Origins of Environmentalism, 1600–1860*. Cambridge: Cambridge University Press, 1995.

Guha, Ranajit. *Elementary Aspects of Peasant Insurgency in Colonial India*. Delhi: Oxford University Press, 1983.

Head, Bessie. *Where Rain Clouds Gather*. New York: Heinemann, 1996.

Kane, Cheikh H. *Ambiguous Adventure*. Trans. Katherine Woods. New York: Heinemann, 1972.

Kane, Joe. *Savages*. New York: Knopf, 1995.

Kincaid, Jamaica. "Alien Soil." In *The Best American Essays*, ed. Tracy Kidder. Boston: Houghton Mifflin, 1994.

———. *My Garden*. New York: Farrar, Straus, Giroux, 2001.

———. *A Small Place*. New York: Farrar, Straus, Giroux, 1988.

Kumar, Amitava. *Passport Photos*. Berkeley: University of California Press, 2000.

Leopold, Aldo. *Game Management*. 1933. Madison: University of Wisconsin Press, 1986.

Lester, Yami. *Yami: The Autobiography of Yami Lester*. New York: Iad, 2000.

Mabey, Richard. *Landlocked: In Pursuit of the Wild*. London: Sinclair Stevenson, 1994.

Malcomson, Scott. *Tuturani*. New York: Poseidon, 1990.

Mitchell, Timothy, ed. *Questions of Modernity*. Minneapolis: University of Minnesota Press, 2000.

Munif, Abdelrahman. *Cities of Salt*. Trans. Peter Theroux. New York: Vintage, 1987.

Murphy, Patrick. *Further Afield in the Study of Nature-Oriented Literature*. Charlottesville: University of Virginia Press, 2000.

Naipaul, V. S. *The Enigma of Arrival: A Novel*. New York: Knopf, 1987.

Oelschlaeger, Max. *The Idea of Wilderness: From Prehistory to the Age of Ecology*. New Haven, CT: Yale University Press, 1991.

Olafioye, Tayo. *A Carnival of Looters: Poems*. Ibadan, Nigeria: Kraft, 2000.

Owolabi, Kolawole. *Because of Our Future: The Imperative for an Environmental Ethic for Africa*. Ibadan: IFRA/African Book Builders, 1996.

Payne, Daniel G. *Voices in the Wilderness: American Nature Writing and Environmental Politics*. Hanover, NH: University Press of New England, 1996.

Robinson, Marilynne. *Mother Country*. New York: Faber, 1989.

Rodriguez, Richard. *Days of Obligation: An Argument with My Mexican Father*. New York: Viking, 1992.

———. "True West." In *The Anchor Essay Annual: The Best of 1997*, ed. Phillip Lopate. New York, 1998.

Roy, Arundhati. *The Cost of Living*. London: Modern Library, 1999.

Saro-Wiwa, Ken. *A Month and a Day: A Detention Diary*. London: Penguin, 1995.

———. *Nigeria: The Brink of Disaster*. Port Harcourt, Nigeria: Saros International Publishers, 1991.

Sawyer, Suzana. "The Politics of Petroleum: Indigenous Contestation of Multinational Oil Development in the Ecuadorian Amazon." *MacArthur Consortium Occasional Papers Series*. MacArthur Program, University of Minnesota, 1997.

Scarce, Rick. *Eco-warriors: Understanding the Radical Environmental Movement*. Chicago: Nobel, 1990.

Selverston, Melina. "The 1990 Indigenous Uprising in Ecuador: Politicized Ethnicity as Social Movement." *Papers on Latin America, no. 32*. New York: Columbia University Institute of Latin American and Iberian Studies, 1993.

Sinclair, Upton. *Oil!* 1926. Berkeley: University of California Press, 1997.

Slaymaker, William. "Echoing the Other(s): The Call of Global Green and Black African Responses." *PMLA* 116, no. 1 (2001): 129–44.

Slovic, Scott. "Forum on Literatures of the Environment." *PMLA* 116, no. 5 (1999): 1089–1106.

Solnit, Rebecca. *Savage Dreams: A Journey into the Landscape Wars of the American West*. Berkeley: University of California Press, 1999.

Soyinka, Wole. *The Swamp Dwellers. In Collected Plays*. Oxford: Oxford University Press, 1973.

Spivak, Gayatri Chakravorty. "Attention: Postcolonialism!" *Journal of Caribbean Studies* 12, nos. 2–3 (1997–98): 159–79.

———. *The Post-colonial Critic: Interviews, Strategies, Dialogues*. New York: Routledge, 1990.

Thiong'o, Ngugi wa. *Grain of Wheat*. New York: Heinemann, 1994.

Williams, Raymond. *The Country and the City*. New York: Oxford University Press, 1973.

———. *Towards 2000*. London: Chatto and Windus, 1983.

Chapter 19

Anna Lowenhaupt Tsing

NATURAL UNIVERSALS AND
THE GLOBAL SCALE

To see a World in a Grain of Sand
And a Heaven in a Wild Flower,
Hold Infinity in the palm of your hand
And Eternity in an hour.
　　　　　—from William Blake,
　　　　　"Auguries of Innocence"

Generalization. The action or process of generalizing, i.e. of forming, and expressing in words, general notions or propositions obtained from the observation and comparison of individual facts or appearances; also, an instance of this.[1]

MANY THINGS ARE SAID to be universal: freedom, money, love. But the two most historically successful universal claims—which continue to form exemplars for all universality—are still God and Nature. The universality of God and the universality of Nature are historically connected; in the European Renaissance, the stirrings of modern science conceived the latter on the model of the former. Only because God was known to be universal could Nature be depicted that way. The connection between God and Nature has continued to inspire the musings of theologians, scientists, and naturalists, reminding us of the importance of reason and mystery in appreciating each domain. Yet readers interested in how God came to be universal will have to consult other texts. This chapter enters the story midway to ask about the universality of capital-N Nature, that is, the awe-inspiring, lawlike system-aticity of the cosmos and of life on earth.

Nature and the globe have helped make each other. Today's most powerful claims about the nature of the globe refer us to global Nature: If universal laws of Nature can be established, then the globe forms an orderly part of them. The globe is a node for the expression of universal logic. Scale-making, in turn, is a foundational move in establishing the neutrality and universalism of Nature; only if observations are compatible and collapsible across scales can they be properly described by a universal logic. Yet to "think globally" is no easy task. To recognize the globe as the relevant unit for our imaginations requires work. Moreover, establishing Nature has never been simple.

How does the universality of Nature operate in a world of friction? I approach this question through looking at the process of "generalization," in which small details support great visions and the universal is discovered in particularities. Two features of generalization intrigue me. First, generalization to the universal requires a large space of compatibility among disparate particular facts and observations. As long as facts are apples and oranges, one cannot generalize across them; one must first see them as "fruit" to make general claims. Compatibility standardizes difference. It allows transcendence: the general can rise above the particular. For this, compatibility must pre-exist the particular facts being examined; and it must unify the field of inquiry. The searcher for universal truths must establish an *axiom of unity*—whether on spiritual, aesthetic, mathematical, logical, or moral principles.

Second, tentative and contingent collaborations among disparate knowledge seekers and their disparate forms of knowledge can turn incompatible facts and observations into compatible ones. Just as tiny convergences in incompatible testimonies at a criminal trial can establish a line of truth, the founding lines through which we learn to recognize Nature are often established in convergent opinions. Convergences offer legitimacy and charisma to nascent categories. They offer bridges over unrecognizable difference. Convincing universals must be able to travel with at least some facility in the world, and this requires negotiations across incompatible difference. Upon occasion, these give rise to collaboratively agreed upon Natural objects. The unfamiliar becomes the familiar through this process, and generalization can occur.

What is most striking to me about these two features of generalization is the way they cover each other up. The specificity of collaborations is erased by pre-established unity; the a priori status of unity is denied by turning to its instantiation in collaborations. Buoyed by axioms of unity, collaborations create convincingly agreed upon observations and facts that then appear to support generalization *directly*, that is, without the prior mediation of the collaboration. The contingency of the collaboration, and its exclusions, no longer seem relevant because the facts come to "speak for themselves." The pre-evidential status of the axiom of unity fades into the background, too, when facts naturalized through collaboration can be called on as the natural basis of generalization.

Generalization to the universal is at the heart of much analytic work; it makes it possible to devise market principles from particular transactions, to interpret events within Biblical prophecy, to mobilize class struggle, and to make scientific observations speak to general laws. No one I know wants to accept every claim made through generalization—or to dismiss them all out of hand. To characterize the process of generalization is not to reject all its products. I am not making fun of this procedure in studying it; I have no interest in ironic dismissals. I write here only about generalizations that I care about.

In this chapter, I illustrate the interplay of the two processes of generalization I have introduced in defining the global scale together with universal Nature. For this, I have chosen discrepant examples: the emergence of botanical science, American nature loving, mathematical climate modeling, and an international forestry accord. Each offers a different axiom of unity through which individual observations are made available for generalization. Botanical science first generalized on the basis of God's will, and only later substituted evolutionary process. American nature loving proposed a spiritual and aesthetic unity for Nature. Climate modeling has offered systems logic. Forest management advocates turned to international politics. Each project, in turn, has built from a divergent history of collaborative relations, such as those that connect botanical collectors across the world, or link nature lovers and promoters of tourism, or join scientists and policy makers. I show how these contingent collaborations are necessary to the process of generalization even as they are covered up by it. Axioms of unity and collaborations both need each other and hide each other; generalization—with its particularistic exclusions and biases—is produced as the product of this interaction.

Naming God's Creations

> [T]he world is a great library, and Fruit trees are some of his Bookes wherein we may read and see plainly the Attributes of God his Power, Wisdom, Goodness, etc.
>
> —R. Austen, *The Spiritual Use of an Orchard*

Botanical classification had a privileged role at the beginning of modern science. Botany pioneered understandings of Nature, showing the potential of a universal science. Botany was perhaps the first science concerned with uniting knowledge from around the globe to create a singular global knowledge. The global scale and the universal were developed and demonstrated for science in this emergent field.[2]

European voyages of discovery in the fifteenth and sixteenth centuries stimulated interest in the diversity of plants around the world. The folk botanies of Europe could not incorporate the wealth of unfamiliar plants that were being described from Asia, Africa, and the New World. In the ensuing excitement about new plants, a universal logic was put forward for the task of ordering global diversity: the logic of God's creation. Plants formed a unified set because God had created them according to His plan. The insight of botanical science was to imagine from this plan a universal *system* of classification. In the nineteenth century, the strength of the system allowed insights about an evolutionary history linking organisms, and only then did a logic *within* Nature usurp God as the unifying source of order of global biology. But by then, plant classification had begun its descent to the lowly scholarly status it occupies today: data collection. Today, newly discovered plants are members of a pre-established scientific set: the plant kingdom, with its constituent families, genera, and species. They are self-evident elements of Nature and thus of little abstract interest. This success in reducing mysteries to facts speaks to the transformation of consciousness involved in making universality, and the global scale, self-evident. Botanical classification was an important catalyst for this transformation.

A key feature of this transformation was the erasure of the collaborations that made global knowledge possible. European botanical knowledge in the sixteenth and seventeenth centuries was gained by learning from Asians, Africans, and indigenous Americans who introduced Europeans to their native plants. Botanical treatises from this period acknowledge the centrality of these knowledge exchanges. As European power grew around the world, however, European botanists came increasingly to imagine themselves as communing directly with plants—and the universality of science—without the mediation of non-European knowledge. The very collaborations that had made this science possible were covered up, and the plants were asked to speak for themselves as elements of Nature. In the history of systematics (the science of classification), universal premises and collaboratively established facts hid each other's work. Given its importance in establishing Nature, it is worth elaborating this story in a little more detail.

Let me return to the moment when plant classification became a site of intellectual discussion throughout Europe—the second half of the sixteenth century. World travelers brought news of unknown and exotic plants from foreign lands. European herbalists were overwhelmed. Thus arose an exciting reconsideration of knowledge, which lasted for two centuries. During this period, plant classification was at the forefront of the development of science. Scholars of the diversity of life worked particularly from two resources: classical treatises, especially the work of Aristotle, and Christian teachings about the workings of God. Both taught of a universal Nature, accessible through reason and by studying life-forms; both suggested the possibility of a singular global system uniting all life. Scholars debated about which was more important: the logical, rational system through which diversity could be charted, or the empirical study of organisms, through which the system could be inductively built. Andrea Cesalpino, a professor at Pisa and papal physician, is known for his early attempt at a universal taxonomy of plants. He relied on Aristotle, as well as his Catholic faith, to construct a rational system to account for diversity. He also developed a dichotomous key to identify plants: On the one hand, it depends on the logic of dichotomy; on the other, it follows the identifying characteristics of real plants, rather than exhausting logical possibilities (Atran 1990: 157). Not much later, Gaspard Bauhin, a Huguenot who presided over the botanical garden at Basel, sought a system of classification through tracing relationships of thousands of plants from around the world (Drayton 2000: 16). Cesalpino has been criticized for being too much of a rationalist; Bauhin has been criticized for not having enough of a logical system. But the concerns about creating a system to understand empirical diversity are clear in each.

Basic to this discussion was the search for universal order, that is, God's order. Cesalpino, for example, classified plants by the organization of their flower and seed parts, not, as modern biologists might, because of the role of these organs in reproductive biology, but rather because he thought these parts were the best exemplification of God's plan (Atran 1990: 152). It turned out that classification through flower and seed worked very well to order global plant diversity; it is because of the effectiveness of this framework that botany was so significant as an emergent science. (Zoology, in comparison, was a mess at the time.) Classification by flower and seed showed the potential of systematization.[3]

God could be known through reason or through observation, but there was no question about the underlying divine plan that would be revealed. Catholics and Protestants had their differences, but both read the world as God's book. Among botanists, differences between those who stressed reason versus empirical study were expressed in arguments about the relative priority of the "genus"—a classificatory category that grouped closely related types of plants—versus the "species"—the basic plant type. But arguments for each depended on the stability of God's plan. He created the species, and told humans to name them. He created the logic of genus, which allowed species to develop, each to its proper place. "The Creator of all things, who gave us the faculty for giving names to plants, places in the plants themselves signifying marks" (Tourefort 1719: 54, quoted in Atran 1990: 166).

This search for the universal—in marks on the plants themselves, and in underlying logics of plant relationships—drew attention away from the knowledge about plants that was learned in dialogue between Europeans and non-Europeans. It might have been possible for Europeans to learn about plants merely by stumbling upon them, but, in fact, they took the easier route of learning about them from other people.

Historian Richard Grove has described two books about plants in India that drew explicitly from such interactions. Garcia de Orta, a Portuguese doctor in Goa, wrote a treatise on botany in 1563; it was quickly translated into Latin and incorporated into European natural history. The treatise is written as a dialogue between Orta, speaking for the importance of the indigenous knowledge of Goa, and a skeptical interlocutor. Grove writes: "In general the text is remarkably subversive and even hostile to European and Arabic knowledge, regarding it as superfluous in the face of the wealth of accurate local knowledge" (1995: 81). European knowledge was not globally dominant at this period. "Far from imposing European systems of classification and perception on South Asia, the invention of printing and the collation of regional botanical knowledge actually provided an opportunity for the diffusion of indigenous South Asian methodologies of classification throughout the European world, rather than the reverse" (Grove 1995: 80). When the Dutch botanist Hendrik van Reede tot Drakenstein made a new compilation of useful plants of Malabar a century later, he assumed a similar respect for indigenous knowledge. His botanical illustrations were annotated in five languages, including the local Malayam, Arabic, and Latin (Drayton 2000: Plate 3). His text discusses his special reliance on Ezhava collectors of the "toddy-tapper" caste, who were adept at medical knowledge as well as identification of plants. His classifications, which feature Ezhava knowledge, were readily absorbed into European discussions.

Yet discussions among Europeans refused to acknowledge this global sharing of knowledge. Instead, they focused on the formation of a universal system of classification. John Ray, known for his "grammar" of botany (Atran 1990: 61), obviously read van Reede: "Who could believe that in one province of Malabar, hardly a vast place, there could be three hundred unique, indigenous species of trees and fruit?" (Ray 1686: sig. A3v quoted in Drayton 2000: 18). Yet he attributed no importance to the Ezhava dialogue that brought those species to him. The system itself was knowledge, not its component parts.

Carl Linnaeus, known as the father of modern biological classification, explained the importance of the system in unifying and ordering a singular global knowledge:

> The system is for botany the thread of Ariadna, without which there is chaos. Let us take, for example, an unknown plant of the Indies, and let a botanophile leaf through descriptions, figures, every index; he will not find it unless by chance. But a systematist will determine it straight away, be it old or new. . . . The system indicates the plants, even those it does not mention; this, the enumeration of a catalog can never do.
>
> (Linnaeus 1751: sec. 156, quoted in Atran 1990: 170–71)

The system takes precedence over the plant, as well as the process through which that plant was gathered "out there." Linnaeus unselfconsciously adopted van Reede's Malabar classifications without noting them as foreign (Grove 1995: 90). For him, all correct knowledge could be united through the use of a universal method. The method is the key to Nature. "Nowhere has the Supreme Creator exposed as many objects to the senses of man as in the Plant Realm, which covers and fills the globe we inhabit. Thus, if there be anywhere a proper method, it is that whereby we may hope to obtain a clear idea of Plants" (Linneaus 1737, quoted in Atran 1990: 151). Since it uncovers the handiwork of God, the system of classification must form a unified, homogeneous whole. There is no understanding here of knowledge as gained in dialogue—and certainly not dialogue between Christians and non-Christians.

As European hegemony grew, European knowledge increasingly directed global programs. If botanists came to see themselves as alone with Nature, it was because of this political power as well as the insight of "the system" in which all knowledges could be absorbed. Scholars of colonialism have pointed to the texts of eighteenth- and nineteenth-century European botanists, gathering plants in non-European locales, as models for imperial consciousness. In contrast to the earlier period, European botanists wrote of the plants but not the people. Their texts emptied the landscapes they studied of human inhabitants, making them appropriate for European settlement and conquest (Pratt 1992; Carter 1987). In the process, they suppressed attention to the practices in which at least some of their knowledge was gained.

Contemporary efforts to describe plants around the world continue to rely on this emptying out of Nature: Although they often depend on folk experts familiar with local flora, they disavow collaboration except among scientists. Celia Lowe (1999) has studied the species-collection activities of a conservation organization in the Indonesian Togean Islands. She found that English-speaking foreign volunteers objected to learning native names; they imagined their task in finding Nature to be the direct matching of organisms and internationally recorded Latin species names. Their Indonesian hosts and guides juggled local, national, English, and Latin species names, and they used their familiarity with multiple systems to identify species. But they, too, favored Latin names to show their affinities with international science; in their reports, only Latin names counted. This use and disavowal of cross-cultural collaboration also characterizes commercial bioprospecting. In her study of pharmaceutical bioprospecting in Mexico, Corinne Hayden (2003) found that researchers depended upon folk knowledge of plants to acquire biologically active samples. The researchers she studied bought plants from market vendors, who described for them herbs used within Mexican folk medicine. However, it was protocol that samples forwarded to their North American partners for further testing be divested of this folk medical information. To count as scientific samples, the biological material was purified from the history of its discovery.

This is a very specific Nature. As the touchstone of biodiversity discourse, it is a resource for environmental politics, and it is one way of encompassing the local within the globe. It also can be criticized for its imperial gaze. Might it be possible to attend to Nature's collaborative origins without losing the advantages of its global reach?

Meanwhile, there are other possibilities for uniting God and Nature. I turn to a different way to the universal, and to the local in the global.

Nature Located—in a Global Gaze

> [W]hen we contemplate the whole globe as one great dewdrop, striped and dotted with continents and islands, flying through space with other stars all singing and shining together as one, the whole universe appears as an infinite storm of beauty.
>
> —John Muir, *Travels in Alaska*

Nature soared in Europe and North America in the second half of the nineteenth century—in the gaze of educated travelers, in amateur and professional natural history, in emergent natural sciences, in philosophy, and in poetry. Looking back at this period, contemporary environmentalists single out Scottish-American nature writer John Muir as a prophet of Nature. Muir was a master of rhetoric who conjured reverence for Nature and zeal in protecting its significant wild places. In these wild places, he argued, the global force of Nature is condensed and made available in all its beauty and power for the appreciation of the cosmopolitan pilgrim.

This vision of a condensed and located global Nature moved a public, who, like Muir, imagined themselves as travelers in a wide and astonishing world. Muir's rhetoric galvanized an emergent movement of nature appreciators, bringing together natural scientists and lay people to create a new kind of public advocacy. Together with businessmen who promoted tourism and patriots who imagined U.S. wilderness as an equivalent to European monuments, these nature appreciators invented the idea of national parks, an idea that proved charismatic enough to spread around the world. The national park idea catered to a model of citizenship that privileged those who imagined themselves as cosmopolitan and civilized travelers, and thus potential park visitors. Wild nature would teach and refresh the cosmopolitan heart. Without a coalition of public forces, this vision would never have flourished.

Yet its focus on personal inspiration in the encounter between an individual and Nature denied all social mediation.

As in my previous example, the collaborative construction of Natural facts—here including inspiration—was shrouded by an axiom of unity in which individual experiences and observations could be referred directly to the universal. Here, too, the axiom of unity depended on the interplay of Nature and God. Yet Muir's God was personal and pantheistic, leading him to discover not the system behind all diversity but rather the totality in the local, the global at home. The collaborations on which it depended (and which it hid) did not cross oceans but instead forged a cosmopolitanism ready to rebuild the nation. This coalescence, with its wide-reaching effects on global nature loving [. . .], is worth exploring in more depth.

John Muir grew up with a potent mixture of Nature and God. His father was a strict and zealous Christian who, in pursuit of religious mission, moved the family from Scotland to rural Wisconsin. Muir recalls his childhood there as full of discipline and pioneer challenges. As a young man, Muir spent some time at the University of Wisconsin, where he was introduced to transcendentalist philosophy and botany. Evading the draft, he spent two years in search of rare plants in Canada. He returned to the United States to work in a factory in Indianapolis, where an industrial accident blinded him temporarily. In his recollections, Muir credits the accident for turning his path more fully toward Nature—as God. "I bade adieu to all my mechanical inventions, determined to devote the rest of my life to the study of the inventions of God" (Lankford 1991: 46).

In 1867, at the age of 29, Muir traveled south, determined to see the grandeur of Nature in South America as described by world explorer Alexander Humboldt. "How intensely I desire to be Humboldt!" he wrote to a friend (Fox 1981: 47). But a bout of malaria in Florida convinced him to travel west instead of south. He took a boat to California and walked east toward the Sierra Nevada Mountains. When he recalled his first glimpse of the Sierras later, it was with that potent religious vision of Nature that characterized so much of his writing. Starting from the western mountains, he looked east over California's Central Valley, which at that time was strewn with flowers. "And from the eastern boundary of this vast golden flower-bed rose the mighty Sierra, miles in height, and so gloriously colored and so radiant, it seemed not clothed with light, but wholly composed of it, like the wall of some celestial city" (Muir 1988: 2). He was even more deeply moved upon finding himself in the spectacular Yosemite Valley. "I feel like preaching these mountains like an apostle," he wrote (Fox 1981: 12). Although he later settled in San Francisco, and, after his marriage, on a ranch outside Oakland, it was Yosemite that remained the center of his gaze.

Muir's descriptions of Yosemite helped others see Nature's power. Some of these were men of influence: philosopher Ralph Waldo Emerson; future president Theodore Roosevelt. Others were friends and colleagues. Muir cofounded the Sierra Club, bringing together nature lovers, scientists, and advocates for the preservation of nature, and thus crystallizing that amateur-professional-activist synthesis that still invigorates environmentalism today. Meanwhile, Muir's writing mobilized an American love of Nature. One result of this mobilization was legislation designed to protect Yosemite Valley—passed first by California and then by the federal government to designate it a national park. Muir, then, is credited with inspiring the national parks movement that spread in and beyond the United States.

Muir's message depended on dramatic, emotionally charged modes of expression, infused with religious rhetoric. Consider Muir's famous indictment of those who would dam Yosemite's Hetch Hetchy Valley for a water reservoir: "The temple destroyers, devotees of raging commercialism, seem to have a perfect contempt for Nature, and, instead of lifting their eyes to the God of the mountains, lift them to the Almighty Dollar. Dam Hetch Hetchy! As well dam for water-tanks the people's cathedrals and churches, for no holier temple has ever been consecrated by the heart of man" (Smith 1987: 177). This passage is characteristic of Muir's identification of Nature as a focus of religious devotion. It mobilizes an advocacy for the sacred, and for the locally sacred—our church—as well as the universal religion it represents. Nature is God, in Hetch Hetchy and beyond. Muir was a priest of Nature, bringing it devotees. On meeting Emerson, Muir wrote: "I invite you to join me in a month's worship with Nature in the high temples of the great Sierra Crown beyond our holy Yosemite. . . . With most cordial regards I am yours in Nature, John Muir" (Fox 1981: 5). Scholars of Muir have noted that Muir's identification of God and Nature is hardly Christian orthodoxy.[4] However, Muir's worship of Nature shares much with the heterodox Protestant Christianity he knew best. Nature, like God, forms the basis of a universal Truth, accessible through direct experience and study. To study a particular instance offers a window into the universal. The local enfolds into the global and the universal; our devotions must simultaneously know the local and its transcendence.

Muir worked back and forth between evoking global Nature and its local instances. One interpreter of his writing speaks of the ubiquity of "planetary passages," in which references to the "earth-planet" offer a heightened emotional charge to landscape descriptions (Lankford 1991: 35).[5] Yosemite thus instantiated global space and time.

> Yosemite temples will be the more enjoyed by those who have traced . . . the crystallization of the granite in the dark, thousands of centuries before development, and who know how in the fullness of time the sun called to lift water out of the sea in vapor which was carried by the winds to the mountains, crystallized into snow among the clouds, to fall on the summits, form glaciers, and bring Yosemite Valley . . . to light.
>
> (Muir quoted in Lankford 1991: 41)

Muir's Nature—and his Yosemite—are forged in a scale-making project in which the local and the global are wrapped together and charged by the principles of the universal. Yosemite stood for the possibility of individual contact, through study and experience, with the hugeness of a global and universal Nature. Not any individual, however, can achieve this gaze. The subject who can grasp Nature here is the cosmopolitan traveler. Muir's use of travel writing as the genre in which he conveyed his sense of Nature's wonders is not incidental. Like Humboldt who inspired him, Muir appeals to the free metropolitan intellect who can imagine him- or herself in global travel. It is tempting to identify this reader as white, male, and wealthy, but this is not historically accurate. White women were among the most enthusiastic audiences for Muir's writing, and women's clubs energized the movement to create parks and nature reserves (Smith 1987).[6] Moreover, Muir projected an ambiguous or androgynous gender identification in his writing, drawing female readers and gentle men (Jespersen 1997). Indeed, Muir's opponents weakened him by portraying his cause as feminine; some scholars have argued that this feminization of nature protection kept environmentalism at a low profile through the first half of the twentieth century (Smith 1987). Race and class are also ambiguously implicated. Rather than reduce him to a "type," it is useful to look at who joined this collaborative momentum.

Consider, then, Muir's most powerful allies: scientists, nature lovers, and a certain set of entrepreneurs and politicians. Each of these was invested in the cosmopolitan gaze upon Nature. In science, Muir's affinities were with scientists who themselves were working through the relation between local and global instances of universal Natural law. Muir's study of glaciation in Yosemite Valley was in direct dialogue with Louis Agassiz, a Harvard naturalist who studied the chronology of rock strata as evidence of a global era of glaciation. Muir also worked with evolutionary biologist Asa Gray in collecting Western flora. In studies of glaciation and botany, Muir's sense that Nature formed a book that could be read—a global/local instancing of the universal—brought him inside an important current of nineteenth-century naturalism.

Muir's most enduring fans have been nature lovers and environmentalists. It is only because of their efforts that his legacy continues to be important today. Even during Muir's lifetime, they came in different sorts, from the activist hikers of the Sierra Club, to the women's clubs already mentioned, to tourists, scholars, and publishers. Despite their differences, the Californians among these nature lovers shared certain orientations: California was a new state, still at the edge of being a colonial territory. Through much of the nineteenth century, "science" in California consisted mostly of military surveys, commissioned for the purpose of securing administrative control. Muir formed part of a change in which science and nature loving signaled a more civilian form of citizenship. The settlers became citizens through their love of the land. Muir's evocation of Nature helped to secure this form of settler consciousness (Smith 1987).[7]

The support of these groups only translated into political effectiveness, however, because of influential allies: the bosses of the Southern Pacific Railroad. Muir formed a friendship with railroad baron E. H. Harriman, who convinced the U.S. Congress to designate Yosemite a national park (Fox 1981). The railroad was interested in the development of tourism since tourists came to the western United States mainly by train. Larger issues of what it meant to be a citizen were also at stake. The railroad block promoted notions of citizenship in which cosmopolitan travelers—people on the move—were the quintessential U.S. citizens. These people could benefit from encounters with Nature; indeed, these mobile and malleable citizens could be made as such in encounters with Nature. The railroad bosses fought for a particular point of view in the making of the western United States, and Muir's version of Nature supported their struggle.

Muir's articulation also created opponents and areas of invisibility. Ranchers were Muir's most explicit enemies; ranchers *used* the wilderness rather than experiencing or studying it. They were cut off from the universal; they destroyed it through inattention. Ranchers became the icon of one side of a dichotomy dividing the exploitation of Nature from its study and protection.

This dichotomy forms the basis of the most well-known divide in U.S. environmental politics: the divide between "conservation" and "preservation." (These terms take on particular meanings for this debate; after discussing the debate I return to using the term "conservation" much more broadly.) Histories of U.S. environmentalism often begin with Muir's disagreements with Gifford Pinchot, who became the first head of the U.S. Forest Service.[8] Pinchot, educated in the emerging European science of scientific forestry, believed that forests should serve economic and state-administrative interests. Ranching, timbering, and other forms of commercial use were a proper part of forest management; the goal of forestry was to maintain a national stock of forest lands precisely for such uses. Pinchot here stands for a view of the forests that combines utilitarian use and bureaucratic control, in this story called "conservation." Muir, in contrast, stands for the full protection of Nature for its own sake.

Both sides of this debate formed their momentum through culturally specific claims about the universal that blocked attention to the sometimes discordant collaborations that enlivened each agenda. Scientific forestry promoted universals of rationalism and profit. The uses of nature could be planned through a calculus of management. This agenda drew bureaucrats and businessmen. It also appealed to popular democracy: people should *use* forests. In this spirit, small as well as large users have been drawn to the resource management agenda. However, it is useful to remember that the legacies of both Pinchot and Muir articulate problematic universals and draw dangerous allies into the struggle for environmental well-being.

The debate reminds us why Muir's vision continues to inspire. In contrast to the resource managers, Muir tells us that Nature cannot be reduced to the needs of capitalism and the state. Nature deserves protection for itself. Here too are the shortcomings of the collaborative legacy of Muir's vision. The nature protection that Muir stimulated has not done well in forming alliances with local residents, who tend to be dismissed as users and therefore despoilers of nature. It has been easier to gain the support of distant corporate sponsors, who, like Muir's railroad friends, support nature tourism, rather than resident communities. As the national park idea spread around the world, parks advocacy formed even more problematic alliances with colonial heritages of resettlement and the displacement of indigenous residents. Residents have been evicted from nature reserves by force; local livelihoods have been disrupted. Recent environmental scholarship is full of documentation on the conflicts between residents and parks.[9] The challenges loom large.[10]

These alliances and enmities are the collaborative legacy John Muir set into motion. They form the power and the danger of this legacy; they set an awkward agenda. Yet nature lovers rarely acknowledge these issues; certainly Muir himself did not. Why? Muir's vision of Nature itself shut out the possibility that collaborations were important. Nature was knowable through direct experience. We need no conversations to make Nature come to life; we want direct access to the universal text. "The clearest way into the Universe is through a forest wilderness" (Muir quoted in Lankford 1991: 38). Environmentalists and nature lovers must struggle with this legacy, which offers both the transcendent power of Nature and the inability to know one's own collaborative positions.

Meanwhile, the United States launched other understandings of the globe. After World War II, U.S. military intelligence research was responsible for new kinds of globalisms, in which a mechanical vision of the relations of the parts to the whole replaces God as the author of universal laws. Cybernetics, systems dynamics, systems ecology, and circulation models were developed from the insight that systems create their own dynamics. Information about the interrelationship of elements within a system can generate knowledge of the whole. In contrast to Muir's endorsement of the global condensed in the local, these models bypass locality completely, except as an unmarked moment in scaling up and down. The system of flow and feedback takes precedence to any internal point. The global emerges as a node of systematicity. A key example is the model-making at the heart of public and scientific discussion of global climate change. My focus here is not the making of a universal logic but rather its use in the construction of a new kind of global scale. Collaborations across difference are both demanded and denied in this process.

Global Climate is a Model

Developing a predictive understanding of global environmental change in order to provide a scientific basis for national and international policy and decision making requires a comprehensive, interdisciplinary approach to studying the total Earth system.

—SEDAC, Consortium for International Earth Science
Information Network, "a part of NASA's Earth Observing System Data
and Information System," 1993 brochure

In the 1990s, global climate change was the center of what environmentalists, and the inter-ested public, thought about when they imagined environmental issues as global. When envi-ronmental organizations wanted to prove that they were tapped into transnational networks, they mentioned global climate change. Government officials and businesses pointed to global climate change to index the common problems of the world. One kind of globality, or at least multilocality, of climate change, then, is its multiple referencing by groups in varied social and physical locations.

Climate change seemed "global" to the public, too, because the issue was introduced during a period of concern about transboundary environmental issues: species loss, water pollution, acid rain, radioactivity. In the United States, a hot, dry summer in 1988 corre-sponded to the peak of public concern about the destruction of the rainforests in Amazonia. The emission of greenhouse gases (carbon dioxide and other gases whose increase in concen-tration is causing global warming) linked the U.S. climate and the loss of the Brazilian forest. The world was losing the carbon sink of the forests, while the burning of the forests produced more greenhouse gases. The idea of global climate change articulated the new realization that places far apart from each other were still connected for their basic survival, especially through the circulation of air and water.

The most easily identified "globality" of this realization, however, has been in the model that climate experts promoted to explain and predict climate change. General Circulation Models (GCM) use the laws of circulation of air and water to generate an abstraction we might call global climate. These models are self-conscious representations. They do not purport to describe the globe but rather to picture it in the model. They simplify and reduce the social and natural world to geophysical laws. In the process, they develop a globe that is unified, neutral, and understandable through the collection and manipulation of information.[11]

This is a specific—even a peculiar—kind of globe. The global scale is privileged above all others. In contrast to Linnean plant classification or Muir-inspired nature appreciation, the global scale is the locus of prediction as well as understanding. Local conditions can be predicted from the global model; that is the point of its globality. Local data may adjust the global model but never defy it. Its globality is all-embracing.

The model declares itself continually to be science. It is expert, neutral, rational, and empirically grounded. We know this, in part, because the model is complex and constantly under revision. It requires the computational prowess of computers because it integrates many factors. It admits to many uncertainties. Because of all the uncertainties integrated into it, using it requires great skill. Experts must train as part of a "community" of model users; they must develop common standards and trust. They should also communicate with the public. Experts use the models to tell the public about risks; public representatives can then debate what to do about these risks. "Uncertainties," "trust," "risk": These terms circle in the model's orbit. Through them, the model both secures its place as science and stimulates debate. The model unleashes its own dangers: This is its goal. Neither botanists nor nature lovers have used globality to push potential collaborators to the negotiating table, but climate modelers do just that.

It is my contention that the global commitments of the model are strategic: They are tuned to stimulate international dialogue. They also cover up dialogue through reference to the unified globe of the model. Model-building practitioners are self-conscious about the effects of their models on policy makers and the public. They want to create collaborations, and they know what kind they want. They want their models to show the way to global stand-ards and structures of management. Their models show that only such standards and struc-tures will promote survival. The model-makers want to bring policy makers into the modeling effort. They want policy makers to be future-oriented global citizens. The model is an attempt to make this happen by denying pre-existing interests and identities—and thus the necessity of negotiation within the collaborations they endorse. The global unit super-cedes nations, classes, cultures, or specific business interests. The model's generalizations promote negotiation by making its necessity disappear into a seamless globe.

The models incorporate strategy through the forms of global Nature they delineate. To see this, it is useful to examine the culture of modelers. First impressions, imbued with the shock of cultural difference, can perhaps convey this culture's strangeness and specificity. I offer an ethnographic arrival story.

I had my first taste of global climate models, and their makers, at the "First Open Meeting of the Human Dimensions of Global Environmental Change Community" in 1995 at Duke University in Durham, North Carolina. This was a very specific segment of the "community": the meeting was organized by political scientists, who have their own global agendas; the modelers present were those most interested in socioeconomic rather than geophysical data. Yet if I ignore the political science and focus on the surprises of my first impressions of modeling, I can introduce some recurrent cultural features.

For me, everything seemed exotic: the incessant clicking of laptops in the lecture halls; the parade of computer projections; the use of acronyms; the programmatic nature of much of the research, in which results were just an example of potential. It seemed that U.S. modelers wore dark, drab suits and armed themselves with piles of overheads, while Europeans wore bright jackets and flamboyant ties and spoke of creativity and culture. Women appeared as representatives of official organizations; they hid behind charts. Used to the informality of scholars who imagine themselves as of little public importance, I could tell I had entered an unfamiliar scene of action and effectiveness. Details of dress and presentation were geared for particular policy audiences. More so the models, which, through the ways they surprised me, instructed me in fundamentals.

I recall my first surprise: *The global scale takes precedence—because it is the scale of the model.* A geographer showed us how to use climate models for social science research. We needed to understand the procedures for "downscaling" from the global model to predict local envi-ronmental impacts. He used his computer to demonstrate for us how to predict the weather in one Swiss canton two hundred years in the future.

At first, I was just shocked by the temerity of predicting the local from the global. What happened to the social and natural landscape of that canton? Could it mean nothing? Then I did see that his demonstration was not just a direct downscling. One can "nest" a limited-area atmospheric model within the global climate model, thus including a certain amount of local information. Smaller scale information can be incorporated in global climate models in a number of ways. "Parameters" are introduced into the global model from regional and local empirical studies; these keep the model closer to accepted descriptions of reality. Model users may add data from other sources to create regional and landscape scale predictions. There is considerable interest in "meso-scale" modeling. Finally, there is much discussion among modelers about problems of scale. In a special issue of *Science* on global environmental problems, for example, two scientists argue that neither "scale-up" nor "scale-down" research paradigms can provide reliable ecological assessments. They advocate "strategic cyclical scaling," which integrates regional and local empirical data into global models, correcting global projections with the results of smaller-scale monitoring and evaluation of actual effects (Root and Schneider 1995).

Within these nuances, a set of assumptions about scale remains. Scales ought to fit neatly inside each other, the small inside the large, each neutral and fully encompassed by the next scale up. If they don't, we must fiddle, looking for a more realistic fit. The incompatibility of scales is a practical problem. It does not challenge the principles of the model, which requires that the local disappear compatibly inside the global.

My second surprise: *Models breed more models*. One man lectured on the modeling of uncertainty. It was one of the more unusual kinds of social science I had seen. He discussed, for example, the degree of trust that different climate scientists had in the global climate model, based on a survey. He then correlated their trust with personal characteristics, such as whether they smoked. I thought at first it was a joke, but I hadn't been around the discussion of uncertainty, or modeling. Models are made more reliable by incorporating uncertainties into the model, that is, by modeling them.

Since the emergence of global climate models, much concern has been expressed about the fact that the GCM does not include social information: The world is reduced to physical laws. Modelers have responded by developing more extensive models that incorporate everything. This is called *integrated assessment* (IA), and it requires combining rather different kinds of models. Social features of the globe are usually modeled using systems dynamics models, which are then combined with geophysical circulation models. Other kinds of modeling may be brought in as well. Since it is not clear how to do this, many forms of integrated assessment compete for attention. Everyone wants to include population and land use, but there are many other categories; some have even tried adding "culture" to that which can be modeled. The common assumption is that everything can be quantified and located as an element of a system of feedback and flow.

"Uncertainties" pile up. One IA project admits, "In view of the accumulation of uncertainties, the interpretative and instructive value of the . . . model is far more important than its predictive capacity, which is limited by the incomplete science upon which it is constructed" (Rotmans 1995b: 3). Is modeling a teaching practice or a predictive science?

Another surprise: *Models must be charismatic and pedagogical*. One modeler compared the success of European modeling with the failures of U.S. counterparts. He explained that the first success of climate modeling in Europe occurred as a result of concerns over acid rain. The European Union was just emerging, with transboundary issues as its reason to exist. The modelers brought policy makers from the EU into their modeling efforts. They let them design simulations. The policy makers became involved; they integrated the models into their positions. In contrast, he argued, U.S. modelers have had much less success. Their models are too complex and too academic; policy makers aren't attracted to them. Modeling, he argued, is a tool, not a declaration of truth.

The embedding of smaller scales into the global; the enlargement of models to include everything; the policy-driven construction of the models: Together, these features make it possible that models can bring diplomats to the negotiating table. Indeed, the models have helped stimulate negotiations, as in Rio in 1992 and in Kyoto in 1997. Yet, rather than the consensus that modelers hoped for, these negotiations have been arenas of conflict. Two conflicts have dominated the field: differences between representatives of the global north and south, and differences between the United States and Europe. The former takes the unified globe of the models apart, dividing it into sectors with dissimilar interests. The latter disputes environmental science, arguing for other forms of knowledge. Each reveals the collaborative structure of modeling through claims of being excluded.

Spokespeople for the global south argue that global climate models are an articulation of northern interests. Global climate models show everyone invested in the same reductions of greenhouse gases; they cover up the fact that most of these gases are emitted in northern countries. In blaming southern countries for a share of the greenhouse gas problem, the models also obscure differences between northern and southern emissions. Many greenhouse gases emitted in southern countries are "subsistence emissions," in contrast to the "luxury emissions" of northern countries. Global modeling, they imply, is not neutral but rather positioned with those wealthy nations who can cut emissions—but want others to help them. In international negotiations before the 1992 Rio Earth Summit, this argument was convincing enough to be incorporated into the United Nations Framework Convention on Climate Change.[12]

This north-south separation was one reason anti-environmental politicians in the United States criticized climate change negotiations, and, in the face of international disapproval, withdrew from the Kyoto Protocol in 2001. U.S. politicians have advocated a different form of universals through which they imagine the globe: private property, free trade, and the entrepreneurial spirit. U.S. negotiators had already done their best to bring these business-oriented perspectives into discussions of climate change.[13] Yet the models of global change that informed climate negotiations still privileged the environment for itself. These environmental universals had not won over U.S. politics.

U.S. intransigence warns us against the glorification of incompatibility; when claims of difference are combined with unilateral power, they can be ugly. Whereas representatives of the south asked for revisions of the model, the most powerful nation of the north merely refused to discuss it. Powerful blocs have worked hard to stop global agreements based on international cooperation and amity. The expertise of modelers has formed defensive walls against such power plays, but generalizations more directly dependent on international politics have had fewer defenses.

The recognition of environmental crisis has brought nations to the negotiating table to talk about a variety of universal standards. But not all negotiations result in effective generalization. Negotiators must agree upon common objects. As long as they refuse all compatibility, generalization is impossible. The troubled progress of international negotiations illuminates the specificity of the generalization process, in which productive collaborations and sincerely endorsed axioms of unity are not easy achievements. I turn to these troubles.

A Universal Regime?

> The ITTO's underlying concept is to sustainable development of tropical forests by encouraging and assisting the tropical timber industry and trade to manage and thus conserve the resource base on which they depend.
> —International Tropical Timber Organization, "What Is the
> International Tropical Timber Agreement?"

The combination of trade promotion and conservation is a heady brew for international politics. Nowhere has this been more important than in the International Tropical Timber Organization, better known as the ITTO. With this combination brewing, the dream of a global management regime was born. Could forest protectors and exploiters, and wood producers and consumers, come together to form universal standards, governance procedures, and expectations about the use of forests?[14]

The ITTO's hopes for forming universal standards came to life around the concept of "sustainable forest management." Sustainable management emerged at the intersection of varied concerns about "protection": of wood supplies for consumer industry; of state forestry institutions; of wood prices for timber companies; of the reputation of the forest-products trade; and, of course, of forests themselves. Sustainable management showed the potential to reshape conservation, trade, forestry, and industry, so that they formed a common trajectory in a commitment to a managed global Nature. Sustainable management could be the cornerstone of a new governmentality. Yet the most exciting thing about the ITTO turned out to be its failure. Everyone saw quickly that "sustainable management" was an empty concept. The ITTO stayed on, but the action, emerging from other sites, swirled around it. The ITTO took up the defensive role of managing participants' agendas in the light of what was happening elsewhere.

This section, then, turns from relatively successful agendas for global Nature to consider a relatively unsuccessful one. A coalition politics continues to sustain the ITTO, but it is not a coalition that has forged effective collaborations. Some participants hang in, hoping to exert influence on other players and on international programs. They advocate global accord for the name, not the substance; they are most involved in their separate mandates. In their still-strident efforts, global Nature stutters, and falls silent. Why?

The ITTO was imagined as a forum in which compromises might bridge disagreements among dissimilar parties. Even while claiming to search for common ground, the organization worked assiduously to maintain these globe-ripping divides. The ITTO began as a Japanese dream, suggested to the UN Conference on Trade and Development in 1977. The Japanese representatives said they were concerned about the stability of the tropical timber trade, for which Japan was the most prominent consumer. Conservationists and foresters had pointed to evidence of rapid deforestation; supplies in key Japanese source areas, such as the Philippines, were already running out. The Japanese plan blocked other possibilities. Sporadic discussions among tropical wood producing countries had generated speculation that a cartel might form to influence supply and pricing. It also seemed possible that conservationists, concerned about the rapid loss of tropical forests, might themselves succeed in forming international forestry standards. In either case, Japan's business profits would suffer. These concerns informed several years of discussion of the proposal. In 1983, an International Tropical Timber Agreement (ITTA) was signed, to take effect in 1985. The agreement formalized the dialogue between tropical wood producing countries and consuming countries. It included conservation as well as trade promotion goals. The agreement also formed the ITTO.

Bureaucratic structure seems cut and dry; but much agonizing and struggle went into settling the structure of the ITTO. Who would participate? What global, national, or business commitments would dominate the agenda? These were questions hammered out in the organizational structure. The ITTA made a start. The organization would be divided into moieties, consisting of representatives of nation-states, and identified respectively as "producers" and "consumers"—thus assuring that the ITTO would function neither as a price-setting cartel nor as a forum for global citizens. Votes were to be distributed in proportion to a nation-state's "involvement" with the tropical timber trade; countries that either bought or sold more tropical wood received more votes. As one critic points out: "The net result is that the more a country destroys tropical forests, the more votes it gets. The voting structure ensures that the ITTO's primary role of promoting the timber trade heavily outweighs its secondary conservation role" (Colchester 1990: 167).

These arrangements meant that the struggle over the organization's goals was played out in relation to the representation of different countries. Forest conservation objectives became identified with countries such as the United Kingdom and the Netherlands; the voice of the wood-products industry was heard from Japan; the defense of national sovereignty and rights to destroy the forests became identified with Indonesia and Malaysia. Thus, too, the struggle over which nation would supply the Executive Director and where the secretariat would be seated was a struggle over organizational definition. The battle was heated. Finally, the Japanese government offered to fund the ITTO in exchange for gaining the secretariat. Japanese support then boosted a Malaysian forester, Dr. Freezailah, to the post of Executive Director (Colchester 1990).

Despite this alignment of Japanese and Malaysian interests in rapid timber exploitation, conservationists hung on. Getting forest conservation goals into a mandate that had begun as a trade agreement was a victory; they were not about to retreat. For nongovernmental organizations, the goal of participating at all in ITTO negotiations seemed overwhelmingly important. In Indonesia, for example, environmental NGOs were just then struggling for a voice in the nation—in the legal system, in forestry, and in public culture. Indonesia was a major player in the ITTO, and NGOs wanted to be involved.[15]

In other arenas—including global climate change—agreement among experts has sparked intergovernmental cooperation. Not so for forest protection. Experts are differently aligned. Foresters have been trained to work with the timber industry, not the environmental movement; in contrast, conservation biologists, often spokespersons for environmentalism, may oppose logging. Anthropologists, who may speak up for forest-dwelling peoples, are rarely given credence by either foresters or biologists. Economists are given much credence although they may know nothing about forests. Agendas for forest management thus multiply. Most experts adopt a rhetoric of concern for forests, whether they propose to stay or hasten their disappearance. The 1992 UN Earth Summit at Rio produced a set of principles on forests that affirm state sovereignty and promote free trade; what does this have to do with forest protection?[16] Thus, too, the ITTO combines and juxtaposes agendas that, everyone admits, contradict each other.

Sustainable management holds the mix together. But it is not enough. The ITTO promotes sustainable management of forests. But, given the self-conscious reliance on contradictory programs, it is difficult for the organization to define the term substantively. Here is the organization's formal definition:

> Sustainable forest management is the process of managing forest to achieve one or more clearly specified objectives of management with regard to the production of a continuous flow of desired forest products and services without undue reduction of the inherent values and future productivity and without undue undesirable effects on the physical and social environment.[17]

This is obviously a compromise between sustainable *yield*—the foresters' dream of stable timber production ("a continuous flow of desired forest products")—and sustainable *ecological function*—the environmentalists' goal ("inherent values," "undesirable effects"). The product is almost incomprehensible. Furthermore, no one knows how to do it. No one, even industry experts, thinks that current tropical logging techniques are allowing the forest to regenerate—even for timber.

Two paths present themselves as ways out of this conundrum. One could use the term as public relations rhetoric to defend the reputation of current logging practices, taking them out of the opprobrium of environmentalist criticism. The advantage here is that it doesn't matter if the definition is incomprehensible. Alternatively, one could focus on *management* itself as the true objective. By rationalizing data collection and bureaucratic structures for forestry while at the same time highlighting technical training, one might achieve some goals, even if they might not be forest protection ones. After all, the definition says that sustainable management is meeting the specified objectives of management. It is management itself that must be sustainable. The ITTO has worked back and forth between these two paths.

Throughout the 1990s, the highest profile program of the ITTO was the "Year 2000 Objective," the promise to limit trade in tropical timber to supplies from sustainably managed forests by the year 2000. The promise was passed as a producer-countries' resolution in 1991, with participating environmental organizations, and even some representatives from consumer countries, bewildered about just what this promise meant. The first possibility that occurred to critics is that the promise meant nothing at all: "In fact, 'Target 2000' will present the timber industry with few difficulties, for, according to the rhetoric of the producers and traders, logging as practiced *already is sustainable*" (Colchester 1990: 169). As 2000 approached, the organization began to suggest that the Year 2000 Objective was rhetoric: "The . . . ITTO has done more in the 15 years of its existence than any other organization to advance the idea of sustainable tropical forest management" (ITTO 2000). Spreading the *idea* of sustainable management is enough.

Meanwhile, the organization sponsored a variety of technical studies and data collection exercises, some of which might lead to more, if not better, management. Guidebooks for standards of forestry are being published. "Reduced impact logging" offers the solution of managing timber industry workers to address the problem of logging's destructive impact. Other ITTO grants sponsor studies of illegal logging—one of the few evils on which state bureaucracies, the timber industry, and tree-counting conservationists can agree. These activities advance the bureaucratic ideal; however, little effort has gone into addressing the problems of *legal* logging, the loss of local livelihoods, and the opening of forests to destructive forms of settlement and mining. The technical solutions of ITTO programs do not address either ecological or social questions. Sustainable forestry management is self-contained—an "anti-politics machine" that converts social issues into technical ones.[18]

The machine asserts its globality mainly as a rampart against attacks from other transnational sources. The ITTO's major activity has involved neutralizing other initiatives for tropical forest management. It has been particularly active against environmentalist initiatives, such as tropical wood boycotts to protest destructive logging. ITTO fought the concept of wood-products labeling as well as certification, which environmentalists proposed as a way of identifying better and worse timber sources. When it became clear that labeling and certification were ideas that would not go away, the ITTO then rushed in to create its own profit-friendly programs.[19]

Meanwhile, the ITTO has taken a stand for particular governments against international pressure. In 1989, at the height of the international campaign against the logging of Sarawak, Malaysia, the ITTO sent an official mission to assess "the sustainable utilization and conservation of tropical forests" there (ITTO 1990: 2). The mission made no attempt to meet with indigenous protestors or environmentalist critics; instead it limited its vision to the formal aspects of forest management. "The mission inverts the priorities of Sarawak's forest policy, putting the production of timber above local needs," environmentalists proclaimed (Rowley 1990). Meanwhile, the Sarawak government touted the ITTO mission's regard as an endorsement of its sustainable forest management.

None of this is doing the tropical forests much good. The conditions of tropical forests have only deteriorated since the formation of the ITTO, and no amelioration seems in sight. Nor has there been much success in forming global accord. No mechanisms have been set for compliance with forestry standards, should meaningful standards be suggested. Everyone who knows about the problems of forestry on the ground—from local foresters, to residents, to spokespeople for wildlife—has been excluded. Practical forestry solutions would look quite different with their input.

These failures show the weakness of the process of generalization the ITTO put in motion. International cooperation did not prove a convincing axiom of unity. The ITTO's retreat to technical rhetoric is an exemplar of the weakness of contemporary international politics in forging a "universal regime." Yet, given its penchant for blocking more meaningful forest solutions, the organization's ineffectiveness is perhaps its best quality.

Nature and the Globe

Making the globe our frame of reference is hard work. This chapter has explored projects for making global commitments that rely on Nature as a set of universal, orderly, and inspiring laws. Looking at universals, I find that they include contrasting sources of knowledge and define varied kinds of participants in the knowledge-making process. Their quiet exclusions, and their heralded opponents, are equally varied. Yet they rely on a common process: Global Nature both facilitates and obscures worldwide collaborations.

Nature offers various kinds of commitment to a global scale. Global Nature can collate facts from around the world. In forming a plant classification system, global Nature made the knowledge of varied localities compatible. It offered a universal system to bring together local knowledges. Global Nature can inspire moral views and actions. In nature appreciation and the parks model, localities are charged with global insight; they are microcosms of universal knowledge. Global Nature can also form a common object for the formation of international standards. In global climate models, the material primacy of the globe seen in the model can impel the urgency of international negotiation. And global Nature can facilitate governance regimes, making technical standardization an international imperative. The sustainably managed forests of the International Tropical Timber Organization are leaky boats for Nature. But, like the other projects introduced here, they are claims about Natural universals that make the globe the relevant forum.

These forms of global Nature are resources for everyone involved in using or advocating for the environment. They make it possible to make claims for Nature, and for the globe. The cultural specificity of their universals does not, in itself, make them wrong. However, claims of universality do make it hard for us to see just who can imagine themselves inside, and who is out.

The projects for making nature and scale that I describe in the rest of this book draw on these cultural resources. You will hear more about botanizing as a moment of cultural sharing, about nature loving in the legacy of Muir, about the dreams and models of environmental science, and about heated debates over the protection of tropical forests. These projects are deployed and transformed in varied social contexts—making and remaking the variety of small-n nature.

For this task, however, I need a different approach than I have used in this chapter. To see practices of nature and scale-making in their variety, I can't just work with famous examples; I need to investigate more ordinary environmental politics. Instead of beginning with successful globe-making projects and ferreting out their collaborators, I must proceed the other way around. I must follow the articulative process, however partial and incomplete its results. I dip into the cultural resources I have introduced here, but I do not privilege their globe-making perspectives. Instead, I track globe-making interactions much closer to the ground.

Notes

1   *Oxford English Dictionary*, 2d ed. s.v. "generalization."
2   I am indebted to Atran (1990); Drayton (2000); and Grove (1995) for my understanding of the emergence of botanical classification.
3   Nineteenth-century evolutionary theory, indeed, retained the priority of flower and seed in the secular universal it substituted for God's plan. This happy conjunction strengthened convictions about the universal order of Nature as revealed through plants.
4   Fox (1981) calls it pantheism.
5   Muir signed one work with a global address: "John Muir, Earth-Planet, Universe" (Lankford 1991: 36). Lankford also quotes Muir explaining his commitment to moving back and forth between tiny details and the grand scheme of Nature: "If my soul could get away from this so-called prison . . . I should hover over the beauty of our own good star. I should study Nature's laws in all their crossings and unions . . . But my first journey would be into the inner substance of flowers" (38).

6   Limbaugh (1991) discusses Muir's friendship with Sarah McChesney, a leader of feminist animal rights activists. Muir's stories of the moral behavior of animals were written to this audience.

7   Muir's vision of Nature seemed powerful and convincing in part because it helped resolve an imperial problem: Was California a part of the U.S. nation or part of its global empire? Yosemite National Park was a firm claim to the national status of the still-wild western states. Nationalizing nature brought the global-imperial agenda of travel, conquest, and awe into domestic, national space. Muir himself did not focus on this national problem; arriving in California on a boat, he could have been arriving in South America. He was not invested in the national project, but his vision articulated a new national presence for California. One reason that the parks model took off around the world is that it showed one way nation-states could incorporate the wild frontiers of their imperial ambitions.

8   See Smith (1987) and Fox (1981) for versions of this story.

9   Neumann (1998) explores African examples. Stevens (1997) offers cases that work toward dialogue.

10   The question of indigenous residents has been one of those challenges. Can advocates for nature move beyond Muir's problematic relationship with Native Americans? Native Americans enter Muir's vision in several ways. First, they are a troubling absence: the haunting absence of the dead. The genocidal murder of Native Americans in California contributed to the emptiness of Nature that Muir appreciated as the window to sacred presence. Native Americans had been hunted down and murdered; remnant groups were rounded up and forced into forts and resettlement areas, where many died. Only then could the environment to which native livelihoods contributed come to seem the exclusive handiwork of God, laid out for the gaze of settlers. Second, Muir was not sympathetic to those Native Americans who remained. Yosemite Indians—so called by neighboring enemies— still inhabited the valley, although in small numbers. Muir's writing contains only derogatory mention of them (Lankford 1991: 234). Besides being non-Christians, the native population joined white ranchers as users, rather than students, of nature. The reservation of the valley as a park did not help the native residents. Federal marshals rounded up the native population and evicted them from their lands. Yet, third, Muir scholars have argued that Native American philosophies inspired Muir's vision of Nature. (See Fleck 1985.) This brings up contemporary challenges for the Muir legacy. In stating their support for indigenous communities, advocates of nature protection so often go directly to native philosophies. Other issues—such as subsistence and survival—are easily ignored. Indigenous leaders willing to endorse nature philosophies do well with nature protection groups; those who stress community development and resource use are drawn, instead, to alliances with developers. The common split within communities with some leaders arguing for support of environmentalists and others siding with developers is a piece of this legacy.

11   The climate change models discussed in this section are those that were widely discussed in the mid-1990s, during a period of great hopefulness for international cooperation on environmental issues. The more blatant U.S. endorsement of imperial claims in the twenty-first century has dampened these hopes and reduced the public prominence of climate modeling. To evaluate the models' use of universal frames and the global scale, I focus on the period when the models seemed most charismatic.

12   Northern industrial countries were singled out as "Annex I countries" and asked, as a nonbinding target, to scale back greenhouse gas emissions by 2000 to 1990 levels. This separation between northern and southern countries was continued in the 1997 Kyoto Protocol, which, responding to the fact that no nation had met its Rio pledges, set comprehensive greenhouse gas emission targets. Demeritt (1999) offers an insightful analysis.

13   The Kyoto Protocol goes far in converting environmental values into business values. The Protocol allows countries to lower their emissions through business rather than environmental accounting: They can trade in emission reductions by buying figures showing reduced rates from other countries ("international emissions trade") or by supporting emissions reductions wherever they are cheapest ("joint implementation"). However, for many business leaders, these concessions were not enough. See Demeritt (1999).

14   Gale (1998) offers a comprehensive history of the ITTO in the 1990s.

15   Many conservation organizations also believe in logging as a route to forest preservation. First, it adds economic value to forests, creating the will of governments and investors to maintain forests. Second, by working with timber harvesters and wood product industries, conservationists might have the ability to influence the forest practices in which these users engaged. To withdraw from interaction would be to give up the possibility of leverage. Some conservationists also hope to insert other small conservation goals—such as the establishment of nature reserves or parks—into the forest management agenda. Despite these incentives to stay with the ITTO process, however, many environmental NGOs turned against the ITTO in the mid-1990s.

16   This was the "Non-Legally Binding Authoritative Statement of Principles for a Global Consensus on the Management, Conservation, and Sustainable Development of All Types of Forests." Even supporters of the document agree that the principles have more to do with détente than with a forest program. See Fletcher (1995).
17   The definition is repeated in many organization publications. See ITTC (1992).
18   The term is from James Ferguson (1994), writing of international development.
19   On the turnaround, see Sizer and Plouvier (1997); on the new programs, see Atya and Simula (2002). WTO and GATT bans on trade restrictions have been important presences in the negotiations.

References

Atran, Scott. 1990. *Cognitive foundations of natural history*. Cambridge: Cambridge Univ. Press.

Atya, Richard Eba'a, and Markku Simula. 2002. *Forest certification: Pending challenges for tropical timber*. ITTO Technical Series 19.

Austen, Ralph. 1653. *A treatise of fruit trees. . . . together with The spiritual use of an orchard . . .* Oxford: Tho. Robinson.

Blake, William. 1982. Auguries of innocence. In *The rattle bag*, eds. Seamus Heaney and Ted Hughes, 47–50. London: Faber and Faber.

Carter, Paul. 1987. *The road to Botany Bay*. London: Faber.

Colchester, Marcus. 1990. The International Tropical Timber Organization: Kill or cure for the rainforests? *The Ecologist* 20 (5): 167.

Drayton, Richard. 2000. *Nature's government: Science, imperial Britain, and the 'improvement' of the world*. New Haven, CT: Yale Univ. Press.

Ferguson, James. 1994. *The anti-politics machine*. Minneapolis: Univ. of Minnesota Press.

Fleck, Richard. 1985. *Henry Thoreau and John Muir among the Indians*. Hamden: Archon Books.

Fletcher, Susan. 1995. International forest agreements: Current status. *Congressional Research Service Report for Congress, 95–960 ENV*, September 11. National Council for Science and the Environment.

Fox, Stephen. 1981. *The American conservation movement: John Muir and his legacy*. Madison: Univ. of Wisconsin Press.

Grove, Richard H. 1995. *Green imperialism: Colonial expansion, tropical island edens, and the origins of environmentalism*, 1600–1860. Cambridge: Cambridge Univ. Press.

Hayden, Corinne. 2003. *When nature goes public: The making and unmaking of bioprospecting in Mexico*. Princeton, NJ: Princeton Univ. Press.

ITTO (International Tropical Timber Organization). 1990. The promotion of sustainable forest management: A case study in Sarawak, Malaysia. Report submitted to the International Tropical Timber Council VIII (7, May 7).

———. 2000. Measuring up: Assessing progress toward sustainable forest management in the tropics.

Jespersen, Christine. 1997. *Engendering adventure: Men, women, and the American 'frontier,' 1880–1927*. Ph.D. diss., Rutgers Univ.

Lankford, Scott. 1991. *John Muir and the nature of the West: An ecology of American life, 1864–1914*. Ph.D. diss., Stanford Univ.

Limbaugh, Ronald H. 1991. Stickeen and the moral education of John Muir. *Environmental History Review* 15 (1): 25–45.

Lowe, Celia. 1999. *Cultures of nature: Mobility, identity, and biodiversity conservation in the Togean Islands of Sulawesi, Indonesia*. Ph.D. diss., Yale Univ.

Muir, John. 1915. *Travels in Alaska*. Boston: Houghton Mifflin.

Neumann, Roderick. 1998. *Imposing wilderness: Struggles over livelihood and nature preservation in Africa*. Berkeley: Univ. of California Press.

Pratt, Mary Louise. 1992. *Imperial eyes*. London: Routledge.

Ray, John. 1686. *Historia plantarum generalis*, I. London.

Rotmans, Jan. 1995b. *Targets in transition*. Pamphlet issued by Rijksinstituut voor Volksgezondheid en Milieu (National Institute of Public Health and the Environment). Bilthoven, The Netherlands: GLOBO.

Rowley, Anthony. 1990. Logged out: Sarawak report criticized by conservationists. *Far Eastern Economic Review* (December 13): 72–74.

Sizer, Nigel, and Dominick Plouvier. 1997. Increased investment and trade by transnational logging companies in ACP countries: Implications for sustainable forest management and conservation. Draft of a Joint Report of WWF-Belgium WRI and WWF-International, 1997.

Smith, Michael L. 1987. *Pacific visions: California scientists and the environment, 1850–1915*. New Haven, CT: Yale Univ. Press.

Stevens, Stan, ed. 1997. *Conservation through cultural survival*. Washington, DC: Island Press.

Tourefort, J. P. 1719. *Institutiones rei herbariae*. 3rd ed. Paris: Imprimerie Royale.

Chapter 20

Bruno Latour

WHAT IS TO BE DONE? POLITICAL ECOLOGY!

TO OFFER POLITICAL ECOLOGY a legitimate place, it sufficed to bring the sciences into democracy.

Throughout the present book, I have had to propose this solution while using outmoded terms: "speech," "discussion," "Constitution," "Parliament," "house," *logos*, and *demos*. As I am well aware, I have expressed only one particular viewpoint, one that is not simply European but French, perhaps even social democratic, or worse still, logocentric. But where has anyone seen a diplomat who did not bear the stigmata of the camp he represents? Who does not put on the livery of the powerful interests that he has chosen to serve and thus to betray? If we have to call upon parliamentarians, it is precisely because there is no vantage point on Sirius from which judges could assign faults to the various parties. Am I therefore limited to my own point of view, imprisoned in the narrow cell of my own social representations? *That depends on what follows.* It is true that diplomats do not benefit from the privileges granted by the Heaven of Ideas, but they are not prisoners of the dark Cave, either. They are beginning to parley, wherever they are, with the words they have inherited. They present themselves with these formulas to others who have no better ones, no more definitive ones, and who are also leaving the narrow confines where they were born. For a diplomat, the first words do not count, but only those that follow: the first stitch in the common world that their fragile terms are going to make it possible to knit. Everything is negotiable, including the words "negotiation" and "diplomacy," "sciences" and "democracy"—simple white flags waved at the front to suspend hostilities.

If I have sometimes offended against good sense, it is because I wanted to rediscover common sense, the sense of the common. People who speak of nature as if it were an already constituted unity that would make it possible to throw back onto social representations everything that calls for disunion—such people *exercise a kingly power*, the most important of all, a power superior to all the purple mantles and all the gilded scepters of civil and military authorities. I ask no more of them than one minuscule concession: since you have granted yourselves the power to define what unites us and what drives us apart, what is rational and what is irrational, show us also the proofs of your legitimacy, the traces of your election, the motivations for your choices, the institutions that permit you to exercise these functions, the *cursus honorum* through which you have had to make your way. Starting from the moment when you agree to redefine public life as the progressive composition of the common world, you can no longer exercise this power under cover of the "indisputable laws of nature." If there are laws, there has to be a Parliament. "No reality without representation." No one is asking you to abandon all power, but simply to exercise it *as a power*, with all its precautions, its slowness, its procedures, and especially its checks and balances. If it is true that absolute power corrupts absolutely, then the power that made it possible to define the common world under the auspices of nature corrupted you more than any other. Is it not time to free yourselves of that absolutism by rising to the dignity of representatives, each of whom must learn to doubt?

The science wars bring us back today to the situation of the religious wars that forced our predecessors in the seventeenth century to invent the double power of politics and Science, while thrusting faith back into the inner self. When each reader of the Bible, in direct contact with his God, could come to reverse the established order in the name of his own interpretation, it spelled the end of public order. There was no more common world. That is why our ancestors had to secularize politics and relativize religion, which had become a simple private conviction. Must we carry out the same neutralization, now that each of us can rise up against public authority with his or her own interpretation of nature in the name of direct contact with the facts? Can we secularize the sciences as we have secularized religion and make of exact knowledge an opinion that is respectable, to be sure, but private? Must we imagine a State that would guarantee nothing other than the freedom to practice the scientific rites freely *without supporting a single one of them?* As soon as it is formulated, the solution appears aberrant, since morality and religion have been successfully secularized only thanks to that assurance of an already-accomplished unity that Science used to hand us on a platter. Agnostic in Science and religion both, the secular Republic would be emptied of all substance. So far as the common world is concerned, it would rest on the least interesting and most arbitrary of smallest denominators: the king-self.

I have sought to explore a different solution. Instead of eliminating the requirements that bear on the constitution of the facts by sending them back to the private sphere, why not, on the contrary, *lengthen the list* of these requirements? The seventeenth-century solution, the simultaneous invention of indisputable *matters of fact* and of endless discussion, ultimately did not offer sufficient guarantees for the construction of the public order, the *cosmos*. The two most important functions were lost: the capacity to debate the common world, and the capacity to reach agreement by closing the discussion—the power to take into account along with the power to put in order. Even though no pontiff can now say *"Scientia locuto est, causa judica est,"* the loss of authority turns out to be compensated a hundredfold by the possibility of exploring in common what a *good* fact is, what a *legitimate* member of the collective is. If we need less Science, we need to count much more on the sciences; if we need fewer indisputable facts, we need much more collective experimentation on what is essential and what is accessory. Here, too, I am asking for just a tiny concession: that the question of democracy be extended to nonhumans. But is this not at bottom what the scientists have always most passionately wanted to defend: to have absolute assurance that facts are not constructed by mere human passions? They believed too quickly that they had reached this goal by the short-cut of *matters of fact* kept from the outset apart from all public discussion. Can one not obtain—more painfully, more laboriously, to be sure—a quite superior guarantee if humans are no longer alone in elaborating their Republic, their common *thing?*

I do not claim that politics once translated into ecology will be easier. On the contrary, it is going to become more difficult, more demanding, more procedural, indeed, more bureaucratic, and, yes, groping. We have never seen the establishment of a State of law simplify life for those who were used to the conveniences of a police state. Similarly, imagining a "State of law of nature," a *due process* for the discovery of the common world, is not going to make life easier for those who claim to be sending back to the nonexistence of the irrational all the propositions whose looks they do not like. They are going to have to argue and come to terms, without skipping any of the steps we have covered in the preceding chapters. But, as we have seen many times, by losing nature, public life also loses the principal cause of its paralysis. Freed from transcendences that are as inapplicable as they are beneficial, politics breathes more freely. It no longer lives in the shadow of the sword of Damocles, the threat of salvation from elsewhere. Agreement is going to have to be reached.

Is the hypothesis I have developed normative or descriptive? I have proceeded as though the new Constitution described a state of things that is already in place, lacking only certain adequate terms to become self-evident to those best prepared to see it. This was the only way to rejoin common sense. The difference between the descriptive and the normative depends, moreover, on the distinction between facts and values: thus I could not use it without contradicting myself. There is in "mere description" an overly powerful form of normativity: what *is* defines the common world and thus all that *must* be—the rest having no existence other than the nonessential one of secondary qualities. Nothing is more anthropocentric than the inanimism of nature. Against the norm dissimulated in the politics of *matters of fact*, then, we had to be even more normative. For the rest, there is nothing less utopian than an argument that aims at nothing but putting an end to that utopia, the modernist eschatology that is still expecting its salvation from an objectivity originating elsewhere. It is to the *topos*, the *oikos*, that political ecology invites us to return. We come back home to inhabit the common dwelling without claiming to be radically different from the others. In any event, having arrived much later than the avant-garde, a little earlier than Minerva's owl, intellectual workers can never do much better than to help other intellectuals, their readers, rejoin what the *demos* already brought into the state of things some time ago.

Someone will object that it is necessarily a question of a utopia, since power relations will always come to break up the State of law and oppose to the delicate procedure deployed here the wordless brutality of the established order. It is true that I have not made use of the resources offered by critical discourse. I have unmasked only one power, that of nature. I had a very powerful reason to do so: society plays the same role in critical discourse that nature plays in the discourse of the naturalizers. *Societas sive natura.* To assert that underneath legitimate relationships there are forces invisible to the actors, forces that could be discerned only by specialists in the social sciences, amounts to using the same method for the metaphysics of nature as was used for the Cave: it amounts to claiming that there exist primary qualities—society and its power relations—that form the essential furnishings of the social world, and secondary qualities, as deceitful as they are intensely experienced, that cover with their mantle the invisible forces one cannot see without losing heart. If the natural sciences have to be rejected when they employ that dichotomy, then we have to reject the social sciences all the more vigorously when they apply it to the collective conceived as a society. If the common world has to be composed progressively along with the natural sciences, let us be careful not to use society to explain the actors' behavior. Like nature, and for the same reason, society finds itself at the end of collective experimentation, not at the beginning, not all ready-made, not already there. It is only good for attempting to take power—without ever managing to exercise it, since it is even mistaken about its own strength.

The social sciences—economics, sociology, anthropology, history, geography—have a much more useful role than that of defining, in the actors' place and most often against them, the forces that manipulate them without their knowledge. The actors do not know what they are doing, *still less* the sociologists. What manipulates the actors is unknown *to everyone*, including researchers in the social sciences. This is even the reason there is a Republic, a common world still to come: we are unaware of the collective consequences of our actions.

We are implicated by the risky relations of which the provisional ins and outs have to be the object of a constant *re*-presentation. The last thing we need is for someone to compose in our stead the world to come. But to inquire into what binds us, we can count on the human sciences' offering the actors multiple and *rapidly revised* versions that allow us to understand the collective experience in which we are all engaged. All the "-logies," "-graphies," and "-nomies" then become indispensable if they serve to propose constantly, to the collective, new versions of what it might be, while keeping track of the singularities. With the social sciences, the collective can finally *collect itself again*. If quite ordinary minds are capable of becoming precise and meticulous scientists, thanks to their laboratory equipment, we can imagine what ordinary citizens might become if they benefited, in order to conceive of the collective, from the equipment of the social sciences. Political ecology marks the golden age of the social sciences finally freed from modernism.

May I keep the expression "political ecology" to designate that sort of state of war? I am aware that the connection with the "green" parties remains very tenuous, since I have done nothing but criticize the use of nature by showing that it paralyzed the combat of the ecology-minded. How can I keep the same term, political ecology, to designate the *Naturpolitik* of the ecologists who claim to be bringing nature back into politics, and to designate a public life that has to get over its intoxication with nature? Am I not abusing the term here? If I have allowed myself to lack respect for the political philosophy of ecology, it is because it has made very little use up to now of the combined resources of the philosophy of the sciences and comparative anthropology, both of which [. . .] require us to give up nature. In contrast, I have not ceased to do justice to the burgeoning practice of those who discover behind every human being proliferating associations of nonhumans and whose tangled consequences make the old division between nature and society impossible. *What term other than ecology would allow us to welcome nonhumans into politics?* I hope I may be pardoned for shaking up the wisdom of ecology in the hope of ridding it of some of its most flagrant contradictions. To speak of nature without taking another look at the democracy of the sciences did not make much sense. And yet if we assure ourselves that humans no longer engage in their politics without nonhumans, is this not what the "green" movements have always sought, behind awkward formulas involving the "protection" or the "preservation" of "nature"?

A delicate question remains: Does political ecology have to inherit the classic political divisions? The parties that lay claim to political ecology, as has often been noted, have trouble telling their left from their right. But left and right depend on the Assembly that brings together the parliamentarians, on the organization of the rows, on the form of the amphitheater, on the position of the president, on the podium where the speaker presides. Political ecology is seeking not to choose a place within the old Constitution, but to convene a collective in a different assembly, a different arena, a different forum. Left and right will no longer reproduce the old divisions. No prewrapped package will permit the forces of Progress and the forces of Reaction to confront each other any longer, as if there were a single front of modernization that would make the Enlightenment, secularization, the liberation of morals, the market, the universal all walk in step. The divisions within the parties have been superior to what unites them for a long time now.

What is to be done with the left and the right if progress consists in going, as we have seen, from the tangled to the more tangled, from a mix of facts and values to an even more inextricable mix? What if freedom consists in finding oneself not free of a greater number of beings but attached to an ever-increasing number of contradictory propositions? What if fraternity resides not in a front of civilization that would send the others back to barbarity but in the obligation to work with all the others to build a single common world? What if equality asks us to take responsibility for nonhumans without knowing in advance what belongs to the category of simple means and what belongs to the kingdom of ends? What if the Republic becomes at once a very old and very new form of the Parliament of things?

For the triage of possible worlds, the left-right difference appears very awkward indeed. At the same time, it is unthinkable to come to an agreement by outstripping that opposition through a unanimous power, since nature is no longer there to unite us without lifting a finger. I am not too worried about this difficulty. Once assembled with its own furnishings, political ecology will quickly be able to identify the new rifts, the new enemies, the new fronts. There will be time enough then to find labels for them. Most are already right here in front of us. Surprising in the eyes of the Old Regime, these regroupings will appear banal for the new one. Let us not hurry, in any case, to inherit old divisions.

Are there really any solutions, moreover, besides political ecology? Ultimately, what do you want? Can you really say, without blushing, still believing it, that the future of the planet consists in a melting away of all cultural differences, in the hope that they will gradually be replaced by a single nature known to universal Science? If you are not that bold, then be honest: Will you have the nerve to admit, conversely, that you are resigned to the idea that cultures, although inessential, should become as many incommensurable worlds, added mysteriously to a nature that is at once essential and devoid of meaning? And if you do not pursue that goal either, if mononaturalism combined with multiculturalism strikes you as an imposture, if you really no longer dare to be modern, if the old form of the future really has no future, then must we not put back on the table the venerable terminology of democracy? Why not try to put an end to the state of nature, to the state of war of the sciences? What risk do we run in trying out a politics without nature? The world is young, the sciences are recent, history has barely begun, and as for ecology, it is barely in its infancy: Why should we have finished exploring the institutions of public life?

Chapter 21

Timothy Morton

IMAGINING ECOLOGY WITHOUT NATURE

I am here, sitting by the fire, wearing a dressing gown, holding this page in my hand.
— DESCARTES, *MEDITATIONS*

[T]HE PREVIOUS CHAPTER] COULD LEAVE us in a state of cynicism. On some days, environmentalist writing seems like patching up the void with duct tape. So many solutions seem either out of date or inadequate in their attempt to generate different ways of making us feel about the state we are in, without changing it. But all cultural forms lag behind processes of production. Environmental art and politics are no exception. Moreover, certain radical or avant-garde practices have come more up to date with the current moment. The Paris Communes were experiments in the production of social space, documented by poets such as Rimbaud. The revolutionary space mobilized the floating world of the *flâneurs* and their psychic disposition of boredom, opening up desires for Utopian "free space" that sounds much like the wilderness.[1] The Situationists in 1960s Paris and other experimenters in "psychic geography" have struggled to keep abreast of the productive forces:

Remaining in cynicism is a habit of the beautiful soul. Our choice is false if it has been reduced to one between hypocrisy and cynicism, between wholeheartedly getting into environmental rhetoric and cynically distancing ourselves from it. In both cases, we would be writing liturgies for the beautiful soul. Although it is "realistic" to be cynical rather than hypocritical, we do not wish to reinforce the current state of affairs. Our answer to the ruthless ransacking of nature, and of the idea of nature, must be yes, we admit to the reality of the situation. And no, we refuse to submit to it.

Instead of serving up lashings of guilt and redemption, might ecological criticism not engage the ideological forms of the environment, from capitalist imagery to the very ecocriticism that opposes capitalism? Eco-critique could establish collective forms of identity that included other species and their worlds, real and possible. It would subvert fixating images of "world" that inhibit humans from grasping their place in an already historical nature. Subverting fixation is the radical goal of the Romantic wish to explore the shadow lands. The hesitations of a Wordsworth, the unreliable narrators of a Mary Shelley— the whole panoply of irony and linguistic play is not marginal, but central to Romanticism.

Subversion of identity fixations is what Alain Badiou calls a truth process, a rigorous and relentless distinction of the subject from its identifications.[2] It is valid both to say that subjectivity is profoundly Romantic, and to claim that we haven't attained it yet. Indeed, an ecological collective to come would definitely not look like the nature-nation construct with its fascist-tending ideal of work and wholeness. It would be more like Jean-Luc Nancy's society of "unworking," and in this sense, the "unintention" and openness of ambient art hold out a promise of an almost unimaginable kind of being together.[3]

The environment was born at exactly the moment when it became a problem. The word *environment* still haunts us, because in a society that took care of its surroundings in a more comprehensive sense, our idea of environment would have withered away. The very word *environmentalism* is evidence of wishful thinking. Society would be so involved in taking care of "it" that it would no longer be a case of some "thing" that surrounds us, that environs us and differs from us. Humans may yet return the idea of the "thing" to its older sense of *meeting place*.[4] In a society that fully acknowledged that we were always already involved in our world, there would be no need to point it out.

At the Looking Glass House

The more strenuously we try to exit the Looking Glass House of the beautiful soul, the more we end up back at square one. If we leave the beautiful soul bleeding in the street, have we really transcended it? Instead of trying to fight it, that is, to burst its bounds on its own terms, a more subtle, nonviolent, judo-like approach is in order. There is a rich vein of thinking on how to get out of beautiful soul syndrome.[5] Forgiveness is the key. But as Derrida has shown, forgiveness is an infinitely rich, difficult, and complex subject.[6] It has to do with acknowledging the gap between, the difference between, ideas and signs, between selves, and the gap between beautiful soul and "beautiful Nature." Ecology wants to go from dualism to monism, but not so fast! Rather than seeking some false oneness, acknowledging the gap is a paradoxical way of having greater fidelity to things. We will be exploring this later under the heading of "dark ecology."

To think in terms of either crude action or pure ideas is to remain within the prison of the beautiful soul. Oppositional consciousness is blessed and cursed with beautiful soul syndrome.[7] *Ecology without Nature* certainly suffers from it. The world of nature writing shimmers "over there" while we remain here safe (or stuck) in our critical mode. We cannot remain on the fence. But the possibilities are restricted: there is a strong gravitational pull toward the "new and improved" world of commodified solutions to a commodified world. The siren song of the beautiful soul exerts a fascination that could falsely induce one to think that one had transcended it. There is something of the "I can't go on . . . I'll go on" quality found in Adorno and Beckett about this part of our investigation.

The shape of this chapter is twofold. In the first few sections, I will consider some possibilities for a critical ecomimesis. Ambience may have a liberating potential. It is a candidate for what Benjamin called a "dialectical image," a form that looks both toward oppression and toward liberation, like the two-headed god Janus. On the one hand, ambient rhetoric provokes thought about fundamental metaphysical categories, such as inside and outside. On the other hand, if ambience becomes a resting place, a better version of the aesthetic dimension, then it has abandoned its liberating potential. If we find no resting place in ambience, no new religion or territory upon which to pin our flag, then ambience has helped to liberate radical thinking.

Our analysis needs to return to Romanticism, for Romantic experiments had already surpassed the conundrum of how embedding yourself in reality can also produce the opposite, a sublime aesthetic distancing. This is the problem that haunts David Abram's utopian prose. The self-defeating routine of puncturing the aesthetic veil, only to have it grow back even stronger, is why some Romantic writers, in their different ways, experiment with ecomimesis. They open up the rendered environment to the breeze of the cosmic, the historical, the political. Moreover, they turn the anti-aesthetic of ecomimesis around on itself. This is only possible because of the intrinsic playfulness and reversibility of language, and because of the inherent qualities of the perception dimension that, as we shall discover, makes *perception* diverge from the *aesthetic* (too often its analogue). The first sections consider two ways of solving the problems of ambience. First, I will investigate the possibility of dissolving the solidity of perception, either through juxtaposition, or through a redefinition of the aesthetic dimension itself. Second, the idea of *place* subtending the aesthetic will be deconstructed.

As Heidegger, Merleau-Ponty, and Derrida remarked in their very different ways, perception contains nonidentity like a carpet contains holes, or as a text is shot through with nothingness. We cannot see ahead, what we see behind us is only a surmise, and what we see in front of us is fleeting and illusory. The specter of a trickster nature, which is precisely what these theories of perception generate, is surprisingly what Abram finally wards off in his evocation of a monist spirit that rolls through all things. And ironically this trickster is available through the study of deconstruction, so our way out of the beautiful soul may seem like going further into it.

In the remaining sections of this chapter, I show how the idea of place is not single, independent, and solid. This leads to developing a new way of doing ecological criticism, which I call *dark ecology*. Dark ecology acknowledges that there is no way out of the paradoxes outlined in this book. Far from remaining natural, ecocriticism must admit that it is contingent and queer. I conclude by asserting that ecocritique, far from being hostile to deep ecology, is a form of "really deep ecology."

Juxtaposition as Ecocritique

Ecomimesis is above all a practice of juxtaposition. Avant-garde art values juxtaposition as collage, montage, bricolage, or rhizomics. But it all very much depends upon what is being juxtaposed with what. If it is to be properly critical, montage must juxtapose the contents with the frame. Why? Simply to juxtapose contents without bringing form and subject position into the mix would leave things as they are. As we have seen, just adding items to a list (such as adding polluting factories to a list of things in "nature") will not entirely do. The most extreme example of "contents" would be the writing quality of writing. The most extreme example of "frame" would be the ideological matrix that makes things meaningful in the first place. Ambient art gestures toward this (dialectical) juxtaposition of writing with the ideological matrix. By presenting objects without a frame (clumps of "stuff" in a gallery, for instance) or frames without an object (white canvases, empty frames, and so on), ambient art questions the gap between contents and frame.

To juxtapose contents and frame, one must preserve the gap between them, even though ambient rhetoric screams (quietly) that the gap has been abolished. There is a gap between the particular and the general. If there were no gap then infinity would be merely another number—just an extremely high one. But infinity is radically beyond number; otherwise we fall back into the problem of "bad infinity"—an infinity that is ultimately countable. The frame is not just another element. Ambient art plays with what "counts" as either frame or contents, through the play of the re-mark. The re-mark establishes (and questions) the differences between, for example, graphic mark/sign, noise/sound, noise/silence, foreground/background. To reiterate Chapter 1 [of Mortons original text (to which all additional chapter references by Morton refer)], there is *nothing* in between; literally nothing, not even space, since space is also subject to these distinctions. Something is *either* a noise *or* it is sound. (The ideological fantasy of ecomimesis and especially ambience, *seems* to suggest that something could be both.)

In the universe according to quantum mechanics, things can be either particles or waves, but not both simultaneously. It is not even appropriate to say that "energy" can be either a particle or a wave. There is nothing behind these in the standard model that can be either, or worse, both at once. Similarly, contemporary neuroscience argues that experience comes in discrete quanta that are then blended to appear continuous. Perception may well be made up of moments rather than continua, as the theoretical exploration in Chapter 1 suggested.[8] Despite the fact that many green thinkers have relied on it, almost as a form of automated philosophy (the ontology of physics does it for you! Relax!), the Standard (Quantum) Model does not abolish subject–object dualism.[9] If anything, quantum theory demonstrates the persistence of this conundrum.

The aesthetic dimension is frequently posited as existing between subject and object; so do ecological dimensions. Consider the idea of "mesocosm," developed in studies of food webs by Gary Polis.[10] The mesocosm—a "medium-sized ecosystem"—functions in ecological science in experiments whose conditions simulate real life as closely as possible. Mesocosms exist between microcosm and macrocosm. Practically speaking, mesocosms may be beneficial scientific concepts. Magically, all animals and plants, and ultimately everything else, might find a place in them (or it?). The mesocosm swallows everything. Phenomena become equally meaningful, and thus meaningless, like a 1.1 map of reality. One reason why studying ambient poetics subverts aestheticization is that the re-mark signals a difference that is irreducible—it is not made out of anything smaller or more general. Either that, or everything is "between" and there is no definition. You will never find a thing between noise and sound, or between noise and silence. The re-mark is a quantum event. There is nothing between background and foreground. And there is nothing between frame and contents. Radical juxtaposition plays with the frame and its contents in such a way as to challenge both dualism (their absolute difference) and monism (their absolute identity). Dialectics is shorthand for a play back and forth between contents and frame.

Ekphrasis suspends time, generating a steady state in which the frequency and duration of the form floats wildly away from the frequency and duration of the content. Abram's hyperekphrasis means to transport us to this world—a bubble in the onward flow of the argument, a little island of fantasy. Indeed, there are bubbles within bubbles in the passage quoted in Chapter 2—we get from the present of enunciation "As I write" to the deer tracks the narrator "follows" by the end, via a paragraph break that forces the reader to step further into the fantasy world by tracking the text with his or her descending eyes. Recalling that Abram compares writing with following tracks, we should not be surprised that the narrative-within-a-narrative that is the second paragraph ends with the image of following tracks rather than writing.[11] Even the narrator's act of inscription itself has become attentiveness to the divine other, an attunement, a *Stimmung*. Everything is automated, and everything is seen from the outside and exoticized, in the very gesture of embedding us in a deep, dark inside.

The prose seems to stand up and arrest our progress through the argument's propositions. The passage is coordinated with the tissue of the surrounding text. In an invagination where form plays the opposite role from content, the passage's content surrounds the content of the argument (as I write the world goes on around me), just as the actual text is embedded with it (the reader must pause to take in an inset narrative). But what if a writer were to present this ekphrastic suspension on its own, to decontextualize it, like those modern artists who present lumps of something or other in a gallery without a frame around it?

One approach would be isolating the fantasy object of ecomimesis, leaving it high and dry. It is what Leigh Hunt tries in "A Now, Descriptive of a Hot Day."[12] Hunt's essay is an instance of Cockney ecomimesis—a suburban picture of suspended time interrupted not at the beginning, but at the end, by the notion that the writer is embedded in the scene. The inversion of the order, so that the metonymic exorbitancy comes first, and the "as I write" comes last, undermines naturalization. The last glimpse of the scene is of the author's pen, which waves away the fantasy's compelling quality in a reverse sleight of hand as we realize that the subject of the enunciated is also the subject of enunciation. The narrator takes responsibility for the fantasy—instead of using it as a treasure trove of his beautiful soul, he undermines the distance toward it that maintains the objectification and *vraisemblable* of the narrative world. The mixed-media art of David Robertson likewise juxtaposes everyday texts such as a deck of cards or a newspaper with existential-religious musings and quantum theory, as it takes the reader on a nonholistic ecological tour.[13]

The privileged attention of Abram's narrator is also the fortunate position of the framing narrator of Wordsworth's *The Ruined Cottage*. Wordsworth embeds a narrator—the Pedlar and his tale of Margaret and her husband who went to war and never came back—within another narration. The apparently simple act of double framing induces a sense of hesitation. Can we trust where the frame stops and where the next one starts, what is inside the frame, how truthful it is? The aesthetic, and aestheticizing, frame undermines the necessarily comfortable aesthetic distance with which to accept the poem as a soothing aesthetic-moral lesson. Wordsworth destabilizes the supposed neutrality of the medium in which we glimpse events. The introductory verse paragraph contains instructions on how to read the rest of the poem:

> 'Twas summer and the sun was mounted high;
> Along the south the uplands feebly glared
> Through a pale steam, and all the northern downs,
> In clearer air ascending, shewed far off
> Their surfaces with shadows dappled o'er
> Of deep embattled clouds: far as the sight
> Could reach those many shadows lay in spots
> Determined and unmoved, with steady beams
> Of clear and pleasant sunshine interposed;
> Pleasant to him who on the soft cool moss
> Extends his careless limbs beside the root
> Of some huge oak whose aged branches make
> A twilight of their own, a dewy shade
> Where the wren warbles while the dreaming man,
> Half-conscious of that soothing melody,
> With side-long eye looks out upon the scene,
> By those impending branches made more soft,
> More soft and distant. Other lot was mine.
>
> (1–18)[14]

The lines juxtapose a panoramic view with a more specific one. Details alert us to the idea that we are being let in on a clue. The sun "was mounted" (1)—like the word "sun," itself mounted high on the page. At first, the shadows "lie" on the surface of the land like the words on the page (7), loosely associated in the most open form available to Wordsworth (blank verse). The imagery is pale and minimalist, inviting our closer scrutiny at the very moment at which it seems to offer a relaxing ease. The repetition of "pleasant" (9–10) creates a tiny ripple on a smooth surface, to which our suspicion is drawn. We find ourselves embedded in the poem, via the semicolon (9) that hesitates before we find ourselves placed ("Pleasant to him," 10). This virtual reader, the "dreaming man," both is and is not the reader. Wordsworth is careful not to identify us absolutely with this figure. We are involved in the scene, yet critically so—our view seems to oscillate between a particular point of view within it, and a more general view outside it. This oscillation repeats itself on the very inside itself. The man "looks out" with "side-long eye"—he views the scene anamorphically, from an unexpected vantage point.

By the time we arrive at the quiescence of "more soft, / More soft and distant" (17–18), the scene has become far from an aesthetic blur. We want to peer into the softness, we are disturbed by the distance. All this takes place before we are pulled up short, anyway, by "Other lot was mine" (18). The very beauty of the exorbitant growth around the cottage—like the endless lines of blank verse silent before us on the page—haunts us with the possibility of pain and with the history of other places, other times that impinge intensely on this one. Instead of embedding the narrator in an othered war, *The Ruined Cottage* embeds the war in our experience of reading. In its very tranquility, it is one of the most powerful antiwar poems ever written.

Writing during another moment of oppressive imperialism, the First World War, Edward Thomas juxtaposes content and frame:

> Tall nettles cover up, as they have done
> These many springs, the rusty harrow, the plough
> Long worn out, and the roller made of stone:
> Only the elm butt tops the nettles now.
>
> This corner of the farmyard I like most:
> As well as any bloom upon a flower
> I like the dust on the nettles, never lost
> Except to prove the sweetness of a shower.[15]

It would be easy to say that the quietism and minimalism evoke the absent presence of Edwardian Englishness, an internal distance toward the pomp and circumstance of state affairs that only serves to throw that state into greater relief. The "corner," the neglected and unlovely plants (a Wordsworthian de-aestheticization), the "dust on the nettles"—in all these images *nature* seems very close to *nation*. This is miniaturized wildness, not the open frontier of manifest destiny, but a little corner of unreconstructed wilderness; even of atavism, a Romantic backsliding into a world before the domination of nature, figured by the rusting farm tools. As surely as do Heidegger's peasant shoes, these broken pieces of abandoned equipment open up the environment, cultural, meteorological, agricultural, and biological.

If tropes are flowers ("the flowers of rhetoric") then the tall nettles are wild tropes: ecomimesis. The poem holds something in reserve, something Blanchot calls the "interminable" of writing, figured in the nettles. At the end the dust, an image of stasis, is "lost" to the rain's "sweetness," a powerfully weak image, if that is not too oxymoronic. The reserve is barely encapsulated in the most imperceptible of things. But its trace is everywhere, on edges and corners—ambient. Thomas's poem is a quiet resistance to imperial poetics, with its corners of foreign fields that will be forever England. It plays with the idea of *world* like Wilfred Owen, who in "Anthem for Doomed Youth" juxtaposes the screams of war materiel (2–7) with "bugles calling for [the dead] from sad shires" (8), a line that never fails to evoke a visceral reaction as it suddenly reconfigures the viewpoint from No-Man's Land back to the grieving families: "Their flowers the tenderness of silent minds, / And each slow dusk a drawing-down of blinds" (13–14).[16] The shifts and turns are Wordsworthian, as is the writing of W. G. Sebald, whose *On the Natural History of Destruction* positions us in an impossible, almost unspoken point of view, as fictional as it is urgent, inside Dresden and Hamburg as they are being bombed to smithereens at the end of the Second World War.[17]

"To see a World in a Grain of Sand" is to juxtapose the content with the frame in a highly critical manner. Writing "Auguries of Innocence" in a time of almost totalitarian surveillance and paranoia, during a particularly oppressive moment of the Napoleonic Wars, Blake imagines how the tiniest particularity can relate to the grandest generality: "A Robin Red breast in a Cage / Puts all Heaven in a Rage" (5–6); "A dog starvd at his Masters Gate / Predicts the ruin of the State" (9–10).[18] The poem sustains an almost static tone, reading the general in the particular over and over in simple AABB rhyming that only changes by increasing in intensity toward the end (tending toward AAAA). This feels like braking. I am reminded of Benjamin's comment that socialism is not so much a progression as the application of the emergency brake.[19] An augury is a prophecy written in the tea leaves, in the guts of a bird, in the real— ecomimesis. It is knowledge that is somehow imprinted in the real.

A stain on the horizon announces the presence of a significant Beyond. But this Beyond is sick: we can read it in the tea leaves. This is an everyday experience for people living in a time of intense war. Jane Austen's novels are saturated with the presence of the war, which appears every day in the paper on the breakfast table.[20] In this atmosphere, it is a supreme political act to de-objectify the world, which is what happens here, especially in the "AAAA" section. It contains its own negation within itself, its own nonidentity:

> Some to Misery are Born
> Every Morn & every Night
> Some are Born to sweet delight
> Some are Born to sweet delight
> Some are born to Endless Night
> We are led to Believe a Lie
> When we see not Thro the Eye
> Which was Born in a Night to perish in a Night
> When the Soul Slept in Beams of Light
> God Appears & God is Light
> To those poor Souls who dwell in Night
> But does a Human Form Display
> To those who Dwell in Realms of day
> (120–32)[21]

The evocation of the impermanence of perception ("Which was Born in a Night to perish in a Night") breaks up the rhythm into rapid pyrrhics that undermine the solidity of the basic pulse. Seeing becomes not a view of the Beyond (sick or not) from a local vantage point, for the local has swallowed up everything in the human form divine: a hard-won victory in which the narrator generalizes the passionate militancy of what is "in his face" against the shadow play of state terror. This is ecological politics, and it is no surprise that violence toward animals makes an appearance as Blake enumerates canaries in the coal mine of institutionalized violence. Blake's radical leaps are a surprising form of realism. In contemporary Colorado, the nuclear "missile field" exists amidst real estate. Some people actually have missile silos in their backyards, complete with soldiers on hair-trigger alert. The state jams up against civil society just like the couplets of Blake's poem.

We have read four war poems that have something to say about to an age of war against life forms. It is almost possible to show how any text could deliver a radical message, not because of the presence of some special property in the text (the literalism of ecomimesis, for example), but because of the *absence* of one. *Almost* possible, not only because it seems like hard work getting certain texts to read this way (*Mein Kampf*, a bus ticket), but because this proposition might presuppose the very radicalism it is "finding" in the text as an object of ideological enjoyment. These problems inhere in Benjamin's montage technique. In his (non)monumental study of the space of consumerism in early nineteenth-century Paris, the *Arcades* project, Benjamin shows how sheer juxtaposition can speak volumes. Benjamin practices a form of environmental criticism—not of bunnies and butterflies, but of the distracting, phantasmagoric spaces produced by modern capital. Yet there is a sense of predetermination, of knowing already what we will find.

The text's non-coincidence with us is what is significant. Likewise, the text of nature—it is the silence of the owls that speaks volumes about the environment in Wordsworth's "There was a Boy." Nevertheless, these radicalizations of ecomimesis hold open the aesthetic dimension even as they seek to abolish aestheticization. In an era when the aesthetic has been commodified, and the commodity has been aestheticized, an empty frame or frameless unformed stuff retains the possibility of other ways of being. At a moment such as ours, radical ecomimesis can only honestly appear as sheer negativity.

Radical Ecological Kitsch

Finding out where your breakfast came from can reveal social patterns on a global geographical scale. When it comes to delineating the environment, simple materialism has a lot going for it. Living beings all exchange substances with their environment(s). Any field of study that takes metabolism as one of its objects is bound to generate straightforward environmental images. This includes the study of food and diet. "Oh! for a beaker full of the warm south" says Keats ("Ode to a Nightingale," 15), depicting the idea of *terroir*, the notion that grapes taste of where you grow them.[22] For all his mysteriousness, Heidegger offers an ambient materialism in his idea of *Umwelt:* "in the ontological doctrine of Being's priority over thought, in the 'transcendence' of Being, the materialist echo reverberates from a vast distance."[23]

Areas such as food studies, emerging by the side of traditional work in the humanities, and sometimes connected to the sciences, are to be encouraged. A direct approach to the object—where did it come from, where is it going?—will help people understand ecological politics, without appealing to abstract nature. But this materialism is prone to monism: reducing the world of two to that of one. Monism is not a good solution to dualism. We still need to establish a subtler sense of what "body," "mass," and "matter" might mean; and for that matter, materialism.[24] Idealism and materialism can both generate flat worlds in which there is no otherness. If ecology without nature has taught us anything, it is that there is a need to acknowledge irreducible otherness, whether in poetics, ethics, or politics.

Ecomimesis wants us to forget or lay aside the subject-object dualism. Ecomimesis aims for immediacy. The less thinking or mediating we do, the better. Lest we scoff, notice that such notions are present in high experimental art, not just in kitsch. One of Alvin Lucier's early experiments involved using electrodes to pick up alpha waves in his brain, which activated various instruments. Or think of action painting, drip painting, happenings.

A beer mug in the shape of a president's head, a tea cup with a swastika on it, a tiny ceramic model of a Bambi-eyed fawn; such objects are mind-bogglingly inconsistent, and, as Clement Greenberg pointed out long ago, can supply the kernel of powerful ideological fantasies, by no means limited to fascism.[25] Ecomimesis evokes a sense of "sheer stuff," of sprouting enjoyment—the sinthome. Sheer stuff, historically, is *for* someone: the name we give to it is kitsch, which is really a way of saying "other people's enjoyment." Though the German etymology is obscure, consider the high-handed dictionary definition: "Art or *objets d'art* characterized by worthless pretentiousness."[26] I use *kitsch* in contradistinction to *camp.* Some people confuse the two. While *camp* refers to an "ironic" (distanced) appropriation of a bygone aesthetic commodity, *kitsch* indicates the unalloyed enjoyment of an object not normally considered aesthetic in a "high" sense. Commodities pass through different phases. Some objects are born camp, some achieve it, and some have camp thrust upon them.[27]

Kitsch is unashamed about its status as a mass-produced commodity. And many works that have been mechanically reproduced would count as kitsch. How many student dorm rooms are adorned with that classic example of ecomimesis, a Monet water lilies painting? How many modern shopping malls feature a deconstructed look, where we can see the pipes? Kitsch exerts a fascinating, idiotic pull. It is often synesthetic, and it has no power except for the love we invest in it. Kitsch is the nearest thing in modern culture to the shamanic ritual object. Kitsch is immersive. It is a labor of love: you have to "get into it." It poses the problem of how the subject relates to the object in a striking manner. Kitsch is based on the idea that nature can be copied, and thus on the notion of ecomimesis.[28] For Adorno, "nature" denotes a phase of existence that is both dominating and dominated: "The song of birds is found beautiful by everyone; no feeling person in whom something of the European tradition survives fails to be moved by the sound of a robin after a rain shower. Yet something frightening lurks in the song of birds precisely because it is not a song but obeys the spell in which it is enmeshed."[29] The copying of nature, on this view, is the domination of nature— but also, in a dialectical twist, a condition of being spellbound by its dominating quality.

Kitsch is the object of disgust.[30] It must fall out of the aesthetic for aesthetic judgment to mean anything. He likes kitsch, your nature writing is distasteful, whereas my ambience is richly ambiguous and full of irony. The journal mode tries to drop out of the aesthetic dimension altogether, to subvert the panoply of aesthetic distinctions, and to regain a purposive aspect that Kant ruled out of the aesthetic proper. There is a point to nature writing. It wants to make us love nature. All that prose and all those illustrations in *A Sand County Almanac* are meant to melt our hearts. There is something of the fetish in kitsch. It only maintains the powers invested in it, like a souvenir. Nowadays, what separates high art from kitsch is often just the price of admission to a gallery, not even a recherché one. Through the tiny gestures of the re-mark, high environmental art polices the boundaries between itself and kitsch. Witness the gyrations in *The Wire* magazine, a journal about contemporary avant-garde and pop music. The sleeve notes to Brian Eno's *Ambient 1: Music for Airports* attempts to distinguish "ambient" music from Muzak, which he describes as "familiar tunes arranged and orchestrated in a lightweight and derivative manner":

> Whereas the extant canned music companies proceed from the basis of regulating environments by blanketing their acoustic and atmospheric idiosyncracies, Ambient Music is intended to enhance these. Whereas conventional background music is produced by stripping away all sense of doubt and uncertainty (and thus all genuine interest) from the music, Ambient Music retains these qualities. And whereas their intention is to "brighten" the environment by adding stimulus to it (thus supposedly alleviating the tedium of routine tasks and levelling out the natural ups and downs of the body rhythms) Ambient Music is intended to induce calm and a space to think.[31]

Decades beforehand, Jean Cocteau and Erik Satie had already deconstructed the difference Eno struggles to maintain. Powerful computers and music software such as Pro Tools and Reason have reduced or eliminated the distinction between high and low sound art. Minimalism is now a way of decorating suburban kitchens. Bamboo has become popular in British gardens for its sonic properties.

Adorno commented on such experimentation by linking it specifically to a form of "naturalism," produced "in spite of the absence of representational objectivity and expression":

> Crudely physicalistic procedures in the material and calculable relations between parameters helplessly repress aesthetic semblance and thereby reveal the truth of their positedness. The disappearance of this positedness into their autonomous nexus left behind aura as a reflex of human self-objectification. The allergy to aura, from which no art today is able to escape, is inseparable from the eruption of inhumanity. This renewed reification, the regression of artworks to the barbaric literalness of what is aesthetically the case, and phantasmagorical guilt are inextricably intertwined. As soon as the artwork fears for its purity so fanatically that it loses faith in its possibility and begins to display outwardly what cannot become art—canvas and mere tones—it becomes its own enemy, the direct and false continuation of purposeful rationality. This tendency culminates in the *happening*.[32]

High experimental art becomes its opposite—a "second naturalism"—despite itself. Adorno is addressing a consequence he identifies in Benjamin's criticism of the "aura" of high art. In its worry about the aura of lofty and commodified artworks, art tries to de-reify itself, to jump off the canvas and out of the concert hall. But in doing so, it finds that it has reduced itself to an even more reified thing, "the barbaric literalness of what is aesthetically the case." Atmosphere, environment, becomes a specific vibration. We could even measure it with subsonic microphones and speed it up to within the range of human hearing. My own procedures—a literalist view of what tone is, for instance—are hopelessly guilty as charged. Is experimental art already aware that it is kitsch, the naturalism Adorno speaks about? Or is this kitsch quality a retroactive effect? Do some works achieve kitsch while others are just born that way? And can kitsch be radical as kitsch? The liner notes to my copy of Lucier's *I Am Sitting in a Room* suggest that it is high kitsch: "[it] pulls the listener along with a process that, whether understandable nor not, seems perfectly natural, totally fascinating, intensely personal, and poignantly musical."[33]

There seems to be no getting around it. The aesthetic itself is, on this view, just a disavowal of kitsch that is, uncannily, its inner essence.[34] Nature writing is easy to dismiss as lowbrow, bad taste, unhip. But in doing so we simply adopt a speculative distance, a distance that actually maintains the object of desire (or disgust). In this way, new historicism is in danger of re-establishing the very aesthetic dimension that it considers public enemy number one. By holding the art object at a distance—it is locked in a past whose otherness we are obliged to describe carefully; it is contaminated with aesthetic strategies that erase history—its power as an object is magnified, because the aesthetic is indeed that which holds things at a distance. The problem with new historicism is exactly the reverse of what ecocriticism is afraid of. Far from contaminating the beautiful art object, it raises the object's aesthetic power to a level of phobic fascination. All art becomes (someone else's) kitsch.

It would be very easy, and highly ineffective, to denounce nature writing as sheer cheesiness without the "class" of proper (aesthetic) writing. This denunciation would reproduce aesthetic distancing. If ecology is about *collapsing* distances (between human and animal, society and natural environment, subject and object), then how much sense does it make to rely on a strategy of reading that keeps reestablishing (aesthetic) distance? Adorno makes a poignant observation about the hypocrisy of high art:

> The hardly esoteric judgment that paintings of the Matterhorn and purple

heather are kitsch has a scope reaching far beyond the displayed subject matter: what is innervated in the response is, unequivocally, that natural beauty cannot be copied. The uneasiness this causes flares up only in the face of extreme crudeness, leaving the tasteful zone of nature imitations all the more secure. The green forest of German impressionism is of no higher dignity than those views of the Königssee painted for hotel lobbies.[35]

Kitsch, says Adorno, is common to both "high" and "low" art forms, such that the "tasteful zone" of the officially sanctioned aesthetic gets a pass. In general, however, Adorno wants to exercise an ecology of cleanliness to filter the "poisonous substance" of kitsch out of art.[36]

This is not to say that we should throw away our copies of *The Norton Anthology of Poetry* and start reading books with embossed covers, as if that would save the earth. Throw away the Turner paintings, dust off the cute porcelain models of cows. I am trying not to say that kitsch is a "new and improved" version of the aesthetic. In rendering nature, nature writing tries to be a "new and improved" version of normal aesthetic forms. But, like Lyotard's "nuance," it just ends up collapsing into the aesthetic. There appears to be no way out. Trying to get out by the roof (high critique such as historicism) commits us to the distancing that re-establishes the aesthetic. And trying to get out via the basement (delving into kitsch) just widens the aesthetic dimension, generating a world of sentimental-sadistic sensations. We are going to have to admit it: we're stuck.

In its attempt to outflank aestheticized ambience (both the ecocritical and postmodern kinds), *Ecology without Nature* itself risks becoming a "super-new, ultra-improved" version of the syndrome it has been exploring all this time, consumerist appreciation for the reified world of nature. In so doing, it would ironically become another form of kitsch. Instead of trying to escape kitsch only to be sucked back into its gravitational field, we should try another approach. This would be the paradoxical one of thoroughly delving into, even identifying with, kitsch, the disgusting-fascinating sinthome of high, cool, critical art theory and theory-art.

Terry Eagleton asks how different literary theories would deal with *Finnegans Wake*.[37] One of the tests I applied consistently to theories under analysis in this study was to ask how they would cope with a snow globe of one of the Elves in *The Lord of the Rings* movies. Is it possible for sentimentalism and critique to exist together? I am not talking about the ironization of kitsch as *camp*, because that would be just another aesthetic pose. For kitsch to be critical, it would have to remain kitsch, and not be hollowed out and worn as a design on a T-shirt. Its sentimental qualities would have to persist, along with its objectal properties.

Could there be such a thing as critical kitsch? Children's stories certainly often count as sparkling kitsch fantasy objects. William Blake wrote children's songs and stories that turn out to be for adults. With its detailed, cartoonish watercolor illustrations, *The Book of Thel* approaches kitsch, although its distinctly non-mass-produced form denies it. Blake tells the story of a young girl who does not know her place in life. She lives a pastoral existence in a blissful idyllic landscape, but is somehow afflicted with melancholy sadness. What is the matter with her? Blake's Thel describes herself in natural terms, but those terms are ingrained with figurative, deceptive properties. These terms are also ambient. In a paratactic list, a plateau of tone that is a perverse ecorhapsody, Thel describes herself as various tricksterish forms of environmental anamorphic shape ("Thel is like . . . a reflection in a glass . . . like music in the air" (1.8–11)). Thel is like the beautiful soul, whose certainty Hegel brilliantly describes as "changed immediately into a sound that dies away."[38] She is all dressed up with nowhere to go.

Those with whom Thel converses—a flower, a cloud, a worm, and a clod of clay—describe themselves as natural: "naturally" interpellated into ideological consistency by the penetrative hailing of God's word. They know who they are, paradoxically, insofar as they take delight in their own insertion into their environments. The cloud falls as rain. In a Hegelian world, even nonidentity can be made into identity. In this "ecologocentric" realm, a restricted economy in which elements of the ecosystem are fed back perfectly into it without excess, Thel is a question mark amidst affirmative exclamations. Ambiguity itself can be aesthetically contained. The clod of clay "ponders" its existence (5.6), but this pondering is elevated to a second power as a Heideggerian rumination upon destiny. At the end Thel encounters her "own" voice as a disembodied sound emanating from her grave, from the earth. The voice asks a series of disturbing rhetorical questions that evoke both the materiality of the body and the deceptiveness of perception. Thel screams and flees "back" to her original state (6.22). Has nothing changed?

The juxtaposition of Thel's and her interlocutors' views is a form of ecocritique. Which side is more "ecological," the creatures', as in the standard reading, or Thel's? Most readers end up telling Thel, in the Midwestern vernacular, to shit or get off the pot. Is the poem an erotic version of a "Barbauldian moral hymn"³⁹ Or are Thel's disembodied questions, and the question of her disembodiment, in fact theoretical reflections that productively trouble the still waters of ecologocentric identity? Here is a paradox. To condemn Thel would be to inhabit the very position of the beautiful soul that she so poignantly articulates. "That stupid girl Thel. I myself am reconciled to the world with its cycles of life and death." In the beautiful soul's world there is a place for everything except uncertainty. Thel is a figure for ecocritique.⁴⁰ Her melancholia is an ethical act of absolute refusal, a series of *no*'s that finally erupt in a bloodcurdling scream. By operating as a modern trickster, ecocritique is paradoxically closer to nature. But nature by now has been deformed into something deceptive, something queer. Thel is a sentimental figure who is nevertheless critical of her ideological world.

For the *flâneur*, all objects achieve the status of kitsch. Consumerism tends to turn every object into the embodiment of the enjoyment of the other—even when it is the consumer's "own" thing. Benjamin was obsessed with phantasmagoria and the lurid kitsch of the Arcades. Wordsworth's response to the Panoramas in London deserves comparison. Wordsworth was far from simply disgusted with these immersive forms of "casual enjoyment," gigantic depictions of landscapes without aesthetic distance, enveloping viewers up and down a spiral staircase.⁴¹ Wordsworth maintained that art could be as immersive as this, and still permit one to think and reflect. His style bears uncanny similarities to the mass entertainment in Leicester Square. Late Wordsworth poems, in their miniaturized triteness, seem to aim for kitsch from another direction—the small rather than the outlandishly large. They are deceptively simple, often turning out to be little essays in poetics. "This lawn, a carpet all alive" offers a mundane garden lawn for our close-up inspection, destroying the aura of the aesthetic object by bringing it into a proximity in which it dissolves into a dancing field of ambiguous signs. To choose a lawn rather than a mountain range is itself significant—we have established that they are the inverse of one another. But to delve into the lawn in the way Wordsworth manages is extraordinary.⁴²

Coleridge's *The Ancient Mariner* suggests an ecological approach that we could call an ethics of kitsch. Kant's position is that pure art is nonconceptual. This nonconceptuality has been the basis of radical aesthetics.⁴³ Could kitsch, with its affective glow, also have a non-conceptual aspect that is even more radical? It is only at the point of utter exhaustion that the Mariner gives up the notion of imposing conceptuality onto the real. This imposition has been read as falling within the territorializing logic of imperialism (see the discussion of the poem in Chapter 2). Alan Bewell argues that colonialism and imperialism in the Romantic period produced tremendous anxiety about, fascination with, and desire to dominate the earth's life-forms. *The Ancient Mariner* deals a swift blow to the aesthetics of wilderness. The Mariner shoots the albatross; the Death Ship takes his men's souls; he is left "Alone, alone, all, all alone" in a vast, panoramic ocean (4.232); "And a thousand thousand slimy things / Lived on; and so did I" (4.238–39).[44] The Mariner embodies all those conscious beings stricken with continuation of poisoned life. The Mariner's conceptuality is resonant in the sliminess of "a thousand thousand slimy things," a register reused in Sartre's disturbingly phobic *Being and Nothingness*.[45] The slimy things absorb the gaze into a teeming infinity and collectivity (Sartre: "a sly solidarity"). At this very moment, however, the Mariner experiences some relief from the burden of his guilt: "Blue, glossy green, and velvet black, / They coiled and swam" (279–80). The snakes are still slimy, but they are not to be abjected (and subsequently objectified). Their sliminess is not only the revenge of objectivity (Sartre: "the revenge of the In-itself"), but also an invitation to look more carefully, to wonder. The "things" become "snakes." As Stanley Cavell declares, the Mariner "accepts his participation as a being living with whatever is alive."[46] The "whatever" is crucial. Ecology without nature needs the openness of this whatever, probably pronounced with the distracted yet ironic casualness of a Californian high school student. Otherwise the ecological collective to come will be captured by the fantasies of nation building that have haunted the concept of nature.

When the Mariner blesses the snakes "unaware" (4.287), does that mean that he appreciates them aesthetically first? Despite his state of mind, it seems, he blesses what before he found slimy and disgusting. What is the place of the aesthetic here? Is it being transcended, reinforced, or subverted in some other way? I am sucked into a culinary reference, especially as it pertains to Coleridge's Romantic opposition between poetic *hypsilatos* (sublimity, power) and *gluchotes* (sweetness), also used in his antislavery writing on sugar. Sartre declares that the revenge of the In-itself is threatening to the masculine subject: "the sugary death of the For-itself (like that of a wasp which sinks into the jam and drowns in it)."[47] The Mariner's temporary solution to the problem of his guilt and isolation is an immersion in the aesthetic experience of *gluchotes*: a sugary sentimentality whose gaze is down, as opposed to the sublime upward gaze of the masculine mountain-climber. This solution is fresh, given Coleridge's linkage, in the mid-1790s, of sugar with softness, artifice, luxury and cruelty.[48] *The Ancient Mariner* and *Frankenstein* are gothic and tacky. The tacky is the anaesthetic (un-aesthetic) property of kitsch: glistening, plasticized, inert, tactile, sticky—compelling our awareness of perception; too bright, too dull, too quiet, too loud, too smelly, not smelly enough—subverting aesthetic propriety. Coleridge respected the tacky; he appreciated the ethics of calling sugar the crystallized blood of slaves.[49] So did Mary Shelley: her monster story undermines the myth of Romantic genius. Both stories are about excessively material stuff, art-matter as pure extension.

The Ancient Mariner is compelled to repeat. We become infected with his tacky "rime"—sound pattern or hoar frost? The hoary, frosty quality of the poem is an allegory for the way the environment changes the object. Is the point to digest his story (moral: don't shoot albatrosses!)? Or is it to infect others? Coleridge models the ultra-slow-motion way of falling in love with your world. "He prayeth well, who loveth well / Both man and bird and beast" (*The Ancient Mariner* 7.612–13). *Love itself is* the true form of prayer, rather than: "you'll get the fast dialup speed to God if you are nice to animals." Being nice *is* the fast dialup. It goes beyond refraining from shooting albatrosses; beyond the "Hermit good" who is already way beyond the church on his "rotted old oak-stump" (7.514, 522). In the same way, *Frankenstein* transgresses advanced republicanism (the doctor is already one of those). Nature is not just an Alpine place where everything is equally splendid and sublime.

The problem of human beingness, declared Sartre and Lacan, is the problem of what to do with one's slime (one's shit): "The slimy is *myself*."[50] Ultimately, is sliminess not the sacred, the taboo substance of life itself? One word for this is Kristeva's *abject*, the qualities of the world we slough off in order to maintain subjects and objects.[51] Ecological politics is bound up with what to do with pollution, miasma, slime: things that glisten, schlup, and decay. Should radioactive waste from the nuclear bomb factory at Rocky Flats be swept under the Nevada carpet of an objectified world, a salt deposit that was declared in the 1950s to be safe, but in the 1990s had been found to leak (the Waste Isolation Pilot Project, or WIPP)? How about the planned destination for spent fuel rods from reactors, Yucca Mountain in New Mexico? What does one do with the leakiness of the world? Deep green notions such as Nuclear Guardianship (advocated by Joanna Macy) assert that substances like the plutonium whose release of poisoned light takes tens of thousands of years to cease, should be stored above ground in monitored retrievable storage; moreover, that a culture, indeed a spirituality, would have to grow up around the tending of this abject substance.[52]

Nuclear Guardianship politicizes spirituality as not an escape from, but a taking care of, the abject. Beyond its cuteness (a reified version of Kantian beauty), an element in kitsch ecological imagery maintains this abjection, a formless, ambient element, Bataille's *informe*. Milan Kundera says that kitsch holds shit at bay.[53] But (other people's) kitsch *is* shit. The bourgeois subject would rule forever if fascination and horror *always* resulted in spitting out the disgust object. Ecological art is duty bound to hold the slimy in view. This involves invoking the underside of ecomimesis, the pulsing, shifting qualities of ambient poetics, rather than trying to make pretty or sublime pictures of nature. Instead of trying to melt it away, radical kitsch exploits dualism, the difference between "I" and "slimy things." The view of nature according to the ethics of kitsch has more in common with the standard Cartesian dualism than New Age or Deep Ecology. While in these views, nature is a mysterious harmony, kitsch ecology establishes an existential life substance.[54] *Ecology without Nature* has argued consistently that the phenomenological and existential approaches flesh out, rather than make obsolete, the Cartesian view of nature as an automatic machine, a universe of mechanical reproduction.

Picking up Bad Vibrations: Environment, Aura, Atmosphere

Although environmental writing is historically determined, and although it has been the tool of many a potent ideology, ecomimesis can allow speculation on other, more free and just, states of affairs, if only in the negative. This is far from saying that it could be our salvation or medicine. Ecological criticism wants desperately to market new brands of medicine. The qualities of ecomimesis affect our ideas of what "negative" or "critical" means. If all forms of positive ecological poetry are compromised by setting up an idea of nature "over there," how about trying a negative path? This is also problematic. Claiming that valid ecological art falls short of a nature that necessarily cannot be included within it makes a success of failure—a Romantic solution that makes the earth as impenetrably real, and as distant and intangible, as the modern forces against which it is raging.[55] In Derrida's words, negative theology establishes a *hyperessential* being beyond being itself.[56]

Delving into ambience is about exploring the aesthetic, since aestheticization maintains the beautiful soul—hence its apparent *beauty* (of course Hegel means this ironically). The beautiful soul holds all ideas at a distance. Aestheticism is the art-religion of distance. Collapse the distance, and beautiful soul syndrome is cut at the root. This argument itself entirely runs the risk of beautiful soul syndrome. It could see all positions as flawed, except its own, and remain untouched in perfect, beautiful isolation, safe in the (non)position that is its own resistance to coming down firmly somewhere or other. The collapse of distance would consist in owning up to the contingency of one's own ecological desires.

Benjamin and Adorno raised ambience to a new, potent pitch. The idea of *field* explored

in Chapter 2 gains a much more fruitful resonance in Benjamin, who politicizes it: the potential for political action is a field of vectors. The idea of a historical "moment" grasps the
importance of momentum. The peculiarly charged atmosphere Benjamin detects in modern
cultural forms is what he and Adorno call *force field*—a cluster of apparently unrelated
elements that resonates with significance.[57] This *Jetztzeit* or nowness is an intense signifying
atmosphere that erupts out of the "homogeneous empty time" of official reality, even when
the ideological machinery is running smoothly.[58] All is not lost in a consumerist universe, if
only because the junk that surrounds us is so inconsistent. Its inconsistency has the quality of
a clue. This clue is the secret of suffering curled up inside the very dimension of the object.

For conservative ecocriticism, the author, the literal content of the text, the referent,
are all celebrated unequivocally, as if what "postmodern theorists" needed was a thorough
soaking in a midwestern thunderstorm, as the introduction to Karl Kroeber's *Ecological
Literary Criticism* puts it.[59] The authority of nature, especially of "place," is uncritically
celebrated. A biological basis is sought for social forms: reading Jane Austen becomes an
adaptive survival trait.[60] Ecofeminism, apparently the most progressive ecocritical genre,
tends toward biological essentialism; though the radical utopianism of 1970s ecofeminism is
surely better than the rather watered-down Habermasian version that is now emerging.
Coupled with this enforcement of reality is a repetitive claim to be able to spy ecotopia, to
be able to see the future—an augury of experience as opposed to innocence. Even ecological
apocalypticism has a streak of wishful thinking. At least we can witness the disaster occurring.
Is it too much to suggest that we may even take pleasure in it?

Conservative ecocriticism translates ecological crisis into a program for reading the text.
The text's significance is conceived as a scarcity that must be conserved. Postmodernism
generates a population growth of different and deviant interpretations that must be curbed.
Left eco-criticisms have not developed properly yet. There are some skeptical comments on
ecocriticism, for instance, in Dana Phillips's *The Truth of Ecology*. But skepticism does not
imagine alternatives. Moreover, ecocriticism has either not engaged with, or has positively
shunned, "theory"—notably deconstruction. What better time, then, to focus upon
Benjamin, who has been claimed variously by deconstruction and Marxism, as a theorist with
whom ecocritique could engage productively. Just as Thomas De Quincey, the Romantic
consumerist par excellence, is ironically a superb theorist of environmental art, so Benjamin,
fascinated with the consumerism that brought De Quincey to prominence, is an ally of
ecocritique. Ecocritique needs a figurehead as significant on the left as Heidegger has been on
the right. It needs to be able to argue for a progressive view of ecology that does not submit
to the atavistic authority of feudalism or "prehistoric" primitivism (New Age animism). It
requires, instead, that we be nostalgic for the future, helping people figure out that the
ecological "paradise" *has not occurred yet.*

At least two terms Benjamin developed are relevant to the study of aesthetics and atmosphere. An ecological-critical use of Benjamin would develop his key notions of *aura* and
distraction (Zerstreuung). The tantalizingly brief and very suggestive remarks on aura in
Benjamin's writing on technical reproducibility use the analogy (but is it an analogy?) with an
(aesthetic) experience of the natural world. The aura is a form of ambience that attaches to
works of art, an atmosphere of veneration and value in which they are bathed. The environment evoked in nature writing is itself this aura. Benjamin's definition of aura is, precisely,
also a definition of hypostasized Nature (with a capital n). The definition is chiastic, evoking
nature in describing artifice: "We define the aura . . . as the unique phenomenon of a distance,
however close [the object] may be. If, while resting on a summer afternoon, you follow with
your eyes a mountain range on the horizon or a branch which casts its shadow over you, you
experience the aura of those mountains, of that branch."[61] Benjamin evokes ecological representation. Since we are not living in the mountains, distracted in them by day-to-day tasks,

we can be aesthetically captivated by them, as we can by an auratic work of art. The aura is in peril, says Benjamin, because "contemporary masses" wish "to bring things 'closer' spatially and humanly . . . Every day the urge grows stronger to get hold of an object at very close range by way of its likeness, its reproduction."[62] All realms of art are affected. Sampling and recording has done for music what photography did for painting. Chaplin lamented the introduction of sound into cinema, because it decisively altered the audience's distance toward the film, bathing the picture in an aquarium of sound. In particular the role of the acousmatic voice, which we explored in Chapter 1, is startlingly uncanny.[63]

Zerstreuung, on the other hand, de-distances and thus de-aestheticizes the object, dissolving the subject-object dualism upon which depend both aestheticization and the domination of nature. *Zerstreuung* also undermines the capitalist-ideological difference between work and leisure, which attenuates the notion of labor and is a reflection of alienated labor. When people are involved in their work, they experience, and produce, and produce *as* experience, a dissolution of the reified object and, for that matter, the reified subject. Involvement in the world is a negation process, a dissolving. There is no such "thing" as the environment, since, being involved in it already, we are not separate from it. Art as distraction does not obey the normative post-Romantic distinction between art, kitsch, and "schlock"; things are not even kitsch, but decidedly non-auratic, functional-technical objects that are seized and enjoyed and discarded without "respect." I am loath to say that *Zerstreuung* puts back together art and craft, which Romanticism had split apart, for craft now has a Romantic aura all its own; for instance, in the medievalism of a William Morris. A rigorous recycling policy would enable rather than hinder the "disrespectful" tossing away of ecological schlock.

Zerstreuung is the synesthetic mixture of "half-conscious" hearing and soft gazing and "careless" physical absorption of the "dreaming man" in the evocative opening paragraph of Wordsworth's *The Ruined Cottage* (11,14,15). *Zerstreuung* invites relaxed but critical awareness. Wordsworth shows us how to look "side-long" (16), how to maintain a critical sense even in the very moment of perceiving things as "soft" and "distant" (17–18)—as auratic and aestheticized. Wordsworth's narrator models for us something that is not so easy to think: an intelligent absorption that inoculates us against the aesthetic moralizing of the awful story of Margaret and her husband which the poem also includes, in its capacious ability to explore all kinds of ways of perceiving war and nature and social conditions. *The Ruined Cottage* is a scream whose very quietness and meditative absorption make it terribly loud. Ambience, as distraction, can indeed function in a powerfully critical way.

Like the meditation described by Trungpa Rinpoche in Chapter 2, *Zerstreuung* is a way of getting over deception, rather than falling more deeply into it. *Zerstreuung* thus contrasts sharply with the meditative bliss (Simpson: "happy situatedness") of Heidegger's peasant woman, a condition that anthropology applied to the "primitive" other.[64] Amazingly, *Zerstreuung* is a fundamental quality of Heidegger's *Dasein*, but Heidegger resists the implications of this distraction, dissemination, or dispersal. *Zerstreuung* does not imply pacifying intellectual productivity or reflexive phenomena such as irony.[65] *Zerstreuung* is the product of contemporary capitalist modes of production and technologies. Yet precisely for this reason it holds a utopian aspect, a quality of nonstupefied absorption in the environment, conceived not as reified nature "over there" outside the city or the factory gates, but "right here"—I put the phrase in quotation marks since we will see the extent to which *here* is both objectively and ontologically *in question*.

The haunting ambience typified in the space of Benjamin's Arcades is a dialectical image. Ever since the Romantic period, ambience, a complex product of automation, private property, collectivity, and new media, has generated ever more virulent forms of aestheticization. The "embedded" reporters in Iraq were virtual couch potatoes passively contemplating the aesthetics of the panoramic, ambient sound of bullets ripping through human flesh. Technology and ideology strive hand in hand to produce forms that unmercifully de-distance the object, only to reify that very de-distancing (reality TV, ambient music in corporate space). The most extreme example would be Adorno's: the "musical accompaniment" that masked the screams in the concentration camps, which he takes as an analogue for the way in which one might try to avoid measuring concepts by the "extremity" that eludes them.[66] But there is another aspect of ambience, one that precisely points out our failure

to grasp something. Ambience contains unfulfilled promises of a world without boundaries, a de-aestheticized but nevertheless perceptually vivid world, in which the productive energies of boredom, distraction, irony, and other waste products of capitalism are released. A brief summary of these energies would be the notion of "unworking" (*désoeuvrement*) developed in Scott Shershow's reading of Jean-Luc Nancy and Blanchot. One glimpses in radical environmental art the possibility of a radical openness to other beings, without goal.

By connecting what ecocriticism forbids us to connect—consumerism and environmentalism, even the "deep" sorts—we could do fresh ecological criticism, awake to the irony that a national park is as reified as an advertisement for an SUV. Ecocritique should aim not only at globalized capitalism, but also the "Nature" that gets in the way of looking out for actually existing species, including the human species. In a splendid irony, the theorist of technological development par excellence supplies thinking with resources for ecological critique. Distraction hesitates between a form of politicized consumerism—*flâneurs* against the machine—and a quotidian response to modern sensory input.

Just as the beautiful soul is the subjective form of ambience, so distraction is the subjective form of the collapse of aesthetic distance. There are two types of distraction, and there is a knife-edge of discrimination between them. This makes distraction a very dangerous concept.[67] But distraction is nevertheless something we must explore. Anyway, all aesthetic solutions to the problems posed by the modern world end up reproducing the commodity form.

The first type of distraction is the ignorance born of living in a channel-surfing, easy-clean environment. Ignorance is one of the central ways in which ideology is enforced in the modern world and the United States has pioneered experiments in just how much ignorance people can tolerate. In this state of affairs, escapism proves to be more radical than sheer avoidance. At least art offers the possibility that things might be otherwise. The basic complaint against distraction, asserts Benjamin, is the "commonplace" "that the masses seek distraction whereas art demands concentration from the spectator."[68] This applies to ecology and anti-consumerism. The contemporary "slow movement," an impulse that is more arts-and-crafts than Luddite, which praises the idea of deceleration in "appreciating life," is a contemplative approach that is ultimately aesthetic rather than ethical or political—concentrating rather than being distracted. The aggressive speed of modern technological existence *is* destroying the planet as we knew it. But reclining our aircraft seat to contemplate this is not a good solution. Far from giving us a smoother ride, the deceleration process that is ecocritique makes us notice contradictions and inconsistencies.

The second type of distraction is critical absorption.[69] This form is enabled by two phenomena: synesthesia and the inherent emptiness of the perception dimension. Children's toys are good examples of synesthetic things, evoking a range of responses from eyes, ears, touch, and smell all at once. Food is profoundly synesthetic. It goes in our mouths while we look around the table. The synesthetic manifold makes it impossible to achieve the distance necessary to objectify and aestheticize the object. Far from generating the smoothness of the Wagnerian total work of art, where music, theater, and other media are fused together to create a compelling phantasmagorical sheen, synesthesia makes clear that experience is fragmented and inconsistent. Benjamin's argument about art in our times works its way through the aesthetic dimension all the way to the perceptual level. Aesthetics derives from perception (Greek *aisthanesthai*, "to perceive"). But the history of the aesthetic has been the story of how bodies, and especially nonvisual sense organs, have been relegated and gradually forgotten, if not entirely erased. Benjamin claims that "the tasks which face the human apparatus of perception at the turning points of history cannot be solved by optical means, that is, by contemplation, alone. They are mastered gradually by habit, under the guidance of tactile appropriation." "Reception in a state of distraction" would be more akin to walking through a building than to contemplating a canvas.[70]

Perceptual events only appear in difference to one another. Phenomenology has delineated how perception involves a dynamic relationship with its objects. Current neurophysiology is developing a quantum theory of perception, borrowing the Gestalt idea of the phi phenomenon—the way the mind joins up strobing, flickering images to obtain the illusion of movement. But instead of confirming a holistic world in which object and subject fit each other like a hand in a glove, the reduction of perception to a sequence of dots enables us to demystify it. The perception dimension is effectively devoid of independent, determinate conceptual contents.

In his project for an aesthetics of nature, Gernot Böhme has suggested that "atmosphere" is inherently differential. By moving from one atmosphere to another we become aware of them.[71] This is not rigorous enough. Since atmosphere, as Böhme allows, is a phenomenological thing—since it involves consciousness as well as an object of some kind, which is itself a manifold of bodily sensation and events happening outside the body—then it is inevitably not only spatial but also temporal. A shower of rain is atmospherically different if you stand in it for two hours, as opposed to five minutes. The "same" atmosphere is never the "same" as itself.

This is a matter not of ontological nicety, but of political urgency. The notion of atmosphere needs to expand to include temporality. *Climate* (as in climate change) is a vector field that describes the momentum of the atmosphere—the rate at which the atmosphere keeps changing. A map of atmospheric momentum would exist in a phase space with many dimensions. The neglect of temporality in thinking about the weather is why it is practically impossible to explain to people that global warming might result in pockets of cooling weather.

Even more strictly, atmosphere is subject to the same paradox as identity—it does for the weather what identity does for the idea of self. For something to resemble itself it must be different—otherwise it would just *be* itself and there would be no resemblance. Identity means "being the same as" oneself (Latin *idem*, "the same as"). Since an atmosphere requires a perceiver, just as a text requires a reader, its identity is always a matter of resemblance. The re-mark, which differentiates between what is inside and outside its frame, also appears on the inside of the frame. A cloud of flower scent is only "an" atmosphere (consistent and unique) because an act of framing differentiates itself from the other smells that are pervading the vicinity. In this respect, the ambient stasis we were examining in Chapter 1 is yet another example of an illusion of something lying "in between"—a moving stillness. Even conventional visual art, which is read over time, is not utterly still.

Perception is a process of differentiation. It involves Derridean *différance*, that is, both differing and deferment. There is a quality of "to come" built into hearing, touching, seeing, tasting, smelling. Perception appears utterly direct: this is a red ball; that is a quiet sound. But a process by which objects of sense perceptions differ from each other, like words in a text, underpins this directness. Our capacity to "make things out" is also an ability to hold things in abeyance; we can't tell what something "is" yet; we need to keep looking. Thinking like this retains aesthetics as a basis for ethics, but in a paradoxical way.[72] Curiously, the emptiness of perception guarantees that perceptual events are not just nothing. A certain passion and desire are associated with perception. In the perception dimension, belonging has dissolved into longing.

Unless we are rigorous about perception and the philosophy and politics of distraction, it is likely that distraction will become a political version of the "new and improved" syndrome. We could regard distraction as a special aesthetic appreciation, hovering nicely in between aestheticizing objectification and tuning out altogether. Any critical bite would be lost. This is urgent, since art is now being produced that wants to internalize distraction. Ambient music is music you do not have to listen to front and center. You cannot take in an installation like a painting on a wall. And, at the level of ecology, we are being asked to bathe in the environing ocean of our surroundings as a means to having a better ethical stance toward species and ecosystems. "Automated" critique—sitting back, relaxing, and letting the system do it for you—is just ignorance, the first kind of distraction. At some level, respecting other species and ecosystems involves a choice. This choice is saturated with contingency (it is our choice) and desire (we want something to be otherwise). There is no place outside the sphere of this contingent choice from which to stand and assess the situation—no "nature" outside the problem of global warming that will come and fill us in on how to vote. Ecology has taken us to a place of "no metalanguage," in the strong Lacanian sense. Even the position of knowing *that* cannot exist outside the dilemma we are facing. This is elegantly summed up by Bruno Latour, writing on the 1997 Kyoto meetings to tackle global warming: "Politics has to get to work *without* the transcendence of nature."[73]

To dissolve the aura, then, is rigorously to interrogate the atmosphere given off by ecomimesis. In Romantic, modern, and postmodern hands, ecomimesis is a "new and improved" version of the aesthetic aura. By collapsing the distance, by making us feel "embedded" in a world at our fingertips, it somehow paradoxically returns aura to art with a vengeance. If we get rid of aura too fast, the end result is abstract expressionist eco-schlock that would look good on the wall of a bank. But what would a slow-motion approach to aura look like? We could start by ruthlessly standing up to the intoxicating atmosphere of aura. Seeing it with clear, even utilitarian eyes, lyrical atmosphere is a function of *rhythm:* not just sonic and graphic rhythm (the pulse of marks on the page and sounds in the mouth), but also the rhythm of imagery, the rhythm of concepts. The juxtapositions in Wordsworth and Blake set up complex rhythms between different kinds and levels of framing device. If atmosphere is a function of rhythm then it is literally a *vibe:* a specific frequency and amplitude of vibration. It is a material product rather than a mystical spirit—it is as mystical as a heady perfume or narcotic fumes.

This takes us to a strange point, an intersection between Benjamin, relentless critic of the aura, and Adorno, paradoxical champion of aura. Adorno insists that we not get rid of aura too soon, for precisely the reason that it may return with a vengeance, in an even more corn-modified, "culinary" form. Strangely, a careful appreciation of aura can open up the *Erschütterung* or "shaking" of the subject, the lyrical "I." In the words of Adorno and Robert Kaufman, this tremor of subjectivity "can break down the hardening of subjectivity . . . [dissolving] 'the subject's petrification in his or her own subjectivity' and hence can allow the subject to catch . . . the slightest glimpse beyond that prison that it [the 'I'] itself is', thus permitting 'the "I," once 'shaken, to perceive its own limitedness and finitude' and so to experience the critical possibility of thinking otherness."[74] In Adorno's words, "The aesthetic shudder . . . cancels the distance held by the subject"—"For a few moments the I becomes aware, in real terms, of the possibility of letting self-preservation fall away."[75]

Adorno probably would have gone crazy at the mere thought of it, but I am suggesting here that the strictly vibrational *rhythm* of atmosphere is the material induction of this shudder. Contra Heidegger, the earth does not stand still in lyric. It does not reveal a world or a destiny. If it opens, it opens much too much, swallowing us up. This is the very quality that Blanchot calls the "earth" of poetry.[76] Embodied in the sonic and graphic materiality of the text, the earth quakes, setting up a subject quake, a tremor of the "I." What remains after our long delve into the fake otherness of ecomimesis is the fragility of an "I" that we can't quite get rid of, but that at least can be made to vibrate, in such a way that does not strengthen its aggressive resolve (like a hammer or a boot), but that dissolves its form, however momentarily.

Notes

1   Kristin Ross, *The Emergence of Social Space: Rimbaud and the Paris Commune* (Minneapolis: University of Minnesota Press, 1988), 47–74, 102.

2   Alain Badiou, *Ethics: An Essay on the Understanding of Evil*, trans. and intro. Peter Hallward (London: Verso, 2001), 40–57.

3   Scott Shershow has powerfully demonstrated this linkage. *The Work and the Gift* (Chicago: University of Chicago Press, 2005), 193–205. See Jean-Luc Nancy, *The Inoperative Community*, trans. Peter Connor et al. (Minneapolis: University of Minnesota Press, 1991).

4   Martin Heidegger, "Building Dwelling Thinking," in *Poetry, Language, Thought*, trans. Albert Hofstadter (New York: Harper and Row, 1971), 143–61 (153). See also "The Thing," in *Poetry, Language, Thought*, 163–86 (174). This is not just a matter of Old English but also of Latin. The *res* in *res publica* (republic) is the public "thing," that is, the transactions of an assembly. The resonance of *res* is both "object" and "circumstance," as well as "dealings" (Ethan Allen Andrews, *A Latin Dictionary: Founded on Andrews' Edition of Freund's Latin Dictionary*, rev. and enl. Charlton T. Lewis [Oxford: Clarendon Press, 1984]). See Bruno Latour, *Politics of Nature: How to Bring the Sciences into Democracy* (Cambridge, Mass.: Harvard University Press, 2004), 54.

5   See for example Emmanuel Levinas, "Ethics and Politics," in *The Levinas Reader* (Oxford: Blackwell, 1989), 289–97 (294); *Totality and Infinity: An Essay on Exteriority*, trans. Alphonso Lingis (Pittsburgh, Penn.: Duquesne University Press, 1969).

6   Jacques Derrida, "Hostipitality," in *Acts of Religion*, ed., trans., and intro. Gil Anidjar (London: Routledge, 2002), 356–420.

7   Robert Bernasconi, "Hegel and Levinas: The Possibility of Forgiveness and Reconciliation," *Archivio di Filosofia* 54 (1986): 325–46; "Levinas Face to Face with Hegel," *Journal of the British Society for Phenomenology* 13 (1982): 267–76.

8   Christof Koch, *The Quest for Consciousness: A Neurobiological Approach* (Englewood, Colo.: Roberts & Co., 2004), 33, 35, 83–84, 140–44, 250–55, 264–68.

9   See for example John M. Meyer, *Political Nature: Environmentalism and the Interpretation of Western Thought* (Cambridge, Mass.: MIT Press, 2001), 47.

10   See for example Gary Polis, ed., *Food Webs at the Landscape Level* (Chicago: University of Chicago Press, 2004).

11   That is, with reading. See David Abram, *The Spell of the Sensuous: Perception and Language in a More-Than-Human World* (New York: Pantheon, 1996), 131, 282n2.

12   James Henry Leigh Hunt, "A Now, Descriptive of a Hot Day," *The Indicator* 1 (1820): 300–302.

13   See for example David Robertson, *Ecohuman's Four Square Deck/Deal* (Davis, Calif.: Printed for the author, 2002), a deck of fifty-two cards like a deck of playing cards, which can be shuffled to give various instructions and observations concerning a tour beginning in Europe and ending in New York City; and *Freakin Magic Playing Cards* (Davis, Calif.: Printed for the author, 2003), based on a circumambulation of Yucca Mountain. Or see http://www.davidrobertson.org/

14   William Wordsworth, *"The Ruined Cottage" and "The Pedlar*," ed. James Butler (Ithaca, N.Y.: Cornell University Press, 1979).

15   Edward Thomas, *The Collected Poems of Edward Thomas*, ed. R. George Thomas (Oxford: Oxford University Press, 1981). By permission of Oxford University Press.

16   Wilfred Owen, *The Complete Poems and Fragments*, ed. Jon Stallworthy, 2 vols. (London: Chatto & Windus, 1983).

17   W.G. Sebald, *On the Natural History of Destruction*, trans. Anthea Bell (1999; repr., New York: Random House, 2003).

18   William Blake, *The Complete Poetry and Prose of William Blake*, rev. ed., ed. D. V. Erdman (New York: Doubleday, 1988).

19   Walter Benjamin, "Notes to the Theses on History," in *Gesammelte Schriften*, ed. Theodor Adorno and Gersshom Scholem, 7 vols. (Frankfurt am Main: Suhrkamp, 1972–89), 1.1232.

20   Mary Favret, "War, the Everyday, and the Romantic Novel," paper given at "New Approaches to the

Romantic Novel, 1790–1848: A Symposium," the University of Colorado, Boulder, October 5–6, 2001.

21   William Blake, "Auguries of Innocence," in *The Complete Poetry and Prose of William Blake*.

22   James E. Wilson. *Terroir* (Berkeley: University of California Press; San Francisco: Wine Appreciation Guild, 1998); Patrick Bartholomew Reuter, "Terroir: The Articulation of Viticultural Place" (Master's Thesis, University of California, Davis, 1999).

23   Theodor W. Adorno, *Negative Dialectics*, trans. E. B. Ashton (New York: Continuum, 1973), 200.

24   For a decisive account, see Marjorie Levinson, "Pre- and Post-Dialectical Materialisms: Modeling Praxis without Subjects and Objects," *Cultural Critique* (Fall 1995): 111–20.

25   Clement Greenberg, "The Avant-Garde and Kitsch," in Gillo Dorfles, ed., *Kitsch: The World of Bad Taste* (New York: Bell, 1969), 116–26.

26   *Oxford English Dictionary*, "kitsch." German philology speculates that *kitsch* derives from the English "sketch," though there is little or no evidence to prove it (Winfried Schleiner, private communication). The modern edition bundles *A Sand County Almanac* with *Sketches Here and There*, which turn out to be anything but sketchy in their outlining of the land ethic. *Kitsch* stems from the verb meaning "to put together sloppily." For a decisive analysis see Susan Stewart, *On Longing: Narratives of the Miniature, the Gigantic, the Souvenir, the Collection* (Chapel Hill, N.C.: Duke University Press, 1993), 166–69.

27   Arjun Appadurai, ed., *The Social Life of Things: Commodities in Cultural Perspective* (Cambridge: Cambridge University Press, 1986), 13, 15–17; Susan Sontag, "Notes on 'Camp,'" in *Against Interpretation* (1966; repr., New York: Doubleday, 1990), 275–92; Andrew Ross, "Uses of Camp," in *No Respect: Intellectuals and Popular Culture* (London: Routledge, 1989), 135–70.

28   Theodor Adorno, *Aesthetic Theory*, trans. and ed. Robert Hullot-Kentor (Minneapolis: University of Minnesota Press, 1997), 67.

29   Ibid., 66.

30   Yve-Alain Bois and Rosalind Kraus, *Formless: A User's Guide* (New York: Zone Books, 1997), 117–24.

31   Brian Eno, *Ambient 1: Music for Airports* (EG Records, 1978), sleeve note.

32   Adorno, *Aesthetic Theory*, 103.

33   Nicholas Collins, sleeve note in Alvin Lucier, *I Am Sitting in a Room* (Lovely Music, 1990).

34   Paul Hamilton, *Metaromanticism: Aesthetics, Litertature, Theory* (Chicago: University of Chicago Press), 102–4.

35   Adorno, *Aesthetic Theory*, 67.

36   Bois and Kraus, *Formless*, 118.

37   Terry Eagleton, *Literary Theory: An Introduction* (1983; repr., Oxford: Basil Blackwell, 1993), 82.

38   Georg Wilhelm Friedrich Hegel, *Hegel's Phenomenology of Spirit*, trans. A.V. Miller, analysis and foreword by J.N. Findlay (Oxford: Oxford University Press, 1977), 399.

39   David V. Erdman, *Blake: Prophet Against Empire*, 2nd ed. (New York: Dover, 1991), 133; see also 123–24.

40   Gerda Norvig has read Thel as a figure for theory: "Female Subjectivity and the Desire of Reading in(to) Blake's *Book of Thel*," *Studies in Romanticism* 34.2 (1995): 255–71.

41   William Galperin, *The Return of the Visible in British Romanticism* (Baltimore, Md.: Johns Hopkins University Press, 1993), 13, 53–55, 71; Jennifer Jones, "Virtual Sublime: Sensing Romantic Transcendence in the Twenty-First Century" (Ph.D. dissertation, University of California, Santa Barbara, 2002).

42   See Timothy Morton, "Wordsworth Digs the Lawn," *European Romantic Review* 15.2 (March 2004): 317–27.

43   Adorno, *Aesthetic Theory*, 67.

44   Samuel Taylor Coleridge, *Coleridge's Poetry and Prose*, ed. Nicholas Halmi, Paul Magnuson, and Raimonda Modiano (New York: Norton, 2004).

45   Jean-Paul Sartre, *Being and Nothingness: An Essay on Phenomenological Ontology*, trans, and ed. Hazel Barnes (New York: The Philosophical Library, 1969), 601–15. Sartre's view of woman/sex as a "hole" (613–14) is relevant to the earlier discussion of space as invaginated sinthome. For parallels between Romantic and existential disgust, see Denise Gigante, "The Endgame of Taste: Keats, Sartre, Beckett," *Romanticism on the Net* 24 (November 2001), http://users.ox.ac.uk/~scat0385/24gigante.html.

46   Stanley Cavell, *In Quest of the Ordinary: Lines of Skepticism and Romanticism* (Chicago: University of Chicago Press, 1988), 61.

47   Sartre, *Being and Nothingness*, 609.

48   Timothy Morton, "Blood Sugar," in Timothy Fulford and Peter Kitson, eds., *Romanticism and*

Colonialism: Writing and Empire, 1780–1830 (Cambridge: Cambridge University Press, 1998), 87–106.

49   Samuel Taylor Coleridge, *The Collected Works of Samuel Taylor Coleridge*, vol. 1 *(Lectures 1795 on Politics and Religion)*, ed. L. Patton and P. Mann (London: Routledge and Kegan Paul; Princeton, N.J.: Princeton University Press, 1971), xxxviii, 235–37, 240, 246–48, 250–51.

50   Sartre, *Being and Nothingness*, 609.

51   Julia Kristeva, *Powers of Horror: An Essay on Abjection* (New York: Columbia University Press, 1982), 1–31.

52   See *http://www.joannamacy.net/html/nuclear.html*.

53   Milan Kundera, *The Unbearable Lightness of Being* (New York: Harper, 1999), 248.

54   Slavoj Žižek, *The Indivisible Remainder: An Essay on Schelling and Related Matters* (London: Verso, 1996), 218–20.

55   See for example Kate Rigby, "Earth, World, Text: On the (Im)possibility of Ecopoiesis," *New Literary History* 35.3 (2004): 439.

56   Jacques Derrida, "How to Avoid Speaking: Denials," in *Derrida and Negative Philosophy*, ed. Harold Coward and Toby Foshay (Albany: State University of New York Press, 1992), 74.

57   Martin Jay, *Force Fields: Between Intellectual History and Cultural Critique* (New York: Routledge, 1993), 1–3, 8–9.

58   Walter Benjamin, "Theses on the Philosophy of History," in *Illuminations*, ed. Hannah Arendt, trans. Harry Zohn (London: Harcourt, Brace and World, 1973), 253–64 (261).

59   Karl Kroeber, *Ecological Literary Criticism: Romantic Imagining and the Biology of Mind* (New York: Columbia University Press, 1994), 42.

60   Joseph Carroll, *Evolution and Literary Theory* (Columbia: University of Missouri Press, 1995), 2.

61   Walter Benjamin, "The Work of Art in the Age of Mechanical Reproduction," in *Illuminations*, 222–23.

62   Ibid., 223.

63   Slavoj Žižek, "The One Measure of True Love Is: You Can Insult the Other," interview with Sabine Reul and Thomas Deichmann, *Spiked Magazine*, November 15, 2001, *http://www.spiked-online.com/Articles/00000002D2C4.htm*.

64   Martin Heidegger, "The Origin of the Work of Art," in *Poetry, Language, Thought*, 34.

65   See David Simpson, *Situatedness, or, Why We Keep Saying Where We're Coming From* (Durham, N.C.: Duke University Press, 2002), 234. Simpson compares Heidegger's peasant with Malinowki's primitivist image of Pacific islanders.

66   Adorno, *Negative Dialectics*, 365.

67   See Howard Eiland, "Reception in Distraction," *boundary 2* 30.1 (Spring 2003): 51–66.

68   Benjamin, "Work of Art," 239.

69   Eiland, "Reception in Distraction," 60–63.

70   Benjamin, "Work of Art," 240.

71   Gernot Böhme, *Atmosphäre: Essays zur neuen Ästhetik* (Frankfurt am Main: Suhrkamp, 1995), 66–84.

72   Robert E. Norton, *The Beautiful Soul: Aesthetic Morality in the Eighteenth Century* (Ithaca, N. Y.: Cornell University Press, 1995), 1–8, 277–82.

73   Latour, *Politics of Nature*, 56.

74   Robert Kaufman, "Aura, Still," *October 99* (Winter 2002): 45–80 (49). Kaufman quotes Adorno, *Aesthetic Theory*, 269, 245.

75   Adorno, *Aesthetic Theory*, 269, 245.

76   Maurice Blanchot, *The Space of Literature*, trans. Ann Smock (1955; repr., Lincoln: University of Nebraska Press, 1982), 224.

Chapter 22

Dana Phillips

EXPOSTULATIONS AND REPLIES

Books! 'tis a dull and endless strife:
Come, hear the woodland linnet,
How sweet his music! on my life,
There's more of wisdom in it.

And hark! how blithe the throstle sings!
He, too, is no mean preacher:
Come forth into the light of things,
Let Nature be your teacher.
                William Wordsworth,
            "Expostulation and Reply"

The World, the Text, and the Ecocritic

BECAUSE AMERICAN ECOCRITICISM, as a movement, is only about a dozen years old, generalizations about it are hard to make and still harder to validate.[1] So I want to begin, not by describing the principles and practices of ecocriticism in any detail [. . .], but by looking at what seems to be, for many of its adherents, ecocriticism's moment of origin, which is threefold in its implications. This moment takes the form of an epiphany: of a discovery, or a renewal, of faith in all things green, just as the bewildered ecocritic emerges from the vale of all things black and white. The ecocritic's epiphany seems to make the newly enlightened student of literature and culture feel a lot better, at least for a moment, but it is actually an ambivalent experience and soon gives rise to a corrosive negativity. As interpreted by those who claim to have had it—and to judge from the evidence presented so far—the ecocritic's epiphany can be summed up by the propositions (1) that nature, which is refreshingly simple, is good; and (2) that culture, which is tiresomely convoluted, is bad; or (3) at least not so good as nature. And insofar as the ecocritic's epiphany inspires such thoughts, its implications are largely reactionary. This becomes increasingly clear as soon as one begins to view ecocriticism's moment of origin in its broader cultural and intellectual context (as I will do, more or less systematically, in the second half of this chapter).

The following passage, which I quote from Frank Stewart's book *A Natural History of Nature Writing*, can stand as a fair example of the more or less embittered way in which ecocritics interpret their epiphanies and begin their new careers as academic Jeremiahs and John Muirs:

> On a morning several summers ago, as I glanced up from researching the post-modern poets and critics, through the narrow window above my head I saw that the brightening dawn had made my reading lamp unnecessary. A pale mist hung like a veil over the deep meadow outside, and the violet morning colors were tinting the ends of the long grasses.

Unlike Zarathustra, the author of this passage does not emerge at dawn after a restful, strength-restoring sleep. This nascent ecocritic has been up early wrestling with abstruse, difficult texts, and once he has seen the light of day and the Wordsworthian "light of things," these "postmodern" texts will figure not as part of the solution, nor as part of the problem, but quite simply *as the* problem he must resolve or, in a concession of defeat, push to one side. Only then can he answer the beckoning call of morning mists and tinted grasses, having decided that "literary theorists and academics" tend to "distance the humanities and the literary arts from the natural world outside their offices," something he no longer wishes to do.[2]

Not that resisting the temptation to theorize is going to be as simple a matter as getting up and walking outdoors into the sunshine: the coils of culture, ecocritics like to remind themselves, are not to be shuffled off with an easy shrug. As Stewart puts it, "What we always see when we look at nature is our own eyes looking back at us, filtering and altering what we choose to perceive, what we emphasize or ignore, what questions we ask and pursue."[3] Thus the ecocritic's epiphany initiates a process of reflection (of an implicitly and ironically theo-retical character), which seems to give the pursuit of the ecocritical vision a certain moral and philosophical grandeur.

A crisis of conscience and of consciousness similar to Stewart's is described in many of the ecocritical essays and monographs published since the late 1980s. This suggests that for ecocritics, invoking their epiphanies has become a ritual by means of which they can display their professional bona fides and, at the same time, register their critical opinions not only of literature and culture but of the academy, too. Quite possibly this ritual has become a signa-ture feature setting ecocriticism apart as a minor genre all its own; much that calls itself ecocriticism may strike outsiders as having more in common with the personal essay than with literary and cultural criticism as currently practiced in the academy, and for the good reason that escape from academic constraints is one of ecocriticism's central themes. For instance, the ecocritic Patrick Murphy writes: "One day, while I was attending a seminar on Menippéan satire, the whole literary-criticism game became transparently irrelevant to events in the world." It was many years, he says, before his realization of the irrelevancy of "the whole literary-criticism game" got cashed out in the form of ecocriticism.[4] Another ecocritic, SueEllen Campbell, reports feeling pulled in different directions by her attraction to theory on the one hand, and to narratives of wilderness adventure and nature writing on the other. She claims to have reconciled the two kinds of texts by pursuing a vigorous program of reading—and an equally vigorous program of backcountry hiking in the Colorado Rockies.[5]

That the ritual invocation of the moment of epiphany is centrally important to eco-criticism is also borne out by the work of Lawrence Buell, who since the publication of his book *The Environmental Imagination* in 1995 has emerged as a de facto spokesman for the movement. Like Stewart and many others, Buell argues that engrained mental habits and the forces of institutional inertia must be overcome before an ecocritic can kick free of the shackles of academic training and university life. Otherwise the longed-for epiphany may not occur, or when it does occur, it may have a decidedly bookish flavor—as it does when, describing a dawning of insight similar to the one described in the passage from Stewart's book that I quoted above, yet different from it in distinctive ways, Buell writes:

> The grove of second-growth white pines that sway at this moment of writing, with their blue-yellow-green five-needle clusters above spiky circles of atro-phied lower limbs, along a brown needle-strewn ridge of shale forty feet from my computer screen—this grove can be found in the pages of American litera-ture also, but it is not the woods imagined by American criticism.[6]

As this passage illustrates, odd wrinkles tend to creep into the fabric of the quintessential ecocritical experience, which isn't as decisive as ecocritics would like it to be. Here we are not confronted with a (relatively) clear-cut distinction between text and world—between postmodern poetry and criticism lit by electric lamplight, and pale mist and grasses illumi-nated by the morning sun. Instead, Buell presents us with a scenario in which an exemplary grove of white pines does not stand juxtaposed with and in indictment of the diminished and diminishing world of words, but is said to be in two places at once: forty feet from a computer screen, and "in the pages of American literature," where literary critics have ignored it, culpably so.

Several pages earlier, anticipating the charge of negligence he is about to lodge against his fellow critics, Buell writes: "When an author undertakes to imagine someone else's imag-ination of a tree while sitting, Bartleby-like, in a cubicle with no view, small wonder if the tree seems to be nothing more than a textual function and one comes to doubt that the author could have fancied otherwise."[7] Well, small wonder indeed, or so it seems to me, since this view of the tree, which in this case is without doubt a purely imaginary entity ("someone else's imagination of a tree"), is an eminently commonsensical one. The scenario Buell has sketched, both here and in the first passage I quoted, is much less scandalous than he seems to think it is, if it is scandalous at all.

I suspect that what really concerns Buell and his fellow ecocritics is the architecture and the interior design of the contemporary academy, where many of the rooms afford their tenants impoverished views of the extramural world. Ecocriticism has been eager to redirect its gaze toward this world, and understandably so. But its practitioners have been hasty in formulating their arguments about what it takes to shift the focus of our gaze, both individu-ally and collectively, especially where the specifics of literary criticism and literary theory are concerned. The questions we need to ask of them, and of ecocriticism as a movement, with regard to those specifics, are these: We know you told us that it's a window, but isn't that actually a looking glass hanging there on your wall? Couldn't that explain why, when you try to look through it, what you see are your own eyes looking back at you, just as one of you (Stewart) has admitted?

To get a sense of the difficulties ecocritics will have when they try to answer these ques-tions, it will help if we return to Buell's description of the vista he enjoys (as one of the lucky few) from his workstation. As I've suggested, the epiphany of the second-growth white pines is an odd one: in it, the pines figure as guidebook-perfect exemplars of their species. This is an impressive feat, given the vagaries of a pine tree's life in the open air and given the appear-ance of these particular pines "at this moment of writing," just when an apt illustration of the point being pressed is needed. Rhetorically, these are very convenient and uncannily obliging pines, "with their blue-yellow-green five-needle clusters above spiky circles of atrophied lower limbs." Most uncanny of all, I think, is their dual citizenship as inhabitants of the "brown needle-strewn ridge of shale" and of the pages of American literature. They are the ultimate screen saver for the writer eager to chastise his fellow critics, and fellow authors of criticism, for imagining that trees can serve literature only in the guise of textual functions.

Yet textual functions, in the form of words or phrases postulating an imaginary object, describing an imaginary setting, or suggesting a vaguely personified imaginary entity (such as the woods that we encounter in fairy tales), is surely what trees must be, and can only be, insofar as they figure "in the pages of American literature." It seems not so much naïve as occult to suppose otherwise. I wonder how we should regard trees that are *in literature* as something other than textual functions: I wonder what species of trees they might be, and by what right they will have acquired their unusual standing. Is Buell merely making a claim about the power of description or does he have something more iconic, or metaphorical and symbolic, in mind?

Given how his argument develops over the course of *The Environmental Imagination*, Buell seems to want there to be a relationship between trees in literature and trees in the world closer than a relationship of mere semblance would be, whether that semblance is descriptive, iconic, or metaphorical and symbolic. Such, at least, is the trend of his rhetoric, which throughout his book reveals an inchoate and perhaps not fully conscious desire for a literature of presence. This desire isn't nostalgic, since in truth it is a desire for a literature the likes of which we've never seen before, however much it may have been intimated in the works of writers like Thoreau (whose admiration for white pines was unparalleled). If I follow Buell's arguments, this literature would be "environmental." It would evoke "the natural world through verbal surrogates," and would thereby attempt "to bond the reader to the world as well as to discourse." Most remarkably, it would enable the reader "to see as a seal might see."[8] But why environmental literature should be deputized to make the presence and reality of the natural world available to us by proxy, when that world lies waiting to be explored by bookworms and bold adventurers alike, is a question insufficiently mooted in *The Environmental Imagination*, and in ecocriticism generally speaking. Devoting our time and energy to the perusal of environmental literature would seem to be a roundabout way for us to secure a bond with the earth: it's as if we should spend our time poring over the personal ads, instead of striking up a conversation with the lonely heart next door.

In raising these questions about the status of trees and of the world in literature, questions about *mimesis* (and Buell does insist on using that term), I am broaching what has been a pivotal issue in American ecocriticism, one I would like to lay to rest, if I can, over the course of this book.[9] But first I should make my own position as clear as possible, since it is apt to be misunderstood: I am a sort of agnostic. I think we need to cure ecocriticism of its fundamentalist fixation on literal representation, and shift its focus away from the epistemological to the pragmatic. For a garden-variety pragmatist of the sort I think ecocritics ought to be, to assert the imaginary status of the things we find depicted in literature raises no issues of belief or of professional relevance. It's something we can do without positing anything controversial about either the world or the text, most especially the text, which if it is literary must be imaginative by definition and well-established convention. Otherwise the garden-variety pragmatist is perfectly happy to take the representational powers of language for granted, much in the same carefree way that the force of gravity is taken for granted. Not that the garden-variety pragmatist would deny that there are important questions to be asked about representation and gravity once we depart from the workaday realm of common sense: that's something we are compelled to do sometimes, if we happen to be literary critics, philosophers, physicists, or rocket scientists, who can't always be insouciant about such matters for professional reasons.

While lodging its complaints about the limitations of literary study, ecocriticism has regularly gone well beyond the realm of the plausible in its declarations about what literature can and ought to do. It needs to be reminded that the difficulty of making a case for mimetic representation is not solely a freakish by-product of the strange weather of recent academic debate over the latest theories: in certain quarters, mimetic representation has been regarded as a dubious idea all along. In a 1980 essay on the supposed "crisis of representation" in contemporary culture, Umberto Eco writes:

> Even assuming that whoever speaks of it has a definition of representation (which is often not the case), if I rightly understand what they're saying—namely that we are unable to construct and exchange images of the world that are certainly apt to convey the form, if there is one, of this world—it seems to me that the definition of this crisis began with Parmenides, continued with Gorgias, caused Descartes no small amount of concern, made things awkward for everyone thanks to Berkeley and Hume, and so on, down to phenomenology. . . . Those who rediscover the crisis of representation today seem to have charmingly vague ideas about the continuity of this discussion.[10]

With the continuity Eco describes in mind, I think we are entitled to ask just how viable ecocriticism's rehabilitation of mimesis is likely to be. It may be possible to qualify the idea of representation-of-things-just-as-they-are so as to make it seem at least reasonable (as Eco argues). Then we might buy into the idea but at a steep discount, recognizing the relative efficacy of language in depicting some parts or even the whole of the world, in response to specific and clearly articulated needs—ordering lunch, for instance, or planning the launch of a mission to Mars. Should we choose to do this, however, we will have to gut the idea of mimesis of most of its content, consigning the strict sense of the term to the history of philosophy, which is where it belongs. As a result, mimesis will come to seem devoid of literary interest, and we will have gained nothing, except perhaps for a short-lived peace of mind and a meaningless rearrangement of our definitions.

I think this is precisely the quandary ecocriticism has put itself in with regard to mimesis, or the representation-of-things-just-as-they-are. Realistic depiction of the world, of the sort that we can credit as reasonable and uncontroversial, is one of literature's more pedestrian, least artful aspects. It comprises, for example, such basics of technique as description. Those who are sticklers for precision and conversant with the long traditions of literary theory and philosophy can see no good reason why we should use a highly contested and highly charged word like "mimesis" to talk about matter-of-fact depiction of the descriptive sort, since doing so raises hackles and inspires distrust. To these sticklers, the issue of mimesis simply does not seem to be a live one. And ironically enough, ecocritics do acknowledge that this is, in fact, a closed file whenever they describe ecocriticism as a revival of mimesis and a counterinsurgency. The romantic appeal of opening a closed file is difficult for others to see.

To make the assertions I've just made is to slight neither art nor the world, though it may suggest that literary criticism still needs to be brought to heel. Consider, by way of illustration of my argument, a case of "dual citizenship" that I think is parallel to the one described by Buell, even if in formulating it I have stacked the deck differently than he has, and even if I am dealing from the bottom of the deck, where things become more obviously fictional and where there are, perhaps, fewer trees. An expatriate American in Paris is an expatriate American in Paris, but if his name happens to be "Jake Barnes," he won't need a visa, a passport, and a birth certificate in order to establish his true national identity. He won't have one, however rounded his character may seem to Hemingway's readers, because identities are things had only *in the world*, a place where the preposition at issue ("in") seems un-problematic.

By the same token, I think it is obvious that trees can never be, as Buell insists they are, *in literature*, and least of all *in a novel*, however much they may be "in" it figuratively and even if it is true that because books are made from paper, and paper from pulpwood, trees are in our books (and thus make up the sort of content more suited to chemical than literary analysis).

To insist that trees must be present *in literature*, just because they happen to be mentioned and described or even celebrated there, seems hostile to the very possibility of imagination, which pays its dividends in the coin of figuration, not representation. And to persist in thinking that trees might somehow be present in literature after all, despite the strictures of recent literary theory (and at least two thousand years of philosophy), is uncritical and, worse, hostile to criticism. If we cannot be imaginative, and we cannot be critical, then our only alternative, a poor one, is to be cryptic. Or sentimental, in a Joyce Kilmer-like way: as the reader may have surmised, the poet and author of "Trees" is one of the shadowy figures lurking in the background of this discussion. Another of those shadowy figures is the linguist Ferdinand de Saussure, who drilled his students in the arbitrariness of the sign and thereby helped to found much of what is now thought of as literary theory. It's a nice coincidence that Saussure's key example of the arbitrariness of the sign just happens to be the French word for tree (*le arbre*).

The critic and theorist who has put Saussure's linguistics to the most interesting use may be Roland Barthes, who in his essay "Myth Today" explains the concept of the arbitrariness of the sign as follows: "Nothing compels the acoustic image *tree* 'naturally' to mean the concept *tree*: the sign, here, is unmotivated." And in a passage even more directly relevant to the present discussion, Barthes writes:

> Every object in the world can pass from a closed, silent existence to an oral state, open to appropriation by society, for there is no law, whether natural or not, which forbids talking about things. A tree is a tree. Yes, of course. But a tree as expressed . . . is no longer quite a tree, it is a tree which is decorated, adapted to a certain type of consumption, laden with literary self-indulgence, revolt, images, in short with a type of social *usage* which is added to pure matter.

Viewed in Barthes's terms, Buell's suggestion that trees can occur *in literature* as something more vital than textual functions must be regarded as an attempt to supply a motivation for literary trees other than a social one. To attempt something like this, Barthes says, is the essential technique of ideology. He writes: "The passage from the real," by which he means the socially real, "to the ideological is defined as that from an *anti-physis* to a *pseudo-physis*." The latter is precisely the hallucinatory stuff that trees-in-literature would have to be made of (if, that is, they are not so to speak "made of" images, ideas, concepts, and the like, as I am arguing they must be). The logic of the passage from social reality to ideology (or to myth) is, Barthes says, tautological, as when one righteously insists, "A tree is a tree," and means by that to include the tree even "as expressed." "Tautology is a faint at the right moment, a saving aphasia, it is," Barthes writes, "the indignant 'representation' of the *lights* of reality over and above language," and it "testifies to a profound distrust of language."[11] Barthes's point isn't that a critic should have no distrust of language whatsoever, but rather that this distrust should not be so extreme as to make the critic impatient with and dismissive of the niceties of language, oral or written, in particular those niceties having to do with verbal reference to things in the world. The critic needs to bear in mind a point that Barthes makes in his essay on "The Death of the Author," a point consistent with the arguments about the representational function of language often made by pragmatists: "As soon as a fact is *narrated* no longer with a view to acting directly on reality but intransitively, that is to say, finally outside of any function other than that of the very practice of the symbol itself, this disconnection occurs, the voice loses its origin, the author enters into his own death, writing begins."[12]

Clearly, only the kind of author who is also a critic and for whom writing truly never seems to end, so that it constitutes a sort of living death (here I speak advisedly), would spend time trying "to imagine someone else's imagination of a tree," to recall Buell's sketch of the critic's way of life. To spend time in this fashion already seems wasteful enough to those who think our turf ought to be literally turf, and who disapprove of the critic's lifestyle. This life-style dictates a daily return to the desk in much the same way that the vampire's ghoulish condition dictates a return, each dawn and for all eternity, to the coffin. I see no good reason to indict the oddball activity of criticism still further, on the additional grounds of its somehow being a slight to those splendid trees growing on that ridgeline over yonder—about which criticism probably has nothing pertinent to say, condemned as it is to approach to the world crabwise and confining itself to the shadows of print.

Confusing actual and fictional trees, or trying to conflate them (however rhetorically and provisionally), would seem to be a primitive error, both in the sense of its being the sort of error that perpetuates myth (or ideology) and in the sense that it occurs at a level of such fundamental philosophical importance as to lead anyone who makes it astray, sooner rather than later. In short, it is a critical error. To cite yet another observation made by Barthes, it overlooks the fact that while "the work is a fragment of substance, occupying a part of the space of books (in a library for example), the Text is a methodological field." It is "held in language," not "in the hand."[13]

Ecocriticism has been staunch in its refusal to view the text in this light. Buell insists that "to posit a disjunction between text and world is both an indispensable starting point for mature literary understanding and a move that tends to efface the world."[14] Frankly, I don't see how the second of these assertions follows at all from the first: the world isn't so easily effaced, unless one has very little faith in it to begin with. I think asserting that the text somehow contains the world or some selected portion of it is "a move that tends to efface the world," portion and all, albeit only *imaginatively*, and not *really*.[15] I can see no reason why the ecocritic should be filled with a burning desire to save the text before the world: texts are disposable, whereas the world is not. And I can see every reason why the ecocritic needs to have a perspicuous sense of the difference between words and things, if only to keep from bumping into the latter unexpectedly. To approach either text or world without a sense of this difference is to attempt the view through the looking glass, and we all know what you are going to see when you attempt this view. That is why the ecocritic's epiphany is more self-revelatory than revelatory of the world: the world, that is, of both words and things.

Notes

1   For overviews of the field and a representative sample of essays in ecocriticism, see *Earthly Words; Essays on Contemporary American Nature and Environmental Writers*, ed. John Cooley (Ann Arbor: The University of Michigan Press, 1994); *The Ecocriticism Reader; Landmarks in Literary Ecology*, ed. Cheryll Glotfelty and Harold Fromm (Athens: University of Georgia Press, 1996); the selected papers from the first conference held by the Association for the Study of Literature and Environment in 1995, published as *Reading the Earth; New Directions in the Study of Literature and the Environment*, ed. Michael Branch, et al. (Moscow, Idaho: University of Idaho Press, 1998); *Writing the Environment; Ecocriticism & Literature*, ed. Richard Kerridge and Neil Sammells (London: Zed Books, 1998); the special issue on ecocriticism published in the summer of 1999 by the journal *New Literary History*; and the contributions to a "Forum on Literatures of the Environment," *PMLA* 114,5 (October 1999): 1089–1104.

2   Frank Stewart, *A Natural History of Nature Writing* (Washington: Island Press, 1995), 222, 221. Unlike other ecocritics, Stewart invokes his moment of epiphany retrospectively, at the end of his book.

3   Stewart, *A Natural History of Nature Writing*, 229.

4   Patrick Murphy, *Farther Afield in the Study of Nature-Oriented Literature* (Charlottesville: University Press of Virginia, 2000), x.

5   See SueEllen Campbell, "The Land and Language of Desire; Where Deep Ecology and Post-Structuralism Meet," in *The Ecocriticism Reader*, 124–36.

6   Lawrence Buell, *The Environmental Imagination; Thoreau, Nature Writing, and the Formation of American Culture* (Cambridge: Harvard University Press, 1995), 10.

7   Buell, *The Environmental Imagination*, 5.

8   Buell, *The Environmental Imagination*, 102: The seal's point of view is one that Barry Lopez tries to imagine in his book *Arctic Dreams*, in a passage to which Buell is alluding.

9   I should note that American ecocritics are not alone in their assumption that realism is somehow a crucial issue ecologically and environmentally. "The real, material ecological crisis," according to the British ecocritic Richard Kerridge, "is also a cultural crisis, a crisis of representation." He also suggests that ecological crisis is caused by "a failure of narrative" ("Introduction," in *Writing the Environment*, 4).

10   Umberto Eco, "On the Crisis of Representation," in *Travels in Hyperreality*, trans. William Weaver (New York: Harcourt Brace Jovanovich, 1986), 126–27.

11   Roland Barthes, "Myth Today," in *Mythologies*, trans. Annette Lavers (New York: Hill and Wang, 1972), 126, 109, 142, 152–53. Italics in original.

12   Roland Barthes, "The Death of the Author," in *Image Music Text*, trans. Stephen Heath (New York: Hill and Wang, 1977), 142. Italics in original.

13   Barthes, "From Work to Text," in *Image Music Text*, 156–57, 157.

14   Buell, *The Environmental Imagination*, 5.

15   In an essay critical of versions of ecocriticism like Buell's, Bonnie Costello writes: "A rhetorically oriented criticism is aware of the text (and indeed all mediating forms) less as a statement about reality than as a series of motivated strategies and structures that communicates to an audience or makes something happen imaginatively. A rhetorical criticism does not necessarily lead to a thesis about the primacy of the imagination, mind, or culture, as ecocriticism has charged" ("'What to Make of a Diminished Thing': Modern Nature and Poetic Response," *American Literary History* [Winter 1997]: 574).

Chapter 23

Kate Soper

THE DISCOURSES OF NATURE

IN ITS COMMONEST and most fundamental sense, the term 'nature' refers to everything which is not human and distinguished from the work of humanity.[1] Thus 'nature' is opposed to culture, to history, to convention, to what is artificially worked or produced, in short, to everything which is defining of the order of humanity. I speak of this conception of nature as 'otherness' to humanity as fundamental because, although many would question whether we can in fact draw any such rigid divide, the conceptual distinction remains indispensable. Whether, for example, it is claimed that 'nature' and 'culture' are clearly differentiated realms or that no hard and fast delineation can be made between them, all such thinking is tacitly reliant on the humanity–nature antithesis itself and would have no purchase on our understanding without it. The implications of this are not always as fully appreciated as they might be either by those who would have us view 'nature' as a variable and relative construct of human discourse or by those who emphasize human communality with the 'rest of nature', and I shall have more to say on this in the following chapter. Suffice it to note here that an *a priori* discrimination between humanity and 'nature' is implicit in all discussions of the relations between the two, and thus far it is correct to insist that 'nature' is the idea through which we conceptualize what is 'other' to ourselves.

But for the most part, when 'nature' is used of the non-human, it is in a rather more concrete sense to refer to that part of the environment which we have had no hand in creating. It is used empirically to mark off that part of the material world that is given prior to any human activity, from that which is humanly shaped or contrived. This is the sort of distinction which John Passmore makes central to his work on *Man's Responsibility for Nature*, where he writes he will be using the word 'nature'

> so as to include only that which, setting aside the supernatural, is human neither in itself nor in its origins. This is the sense in which neither Sir Christopher Wren nor St Paul's Cathedral forms part of 'nature' and it may be hard to decide whether an oddly shaped flint or a landscape where the trees are evenly spaced is or is not 'natural'.[2]

Passmore himself admits that this is to use the term in one of its narrower senses; yet it is also, I think, to use it in the sense which corresponds most closely to ordinary intuitions about its essential meaning. The idea of 'nature' as that which we are not, which we are external to, which ceases to be fully 'natural' once we have mixed our labour with it, or which we have destroyed by our interventions, also propels a great deal of thought and writing about 'getting back' to nature, or rescuing it from its human corruption. Ecological writing, for example, very frequently works implicitly with an idea of nature as a kind of pristine otherness to human culture, whose value is depreciated proportionately to its human admixture, and this is an idea promoted by Robert Goodin, in his attempt to supply a 'green theory of value'. What is crucial to a 'green theory of value', argues Goodin, is that it accords value to what is created by natural processes rather than by artificial human ones; and he employs the analogy with fakes and forgeries in art to argue that replications of the environment by developers, even if absolutely exact, will never be the same, or have the same value, precisely because they will not be independent of human process:

> . . . a restored bit of nature is necessarily not as valuable as something similar that has been 'untouched by human hands'. Even if we simply stand back and 'let nature take its course' once again, and even if after several decades most of what we see is the handiwork of nature rather than of humanity, there will almost inevitably still be human residues in its final product. Even if we subsequently 'let nature take its course', *which* course it has taken will typically have been dictated by that human intervention in the causal history. To the extent that that is true, even things that are largely the product of natural regeneration are still to some (perhaps significant) degree the product of human handiwork. And they are, on the green theory of value, that much less valuable for being so.[3]

But persuasive as these approaches may seem, in some ways, there are a number of reasons to question their tendency to elide 'nature' defined as that 'which is human neither in itself nor its origins' with 'nature' defined as that part of the environment which is humanly unaffected. Much, after all, that is 'natural' in the first sense is also affected by us, including, one may argue, the building materials which have gone into the making of St Paul's Cathedral. On the other hand, if 'nature' is identified with that part of the environment that is humanly unaffected, then, as Passmore rightly notes, it is being defined in such a way as to leave us uncertain of its empirical application, at least in respect of the sort of examples he gives: the oddly shaped flint, the landscape where the trees are straight, and so on. The fact that we may not be able concretely to determine what is or is not 'natural' in this sense is no objection, of course, to its conceptualization as that which is unaffected by human hand; but when we consider how much of our environment we most certainly know *not* to be 'natural' in this sense, and how much of the remainder we may be rather doubtful about, we may feel that the conceptual distinction, though logically clear enough, has lost touch with the more ordinary discriminations we make through the idea of 'nature' – as between the built and unbuilt environment, the 'natural' and the 'artificial' colouring, the 'Nature' park and the opera house, and so forth.

If we consider, that is, the force of Marx's remark that: 'the nature which preceded human history no longer exists anywhere (except perhaps on a few Australian coral-islands of recent origin)';[4] and if we then consider the human 'contamination' to which these possible 'exceptions' have been subject since he wrote, then it is difficult not to feel that in thinking of 'nature' as that which is utterly unaffected by human dealings, we are thinking of a kind of being to which rather little on the planet in reality corresponds. Now this, it might be said, is precisely the force of so construing it, namely that it brings so clearly into view its actual disappearance; the extent, that is, to which humanity has destroyed, nay obliterated, 'nature' as a result of its occupation of the planet. This certainly seems to be the kind of prescriptive force that Goodin, and some of those associated with a 'deep ecology' approach, would wish to draw from it, insofar as they present human beings as always desecrating nature howsoever they intervene in it.[5]

But to press this kind of case is inevitably to pose some new conceptual problems. For it is to present humanity as in its very being opposed to nature, and as necessarily destroying, or distraining on its value, even in the most minimal pursuit of its most 'natural' needs. Since merely to walk in 'nature', to pluck the berry, to drink the mountain stream, is, on this theory of value, necessarily to devalue it, the logical conclusion would seem to be that it would have been better by far had the species never existed. But, at this point, we might begin to wonder why the same argument could not apply to other living creatures, albeit they are said, unlike ourselves, to belong to nature, since they, too, make use of its resources, destroy each other, and in that sense corrupt its pristine paradise. In other words, we may ask what it is exactly that makes a human interaction with 'nature' intrinsically devaluing, where that of other species is deemed to be unproblematic – of the order of nature itself. If humanity is thought to be an intrusion upon this 'natural' order, then it is unclear why other creatures should not count as 'intrusions' also, and inanimate 'nature' hence as better off without them. We may begin to wonder what it is exactly that renders even the most primitive of human dwellings an 'artificial' excrescence, but allows the bee-hive or ant-heap to count as part of nature; or, conversely, whether the humanity–nature relationship is not here being conceived along lines that might logically require us to question the 'naturality' of species other than our own. Or to put the point in more political terms: we may suspect that this is an approach to the 'value' of nature that is too inclined to abstract from the impact on the environment of the different historical modes of 'human' interaction with it, and thus to mislocate the source of the problem – which arguably resides not in any inherently 'devaluing' aspect of human activity, but in the specific forms it has taken.

But rather than pursue these issues further here, let me return to the point I earlier raised concerning ordinary parlance about 'nature'. For there is no doubt that any definition of nature as that untouched by human hand is belied by some of the commonest uses of the term. In other words, if we count as 'nature' only that which preceded human history, or is free from the impact of human occupancy of the planet, then it might seem as if we were committed to denying the validity of much of our everyday reference to 'nature'. To speak of the 'nature walk' or 'Nature Park'; of 'natural' as opposed to 'artificial' additives; of the 'natural' environment which we love and seek to preserve – all this, it might follow from this approach, is a muddle; and a muddle, it might be further argued, that we ought to seek to correct through an adjustment of language. But tempting as it might seem, in view of the conceptual imprecision of ordinary talk of 'nature', to want to police the term in this way, there are a number of reasons to resist the move. In the first place, talk of the country-side and its 'natural' flora and fauna may be loose, but it still makes discriminations that we would want to observe between different types of space and human uses of it. If ordinary discourse lacks rigour in referring to woodland or fields, the cattle grazing upon them, and so forth, as 'nature', it is still marking an important distinction between the urban and industrial environment. [T]he criteria employed in such distinctions may be difficult to specify, but the distinctions are not of a kind that we can readily dispense with, or that a more stringent use of terminology can necessarily capture more adequately. Or to put the point in more Wittgensteinian terms, it may be a mistaken approach to the meaning of terms to attempt to specify *how* they should be employed as opposed to exploring the *way* in which they are actually used. The philosopher's task, suggested Wittgenstein, was not to prescribe the use of terms in the light of some supposedly 'strict' or essential meaning, but to observe their usage in 'ordinary' language itself; and it is certainly in that spirit that much of my pursuit here of the 'meaning' of nature will be conducted, even if that only serves to expose its theoretical laxity relative to any particular definition we might insist it ought to have. Indeed, there is perhaps something inherently mistaken in the attempt to define what nature is, independently of how it is thought about, talked about and culturally represented. There can be no adequate attempt, that is, to explore 'what nature is' that is not centrally concerned with what it has been *said* to be, however much we might want to challenge that discourse in the light of our theoretical rulings.

Cosmological 'Nature'

These, then, are some of the reasons for questioning the adequacy of any attempt to conceptualize 'nature', even when we are thinking primarily only of the 'natural' environment, as that which is wholly extraneous to, and independent of, human process. Moreover, of course, we do not simply use the term 'nature' to refer to an 'external' spatial domain, from which we and our works are clearly delineated. We also use it in reference to that totality of being of which we in some sense conceive ourselves as forming a part. We have thought, that is, of humanity as being a component of nature even as we have conceptualized nature as absolute otherness to humanity. 'Nature' is in this sense both that which we are not *and* that which we are within.

When the order of 'Nature', for example, was conceived as a Great Chain of Being, as it was in the physico-theology which prevailed from the early Middle Ages through to the late eighteenth century,[6] humanity was thought of very definitely as occupying a place within it, and a rather middling one at that. Based on the Neoplatonist principles of plenitude (the impossibility of a vacuum or 'gap' in being), hierarchy and continuity, the Great Chain of Being perceived the universe as:

> composed of an immense, or – by the strict if seldom rigorously applied logic of the principle of continuity – of an infinite, number of links ranging in hierarchical order from the meagerest kind of existents, which barely escape non-existence, through 'every possible' grade up to the *ens perfectissimum* – or, in a somewhat more orthodox version, to the highest possible kind of creature, between which and the Absolute Being the disparity was assumed to be infinite – every one of them differing from that immediately above and that immediately below it by the 'least possible' degree of difference.[7]

Or, as Pope expressed it in his *Essay on Man*:

> Vast Chain of being! which from God began,
> Natures aethereal, human, angel, man,
> Beast, bird, fish, insect, what no eye can see,
> No glass can reach; – On superior pow'rs
> Were we to press, inferior might on ours;
> Or in the full creation leave a void,
> Where, one step broken, the great scale's destroy'd;
> From Nature's chain whatever link you strike,
> Tenth, or ten thousandth, breaks the chain alike.[8]

Pope in the eighteenth century is emphasizing the coherence of the 'natural' cosmos and chaos that would ensue from breaking its 'chain', where as the stress of Mediaeval thought was on the creative and generative power of God's love in divinely willing the fullest of universes.[9] But the essential idea that humanity is within this order of 'Nature', and indeed occupies a fairly modest rung in its hierarchy of being, remains common to both. Humanity is thought of as infinitely inferior to the deity, but also to all those aethereal spirits, angels, possibly more sublime mortals elsewhere in the universe, who people the myriad degrees of difference within the abyss which yawns between man and God. When 'Nature', then, is conceived in cosmological terms as the totality of being, humanity is neither opposed to it nor viewed as separable from it. This is not to deny that there is much in the conception of the Chain that directly encouraged the idea of human lordship over the rest of animal (and vege-table) life. The teleological purposes it attributed to a deity, who had so designed all things and laws of nature as to place them at the service of his human servant, were frequently used to justify a dominion over all those creatures below us in the Chain, and an instrumental use of earthly resources. In the words of a key text of Scholastic philosophy: 'As man is made for the sake of God, namely, that he may serve him, so is the world made for the sake of man, that it may serve him',[10] and this was echoed in many other expressions of a similar compla-cency over the ensuing centuries. The increasingly ingenious and anthropocentric use of Christian doctrine by English preachers and commentators prior to the Reformation to support an instrumental use of nature has been charted by Keith Thomas, who concludes his survey by suggesting that 'a reader who came fresh to the moral and theological writings of the sixteenth and seventeenth centuries could be forgiven for inferring that their main purpose was to define the special status of man and to justify his rule over other creatures'.[11] In this sense, the idea of the Chain supported those currents of Enlightenment thought which emphasized our difference from, and right to exploit, 'nature', and operated as a kind of theological complement to their secular and temporalized teleology.

All the same, we should note that when conceived as a way of considering the question of 'Man's place in Nature', the cosmology of the Great Chain of Being can by no means be viewed as supplying a straightforwardly anthropocentric answer, and this is particularly true of the inflections it acquired in the age of Enlightenment itself. Descartes, Spinoza and Liebniz had all agreed to the principle that *non omnia hominum causa fieri* ['not everything is created for human ends'],[12] and Locke, Kant, Addison, Bolingbroke, and many others, were to invoke the idea of the Chain as a reminder of the numerous creatures superior to man, and as a caution against arrogant assumptions of human dominance within 'Nature'. Addison wrote, for example, that the difference of species 'appears, in many instances, small, and would probably appear still less, if we had means of knowing their motives'. Thus, if under one aspect man is associated with the angels and archangels, under another he must 'say to Corruption, Thou art my Father, and to the worm, Thou art my sister'.[13] In similar vein, Bolingbroke argued that superior as man was, he was nonetheless:

> . . . connected by his nature, and therefore, by the design of the Author of all Nature, with the whole tribe of animals, and so closely with some of them, that the distance between his intellectual faculties and theirs, which constitutes as really, though not so sensibly as figure, the difference of species, appears, in many instances, small, and would probably appear still less, if we had the means of knowing their motives, as we have of observing their actions.[14]

We may say, then, that, although the Promethean assumptions of human separation from and superiority over 'Nature' do eventually triumph over the idea of our 'middling' rank within its overall cosmology, they were nonetheless continually countered by less confident assump-tions, deriving from the Mediaeval theology, about humanity's place within this order. Worth noting, moreover, in this connection are the quite striking similarities between the contemporary ecological emphases on humanity's continuity with nature and place 'within' it, and those of the Great Chain of Being. Of course, there can be no direct analogue between a secular critique of instrumental rationality and of a 'technical fix' approach to nature, and a Neoplatonist theology which grounds its demand for human humility in the distance which separates man from the lowliest of divine beings. Ecology, moreover, is generally opposed to the hierarchical ranking of species that is the organizing principle of the Great Chain. But if we extrapolate the cosmological principles from their theological trappings, and focus simply on the idea of plenitude, diversity and organic interconnection informing the idea of the Chain, then there would at least seem some parallel here with current arguments concerning the interdependency of the eco-system, the importance of maintaining bio-diversity, and the unpredictable consequences of any, however seemingly insignificant, subtraction from it. Moreover, there is no doubt that, in a general way, ecology would have us revise our attitudes to 'nature' and the place of humanity within it, along lines that would reintroduce some of the conception of the Chain; rather than view 'nature' as an external and inorganic context, we should regard the eco-system as a plurality of beings each possessed of its particular function and purpose in maintaining the whole.

Human 'Nature'

The limitations of thinking of 'nature' as that which is independent of us, and external to us, are also brought into view when we consider the way in which we use the term in reference to ourselves. For we, too, it is said, are possessed of a 'nature', and may behave in more or less 'natural' ways. Now, it might be argued, that all that we should read into this vocabulary is the idea that human beings possess properties which are of their 'essence', with no presumption being made about their 'naturality' in any other sense. In other words, in speaking of 'human nature' we are not necessarily implying that human beings participate in the 'nature' we ascribe to animality or pointing to the continuity of their being with that of the 'natural' world. On the contrary, it might be said, we are precisely designating those features which are exclusive to them, and mark them off from 'nature' conceived on the model of 'animality'. Certainly, it is true that the idea of 'human nature' is very often used to emphasize our difference from 'natural' species, as when it is said, for example, that human beings are 'by nature' rational and moral beings in a way that no other species are, that it is against their 'nature' to behave 'like animals', or that in taking 'nature' as a model they are precisely reneging on what is true to their own.

It is in line with this view of 'human nature' that John Stuart Mill in his essay on 'Nature' denounces the immorality of following the course of nature and rejects any consecration of instinctual action. Since natural phenomena, he argues, are 'replete with everything which when committed by human beings is most worthy of abhorrence, any one who endeavoured in his actions to imitate the natural course of things would be universally seen and acknowledged to be the wickedest of men.'[15] Coming at the issue from a very different political perspective, Baudelaire employs a similar vocabulary in denouncing Romantic conceptions of 'nature' as a model of human beauty and goodness. 'Nature,' he writes, 'cannot but counsel that which is criminal . . . [In] all the actions and desires of the purely natural man, you will find nothing that is not ghastly.'[16] Yet there would be little point in moving these arguments were it thought that human beings are 'by nature' incapable of following the 'counsel' of nature, and their point, in fact, is not so much to assert the actual impossibility as to emphasize the immorality or cultural degeneracy of doing so. What is being disputed here is not so much the human possession of instinct or 'animal' desire, but the ethics of human conduct, and specifically the extent to which 'nature' offers itself as an appropriate guide to this; in other words, whether it is conceived essentially as a source of virtue or of vice, and thus as a mode of being we should seek to emulate or disown. Clearly, as Mill himself in effect points out,[17] there is little point in recommending that human beings either follow or reject the model of 'nature' if nature is here being construed as a set of powers or properties that they have no choice but to comply with. Admonitions of this kind implicitly reject a deterministic conception of 'human nature' even as they advocate a certain view of its 'order' and propriety. To suggest, for example, that 'human nature' is betrayed by following the course of 'animal' nature is paradoxically to acknowledge that human beings are capable of defying their 'nature' in ways denied to other animals. It is to suggest, in effect, that 'human nature' is such as to be realized only in compliance with a certain order of 'conventions' of a kind that no other creature can be expected to recognize or would require its fellows to observe. As Empson wryly notes, the animal 'is at least unconventional in the sense that it does not impose its conventions.'[18]

Yet there is no doubt, too, that the idea of a 'human nature' cannot be so readily divorced from the assumption of humanity's sameness with the animal world and rootedness within the order of nature. This is in part because the notion of our having a 'nature' carries with it something of that same necessity we attribute to animal and inorganic modes of being: to speak of 'human nature' is to imply that we are possessed of preordained features, and subject to their order of needs in the way that other creatures also are. These features may be supposed to be very different from those of animals, but in describing them as 'natural' to us we are imputing a similar determination and necessity to them.

But we should note, too, the way in which the idea has been used to condemn the 'perversity' of human behaviour where it is thought to *diverge* from that of other animals – as in the case, most notably, of certain forms of sexual practice. The 'convention' through which homosexuality has been perennially condemned as a 'crime' against nature would have us conform to, rather than contravene, a supposed 'norm' of animal conduct; and a similar rationale is at work in the condemnations of much else that is thought 'perverse' in our own behaviour: here the point is to exclude those human modes of conduct that have been deemed (though often mistakenly in fact) *not to conform* to those of other animals.

But against all those cases in which the 'healthy' human norm is established by reference to the custom of nature, must, of course, be set all those numerous others in which we become creatures of 'nature' in failing to conform with the custom of humanity. The conception of what is proper to human nature is thus arrived at both in approval and in rejection of what is thought 'spontaneous' or 'instinctual', and it is this ambivalence of attitude that Edmund in *King Lear* turns powerfully to his own account in calling upon God to stand up for the bastards bred in the 'lusty stealth of Nature' rather than for the 'tribe of fops' who are got in the 'dull stale tired bed' of matrimony.[19] (Although we might note that what God is to stand up for are rights of inheritance to land which no 'lusty Nature' ever bestowed.)

The history of the ways in which the idea or model of nature has figured in human self-conceptions is extraordinarily complex, and there can be no question of offering more than the sketchiest account of its convolutions in this context.[20] But one of the main divisions which can be drawn is between those ethical, political and aesthetic arguments that are constructed upon a view of culture as offering an essential corrective to 'nature', or providing the milieu in which alone it acquires any definitively human form, and those that view nature as releasing us from the repressions or deformations of culture and as itself a source of wisdom and moral guidance. The former regard human 'nature' as appropriately and fully reflected only in those achievements of 'civilization' that distance us from the sinfulness or naivety or crudity of 'nature'; the latter would have us see the very process of authentic human fulfilment as jeopardized or distorted by the corrupting effects of cultural 'progress'. In the one conception, the emphasis falls on those human powers in which we transcend 'nature', and on the moral goodness which is realised only in our freedom from its order; in the other on the 'nature' within us that is the well-spring of human virtue and thus of social regeneration.

Broadly speaking, we can say that the one provides the animating idea of the high Enlightenment, the other of the Romantic reaction to its economic and social consequences. In releasing humanity from a Deist conception of the order of Nature as hierarchically fixed or Providentially designed to secure the 'best of all possible worlds', the Enlightenment sought to realize the inherent dignity of the individual as a self-motivating rational and moral being: the progressive development of art, science and culture is thus viewed as the vehicle for the realization of a 'human nature' previously held in thrall to superstitious fears of 'nature' and theological bigotry. In the Romantic reaction, which is profoundly influenced by Rousseau's summons to attend to conscience as the 'voice of nature' within us, the integrity of nature is counterposed to the utilitarianism and instrumental rationality through which the Enlightenment ideals were practically realized and theoretically legitimated: the point is not to return to a past primitivity, but to discover in 'nature', both inner and outer, the source of redemption from the alienation and depredations of industrialism and the 'cash nexus' deformation of human relations. In the aesthetic theory of the Romantic movement the artistic or poetic imagination is charged with the task of expressing this latent and occluded force of nature as redemptive resource, and this idea remains central to the forms of expressivism into which it subsequently flows. In social theory, the Romantic critique receives its most powerful elaboration in the argument of the Frankfurt School critical theorists: 'instrumental rationality', in oppressing nature, cuts us off from it as a source, and thus betrays its original promise to release us from thraldom to a Deistic order by entrapping us in relations to nature that are deeply oppressive of ourselves as well.[21]

Let it be said immediately, however, that this is to offer only a very general framework of opposing viewpoints, both of which are subject to numerous mutations and inflections, and neither of which provide compartments into which we can readily slot the argument of particular writers. The argument of Descartes and Locke, for example, was crucial in laying the foundations of the Enlightenment idea of subjectivity, but remained committed to Deistic or Providential conceptions of the social whole. Kant is a major architect of the Enlightenment conception of the autonomous subject, but exerts a lasting influence on Romanticism in rejecting the utilitarian ethic and the 'civilization' that 'progresses' in accord with it; Marx combines a Promethean aspiration to transcend all natural limits on human self-realization with a quasi-Romantic critique of alienation; and there are many other examples one might give of such hybrid modes of thinking and lines of influence.

We must allow, too, that very divergent and often antithetical moral postures and political ideologies can be defended from either of these perspectives on the model offered by 'nature'. An Enlightenment conception of our 'nature' as 'improvable' has been of critical importance to the promotion of the ideals of equality, justice and freedom which have come to ground the Western conception of progress. The (alas, continuing) horrors of the twentieth century have severely dinted the faith in the ameliorative powers of 'civilization', but in a sense this itself speaks to a presumption that our 'human nature' is such as to allow and require us to act in ways that transcend 'nature': to act in accordance with justice and to observe a system of rights. Moreover, the importance attached by a *tabula rasa* conception of nature to providing the appropriate cultural and physical milieu for human growth and self-realization has issued in some of the most progressive programmes of social reform.

On the other hand, it must be recognized that the emphasis on the role of culture in the formation or improvement of human nature can lend itself both to enlightened forms of educational and social policy and to the crudest forms of 'social engineering' and technocratism. The Enlightenment acclamation of human freedom and autonomy, moreover, carries within it a potentially repressive legacy of the modes of thought from which it breaks in the form of a continued elevation of mind over body, the rational over the affective. Though pitted against the more puritanical suppressions of bodily appetite and 'animal' instinct sustained in Christian dogma, the rationalist element of Enlightenment thinking may also be charged with fostering modes of 'corrective' education and regulation that have denied self-expression and served as the continued prop of class, race and gender divisions.

In view of this, it is not surprising that the Romantic conception of 'nature' as an essentially innocent and benevolent power has played such a key role in the discourses of sexual and social emancipation from the time of Blake and Shelley through to the 'flower power' politics of the sixties and much of the ecological argument of our own time. Liberating the 'nature' within or without us has been a constant theme of emancipatory discourse (and one might argue, some reference to a 'repressed' nature is a condition of the coherence of any such talk). But we should not forget the irrationalities and repressions to which this 'nature libertarianism' can also lend itself. Romantic conceptions of 'nature' as wholesome salvation from cultural decadence and racial degeneration were crucial to the construction of Nazi ideology, and an aesthetic of 'nature' as source of purity and authentic self-identification has been a component of all forms of racism, tribalism and nationalism. Equally, of course, the appeal to the health, morality and immutability of what 'nature' proposes has been systematically used to condemn the 'deviants' and 'perverts' who fail to conform to the sexual or social norms of their culture.

Finally we might note the ways in which some of these inflections of the pro-nature ethic have prompted a series of counter-Romantic denunciations of the quest for humanist redemption through 'nature', ranging from T. E. Hulme's rejection of any Rousseauan confidence in human amelioration and preference for all that is 'life-alien', to Baudelaire's protestations against 'ensouled vegetables';[22] from Oscar Wilde's professions of hatred for nature, to Foucault's conventionalist leanings towards an erotic-aesthetic of 'cruelty' and 'dandyist' ethic of style.[23] In these voices we encounter some of the more 'violent' attacks on the 'violence' of 'nature' and a systematic refusal to endorse its truth, authenticity or regenerative powers. But we should note that they also give expression to a form of resistance common to all those who have challenged the appeal to 'nature' to legitimate and preserve a status quo, whether of class relations, patriarchy, sexual oppression or ethnic and racial discrimination. What is put in question through such challenges is precisely the extent to which what is claimed to be 'natural' is indeed a determination of 'nature', and hence a necessity to which we must accommodate, as opposed to a set of conventional arrangements, which are in principle transformable. In the case of many of these expressions of dissent, however, it is not so much *any* invocation of nature that is rejected, but that construction of it which has pre-empted or distorted the potential forms in which it might be realized.

Within the general opposition to the naturalization of the social, therefore, we may distinguish between two rather differing types of claims: between those that reject the specific accounts that have been given of what is 'natural' in the name of the equal or more authentic 'naturality' of what they seek to institute; and those that insist on the non-natural, or normative, or culturally-constructed quality of all social arrangements, practices and institutions. Whereas the former position retains the idea of there being some sort of 'natural' order in human society, which if instituted will guarantee the well-being of its members and allow them to realise their essential 'nature' as persons, the latter emphasizes the discursive and revisable quality of what is claimed to be 'natural' to human beings and their societies at any point in history. For the latter position, then, 'nature' in human affairs is a concept through which social conventions and cultural norms are continuously legitimated and contested; it does not refer us to an essential or true mode of being from which we may think of ourselves as being culturally alienated at any point in time, or as having realized in some historical past, or as able potentially to realize in the future. The concept of 'nature' according to this 'culturalist' argument is certainly always employed *as if* it referred us to what is 'essential', 'true' or 'authentic' to us, but it is a usage that at the same time necessarily denies the historicity of what has been believed at any time to be the dictate of nature. Since 'progressive culture' has constantly re-thought the limits it has imposed on what is 'natural' or 'proper' to human beings and their society, the use of 'nature' as if it referred to an independent and permanent order of reality embodies a kind of error, or failure to register the history of the legitimating function it has played in human culture. From this 'culturalist' perspective, then, 'nature' is a kind of self-denying concept through which what is culturally ordained is presented as pre-discursive external determination upon that culture. From a 'realist' perspective, by contrast, nature refers to limits imposed by the structure of the world and by human biology upon what it is possible for human beings to be and do, at least if they are to survive and flourish. It is an order of determinations that we infringe only at the cost of a certain 'loss' of self or 'alienation' from what is true to ourselves, and in this sense provides the essential gage by which we may judge the 'liberating' or 'repressive' quality of human institutions and cultural forms, including those through which we relate most directly to the environment and other creatures.

The essential difference or tension is, then, as suggested, between a generally 'nature-endorsing' and a generally 'nature-sceptical' response. For the former, which may take either conservative or progressive forms, 'nature' is appealed to in validation of that which we would either seek to preserve or seek to instigate in place of existing actuality; for the latter, which is usually advocated as progressive, but may be charged with conservatism in the free hand it gives to cultural determination, the appeal is always to be viewed as a dubious move designed to limit and circumscribe the possibilities of human culture.

Notes

1   In his essay on 'Nature' John Stuart Mill speaks of nature in this sense as 'what takes place without the voluntary and intentional agency of man'. See Mill, *Three Essays on Religion* (Longman, London, 1874), pp. 3–65.
2   John Passmore, *Man's Reponsibility for Nature*, 2nd edn (Duckworth, London, 1980), p. 207.
3   Robert E. Goodin, *Green Political Theory* (Polity Press, Oxford, 1992), p. 41; cf. pp. 30–40.
4   Karl Marx, *The German Ideology* (Progess Publishers, Moscow, 1968), p. 59. The observation is illuminatingly discussed by Neil Smith in *Uneven Development: Nature, Capital and the Production of Space* (Blackwell, Oxford, 1984), p. 54f. The idea of 'nature' as 'cultural construction' is more fully discussed in chapter 5.
5   Thus Goodin's general claim is that pristine nature is always to be preferred to that which has been tampered with, however congenial the effect. More specifically he argues that, if faced with the choice between a small-scale English village 'more in harmony with nature' and 'postmodern' Los Angeles, we must always opt for the former. All the same, 'grubbing out' nature to build even the most harmonious hamlet is a less acceptable option than leaving nature in its original state. See *Green Political Theory*, pp. 51–52.
6   The classic work on the subject is that of A. O. Lovejoy, *The Great Chain of Being* (Harvard University Press, Cambridge, Mass. and London, 1964) where it is argued that it is only in the late eighteenth century that the idea attains its widest diffusion. See esp. p. 183.
7   Ibid., pp. 59–60.
8   Alexander Pope, *An Essay on Man*, Epistle 1, 237–46 (Methuen, London, 1950), pp. 44–45.
9   Lovejoy, *Great Chain*, p. 67f.
10 *Libri Sententiarum*, II, 1, 8, cited in Lovejoy, *Great Chain*, pp. 186–87.
11 Keith Thomas, *Man and the Natural World* (Allen Lane, London, 1983), p. 25. In his preceding survey (pp. 17–24), Thomas cites, as instances of such anthropocentric ingenuity, the suggestion that horse-flies had been created 'that men should exercise their wits and industry to guard themselves against them'; that apes had been designed 'for man's mirth'; and the argument of the Elizabethan, George Owen, concerning the multiple purposes of the lobster: that it provided food to eat, exercise in cracking its legs and claws, and an object of contemplation in its wonderful suit of armour.
12 Lovejoy, *Great Chain*, p. 188f.
13 Ibid., p. 195.

14   Ibid., p. 196.
15   J. S. Mill, 'Nature' in *Three Essays on Religion*, p. 65.
16   Quoted in Charles Taylor, *Sources of the Self* (Cambridge University Press, Cambridge, 1989), p. 434.
17   J. S. Mill, *Nature*, pp. 13–19.
18   Willam Empson, *Some Versions of Pastoral* (Harmondsworth, Penguin, 1966), p. 212.
19   Shakespeare, *King Lear*, I, ii. Cf. John F. Danby, *Shakespeare's Doctrine of Nature* (Faber and Faber, London, 1949), esp. parts I, II.
20   One of the most illuminating and discriminating accounts of the role played by the idea of nature in shaping conceptions of human subjectivity is to be found in Taylor, *Sources of the Self*, especially parts IV and V. My discussion here draws extensively on this work.
21   The seminal text here is Theodor Adorno and Max Horkheimer, *Dialectic of Enlightenment* (Verso, London, 1979). For a full bibliography on the Frankfurt School, see David Held, *Introduction to Critical Theory* (University of California Press, Berkeley, 1980).
22   On both, see Taylor, *Sources of the Self*, pp. 426–29, 434–42, 459–63.
23   For an illuminating tracing of these veins of Foucaultian resistance to 'nature', see James Miller, *The Passion of Michel Foucault* (Harper Collins, London, 1993).

Chapter 24

Gabriel Egan

ECOPOLITICS/ECOCRITICISM

To SEE HOW ECOPOLITICAL insights can inform critical readings of Shakespeare, it is necessary to survey briefly the origins of the Green movement and in particular the twentieth-century scientific and industrial developments that it defined itself in opposing. In the summer of 1942 Edward Teller, one of J. Robert Oppenheimer's team building the first atomic bomb, calculated what would happen in the first few millionths of a second after detonation. Enrico Fermi was worried that the new weapon might disastrously replicate the conditions inside the Sun, and Teller's new calculations started to convince Oppenheimer's team that merely testing the bomb 'might ignite the earth's oceans or its atmosphere' (Rhodes 1986, 418). Unknown to the Americans, in June 1942, the theoretical physicist Werner Heisenberg expressed to Hitler, via Albert Speer, the same fear about Germany's atomic programme (Rhodes 1986, 404–5). The night before the first Manhattan Project test, Fermi offered to take bets on whether the atmosphere would catch fire, and Teller wondered if he was right (Rhodes 1986, 664–65). Stunned by the brightness of the flash, Oppenheimer's colleague Emilio Segrè feared that the worst had indeed happened (Segrè 1970, 147). The scientists who performed the first atomic test believed it carried a small, but quite real, chance (about one-in-fifty, some of them thought) of instantly igniting the world, and they decided to risk it.

Among other things, the international Green movement is a response to the rapid increase in the power of human technologies and the hubris of the scientists and technocrats in charge of them. All life on Earth is a direct expression of the energy released by thermo-nuclear reactions inside the Sun and, ironically, the means to initiate such reactions on Earth made Oppenheimer's the first generation capable of ending all life. Over the succeeding decades, the nuclear states developed the technologies with which to threaten doing this, each fearing another gaining a technical advantage that would upset the balance of terror. This fear was acute in the 1960s when intercontinental ballistic missiles (ICBMs) became too fast for the available computers to track reliably, raising the possibility that a sneak attack might overwhelm an opponent before retaliation could be mounted.

One of the breakthroughs that restored the balance came from, of all places, the technique of lithography used in commercial book publishing and refined into a fine art by Henri de Toulouse-Lautrec and Paul Gauguin. Rather than wire individual components together, transistors, diodes, capacitors, and resistors of microscopic size could be lithographically printed directly onto semiconductor material, to make an integrated circuit, or microchip. Computing devices shrank in size and cost, and rose exponentially in power. A second break-through was the distributed networking of computers invented by Paul Baran of the Rand Corporation, which showed that 'highly survivable system structures can be built, even in the thermonuclear era' (Baran 1964, 4). The Advanced Research Projects Agency Network (ARPANET) embodying this technology first connected four university computer sites in 1969, and in 1972 it explicitly acquired the adjective 'defense' to become DARPANET, which became the Internet. Epitomizing the beauty of the swords-into-ploughshares prin-ciple, the Internet is now the primary means by which Green activism communicates with itself and the wider political domain.

A certain kind of political idealism and activism driven by global thinking came to an end in 1968 as within a few months Martin Luther King and Robert Kennedy were assassinated, anti-Vietnam demonstrations were suppressed, the French uprising collapsed and Charles de Gaulle won a landslide victory, the Civil Rights movement in Northern Ireland was violently crushed, and Warsaw Pact forces invaded Czechoslovakia and stayed there to ensure that Alexander Dubček's political and social reforms were cancelled. One strand of activism turned from the global to the local, producing the communes and self-help groups of the early 1970s, but at the same time a new kind of global thinking emerged to replace the old. In September 1969, Friends of the Earth was formed by David Brower in San Francisco and the following year it was transformed into an inter-national Organization with affiliated groups forming first in France (1970) and the United Kingdom (1971). In 1970, Friends of the Earth began to publish the journal *Not Man Apart* that outlined its core campaign topics: the fur trade, preservation of rivers, pollution from supersonic flight, and whaling.

The international organization Greenpeace arose from protests against American under-ground nuclear bomb tests. In 1970 three Canadian activists, Jim Bohlen, Irving Stowes, and Paul Cote, formed the Don't Make a Wave committee to prevent nuclear testing on the island of Amchitka, one of the Aleutian Islands off the west coast of Alaska. The name alluded to the danger of triggering a tsunami, for Amchitka is a few miles from a geological weakness that leads to the Californian San Andreas Fault. The youngest member of the committee, Bill Darnell, suggested that 'Green Peace' captured the group's philosophy and should be the name of their boat. In the event the trip failed to prevent the test, but brought extensive media coverage, following which the future, bigger tests at Amchitka were cancelled (Hunter 1979, 11–118; Brown and May 1989, 7–15).

Yet another strand of the new movement arose within the academy. The phrase 'animal liberation' – with an exclamation mark to indicate the novelty – first appeared in print on the cover of the 5 April 1973 issue of the *New York Review of Books* to advertise that within was Peter Singer's review of a collection of essays on the maltreatment of 'non-humans' (Godlovitch, *et. al.* 1971; Singer 1973). Singer, a philosopher of the preference utilitarian school, approvingly quoted Jeremy Bentham's assertion that what mattered when deciding how much value to place on individuals' interests was not 'Can they *reason*? nor, Can they *talk*? but, Can they *suffer*?' (Bentham 1789, 309n). Singer coined the expression 'speciesism' to liken the unthinking assumption of human superiority to the long-standing but recently challenged assumption of racial superiority by whites and of gender superiority by men. Singer developed his review into a full-blown utilitarian argument for the capacity to suffer, rather than membership of a particular species, being the primary criterion by which to weigh the good or harm of any of our interactions with humans and other animals (Singer 1975). Looked at this way, a severely mentally disabled person incapable of preferences and protected from pain has less right to life than a healthy chimpanzee with rudimentary sign-language skills, a well-developed social network, and a degree of self-consciousness, as Singer argues in his book *Practical Ethics* (Singer 1979, 93–105, 127–57).

These roots of the Green movement are worth tracing because they counter the common misconception that ecopolitical thinking arose only after the collapse of communism. In truth, it was an active force in the extraordinary events of 1989–90. The final decline of the Soviet Union was triggered by Mikhail Gorbachev's refusal to assist Erich Honecker's government in suppressing the fledgling ecology-and-peace movement in the German Democratic Republic. This movement was inspired by the West German Green Party founded by Herbert Gruhl and Petra Kelly in 1979, whose programme called for the demilitarization of Europe by dissolving the NATO and Warsaw Pact agreements, the closure of nuclear power plants, rigorous state control of polluting industries, and economic advantages being given to small-scale businesses over large corporations. The connection between nuclear power and pollution was especially urgent after the explosion of the Ukrainian nuclear electricity generator at Chernobyl in April 1986 spread radiation clouds across Western Europe as far as Ireland. This outcome contrasted with the narrow escape from a similar reactor core meltdown at the Pennsylvanian Three Mile Island nuclear electricity generator in 1979, strengthening a perception of communist technological inferiority rooted in political and economic inferiority. Chernobyl bolstered the nascent Ukrainian independence movement which achieved its goal when Gorbachev's government in Moscow collapsed in August 1991.

It is clear, then, that ecopolitics has operated strategically at key moments in recent world history. What are the consequences of this for literary criticism? By analogy with the politics of class, race, and gender, it would seem that ecopolitics will necessarily have things to teach us about literary criticism, but it is far from clear what those lessons might be. Virtually every dramatic character, like every reader and theatre spectator, has an identifiable class, a race, and a gender and it is abundantly clear that politicized criticism can investigate how these classifications arise, how they are figured in oppression, and how they might be transfigured in the future. By analogy with these, ecocriticism would seem to lack an oppressed subject, unless it take up something as potentially risible as the Earth's point of view, or the animals'. I will suggest some means by which ecopolitical concerns can be projected into the domain of criticism, despite the absence of an oppressed subject on whose behalf a political struggle could be mounted. For this, a little more popular science must be essayed before we return to the literary and the dramatic.

The Earth is effectively a sealed system, bombarded by energy from the Sun but closed in the sense that (barring a few trivial exceptions) we and our products cannot leave. Whatever we make here stays here, and the only replenishment of spent energy is in the form of sunlight. This insight is largely absent from mainstream Marxist analysis, which treats the Earth as an infinitely rich supplier of raw materials and an infinitely capacious sink for wastes. This is a surprising oversight, since one of the central principles of Marx's analysis of capitalism was that the extraction of surplus value from producing workers leaves them too poor to buy back what they have made, so capitalism is forced to scour the world for new markets and new workforces (Marx 1954, 713 15; Marx and Engels 1974, 58) and must eventually come up hard against the Earth's finitude: at some point it will exhaust the last market and the last free worker. Since this is a central principle, acknowledging the finite ought really to be habitual for Marxists. The ever-increasing productive forces of humankind cannot go on indefinitely even if the systems of production and exchange are revolutionized, since the Earth's resources are finite. Marx, however, chose to focus on the vast and as-yet untapped resources of the Earth and the fact that individual productivity has always increased more quickly than population, which is why humankind's capacity to feed itself has never faltered. (As is well known, distribution rather than production is the cause of majority world hunger:

more than enough food is produced each year to feed the world's population.) Engels was explicit about what keeps productivity ahead of consumption: 'science – whose progress is as unlimited and at least as rapid as that of population' (Marx 1977, 176).

The rapidly expanding production of the Industrial Revolution, also enabled by a mistaken sense of the Earth's infinitude, was undergirded by a new conception of nature that arose in the second half of the seventeenth century. It was, in essence, the replacement of a vitalistic model with a mechanistic model. Instead of the natural state of things being movement, as Aristotle articulated in his *Physics* (Aristotle 1930, 184a–267b), it was inertia, as Isaac Newton proved; the transition is neatly summarized by R. G. Collingwood in *The Idea of Nature*. Throughout the drama of Shakespeare, characters speak of the world around them as though it is alive, and this view is put into conflict with the emergent mechanistic view, as we shall see. As Collingwood points out, 'The naturalistic philosophies of the fifteenth and sixteenth centuries attributed to nature reason and sense, love and hate, pleasure and pain, and found in these faculties and passions the causes of natural process' (Collingwood 1945, 95). In an essentially clockwork universe, on the other hand, the Earth is merely an instrument of human self-fulfilment.

The twentieth-century field of cybernetics bridges these different conceptions of the world in its concern with communication and control systems in living organisms and machines, and its origins can be traced to the eighteenth-century invention of mechanical self-regulation modelled on living organisms. The key notion is feedback: the connection of the outcome of an event or process with the originating conditions. Contrary to everyday use of the term, positive feedback is often a bad thing and negative feedback often a good one. In positive feedback, the outcome of a process reinforces the originating conditions so that the system accelerates, as when a snowball rolls downhill, a debt accumulates compound interest, or the subatomic particles ejected in a chain reaction excite yet more particles. Exponential growth is the characteristic outcome of positive feedback. In negative feedback, however, the outcome diminishes the originating conditions so that the system achieves a dynamic equilibrium, and if perturbed by an external force (so long as it is not too great) the system is able to restore its equilibrium.

The ecological processes with which Green politics are concerned are chiefly examples of either of these two conditions: explosive growths (bombs, populations, atmospheric gases) and the countervailing systems of self-regulation. The ozone layer problem identified in the 1980s has been solved by banning chlorofluorocarbons. A zone of partial ozone depletion over the Antarctic remains, but will disappear in about 50 years because of what atmospheric chemists – a group not given to excessive anthropomorphism – call the self-healing effect, a classic negative-feedback loop. The ozone layer is created in the upper atmosphere by the bombardment of solar ultraviolet radiation that turns O_2 (oxygen) molecules into O_3 (ozone) molecules that block the radiation from reaching the Earth's surface. Where ozone depletion occurs, solar radiation penetrates further, but in doing so it creates fresh ozone at the lower level and backfills the hole.

On the other hand, the accumulation of greenhouse gases from human activity starts a positive-feedback reaction. The northern polar ice cap floats on an ocean, so as it melts it occupies the volume it formerly displaced, leaving the sea-level unchanged. The southern ice cap, however, rests on land and as it melts it exposes dark soil where there was previously white ice, lowering the Earth's capacity to reflect sunlight and thereby accelerating the absorption of heat and the melting. The key determinate of whether humankind survives the next 100 years is whether our perturbations of the Earth's self-regulating systems have exceeded its capacity to restore an equilibrium, or, to be more precise, whether the new equilibrium state that emerges can support human life. In these debates, distinctions between organic and inorganic processes begin to break down, as we shall see.

The most famous early example of a machine emulating organic self-regulation was James Watt's steam engine governor of 1769, which made an engine run at a constant speed irrespective of the load applied to it. The collar is connected to the engine's throttle, so if the speed rises, the balls rise under centrifugal force and pull the throttle closed, thus lowering the speed; if the speed falls, the balls descend and so open the throttle to raise the speed.

For Charles Dickens, such regulatory devices made for fearful hybrid creatures, animal yet robotic, that mocked human labour in the fictional Coketown of *Hard Times*:

> But no temperature made the melancholy mad elephants more mad or more sane. Their wearisome heads went up and down at the same rate, in hot weather and cold, wet weather and dry, fair weather and foul. The measured motion of their shadows on the walls, was the substitute Coketown had to show for the shadows of rustling woods; while, for the summer hum of insects, it could offer, all the year round, from the dawn of Monday to the night of Saturday, the whirr of shafts and wheels.
>
> (Dickens 1854, 132–33)

Positive and negative feedback loops are common to organic and inorganic systems, and a full understanding of them is a key difference between our times and Shakespeare's. They nonetheless appear in the plays and are treated as paradoxical situations that might be understood mystically, although particular characters attempt to offer materialist accounts of them and rightly perceive negative feedback to be one of the reasons that the world is, in important respects, essentially unchanging. In teasing out the range of ideas about feedback presented in the plays, and the characters' efforts to make sense of them as vitalistic or mechanical phenomena, we are exploring their capacity to understand the world around them.

This project of mapping how Elizabethans made sense of the world takes us to the second specific insight that ecological thinking can bring to criticism. In his model of what he called the Elizabethan World Picture, E. M. W. Tillyard characterizes the set of beliefs, assumptions, and habits of mind that a typical educated person might hold as a cobbled-together patchwork of medieval commonplaces and newly minted explanations (Tillyard 1943, 1–6). The Picture itself has been widely criticized by historians of science and philosophy for its oversimplification of belief systems, its understatement of scepticism and dissent, and most of all for its claim that despire the obvious disorderliness of Elizabethan drama, 'the conception of order is so taken for granted, so much part of the collective mind of the people, that it is hardly mentioned except in explicitly didactic passages' (Tillyard 1943, 7). A central element of Tillyard's Picture is a system of alleged correspondences between the celestial bodies, social relations, and human biology (Tillyard 1943, 77–93), which Elizabethan prose and verse art endlessly returned to for analogies.

The focus of the attack on Tillyard has been that Elizabethans did not actually believe the picture he outlined, but for our purposes that question may be somewhat beside the point. Like witchcraft or alien-abduction for us, the account of the universe that the Picture embodied was available for use in plays and poems. Characters in Shakespeare speak meaningfully about comets presaging disaster and about the music of the spheres, and unless we suppose that these lines elicited derisive laughter from the theatre audiences we have to accept that such things were within the realm of the believable even if not widely believed. This alone gives us cause enough to study Tillyard's Picture, but in fact (and unlike witchcraft and alien-abduction) his model of reality might also in some surprising ways be objectively true. A macrocosm/microcosm correspondence need not of itself run counter to the particularities of life as it is lived on Earth and events in the wider universe.

To see why, we should recall that Newton's great discovery, announced in *Philosophiae Naturalis Principia Mathematica* (1687), was that what happens to the largest heavenly bodies is governed by the same mechanics that control what happens on Earth. This development could easily be taken as confirming macrocosm/microcosm correspondence rather than displacing it: the universe's condition, Newton proved, really was the earthly condition writ large. The telescope had shown that the planets were imperfect, like the Earth, and the microscope showed that processes occurring within organisms invisible to the naked eye were the same as the processes occurring in larger creatures. The corresponding phenomena on different scales were to a considerable degree real, not superstition, nor mere analogy.

The twentieth-century sciences of holograms and fractals have advanced this principle of correspondences between phenomena on different scales to an extraordinary degree.[1] When a glass hologram is smashed, each resulting shard contains the full image rather than a fraction of it, and this image can be shattered again to produce yet smaller versions. A fractal is a mathematically defined curve that also exhibits this principle of diminishing self-similarities: any part of it, when enlarged, is the same shape as the original. These curves occur in non-organic and organic nature, such as the snowflake and the fern leaf.[2]

From the new perspectives provided by holograms, fractals, and genetics, Tillyard's version of an alleged Elizabethan concern for macrocosmic/microcosmic correspondences looks considerably less naive than critics have given him (and, indeed, the Elizabethans) credit for. Such correspondences are how the world is, and as we shall see, they are the bases for sophisticated analogical thinking that we must not dismiss out of hand.

Previous generations of critics had a firmer grasp of this point than recent ones. For all their differences over the proper approach to literature, old historicists such as Tillyard and Lily B. Campbell shared with their contemporary New Critics the principle that a fragment of a literary work might operate as a miniaturized version of the whole. Writing about *Macbeth*, for example, the founding father of New Criticism Cleanth Brooks considers the images of the naked babe (1.7.21–22) and clothed ('breeched') daggers (2.3. 115–16) to be 'two of the great symbols which run throughout the play' and 'so used as to encompass an astonishingly large area of the total situation' (Brooks 1947, 49). For the New Critics, the compression of meaning in, for example, an image was the essential quality of literary writing, and it was this forcing of so much into so little that made the words on the page (as opposed to the collateral knowledge about the writer's biography and historical context) all one needed to do criticism.

The compression need not happen via imagery; according to the English New Critic William Empson[3] it could be a matter of surprisingly awkward syntax or diction. However achieved, it was the compression that made the text literary:

> When you are holding a variety of things in your mind, or using for a single matter a variety of intellectual machinery, the only way of applying all your criteria is to apply them simultaneously; the only way of forcing the reader to grasp your total meaning is to arrange that he can only feel satisfied if he is bearing all the elements in mind at the moment of conviction; the only way of not giving something heterogeneous is to give something which is at every point a compound.
>
> (Empson 1930, 302)

Approaching literature from entirely the opposite angle – 'I do not believe that a poet exists in a vacuum, or even that he exists solely in the minds and hearts of his interpreters' – Lily B. Campbell nonetheless shares the New Critics' convictions that the poet, because a poet, relates the microcosm to the macrocosm:

He is inevitably a man of feeling. If, however, he is not merely a poet but a great poet, the particulars of his experience are linked in meaning to the universal of which they are a representative pan. . . . the greatest poets . . . have seen life as a whole, not in fragments.

(Campbell 1947, 6–7)

Hugh Grady observes that uniting the disparate modernist approaches to Shakespeare was a faith in the organic unity of art and a respect for hierarchy, both of which he hopes can be swept away by postmodernism:

The relevant characteristics are the abandonment of organic unity as an aesthetic value and practice and the overthrow of a series of formerly privileged hierarchical oppositions through a Postmodernist anti-hierarchical impulse (as, for example in the collapse of the High Modernist distinction between 'art' and 'popular culture' or in the championing of the various Others of Western rationality like women and Third World peoples).

(Grady 1991, 207)

Understandably, Grady worries that any new mode of literary analysis might become just as easily professionalized, and hence made safe for mass dissemination in English studies, as the old ones have (Grady 1991, 213–14); indeed, some deconstruction can seem remarkably like New Criticism, However, I wish to argue that the abandonment of 'organic unity as an aesthetic value' is a mistake and that ecopolitics shows why. Insisting on the value of various kinds of unity can be a powerful solvent of the fracturing impulses of late industrial capitalism, not least of all in the case of the unitary Earth.

Drawing on the principle of feedback, the final example of what ecological thinking can bring to criticism is the notion of a unitary Earth, or Gaia. In essence, this holds that the Earth is a single organism comprised of the obviously alive biota (the life forms we recognize) and the parts that we have previously treated as inorganic, the background environment such as the rocks, oceans, and atmosphere – that is, the latter parts are, in a sense, as alive as the former. The hypothesis was first formally presented by the chemist James E. Lovelock (Lovelock 1972), subsequently expanded upon in collaboration with a biologist (Lovelock and Margulis 1974a; Lovelock and Margulis 1974b), and finally submitted as a cybernetic proof using fundamental principles of physics and natural selection (Lovelock 1983). Lovelock's simplified DaisyWorld model illustrates that regulation of an entire planet's temperature can occur merely from competition between two kinds of plants, one dark and hence absorptive of heat and the other light and hence reflective of heat; over time their population ratios alter to keep their planet comfortable. The details of Gaia need not detain us, and the essential point is Lovelock's demonstration that the entire Earth exhibits a characteristic (temperature regulation) that we have, since the Enlightenment, attributed only to individual living creatures. It is a disturbing thought for us, but if Tillyard's model of the Elizabethan World Picture is even faintly close to the habits of minds of Shakespeare's first audiences and readers, that is to say, if it was thinkable as a model of the world even as it was dismissed as official propaganda, then the Gaia hypothesis would have appeared unremarkable to them.

A belief in the connection between the affairs of human beings in the sublunary sphere and occurrences among the higher layers (the sky, planets, and beyond) was firmly, and it seemed at the time irrevocably, ruptured in the eighteenth century. Modern science seems to be restoring this belief, and there are two ways we may respond to this development. One is to accept that aspects of Enlightenment thinking were excessively particularizing and, in ways that suited the Industrial Revolution, overlooked connectivities that we find obvious. Had factory owners been forced to site their fresh water intake pipes downstream of their waste-water discharge pipes, for example, the idea that inputs come from an unlimited pure source and that outputs can be sent to an infinitely capacious 'sink' would not so easily have persisted. That is to say, certain rational responses to the practices that flowed from Enlightenment habits of mind might quickly have identified the discrepancies between theory and reality.

An alternative response to the new sciences is to find in them cause to reject reason, rationality, and the Enlightenment *tout court*. One of the most noticeable cultural developments in the Western world in the past 30 years has been the rise of an anti-rationalistic, alternative culture that embraces the New Age movement, complementary medicine, and forms of holistic spiritualism, and which links these to the broader anarchist and animal rights movements. For an apparently rising number of people the Enlightenment itself should be dismissed as an illusory detour into hyper-rationality. For such people, the cosmic connectedness voiced in Elizabethan drama and poetry offers a sociable spirituality already packaged within a rich supply of artistic works that are central to Western culture.

This latter response is, of course, delusional and riven by contradiction: the new sciences themselves are founded on reason and cannot simply be co-opted to irrationality. This Alan Sokal and Jean Bricmont brilliantly demonstrate in their book *Intellectual Impostures* about certain postmodernists' exploitation of the myth that science is coming around to accept irrationality (Sokal and Bricmont 1998). The proper way to understand the new sciences in relation to artistic culture is to respect their counter-intuitive claims while exploring how these throw light on past works of art. This can be illustrated by considering Shakespeare's characters' understanding of why black people are black, which is essentially correct (the sun makes them black) but for the wrong reason.

An early modern conception of racial blackness is expressed by characters such as the prince of Morocco in Shakespeare's *The Merchant of Venice* who assumes (correctly, it turns out) that Portia is racist:

> MOROCCO (*to Portia*)
> Mislike me not for my complexion,
> The shadowed livery of the burnished sun,
> To whom I am a neighbour and near bred.
> (*The Merchant of Venice* 2.1.1–3)

On the inside, he insists, his blood is as red as anyone else's, even though he is coated with blackness (a 'shadowed livery') caused by living in a sunny country. Desdemona's father uses the same idea of a burnt coating that should have revolted his daughter, and that hence magic must have been used to make her 'Run from her guardage to the sooty bosom | Of such a thing as thou' (*Othello* 1.2.71–72). Othello comes to share this sense of his blackness as a coating: convinced that Desdemona is unfaithful he says 'My name, that was as fresh | As Dian's visage, is now begrimed and black | As mine own face' (3.3.391–93).

Likewise, in the very act of denying that blackness can wash off, Aaron in *Titus Andronicus* imagines it not as an innate colour but a coating:

> [AARON]
> Coal-black is better than another hue
> In that it scorns to bear another hue;
> For all the water in the ocean

Can never turn the swan's black legs to white,
Although she lave them hourly in the flood.

(*Titus Andronicus* 4.2.98 102)

Washing the Ethiop (or blackamoor) white was, of course, proverbial in Shakespeare's time (Dent 1981, Appendix A, E186). What conceptions about the world gave rise to the idea that blackness is a coating? For a white actor playing Morocco, Othello, or Aaron the character's sense of his blackness as a coating is, of course, literally true: excluding the unlikely possibility that a black actor worked in Shakespeare's company (about which we would expect there to be some record), a white actor would have 'blacked up' as preparation for the performance. The part, then, with its references to blackness as a coating, suits the particulars of the theatre's impersonation of blackness, which is far from real blackness, and this adds support to the argument made by the Ghanaian actor Hugh Quarshie that black actors should not play Othello, or at least not without major reworking of the play (Quarshie 1999).

Elizabethans noticed that black people live in hot countries and since skin darkens in the sun it was reasonable to suppose that they simply had deep tans. Certainly, the melanin pigment that tanning brings to the surface is the same in all humans, but colour differences between races are an effect not of any one person's tanning but a phenomenon operating across whole populations. In countries where sunshine is strongest, humans whose melanocyte cells produce much melanin are less likely to get skin cancers than those whose cells produce little because the pigment absorbs harmful ultraviolet light before it penetrates too far into the body, and hence natural selection favours dark skins. If humans first evolved in Africa, as seems likely, then those who migrated to colder northerly climates no longer needed to make so much melanin, and indeed making too much would carry an evolutionary penalty since it costs energy that were better spent elsewhere in the body. Hence, over evolutionary time, people in the cold climates turned white. Sunshine is the explanation of blackness (and indeed whiteness) in humans, just as it is – and by precisely the same genetic pressures in Lovelock's model of light and dark daisies changing the face of DaisyWorld. Disturbing as it is to our post-Enlightenment sensibilities to acknowledge, the Elizabethans, while not exactly right about blackness, had a fair inkling of what was going on.

There is, of course, no simple continuity between Renaissance habits of mind and our own. We might nonetheless share ideas with the Renaissance by the indirect route: we may find ourselves returning to consider their commonplaces in the light of new science and philosophy that rational study has made possible. Large-scale systems thinking and correspondences between processes at the micro- and macro-levels are not to be ruled out as archaisms. This is one of the fundamental insights of ecological thinking and it has practical, political, consequences. The Internet, the cellular telephone network, franchised corporations, and indeed terrorist networks share design principles from nature that humankind has not hitherto emulated. The topologies of such networks make for peculiar (frequently, counter-intuitive) relationships between the part and the whole, and although we encounter them in structures we have made, Shakespeare's contemporaries encountered them in the natural world. For example, we know from genetics that in response to the human migration from its birthplace in Africa to colder climates, no individual got paler or shorter or rounder (the physical attributes better suited to cooler climates), but, considered collectively, human beings did.

In the twentieth century several of the central mysteries of life ceased to be mysteries, as the mechanical processes of sexual reproduction and its relation to heredity became explicable in terms of interactions among proteins. Although there remains considerable ignorance of the detail, organic processes, it seems, can be understood in mechanical terms.

A corollary of this dissolving of the organic/mechanical binary, and one that criticism has yet to fully encompass, is that organic explanations for mechanical processes can be perfectly valid too: it is reasonable to say that DaisyWorld, treated as a singularity, cools itself down by changing colour just as humankind, treated collectively, changed skin colour to suit local climates. Post-Enlightenment science has long treated such metaphors as intentionalist errors deriving ultimately from Aristotle's personification of matter in his *Physics*, which explained things coming to rest because getting tired is the way of the world. Virtually all Shakespeare criticism has been written according to the Enlightenment's scientific principles, and these are currently being revised. It is worth taking notice of the revision.

*

A generation ago, the first academic refuge of the intellectual out of touch with his times was the Department of the Classics. It is now above all the Department of English.

(Wiener 1950, 158 9)

Norbert Wiener's complaint that English is a subject out of touch with life and recent history made perfect sense when written in 1950, in the heyday of New Criticism, and it makes perfect sense now at the tail end of post-structuralism. It would, however, have seemed itself acutely out-of-touch with the subject between the late 1960s and the late 1980s when the relevance of the subject *was*, for the most part, the subject. I share with Wiener the conviction that not engaging with 'the main facts concerning science and machinery' (Wiener 1950, 163) is a dereliction of critical duty. At the start of the twenty-first century, that engagement is ecocriticism.

The term ecocriticism was first used in the essay 'Literature and ecology: An experiment in ecocriticism' (Rueckert 1978) and most simply it expresses a desire to bring to the study of literature the concerns of ecopolitics. Ecocriticism is not yet codified or institutionalized sufficiently to prescribe how this might be done. Those who object to the destruction of forests, animals, and waterways might well find themselves attracted to literary works about, those things, as opposed to, say, Fyodor Dostoyevsky's novels of life in nineteenth-century Saint Petersburg. Much ecocriticism has been concerned with nature writing – prose and poems about walks in remote and beautiful places – by English Romantics such as William Wordsworth and Samuel Taylor Coleridge and the American Transcendentalists such as Ralph Waldo Emerson and Henry David Thoreau and their followers. There are at least two good reasons not to confine ecocriticism within these bounds, however.

The first is that the history of politicized criticism teaches us to move from the obvious cases to the not so obvious. Feminist criticism began with analysis of female characters in novels, poems, and drama, and with female writers, but produced its most compelling work when it moved from this marginal position to look at male characters and writers, from which perspective it could discover the concealed sexism that made female desires, experiences, and creativity marginal in the first place. In Shakespeare studies this involved a move from harping on daughters, as Lisa Jardine's landmark book of the first kind called it (Jardine 1983), to Catherine Belsey's analysis of how Shakespeare's comedies call into question 'that set of relations between terms which proposes as inevitable an antithesis between masculine and feminine, men and women' (Belsey 1985, 167). By analogy, ecocriticism could concern itself with the relations that propose an inevitable antithesis between nature and culture.

Similarly, gay studies (later subsumed into queer theory) began its critique of canonical heterosexism first with a purchase on writers and characters whose homoeroticism was fairly obvious (say, Oscar Wilde or Patroclus in Shakespeare's *Troilus and Cressida*) and moved from there to an analysis of how far sexual orientation itself might be a category of human personality that emerged under particular historical circumstances (Bray 1982). By these models, ecocriticism could attend to positive representations of nature but should not confine itself to these, for its proper purview is all that happens in literary culture that tends to create or sustain the political, social, and cultural conditions that ecopolitics seeks to change.

A second reason why ecocrticism should not confine itself to nature writing is that the English Romantics and American Transcendentalists themselves did not do so, unless we exclude such obvious members as William Blake from the first group and Margaret Fuller, historian of the Italian revolution, from the second (Mehren 1994). When Blake writes what seems to be a paean to the pastoral life, the activities of the city enter as a means of communicating the life:

> Piper sit thee down and write
> In a book that all may read—
> So he vanish'd from my sight.
> And I pluck'd a hollow reed.
>
> And I made a rural pen,
> And I stain'd the water clear,
> And I wrote my happy songs
> (Blake 1789, 'Introduction')

For all that it is a 'rural' pen, the clear stream water has to be stained to make ink and the book of paper must have been manufactured somewhere other than the countryside.

In a similarly worldly-wise vein, Blake's questions about the origins of tigers are as much metallurgical as biological:

> What the hammer? what the chain,
> In what furnace was thy brain?
> What the anvil? what dread grasp,
> Dare its deadly terrors clasp!
> (Blake 1789, 'The Tyger')

The Romantic poets' own representation of nature as a domain of solace and respite from the depredations of industrialization has long been understood as subjected to critique from within that movement itself: Blake's tiger is more fashioned (by 'hammer', 'furnace', and 'anvil') than reared.

Such critique of romanticizing about nature and the countryside can also be found in Wordsworth and Coleridge's *Lyrical Ballads*, whose oxymoronic title was as self-contradictory as the literary manifesto, the second edition's preface, which was produced two years after the poems it sought to introduce (Wordsworth and Coleridge 1800, v–xlvi). Wordsworth opposes the natural, unmannered life of the country to 'encreasing accumulation of men in cities' that coarsens appetites so that Shakespeare and Milton are neglected in favour of 'frantic novels, sickly and stupid German Tragedies, and deluges of idle and extravagant stories in verse' (Wordsworth and Coleridge 1800, xviii–xix). The city is the place of artifice and the country the place of emotional and linguistic origins and hence Wordsworth concerns himself with the latter (Wordsworth and Coleridge 1800, xvi–xvii).

This assertion that rural people and behaviours have an inherent dignity was a radical statement at the time, but the obvious question that follows from such a digging below artifice in search of natural purity is why, then, use verse at all? Wordsworth did not shy away from that question and gave an answer which might have surprised himself as much as it does us:

> The end of Poetry is to produce excitement in coexistence with an over-balance of pleasure. . . . But if the words by which this excitement is produced are in themselves powerful, or the images and feelings have an undue proportion of pain connected with them, there is some danger that the excitement may be carried beyond its proper bounds. Now the co-presence of something regular [that is, metre], something to which the mind has been accustomed when in an unexcited or a less excited state, cannot but have great efficacy in tempering and restraining the passion by an intertexture of ordinary feeling.
>
> (Wordsworth and Coleridge 1800, xxx–xxxi)

The value of verse, then, is to restrain the over-excitement the readers might suffer if the poet immoderately exploited the power of everyday language. As well as clipping the peaks of excitement, metre can ameliorate the boredom 'if the Poet's words should be incommensurate with the passion' (Wordsworth and Coleridge 1800, xxxi), and thereby it evens out the readerly experience. Thus artifice retains its place as the necessary mediator within a literary manifesto of the man who has been most widely received, and by this manifesto promoted himself, as the poet of simple nature.

The Romantic poets are a good place to start thinking about the relationship between ecological politics and art, not only because their poems so often invoke the natural world but also because as poets they (conveniently for our purposes) took pains to explain themselves in political terms. Percy Bysshe Shelley's *Defence of Poetry* was among other things a politicized response to Philip Sidney's book of the same name of 230 years earlier that had patiently refuted Plato's dismissal of fiction-makers as liars and made a modest claim for the good poets do. Contrary to Plato's view that poets copy objects from nature, which are themselves only copies of Ideas, Sidney characterizes as poetic mimesis the relationship between the Idea and its natural manifestation. This manoeuvre disables the objection to poetic copying of reality with the insistence that since reality is a copy, poets are something like makers of reality (Sidney 1595, B4v–C1r; Egan 2005, 69–71). Alexander Pope makes precisely this case in relation to Shakespeare:

> His *Charadas* are so much Nature her self, that 'tis a sort of injury to call them by so distant a name as Copies of her. . . . every single character in Shakespear is as much an Individual, as those in Life itself.
>
> (Shakespeare 1725, ii–iii)

No such half measures suited Shelley, whose extraordinary closing assertion is that, as mouthpieces of the best thoughts of an age, poets are the 'unacknowledged legislators' of the world.

Before reaching this point, Shelley argues that poetry is merely one aspect of the general human love of order and beauty that makes us arrange the things at our disposal in pleasure-giving ways. Like Wordsworth, Shelley claims that the capacity to be poetic is shared by everyone, albeit to different degrees, and is manifested in a capacity to create language that 'marks the before unapprehended relations of things and perpetuates their apprehension' (Shelley 1840, 5). This, rather than any arbitrary distinction between verse and prose, was for Shelley the essence of poetry, and in this mind-expanding role it finds its true power:

It awakens and enlarges the mind itself by rendering it the receptacle of a thousand unapprehended combinations of thought. Poetry lifts the veil from the hidden beauty of the world, and makes familiar objects be as if they were not familiar; it reproduces all this it represents, and the impersonations clothed in its Elysian light stand thence-forward in the minds of those who have once contemplated them, as memorials of that gentle and exalted content which extends itself over all thoughts and actions with which it coexists.

(Shelley 1840, 16–17)

Thus poetry is necessarily social, not individualistic, for it enables a man to 'put himself in the place of another and of many others; the pains and pleasures of his species must become his own' (Shelley 1840, 17).

Raymond Williams observes that in redefining the artist as a person with a special sensibility and special powers of expression rather than just special manufacturing skills (the earlier meaning of 'artist'), the Romantics enabled a one-way traffic between art and life. The dehumanizing effects of increasing industrialization and the degradation of the urban and rural poor, it was imagined, could be ameliorated by literature expressing repugnance at this and revealing the finer thoughts that even ordinary people speaking ordinary language are capable of. This humanizing impulse should not be confined to art, Williams argues, else art becomes an isolated mode of resistance; rather the resistance to dehumanization has to be part of a full social response (Williams 1958, 43–46). That is to say, for Williams it is not enough to find comfort, as Wordsworth allegedly did, in country walks that inspire eulogies to the daffodil, nor in encouraging the masses to take such walks when they can get them and to obtain the same pleasure vicariously when they could not. Yet such a view of the value of literature is offered by the most widely read modern critic of Romanticism and ecology, Jonathan Bate:

This book is dedicated to the proposition that the way in which William Wordsworth sought to enable his readers better to enjoy or endure life was by teaching them to look at and dwell in the natural world. . . . most people know two facts about Wordsworth, that he wrote about daffodils and that he lived in the Lake District, and these two facts would seem to suggest that he was a 'nature poet'. . . . this book will argue that, unfashionable as that way [of seeing him] is in literary circles, it might just be the most useful way of approaching Wordsworth in the 1990s and the early twenty-first century.

(Bate 1991, 4)

For Bate the English proto-socialism of John Ruskin and William Morris stands at odds with Marxist theory, for it recognized that the real basis of 'political economy was not money, labour, and production, but "Pure Air, Water, and Earth"' (Bate 1991, 59). We should not, Bate argues, deconstruct out of existence the difference between human artifices such as class and city and the non-human given of nature – as Cultural Materialism in particular is apt to do – because 'Whatever our class, nature can do something for us' (Bate 1991, 56).

Bate's opposition between politics and nature is false because class struggle is in fact concerned with the enjoyment of those things that nature can do for us, and it is only class (the category that Marxism seeks to do away with) that keeps nature's bounty from the majority of the world. Bate rightly points to an important political consequence of industrialization in eastern Europe – 'Where capitalism has its Three Mile Island, Marxist-Leninism has its Chernobyl' (Bate 1991, 57) – but seems to think that this was because capitalist industrialization was somehow inherently cleaner, brighter, and more safety-conscious than communist industrialization. The truth is that governmental restraints on capitalist rapacity were won by campaigning workers, not beneficently granted by self-restraining energy companies, so that we have the workers not the bosses to thank for the marginally safer conditions in American nuclear power plants.

In his landmark publication of ecocriticism *avant la lettre, The Country and the City*, Williams points out that the sense of a bucolic paradise lost in the recent past can be detected in the literary work of each generation, reaching back through Edwardian, Victorian, Romantic, Augustan, Restoration, Renaissance, and late medieval writers. To avoid mistaking this impulse for a real loss, 'we must get off the escalator' of Edenic yearning and consider its general movement (Williams 1973, 12). For Williams the only way to make sense of this is within the phases of capitalism:

> I am then very willing to see the city as capitalism, as many now do, if I can say also that this mode of production began, specifically, in the English rural economy, and produced, there, many of the characteristic effects — increases of production, physical reordering of a totally available world, displacements of customary settlements, a human remnant and force which became a proletariat — which have since been seen, in many extending forms, in cities and colonies and in an international system as a whole. . . . What the oil companies do, what the mining companies do, is what the landlords did, what plantation owners did and do.
>
> (Williams 1973, 292–93)

The shared sense of lost innocence comes from the shared experience of increasing forces of production, and hence, as a way of understanding change, historical materialism – the explanation of the world that posits the increasing forces of production as the engine of everything else (Egan 2004, 25–26, 38–39, 54–57) – dissolves all hard distinctions between country and the city, and specifically between 'the country as cooperation with nature, and city and industry as overriding and transforming it' (Williams 1973, 293). From this point of view, Shakespeare's works are particularly of interest because they appeared during a crucial transition from nascent to full-blown early capitalism, as joint-stock companies of players as well as buccaneers and merchant traders gained royal monopolies that enabled them to accumulate capital at rates quite impossible within guild regulation. There will be more to say about this shortly.

Even ecocritics such as Bate who are familiar with and apparently approving of Williams's work tend to reinforce the false distinction between urban capitalization and rural pastoralism in its literary form, thinking of country walks as a balm to soothe the troubled mind. Of course, country walks *are* such a balm and in Britain the right to use public footpaths formerly (illegally) closed by landowners was established by a series of mass trespasses organized by the founders of the Ramblers' Association, which itself arose out of informal workers' walking clubs (Stephenson 1989). To see Wordsworth as an early popularizer of the pleasures of walking, however, it is not necessary to hold that an arbitrary division of time between work and leisure is inevitable. Those who are able to afford to live in the country because they like it, while working in a city because they need to, can easily come to see ' "the state" or "the planners" as their essential enemy, when it is quite evident that what the state is administering and the planners serving is an economic system which is capitalist in all its main intentions, procedures and criteria' (Williams 1973, 294).

Norbert Wiener, the founder of cybernetics and writer of this section's epigraph, saw this too and observed of his New Hampshire farmhouse:

it is all very well for me to wish to enjoy the amenities of life which still remain in a country community of this sort. I must, however, realize that whereas in the old days the New England cities were tributary to this community and to communities like it, nowadays these communities represent nothing more than economic extensions of our cities. The *Saturday Evening Post* cover is not an adequate representation of the facts of modern life.

(Wiener 1950. 57)[4]

Williams observes that Wordsworth had been aware of retreat into 'deep subjectivity' as one of the responses to our modern way of living among strangers whose behaviour, for all its anonymity, affects us. Alternatively, we

look around us for social pictures, social signs, social messages, to which, characteristically, we try to relate as individuals but so as to discover, in some form, community. Much of the content of modern communications is this kind of substitute for directly discoverable and transitive relations to the world.

(Williams 1973, 295)

Shakespeare wrote nothing that we can directly call a city comedy, but he wrote of people leaving cities and constructing alternative communities elsewhere, and he wrote of people confronting the paradoxical isolation of city life. Indeed, the impulse to create communities impinged on his professional life. It is well known that there was no city guild for early modern actors, but Roslyn Knutson suggests that they formed their own guild-like communities in response to this economic isolation (Knutson 2001). That is to say, rival playing companies might not have been as competitively cut-throat as we have imagined. On the other side of the equation, it is easy to overstate the sense of community among those in a guild. As Zachary Lesser has shown, within the Stationers' Company the printers were greatly inferior to the book-sellers and publishers, and from 1603 the leading stationers created a joint-stock company within the guild, operating with royal monopoly just like the theatre troupes and the buccaneers (Lesser 2004, 26–51).

   In his second work of ecocriticism, Jonathan Bate develops his thesis, contra Williams, that reading about wandering as lonely as a cloud might fruitfully offer a recreational escape from urban life, that poems 'may create for the mind the same kind of re-creational space that a park creates for the body' (Bate 2000, 64). This kind of thinking easily descends into risible sentimentality – 'Nature is calling to us in a voice like that of our primal mother' (Bate 2000, 67) – and it does not even make for convincing criticism of Bate's favourite neglected poet, John Clare. Bate reproduces Clare's poem 'The Pettichap's Nest', which ostensibly describes the finding of a nest with 'scarce a clump of grass to keep it warm | . . . Or prickly bush to shield it', and 'Built like an oven with a little hole' (Bate 2000, 158–60). Unencumbered by a post-Freudian suspicion that Clare's choice of words might speak of concerns of which the poet was unaware, Bate does not connect this vaginal imagery to the little-man phallus of the title, even when the poet speaks of the nest being concealed, its entrance 'Scarcely admitting e'en two fingers', and the wider space inside being 'full of eggs'. Bate appreciates in Clare his ability to just be in the countryside, soaking it up rather than thinking too hard about it. Despite Bate's claim to theoretical sophistication in this book (Jensen 2003–4, 113), it offers little more than the dumbstruck peasant awe that Terry Eagleton pointed out was the logical conclusion of the ideas of Bate's favourite philosopher, Martin Heidegger (Eagleton 1983, 62–66).

   In a final programmatic chapter called 'What are poets for?' Bate uses the idea from Heidegger (and, indeed, Hans-Georg Gadamer, although Bate does not credit him) of a reader's and a writer's horizons of experience meeting in the text (Bate 2000, 243–83). The idea is that a poem gives us an experience of another's way of being in the world, another's attitude towards it, that we share when we read it, and that this experience can be a dwelling 'at home', as it were, in the work. Bate thinks that Heidegger's writings about the nature of technology and the storing of energy showed why windmills are safe but large dams are not, but this is of course nonsense. No one would object to nuclear power if it were in fact clean.[5] It is not the particular means of generating power that people object to in principle, it is the real danger they present and the damage that they cause in their processes. An exception to this point might be made for those extraordinary country-dwellers who oppose the construction of onshore windfarms, for whom the obvious solution to the nation's rising energy needs is not they should put up with living near windmills but that someone else, somewhere else, should put up with living near a coal mine or a nuclear power station.

A guiding theme of Bate's book is that language is our means to reconnect with nature, and yet language is the acme of human artifice, the triumph of the cultural over the natural. This presents an ecocritical dilemma: the poetry and the criticism are at a remove from the pure experience of nature that they seek to articulate. Bate's tackling of, and solution to, this dilemma are reminiscent of Wordsworth's wrestling in the preface to *Lyrical Ballads* with the related problem of complex and artificial verse being in the service of plain speaking. For Bate, the solution comes in a kind of low-impact poetry that does as little reasoning and exhorting as possible and seeks instead to emulate the natural world in itself.

Such poetry should be read in a gentle, awestruck, and non-political, way:

> The poet's way of articulating the relationship between humankind and environment, person and place, is peculiar because it is experiential, not descriptive. Whereas the biologist, the geographer and the Green activist have *narratives* of dwelling, a poem may be a *revelation* of dwelling. Such a claim is phenomenological before it is political, and for this reason ecopoetics may properly be regarded as pre-political. . . . Marxist, feminist and multiculturalist critics bring explicit or implicit political manifestos to the texts about which they write. They regard their work as contributing towards social change. Green critics have a difficulty in this respect: it would be quixotic to suppose that a work of literary criticism might be an appropriate place in which to spell out a practical programme for better environmental management. . . . Ecopoetics must concern itself with consciousness. When it comes to practice, we have to speak in other discourses.
>
> (Bate 2000, 266)

This is simply a new way to formulate the old cry that politics should stay out of literary studies, which plea the Romantic poets would scarcely have credited as arising from their work.

In the latest literary scholarship too, such a split between consciousness and social practice has been discredited. On principle, a feminist critic must be in favour of equal pay for women (since a founding principle is that sex discrimination is unfair) and there is no conflict between this pragmatic concern and the feminist analysis of the kinds of consciousness evident in the poems under discussion. Indeed, the greatest critical dividends occur when one can show how the two discourses, the literary and political, are mutually reinforcing: low social status has long degraded women and the internalizing of this degradation (including its literary versions) has added to women's reluctance to fight their employers, which is why raising consciousness has been part of the feminists' political struggle.

Bate's claim that ecocriticism should necessarily be non-(or in his phrase, pre-) political is as absurd as it would be in the fields of Marxist, feminist, postcolonial, and queer criticism. Having kicked away the political leg upon which ecocriticism might stand, one could expect Bate to lean rather more heavily upon the other leg, science, but his grasp of neo-Darwinism is shaky too:

> There is no such thing in nature as what Thoreau in the section of *Walden* entitled 'Shelter' calls 'superfluous property'. The savage has his shelter, writes Thoreau, the birds their nests and the foxes their holes, but 'in modern civilized society not more than half the families own a shelter'. 'Civilization' creates laws which prevent the 'natural' process whereby shelter superfluous to the necessities of one individual animal or animal-family is swiftly occupied by others. . . . In the natural world, different species fight for territory between each other and among themselves, but each must share its ecosystem with other species.
>
> (Bate 2000, 279)

It is tempting to respond that urban squatters fill the gap in civilization that Bate has identified, but more importantly his model of natural sharing is entirely sentimental. Genes are in competition with one another and this causes the organisms they create to share nothing with other individuals in the same species, let alone other species, except inasmuch as doing so furthers their own chances of replication. [T]he proper use of the analogy of human cooperation with cooperation elsewhere in the natural world is that altruism can nonetheless emerge from competition between genes.

In a book-closing swipe at the latest manifestations of the modern, Bate complains about the insidious 'susurrus of cyberspace' that threatens to drown the grasshopper and the cricket (Bate 2000, 282). This is a remarkable objection to a technology that has put means for the dissemination of writing into the hands of millions who otherwise would never have learned to type, and irony is piled upon irony when we reflect that the Internet, far from silencing insects, achieves mass dissemination of words without cutting clown trees to make the sheets of compressed wood-pulp upon which, regrettably, Bate's words (and my own) have to appear.

*

Let us retreat from the blind alley of treating of ecocriticism as the study of nature writing and consider again Williams's deconstruction of the distinction between country and city. The word 'ecology' was coined in the late nineteenth century to mean 'that branch of biology which deals with the relations of living organisms to their surroundings' (OED ecology 1), from the Greek word 'οἶκ-ος' (house) and the Greek suffix '-logy', which had by then come to be used for 'departments of study' (OED-logy). The model for this formation was 'economy', the sixteenth-century meaning of which was the art of managing a household (OED economy 1a), and which by analogy between the domestic and the social came in the seventeenth century to mean the management of a community's affairs (OED economy 2a). Economics and ecology are not antithetical but cognate. An ecocriticism that drew on this shared origin in 'home' would have a wide remit indeed, for that word has always meant not just one's particular dwellings but also the collection of dwellings of which it is a part, and the native land (country) where that collection is located (OED home *n.*[1] 1, 2, 6).

In relation to Renaissance drama, a concern for place has lately driven attempts to connect the plays to their first home, the cultural phenomenon of London theatre that arose in a particular location at a particular time. Drawn on a map of early modern London such as Steven Mullaney provides (Mullaney 1988, 28–29), the open-air amphitheatres encircle but do not encroach upon the central area, the city, controlled by the London corporation; this central area, like its analogues in New York and Tokyo, is now one of the vital organs of international capitalism.

In Mullaney's analysis, the laminal zone around the central area was special because it was not quite within nor was it without the privileged centre:

> the ideological and topological structure of the walled medieval and Renaissance city was a tertiary rather than a binary one; long before the emergence of popular drama, the Liberties of London had served as a transitional zone between the city and the country, various powers and their limits, this life and the next – as a culturally maintained domain of ideological ambivalence and contradiction, where established authority reached and manifested, in spectacular form, the limits of its power to control or contain what exceeded it.
>
> (Mullaney 1988, viii–ix)

Approaching London from the countryside, this outer zone of suburbs might be as far as many would-be immigrants could reach. Conversely, viewed from within, it was the place to which the city expelled what was unwanted: lepers (for hospitalization), felons (for incarceration or execution), and actors (for whatever it is they do).

The last group, at least, could exploit their marginality:

> Secular drama in the city often played with the festive inversion of cultural norms, but rituals of misrule, dramatic and otherwise, are precisely what their name implies: misrule, defined against and delimited by proper rule, its reigning antithesis. The public playhouses were born, however, at a time when traditional hierarchies were breaking down, and neither they nor the plays they fostered were thus contained by the customary antithesis of rule and misrule, order and disorder, everyday and holiday. With their advent we are no longer concerned with an interstitial stage, but with what we might can an *incontinent* one.
>
> (Mullaney 1988, 49)

Playhouses were physically dangerous because of thieves and morally (as well as physically) dangerous because of prostitutes, but they were also socially dangerous because on their stages ordinary men broke the dress codes that applied everywhere else (the sumptuary laws) by appearing as aristocrats, princes, and monarchs (Hunt 1996, 295–324), and because within them gathered thousands of workers who should, at 2 p.m. on a weekday afternoon when the performances began, be at their jobs.

In Mullaney's view, the plays are self-consciously concerned with their liminal powers and use them to explore the basis of every aspect of Elizabethan ideology, including the right to govern others, the differences between men and women, and the lessons to be drawn from the past for deciding how things should happen in the future. As such, they were inherently political:

> The public playhouses were not a minor irritation to London: they represented a threat to the political well-being and stability of the city. Their rise and continued existence marked a radical shift in the delicate balance between the city and the Court – a balance that had been graphically enacted in the past at the point where civic and royal authorities met and in a sense combined, to display their mutual limits and limitations through the vehicle of marginal spectacle.
>
> (Mullaney 1988, 53)

The radical shift referred to here was the granting of royal monopolies to joint-stock companies such as the acting troupes and the East India Company that, this dispensation notwithstanding, operated as free-enterprise rather than guild-regulated industries.

Granted the epitome of control – royal patronage – the Shakespearian drama paradoxically gained a licence to reflect upon wider society as well as upon its own conditions of possibility. Being based in the liminal environment of the Liberties, traditional places of licence, 'The stage decentered itself, and its displacement provided it with something approaching an exterior vantage point upon the culture it was both a part of, yet set apart from' (Mullaney 1988, 54).

Attractive as Mullaney's hypothesis is, and however appealing its relation of the drama's ideological interrogations to the geographical situation of the playhouses, there are important qualifications to be made. Throughout *The Place of the Stage* Mullaney calls the marginal zone beyond city authority the Liberties, as though the mere fact of being outside made for freedom of expression. In fact, a Liberty meant any place that would normally be subject to city authority were it not exempted by special licence. The freedoms enjoyed by the theatres of London's South Bank were not due to the city's authority ending at the water's edge on the northern shore (it did not), but because they were within specific. places, the Liberties of the Clink and Paris Garden, that were (because Liberties) exempt from city control despite where they stood.

This matters because Liberties were not necessarily geographically marginal at all: the indoors Blackfriars theatre was in the heart of the city, on the site of a former Dominican monastery that had Liberty status. Far from relishing their marginal status in demotic open-air amphitheatres in the suburbs, the players always wanted to play indoors to rich patrons in the city and did so whenever they could, for example in the city inns before the ban of 1594. In 1596 James Burbage purchased the Blackfriars building as a new home for his son Richard's troupe, but they were prevented from using it by a petition raised by the residents of this select district.

Until 1608 most of the opportunities to play indoors were in temporarily adapted halls rather than permanent structures. When the boy players who were using the Blackfriars once a week for semi-public performances were forced to cease in 1608, Shakespeare's company took possession of the building and achieved their goal of playing indoors to rich patrons. They kept their open-air Globe amphitheatre going too, in the summer, probably not because they could afford to be profligate nor, as Andrew Gurr suggests, because they had a nostalgia for the pre-1594 habit of touring the suburban amphitheatres in the summer and then moving into the warm city inns in the winter (Gurr 1988, 10). A more likely reason for running two theatres at once was that, although their Blackfriars survived on this occasion, the ending of the privileges of the Liberties in 1608 made them wonder if their prized foothold in the city might be lost yet again, as it had been in 1594 and 1596. Only if their royal patronage failed the King's Men would the advantage of being distant from central authority outweigh the cost of being distant from the most lucrative market for playing, which was in the heart of the city. Mullaney's model of a liminal space between country and city is insufficiently attentive to the dynamic equilibrium by which are balanced these changeable centripetal and centrifugal forces.

In *Theatre, Court and City, 1595–1610*, Janette Dillon gives Mullaney's geopolitical domain a finer reticulation by using Henri Lefebvre's theory of place (Lefebvre 1991), tying locations to their effects on the psyche:

> The concept of 'place' . . . needs to be understood as both topographical and conceptual. Particular locations in London may emblematically represent particular activities (the Royal Exchange, for example, may stand for commercial transaction), but the inhabitants of the city who do not experience those aspects of city life only within those special locations. They carry their

experience of the city in all its aspects with them, experiencing their own subjectivities as the sum (and conflict) of those various locations and activities.

(Dillon 2000, 6–7)

In London a new kind of space opened up in the early seventeenth century when buildings appeared on the Strand running between the city of London and the courtly centre in Whitehall, forming a new district called 'the town' as a shopping location, especially once Robert Cecil's New Exchange was opened there in 1609 with a performance written by Ben Jonson (Dillon 2000, 9–10). More complex than Mullaney's model of centricity, Dillon's account helps us see that the city's boundaries were not clearly marked its power had long extended beyond the walls – and the word 'court' too embodied a slippery notion of place, for it meant (and still means) wherever the monarch happens to be residing. In Marxist theoretical terms, one of capitalism's abiding characteristics is reification, the turning of the immaterial into something material (Egan 2004, 28–38), but it can also accomplish the opposite transformation, which we might call virtualization. The word 'market' had, in medieval times, denoted the place where transactions took place, but in Shakespeare's time it came to acquire its modern sense of the placeless domain within which exchange occurs. The theatre came to see itself as a market, 'a place when· values may be tested in relation to one another' (Dillon 2000, 11).

These ideas about how early moderns experienced the city provide a useful bridge between ideas about urban alienation (from Lefebvre) and Edenic yearning (from Williams) and our present concerns with destruction of the natural environment. Late sixteenth- and early seventeenth-century London underwent a population explosion despite the death rate outstripping the birth rate, because thousands of immigrants came from the rest of the country and from abroad (Dillon 2000, 23 5). Most Londoners were born in the countryside, so naturally their ideas of it were bound up with thoughts of their own childhoods. Dillon rightly insists that although they seldom represent city life directly, Shakespeare's plays show urban concerns, as when in *Love's Labour's Lost* the young men form what is effectively a new city: their academy is bound by oaths, statutes, and signatures, it requires surveillance, and it is subject to intrusion and disruption. Even the oath they take is effectively that of an apprentice: stay put for a fixed term, live-in, work hard, and do not marry (Dillon 2000, 67). Characters in Shakespeare seek, construct, fly from, and attempt to destroy formal and informal communal Structures, and they do these things in the countryside and in the cities.

The readings that follow draw nothing from such sentimentalities as the idea that there exists, among certain people who tend not to inhabit the cities of the industrialized world, something called ecological wisdom, nor that 'poetry is the place where we save the earth' (Bate 2000, 283), to which Bate's flight from politics leads him. Political action is where we save the Earth, and analysis of poetry can be where we wield ecopolitical insights to re-examine past representations of analogous situations, and indeed to see how past understandings of the world gave rise to the conditions of the present. Although he would not, of course, have used these terms, Shakespeare's plays show an abiding interest in what we now identify as positive- and negative-feedback loops, cellular structures, the uses and abuses of analogies between natural and social order, and in the available models for community. Characters in Shakespeare display an interest in aspects of this natural world that are relevant for us, and if we take that interest seriously we find that there is nothing childlike or naive about their concerns.

Notes

1   In 1948 the Hungarian scientist Dennis Gabor invented a means of improving the resolving power of the electron microscope by photographing not the image produced by the beam of electrons bouncing

off an object but instead the interference pattern between this beam and a beam reflected by the object's background. Viewed in a coherent light (that is, one with its waves in phase), this photograph reveals depth-information about the object, making a three-dimensional picture rather than a two-dimensional picture. With the development of lasers as sources of bright, coherent light in the 1960s it became possible to make three-dimensional pictures stored on two-dimensional planes of glass: holograms.

2   In the snowflake, the Star of David pattern of two overlapping triangles governs the overall shape and is fully repeated, at a small scale, in each of the corners. Each of these six corners is itself made of a further six Star of David patterns, and so on down through the scale. Expressed as a mathematical function, this principle of self-repetition goes on indefinitely. In the example of the fern too, the overall shape of the leaf is repeated in each petal of the leaf, and each petal is made of still smaller versions of the same shape. The example of the fern leaf is particularly instructive because it indicates the informational economy of reusing at different scales a single set of genetic instructions for growth, which brevity is doubtless advantageous to an organism. Similarly, as Richard Dawkins showed, the simple instruction for a growing limb to branch can be reused throughout an organism to produce the great variety of physical structures that we see in living things (Dawkins 1986, 43–74). In another way too, the Tillyardian holographic principle applies to biology. Every cell in the human body contains a full set of instructions, genes, necessary for making the whole body. Indeed, each contains not only the instructions for making the individual but also the instructions (inherited from the parent of the opposite sex) for making body parts the individual does not possess but which will be needed by his or her child of the opposite sex. Men carry unexpressed genes for making breasts, ovaries, and a womb, and women carry unexpressed genes for making a penis and an Adam's apple. Each of us contains information that is redundant to ourself as an individual and that expresses our place in a lineage of genes, for the correct way to think about it is not that we carry genes in order to propagate ourselves but that the genes made us (in two kinds) to carry and propagate them.

3   It could be argued that calling Empson a New Critic understates the degree to which he was his own man. However, as a recent biography of Empson up to the age of 33 makes clear, his dependence upon the ideas of his tutor I. A. Richards (for example in claiming that literary meaning is inherently overdetermined) was extensive (Haffenden 2005). While the differences between Richards, Empson, and F. R. Leavis were as important as their collective differences from the American branch of New Criticism, what this generation of critics had in common and differentiated them from previous generations is coherent enough to form a family resemblance and hence a single label.

4   Wiener's comments on modern country life occur in the midst of an argument that in a sense we all live on borrowed time because we rely on technological solutions not yet invented to ensure that our children have a future (Wiener 1950, 20–58). This was also the insight of Jay Wright Forrester's modelling that underlay the alarming Club of Rome report *Limits to Growth*, which commented that 'Applying technology to the natural pressures that the environment exerts against any growth process has been so successful in the past that a whole culture has evolved around the principle of fighting against limits rather than learning to live with them' (Meadows et al. 1972, 150).

    The danger of what the report's authors call 'technological optimism' (Meadows et al. 1972, 154) is easily illustrated from the nuclear power industry, which, having no means to render harmless its waste products, buries them in the ground in the hope that either these burial sites will remained undisturbed for the thousands of years necessary for the radiation to decay to natural levels, or that new technologies will be invented to hasten the process. It is salutary to recall that although we can (just about) read papyri from 3,000 years ago, data written to computer storage media such as magnetic disks as recently as the 1970s are quite unrecoverable now, even using machines preserved in science museums. Writing the locations of nuclear dumps on paper might, for all this technological optimism, be the safest way to preserve such valuable knowledge.

5   This point is humorously made by the visiting alien in the television comedy *Mork and Mindy*, who cannot comprehend his human girlfriend's objection to the construction of a nearby nuclear power station, since any accidental spills can easily be removed with the everyday cleaning product 'Nuke-Away'. Horrified to learn that humankind has no 'Nuke-Away', Mork protests that without it nuclear power is the height of recklessness.

References

Aristotle (1930) The Works, David Ross (ed.), Vol. 2: PHILOSOPHY OF NATURE: *Physica; De Caelo; De Generatione et Corruptione*, 12 vols, London: Oxford University Press.

Baran, Paul (1964) 'On Distributed Communications Networks', *Institute of Electrical and Electronic Engineers Transactions on Communications* 12: 1–9.

Bate, Jonathan (1991) *Romantic Ecology: Wordsworth and the Environmental Tradition*, London: Routledge.

—— (2000) *The Song of the Earth*, London: Picador.

Belsey, Catherine (1985) 'Disrupting Sexual Difference: Meaning and Gender in the Comedies', in *Alternative Shakespeares*, John Drakakis (ed.), New Accents, London: Routledge, 166–90.

Bentham, Jeremy (1789) *An Introduction to the Principles of Morals and Legislation*, London: T. Payne and Son.

Blake, William (1789) *Songs of Innocence and of Experience, Shewing the Two Contrary States of the Human Soul*, London: William Blake.

Brooks, Cleanth (1947) *The Well Wrought Urn: Studies in the Structure of Poetry*, New York: Reynal and Hitchcock.

Brown, Michael and John May (1989) *The Greenpeace Story*, London: Dorling Kindersley.

Campbell, Lily B. (1947) *Shakespeare's 'Histories': Mirrors of Elizabethan Policy*, San Marino CA: Huntington Library.

Collingwood, R. G. (1945) *The Idea of Nature*, Oxford: Clarendon Press.

Dawkins, Richard (1986) *The Blind Watchmaker*, Harlow: Longman.

Dent, R. W. (1981) *Shakespeare's Proverbial Language: An Index*, Berkeley CA: University of California Press.

Dickens, Charles (1854) *Hard Times: For These Times*, London: Bradbury and Evans.

Dillon, Janette (2000) *Theatre, Court and City, 1595–1610: Drama and Social Space in London*, Cambridge: Cambridge University Press.

Eagleton, Terry (1983) *Literary Theory: An Introduction*, Oxford: Basil Blackwell.

Egan, Gabriel (2004) *Shakespeare and Marx*, Oxford Shakespeare Topics, Oxford: Oxford University Press.

—— (2005) 'Platonism and Bathos in Shakespeare and Other Early Modern Drama', *Refiguring Mimesis: Representation in Early Modern Literature*, Jonathan Holmes and Adrian Streete (eds), Hatfield: University of Hertfordshire Press, 59–78.

Empson, William (1930) *Seven Types of Ambiguity*, London: Chatto & Windus.

Godlovitch, Stanley, Rosalind Godlovitch and John Harris (eds) (1971) *Animals, Men and Morals: An Enquiry Into the Maltreatment of Non-humans*, London: Gollancz.

Grady, Hugh (1991) *The Modernist Shakespeare: Critical Texts in a Material World*, Oxford: Clarendon Press.

Gurr, Andrew (1988) 'Money or Audiences: The Impact of Shakespeare's Globe', *Theatre Notebook* 42: 3–14.

Haffenden, John (2005) *William Empson*, Vol. 1: Among the Mandarins, 2 vols, Oxford: Oxford University Press.

Hunt, Alan (1996) *Governance of the Consuming Passions: A History of Sumptuary Law*, Basingstoke: Macmillan.

Hunter, Robert (1979) *The Greenpeace Chronicle*, London: Pan.

Jardine, Lisa (1983) *Still Harping on Daughters: Women and Drama in the Age of Shakespeare*, Hemel Hempstead: Harvester Wheatsheaf.

Jensen, Michael P. (2003–4) 'Talking Books with: Jonathan Bate', *Shakespeare Newsletter* 53: 113–14.

Knutson, Roslyn Lander (2001) *Playing Companies and Commerce in Shakespeare's Time*, Cambridge: Cambridge University Press.

Lefebvre, Henri (1991) *The Production of Space*, Donald Nicholson-Smith (trans.), Oxford: Blackwell.

Lesser, Zachary (2004) *Renaissance Drama and the Politics of Publication: Readings in the English Book Trade*, Cambridge: Cambridge University Press.

Lovelock, James E. (1972) 'Gaia as Seen Through the Atmosphere', *Atmospheric Environment* 6: 579–80.

—— (1983) 'Daisy World: A Cybernetic Proof of the Gaia Hypothesis', *Coevolution Quarterly* 38: 66–72.

Lovelock, James E. and Lynn Margulis (1974a) 'Atmospheric Homeostasis by and for the Biosphere: The Gaia Hypothesis', *Tellus* 26: 2–9.

—— (1974b) 'Biological Modulation of the Earth's Atmosphere', *Icarus* 21: 471–89.

Marx, Karl (1954) *Capital: A Critical Analysis of Capitalist Production*, Frederick Engels (ed.), Vol. 1, 3 vols, London: Lawrence & Wishart.

—— (1977) *Economic and Philosophical Manuscripts of 1844*, London: Lawrence & Wishart.

Marx, Karl and Frederick Engels (1974) *The German Ideology*, C. J. Arthur (ed.), London: Lawrence & Wishart.

Meadows, Donella H., Dennis L. Meadows, Jorgen Randers, and William W. Behrens III (1972) *The Limits to Growth: A Report for the Club of Rome's Project on the Predicament of Mankind*, London: Earth Island.

Mehren, Joan von (1994) *Minerva and the Muse: A Life of Margaret Fuller*, Amherst MA: University of Massachusetts Press.

Mullaney, Steven (1988) *The Place of the Stage: License, Play, and Power in Renaissance England*, London: University of Chicago Press.

Quarshie, Hugh (1999) *Second Thoughts About Othello*, International Shakespeare Association Occasional Papers, 7, Chipping Campden: International Shakespeare Association.

Rhodes, Richard (1986) *The Making of the Atomic Bomb*, New York: Simon & Schuster.

Rueckert, William (1978) 'Literature and Ecology: An Experiment in Ecocriticism', *Iowa Review* 9(1): 71–86.

Segrè, Emilio (1970) *Enrico Fermi, Physicist*, Chicago IL: University of Chicago Press.

Shakespeare, William (1725) *The Works*, Alexander Pope (ed.), Vol. 1: Preface; *The Tempest; A Midsummer Night's Dream; The Two Gentlemen of Verona; The Merry Wives of Windsor; Measure for Measure; The Comedy of Errors; Much Ado About Nothing*, 6 vols, London: Jacob Tonson.

—— (1986) *The Complete Works*, Stanley Wells, Gary Taylor, John Jowett, and William Montgomery (eds), Oxford: Oxford University Press.

Shelley, Percy Bysshe (1840) *Essays, Letters from Abroad, Translations and Fragments*, Mary Shelley (ed.), Vol. 1, 2 vols, London: Edward Moxon.

Sidney, Philip (1595) *The Defence of Poesie*, STC 22535, London: [Thomas Creede] for William Ponsonby.

Singer, Peter (1975) *Animal Liberation: A New Ethics for Our Treatment of Animals*, New York: New York Review.

—— (1979) *Practical Ethics*, Cambridge: Cambridge University Press.

Sokal, Alan and Jean Bricmont (1998) *Intellectual Impostures: Postmodern Philosophers' Abuse of Science*, London: Profile.

Stephenson, Tom (1989) *Forbidden Land: The Struggle for Access to Mountain and Moorland*, Ann Holt (ed.), Manchester: Manchester University Press.

Tillyard, E. M. W. (1943) *The Elizabethan World Picture*, London: Chatto & Windus.

Wiener, Norbert (1950) *The Human Use of Human Beings: Cybernetics and Society*, London: Eyre & Spottiswoode.

Williams, Raymond (1958) *Culture and Society*, 1780–1950, London: Chatto & Windus.

—— (1973) *The Country and the City*, London: Chatto & Windus.

Wordsworth, William and Samuel Taylor Coleridge (1800) *Lyrical Ballads, with Other Poems*, second edition, Vol. 1, 2 vols, London: T. N. Longman and O. Rees.

Chapter 25

Alfred K. Siewers

READING THE OTHERWORLD ENVIRONMENTALLY

IN THE EARLY IRISH story *Tochmarc Étaíne* ("The Wooing of Étaín"), the Otherworld ruler Midir and his former wife Étaín are reunited, a millennium after magic had broken up their marriage, near the royal mounds at Temair (Tara) where she lived with her husband, the high king of Ireland. Midir reminds Étaín, who has been reborn in cycles of new life, of his Otherworld realm in the landscape of Ireland and her old name in it, Bé Find, or "fair lady."

> A Bé Fhind, in ragha lium.
> a tír n-ingnadh i fil rind.
> is barr sobairci fol and.
> is dath snechta for corp slim.
>
> Is ann nád bí muí na tuí.
> gel ded and dubai a brai.
> is lí sula lín ar sluag.
> is dath síon and gach gruadh.
>
> Is corcair muighi cach muín.
> is lí sula ugai luin.
> cidh cain deicsiu Muighe Fail.
> anam iar ngnais Muigi Mair.
>
> Cidh caín lib coirm Insi Fail,
> is mescu cuirm Thiri Mair.
> amrai tíre tír asber.
> ni théid óc ann ré sén.
>
> Srotha téith millsi tar tír.
> rogha dé midh ₇ fin.
> daine delgnaide cen ón
> combart cen pecadh cen chol.

Atchiam cach for cach leath.
₇ nícon aice nech.
teimel imorbuis Adaim
dodonarcheil ar araim.[1]

[Bé Find will you go with me
to a strange land where there is harmony?
Hair there like primrose,
color of snow on a smooth body;

Neither mine nor yours there;
white tooth, dark brow;
The troop of our hosts gladdens the eye—
color of foxglove on each cheek.

As flowers of the plain, pink each neck,
blackbird's eggs, joy of eye;
Though Mag Fáil be fair to see,
it is desolate after experiencing Mag Már;

Though fair be the ale of Inis Fáil,
more confounding that of Tír Már;
Miraculous of lands, the land of which I tell:
youth not leading to ancientness there.

Warm, sweet currents over the land,
choicest of mead and wine;
Outstanding human beings, not disfigured,
procreation without sin or illegality.

We see each one on every side,
and no one sees us;
The shadow of Adam's sin
prevents our being reckoned right.][2]

The story forms a part of what modern scholars call the Irish Mythological Cycle, as well as an important prequel to the Ulster Cycle in early Irish fantasy history and foundational text of the Otherworld as landscape trope, highlighting as it does a network of ancient mounds in the Irish countryside. The reconstructed story, based on the text in the Yellow Book of Lecan, stitches together three narrative panels covering more than one thousand years of plot that apparently end in the first century BCE, although the texts themselves probably date to the eighth or ninth century CE.[3]

    In his poetic wooing, Midir juxtaposes references to names for the physical land of Ireland that have fantasy Otherworld associations (Mag Fáil and Inis Fáil) with names of otherworldly landscapes of the imagination that seem to mirror physical Ireland (Mag Már and Tír Már). His words imply that the realm from which he comes is present all around the Irish Sea archipelago and beyond, associated with the biblical Paradise although full of both sensual and artistic delights in the natural world, and of plenty shared among all people. Yet one enters it throughout the narrative via particular portals: the síde (the singular síd also meaning "peace" in the early Irish period[4]), or mounds still locatable in Irish topography and often dating to the Neolithic era. Thus Midir lives at the mound of Brí Léith (Ardagh Hill in County Longford, Leinster), Étaín's apparent otherworldly home was at Síd Ban Find or Síd ar Femuin (on the plain of Cashel in Munster), and they reunite as a couple at the otherworldly mound-portal of Temair (in County Meath), only to fly as swans to the Munster portal while her husband, the king, Eochaid Airem (associated by the story with a new form of ploughing), vainly tries to dig up mounds to find them. The story begins with a focus on the famous Neolithic mound site of Bruig na Bóinde (in County Meath) on the bend of the Boyne River (usually identified with Newgrange but part of a complex of mounds also including Dowth, and Knowth) as an Otherworld portal to which the plot returns twice. And across this and a number of early narratives, other cosmographic features such as rivers, wells, the sea, and sky are referenced also as Otherworld portals.

This chapter will argue that such tales participated in and helped to shape narrative environmental landscapes in a non-modern sense of ecoregion as story. In laying the philosophical groundwork for the modern concept of "bioregion" or "ecoregion," Martin Heidegger articulated personal place as event, as a confluence of what he called the hidden-yet-appearing, singular-yet-multiple, "four-fold" of earth, sky, mortals, and gods, which associated both past and future with "the thing" being experienced as place. He compared this experience of a place as imaginative art to a dance or multiple mirroring, which expresses connections between environment, self, and other. Of this sense of place as relational process, Heidegger wrote, "thinging is the nearing of the world."[5] He then extended this definition of place to a regional fourfold. This included not only the experience of "the thing" as place, but also "openness" interconnecting a region of places, which relates the thing and the human, shapes human cultural dialogue with the thing, and reshapes inter-human relations in the process.[6] "Place opens a region by every time gathering things into their belonging together," he concluded.[7]

Ecoregion today means an assemblage of natural communities sharing relational patterns of species and ecological processes, environmental conditions, and symbiotic interrelationships.[8] Yet these are in turn reciprocally defined and influenced by human cultural patterns articulated in narrative. Two textual "maps" in this chapter highlight alternate routes to experiencing the Otherworld as regional landscape in an environmental sense. Thematic categories from landscape studies focus the environmental reading of *Tochmarc Étaíne* as region. Tracing Christian and native pagan meanings in the topography of Wales highlights the Welsh *Mabinogi* as a dynamic image of region resisting political domination of landscape. In the stories, dynamic places such as the *síde* of *Tochmarc Étaíne* or the *gorsedd* (probably a linguistically related Welsh term) of Arberth in the *Mabinogi* help constitute culturally imaginative place-regions for eastern Ireland and southern Wales in the early Middle Ages.[9] These narrative regions reciprocally mediate between places and larger spaces in the culture and environment, such as all of Wales or all of Ireland, the Irish Sea province, the entire Atlantic archipelago of Europe, the mainland continent, and so on—overlapping into Creation at large in a "rhizomic" network.[10] These landscapes generated both place and space, articulating through story how that which is given by the environment entwines that which is shaped by human narrative, mutually reforming one another, involving both grace from a theophany of landscape and earthly struggle to participate in it.[11]

In these stories, human place becomes the experience of difference: Experience of different temporalities associated with different cosmic environments coming together in the same topography, as in the mound-portals of Ireland in *Tochmarc Étaíne* and in the reuniting of Étaín with Midir after a thousand years through those portals; and experience of different types of being, such as the human-born Étaín's transformation into nonhuman forms associated with nature, her human rebirth, and ultimate move into the Otherworld, as humans interact with characters who represent old native gods and otherworldly rulers such as Midir.

This all reflects the probable origins of the Otherworld in pre-Christian symbolism for nonhuman time in the world (the temporality of trees, plants, animals, seasons, stars, rivers, the sea, and topography) related to ancestral memory.

The alternate time and memory of the Otherworld are associated with the dynamic border between eternity and time, emanating in biblical terms from an antediluvian Paradise near the epoch of Creation. It is a native ancestral realm akin to the world of Genesis before the Flood, when giants walked the earth. Yet it also intersects with the eternal realm of spiritual Creation. Just as Creation means both event and continuing landscape, so the Greek *aion* in Christian scripture, meaning created interval, can be translated both "age" and "world." This articulates an enfolded space–time of eternity figured by the Otherworld in narratives, framed by a patristic sense of an uncreated everlasting beyond eternity. The environmental phenomenologist Erazim Kohák describes a "natural time" of the earth that goes beyond either subjective or objective human temporalities and overlaps with a distinctively human experience of eternity. Such natural time is "set within the matrix of nature's rhythm which establishes personal yet nonarbitrary reference points." Experience of eternity involves "awareness of the absolute reality of being, intersecting with the temporal sequence of its unfolding at every moment . . . nontemporal reference . . . grasping the moral, non-instrumental value of being,"[12] Their interweaving establishes a dynamic sense of region in a larger cosmic context. And that overlapping of reader, modes of being, time and non-time, and topography in storytelling as landscape here becomes iconographic itself, participatorily symbolic of the flow of everlasting uncreated divine energies amid the interaction of time and eternity, as in John Scottus Eriugena's philosophy of theophanies infusing the earth [. . .].

Feedback between human culture and environment in such story becomes a narrative process akin to Evan Thompson's image of forming a path while walking, which can physically shape an ecoregion.[13] American Indian cultural traditions shaped prairie and oak savannah ecosystems of the upper Midwest, whose remnants today engage environmental restorationists in shaping their own narratives for tending and reviving old prairie groves.[14] Irish Sea texts such as *Tachmarc Étaíne* and the *Mabinogi* engaged readers in empathy with nonhuman realms, reflecting communal ascetic ethics and relational land practices resisting a centrally controlled landscape. Such narratives of environmental landscape, however different in context, share a radical intertextuality incorporating topography with story and cultural practice. Gilles Deleuze and Félix Guattari wrote that through experience of a regional "opening" brought by such art, "The landscape sees."[15] Art (including narrative) allows us first to experience immanence reconnecting us with our body through sensations that, combined, in turn evoke a "becoming-animal" experience of imagination finally "opening" landscape to its own subjectivity. Philip Goodchild in glossing Deleuze and Guattari concludes: "The work of art opens thought onto the body and landscape, so as to give a voice to the body before all words," and ultimately to landscape as well, from relationship with it.[16] Ultimately, through narrative relating body to land, the landscape speaks as a story beyond words, too, and in effect looks out, as if an icon, at us.

The Ulster Cycle as Regional Landscape

A brief landscape survey based on the Ulster Cycle can outline this sense of regional narrative before exploring *Tochmarc Étaíne* in detail. At the climax of the Cycle's central work, *Táin Bó Cúailnge* ("The Cattle Raid of Cooley") in the version from the Book of Leinster, the otherworldly Brown Bull of Cooley ends up in northwest Ireland. When the bull sees "the beautiful strange land" (*in tír n-álaind n-aneóil*) of Connacht,[17] the realm of the quasi-goddess

Queen Medb,[18] he bellows three times loudly. His counterpart, the white bull of Connacht, answers. The two begin a mutual struggle to the death. Their battle shapes and gives names to terrain, but also ends the foundational twelfth-century text by signaling the inability of the best warriors of Ireland to possess the creatures for whom they had fought at great cost. The ending marks the exhaustion of the old order of pagan warrior realms just before the coming of Christ. It also reveals the landscape of Ireland, by synecdoche in the bulls, as central character in a complex narrative that developed during at least four centuries of storytelling. A "prequel" to the main story describes the bulls as shape-shifting herdsmen of otherworldly rulers who inhabit Neolithic mounds, portals to the ancestral landscape of the Otherworld.[19] Other early lore suggests that the bulls bore the names of twins born to the goddess Macha, whose own name probably derived from *mag* or "field" or "plain," as a goddess of the land.[20] And the struggle of the twin bulls, light and dark, suggests seasonal cycles of change, reinforced by the timing of the *Táin* across the winter season into the spring, from the quarter holiday of Samain to that of Imbolc, with an aspect of sexual difference because one of the bulls is identified with a kingdom led by a woman and the other with a kingdom led by a man.[21] Topographically, Macha is associated with the prehistoric mound complex Emain Macha, legendary center of the warriors who fight vainly to keep the Brown Bull as property of their realm. That site features twinned mounds matching her twin offspring. Macha's curse, related to disrespect of the land goddess by the hypermasculine Ulstermen at the time of the birth of her twins, keeps the warriors apparently suffering like women in labor during the first part of the action as the forces of the goddess-like figure Medb of Connacht attack their realm.[22]

In this region of landscape-story, the twin-hilled site at Emain Macha (itself containing other twinned features as well[23]) in turn is complexly twinned topologically with another mound complex at Ard Macha or Armagh, just two miles to the east. There an old pagan center on Cathedral Hill became the legendary base for St. Patrick and later focus of ecclesiastical power struggles that probably played a role in shaping the *Táin* narratives [. . .]. Emain Macha and Ard Macha were, in effect, the topographical Old and New Testaments framing the Ulster Cycle.[24] (Another famous twinned hill site in an opposite part of Ireland was known as the Paps of Anu, breasts of a fertility goddess; perhaps a similar pre-Christian tradition once held sway at the twin mounds of Emain Macha?)

But there are still more entwined filaments to this regional landscape of stories. Not far to the south of Emain Macha, along a curve of the Boyne River (the source of which, in a well associated with the sea, purportedly boasted hazel trees dropping nuts of wisdom to magic salmon[25]), sits the island's premiere Neolithic mound complex including Brúig na Bóinde, featured in certain prequel tales to the *Táin* cycle including *Tochmarc Étaíne*. This complex was in ancient times part of a fertile prehistoric valley civilization, and is located near what later became other early Patrician Christian sites. It formed one of many vestibules between everyday life and otherworldly beings: either old gods or conquered earlier inhabitants haunted the land, perhaps one and the same. By design of the original builders, each winter solstice the sun shines into the passageway mound of Newgrange there, illuminating inner chambers and stone carvings upon them. The Neolithic curves of that art (emplaced patterned movements sometimes interpreted as an image of Creation) reappear in both Christian sculpture and the illustrations of the gospel Book of Kells and other illuminated manuscripts from the Irish Sea zone millennia later.[26]

That leads us to a third dimension of these regional narratives, beyond the presentation of a quasi-historical region of Ulster and the Otherworld landscape of Ireland, namely an environmental textuality. The visual style of the famous *Chirho* page of the Book of Kells shares an exteriorized iconographic style with the Otherworld trope. Some suggest that this illuminated book art could be stereoscopic in intent.[27] Its imagery cues a "pop-up" effect, resisting any interiorized illusion of *trompe l'oeil* "realism." The effect cues the reader-viewer's focus into a relational, quasi-physical medial ground between subject and object. In using such techniques, the art in effect shapes an environmental place in the foreground between it and the viewer. The effect "thrusts focal points out at us," while "reminding us of our distance from heavenly things," as historian James Billington puts it. The image—in this case the textual landscape—again looks out at us. Readers are not meant to go inside and penetrate text that is both topological and topographical, but to negotiate and engage with text in a bodily context of topography. [. . .]

Map 1: *Tochmarc Étaíne*, a Contour Guide to the Otherworld

Tochmarc Étaíne effectively functions as a *remscéla* or prequel to the *Táin Bó Cúailnge*, the central epic of the Ulster Cycle, in that it explains how violation of the contractual agreement between the high king and the Otherworld in effect led to chaos and divisions among a legendary pentarchy of realms.[28] The first of the three main parts of *Tochmarc Étaíne*, based on the Yellow Book of Lecan text, illustrates the power of the Otherworld in shaping time and space in relation to landscape. A dynamic mix of the known and the unknown in birth, love, and death moves behind and roils the complex story line, all in relation to an alternate temporality of landscape that is beyond-human. First, a fertility god, the Dagda (the "good god"), uses deception to sleep at the Bruig na Bóinde mound with a goddess, Bóand. Her name is linked with that of the mound and the Boyne and seems to have a root meaning of "cow."[29] The Dagda, another one of whose names stems from a term for horse, is high king of the people of the Otherworld or Tuatha Dé Danann. He changes the apparent flow of time to hide his affair with Bóand from her husband, Elcmar. Nine months pass as a day, and Bóand gives birth to their offspring, the divine youth Óengus, the Mac ind Óc, or "young son." He is fostered or brought up by Midir, who rules at a mound portal in another part of Ireland. With the assistance of Midir and his father, young Óengus gains control of his mother's Bruig na Bóinde portal from Elcmar on Samain, a liminal festival in autumn (at our modern Halloween) associated with access to the Otherworld. Óengus gains permission to dwell in the mound for a day and a night, and thus for a day and a night perpetually. The Dagda decides in favor of Óengus' right to do so, declaring that Elcmar loved his own life more than his land (*ar ba caime lat do ainim oldas do thír*)[30] when he allowed Óengus to establish a relationship to it for a cycle of time (a day and a night). Midir then visits his foster-son Óengus at his new mound, but is injured by accident in one eye, thus becoming unable to continue as a king under Irish tradition, due to physical imperfection. Óengus arranges for a healer to restore Midir. Then, Óengus agrees to help Midir obtain the beautiful Étaín of the Ulaid (the realm of Ulster) as his queen. She is the daughter of royal Ulster parents who, however, goes through transformations that seem to morph her into an otherworldly figure. Étaín's father gives Óengus (the Mac Óc) seemingly impossible tasks in order to win her, related to shaping the topography of Ulster for the father's rule and providing wealth from the earth in gold and silver equal to his daughter's physical body. This accomplished, she is given to Midir. He takes her home to his *síd* or mound. But Midir already has a wife waiting there. Trained in druidic arts, she transforms Étaín into a magical fly via other forms. This leads to Étaín's rebirth as a human more than a thousand years later.

The second part of the story illustrates further the folded nature of space and time in the Otherworld. It tells of the separation and initial reunion of Midir and Étaín after incredible physical transformations across a millennium. Étaín is reborn as daughter of an Ulster couple. Midir comes to her from the *síde*, later reciting the verses quoted at the beginning of the chapter to win her back. Meanwhile a festival is called for at Temair. However, the new high king Eochaid or Echu Airem (whose name echoes the horse moniker of the Dagda) needs to find a wife in order for him to host the feast, and marries Étaín. Echu's brother Ailill Angubae (who shares a name with Étaín's father in her earlier life) becomes obsessed with his brother's new wife. Ailill wastes away for love of her, and when she finally agrees to meet with him to heal him, he falls into an enchanted sleep. It is Midir (from her previous life) who shows up in his stead. Étaín tells Midir that she will return with him to the Otherworld, but only if her husband King Eochaid grants permission.

The Otherworld provides a larger context of difference that shapes place in the story. Mysteries of life (parentage, sexual difference, love and marriage, life after death) relate creationary moments of landscape to the shaping of order through marriage. On such "an immanent plane of composition," as Goodchild glosses Deleuze and Guattari, "[h]umanity ceases to be alienated from the plane of nature."[31] The conclusion of the story tells of how Étaín and Midir restore their marriage and Eochaid loses his queen. Midir and the king gamble over *fidchell*, a native board game. In their matches Midir must pay back his intentional losses with otherworldly help, to do impossible tasks for the high king related to reshaping the landscape of Ireland. By losing two games, Midir lulls the king into a false sense of security. Midir wins the third game, having secured as a pledge for his winning the promise that he be able to embrace Étaín once. This he does at Temair, surrounded by the king's guards. When the two embrace they transform into swans, and fly away to the network of Otherworld mounds. The king tries fruitlessly to dig up the mounds. Finally, he is promised the opportunity to win Étaín back if he can identify her from a group of seemingly identical women. He ends up choosing his own daughter unknowingly, and has a child with her, setting off a sequence of events that end in sequel stories with the collapse of the high kingship and the apocalyptic epic action of the longer *Táin Bó Cúailnge*. (In some fragments of the story, Eochaid regains Étaín by force, but the disastrous results are similar.[32])

Desire is embodied in landscape that becomes region rather than an object, through Midir's wooing of Étaín and her growing openness to the Otherworld, which together come to embody a reciprocal desire for and by landscape.

Notes

1   Osborn Bergin and R.I. Best, "Tochmarc Étaine," *Ériu* 12 (1938): 180–81 [137–96].

2   For translations, compare John Carey, *Tochmarc Étaíne*, in *The Celtic Heroic Age: Literary Sources for Ancient Celtic Europe and Early Ireland and Wales*, Celtic Studies Publications 1, ed. John T. Koch with John Carey (Malden, MA: Celtic Studies Publications, 1995), p. 149 [135–54]; Jeffrey Gantz, ed. *Early Irish Myths and Sagas* (London: Penguin, 1981), pp. 55–56; and Bergin and Best, "Tochmarc Étaine," p. 181 [137–96].

3   The triptych until the 1930s was only known to modern scholars in fragmentary form from the same manuscript as the First Recension of the *Táin Bó Cúailnge*, the *Lebor na hUidre, ca.* 1100. A complete version was found in the later medieval *Yellow Book of Lecan* manuscript. The edition used here is Bergin and Best, "Tochmarc Étaine," pp. 137–96. As discussed there, the early Celticist Rudolf Thurneysen placed the story's core linguistics in the ninth century, a date related to fragmentary references to elements of it in other texts, but called its current version a late eleventh-century retelling. See Thurneysen, *Die irische Helden- und Königssage bis zum siebzehnten Jahrhundret* (Halle: M. Niemeyer, 1921), pp. 47, 77, 78, Other scholars have placed its origins perhaps in the eighth century, which, significantly in terms of the themes of land and contract as discussed, would parallel the full establishment of Ireland's synthesized seventh-century legal system.

4   E.G. Quin, ed, *Dictionary of the Irish Language Based Mainly on Old and Middle Irish Materials* (Dublin: Royal Irish Academy, 1990), s.v.

5   Martin Heidegger, "The Thing," in Heidegger, *Poetry, Language, Thought*, trans. Albert Hofstadter (New York: HarperCollins, 2001), p. 179 [163–80].

6   Martin Heidegger, "Conversation on a Country Path about Thinking," in Heidegger, *Discourse on Thinking*, trans. J.M. Anderson and E.H. Freund (New York: Harper, 1966), pp. 58–90; and "The

Thing." Jeff Malpas, *Heidegger's Topology: Being, Place, World* (Cambridge, MA: MIT Press, 2007), pp. 195–98.

7   Martin Heidegger, "Die Kunst und der Raum," in Heidegger, *Gesamtausgabe* 13 (Frankfurt: Klostermann, 1983), p. 207 [203–10], trans. Edward S. Casey, *The Fate of Place: A Philosophical History* (Berkeley: University of California Press, 1998), p. 283.

8   World Wildlife Fund, "Ecoregions," at http://www.worldwildlife.org/science/ecoregions/iteml847.html [accessed July 16, 2008].

9   On a possible common root for the Welsh and Irish terms related to "peace" and "settled seat," see John Koch, *Celtic Culture: A Historical Encyclopedia*, 5 vols. (Oxford: ABC-CLIO-2006), vol. 4, p. 1610.

10   On "rhizomic," see Gilles Deleuze and Félix Guattari, *A Thousand Plateaus, Capitalism and Schizophrenia 2*, trans. Brian Massumi (Minneapolis: University of Minnesota Press, 1987), pp. 3–25.

11   Monastic prototypes for that ascetic background can be glimpsed in texts such as Adomnán's Hiberno-Latin *Vita S. Columbae* (*ca*. 700), from the Western Isles of Scotland, and John Climacus' earlier Greek *Ladder of Divine Ascent* (*ca*. 600), from the Sinai Desert. St. John Climacus' work includes an emphasis on the desert, and, as the penultimate of its thirty steps, finding heaven on earth through asceticism. His emphasis on Greek *apatheia* and *hesychia* (dispassion that is a burning love for God, and quietude, respectively) needs to be understood in the context of the "energy theory" discussed in chapter one. Renunciation of the world in that context is renunciation of objectification for uncreated energies of grace by psychosomatic *ascesis* (exercise or struggle). See St. John Climacus, *The Ladder of Divine Ascent*, trans. Archimandrite Lazarus Moore, rev. edn (Brookline, MA: Holy Transfiguration Monastery, 1991).

12   Erazim Kohák, *The Embers and the Stars* (Chicago: University of Chicago Press, 1984), pp. 16, 18.

13   "Laying down a path in walking" (a phrase coined by biologist Francisco Varela) is the dominant metaphor for human development in Evan Thompson, *Mind in Life: Biology, Phenomenology, and the Sciences of Mind* (Cambridge, MA: Belknap-Harvard University Press, 2007). For Thompson's discussion of the role of ecopoesis in this, see pp. 118–22, and 382–411. See also Rebecca Solnit, *Wanderlust: A History of Walking* (New York: Penguin, 2000), p. 13.

14   For examples of traditional Indian cultural narratives in the Great Lakes, see Edward Benton-Benai, *The Mishomis Book: The Voice of the Ojibway* (Hayward, WI: Red School House-Indian Country Communications, 1988); on recent ecological restoration efforts in that region to shape new community narratives, see William K. Stevens, *Miracle Under the Oaks: The Revival of Nature in America* (New York: Pocket Books, 2006).

15   Gilles Deleuze and Félix Guattari, *What is Philosophy?* trans. Hugh Tomlinson and Graham Burchell (New York: Columbia University Press, 1994), p. 169; emphasis in the original.

16   Philip Goodchild, *Deleuze and Guattari: An Introduction to the Politics of Desire*, Theory, Culture & Society (London: SAGE Publications, 1996), p. 190.

17   *Táin Bó Cúailnge from the Book of Leinster*, ed. Cecile O'Rahilly [Dublin: Dublin Institute of Advanced Studies, School of Celtic Studies (henceforth abbreviated as Dublin Institute), 1967], line 4855, p. 143; trans. p. 270. This is the later twelfth-century Second Recension.

18   Erica Sessle summarizes Medb's putative backgrounds in Irish sovereignty goddess mythology in "Misogyny and Medb, Approaching Medb with Feminist Criticism," in *Ulidia*, ed. J.P. Mallory and G. Stockman (Belfast: December Publications, 1994), pp. 135–38.

19   *De Chopur in dá Muccida* ("The Quarrel of the Two Swineherds"), in the Book of Leinster; trans. Thomas Kinsella, *The Táin* (Oxford: Oxford University Press, 1970), pp. 46–51.

20   An early text about Ath Luin refers to the two sons of Crond mac Agnomain, Macha's husband, as Rucht and Rucne, the names of the two swineherds who became the bulls of the *Táin*. Whitley Stokes, "The Prose Tales in the Rennes Dindshenchas," in *Revue celtique* 15 (1894): 466 [272–336, 418–84], and 16 (1895): 31–83, 135–67, 269–312]. Garrett Olmsted notes that this relation of offspring associated with Macha to quadrupeds may be a mythic analogue of portrayals of the Gallo-Celtic horse goddess Epona between two colts, which would link her to the figure Rhiannon in the *Mabinogi*; *The Gods of the Celts and the Indo-Europeans*, Archaeolingua 6 (Budapest: Archaeolingua Alapítvány, 1994), pp. 169–71. There Olmstead also summarizes etymological issues in the relation between Macha and the Irish term *mag* for field or plain, the adoption of which for the figure Macha may have been a secondary development from Emain as a name for a horse goddess meaning "swift one," though later understood in Emain Macha as "twins of Macha."

21   Olmsted in his extensive philological efforts to reconstruct a Celtic pantheon of gods suggested a proto-pantheon of European myth in which the bulls represent varying sides of a shape-shifting deity of tree fruit (hence perhaps the relation to Emain Abhlach with its fruit associations) most often appearing in "bull-like guise" (*The Gods of the Celts and the Indo-Europeans*, p. 269). In his schema the

destruction of the white bull is related to the end of the winter season he associates with the goddess Bóand, whose name means "white cow," for whom the Boyne is named (p. 271). Similarly, the ancient Mediterranean god Dionysos has been described as expressing a bull-associated "two-fold nature" representing winter and summer (Carl Kerényi, *Dionysos: Archetypal Image of Indestructible Life* (Princeton, NJ: Princeton University Press, 1976), pp. 63, 115). See also Caroline Humphrey, "Chiefly and Shamanist Landscapes in Mongolia," in *The Anthropology of Landscape: Perspectives on Place and Space*, ed. Eric Hirsch and Michael O'Hanlon (Oxford: Clarendon Press, 1996), p. 135 [135–62].

22   *Noinden Uled* or *Tochmarc Cruinn ocus Macha*. "The Debility of the Ulsterman" or "The Wooing of Crunn and Macha," ed. and trans. Vernam Hull, *Celtica* 8 (1968): 1–42; "Tochmarc Cruinn," ed. Rudolf Thurneysen, *ZCP* 12 (1918): 251–54; trans. Thomas Kinsella, *The Táin*, pp. 6–8.

23   N.B. Aitchison, *Armagh and the Royal Centres in Early Medieval Ireland* (Woodbridge, UK: Cruithne/ Boydell & Brewer, 1994); and in Alfred K. Siewers, *Stories of the Land: Nature and Religion in Early British and Irish Literary Landscapes*, unpublished PhD dissertation (Urbana, IL: University of Illinois, 2001).

24   See Aitchison, *Armagh and the Royal Centres in Early Medieval Ireland*.

25   Miranda J. Green, *Animals in Celtic Life and Myth* (London: Routledge, 1993), p. 191; "Sinnan," in *The Metrical Dindshenchas*, ed. Edward J. Gwynn, 5 vols (Dublin 1903–35; repr. Dublin Institute, 1991), vol. 3, pp. 292–95; also "The prose tales in the Rennes Dindshenchas," part 2, ed. Whitley Stokes, *Revue Celtique* 15 (1894): 457 [418–84].

26   A potential stereographic effect of illuminated manuscripts such as the Book of Kells is described by Oliver Sacks in his article "Stereo Sue" in *The New Yorker* magazine of June 19, 2006, pp. 64–73. See also Jacob D. Benestein. "Information in the Holographic Universe," *Scientific American* (August 2003): 58–65.

27   Sacks, "Stereo Sue."

28   On the relation of *Tochmarc Étaíne* to the Ulster Cycle, see Joan Radner, "'Fury Destroys the World': Historical Strategy in Ireland's Ulster Epic," *The Mankind Quarterly* 23 (1982): 42–60.

29   A good source for tracing names of Celtic literary characters in relation to mythology and root meanings is Olmsted's *The Gods of the Celts and the Indo-Europeans*; on Dagda and Bóand see pp. 43–45; some of the name interpretations here also draw on Jeffrey Gantz's endnotes to his translation of the story in *Early Irish Myths and Sagas*.

30   Osborn Bergin and R.I. Best, "Tochmarc Étaíne," p. 146.

31   Goodchild, *Deleuze and Guattari*, pp. 194.

32   On that variation, see the background summary and translated version of the story in Tom P. Cross and Clark Harris Slover, *Ancient Irish Tales* (New York: Henry Holt, 1936), pp. 82–92.

Chapter 26

Beth Tobin

TROPING THE TROPICS AND
AESTHETICIZING LABOR

[W]e should not imagine that the world presents us with a legible face, leaving us merely
to decipher it; it does not work hand in glove with what we already know; there is no
prediscursive fate disposing the word in our favour. We must conceive discourse as a
violence that we do to things, or, at all events, as a practice we impose upon them.
　　　　　　　　　　　　　　—*Michel Foucault*, "The Discourse of Language"[1]

J AMES THOMSON'S POEM "Rule, Britannnia!" (1740) celebrates British naval
power, which ensured the expansion and dominance of British commerce across the
globe.[2] As a measure of British rule, the tropics are invoked as a site to be exploited by and
harnessed to British commercial forces:

I see thy Commerce, *Britain*, grasp the world:
All nations serve thee; every foreign flood
Subjected, pays his tribute to the *Thames*.
Thither the golden South obedient pours
His sunny treasures: thither the soft East
Her spices, delicacies, gentle gifts . . .[3]

The warm and fecund regions of the world are Britain's obedient servants, whose tributes are
their natural riches. What constitutes these tributes (aside from the ubiquitous "spices") is
made more explicit in his much longer poem, *The Seasons,* which catalogs the "dreadful
beauty" and "barbarous wealth" (ll. 643–44) found in the tropics. These regions, blessed and
cursed with "returning suns and double seasons" (l. 645), produce not only shining metals
and gems but also exotic fruits, flowers, plants, and animals. Suvir Kaul explains in his reading
of *The Seasons* though the sun is the "source of tropical abundance," it also "turns out to be a
tyrannical and morally corrupting force there."[4] With this ambivalent portrait of the sun's
powers, Thomson conveys the excitement as well as the anxiety generated by Britain's
assumption of imperial authority over the globe's natural resources. As this poem implies,
mastery of tropical nature, and especially its potential for agricultural productivity, became
key concepts in the formation of British imperial identity. This book is about how the tropics,

as a region and as an idea, became central to the way in which Britons imagined their role in the world. I take as my subject the representation of tropical nature and tropical landscapes in a variety of media, from travel writing to botanical treatises and from family portraits to topographical illustrations, as a way to investigate how these modes of representation constructed the tropics as simultaneously paradisaical and in need of British intervention and management.

Bounty and the Tropics

I begin with Captain James Cook's depiction of tropical landscapes in the South Pacific. What is remarkable about Cook is the attention he paid to Pacific Islanders' agricultural practices. As a writer, Cook did not do what most of his contemporaries did when they wrote about tropical nature. He did not recur to pastoral, georgic, or edenic tropes, nor did he aestheticize the worked landscape, transforming it into an object for visual consumption. Nor did Cook use what he had observed as a platform to construct theories about human difference and the civilizing process. Nor did he make extracts from his observations of tropical nature to slot into existing classifying schemas. As James Boswell said of Cook after having met him in 1776, he "was a plain, sensible man with an uncommon attention to veracity" and "did not try to make theories out of what he had seen."[5] Because Cook's writings about tropical landscapes eschew his contemporaries' rhetorical strategies of troping the tropics, aestheticizing labor, and decontextualizing plant life, his descriptions of Pacific gardens are a good place from which to explore the way in which writers and artists in the late eighteenth and early nineteenth centuries depicted the tropics.

In August 1774, Captain Cook, in the second year of his second circumnavigation, guided his ship, the *Resolution,* to Vanuatu, or as Cook called this group of islands, the New Hebrides. Along with his team of artists and scientists, he disembarked to explore the island and take stock of the plants, animals, and people. He wrote the following about the island of Tanna in his journal:

> Here and there we met with a house, some few people and plantations, of these latter we found in different states; some of long standing, others lately clear'd and some only clearing and before any thing was planted. The clearing a peice of ground for a plantation seem'd to me to be a work of much labour, considering the tools they have to work with, which are of the same kind but much inferior to those at the Society Isles. Their methods is however judicious and as expeditious as it can well be. They lop off the small branches of the trees, dig under the roots and there burn the branches or small shrubs and plants which they root up and by this means destroy both root and branch of every thing.[6]

Such a matter-of-fact statement about how Tannese cleared their land for planting appears to contain nothing noteworthy. And yet, Cook's careful observation of how the Tannese worked their land is extraordinary because he is one of the few eighteenth-century European travelers to acknowledge the labor, skill, and knowledge that Pacific Islanders employed when practicing tropical agriculture.[7]

Cook also expressed admiration for the way in which taro was cultivated in New Caledonia, a much drier climate than Tonga or Vanuatu. Noting that one village had "about it a good deal of cultivated land, regularly laid out in Plantations, planted and planting, with Taro or eddy roots, yams, Sugar Cane and Plantains," Cook provided a detailed description of the methods used to plant and water taro: "They have two methods of planting these roots, some are planted in square or oblong plantations which lie perfectly horizontal and sunk below the common level of the adjacent lands, so that they can let in as much Water upon them as they please or is necessary; I have generally seen them covered two or three inches deep, but I do not know that this is always necessary. Others are planted in ridges about 3 or 4 feet broad and 2 or 2½ high, on the middle or top of the ridge is a narrow gutter in and along which is conveyed, as above described, a little rill which waters the roots planted in the ridge of each side of it."[8]

The attention Cook gave to how Pacific Islanders grew the food—taro, yams, plantains, and breadfruit—that these British voyagers depended on for sustenance is unique among those who traveled with him on his three voyages. Even those charged with the duties of naturalist and botanist did not attend to the details of Pacific Islanders' agricultural practices and horticultural techniques the way Cook did. For instance, surprisingly indifferent to Pacific Island agronomy was Sir Joseph Banks, who accompanied Cook on the first circumnavigation and was given permission by the Admiralty to oversee the collection and classification of new plant life. An avid amateur naturalist rather than a professional botanist, Banks financed much of this part of the expedition, employing a professional taxonomist, Daniel Solander, and botanical illustrator, Sydney Parkinson. Banks wrote of the culture of breadfruit trees in Tahiti:

> In the article of food these happy people may almost be said to be exempt from the curse of our forefather; scarcely can it be said that they earn their bread with the sweat of their brow when their cheifest sustenance Bread fruit is procurd with no more trouble than that of climbing a tree and pulling it down. Not that the trees grow here spontaneously but if a man should in the course of his life time plant 10 such trees, which if well done might take the labour of an hour or thereabouts, he would as compleatly fulfull his duty to his own as well as future generations as we natives of less temperate climates can do by toiling in the cold of winter to sew and in the heat of summer to reap the annual produce of our soil, which once gathered into the barn must be again resowd and re-reapd as often as the Colds of winter and the heats of Summer return to make such labour disagreeable. *O fortunati nimium sua si bona norint* may most truly be applied to these people; benevolent nature has not only supplyd them with nescessaries but with abundance of superfluities.[9]

Though in this passage Banks quotes Virgil's *Georgics,* a poem about the necessity of hard labor in husbandry and agriculture, his sentiments belong to the pastoral vision and the belief that nature, at least in these tropical zones, is bountiful. According to this myth, those who dwell in the tropics have nothing more to do than to gather nature's bounty. Banks was convinced that the easy living he thought he observed in Tahiti was due to the abundance of breadfruit. "Idleness the father of Love reigns here in almost unmolested ease, while we inhabitants of a changeable climate are obliged to Plow, Sow, Harrow, reap, Thrash, Grind Knead, and bake our daily bread . . . these happy people whose bread depends not on an annual but a Perennial plant [breadfruit] have but to climb up and gather it ready for baking from a tree."[10] Banks's belief that breadfruit could sustain a large population without requiring labor to produce that food source resulted in one of his earliest and most famous plant transfer schemes, involving Captain Bligh, the ship *Bounty,* and breadfruit seedlings, which ended up being thrown overboard. The mutiny on the *Bounty* thwarted Bligh's first attempt to bring breadfruit to the Caribbean to feed enslaved Africans laboring on sugar plantations, slaves who were starving by the thousands due to the interruption in the flow of foodstuffs from the thirteen colonies during the American Revolution. But Bligh returned to Tahiti and on his second attempt was successful in putting Banks's plan into action. Banks believed that breadfruit could help maintain slave populations, as he thought that the large populations of the "Society Islands" were due, in part, to breadfruit. Banks did not seem to realize that the plentiful food supplies of Tahiti were the product of careful management of resources by skilled agriculturalists. It may seem ironic that Banks, who thought of himself as a naturalist, was oblivious to the skill and labor that went into the making of the tropical landscape. Banks's inability to see labor in a landscape that looked lush and green can be explained, in part, by the European belief that tropical landscapes, given their warmth and moisture, are naturally bountiful.[11]

Even the astute naturalist George Forster, who accompanied Cook on the second circumnavigation, fails in his travel narrative to describe as fully as Cook the agricultural techniques employed by Pacific Islanders. Comparing Cook's description of the taro irrigation system in New Caledonia with Forster's, we find that Cook's is more detailed. Forster notes that the "coco-palms, destitute of fruit, some sugar-canes, bananas, and eddoes" were "supplied with water by several little trenches. Some of the eddoes were actually set under water, in the same manner as is customary throughout the South Sea islands."[12] As we can see from this passage, Forster does indeed note native agricultural practices; however, his description lacks Cook's eye for detail and his appreciation for the islanders' elaborate method of taro irrigation. Perhaps Forster was so heavily invested in current protoanthropological theories about hierarchies of civilization and their relation to agriculture that he underestimated the sophistication of the irrigation systems that Pacific Islanders constructed for their taro gardens.[13] Cook, on the other hand, is generous with his admiration for the ingenuity displayed in these "little rills": "The Taro plantations were prettily watered by little rills continually supplied from the Main Channel, where the Water was conducted by art from a River at the foot of the Mountains. . . . [T]hese plantations are so judiciously laid out that the same stream waters several ridges. These ridges are sometimes the divisions to the horizontal plantations, when this method is used, which is for the most part observed, when a Path way or something of that sort is not necessary, not an inch of ground is lost."[14] In describing the elaborate irrigation systems of New Caledonia as "judiciously laid out," Cook acknowledges native knowledge and agricultural expertise.

To be fair to George Forster's skills as a naturalist, it is important to note that he does indeed notice native horticultural practices and the climatic conditions under which native agriculture is conducted. Forster is consistently much more perceptive about native horticultural practices than the other "gentlemen" on this or the other voyages including his father. The younger Forster recognizes that the tropical climate does not ensure agricultural bounty since pests and weeds are constant threats to food-producing plants in warm and wet regions. He writes, "The excellence of the soil, instead of being an advantage to cultivation in its infant state, is rather of disservice; as all kinds of wild trees, bushes and weeds, are with the greatest difficulty rooted out, and propagate with luxuriance, either from seeds, or from the roots. Cultivated vegetables, being of a more weakly and delicate nature, are easily oppressed and suffocated by the indigenous wild tribes, till repeated labours succeed at last to bring them to a flourishing state" (2:553). Not only does Forster recognize the difficulties inherent in farming in tropical climates, but he, like Cook, is struck with the infertility of New Caledonia: "it was plain they had barely enough for their own subsistence. The soil of New Caledonia is indeed very unfit for agriculture, and poorly rewards the labours which the natives bestow upon it" (2:574). Unlike Banks, who assumed that tropical climates were naturally abundant, Forster recognized the difficulties of growing food-producing plants in the tropics. And yet, Forster was not interested in learning Pacific Islanders' agricultural methods for the sake of knowing this information. Instead, their practices became evidence to support his ideas about climate as the origin of human variation.[15]

In addition to using what he saw in the Pacific to help construct theories to explain the problem of cultural difference, Forster also used tropical landscape as a source of romantic inspiration and aesthetic appreciation. Cook and Forster witnessed the same method of clearing land on Tanna, "a work of much labor" in Cook's description. Forster, in contrast, dwells on himself and the feelings he experienced as he viewed "rich plain" and "vast number of fertile hills" (2:548). Though he begins his description by noting that "I frequently saw the natives employed in cutting down trees, or pruning them, or digging up the ground with a branch of a tree," his imagination is caught when he hears "a man singing at his work" (2:548); his narrative quickly shifts tonal register as it moves into a romantic appreciation of this "rich plain" (2:548):

> Those who are capable of being delighted with the beauties of nature, which deck the globe for the gratification of man, may conceive the pleasure which is derived from every little object, trifling in itself, but important in the moment when the heart is expanded, and when a kind of blissful trance opens a higher and purer sphere of enjoyment. Then we behold with rapture the dark colour of lands fresh prepared for culture, the uniform verdure of meadows, the various tints upon the foliage of different trees, and the infinite varieties in the abundance, form, and size of the leaves. Here these varieties appeared in all their perfection, and the different exposure of the trees to the sun added to the magnificence of the view. . . . The numerous smokes which ascended from every grove on the hill, revived the pleasing impressions of domestic life; nay my thoughts naturally turned upon friendship and national felicity, when I beheld large fields of plantanes all round me, which, loaded with golden clusters of fruit, seemed to be justly chosen the emblems of peace and affluence. The cheerful voice of the labouring husbandman resounded very opportunely to complete this idea.
>
> (2:548)

In Forster's prose, Tanna's gardens become a pleasing prospect, echoing the aestheticizing tropes of harmonized variety and happy husbandmen that frequently structure English georgic poetry. It is a prospect inflected with a romantic sensibility, which transforms beautiful objects into emblems of transcendental feeling. "The mind at rest, and lulled by this train of pleasing ideas, indulged a few fallacious reflections, which encreased its happiness at that instant by representing mankind in a favourable light" (2:549).[16] New Caledonia and Tanna, respectively, become in Forster's journal an opportunity to ruminate on the relationship between agriculture and civilization and to express lofty ideals about intercultural exchange.

Cook's attention to the agricultural practices of Tanna (Vanuatu) and New Caledonia is not only more acute than that of his fellow travelers; it is also typical of his ongoing concern with gardens and gardening in the South Pacific. Though one might not expect a mariner to be so interested in agriculture, Cook himself planted English gardens in New Zealand, gave out seeds for turnips, parsnips, and carrots in Tonga, and tried to stock New Caledonia with pigs. In May 1773, he notes in his journal that "My Self with a party of Men employed digging up ground on Long Island which we planted with Several sorts of garden seeds," and "This day I employ'd in clearing and digging up the ground on Motuara and planting it with Wheat, Pease, and other pulse carrots Parsnips and Strawberries."[17] Maritime historians, who have noticed Cook's enthusiasm for planting gardens in the Pacific, have explained this behavior as altruistic and pragmatic, which is, in fact, the explanation Cook gave in his journals. "We meant to serve," he says of his planting of gardens in New Zealand, and of the seeds he gave to Tongans, he writes, "I probably have added to their stock of Vegetables by leaving with them an assortment of garden seeds and pulses."[18] He sees his acts of plant transfers as benevolent, giving to Pacific Islanders such plants as carrots and turnips, which Europeans have found beneficial. In addition, these gardens were also meant to provide needed nutrition for British mariners, who tended to be dependent on islanders' generosity (and often nonexistent surpluses) to survive the years at sea.[19] In *The Apotheosis of Captain Cook,* Gananath Obeyesekere counters these interpretations that stress Cook's humanitarian motives by arguing that Cook's planting of gardens is driven by an imperialist and expansionist agenda and a Eurocentric dogma that made European-style cultivation the key to the "civilizing" process. The eighteenth-century impulse to conflate English gardens with civilization does indeed haunt Cook's proceedings, but it does not explain Cook's intense interest in how Pacific Islanders grew food-producing plants. The Eurocentric and imperialistic motives that Obeyesekere often justly ascribes to Cook do not in this case allow for Cook's appreciation of native practices and knowledge traditions concerning agriculture. Cook's admiration for the "little rills" so judiciously laid out does not fit into Obeyesekere's paradigm of Cook as an imperialist bent on bringing English values and customs to benighted "savages."[20]

I believe Cook's enthusiasm for planting gardens on various Pacific islands can be explained, in part, by his background.[21] While Cook was growing up, his father had been an agricultural day laborer; he eventually rose into the ranks of farm management as an overseer of the local squire's estate. Cook's ability to see the effects of labor on a landscape, even landscapes of coconut groves and taro patches, can be attributed to his having firsthand knowledge of what was involved in the growing of food-producing plants. That he was able to see that agricultural laborers possessed knowledge and skill in their production of food-producing plants can also be attributed to his limited formal education. With only a few years in a country school, Cook acquired, as an apprentice, the sophisticated skills he needed in mathematics and geography to become the master mariner and navigator that he was. The education that Cook received was, therefore, artisanal, and was not derived from the Latin-driven and classics-based curriculum received by college-educated gentlemen, nor was it informed by a curriculum based in natural philosophy and political economy that was offered by dissenting schools. While it is impossible to know for certain why Cook took such an interest in South Pacific gardens, his lack of a gentleman's polite education may have freed him from serious misconceptions, such as those entertained by Banks, about the edenic nature of the tropics. Cook is unique among his peers in possessing a clarity of vision and understanding when it came to seeing who planted what and how in the Pacific region.

In calling Cook a remarkable observer, I do not mean to suggest that he, unlike the well-educated "gentlemen" who accompanied him, was able to step outside rhetorical conventions and mystifying discourses to see unmediated reality. Rather, I am suggesting that his thinking operated within a different discursive frame, which I will call (in keeping with Marx) "artisanal," a term used by historians of science to distinguish this form of knowing that is embedded in praxis from polite science, which became the dominant scientific mode under Banks's decades-long presidency of the Royal Society. Artisanal science can be thought of as a remnant of pre-Enlightenment engagement with the physical world, based on older systems of knowledge, such as the guild system, where expertise is based on praxis; it can also be thought of as a precondition for Enlightenment science, which, even at its most abstract, was constructed in relation to and even directly derived from work and thought of artisans themselves. The point of comparing Cook's rhetorical strategies with those of the gentlemen scientists on board his ships is to highlight the differences between discursive formations and, for the purposes of this book, to assert that the dominant discourse on the tropics in the late eighteenth century was not Cook's but rather Banks's and Forster's, typified by their use of pastoral and edenic tropes and the deployment of aestheticizing representational practices. This polite discourse on tropicality, in assuming authority and achieving the status of "truth," became "true" and, as such, was used to regulate people and to manage natural resources. Emblematic of how state-sponsored ventures and government policies were constructed wholesale from pastoral visions of tropical nature is Banks's plan to send Bligh to Tahiti for breadfruit. This act signaled the beginning of Banks's busy career orchestrating the movement of plants and people around the globe. Carrying tea plants out of China and planting them in Bihar and Bhutan for British tea drinkers, transplanting breadfruit trees from the Pacific to the Caribbean for starving slaves who produced the sugar for the Briton's tea and jam, and populating Australia with Britain's superfluity of human beings are only a few of the highlights in Banks's long career of managing the globe's resources for Britain's benefit.[22]

Colonizing Nature

Cultivated tropical and subtropical nature is the focus of this book, not the romanticized or spiritualized pristine landscapes of untouched nature, but land that has been harnessed to commercial and market forces. This book is about how a combination of knowledge and ignorance about plants enabled the British to colonize huge parts of the globe, harnessing nature to serve imperial interests. The role of agriculture is undertheorized in the study of colonial expansion.[23] The economics of imperialism is usually discussed in terms of the forging of trade routes, the rise of mercantile capitalism, and the concomitant military conquest of territory. This book insists that agriculture is crucial to understanding the British empire. The vast plantations devoted to the monoculture of sugar in the Caribbean and Pacific, and the cotton, tea, and indigo estates of India not only transformed these regions but also radically altered their populations through genocidal policies and the massive movement of peoples from one region of the globe to another. These agricultural practices also had a huge impact on the social fabric of Britain, shaping daily rituals of consumption central to the formation of a national identity. Because tropical plants as food (such as sugar, tea, chocolate) have been key in the construction of British identity, those who grew the plants in the tropical regions of the empire are therefore implicated in this identity formation. Enslaved Africans and their descendents (and in the postemancipation era, East Indian indentured workers), who labored on West Indian sugar plantations, and South Asians, who grew tea and cotton for British planters, produced commodities that defined British character. As Stuart Hall has said about the centrality of the Afro-Caribbean experience to British life, "I am the sugar in the bottom of the English cup of tea."[24]

My goal is to recover eighteenth-century ideas about the tropics so that we may better understand how Britain came to dominate the global circulation of tropical plants (and people) in the eighteenth and nineteenth centuries. With its sugar plantations in the Caribbean, its domination of India's agriculture and natural resources, and its colonial botanical gardens, Britain made itself the center of a global economy based on agricultural production and exchange, specifically the production of such commodities as sugar, tea, coffee, indigo, and cotton. Though much postcolonial criticism (my own work included) has focused on colonial and postcolonial subjectivity, little attention has been paid to the representation of nature within the colonial context.[25] Only in the field of the history of science, in the subdiscipline of colonial science, are these issues being taken up and discussed with the seriousness they deserve. *Visions of Empire: Voyages, Botany, and Representations of Nature*, a collection of interdisciplinary essays edited by David Philip Miller and Peter Hanns Reill, and Richard Drayton's *Nature's Government: Science, Imperial Britain, and the "Improvement" of the World* represent the best of these efforts to document colonial science and its goal of mastering natural resources for Britain's benefit.[26] While literary critics and art historians have produced extensive studies of the representation of English landscape, few, with the exception of Peter

Hulme, Mary Louise Pratt, and Elizabeth Bohls, have focused their attention on colonial landscapes. Though I draw on Pratt's *Imperial Eyes* and Bohls's *Women Travel Writers* to analyze the rhetorical strategies of natural history and travel writing, my project differs from Pratt's and Bohls's in my combined emphasis on visual and verbal texts, which extend beyond natural history and travel writing to other genres to include georgic verse, the garden conversation piece, and botanical books such as floras and hortuses. I agree with Pratt's brilliant analysis of natural history writing "as a way of taking possession without subjugation and violence."[27] However, I would qualify her characterization of travel writing and natural history as triumphal and dominated by the trope of "master-of-all-I-survey" to suggest that present in the array of visual and verbal texts that represent colonized nature is an anxiety about the potential for failure of the colonial project. What was at stake in the various representations of the tropics was ultimately the question, not necessarily the assertion, of British mastery over the globe's natural resources, a mastery that, though not always complete, was crucial to the formation of British cultural identity and sense of imperial mission.

This book's goal is to call attention to the discursive processes by which labor and history were elided from the representation of tropical nature, and to suggest ways to reconstruct the conditions under which tropical plants, flowers, and fruit as well as landscapes were produced and consumed. Tropicality, the way in which the category of the tropical operates in the European imagination, is touched upon in this book insofar as those European fantasies of fertility and abundance shaped material practices and were deployed in depicting nature. This book critiques the mystifying practices of poets, painters, natural historians, and botanists, their decon-textualizing and aestheticizing practices that, in the process of offering up beautiful images of discrete items, erased the conditions under which tropical commodities were produced, and in the process substituted their own literary and artistic efforts in the place of local producers' work.

Troping the Tropics

Colonizing Nature begins with an examination of the traditional English georgic's capacity to transform physical labor (hoeing and shearing sheep) into its discrete material effects (wheat fields and pastures of sheep). In aestheticizing labor, the georgic and the picturesque shift the emphasis from the agricultural producer to the poet or writer who occupies the subject position in the text. This book also examines the ideological effect of the cataloging that occurs within georgics as well as in natural history and botanical writing. Coupled with the concept of bounty, the catalog decontextualizes tropical nature and erases the material conditions and cultural significance of the local production of tropical commodities. The knowledge and skill of the local producer are lost in the catalog's celebration of nature's bounty and the elevation of the writer as expert about agriculture, botany, geology, and the natural world. Chapter 3, on Anglo-Indian gardens, exposes the processes whereby country house portraits and garden views work to mystify the material conditions that inform landholding practices in Britain and in India. The popularity of the genre of garden conversation pieces with East India Company employees stems from their wishes to be portrayed as if they were the gentry, the garden imagery lending them a landed social status that they coveted as merchants, bureaucrats, and military men. Indian landscape was represented in these garden views as under the command of British authority. In contrast, in the picturesque landscape paintings and topographical prints that William Hodges produced on his tour of Bengal, Bihar, and Oudh, Indian landscape is portrayed as timeless and ancient. The conflict between British and Indian armies for control of these territories is masked by the serenity and stasis of Hodges's picturesque illustrations that fill his book, *Travels in India*. The picturesque banishes labor and history from its frame in much the same way that the georgic, in aestheticizing labor, suppresses the materiality of work.

Genre is key to this study, for genre played an important role in shaping the expectations and desires of artists, natural historians, sojourners, and colonial agents who were confronted with the new and the different in the tropical regions of the world. The central argument of this book is that popular forms of eighteenth-century art and literature played an important role in developing eighteenth-century ideas about land, labor, and natural resources in the tropical regions of the world. Eighteenth-century ways of seeing, describing, and portraying tropical nature were determined, to a large degree, by preexisting notions of what constituted the pastoral and the picturesque. As we have seen, Sir Joseph Banks, gentleman botanist on board Captain Cook's *Endeavour* voyage, saw Tahiti through the lens of pastoral poetry and painting, ascribing to nature's benevolent powers the abundance of breadfruit, taro, and yams that were, in actuality, cultivated by the Tahitians, who were expert agriculturalists, not the leisured swains Banks mistook them for. This way of thinking was shaped, in part, by the locodescriptive poetry of writers such as Pope, Gay, Dyer, and Thomson, by country house portraits both verbal and visual, and by picturesque landscape paintings, drawings, and illustrations. Though these forms of cultural production were distinctly English, growing out of particular sets of social, economic, and artistic concerns that were specific to England at this time, they were used repeatedly by writers and artists to describe regions beyond England's shores, in particular Britain's colonies in the West and East Indies. That poets, painters, travel writers, and naturalists should employ familiar idioms and formal conventions to convey their impressions of these tropical and subtropical regions is not surprising, for, as Giambattisa Vico suggests in *The New Science* (1725), the strange and new can be understood and articulated only within the framework and language of the known and familiar: "poetic geography" is "when people can form no idea of distant and unfamiliar things, they judge them by what is present and familiar."[28] The intellectual and visual mastery of the tropics, as exercised in genres as different as georgic verse, botanical illustrations, and garden views, preceded and accompanied such material appropriations of land, labor, and natural resources as the Pacific voyages of discovery, the sugar plantations in the West Indies, and the indigo, cotton, and tea estates in Bengal.

This book explores the cultural and political work that genre performs by shaping the way in which we think and see. Each genre possesses particular formal codes that operate selectively, organizing that which is being represented, so that an ideologically coherent and aesthetically pleasing visual or verbal image is produced. However, genre, more than a collection of formal features, is also an epistemological tool, a way of knowing and seeing that asserts mastery over the object represented. As Karen O'Brien suggests in her overview of eighteenth-century georgic poetry, "genre is both a set of conventions and mode of social understanding."[29] I use the term "genre" in its most inclusive and expansive form to refer to both a mode of thought and a range of visual and verbal practices that speak beyond the strictly poetical and painterly to social practice and epistemic mastery. I examine the discursive strategies and representational practices that particular genres license and prohibit, focusing on the boundary work that genre performs as it calls into play various tropes and figures in its attempt to give shape and coherence to the new and different.

Though this book is about visual and verbal generic modes and tropes that were prevalent from the 1760s to the 1820s in British colonial settings, the significance of my case studies reaches beyond the long eighteenth century and British studies to have larger implications about cognition and culture. British colonists and travelers, when confronted with the foreign and strange, used familiar tropes and genres to make alien places and people more familiar, more recognizable, and more palatable, or conversely, to dismiss, erase, or contain disturbing differences. For instance, Lady Nugent, wife of the lieutenant governor and commander-in-chief of Jamaica, upon her arrival on that island employed the well-worn pastoral trope of "paradise" to describe the tropical landscape, which, with its mountains, vegetation, sugar estates, and "negro settlements," was "all so new to the European eye." Describing the gardens surrounding the house of a sugar estate, Lady Nugent searches for words to convey what she sees: "it is quite impossible to describe the great variety of beautiful plants, trees and shrubs, that at this moment delight my eyes and regale my nose." Relying on similes and English equivalents, she declares that one plant "is something like the geranium" and another is "like a full blown rose."[30] Using cognitive categories learned at home, these Britons abroad negotiated the otherness presented by the tropical, denying or recognizing the disruptive qualities of difference in ways that assimilated or incorporated the strange and unfamiliar into existing categories of thought. In this book I demonstrate that genres such as the pastoral, the georgic, and the picturesque modes and tropes such as bounty and paradise were integral, even key elements in colonialist ideas about the tropical and subtropical regions of the British empire.

I am aware that some may think that I am claiming too much for the power of literature and art to shape cultural beliefs and practices, that I have got it backwards, as belles lettres and visual culture are superstructural, dependent on the larger determining forces of economics and politics. But, as a cultural materialist, I believe that poetry and painting, which could be dismissed as the most frivolous because the most elite forms of cultural production, can actually shape thought and influence how people interpret the world, and, in turn, can affect the kind of material practices they put into action. As Ernesto Laclau and Chantal Mouffe argue, the assumption that discourse is "mental" and not "material" has led to a dismissive attitude toward the analysis of discourse as a form of meaningful political intervention. They counter such critiques that are often marshaled by traditional Marxists (and by traditional humanists) by insisting on discourse's materiality. Discourse, "embodied in institutions, rituals, and so forth," is "a real force which contributes to the moulding and constitution of social relations." Because social relations are therefore discursively constructed, representational techniques such as metaphor and metonym are not merely "forms of thought that add a second sense to a primary, constitutive literality of social relations; instead, they are part of the primary terrain itself in which the social is constituted."[31] By examining the semantic codes of representational practices, we gain access to social and material relations that informed the colonial project of the eighteenth and early nineteenth centuries.

Notes

1   Michel Foucault, "The Discourse of Language," *The Archaeology of Knowledge and the Discourse on Language,* trans. A. M. Sheridan Smith (New York: Pantheon Books, 1972), 229.
2   As Suvir Kaul convincingly argues, the poem declaims "the coming to global power of a puissant Britain, divinely ordained inheritor of the imperial and civilizational traditions of classical Europe." Suvir Kaul, *Poems of Nation, Anthems of Empire: English Verse in the Long Eighteenth Century* (Charlottesville: University Press of Virginia, 2000), 2.
3   Thomson, "Rule, Britannia!" in *The Complete Poetical Works of Jameson Thomson,* ed. J. Logie Robertson (London: Oxford University Press, 1908), 422.
4   Kaul, *Poems of Nation,* 156.
5   James Boswell, *Boswell: The Ominous Years, 1774–76,* ed. C. Ryskamp and F. A. Pottle (New York: McGraw-Hill, 1963), 308. For Cook's powers of observation, see Roy Porter, "The Exotic as Erotic: Captain Cook in Tahiti," in *Exoticism in the Enlightenment,* ed. G. S. Rousseau and Roy Porter (Manchester Universtiy Press, 1990), 117–44.
6   William Dawson's copy of Cook's *Resolution* journal, entitled "Cap^m Cook's Voyage from the year 1772 to July 1775 Given me by Himself, Bristol," ff. 287–88. Housed at the National Maritime Museum in Greenwich, this manuscript will be referred to as the Greenwich copy in the following citations.

7 My reading of the descriptions of tropical nature produced by naturalists and travelers was developed in conversation with William Cronon's *Changes in the Land: Indians, Colonists, and the Ecology of New England* (New York: Hill and Wang, 1983). Very influential for me was his suggestion that fantasy played an important role in early colonists' perception of Native Americans' relation to the land. The New World had been represented as a place of " 'small labour but great pleasure,' " and, as Cronon argues, "the willingness of colonists to believe such arguments, and hazard their lives upon them, was testimony to how little they understood both the New England environment and the ways Indians actually lived in it" (37). Cronon's analysis of the colonists' perceptions of the New World reveals that pastoral tropes dominated their imaginations, and once they realized the environment was not a perpetual summer, they employed georgic tropes to dispossess Native Americans, who, in their eyes, did not labor, for the colonists did not see that the New England landscape and its productive powers had been managed and tended by Native Americans. "In short, Indians who hunted game animals were not just taking the 'unplanted bounties of nature'; in an important sense, they were harvesting a foodstuff which they had consciously been instrumental in creating" (51). This cognitive failure to recognize the effectiveness of agricultural practices that were different from Europe's was, as I argue, prevalent in British descriptions of the tropics.

8 Greenwich copy, f. 334.

9 J. C. Beaglehole, ed., *The* Endeavour *Journal of Joseph Banks, 1768–1771,* vols. 1 and 2 (Sydney: Angus and Robertson and The Public Library of New South Wales, 1963), 1:341–42.

10 Beaglehole, ed., Endeavour *Journal* 2:330.

11 In arguing that Cook saw that tropical bounty was produced by the labor and skill of Pacific Islanders, I am suggesting that Cook could, unlike Banks, acknowledge that Pacific Islanders possessed valuable horticultural techniques and botanical knowledge. However, Cook's ability to recognize native knowledge traditions did not necessarily extend to other branches of local knowledge, such as navigation. For a complex analysis of why Cook failed to investigate the methods by which Pacific Islanders navigated, see David Turnbull's essay "Cook and Tupaia, a Tale of Cartographic *Meconnaissance?*" in *Science and Exploration in the Pacific: European Voyages to the Southern Oceans in the Eighteenth Century,* ed. Margarette Lincoln (Woodbridge, Suffolk: Boydell Press, 1998), 117–32. Turnbull notes also that Banks valued Tupaia's navigational skills more highly than Cook.

12 George Forster, *A Voyage Round the World,* ed. Nicholas Thomas and Oliver Berghof, 2 vols. (1777; Honolulu: University of Hawai'i Press, 2000), 2:571. Subsequent references to this text will be placed in parentheses following the quotation.

13 See Forster's discussion of the relation between agriculture and the progress of civilization, 2:553–56. George Forster was indebted to his father's thinking on the relationship between climate and civilization; in fact, as Nicholas Thomas and Oliver Berghof contend, "this book was, to some extent, a co-authored work and . . . many broader perceptions expressed here are also enunciated in Forster senior's diary and his *Observations*" (xlvii). For Johann Reinhold Forster's ideas on the role of climate in shaping culture, see his *Observations Made during a Voyage round the World,* ed. Nicholas Thomas, Harriet Guest, and Michael Dettelbach (1778; Honolulu: University of Hawai'i Press, 1996), 191–201. See also the introductory essays in this volume: Nicholas Thomas, "'On the Variety of the Human Species': Forster's Comparative Ethnology," xxiii–xl; Harriet Guest, "Looking at Women: Forster's Observations in the South Pacific," xli–xlv; Michael Dettelbach, "'A Kind of Linnaean Being': Forster and Eighteenth-Century Natural History," lv–lxxiv. For J. R. Forster's journal, upon which his son drew, see *The Resolution Journal of Johann Reinhold Forster, 1772–1775,* ed. Michael E. Hoare, 4 vols. (London: Hakluyt Society, 1982).

14 Greenwich copy, ff. 334–35.

15 For the Forsters' and stagist (or stadial) theories of civilization, see Harriet Guest, "Cook in Tonga: Terms of Trade," in *Islands in History and Representation,* ed. Rod Edmond and Vanessa Smith (London: Routledge, 2003), 95–115. See also Anne Salmond, *The Trial of the Cannibal Dog: Captain Cook in the South Seas* (London: Allen Lane, 2003), chapter 13.

16 These reflections are shattered, however, when he encounters two islanders holding "their dead brethren in their arms" and discovers that the man had been killed by a musketball fired by the ship's sentry. "Thus one dark and detestable action effaced all the hopes with which I had flattered myself" (2:549).

17 Cook, *Resolution* logbook and journal, BL, Add. MS 27,886: f. 107 and f. 108.

18 BL, Add. MS 27,886: f. 164v.; Greenwich copy, f. 119.

19 For interpreting Cook's motives for planting gardens in the Pacific, see J. C. Beaglehole, *The Life of Captain James Cook* (Stanford, Calif.: Stanford University Press, 1974), and Dulcie Powell, "The Voyage of the Plant Nursery, HMS *Providence,* 1791–93," *Economic Botany* 31 (1977): 387–431. For the link between botany and empire in the Pacific, see Alan Frost, *Sir Joseph Banks and the Transfer of*

    Plants to and from the South Pacific 1786–1798 (Melbourne: Colony Press, 1993); John Gascoigne, *Science in the Service of Empire: Joseph Banks, the British State and the Uses of Science in the Age of Revolution* (Cambridge: Cambridge University Press, 1998); David Miller and Peter Reill, eds., *Visions of Empire: Voyages, Botany and Representations of Nature* (Cambridge: Cambridge University Press, 1996).

20   Obeyesekere sees Cook's planting as participating in the larger imperial project of bringing "progress" in the form of "improving" agriculture to the primitive Others of the Pacific. See *The Apotheosis of Captain Cook: European Mythmaking in the Pacific* (Princeton: Princeton University Press, 1992). See Nigel Rigby's thoughtful overview of the problems that attend totalizing historical narratives, such as Obeyesekere's postcolonial approach, and more traditional imperial histories, such as Alan Frost's essay "The Antipodean Exchange," which offer interpretations of British imperial power as unified, rational, and organized. "Although botanical science's important role in empire is being carefully examined, it is also, ironically, being made to seem more efficient, consensual and powerful than it actually was." Rigby, "The Politics and Pragmatics of Seaborne Plant Transportation," in *Science and Exploration in the Pacific,* ed. Margarette Lincoln (Woodbridge, Suffolk Boydell and Brewer, 2001), 100.

21   For a sensitive and persuasive account of Cook's class position and how it affected shipboard dynamics, see Nicholas Thomas, *The Extraordinary Voyages of Captain James Cook* (New York: Walker, 2003).

22   For Banks's plant transfers, see Ray Desmond, *The European Discovery of the Indian Flora* (Oxford: Oxford University Press, 1992), chapters 4, 15, 17, 21. Banks's initial plan for Australia involved moving Pacific Islanders to Australia, primarily from Tahiti, since these islands were to his thinking overpopulated. Of course, with increased contact with Europe, the Pacific Islander population dramatically deceased with the introduction of deadly diseases, including smallpox, and starvation and dislocation due to the restructuring of property relations and agricultural practices. For the impact of European ideas on property and agriculture on Hawai'i, see Lilikalā Kameʻeleihiwa, *Native Lands and Foreign Desires: Pehea Lā E Pono Ai?* (Honolulu: Bishop Museum Press, 1992).

23   Recent work in the history of science, particularly Richard Drayton's *Nature's Government: Science, Imperial Britain, and the "Improvement" of the World* (New Haven: Yale University Press, 2000), and R. H. Grove's *Green Imperialism: Colonial Expansion, Tropical Island Edens, and the Origins of Environmentalism, 1600–1860* (Cambridge: Cambridge University Press, 1995), along with Lucille Brockway's pioneering work, *Science and Colonial Expansion: The Role of the British Botanic Gardens* (New York: Academic Press, 1979), are exceptions to the lack of interest among imperial historians in colonial agricultural practices. Drayton's brilliant work on botanic gardens and the "intellectual history of botany" and his thesis that "sciences shaped the pattern of imperial expansion" (xv) are important contributions to rethinking imperial history.

24   Stuart Hall, "Old and New Identities, Old and New Ethnicities," in *Culture, Globalization and the World-System: Contemporary Conditions for the Representation of Identity,* ed. Anthony King (Binghamton: Department of Art and Art History, State University of New York at Binghamton, 1991), 48. See also Sidney W. Mintz, *Sweetness and Power: The Place of Sugar in Modern History* (New York: Penguin, 1986).

25   Exceptions to this general indifference to the intersection of nature and colonialism are Jill Casid's recent work, "Inhuming Empire: Islands as Colonial Nurseries and Grave," in *The Global Eighteenth Century,* ed. Felicity Nussbaum (Baltimore: Johns Hopkins University Press, 2003), 279–95, and Mimi Sheller's exciting new book, *Consuming the Caribbean: From Arawaks to Zombies* (London: Routledge, 2003).

26   For colonial science and the tropics, see Grove, *Green Imperialism;* Donal McCracken, *Gardens of Empire* (London: Leicester University Press, 1997); Nancy Leys Stephen, *Picturing Tropical Nature* (Ithaca, N.Y.: Cornell University Press, 2001).

27   Mary Louise Pratt, *Imperial Eyes: Travel Writing and Transculturation* (New York: Routledge, 1992), 57.

28   Giambattista Vico, *New Science: Principles of the New Science Concerning the Common Nature of Nations,* trans. David Marsh (1725, 1744; New York: Penguin, 1999). 76.

29   Karen O'Brien, "Imperial Georgic, 1660–1789," in *The Country and City Revisited,* ed. Gerald Maclean, Donna Landry, and Joseph P. Ward (Cambridge: Cambridge University Press, 1999), 160–79, 161.

30   *Lady Nugent's Journal,* ed. Philip Wright (Kingston, Jamaica: Institute of Jamaica, 1966), 25–26.

31   Ernesto Laclau and Chantal Mouffe, *Hegemony and Socialist Strategy: Towards a Radical Democratic Politics* (London: Verso, 1985, 1998), 108–10.

Chapter 27

Robert N. Watson

ECOLOGY, EPISTEMOLOGY, AND EMPIRICISM

THIS BOOK IS THE OFFSPRING of two seemingly incompatible parents: one a desire to bring ecological advocacy into the realm of Renaissance literature (where it has usually been deemed irrelevant at best), the other a desire to articulate the intricate philosophical ironies of Shakespeare's *As You Like It*, Marvell's "Mower" poems, and seventeenth-century Dutch painting. They were brought together by a discovery that what looks to modern eyes like early environmentalist sentiment—what would later evolve into that sentiment—originally functioned as an analogy: civilization is to nature as perception is to reality. Pastoralism was part of a broad primitivism: the nostalgia that appears to concern a lost ecology also laments a lost epistemology. English literature and its cultural contexts during the era of Protestant power running roughly from the destruction of the Armada in 1588 to the Restoration in 1660, which I will be calling the late Renaissance, reveal that the familiar efforts to recover simple experience out in the fields or the wilderness, to re-immerse oneself in the natural order, were partly fueled by a craving for unmediated knowledge in any form. As the persistent references to the Garden of Eden suggest, the movement back to nature was partly a code for a drive back toward some posited original certainty—a drive baffled by paradox and by history, leaving the pastoralist merely posing with his back to nature.

Ecocriticism

Would anyone have bet on horticultural studies as a plausible heir to cultural studies at the forefront of literary criticism in English? Perhaps someone recalling the shift from the divisive Vietnam War protests of the 1960s to the generally cuddlier environmentalism of the 1970s could have foreseen that the next generation of scholars would look back penitently from the ivory tower toward the planted rather than the tented field.[1] In any case, ecocriticism seems to be booming in its test markets (British Romanticism and the literature of the American West), and now stands ready to push its way back into the Renaissance.[2] My goal is to move from the Lake District and Yosemite to Stratford-upon-Avon and Hull—or at least into the Forest of Arden and the fields of the mowers—with due respect for the complexities of literary experience. Though the ecocritical position-papers collected in *PMLA* (October

1999) seem wry and dubious about their ability to colonize Shakespeare, this book finds me in the Greens' camp—perhaps as a Trojan horse, however, since I read *As You Like It* as wry and dubious about the prospects for any authentic involvement with the natural world. Perhaps my view, too, can be historicized, as the critical heir to another form of retreat from the political crises of the late 1960s: the acknowledgment (via Eastern religion or psychedelia) that the mind is its own place and that engagement with the "real world" is a delusion rather than an obligation.

This greening of the literary-critical field generates political as well as philosophical discomforts—especially when regarded through the dark-rose lenses of much Cultural Materialist criticism. The color spectrum on which green and red stand far apart sometimes seems to describe the relationship better than the political spectrum on which they share the left side. Without pursuing the provocative suggestion that the Nazis were the most ecologically minded government of the modern Western world,[3] a critic may still feel swarmed by uneasy questions. Is scarcity (as environmentalists warn) a crucial objective fact about the natural environment, or (from a Marxist perspective) is scarcity itself manufactured to produce value and permit control? Is ecocriticism—like New Historicism, some might argue—mostly an effort of liberal academics to assuage their student-day consciences (and their current radical students) about their retreat into aesthetics and detached professionalism, by forcing literary criticism into a sterile hybrid with social activism? Is environmentalism generally an elitist discourse because it is not obviously relevant to the needs of most city dwellers, misguidedly paternalistic toward rural populations who are directly dependent on hunting, logging, or mining, and structurally unjust to inhabitants of technologically undeveloped societies which consume relatively little yet are being asked to bear the burden of preserving outposts of wilderness for the pastoral contemplation and escape of a patronizing Western aristocracy?[4]

To push the questioning a step further: is ecocriticism the latest resort of identity politics in the academy, a way for those excluded by the usual categories to claim victim status, either by identifying with an oppressed biosphere, in part or in whole, or else by imagining their suffering and extinction in an anticipated ecological catastrophe? Is sentimentality toward nature different from other forms of sentimentality? Is it an effort to have religion without coming to terms with religion's irrational and authoritarian demands, an effort to find an alternative locus for the sacred in an increasingly secular culture—a kind of neutral (if only because infinitely various and infinitely interpretable) object for collective worship, a low common denominator for our experience of Creation?

Is attempting to speak for animals, or trees for that matter, a progressive or an appropriative action? Is it in any way parallel to other efforts in cultural studies to give voice to those who have not been empowered to speak for themselves; or is the parallel I have just proposed itself an offense against social justice, since it echoes pernicious rhetoric associating a human underclass with the so-called "lower forms of life" and encourages a leap beyond issues of social justice that have not yet been effectively addressed? Am I wrong to give a Humane Society money that the human society could use? Do I allay or aggravate this concern by subordinating the environmentalist impulse to more abstract philosophical issues? My questions about ecocriticism in general thus circle back to my speculations about the origins of its current popularity: the search for a politically safe and aesthetically attractive version of late 1960s radicalism may look like a healthy adaptation at one moment, a sinister co-optation at another.

It would be wrong to sophisticate away the growing ecological and environmental mission, all the more wrong because it would be so convenient; wrong to let such important problems slide just because they are ethically and tactically complicated; wrong, also, not to think them through from many angles. If we can understand how some people came to care, in politically and intellectually responsible ways, about present and future life on this planet as a collectivity, we can hope to expand the ecologically minded community and its wisdom. That may in turn expand, in space and time, in however small and gradual a way, the niche in which life makes its beauties and finds its joys.

Overview

This book explores artistic responses to the nostalgia for unmediated contact with the world of nature—a common sentiment focused and magnified by a cultural moment in which urbanization, capitalism, new technologies, and the Protestant Reformation each contributed to anxieties about mediation and the lost sensual past. Behind late-Renaissance efforts to identify with fauna and even flora lies a tendency to view things-in-themselves as the primary object of knowledge and reverence. These anticipations of the Romantic and physicist eras, two hundred and four hundred years later, were already provoking skeptical critiques that alienated humanity from nature and discerned a fundamental indeterminacy in reality. The pursuit of empirical science forced one set of prominent Renaissance thinkers to confront epistemological doubts, while the multicultural upheaval associated with Renaissance humanism threatened to produce a cognitive crisis among another set of thinkers by revealing that the world is less observed than constructed, less an accessible reality than a contingency manufactured by a team of repressed solipsists.

Representation thus became a psychic as well as political crisis in early modern England. Indeed, anxieties about the arbitrary, prejudiced, and unstable character of perception—including both the eccentricities of individuals and the possibility of collective delusion—must have put special pressures on those (particularly in the Parliamentary movement) who were advocating a system of political representatives.[5] Constitutionalism seemed to imply a recognition that all the world is constituted. By the middle of the seventeenth century, both politics and epistemology were increasingly presumed to operate by consent rather than absolutism; that is, reality consisted of what was commonly perceived by human beings, and government consisted of their common interest. The agreement to settle for figurations and approximations of the individual material entity coincided with a similar agreement about the will of the individual citizen. The strenuous and approximate aspects of consensus made it an awkward ally for the dream of government by revelation. While activists, scientists, zealots, philologists, and travelers proclaimed that the rightful truth was ready to manifest itself spontaneously, a repressed fear whispered that it was ever more distant—was, perhaps, nowhere.

The consequent yearning takes many synergistic forms: theological (seeking a new earthly Eden as well as a simpler way to heaven), political (arising from urban afflictions, enclosure controversies, and the sentimental association of political movements with primitive English agriculture), economic (dreaming of a society either fully founded on gold or completely neglectful of it), philosophical (responding to the resurgence of skepticism), philological (attempting to recover a "pure" Latin and an idealized textual past), scientific (seeking a transparent descriptive rhetoric), psychoanalytic (recalling the symbiotic union of breast-feeding—rivers of milk were a pastoral commonplace),[6] painterly (wrestling with the implications of landscape and perspective), and poetic (arising from a sense of artistic belatedness, particularly in the rediscovered pastoral mode). The nostalgia for Eden, for the Golden Age, for an idealized collective-agrarian feudal England, and for a prelinguistic access to reality all come together (notably in Traherne's "Centuries") in fantasies of a liberating regression to garden and wilderness.[7] Titles of important works such as Edward Stillingfleet's *Origines Sacrae* (1662) and Matthew Hale's *Primitive Organization of Mankind* (1677) remind us how eager this culture remained, even as it became scientifically sophisticated, to found truth on some simple and original point—how much the discovery of truth, which for a modern scientific culture is the goal of progress, was then understood as a function of regress. The gaze was so persistently backward (toward ancient paganism and ancient Christianity alike), provoked by the multicultural explosion of the High Renaissance (including the diaspora of scholars, and the voyages of early colonialism and world trade), that I have preferred "late Renaissance" to "Early Modern" in my title.

From the moment of their conception, modern ecological and epistemological anxieties were conjoined twins. Their conjunction brings into alignment a number of important binary oppositions: human/animal, mind/body, self-consciousness/instinct, self/other, art/nature, word/thing, signifier/signified, Symbolic/Imaginary, Platonic shadow/Platonic form, fallen/unfallen consciousness, and even (to the extent that misogynist traditions blame women for alienating men from nature, or make women the repositories or captives of nature) man/woman.[8] Set in parallel series, these polarities conveyed a considerable cultural shock. When Marvell—the great ancestor of Wallace Stevens as a lyricist of self-consciousness—asserts in "The Garden" that "Two paradises 'twere in one/ To live in paradise alone," the patristic resentment of Eve thinly covers the story of another fall, into Cartesian dualism, in which actual nature and perceived nature become distinct, because "a green shade" is never quite identical with the "green thought" that represents it in human consciousness. Renaissance man was post-lapsarian in (among others) a post-structuralist way. How valuable, how viable, is the "Paradise within thee" promised to Milton's Adam and Eve if it misrepresents a paradise that is lost—lost because it can only be misrepresented?[9]

None of this is to claim that these forms of mediation and alienation were entirely new, nor that any period in recorded history has been immune to regrets about a posited lost simplicity. The Middle Ages did not sit comfortably on a firm platform of direct realism. But some late-Renaissance societies nonetheless appear to struggle with a convergence of forces that together raised this familiar cultural problem to the level of crisis, a crisis indirectly narrated by the artists of those societies and formative of the ecological sympathies and epistemological anxieties that now dominate liberal intellectual consciousness, humanistic and scientific alike.[10] My definition of nature may seem to shift among several usages of the term: flora and fauna, the innate character of a being, and the totality of the physical universe. Similarly, my description of a skeptical crisis will sometimes blur the differences among the problem of establishing the existence of material bodies, the problem of discerning essences, and the problem of knowing other minds. My defense in both cases is that this jumbling is exactly what late-Renaissance culture was doing and what permitted it to imagine it could attack the epistemological problems through various forms of pastoral primitivism: "in the state of innocency in the first creation, *Man had perfect naturall knowledge of* all naturall things."[11] Humanity's lost touch with nature is fundamentally a problem of lost knowledge.

Recognizing this amalgamation of issues evokes something new and noteworthy from the individual artworks, which collectively suggest something important about the world that made them and the world we are making. My goal is to apply the stains and the lights that make visible this particular pattern in the grain of cultural history. Moving beyond traditional expositions of the art-nature polarity in this period,[12] I am suggesting homologies among the various causes of this intensified sense of loss and alienation, and suggesting dangerous synergies among the effects. Protestantism sought to restore a direct link between the Savior and the soul through direct reading of the Bible by the sinner, as opposed to the complicated institutional mediations associated with the Catholic version of Christianity; the idea that Protestantism claimed to be returning to the true origins of Christianity, scraping away the accretions which had grown on the Catholic Church like barnacles over time, is so central and so generally acknowledged then and now that I will not linger to offer examples. Peter Sterry, Oliver Cromwell's chaplain, demonstrates how the projects of returning to nature, returning to the origins of Christianity, and returning to Eden could be blended rhetorically into a single inspiring program of Platonist Protestantism: "as Paradise, so the *pure Image* of God in the Soul, seems to some not to be *lost* or destroyed, but *hid* beneath the ruins of the fall. Thus *Knowledg* springing in the Soul, seems to be a *remembrance*, the Life of all good, an awakening by reason of the primitive Image of pure Nature raising itself by degrees, and sparkling through the *Rubbish*, the confusions of the present state."[13] The radical Protestant sects reveal the way this regression toward the primitive church could become a regression toward a thoroughly primitivist absorption in nature. Even allowing for demagogic sensationalism behind reports of nudism among Picardians, Ranters, Adamists, and Quakers, the thematic persistence of such accusations suggest strong atavist and minimalist tendencies in the radical Reformation—a desire to manifest, so to speak, the thing itself.[14] The Ranters were said to believe that "when we die we shall be swallowed up into the infinite spirit, as a drop into the ocean . . . and if ever we be raised again, we shall rise as a horse, a cow, a root, a flower and such like."[15] This is atavism blended into atomism, with overtones of Pythagorean beliefs (about which Jonson's *Volpone*, Donne's *Metempsychosis*, and several of Shakespeare's best-known plays joke uneasily) that proposed a dizzying cycle of origins, back through various other species, for each human soul. The infinite regress pointed not to a Creator, but always further into a void—or at least toward an abysmally low common denominator. Like Darwinism later, Pythagorean metempsychosis was at best an equivocal force in promoting common respect for all forms of life, but it is interesting that resistance to the extreme and casual cruelties toward animals in the period is voiced mostly by Puritans such as Philip Stubbes, William Perkins, Thomas Beard, and George Wither.[16]

Meanwhile, human beings were also imposing new cruelties on each other. Sixteenth-century England was (many economic historians agree) the time and place where wage labor became dominant: segments of the feudal peasantry became a rootless proletariat for hire, alienating workers from their fields and their own bodies in the course of alienating work from product and ownership from object. New channels of money and status carried aristocrats from their country estates to court. Long before industrialism diverted them away from agriculture, capitalism took away Englishmen's proprietary relationship to the earth. Land, labor, and identity were a socio-economic Trinity pulled asunder. Money became an increasingly disturbing and dominant instance of the way that seemingly arbitrary signifiers could come between people and their material world, and periods of rapid inflation drove painfully home how unstable (and therefore contingent) that signification could be. Urbanization, as Barnabe Googe and other pastoralists complained, promoted not only a new kind of anonymity (which wage labor magnified), but also (as in the Hellenistic era) the pangs of alienation from a past more directly linked to the land—and family—that provided life.

Emerging nationalism in the late Renaissance drew heavily on fantasies of origins and of the almost autochthonic "natures" of different peoples. But personal identity—supposedly a truth based in both chief senses of "nature"—became elusive. If inward subjectivity was the rock on which both Montaigne and Descartes would build, outward seeming was therefore all the more opaque. Radical, iconoclastic Reformers such as Andreas Karlstadt argued that there were no external markers of grace. Implicit in this period's anti-theatrical polemics and sumptuary legislation alike was a suspicion that roles and clothes might misrepresent—and thereby alter—the essential nature, the true identity, of a person. Class, gender, even race were at risk of being disguised—which may have been the safe way of saying they were at risk of being exposed as merely costumes, merely constructed.[17] Blaise Pascal comments bitingly on the use of "red robes" to distinguish judges who otherwise have no judgment to distinguish them.[18] Slippage among name, personal appearance, and social place seemed intolerably threatening. The regulations and diatribes were a way of enforcing an illusion of order, not unlike Marvell's mower enforcing, in bad faith, the "pathetic fallacy" (to borrow a useful term from Ruskin's *Modern Painters*) that nature had neglected to sustain once the mower fell into misery. Even the sale of knighthoods and other supposedly hereditary or quality-specific honors by King James would have manifested this split between the nominal and the natural. The fears about lost stability of the social hierarchy and about lost comprehensibility of the material universe—the sociological and epistemological crises—thus inflected and amplified one another. Beneath practical concerns about the current limits of knowledge lurked proto-Kantian concerns about the nature and conditions of knowledge itself. The crises of identity and subjectivity contributed to a fear that representation was not only potentially but inherently a fraud—since (as Greenblatt's argument about self-fashioning suggests) there was also a burgeoning fear that there might be no essence of the self to express or return to, that disrobing after a day of social assertions might be another instance of the onion peeling down to nothing.[19]

Discomfort about how people dressed also reflected discomfort about how they undressed—and nowhere more clearly than in the theater. The fears of unstable selfhood that fueled the sumptuary laws conjoin with a fear of failed erotic teleology in the now-notorious attacks on cross-dressing that featured so prominently in the anti-theatrical tracts.[20] Though literary critics are somehow demographically fated to scoff at this moral indignation, there seems little question that audiences were significantly titillated by the blurring of gender when boys played women's roles. The plays often toy with this open secret, building toward a moment when the genitals would be exposed or involved; think of the tension surrounding the king's order to "Strip that boy" in *Philaster* (5.5), or less directly but with greater complications, the repeated delays in consummating Othello's marriage, and the mixed signals about his wedding sheets. While Othello is being made to wonder whether it is possible that he could ever have Desdemona's maidenhead, or whether it is instead all a cruel joke, audiences are nudged to wonder something similar for a different reason: they too are being cheated, teased with a consummation the playwright could never really give them. Think also about the many plays—especially Jonson's comedies such as *The Alchemist* and *Volpone*—that break off the villains' plot at the moment when the honest woman is finally about to be genitally violated; then consider what Jonson does with this theme in *Epicoene* where a final twist of gender surprises the audience and resolves the plot, and in *Bartholomew Fair* where the puppets finally do what Jonson had so often just barely refused to do: lift up the skirts of the players, only to show the lack underneath. A recent study asserts that the epistemology of cross-dressing on the London stage demonstrates "how in the early modern period sodomy functioned not as an identity, nor even as an activity, but as a site in which the failure of representation produces a desire that has no object."[21] An elusive object, anyway, or a fantastic one. The point of the dramatic tease is precisely that it will not, cannot, be resolved—which leaves gender and sexuality in the same maze of mediations, the same sense of lost contact with both fundamental and biological reality, that I believe haunted so many habitations of Renaissance thought.

The English government, like its citizens, was driven to give up on seeking essences and instead settled for phenomena. A key aspect of the Elizabethan theological compromise was that the state would not "make windows into men's hearts and secret thoughts" to see whether they believed the Protestant doctrine, so long as they complied with it outwardly.[22] This must have left some "Church papists" stewing in their own hypocrisies, and left some Protestants anxious—even more than Jesuit equivocation had already done—about lurking enemies to their beliefs and potentially to their government. The distinction between privacy and disguise dissolved in the corrosive paranoia. As Peter Lake has observed, the emphasis on conformity "opened up a gap between the inward and the outward, the real inner convictions of a person and his or her outward behavior, a space which, it seemed to many contemporaries, could be exploited for all sorts of dissimulation by the faithless and the unscrupulous."[23] These fears were distinctly homologous with the other anxieties this book traces: artistic, scientific, colonial, and sexual exploits in which the gap between the outward manifestation and the inward being could never quite be closed. Precisely because it was so supremely important, doctrinal affiliation became impossible to read. Persons on either side of the religious wars might have found it a delicious relief to slip into a theater where they could hear the soliloquies in which those windows to the private soul flew open and the secret thoughts turned into audible language. This brief reprieve from what philosophers discuss as the problem of other minds—their fundamental inaccessibility—would, moreover, only have emphasized the similar problems of represented reality, of the *theatrum mundi*. The link between a Pyrrhonist resignation to making the best of the appearance of things and the Elizabethan theological compromise becomes visible in a complaint against the Marprelate tracts: "I never entred into other mens hearts to see their consciences: I never looked into their Cofers to see their treasures: I never was desirous to be privie of their secret doings. I must therfore by that I see, heare, and know, judge the best."[24]

Representation

Around the beginning of the seventeenth century, people in England were hearing a crescendo of warnings about the failure of representation—long before it became an explicitly political issue and helped provoke the Civil War (and much earlier than Michel Foucault claims that any fundamental mistrust of resemblance, let alone of representation, could emerge).[25] Developments such as single-point perspective, empirical science, and improved maps and optical devices marked progress; but, as so often, progress brings with it a recognition of limitations. As the technologies get better at replicating reality, it becomes harder to blame them for the imperfection of our representations: it becomes clear that the problem is not one of method. Toward the end of his *History of the Royal Society*, Thomas Sprat warns that if this new collective empirical approach to science were to fail, "They will have reason in all times to conclude, That the long barreness of *Knowledge* was not caus'd by the corrupt method which was taken, but by the nature of the *Thing* itself."[26] Radically improved optics surely promised to make reality more visible; and yet that innovation finally drove reality further off in at least five ways, as it enabled the expanded voyages of discovery and colonization that brought home the dis-eases of multiculturalism, established the unfathomable depth of the physical universe, revealed that organisms were not merely themselves but also colonies of micro-organisms, contributed to the self-conscious fraudulence of perspective painting, and taught scientists lessons about the functioning of human perception that suggest our experience of reality is merely virtual, merely a highly contingent system of mental representation.

The back-to-nature movement of the late 1960s was echoed by a popular song whose refrain ended, "Get back to where you once belonged." By the early 1970s, a more abstract and dubious note had entered, with a chorus that ended instead, "The nearer your destination, the more you're slip slidin' away"[27]—at least, the more you find yourself living in Zeno's paradox instead of Adam's Paradise; Achilles decelerates near the tape, the arrow hovers just short of the bull's-eye. The fantasy of regression to an absolute truth decayed similarly from the mid-sixteenth to the mid-seventeenth century, though Francis Bacon kept bravely assuring his fellow investigators (as if to preclude Paul Simon's wistful warning) that "the nearer it [the investigation] approaches to simple natures, the easier and plainer everything will become."[28] As Pierre Gassendi would demonstrate in the mid-seventeenth century, however, language is a lens that makes close-ups blurry.[29] Leonardo da Vinci, though confident about visual science, characteristically anticipated the problem with scientific language: "the more minute your description the more you will confuse the mind of the reader and the more you will lead him away from the knowledge of the thing described."[30] Francis Quarles warned that "The road to resolution lies by doubt: / The next way home's the farthest way about."[31] There is no direct route to truth; inquiring minds must, as the circumlocuting Polonius advises, "by indirections, find directions out."[32] Sprat observed that "it frequently happens to *Philosophers*, as it did to *Columbus* . . . by prosecuting of *mistaken Causes*, with a resolution of not giving over the persute; they have been guided to the *truth* it self."[33]

Bacon's heirs in the Royal Society were eventually compelled to acknowledge that they could never quite bridge the gap between a highly probable belief about nature and direct knowledge of nature, nor the gap between the sensibly observed properties of an object and the essential identity of that object. When John Locke tries to identify a material essence, he seems to define it by its ability to withstand that endlessly divisive paradox: "Primary qualities . . . are utterly inseparable from the body, in what state soever it be; and such as . . . the mind finds inseparable from every particle of matter, though less than to make itself singly be perceived by our senses: v.g. Take a grain of wheat, divide it into two parts; each part has still solidity, extension, figure, and mobility: divide it again, and it retains still the same qualities; and so divide it on, till the parts become insensible; they must retain still each of them all those qualities."[34] Cream of wheat notwithstanding, this sets a daunting standard for the aspects of nature our senses can truly claim to savor. As Shakespeare's Touchstone reminds his companions (2.4.16–18), the pastoral escapist has to face the fact that he—usually he rather than she—will never really achieve an unselfconscious symbiosis with the fields (at least, not while alive, and especially not while speaking), a fact he could ignore while sitting in the court and the city, the currency exchange and the commodity markets, the scholar's library and the artist's studio, dreaming of escape from the artificial human world.

This version of Zeno's paradox afflicted theological entities as well. The more an image looked like God, the more it threatened to alienate God: Queen Elizabeth placated the Puritans, paradoxically, by replacing the West Cheap Cross with a pagan pyramid, and turning its Virgin Mary into a semi-nude Diana.[35] The zealous Protestant may feel at moments the presence of the divine spirit as intimately as the Catholic may feel the divine body in the Eucharist, but such Protestants were also tortured by the uncertainty and incompleteness of that divine presence: by the way sin, fallen reason, inscrutable predestination, and residual ceremonial structures still somehow remained between themselves and full knowledge of God. Furthermore, the very arguments Luther and his fellow reformers made for a purified text in vernacular tongues finally implied that there could be no meaning independent of context and hence no stable ultimate truth; in the cultural kitchen, philology proved to be less a dishwasher than a mixmaster blender.[36] To use language-study, as Valla did in the fifteenth century, as a tool for exposing the Donation of Constantine as a forgery—a foundational event in Renaissance humanism, and above all an effort to get back to original truth— is finally to expose the internal referentiality and historical instability of any verbal system, a recognition that refutes any lingering hope that words will directly reflect things, uninflected by local circumstances and evolving vocabularies.[37] While Valla's conclusions undermined the legal basis of papal empire, his method—especially in the *Dialectical Disputations*— undermined the Scriptural basis of Protestantism before it began.[38] Absolute truth and origins again recede together. Hence the period's nostalgia for Hebrew, as the true primeval language, rumored to have some pictographic and even magical connection with the things it described (it was speculated "if a child were taught no Language in his Infancy, but left to his own conduct, he would speak *Hebrew*").[39] Ancient Chinese and Egyptian hieroglyphics were attractive for similar reasons: alphabetic writing had some of the disenchanting implications of atomism.[40] To attempt (as Donne, Cudworth, and many others did) to resolve disputes within Christianity by studying its origins in Judaism, however, was to risk heresy and apostasy, to risk dissipating doctrine rather than providing it with stable foundations. Only the paradox by which Christian religion could claim chronological priority over Judaic religion, and the related hermeneutics by which it could convert the Pentateuch into a mere allegorical representation of the New Testament's absolute truth, could keep the hunger for original truth from driving late-Renaissance Christians back into the arms of the Judaic Yahweh.

The art of dialectic itself, which became central to the university curriculum in sixteenth-century England, is a search for truth that systematically defeats, by perpetually deferring, the effort to settle on a truth (even religious truth; no wonder there was a movement back toward Scholasticism in the early seventeenth century). Montaigne ends up arguing that "the opinion of knowledge" is the source of endless human suffering and folly, and that if it would "please nature some day to open her bosom to us . . . what mistakes we should find in our poor science! I am mistaken if it grasps one single thing straight as it is."[41] Along these many different paths, the quest kept turning Quixotic: Cervantes' work captures the paradox of an age that kept finding itself most laughably derivative, most caught up in imaginary sophistications, at the moments it tried hardest to return proudly to the authentic truth of a posited Golden Age.

Notes

1 The first Earth Day was held on April 22, 1970. Less than two weeks later National Guard troops killed four Kent State University students during a war protest; ten days after that, police shot students to death during war protests at Jackson State University. It is not hard to understand why environmentalism, with its far more soothing images and its promise of common ground, became the retreat (in either sense) of many young reformers.

2 McColley, "Milton and Nature," p. 424: "I hope it will become a maxim of literary study and teaching, especially in this age of ecological crisis, that attention to the relations between human beings and the natural world should be included among the principal approaches to literature." Boehrer's *Shakespeare Among the Animals* and his *Parrot Culture* show that such approaches are beginning to reach studies of Renaissance culture. Nonetheless, Estok, "Teaching the Environment," complains that "there has been almost no work done that looks seriously at how representations of the early modern natural environment fit into" other literary-critical discourses, including politicized ones.

3 E.g., Bate's *The Song of the Earth*, p. 267, which also briefly explores the depredations of Social Darwinism. Soper's *What Is Nature?* pursues this anxiety in a more elaborate philosophical vein, while seeking to integrate realist and constructivist assumptions concerning nature.

4 Several different approaches to this question appear in the *Environmental Justice Reader*, ed. Adamson, Evans, and Stein.

5 According to the OED, the use of "representative" in the political sense is a Caroline innovation. Manley, *Convention*, pp. 259–62, offers an admirable discussion of the emerging emphasis on consensus in both politics and natural philosophy. More generally, Manley proposes "Convention" as a third term complicating the nature-art dyad. I believe that—though subsumed by Protestants and empirical scientists into the largely pejorative category of art (whereas it was once synonymous with one sense of "nature")—"convention" recovered its connection to nature as people began to recognize that the Physical reality they perceived was partly constructed and fundamentally probabilistic.

6 E.g., Guarini's *Il pastor fido*, Act 4, and Tasso's *Aminta*, 1.2.320; Samuel Daniel's Pastoral begins, "Oh, happy golden age / Not for that rivers ran / With streams of milk"; cf. McFarland, *Shakespeare's Pastoral Comedy*, pp. 46–47. In Jonson's masque *The Golden Age Restored*, Pallas promises fountains of milk.

7 John Parkinson's 1629 *Paradisi in Sole* is merely one example of the then-widespread notion that humanity could build its own new Edenic gardens; Keith Thomas, *Man and the Natural World*, p. 236, explores the associations between gardens and the lost paradise. Peter Harrison, *The Bible, Protestantism and the Rise of Natural Science*, pp. 237 and 243, offers further examples.

8 Cf. Roberts, *The Shakespearean Wild*, and Ortner, "Is Female to Male as Nature Is to Culture?"

9 John Milton, *Paradise Lost*, 12.58; all citations of Milton's works in this book will be based on *Complete Poems and Major Prose*, ed. Hughes.

10   Though the topic is different, this book may therefore be considered a methodological companion-piece to my study of mortality-anxiety, *The Rest Is Silence*. Having upset some (Foucauldian) readers of that book by discussing the continuities of human experience and other (more traditionalist) readers by discussing the differences in human experience at different cultural moments, I wanted to state explicitly here the kind of argument I will be offering. Again I am trying to highlight a largely transhistorical problem that local circumstances amplified into a crisis, and to encourage close readings and large cultural changes to illuminate each other.

11   Walker, *The History of the Creation* (1641), p. 193; quoted by Harrison, *Rise of Natural Science*, p. 211. My defense thus resembles John Lyly's defense of mixed genre in the prologue to *Mydas*: "If we present a mingle-mangle, our fault is to be excused, because the whole world is become an hodge-podge"; quoted by Manley, *Convention*, p. 199.

12   See, for example, Tayler, *Nature and Art in Renaissance Literature*, and the sophistication of that model by a third term in Manley, *Convention, 1500–1700*.

13   Sterry, *A Discourse of the Freedom of the Will*, p. 99; quoted by Martz, *The Paradise Within*, pp. 35–36. Another intriguing instance is Cotton Mather's assertion that "the first *Age* was the golden *Age*: to return unto *that*, will make a man a Protestant, and, I may add, a Puritan"; quoted by Levin, *The Myth of the Golden Age in the Renaissance*, p. 67.

14   Harrison, *Rise of Natural Science*, p. 233.

15   Clarkson, *Look About You* (1659), p. 98; quoted by Thomas, p. 138. Even if this characterization of Ranter beliefs is unfair, it reflects plausible anxieties about where their beliefs could lead. Thomas Edwards's *Gangraena* (1646), 1:20, suggests that "there is no difference between the flesh of a man and the flesh of a toad"; cited by Thomas, *Man and the Natural World*, p. 166; see also his p. 180.

16   Thomas, *Man and the Natural World*, pp. 156–58, cites these and other strongly Protestant figures strongly protesting cruelty to animals. My chapter 6 below will add several other prominent radical Reformers to the list. Boehrer, *Shakespeare Among the Animals*, p. 192 n. 3, notes that Puritans were prominent opponents of bear-baiting.

17   Along with legislation assorting clothing colors by social rank, and the complaints about gender-bending garb in pamphlets such as *Hic Mulier* and *Haec Vir* (both London, 1620), consider the various costume markers legally imposed on Jews (apparently for fear of mixed marriages), such as the ones described by Janet Adelman, "Her Father's Blood," p. 11: "every Jew shall wear on the front of his dress tablets or patches of cloth four inches long by two wide, of some colour other than that of the rest of his garment."

18   Pascal, *Pensées*, sect. 1, no. 44, p. 40; see similarly sect. 5, no. 87, p.53.

19   Hanson, *Discovering the Subject in Renaissance England*, p. 2, traces an Elizabethan/Jacobean "tendency to construe other people in terms of secrets awaiting discovery." Jonson and his Cavalier followers joke repeatedly about people, especially women, disassembling at home their public selves until nothing remains but a wardrobe and a cosmetic table.

20   For the application of this anti-theatrical rhetoric back to the social practices of gender, see Philip Stubbes's *Anatomie of Abuses* (1583).

21   Sedinger, " 'If Sight and Shape Be True,' " p. 64. The maze is certainly an intricate one, with many entrances and perhaps no exit. Sedinger, p. 69, quotes Thomas Randolph's epigram "*In Lesbiam, & Histrionem*," which speculates why a lesbian would keep a young male actor as a lover. Does theatrical cross-dressing provoke male homoeroticism (as John Rainolds argued in 1599) because the women's clothing allows the men to attach their heterosexual desires to these young male objects, or instead (or also) because that clothing provides repressed homosexual desires with an adequate cover story? In plays such as *The Roaring Girl* and *As You Like It*, the gender-blender is run at high speed, and the results are predictably fluid.

22   Bacon, *Works*, 8:98, attributing this deference to Queen Elizabeth. This remark is often quoted but seldom cited. For confirmation that it reflects Elizabeth's explicit position, see her "Declaration of the Queen's Proceedings" and "Declaration in the Star Chamber," in *Queen Elizabeth's Defence*, pp. 47 and 61. For an indication that Elizabeth did say something of the sort, see Richard Cosin's 1593 defense of church courts, which reports that the queen "*oftentimes caused to bee openly notified in the Starre-Chamber that her gracious meaning is not, to search into mens consciences*" (*Apology*, part 3, chap. 5; 3:50).

23   Lake, "Religious Identities in Shakespeare's England," p. 64.

24   Cooper, *An Admonition to the People of England* (1589), p.113.

25   Foucault, *The Order of Things*.

26   Sprat, *History*, p. 437.

27   "Get Back," Lennon/McCartney, 1969; "Slip Slidin' Away," Paul Simon, 1977.

28   Francis Bacon, *New Organon*, bk. 2, aphorism 8, in Warhaft, p. 384; most of my citations of Bacon

will be based on this widely available edition, though I will use the Spedding et al. *Works of Francis Bacon* (despite the frustrations of dealing with the different organization of volumes in its many editions) for some works that are either not included or not as satisfactorily translated in Warhaft.

29   Kroll, *The Material Word*, p. 119, nicely summarizes Gassendi's point: "Predictably, the moment the world is represented by those mental images is the very moment at which it begins to elude our grasp. The incursion of discrete images—as in Epicurus reflecting the mechanical effects of irreducible and indivisible material atoms—catalyzes the activity of judgment by which we abstract ordinary knowledge in the form of propositions. Thus as knowing creatures, we inescapably operate at an epistemological and perceptual remove from unfiltered sensation."

30   Quoted in Heydenreich, *Leonardo da Vinci*, p. 123.

31   Francis Quarles, *Emblemes* (1635), 4.2.2. John Donne says something similar about religious truth: "on a huge hill, / Cragged and steep, Truth stands, and he that will / Reach her, about must, and about must go" (Satire 3, lines 79–81); all Donne quotations in this chapter and elsewhere in the book, except where noted, are based on *John Donne*, ed. John Carey.

32   *Hamlet*, 2.1.63; all citations of Shakespeare's work in this book are based on *The Riverside Shakespeare*.

33   Sprat, *History of the Royal Society*, p. 109.

34   John Locke, *Essay Concerning Human Understanding* (1690), bk. 2, chap. 8, sec. 9.

35   Phillips, *Reformation of Images*, p. 144; his p. 164 notes that Archbishop Laud allowed some images, but not "the picture of Christ as God the Son . . . for the Deity cannot be portrayed or pictured, though the humanity may." This partly resembles the epistemological limits that prevent human sensation from directly registering the inmost identity of objects in their divine truth, though the objects themselves are visible.

36   See, for example the studies by Kristin Zapalac (1990) and Richard Waswo (1987), as cited by Spolsky, pp. 187–88.

37   Cf. Agrippa, *Of the Vanitie and Uncertaintie of Artes and Sciences* (1530), ed. Dunn, chap. 2, p. 21: "this is the alteration of times, that there are no Letters, no Tongues the whiche at this day doo acknowledge, or understande the forme or manner of their Antiquitee." Greene, *The Light in Troy*, demonstrates the importance of such anxieties for Renaissance poets.

38   Valla can be seen as the first modern critic of the Greek New Testament. Cf. Waswo, *Language and Meaning in the Renaissance*, p. 208: "To open the divine text to the newly historical modes of interrogation was to perceive a temporal semantic fluidity that offered ample scope for competing attempts at determination." The Word could hardly serve as the ultimate stable referent if it proved unstable. No wonder Catholics clung to things commonly accessible to the senses (including the "thingness" of the Vulgate, present for those to whom it made no sense) all the more intensely as Protestants wrestled with the Word.

39   Sibscota, *The Deaf and Dumb Man's Discourse*, p. 24; he evinces the popularity of this theory by striving to refute it scientifically; so does Sprat, p. 96.

40   The dedicatory epistle of John Webb's *Historical Essay* calls Chinese characters a "GOLDEN-MINE of learning, which from all ANTIQUITY hath lain concealed in the PRIMITIVE TONGUE"; quoted in Harrison, *Rise of Natural Science*, p. 251. Sir Thomas Browne preferred the Egyptian option.

41   Montaigne, "Apology for Raymond Sebond," in *Complete Essays*, pp. 359–60 and 400.

References

Adamson, Joni, Mei Mei Evans, and Rachel Stein, eds. *Environmental Justice Reader*. Tucson: University of Arizona Press, 2002.

Agrippa, Henry Cornelius. *Of the Vanitie and Uncertaintie of Artes and Sciences*. 1530. Edited by Catherine M. Dunn. Northridge: California State University, 1974.

Bacon, Francis. *The Works of Francis Bacon*. 14 vols. Collected and edited by James Spedding, Robert Leslie Ellis, and Douglas Denon Heath. London: Longman, 1857–74.

Bate, Jonathan. *The Song of the Earth*. London: Picador, 2000.

Boehrer, Bruce. *Shakespeare Among the Animals: Nature and Society in the Drama of Early Modern England*. New York: Palgrave/St. Martin's Press, 2002.

Clarkson [Claxton], Laurence. *Look About You*. London, 1659.

Cooper, Thomas. *An Admonition to the People of England*. 1589. Edited by Edward Arber. English Scholar's Library of Old and Modern Works, no. 15. Birmingham, 1878.

Cosin, Richard. *An Apologie for Sundrie Proceedings by Jurisdiction Ecclesiasticall*. London: C. Barker, 1593.

Donne, John. *John Donne*. Edited by John Carey. Oxford: Oxford University Press, 1991.

Elizabeth I, Queen of England. In *Queen Elizabeth's Defence*. Edited by W. E. Collins. London: SPCK, 1958.

Foucault, Michel. *The Order of Things*. 1966. Reprint, New York: Random House, 1970.

Greene, Thomas M. *The Light in Troy: Imitation and Discovery in Renaissance Poetry*. New Haven, Conn.: Yale University Press, 1982.

Hanson, Elizabeth. *Discovering the Subject in Renaissance England*. New York: Cambridge University Press, 1998.

Harrison, Peter. *The Bible, Protestantism and the Rise of Natural Science*. Cambridge: Cambridge University Press, 1998.

Heydenreich, I. H. *Leonardo da Vinci*. London: Allen and Unwin, 1954.

Kroll, Richard W. *The Material Word: Literature Culture in the Restoration and Early Eighteenth Century*. Baltimore: Johns Hopkins University Press, 1991.

Lake, Peter. "Puritan Identities," *Journal of Ecclesiastical History* 35 (1984): 112–23.

Manley, Lawrence. *Convention 1500–1700*. Cambridge, Mass.: Harvard University Press, 1980.

Martz, Louis L. *The Paradise Within: Studies in Vaughan, Traherne and Milton*. New Haven, Conn.: Yale University Press, 1964.

McColley, Diane Kelsey. "Milton and Nature." *Huntington Library Quarterly* 62 (1999–2001): 423–44.

McFarland, Thomas. *Shakespeare's Pastoral Comedy*. Chapel Hill: University of North Carolina Press, 1972.

Milton, John. *Complete Poems and Major Prose*. Edited by Merritt Y. Hughes. Indianapolis: Bobbs-Merrill, 1976.

Montaigne, Michel de. *The Complete Essays of Montaigne*. Translated by Donald M. Frame. Stanford, Calif.: Stanford University Press, 1948.

Ortner, Sherry Beth. "Is Female to Male as Nature Is to Culture?" In *Woman, Culture, and Society*, edited by Michelle Zimbalist Rosaldo and Louise Lamphere, pp. 67–87. Stanford, Calif.: Stanford University Press, 1974.

Pascal, Blaise. *Pensées*. Translated by A. J. Krailsheimer. Baltimore: Penguin, 1966.

Phillips, John. *The Reformation of Images: Destruction of Art in England, 1535–1660*. Berkeley: University of California Press, 1973.

Quarles, Francis. *Emblemes*. London, 1635.

Roberts, Jeanne Addison. *The Shakespearean Wild: Geography, Genus, and Gender*. Lincoln: University of Nebraska Press, 1991.

Sedinger, Tracey. "'If Sight and Shape Be True': The Epistemology of Crossdressing on the London Stage." *Shakespeare Quarterly* 48, no. 1 (1997): 63–79.

Shakespeare, William. *The Riverside Shakespeare*. 2nd ed. Edited by G. B. Evans et al. Boston: Houghton Mifflin, 1997.

Sibscota, George. *The deaf and dumb man's discourse, or, A treatise concerning those that are born deaf and dumb, containing a discovery of their knowledge or understanding*. London, 1670.

Spolsky, Ellen. *Satisfying Skepticism: Embodied Knowledge in the Early Modern World*. Burlington: Ashgate, 2001.

Sprat, Thomas. *History of the Royal Society*. 1667. Facsimile edited by Jackson I. Cope and Harold Whitmore Jones. St. Louis: Washington University Studies, 1958.

Sterry, Peter. *A Discourse of the Freedom of the Will*. London, 1675.

Stillingfleet, Edward. *Origines Sacrae*. London, 1662.

Stubbes, Philip. *Anatomie of Abuses*. London, 1583.

Tasso, Torquato. *Jerusalem Liberated* [*Godfrey of Bulloigne*]. 1581. Translated by Edward Fairfax. London, 1600.

Tayler, Edward. *Nature and Art in Renaissance Literature*. New York: Colombia University Press, 1964.

Thomas, Keith. *Man and the Natural World: Changing Attitudes in England, 1500–1800*. New York: Pantheon, 1983.

Walker, George. *The History of the Creation*. London, 1641.

Waswo, Richard. *Language and Meaning in the Renaissance*. Princeton, N.J.: Princeton University Press, 1987.

Chapter 28

Dipesh Chakrabarty

THE CLIMATE OF HISTORY:
FOUR THESES

THE CURRENT PLANETARY CRISIS of climate change or global warming elicits a variety of responses in individuals, groups, and governments, ranging from denial, disconnect, and indifference to a spirit of engagement and activism of varying kinds and degrees. These responses saturate our sense of the now. Alan Weisman's best-selling book *The World without Us* suggests a thought experiment as a way of experiencing our present: "Suppose that the worst has happened. Human extinction is a fait accompli. . . . Picture a world from which we all suddenly vanished. . . . Might we have left some faint, enduring mark on the universe? . . . Is it possible that, instead of heaving a huge biological sigh of relief, the world without us would miss us?"[1] I am drawn to Weisman's experiment as it tellingly demonstrates how the current crisis can precipitate a sense of the present that disconnects the future from the past by putting such a future beyond the grasp of historical sensibility. The discipline of history exists on the assumption that our past, present, and future are connected by a certain continuity of human experience. We normally envisage the future with the help of the same faculty that allows us to picture the past. Weisman's thought experiment illustrates the historicist paradox that inhabits contemporary moods of anxiety and concern about the finitude of humanity. To go along with Weisman's experiment, we have to insert ourselves into a future "without us" in order to be able to visualize it. Thus, our usual historical practices for visualizing times, past and future, times inaccessible to us personally—the exercise of historical understanding—are thrown into a deep contradiction and confusion. Weisman's experiment indicates how such confusion follows from our contemporary sense of the present insofar as that present gives rise to concerns about our future. Our historical sense of the present, in Weisman's version, has thus become deeply destructive of our general sense of history.

I will return to Weisman's experiment in the last part of this essay. There is much in the debate on climate change that should be of interest to those involved in contemporary discussions about history. For as the idea gains ground that the grave environmental risks of global warming have to do with excessive accumulation in the atmosphere of greenhouse gases produced mainly through the burning of fossil fuel and the industrialized use of animal stock by human beings, certain scientific propositions have come into circulation in the public domain that have profound, even transformative, implications for how we think about human history or about what the historian C. A. Bayly recently called "the birth of the modern world."[2] Indeed, what scientists have said about climate change challenges not only the ideas about the human that usually sustain the discipline of history but also the analytic strategies that postcolonial and postimperial historians have deployed in the last two decades in response to the postwar scenario of decolonization and globalization.

In what follows, I present some responses to the contemporary crisis from a historian's point of view. However, a word about my own relationship to the literature on climate change—and indeed to the crisis itself—may be in order. I am a practicing historian with a strong interest in the nature of history as a form of knowledge, and my relationship to the science of global warming is derived, at some remove, from what scientists and other informed writers have written for the education of the general public. Scientific studies of global warming are often said to have originated with the discoveries of the Swedish scientist Svante Arrhenius in the 1890s, but self-conscious discussions of global warming in the public realm began in the late 1980s and early 1990s, the same period in which social scientists and humanists began to discuss globalization.[3] However, these discussions have so far run parallel to each other. While globalization, once recognized, was of immediate interest to humanists and social scientists, global warming, in spite of a good number of books published in the 1990s, did not become a public concern until the 2000s. The reasons are not far to seek. As early as 1988 James Hansen, the director of NASA's Goddard Institute of Space Studies, told a Senate committee about global warming and later remarked to a group of reporters on the same day, "It's time to stop waffling . . . and say that the greenhouse effect is here and is affecting our climate."[4] But governments, beholden to special interests and wary of political costs, would not listen. George H. W. Bush, then the president of the United States, famously quipped that he was going to fight the greenhouse effect with the "White House effect."[5] The situation changed in the 2000s when the warnings became dire, and the signs of the crisis—such as the drought in Australia, frequent cyclones and brush fires, crop failures in many parts of the world, the melting of Himalayan and other mountain glaciers and of the polar ice caps, and the increasing acidity of the seas and the damage to the food chain—became politically and economically inescapable. Added to this were growing concerns, voiced by many, about the rapid destruction of other species and about the global footprint of a human population poised to pass the nine billion mark by 2050.[6]

As the crisis gathered momentum in the last few years, I realized that all my readings in theories of globalization, Marxist analysis of capital, subaltern studies, and postcolonial criticism over the last twenty-five years, while enormously useful in studying globalization, had not really prepared me for making sense of this planetary conjuncture within which humanity finds itself today. The change of mood in globalization analysis may be seen by comparing Giovanni Arrighi's masterful history of world capitalism, *The Long Twentieth Century* (1994), with his more recent *Adam Smith in Beijing* (2007), which, among other things, seeks to understand the implications of the economic rise of China. The first book, a long meditation on the chaos internal to capitalist economies, ends with the thought of capitalism burning up humanity "in the horrors (or glories) of the escalating violence that has accompanied the liquidation of the Cold War world order." It is clear that the heat that burns the world in Arrighi's narrative comes from the engine of capitalism and not from global warming. By the time Arrighi comes to write *Adam Smith in Beijing,* however, he is much more concerned with the question of ecological limits to capitalism. That theme provides the concluding note of the book, suggesting the distance that a critic such as Arrighi has traveled in the thirteen years that separate the publication of the two books.[7] If, indeed, globalization and global warming are born of overlapping processes, the question is, How do we bring them together in our understanding of the world?

Not being a scientist myself, I also make a fundamental assumption about the science of climate change. I assume the science to be right in its broad outlines. I thus assume that the views expressed particularly in the 2007 Fourth Assessment Report of the Intergovernmental Panel on Climate Change of the United Nations, in the *Stern Review,* and in the many books that have been published recently by scientists and scholars seeking to explain the science of global warming leave me with enough rational ground for accepting, unless the scientific consensus shifts in a major way, that there is a large measure of truth to anthropogenic theories of climate change.[8] For this position, I depend on observations such as the following one reported by Naomi Oreskes, a historian of science at the University of California, San Diego. Upon examining the abstracts of 928 papers on global warming published in specialized peer-reviewed scientific journals between 1993 and 2003, Oreskes found that not a single one sought to refute the "consensus" among scientists "over the reality of human-induced climate change." There is disagreement over the amount and direction of change. But "virtually all professional climate scientists," writes Oreskes, "agree on the reality of human-induced climate change, but debate continues on tempo and mode."[9] Indeed, in what I have read so far, I have not seen any reason yet for remaining a global-warming skeptic.

The scientific consensus around the proposition that the present crisis of climate change is man-made forms the basis of what I have to say here. In the interest of clarity and focus, I present my propositions in the form of four theses. The last three theses follow from the first one. I begin with the proposition that anthropogenic explanations of climate change spell the collapse of the age-old humanist distinction between natural history and human history and end by returning to the question I opened with: How does the crisis of climate change appeal to our sense of human universale while challenging at the same time our capacity for historical understanding?

Thesis 1: Anthropogenic Explanations of Climate Change Spell the Collapse of the Age-old Humanist Distinction between Natural History and Human History

Philosophers and students of history have often displayed a conscious tendency to separate human history—or the story of human affairs, as R. G. Collingwood put it—from natural history, sometimes proceeding even to deny that nature could ever have history quite in the same way humans have it. This practice itself has a long and rich past of which, for reasons of space and personal limitations, I can only provide a very provisional, thumbnail, and somewhat arbitrary sketch.[10]

We could begin with the old Viconian-Hobbesian idea that we, humans, could have proper knowledge of only civil and political institutions because we made them, while nature remains God's work and ultimately inscrutable to man. "The true is identical with the created: *verum ipsum factum*" is how Croce summarized Vico's famous dictum.[11] Vico scholars have sometimes protested that Vico did not make such a drastic separation between the natural and the human sciences as Croce and others read into his writings, but even they admit that such a reading is widespread.[12]

This Viconian understanding was to become a part of the historian's common sense in the nineteenth and twentieth centuries. It made its way into Marx's famous utterance that "men make their own history, but they do not make it just as they please" and into the title of the Marxist archaeologist V. Gordon Childe's well-known book, *Man Makes Himself.*[13] Croce seems to have been a major source of this distinction in the second half of the twentieth century through his influence on "the lonely Oxford historicist" Collingwood who, in turn, deeply influenced E. H. Carr's 1961 book, *What Is History?* which is still perhaps one of the best-selling books on the historian's craft.[14] Croce's thoughts, one could say, unbeknown to his legatees and with unforeseeable modifications, have triumphed in our understanding of history in the postcolonial age. Behind Croce and his adaptations of Hegel and hidden in Croce's creative misreading of his predecessors stands the more distant and foundational figure of Vico.[15] The connections here, again, are many and complex. Suffice it to say for now that Croce's 1911 book, *La filosofia di Giambattista Vico,* dedicated, significantly, to Wilhelm Windelband, was translated into English in 1913 by none other than Collingwood, who was an admirer, if not a follower, of the Italian master.

However, Collingwood's own argument for separating natural history from human ones developed its own inflections, while running, one might say, still on broadly Viconian lines as interpreted by Croce. Nature, Collingwood remarked, has no "inside." "In the case of nature, this distinction between the outside and the inside of an event does not arise. The events of nature are mere events, not the acts of agents whose thought the scientist endeavours to trace." Hence, "all history properly so called is the history of human affairs." The historian's job is "to think himself into [an] action, to discern the thought of its agent." A distinction, therefore, has "to be made between historical and non-historical human actions. . . . So far as man's conduct is determined by what may be called his animal nature, his impulses and appetites, it is non-historical; the process of those activities is a natural process." Thus, says Collingwood, "the historian is not interested in the fact that men eat and sleep and make love and thus satisfy their natural appetites; but he is interested in the social customs which they create by their thought as a framework within which these appetites find satisfaction in ways sanctioned by convention and morality." Only the history of the social construction of the body, not the history of the body as such, can be studied. By splitting the human into the natural and the social or cultural, Collingwood saw no need to bring the two together.[16]

In discussing Croce's 1893 essay "History Subsumed under the Concept of Art," Collingwood wrote, "Croce, by denying [the German idea] that history was a science at all, cut himself at one blow loose from naturalism, and set his face towards an idea of history as something radically different from nature."[17] David Roberts gives a fuller account of the more mature position in Croce. Croce drew on the writings of Ernst Mach and Henri Poincaré to argue that "the concepts of the natural sciences are human constructs elaborated for human purposes." "When we peer into nature," he said, "we find only ourselves." We do not "understand ourselves best as part of the natural world." So, as Roberts puts it, "Croce proclaimed that there is no world but the human world, then took over the central doctrine of Vico that we can know the human world because we have made it." For Croce, then, all material objects were subsumed into human thought. No rocks, for example, existed in themselves. Croce's idealism, Roberts explains, "does not mean that rocks, for example, 'don't exist' without human beings to think them. Apart from human concern and language, they neither exist nor do not exist, since 'exist' is a human concept that has meaning only within a context of human concerns and purposes."[18] Both Croce and Collingwood would thus enfold human history and nature, to the extent that the latter could be said to have history, into purposive human action. What exists beyond that does not "exist" because it does not exist for humans in any meaningful sense.

In the twentieth century, however, other arguments, more sociological or materialist, have existed alongside the Viconian one. They too have continued to justify the separation of human from natural history. One influential though perhaps infamous example would be the booklet on the Marxist philosophy of history that Stalin published in 1938, *Dialectical and Historical Materialism.* This is how Stalin put the problem:

Geographical environment is unquestionably one of the constant and indispensable conditions of development of society and, of course, . . . [it] accelerates or retards its development. But its influence is not the *determining* influence, inasmuch as the changes and development of society proceed at an incomparably faster rate than the changes and development of geographical environment. In the space of 3000 years three different social systems have been successfully superseded in Europe: the primitive communal system, the slave system and the feudal system. . . . Yet during this period geographical conditions in Europe have either not changed at all, or have changed so slightly that geography takes no note of them. And that is quite natural. Changes in geographical environment of any importance require millions of years, whereas a few hundred or a couple of thousand years are enough for even very important changes in the system of human society.[19]

For all its dogmatic and formulaic tone, Stalin's passage captures an assumption perhaps common to historians of the mid-twentieth century: man's environment did change but changed so slowly as to make the history of man's relation to his environment almost timeless and thus not a subject of historiography at all. Even when Fernand Braudel rebelled against the state of the discipline of history as he found it in the late 1930s and proclaimed his rebellion later in 1949 through his great book *The Mediterranean,* it was clear that he rebelled mainly against historians who treated the environment simply as a silent and passive backdrop to their historical narratives, something dealt with in the introductory chapter but forgotten thereafter, as if, as Braudel put it, "the flowers did not come back every spring, the flocks of sheep migrate every year, or the ships sail on a real sea that changes with the seasons." In composing *The Mediterranean,* Braudel wanted to write a history in which the seasons—"a history of constant repetition, ever-recurring cycles"—and other recurrences in nature played an active role in molding human actions.[20] The environment, in that sense, had an agentive presence in Braudel's pages, but the idea that nature was mainly repetitive had a long and ancient history in European thought, as Gadamer showed in his discussion of Johann Gustav Droysen.[21] Braudel's position was no doubt a great advance over the kind of nature-as-a-backdrop argument that Stalin developed. But it shared a fundamental assumption, too, with the stance adopted by Stalin: the history of "man's relationship to the environment" was so slow as to be "almost timeless."[22] In today's climatologists' terms, we could say that Stalin and Braudel and others who thought thus did not have available to them the idea, now widespread in the literature on global warming, that the climate, and hence the overall environment, can sometimes reach a tipping point at which this slow and apparently timeless backdrop for human actions transforms itself with a speed that can only spell disaster for human beings.

If Braudel, to some degree, made a breach in the binary of natural/ human history, one could say that the rise of environmental history in the late twentieth century made the breach wider. It could even be argued that environmental historians have sometimes indeed progressed towards producing what could be called natural histories of man. But there is a very important difference between the understanding of the human being that these histories have been based on and the agency of the human now being proposed by scientists writing on climate change. Simply put, environmental history, where it was not straightforwardly cultural, social, or economic history, looked upon human beings as biological agents. Alfred Crosby, Jr., whose book *The Columbian Exchange* did much to pioneer the "new" environmental histories in the early 1970s, put the point thus in his original preface: "Man is a biological entity before he is a Roman Catholic or a capitalist or anything else."[23] The recent book by Daniel Lord Smail, *On Deep History and the Brain,* is adventurous in attempting to connect knowledge gained from evolutionary and neurosciences with human histories. Smail's book pursues possible connections between biology and culture—between the history of the human brain and cultural history, in particular—while being always sensitive to the limits of biological reasoning. But it is the history of human biology and not any recent theses about the newly acquired geological agency of humans that concerns Smail.[24]

Scholars writing on the current climate-change crisis are indeed saying something significantly different from what environmental historians have said so far. In unwittingly destroying the artificial but time-honored distinction between natural and human histories, climate scientists posit that the human being has become something much larger than the simple biological agent that he or she always has been. Humans now wield a geological force. As Oreskes puts it: "To deny that global warming is real is precisely to deny that humans have become geological agents, changing the most basic physical processes of the earth."

> For centuries, [she continues,] scientists thought that earth processes were so large and powerful that nothing we could do could change them. This was a basic tenet of geological science: that human chronologies were insignificant compared with the vastness of geological time; that human activities were insignificant compared with the force of geological processes. And once they were. But no more. There are now so many of us cutting down so many trees and burning so many billions of tons of fossil fuels that we have indeed become geological agents. We have changed the chemistry of our atmosphere, causing sea level to rise, ice to melt, and climate to change. There is no reason to think otherwise.[25]

Biological agents, geological agents—two different names with very different consequences. Environmental history, to go by Crosby's masterful survey of the origins and the state of the field in 1995, has much to do with biology and geography but hardly ever imagined human impact on the planet on a geological scale. It was still a vision of man "as a prisoner of climate," as Crosby put it quoting Braudel, and not of man as the maker of it.[26] To call human beings geological agents is to scale up our imagination of the human. Humans are biological agents, both collectively and as individuals. They have always been so. There was no point in human history when humans were not biological agents. But we can become geological agents only historically and collectively, that is, when we have reached numbers and invented technologies that are on a scale large enough to have an impact on the planet itself. To call ourselves geological agents is to attribute to us a force on the same scale as that released at other times when there has been a mass extinction of species. We seem to be currently going through that kind of a period. The current "rate in the loss of species diversity," specialists argue, "is similar in intensity to the event around 65 million years ago which wiped out the dinosaurs."[27] Our footprint was not always that large. Humans began to acquire this agency only since the Industrial Revolution, but the process really picked up in the second half of the twentieth century. Humans have become geological agents very recently in human history. In that sense, we can say that it is only very recently that the distinction between human and natural histories—much of which had been preserved even in environmental histories that saw the two entities in interaction—has begun to collapse. For it is no longer a question simply of man having an interactive relation with nature. This humans have always had, or at least that is how man has been imagined in a large part of what is generally called the Western tradition.[28] Now it is being claimed that humans are a force of nature in the geological sense. A fundamental assumption of Western (and now universal) political thought has come undone in this crisis.[29]

Thesis 2: The Idea of the Anthropocene, the New Geological Epoch When Humans Exist as a Geological Force, Severely Qualifies Humanist Histories of Modernity/Globalization

How to combine human cultural and historical diversity with human freedom has formed one of the key underlying questions of human histories written of the period from 1750 to the years of present-day globalization. Diversity, as Gadamer pointed out with reference to Leopold von Ranke, was itself a figure of freedom in the historian's imagination of the historical process.[30] *Freedom* has, of course, meant different things at different times, ranging from ideas of human and citizens' rights to those of decolonization and self-rule. Freedom, one could say, is a blanket category for diverse imaginations of human autonomy and sovereignty. Looking at the works of Kant, Hegel, or Marx; nineteenth-century ideas of progress and class struggle; the struggle against slavery; the Russian and Chinese revolutions; the resistance to Nazism and Fascism; the decolonization movements of the 1950s and 1960s and the revolutions in Cuba and Vietnam; the evolution and explosion of the rights discourse; the fight for civil rights for African Americans, indigenous peoples, Indian *Dalits,* and other minorities; down to the kind of arguments that, say, Amartya Sen put forward in his book *Development as Freedom,* one could say that freedom has been the most important motif of written accounts of human history of these two hundred and fifty years. Of course, as I have already noted, freedom has not always carried the same meaning for everyone. Francis Fukuyama's understanding of freedom would be significantly different from that of Sen. But this semantic capaciousness of the word only speaks to its rhetorical power.

In no discussion of freedom in the period since the Enlightenment was there ever any awareness of the geological agency that human beings were acquiring at the same time as and through processes closely linked to their acquisition of freedom. Philosophers of freedom were mainly, and understandably, concerned with how humans would escape the injustice, oppression, inequality, or even uniformity foisted on them by other humans or human-made systems. Geological time and the chronology of human histories remained unrelated. This distance between the two calendars, as we have seen, is what climate scientists now claim has collapsed. The period I have mentioned, from 1750 to now, is also the time when human beings switched from wood and other renewable fuels to large-scale use of fossil fuel—first coal and then oil and gas. The mansion of modern freedoms stands on an ever-expanding base of fossil-fuel use. Most of our freedoms so far have been energy-intensive. The period of human history usually associated with what we today think of as the institutions of civilization—the beginnings of agriculture, the founding of cities, the rise of the religions we know, the invention of writing—began about ten thousand years ago, as the planet moved from one geological period, the last ice age or the Pleistocene, to the more recent and warmer Holocene. The Holocene is the period we are supposed to be in; but the possibility of anthropogenic climate change has raised the question of its termination. Now that humans—thanks to our numbers, the burning of fossil fuel, and other related activities—have become a geological agent on the planet, some scientists have proposed that we recognize the beginning of a new geological era, one in which humans act as a main determinant of the environment of the planet. The name they have coined for this new geological age is Anthropocene. The proposal was first made by the Nobel-winning chemist Paul J. Crutzen and his collaborator, a marine science specialist, Eugene F. Stoermer. In a short statement published in 2000, they said, "Considering . . . [the] major and still growing impacts of human activities on earth and atmosphere, and at all, including global, scales, it seems to us more than appropriate to emphasize the central role of mankind in geology and ecology by proposing to use the term 'anthropocene' for the current geological epoch."[31] Crutzen elaborated on the proposal in a short piece published in *Nature* in 2002:

For the past three centuries, the effects of humans on the global environment have escalated. Because of these anthropogenic emissions of carbon dioxide, global climate may depart significantly from natural behaviour for many millennia to come. It seems appropriate to assign the term "Anthropocene" to the present, . . . human-dominated, geological epoch, supplementing the Holocene—the warm period of the past 10–12 millennia. The Anthropocene could be said to have started in the latter part of the eighteenth century, when analyses of air trapped in polar ice showed the beginning of growing global concentrations of carbon dioxide and methane. This date also happens to coincide with James Watt's design of the steam engine in 1784.[32]

It is, of course, true that Crutzen's saying so does not make the Anthropocene an officially accepted geologic period. As Mike Davis comments, "in geology, as in biology or history, periodization is a complex, controversial art," involving, always, vigorous debates and contestation.[33] The name Holocene for "the post-glacial geological epoch of the past ten to twelve thousand years" ("A," p. 17), for example, gained no immediate acceptance when proposed—apparently by Sir Charles Lyell—in 1833. The International Geological Congress officially adopted the name at their meeting in Bologna after about fifty years in 1885 (see "A," p. 17). The same goes for Anthropocene. Scientists have engaged Crutzen and his colleagues on the question of when exactly the Anthropocene may have begun. But the February 2008 newsletter of the Geological Society of America, *GSA Today*, opens with a statement signed by the members of the Stratigraphy Commission of the Geological Society of London accepting Crutzen's definition and dating of the Anthropocene.[34] Adopting a "conservative" approach, they conclude: "Sufficient evidence has emerged of stratigraphically significant change (both elapsed and imminent) for recognition of the Anthropocene—currently a vivid yet informal metaphor of global environmental change—as a new geological epoch to be considered for formalization by international discussion."[35] There is increasing evidence that the term is gradually winning acceptance among social scientists as well.[36]

So, has the period from 1750 to now been one of freedom or that of the Anthropocene? Is the Anthropocene a critique of the narratives of freedom? Is the geological agency of humans the price we pay for the pursuit of freedom? In some ways, yes. As Edward O. Wilson said in his *The Future of Life:* "Humanity has so far played the role of planetary killer, concerned only with its own short-term survival. We have cut much of the heart out of biodiversity. . . . If Emi, the Sumatran rhino could speak, she might tell us that the twenty-first century is thus far no exception."[37] But the relation between Enlightenment themes of freedom and the collapsing of human and geological chronologies seems more complicated and contradictory than a simple binary would allow. It is true that human beings have tumbled into being a geological agent through our own decisions. The Anthropocene, one might say, has been an unintended consequence of human choices. But it is also clear that for humans any thought of the way out of our current predicament cannot but refer to the idea of deploying reason in global, collective life. As Wilson put it: "We know more about the problem now. . . . We know what to do" (*FL,* p. 102). Or, to quote Crutzen and Stoermer again:

Mankind will remain a major geological force for many millennia, maybe millions of years, to come. To develop a world-wide accepted strategy leading to sustainability of ecosystems against human-induced stresses will be one of the great future tasks of mankind, requiring intensive research efforts and wise application of knowledge thus acquired. . . . An exciting, but also difficult and daunting task lies ahead of the global research and engineering community to guide mankind towards global, sustainable, environmental management.

[""A,"" p. 18]

Logically, then, in the era of the Anthropocene, we need the Enlightenment (that is, reason) even more than in the past. There is one consideration though that qualifies this optimism about the role of reason and that has to do with the most common shape that freedom takes in human societies: politics. Politics has never been based on reason alone. And politics in the age of the masses and in a world already complicated by sharp inequalities between and inside nations is something no one can control. "Sheer demographic momentum," writes Davis, "will increase the world's urban population by 3 billion people over the next 40 years (90% of them in poor cities), and no one—absolutely no one [including, one might say, scholars on the Left]—has a clue how a planet of slums, with growing food and energy crises, will accommodate their biological survival, much less their inevitable aspirations to basic happiness and dignity" ("LIS").

It is not surprising then that the crisis of climate change should produce anxieties precisely around futures that we cannot visualize. Scientists' hope that reason will guide us out of the present predicament is reminiscent of the social opposition between the myth of Science and the actual politics of the sciences that Bruno Latour discusses in his *Politics of Nature*.[38] Bereft of any sense of politics, Wilson can only articulate his sense of practicality as a philosopher's hope mixed with anxiety: "Perhaps we will act in time" (*FL*, p. 102). Yet the very science of global warming produces of necessity political imperatives. Tim Flannery's book, for instance, raises the dark prospects of an "Orwellian nightmare" in a chapter entitled "2084: The Carbon Dictatorship?"[39] Mark Maslin concludes his book with some gloomy thoughts: "It is unlikely that global politics will solve global warming. Technofixes are dangerous or cause problems as bad as the ones they are aimed at fixing. . . . [Global warming] requires nations and regions to plan for the next 50 years, something that most societies are unable to do because of the very short-term nature of politics." His recommendation, "we must prepare for the worst and adapt," coupled with Davis's observations about the coming "planet of slums" places the question of human freedom under the cloud of the Anthropocene.[40]

Thesis 3: The Geological Hypothesis Regarding the Anthropocene Requires Us to Put Global Histories of Capital in Conversation with the Species History of Humans

Analytic frameworks engaging questions of freedom by way of critiques of capitalist globalization have *not*, in any way, become obsolete in the age of climate change. If anything, as Davis shows, climate change may well end up accentuating all the inequities of the capitalist world order if the interests of the poor and vulnerable are neglected (see "LIS"). Capitalist globalization exists; so should its critiques. But these critiques do not give us an adequate hold on human history once we accept that the crisis of climate change is here with us and may exist as part of this planet for much longer than capitalism or long after capitalism has undergone many more historic mutations. The problematic of globalization allows us to read climate change only as a crisis of capitalist management. While there is no denying that climate change has profoundly to do with the history of capital, a critique that is only a critique of capital is not sufficient for addressing questions relating to human history once the crisis of climate change has been acknowledged and the Anthropocene has begun to loom on the horizon of our present. The geologic now of the Anthropocene has become entangled with the now of human history.

Scholars who study human beings in relation to the crisis of climate change and other ecological problems emerging on a world scale make a distinction between the recorded history of human beings and their deep history. Recorded history refers, very broadly, to the ten thousand years that have passed since the invention of agriculture but more usually to the last four thousand years or so for which written records exist. Historians of modernity and "early modernity" usually move in the archives of the last four hundred years. The history of humans that goes beyond these years of written records constitutes what other students of human pasts—not professional historians—call deep history. As Wilson, one of the main proponents of this distinction, writes: "Human behavior is seen as the product not just of recorded history, ten thousand years recent, but of deep history, the combined genetic and cultural changes that created humanity over hundreds of [thousands of] years."[41] It, of course, goes to the credit of Smail that he has attempted to explain to professional historians the intellectual appeal of deep history.[42]

Without such knowledge of the deep history of humanity it would be difficult to arrive at a secular understanding of why climate change constitutes a crisis for humans. Geologists and climate scientists may explain why the current phase of global warming—as distinct from the warming of the planet that has happened before—is anthropogenic in nature, but the ensuing crisis for humans is not understandable unless one works out the consequences of that warming. The consequences make sense only if we think of humans as a form of life and look on human history as part of the history of life on this planet. For, ultimately, what the warming of the planet threatens is not the geological planet itself but the very conditions, both biological and geological, on which the survival of human life as developed in the Holocene period depends.

The word that scholars such as Wilson or Crutzen use to designate life in the human form—and in other living forms—is *species*. They speak of the human being as a species and find that category useful in thinking about the nature of the current crisis. It is a word that will never occur in any standard history or political-economic analysis of globalization by scholars on the Left, for the analysis of globalization refers, for good reasons, only to the recent and recorded history of humans. Species thinking, on the other hand, is connected to the enterprise of deep history. Further, Wilson and Crutzen actually find such thinking essential to visualizing human well-being. As Wilson writes: "We need this longer view . . . not only to understand our species but more firmly to secure its future" (*SN*, p. x). The task of placing, historically, the crisis of climate change thus requires us to bring together intellectual formations that are somewhat in tension with each other: the planetary and the global; deep and recorded histories; species thinking and critiques of capital.

In saying this, I work somewhat against the grain of historians' thinking on globalization and world history. In a landmark essay published in 1995 and entitled "World History in a Global Age," Michael Geyer and Charles Bright wrote, "At the end of the twentieth century, we encounter, not a universalizing and single modernity but an integrated world of multiple and multiplying modernities." "As far as world history is concerned," they said, "there is no universalizing spirit. . . . There are, instead, many very specific, very material and pragmatic practices that await critical reflection and historical study." Yet, thanks to global connections forged by trade, empires, and capitalism, "we confront a startling new condition: humanity, which has been the subject of world history for many centuries and civilizations, has now come into the purview of all human beings. This humanity is extremely polarized into rich and poor."[43] This humanity, Geyer and Bright imply in the spirit of the philosophies of difference, is not one. It does not, they write, "form a single homogenous civilization." "Neither is this humanity any longer a mere species or a natural condition. For the first time," they say, with some existentialist flourish, "we as human beings collectively constitute ourselves and, hence, are responsible for ourselves" ("WH," p. 1059). Clearly, the scientists who advocate the idea of the Anthropocene are saying something quite the contrary. They argue that because humans constitute a particular kind of species they can, in the process of dominating other species, acquire the status of a geologic force. Humans, in other words, have become a natural condition, at least today. How do we create a conversation between these two positions?

It is understandable that the biological-sounding talk of species should worry historians. They feel concerned about their finely honed sense of contingency and freedom in human affairs having to cede ground to a more deterministic view of the world. Besides, there are always, as Smail recognizes, dangerous historical examples of the political use of biology.[44] The idea of species, it is feared, in addition, may introduce a powerful degree of essentialism in our understanding of humans. I will return to the question of contingency later in this section, but, on the issue of essentialism, Smail helpfully points out why species cannot be thought of in essentialist terms:

> Species, according to Darwin, are not fixed entities with natural essences imbued in them by the Creator. . . . Natural selection does not homogenize the individuals of a species. . . . Given this state of affairs, the search for a normal . . . nature and body type [of any particular species] is futile. And so it goes for the equally futile quest to identify "human nature." Here, as in so many areas, biology and cultural studies are fundamentally congruent.[45]

It is clear that different academic disciplines position their practitioners differently with regard to the question of how to view the human being. All disciplines have to create their objects of study. If medicine or biology reduces the human to a certain specific understanding of him or her, humanist historians often do not realize that the protagonists of their stories—persons—are reductions, too. Absent personhood, there is no human subject of history. That is why Derrida earned the wrath of Foucault by pointing out that any desire to enable or allow madness *itself* to speak in a history of madness would be "the *maddest* aspect" of the project.[46] An object of critical importance to humanists of all traditions, personhood is nevertheless no less of a reduction of or an abstraction from the embodied and whole human being than, say, the human skeleton discussed in an anatomy class.

The crisis of climate change calls on academics to rise above their disciplinary prejudices, for it is a crisis of many dimensions. In that context, it is interesting to observe the role that the category of species has begun to play among scholars, including economists, who have already gone further than historians in investigating and explaining the nature of this crisis. The economist Jeffrey Sachs's book, *Common Wealth,* meant for the educated but lay public, uses the idea of species as central to its argument and devotes a whole chapter to the Anthropocene.[47] In fact, the scholar from whom Sachs solicited a foreword for his book was none other than Edward Wilson. The concept of species plays a quasi-Hegelian role in Wilson's foreword in the same way as the multitude or the masses in Marxist writings. If Marxists of various hues have at different times thought that the good of humanity lay in the prospect of the oppressed or the multitude realizing their own global unity through a process of coming into self-consciousness, Wilson pins his hope on the unity possible through our collective self-recognition as a species: "Humanity has consumed or transformed enough of Earth's irreplaceable resources to be in better shape than ever before. We are smart enough and now, one hopes, well informed enough to achieve self-understanding as a unified species. . . . We will be wise to look on ourselves as a species."[48]

Yet doubts linger about the use of the idea of species in the context of climate change, and it would be good to deal with one that can easily arise among critics on the Left. One could object, for instance, that all the anthropogenic factors contributing to global warming—the burning of fossil fuel, industrialization of animal stock, the clearing of tropical and other forests, and so on—are after all part of a larger story: the unfolding of capitalism in the West and the imperial or quasi-imperial domination by the West of the rest of the world. It is from that recent history of the West that the elite of China, Japan, India, Russia, and Brazil have drawn inspiration in attempting to develop their own trajectories toward superpower politics and global domination through capitalist economic, technological, and military might. If this is broadly true, then does not the talk of species or mankind simply serve to hide the reality of capitalist production and the logic of imperial—formal, informal, or machinic in a Deleuzian sense—domination that it fosters? Why should one include the poor of the world—whose carbon footprint is small anyway—by use of such all-inclusive terms as *species* or *mankind* when the blame for the current crisis should be squarely laid at the door of the rich nations in the first place and of the richer classes in the poorer ones?

We need to stay with this question a little longer; otherwise the difference between the present historiography of globalization and the historiography demanded by anthropogenic theories of climate change will not be clear to us. Though some scientists would want to date the Anthropocene from the time agriculture was invented, my readings mostly suggest that our falling into the Anthropocene was neither an ancient nor an inevitable happening. Human civilization surely did not begin on condition that, one day in his history, man would have to shift from wood to coal and from coal to petroleum and gas. That there was much historical contingency in the transition from wood to coal as the main source of energy has been demonstrated powerfully by Kenneth Pomeranz in his pathbreaking book *The Great Divergence*.[49] Coincidences and historical accidents similarly litter the stories of the "discovery" of oil, of the oil tycoons, and of the automobile industry as they do any other histories.[50] Capitalist societies themselves have not remained the same since the beginning of capitalism.[51] Human population, too, has dramatically increased since the Second World War. India alone is now more than three times more populous than at independence in 1947. Clearly, nobody is in a position to claim that there is something inherent to the human species that has pushed us finally into the Anthropocene. We have stumbled into it. The way to it was no doubt through industrial civilization. (I do not make a distinction here between the capitalist and socialist societies we have had so far, for there was never any principled difference in their use of fossil fuel.)

If the industrial way of life was what got us into this crisis, then the question is, Why think in terms of species, surely a category that belongs to a much longer history? Why could not the narrative of capitalism—and hence its critique—be sufficient as a framework for interrogating the history of climate change and understanding its consequences? It seems true that the crisis of climate change has been necessitated by the high-energy-consuming models of society that capitalist industrialization has created and promoted, but the current crisis has brought into view certain other conditions for the existence of life in the human form that have no intrinsic connection to the logics of capitalist, nationalist, or socialist identities. They are connected rather to the history of life on this planet, the way different life-forms connect to one another, and the way the mass extinction of one species could spell danger for another. Without such a history of life, the crisis of climate change has no human "meaning." For, as I have said before, it is not a crisis for the inorganic planet in any meaningful sense.

In other words, the industrial way of life has acted much like the rabbit hole in Alice's story; we have slid into a state of things that forces on us a recognition of some of the parametric (that is, boundary) conditions for the existence of institutions central to our idea of modernity and the meanings we derive from them. Let me explain. Take the case of the agricultural revolution, so called, of ten thousand years ago. It was not just an expression of human inventiveness. It was made possible by certain changes in the amount of carbon dioxide in the atmosphere, a certain stability of the climate, and a degree of warming of the planet that followed the end of the Ice Age (the Pleistocene era)—things over which human beings had no control. "There can be little doubt," writes one of the editors of *Humans at the End of the Ice Age*, "that the basic phenomenon—the waning of the Ice Age—was the result of the Milankovich phenomena: the orbital and tilt relationships between the Earth and the Sun."[52] The temperature of the planet stabilized within a zone that allowed grass to grow. Barley and wheat are among the oldest of such grasses. Without this lucky "long summer" or what one climate scientist has called an "extraordinary" "fluke" of nature in the history of the planet, our industrial-agricultural way of life would not have been possible.[53] In other words, whatever our socioeconomic and technological choices, whatever the rights we wish to celebrate as our freedom, we cannot afford to destabilize conditions (such as the temperature zone in which the planet exists) that work like boundary parameters of human existence. These parameters are independent of capitalism or socialism. They have been stable for much longer than the histories of these institutions and have allowed human beings to become the dominant species on earth. Unfortunately, we have now ourselves become a geological agent disturbing these parametric conditions needed for our own existence.

This is not to deny the historical role that the richer and mainly Western nations of the world have played in emitting greenhouse gases. To speak of species thinking is not to resist the politics of "common but differentiated responsibility" that China, India, and other developing countries seem keen to pursue when it comes to reducing greenhouse gas emissions.[54] Whether we blame climate change on those who are retrospectively guilty—that is, blame the West for their past performance—or those who are prospectively guilty (China has just surpassed the United States as the largest emitter of carbon dioxide, though not on a per capita basis) is a question that is tied no doubt to the histories of capitalism and modernization.[55] But scientists' discovery of the fact that human beings have in the process become a geological agent points to a shared catastrophe that we have all fallen into. Here is how Crutzen and Stoermer describe that catastrophe:

> The expansion of mankind . . . has been astounding. . . . During the past 3 centuries human population increased tenfold to 6000 million, accompanied e.g. by a growth in cattle population to 1400 million (about one cow per average size family). . . . In a few generations mankind is exhausting the fossil fuels that were generated over several hundred million years. The release of SO, . . . to the atmosphere by coal and oil burning, is at least two times larger than the sum of all natural emissions . . .; more than half of all accessible fresh water is used by mankind; human activity has increased the species extinction rate by thousand to ten thousand fold in the tropical rain forests Furthermore, mankind releases many toxic substances in the environment. . . . The effects documented include modification of the geo-chemical cycle in large freshwater systems and occur in systems remote from primary sources.
>
> ["A," p. 17]

Explaining this catastrophe calls for a conversation between disciplines and between recorded and deep histories of human beings in the same way that the agricultural revolution of ten thousand years ago could not be explained except through a convergence of three disciplines: geology, archaeology, and history.[56]

Scientists such as Wilson or Crutzen may be politically naive in not recognizing that reason may not be all that guides us in our effective collective choices—in other words, we may collectively end up making some unreasonable choices—but I find it interesting and symptomatic that they speak the language of the Enlightenment. They are not necessarily anticap-italist scholars, and yet clearly they are not for business-as-usual capitalism either.

They see knowledge and reason providing humans not only a way out of this present crisis but a way of keeping us out of harm's way in the future. Wilson, for example, speaks of devising a "wiser use of resources" in a manner that sounds distinctly Kantian (*SN*, p. 199). But the knowledge in question is the knowledge of humans as a species, a species dependent on other species for its own existence, a part of the general history of life. Changing the climate, increasingly not only the average temperature of the planet but also the acidity and the level of the oceans, and destroying the food chain are actions that cannot be in the interest of our lives. These parametric conditions hold irrespective of our political choices. It is therefore impossible to understand global warming as a crisis without engaging the propositions put forward by these scientists. At the same time, the story of capital, the contingent history of our falling into the Anthropocene, cannot be denied by recourse to the idea of species, for the Anthropocene would not have been possible, even as a theory, without the history of industrialization. How do we hold the two together as we think the history of the world since the Enlightenment? How do we relate to a universal history of life—to universal thought, that is—while retaining what is of obvious value in our postcolonial suspicion of the universal? The crisis of climate change calls for thinking simultaneously on both registers, to mix together the immiscible chronologies of capital and species history. This combination, however, stretches, in quite fundamental ways, the very idea of historical understanding.

Thesis 4: The Cross-Hatching of Species History and the History of Capital Is a Process of Probing the Limits of Historical Understanding

Historical understanding, one could say following the Diltheyan tradition, entails critical thinking that makes an appeal to some generic ideas about human experience. As Gadamer pointed out, Dilthey saw "the individual's private world of experience as the starting point for an expansion that, in a living transposition, fills out the narrowness and fortuitousness of his private experience with the infinity of what is available by re-experiencing the historical world." "*Historical consciousness*," in this tradition, is thus "*a mode of self-knowledge*" garnered through critical reflections on one's own and others' (historical actors') experiences.[57] Humanist histories of capitalism will always admit of something called the experience of capitalism. E. P. Thompson's brilliant attempt to reconstruct working-class experience of capitalist labor, for instance, does not make sense without that assumption.[58] Humanist histories are histories that produce meaning through an appeal to our capacity not only to reconstruct but, as Collingwood would have said, to reenact in our own minds the experience of the past.

When Wilson then recommends in the interest of our collective future that we achieve self-understanding as a species, the statement does not correspond to any historical way of understanding and connecting pasts with futures through the assumption of there being an element of continuity to human experience. (See Gadamer's point mentioned above.) Who is the we? We humans never experience ourselves as a species. We can only intellectually comprehend or infer the existence of the human species but never experience it as such. There could be no phenomenology of us as a species. Even if we were to emotionally identify with a word like *mankind*, we would not know what being a species is, for, in species history, humans are only an instance of the concept species as indeed would be any other life form. But one never experiences being a concept.

The discussion about the crisis of climate change can thus produce affect and knowledge about collective human pasts and futures that work at the limits of historical understanding. We experience specific effects of the crisis but not the whole phenomenon. Do we then say, with Geyer and Bright, that "humanity no longer comes into being through 'thought'"

("WH," p. 1060) or say with Foucault that "the human being no longer has any history"?[59] Geyer and Bright go on to write in a Foucaultian spirit: "Its [world history's] task is to make transparent the lineaments of power, underpinned by information, that compress humanity into a single humankind" ("WH," p. 1060).

This critique that sees humanity as an effect of power is, of course, valuable for all the hermeneutics of suspicion that it has taught postcolonial scholarship. It is an effective critical tool in dealing with national and global formations of domination. But I do not find it adequate in dealing with the crisis of global warming. First, inchoate figures of us all and other imaginings of humanity invariably haunt our sense of the current crisis. How else would one understand the title of Weisman's book, *The World without Us,* or the appeal of his brilliant though impossible attempt to depict the experience of New York after we are gone![60] Second, the wall between human and natural history has been breached. We may not experience ourselves as a geological agent, but we appear to have become one at the level of the species. And without that knowledge that defies historical understanding there is no making sense of the current crisis that affects us all. Climate change, refracted through global capital, will no doubt accentuate the logic of inequality that runs through the rule of capital; some people will no doubt gain temporarily at the expense of others. But the whole crisis cannot be reduced to a story of capitalism. Unlike in the crises of capitalism, there are no lifeboats here for the rich and the privileged (witness the drought in Australia or recent fires in the wealthy neighborhoods of California). The anxiety global warming gives rise to is reminiscent of the days when many feared a global nuclear war. But there is a very important difference. A nuclear war would have been a conscious decision on the part of the powers that be. Climate change is an unintended consequence of human actions and shows, only through scientific analysis, the effects of our actions as a species. Species may indeed be the name of a placeholder for an emergent, new universal history of humans that flashes up in the moment of the danger that is climate change. But we can never *understand* this universal. It is not a Hegelian universal arising dialectically out of the movement of history, or a universal of capital brought forth by the present crisis. Geyer and Bright are right to reject those two varieties of the universal. Yet climate change poses for us a question of a human collectivity, an us, pointing to a figure of the universal that escapes our capacity to experience the world. It is more like a universal that arises from a shared sense of a catastrophe. It calls for a global approach to politics without the myth of a global identity, for, unlike a Hegelian universal, it cannot subsume particularities. We may provisionally call it a "negative universal history."[61]

Notes

This essay is dedicated to the memory of Greg Dening.

Thanks are due to Lauren Berlant, James Chandler, Carlo Ginzburg, Tom Mitchell, Sheldon Pollock, Bill Brown, Françoise Meltzer, Debjani Ganguly, Ian Hunter, Julia A. Thomas, and Rochona Majumdar for critical comments on an earlier draft. I wrote the first version of this essay in Bengali for a journal in Calcutta and remain grateful to its editor, Asok Sen, for encouraging me to work on this topic.

1   Alan Weisman, *The World without Us* (New York, 2007), pp. 3–5.

2   See C. A. Bayly, *The Birth of the Modern World, 1780–1914: Global Connections and Comparisons* (Malden, Mass., 2004).

3   The prehistory of the science of global warming going back to nineteenth-century European scientists like Joseph Fourier, Louis Agassiz, and Arrhenius is recounted in many popular publications. See, for example, the book by Bert Bolin, the chairman of the UN's Intergovernmental Panel on Climate Change (1988–97), *A History of the Science and Politics of Climate Change: The Role of the Intergovernmental Panel on Climate Change* (Cambridge, 2007), pt.1.

4   Quoted in Mark Bowen, *Censoring Science: Inside the Political Attack on Dr. James Hansen and the Truth of Global Warming* (New York, 2008), p. 1.

5   Quoted in ibid., p. 228. See also "Too Hot to Handle: Recent Efforts to Censor Jim Hansen," *Boston Globe,* 5 Feb. 2006, p. E1.

6   See, for example, Walter K. Dodds, *Humanity's Footprint: Momentum, Impact, and Our Global Environment* (New York, 2008), pp. 11–62.

7   Giovanni Arrighi, *The Long Twentieth Century: Money, Power, and the Origins of Our Times* (1994; London, 2006), p. 356; see Arrighi, *Adam Smith in Beijing: Lineages of the Twenty-First Century* (London, 2007), pp. 227–389.

8   An indication of the growing popularity of the topic is the number of books published in the last four years with the aim of educating the general reading public about the nature of the crisis. Here is a random list of some of the most recent titles that inform this essay: Mark Maslin, *Global Warming: A Very Short Introduction* (Oxford, 2004); Tim Flannery, *The Weather Makers: The History and Future Impact of Climate Change* (Melbourne, 2005); David Archer, *Global Warming: Understanding the Forecast* (Malden, Mass., 2007); *Global Warming,* ed. Kelly Knauer (New York, 2007); Mark Lynas, *Six Degrees: Our Future on a Hotter Planet* (Washington, D.C., 2008); William H. Calvin, *Global Fever: How to Treat Climate Change* (Chicago, 2008); James Hansen, "Climate Catastrophe," *New Scientist,* 28 July–3 Aug. 2007, pp. 30–34; Hansen et al., "Dangerous Human-Made Interference with Climate: A GISS ModelE Study," *Atmospheric Chemistry and Physics* 7, no. 9 (2007): 2287–2312; and Hansen et al., "Climate Change and Trace Gases," *Philosophical Transactions of the Royal Society,* 15 July 2007, pp. 1925–54. See also Nicholas Stern, *The Economics of Climate Change: The "Stern Review"* (Cambridge, 2007).

9   Naomi Oreskes, "The Scientific Consensus on Climate Change: How Do We Know We're Not Wrong?" in *Climate Change: What It Means for Us, Our Children, and Our Grandchildren,* ed. Joseph F. C. Dimento and Pamela Doughman (Cambridge, Mass., 2007), pp. 73, 74.

10   A long history of this distinction is traced in Paolo Rossi, *The Dark Abyss of Time: The History of the Earth and the History of Nations from Hooke to Vico,* trans. Lydia G. Cochrane (1979; Chicago, 1984).

11   Benedetto Croce, *The Philosophy of Giambattista Vico,* trans. R. G. Collingwood (1913; New Brunswick, N.J., 2002), p. 5. Carlo Ginzburg has alerted me to problems with Collingwood's translation.

12   See the discussion in Perez Zagorin, "Vico's Theory of Knowledge: A Critique," *Philosophical Quarterly* 34 (Jan. 1984): 15–30.

13   Karl Marx, "The Eighteenth Brumaire of Louis Bonaparte," in Marx and Frederick Engels, *Selected Works,* trans. pub., 3 vols. (Moscow, 1969), 1:398. See V. Gordon Childe, *Man Makes Himself* (London, 1941). Indeed, Althusser's revolt in the 1960s against humanism in Marx was in part a jihad against the remnants of Vico in the savant's texts; see Étienne Balibar, personal communication to author, 1 Dec. 2007. I am grateful to Ian Bedford for drawing my attention to complexities in Marx's connections to Vico.

14   David Roberts describes Collingwood as "the lonely Oxford historicist . . ., in important respects a follower of Croce's" (David D. Roberts, *Benedetto Croce and the Uses of Historicism* [Berkeley, 1987], p. 325).

15   On Croce's misreading of Vico, see the discussion in general in Cecilia Miller, *Giambattista Vico: Imagination and Historical Knowledge* (Basingstoke, 1993), and James C. Morrison, "Vico's Principle of *Verum* is *Factum* and the Problem of Historicism," *Journal of the History of Ideas* 39 (Oct.–Dec. 1978): 579–95.

16   Collingwood, *The Idea of History* (1946; New York, 1976), pp. 214, 212, 213, 216.

17   Ibid., p. 193.

18   Roberts, *Benedetto Croce and the Uses of Historicism,* pp. 59, 60, 62.

19   Joseph Stalin, *Dialectical and Historical Materialism* (1938), www.marxists.org/reference/archive/stalin/works/1938/09.htm

20   Fernand Braudel, "Preface to the First Edition," *The Mediterranean and the Mediterranean World in the Age of Philip II,* trans. Siân Reynolds, 2 vols. (1949; London, 1972), 1:20. See also Peter Burke, *The French Historical Revolution: The "Annales" School, 1929–89* (Stanford, Calif., 1990), pp. 32–64.

21   See Hans-Georg Gadamer, *Truth and Method,* 2d ed., trans. Joel Weinsheimer and Donald G. Marshall (1975, 1979; London, 1988), pp. 214–18. See also Bonnie G. Smith, "Gender and the Practices of Scientific History: The Seminar and Archival Research in the Nineteenth Century," *American Historical Review* 100 (Oct. 1995): 1150–76.

22   Braudel, "Preface to the First Edition," p. 20.

23   Alfred W. Crosby, Jr., *The Columbian Exchange: Biological and Cultural Consequences of 1492* (1972; London, 2003), p. xxv.

24   See Daniel Lord Smail, *On Deep History and the Brain* (Berkeley, 2008), pp. 74–189.

25   Oreskes, "The Scientific Consensus," p. 93.

26   Crosby Jr., "The Past and Present of Environmental History," *American Historical Review* 100 (Oct. 1995): 1185.

27   Will Steffen, director of the Centre for Resource and Environmental Studies at the Australian National University, quoted in "Humans Creating New 'Geological Age,' " *The Australian,* 31 Mar. 2008, www.theaustralian.news.com.au/story/0,23458148–5006787,00.html. Steffen's reference was the Millennium Ecosystem Assessment Report of 2005. See also Neil Shubin, "The Disappearance of Species," *Bulletin of the American Academy of Arts and Sciences* 61 (Spring 2008): 17–19.

28   Bill McKibben's argument about the "end of nature" implied the end of nature as "a separate realm that had always served to make us feel smaller" (Bill McKibben, *The End of Nature* [1989; New York, 2006], p. xxii).

29   Bruno Latour's *Politics of Nature: How to Bring the Sciences into Democracy,* trans. Catherine Porter (1999; Cambridge, Mass., 2004), written before the intensification of the debate on global warming, calls into question the entire tradition of organizing the idea of politics around the assumption of a separate realm of nature and points to the problems that this assumption poses for contemporary questions of democracy.

30   Gadamer, *Truth and Method,* p. 206: The historian "knows that everything could have been different, and every acting individual could have acted differently."

31   Paul I. Crutzen and Eugene F. Stoermer, "The Anthropocene," *IGBP [International Geosphere-Biosphere Programme] Newsletter* 41 (2000): 17; hereafter abbreviated "A."

32   Crutzen, "Geology of Mankind," *Nature,* 3 Jan. 2002, p. 23.

33   Mike Davis, "Living on the Ice Shelf: Humanity's Meltdown," 26 June 2008, tomdispatch.com/post/174949; hereafter abbreviated "LIS." I am grateful to Lauren Berlant for bringing this essay to my attention.

34   See William F. Ruddiman, "The Anthropogenic Greenhouse Era Began Thousands of Years Ago," *Climatic Change* 61, no. 3 (2003): 261–93; Crutzen and Steffen, "How Long Have We Been in the Anthropocene Era?" *Climatic Change* 61, no. 3 (2003): 251–57; and Jan Zalasiewicz et al., "Are We Now Living in the Anthropocene?" *GSA Today* 18 (Feb. 2008): 4–8. I am grateful to Neptune Srimal for this reference.

35   Zalasiewicz et al., "Are We Now Living in the Anthropocene?" p. 7. Davis described the London Society as the "world's oldest association of Earth scientists, founded in 1807" ("LIS").

36   See, for instance, Libby Robin and Steffen, "History for the Anthropocene," *History Compass* 5, no. 5 (2007): 1694–1719, and Jeffrey D. Sachs, "The Anthropocene," *Common Wealth: Economics for a Crowded Planet* (New York, 2008), pp. 57–82. Thanks to Debjani Ganguly for drawing my attention to the essay by Robin and Steffen, and to Robin for sharing it with me.

37   Edward O. Wilson, *The Future of Life* (New York, 2002), p. 102; hereafter abbreviated *FL.*

38   See Latour, *Politics of Nature.*

39   Flannery, *The Weather Makers,* p. xiv.

40   Maslin, *Global Warming,* p. 147. For a discussion of how fossil fuels created both the possibilities for and the limits of democracy in the twentieth century, see Timothy Mitchell, "Carbon Democracy," forthcoming in *Economy and Society.* I am grateful to Mitchell for letting me cite this unpublished paper.

41   Wilson, *In Search of Nature* (Washington, D.C., 1996), pp. ix–x; hereafter abbreviated *SN.*

42   See Smail, *On Deep History and the Brain.*

43   Michael Geyer and Charles Bright, "World History in a Global Age," *American Historical Review* 100 (Oct. 1995): 1058–59; hereafter abbreviated "WH."

44   See Smail, *On Deep History and the Brain,* p. 124.

45   Ibid. pp. 124–25.

46   Jacques Derrida, "Cogito and the History of Madness," *Writing and Difference,* trans. Alan Bass (Chicago, 1978), p. 34.

47   See Sachs. *Common Wealth,* pp. 57–82.

48   Wilson, foreword to Sachs, *Common Wealth,* p. xii. Students of Marx may be reminded here of the use of the category "species being" by the young Marx.

49   See Kenneth Pomeranz, *The Great Divergence: Europe, China, and the Making of the Modern World Economy* (Princeton, N.J., 2000).

50   See Mitchell, "Carbon Democracy." See also Edwin Black, *Internal Combustion: How Corporations and Governments Addicted the World to Oil and Derailed the Alternatives* (New York, 2006).

51   Arrighi's *The Long Twentieth Century* is a good guide to these fluctuations in the fortunes of capitalism.

52   Lawrence Guy Straus, "The World at the End of the Last Ice Age," in *Humans at the End of the Ice Age: The Archaeology of the Pleistocene–Holocene Transition,* ed. Lawrence Guy Straus et al. (New York, 1996), p. 5.

53   Flannery, *Weather Makers,* pp. 63, 64.

54   Ashish Kothari, "The Reality of Climate Injustice," *The Hindu,* 18 Nov. 2007, www.hinduonnct. com/thehindu/mag/2007/11/18/stories/2007111850020100.htm

55   I have borrowed the idea of "retrospective" and "prospective" guilt from a discussion led at the Franke Institute for the Humanities by Peter Singer during the Chicago Humanities Festival, November 2007.

56   See Colin Tudge, *Neanderthals, Bandits, and Farmers: How Agriculture Really Began* (New Haven. Conn., 1999), pp. 35–36.

57   Gadamer, *Truth and Method,* pp. 232, 234. See also Michael Ermarth, *Wilhelm Dilthey: The Critique of Historical Reason* (Chicago, 1978), pp. 310–22.

58   See E. P. Thompson, *The Making of the English Working Class* (Harmondsworth, 1963).

59   Michel Foucault, *The Order of Things: An Archaeology of Human Knowledge,* trans. Pub. (1966; New York, 1973), p. 368.

60   See Weisman, *The World without Us,* pp. 25–28.

61   I am grateful to Antonio Y. Vasquez-Arroyo for sharing with me his unpublished paper "Universal History Disavowed: On Critical Theory and Postcolonialism," where he has tried to develop this concept of negative universal history on the basis of his reading of Theodor Adorno and Walter Benjamin.

Chapter 29

Ursula K. Le Guin

THE CARRIER BAG THEORY OF FICTION (1986)

IN THE TEMPERATE and tropical regions where it appears that hominids evolved into human beings, the principal food of the species was vegetable. Sixty-five to eighty percent of what human beings ate in those regions in Paleolithic, Neolithic, and prehistoric times was gathered; only in the extreme Arctic was meat the staple food. The mammoth hunters spectacularly occupy the cave wall and the mind, but what we actually did to stay alive and fat was gather seeds, roots, sprouts, shoots, leaves, nuts, berries, fruits, and grains, adding bugs and mollusks and netting or snaring birds, fish, rats, rabbits, and other tuskless small fry to up the protein. And we didn't even work hard at it——much less hard than peasants slaving in somebody else's field after agriculture was invented, much less hard than paid workers since civilization was invented. The average prehistoric person could make a nice living in about a fifteen-hour work week.

Fifteen hours a week for subsistence leaves a lot of time for other things. So much time that maybe the restless ones who didn't have a baby around to enliven their life, or skill in making or cooking or singing, or very interesting thoughts to think, decided to slope off and hunt mammoths. The skillful hunters then would come staggering back with a load of meat, a lot of ivory, and a story. It wasn't the meat that made the difference. It was the story.

It is hard to tell a really gripping tale of how I wrested a wild-oat seed from its husk, and then another, and then another, and then another, and then another, and then I scratched my gnat bites, and Ool said something funny, and we went to the creek and got a drink and watched newts for a while, and then I found another patch of oats. . . . No, it does not compare, it cannot compete with how I thrust my spear deep into the titanic hairy flank while Oob, impaled on one huge sweeping tusk, writhed screaming, and blood spouted everywhere in crimson torrents, and Boob was crushed to jelly when the mammoth fell on him as I shot my unerring arrow straight through eye to brain.

That story not only has Action, it has a Hero. Heroes are powerful. Before you know it, the men and women in the wild-oat patch and their kids and the skills of the makers and the thoughts of the thoughtful and the songs of the singers are all part of it, have all been pressed into service in the tale of the Hero. But it isn't their story. It's his.

When she was planning the book that ended up as *Three Guineas*, Virginia Woolf wrote a heading in her notebook, "Glossary"; she had thought of reinventing English according to a new plan, in order to tell a different story. One of the entries in this glossary is *heroism*, defined as "botulism." And *hero*, in Woolf's dictionary, is "bottle." The hero as bottle, a stringent reevaluation. I now propose the bottle as hero.

Not just the bottle of gin or wine, but bottle in its older sense of container in general, a thing that holds something else.

If you haven't got something to put it in, food will escape you—even something as uncombative and unresourceful as an oat. You put as many as you can into your stomach while they are handy, that being the primary container; but what about tomorrow morning when you wake up and it's cold and raining and wouldn't it be good to have just a few handfuls of oats to chew on and give little Oom to make her shut up, but how do you get more than one stomachful and one handful home? So you get up and go to the damned soggy oat patch in the rain, and wouldn't it be a good thing if you had something to put Baby Oo Oo in so that you could pick the oats with both hands? A leaf a gourd a shell a net a bag a sling a sack a bottle a pot a box a container. A holder. A recipient.

> The first cultural device was probably a recipient. . . . Many theorizers feel that the earliest cultural inventions must have been a container to hold gathered products and some kind of sling or net carrier.

So says Elizabeth Fisher in *Women's Creation* (McGraw-Hill, 1975). But no, this cannot be. Where is that wonderful, big, long, hard thing, a bone, I believe, that the Ape Man first bashed somebody with in the movie and then, grunting with ecstasy at having achieved the first proper murder, flung up into the sky, and whirling there it became a space ship thrusting its way into the cosmos to fertilize it and produce at the end of the movie a lovely fetus, a boy of course, drifting around the Milky Way without (oddly enough) any womb, any matrix at all? I don't know. I don't even care. I'm not telling that story. We've heard it, we've all heard all about all the sticks and spears and swords, the things to bash and poke and hit with, the long, hard things, but we have not heard about the thing to put things in, the container for the thing contained. That is a new story. That is news.

And yet old. Before—once you think about it, surely long before—the weapon, a late, luxurious, superfluous tool; long before the useful knife and ax; right along with the indispensable whacker, grinder, and digger—for what's the use of digging up a lot of potatoes if you have nothing to lug the ones you can't eat home in—with or before the tool that forces energy outward, we made the tool that brings energy home. It makes sense to me. I am an adherent of what Fisher calls the Carrier Bag Theory of human evolution.

This theory not only explains large areas of theoretical obscurity and avoids large areas of theoretical nonsense (inhabited largely by tigers, foxes, and other highly territorial mammals); it also grounds me, personally, in human culture in a way I never felt grounded before. So long as culture was explained as originating from and elaborating upon the use of long, hard objects for sticking, bashing, and killing, I never thought that I had, or wanted, any particular share in it. ("What Freud mistook for her lack of civilization is woman's lack of *loyalty* to civilization," Lillian Smith observed.) The society, the civilization they were talking about, these theoreticians, was evidently theirs; they owned it, they liked it; they were human, fully human, bashing, sticking, thrusting, killing. Wanting to be human too, I sought for evidence that I was; but if that's what it took, to make a weapon and kill with it, then evidently I was either extremely defective as a human being, or not human at all.

That's right, they said. What you are is a woman. Possibly not human at all, certainly defective. Now be quiet while we go on telling the Story of the Ascent of Man the Hero.

Go on, say I, wandering off towards the wild oats, with Oo Oo in the sling and little Oom carrying the basket. You just go on telling how the mammoth fell on Boob and how

Cain fell on Abel and how the bomb fell on Nagasaki and how the burning jelly fell on the villagers and how the missiles will fall on the Evil Empire, and all the other steps in the Ascent of Man.

If it is a human thing to do to put something you want, because it's useful, edible, or beautiful, into a bag, or a basket, or a bit of rolled bark or leaf, or a net woven of your own hair, or what have you, and then take it home with you, home being another, larger kind of pouch or bag, a container for people, and then later on you take it out and eat it or share it or store it up for winter in a solider container or put it in the medicine bundle or the shrine or the museum, the holy place, the area that contains what is sacred, and then next day you probably do much the same again—if to do that is human, if that's what it takes, then I am a human being after all. Fully, freely, gladly, for the first time.

Not, let it be said at once, an unaggressive or uncombative human being. I am an aging, angry woman laying mightily about me with my handbag, fighting hoodlums off. However I don't, nor does anybody else, consider myself heroic for doing so. It's just one of those damned things you have to do in order to be able to go on gathering wild oats and telling stories.

It is the story that makes the difference. It is the story that hid my humanity from me, the story the mammoth hunters told about bashing, thrusting, raping, killing, about the Hero. The wonderful, poisonous story of Botulism. The killer story.

It sometimes seems that that story is approaching its end. Lest there be no more telling of stories at all, some of us out here in the wild oats, amid the alien corn, think we'd better start telling another one, which maybe people can go on with when the old one's finished. Maybe. The trouble is, we've all let ourselves become part of the killer story, and so we may get finished along with it. Hence it is with a certain feeling of urgency that I seek the nature, subject, words of the other story, the untold one, the life story.

It's unfamiliar, it doesn't come easily, thoughtlessly to the lips as the killer story does; but still, "untold" was an exaggeration. People have been telling the life story for ages, in all sorts of words and ways. Myths of creation and transformation, trickster stories, folktales, jokes, novels . . .

The novel is a fundamentally unheroic kind of story. Of course the Hero has frequently taken it over, that being his imperial nature and uncontrollable impulse, to take everything over and run it while making stern decrees and laws to control his uncontrollable impulse to kill it. So the Hero has decreed through his mouthpieces the Lawgivers, first, that the proper shape of the narrative is that of the arrow or spear, starting *here* and going straight *there* and THOK! hitting its mark (which drops dead); second, that the central concern of narrative, including the novel, is conflict; and third, that the story isn't any good if he isn't in it.

I differ with all of this. I would go so far as to say that the natural, proper, fitting shape of the novel might be that of a sack, a bag. A book holds words. Words hold things. They bear meanings. A novel is a medicine bundle, holding things in a particular, powerful relation to one another and to us.

One relationship among elements in the novel may well be that of conflict, but the reduction of narrative to conflict is absurd. (I have read a how-to-write manual that said, "A story should be seen as a battle," and went on about strategies, attacks, victory, etc.) Conflict, competition, stress, struggle, etc., within the narrative conceived as carrier bag / belly / box / house / medicine bundle, may be seen as necessary elements of a whole which itself cannot be characterized either as conflict or as harmony, since its purpose is neither resolution nor stasis but continuing process.

Finally, it's clear that the Hero does not look well in this bag. He needs a stage or a pedestal or a pinnacle. You put him in a bag and he looks like a rabbit, like a potato.

That is why I like novels: instead of heroes they have people in them.

So, when I came to write science-fiction novels, I came lugging this great heavy sack of stuff, my carrier bag full of wimps and klutzes, and tiny grains of things smaller than a mustard seed, and intricately woven nets which when laboriously unknotted are seen to contain one blue pebble, an imperturbably functioning chronometer telling the time on another world, and a mouse's skull; full of beginnings without ends, of initiations, of losses, of transformations and translations, and far more tricks than conflicts, far fewer triumphs than snares and delusions; full of space ships that get stuck, missions that fail, and people who don't understand. I said it was hard to make a gripping tale of how we wrested the wild oats from their husks, I didn't say it was impossible. Who ever said writing a novel was easy?

If science fiction is the mythology of modern technology, then its myth is tragic. "Technology," or "modern science" (using the words as they are usually used, in an unexamined shorthand standing for the "hard" sciences and high technology founded upon continuous economic growth), is a heroic undertaking, Herculean, Promethean, conceived as triumph, hence ultimately as tragedy. The fiction embodying this myth will be, and has been, triumphant (Man conquers earth, space, aliens, death, the future, etc.) and tragic (apocalypse, holocaust, then or now).

If, however, one avoids the linear, progressive, Time's-(killing)-arrow mode of the Techno-Heroic, and redefines technology and science as primarily cultural carrier bag rather than weapon of domination, one pleasant side effect is that science fiction can be seen as a far less rigid, narrow field, not necessarily Promethean or apocalyptic at all, and in fact less a mythological genre than a realistic one.

It is a strange realism, but it is a strange reality.

Science fiction properly conceived, like all serious fiction, however funny, is a way of trying to describe what is in fact going on, what people actually do and feel, how people relate to everything else in this vast sack, this belly of the universe, this womb of things to be and tomb of things that were, this unending story. In it, as in all fiction, there is room enough to keep even Man where he belongs, in his place in the scheme of things; there is time enough to gather plenty of wild oats and sow them too, and sing to little Oom, and listen to Ool's joke, and watch newts, and still the story isn't over. Still there are seeds to be gathered, and room in the bag of stars.

Chapter 30

Kate Rigby[1]

WRITING AFTER NATURE

Writing is neither vibrant life nor docile artefact but a text that would put all its money on the hope of suggestion. Come with me into the field of sunflowers is a better line than anything you will find here, and the sunflowers themselves are more wonderful than any words about them.

(Mary Oliver)

HOWEVER THE CRAFT of nature writing might be conceived, there is a sense in which the nature writer is necessarily called to be a follower. Such writing, that is to say, necessarily follows nature: temporally, in that the natural world to which it refers is presumed to pre-exist the written text; normatively, in that this pre-existing natural world is implicitly valued more highly than the text which celebrates it; and mimetically, in that the text is expected to re-present this pre-existing and highly regarded natural world in some guise. Let me stress at the outset, that I am all for the kind of writing (which comes in a wide variety of literary and non-literary genres) that calls upon its readers to revalue more-than-human beings, places and histories. In defence of such writing, along with the more-than-human beings, places and histories to which it bids us turn our concern, I am nonetheless going to argue here that the relation between nature and writing, especially in the literary mode, might best be thought otherwise.[2]

While the ecologically oriented interest in nature writing is a relatively new phenomenon, it is worth recalling that the idea that writing, at least in those genres that we have come to class as literary, should follow nature is positively ancient. In Aristotle's highly influential definition of mimesis, all art and craft, collectively termed *techne*, was said to "imitate" nature (*physis*), while simultaneously accomplishing "what phusis is incapable of effecting," by creating something that does not develop and reproduce itself according to its own indwelling principle, but instead has a determinate form imposed upon it from outside by its human maker (1957, 173). The Aristotelian conception of mimesis, variously inflected, remained predominant in European culture at least up until the late eighteenth century, when it began to be more-or-less radically reformulated in the context of the Romantic movement, to which much contemporary thinking about art and nature remains indebted. This is a complex story, something of which I have endeavoured to tell elsewhere (2004a). Here, I will content myself with recalling just one moment in this historical narrative, by way of beginning to unfold some of the tricky issues that lurk beneath the surface of the beguiling conjunction of nature and writing.

In 1797, Friedrich Schiller famously declared that poets (*Dichter*, a term that then encompassed all creative writers) are, "by their very definition, the guardians of nature. Where they can no longer quite be so and have already felt within themselves the destructive influence of arbitrary and artificial forms or have had to struggle with them, then they will appear as the *witnesses* and *avengers* of nature. They will either *be* nature, or they will *seek* lost nature" (1985, 191). The former, Schiller dubs "naïve": these are above all those ancient writers, whose work, in his analysis, manifested a certain concreteness and sensuous immediacy; the latter were those modern writers of sentiment, whose work tended rather towards imaginative freedom and reflective distance. Whereas ancient poets such as Homer paid little heed to the beauties of the natural world because their culture was still largely integrated into it, Schiller argued, later writers waxed increasingly lyrical about such things as stones, plants, pastoral and, latterly, wild landscapes, in proportion to the disappearance of nature and naturalness from human life. Nature, that is to say, becomes thematic in literature only when it becomes problematic in reality. The boundaries of the 'modern' proving extremely elastic in Schiller's account, this was a phenomenon of which he sees traces in classical Greek times, but which he perceives as having become ever more pronounced in recent centuries.

At least with respect to the German scene, Schiller cannot be classed as a Romantic; but his literary theoretical writing was certainly taken up, and variously reinterpreted, by those who commonly are seen as such (most immediately, and mischievously, in Schiller's view, by the early German Romantics who gathered in Jena in the late 1790s, including Friedrich von Hardenberg ['Novalis'] and the brothers Schlegel). Schiller's essay "On Naïve and Sentimental Poetry," has been also been recalled in recent years in the context of the ecocritical reconsideration of "the place of creative imagining and writing in the complex set of relationships between humankind and environment" (Bate 2000, 72–73; see also Garrard 2005, 44–45 and Rigby 2004a, 93–101). In doing so again here, my purpose is, in the first place, to sound a note of caution: not all talk of nature is necessarily good for the earth. In the conclusion of this article, I will return to Schiller in order to suggest how his reflections on the poet's vocation might be read in a way that is more sympathetic to the project of what, for the moment, I will still term nature writing. What needs to be stressed to begin with, however, is that what looks like a defence of writing in the service of nature actually turns out to be an argument for the subordination of nature to art. As Philippe Lacoue-Labarthe has observed, Schiller cunningly maps the opposition between the 'naïve' and the 'sentimental', both of which are ultimately found wanting, onto the historical sequence of 'ancient' and 'modern' literature in order to propose a new style of writing, in which nature is neither naively embodied nor sentimentally yearned for, but aesthetically transformed (1989, 237). Rather than hankering nostalgically after the 'naturalness' that had been forfeited in the process of civilisation, he suggests, contemporary writers should set their sights on that which was yet to come: an idealised nature, drawn in conformity with the dictates of human reason and the premise of free will.

It appears that Schiller had been goaded into putting in a good word for nature in this essay by his friend Goethe, whom he acclaims as that paradoxical being, a modern genius: a natural talent, that is, whose work testifies to the modern malaise of nature lost (Rigby 2004a, 93). Schiller nonetheless makes it clear that in the interests of safeguarding human liberty, at least *in potentia, poiesis* must be accorded precedence over *physis*, for, as a true heir to the Enlightenment, he held freedom to be grounded in reason, which he assumed to be an exclusively human faculty: normatively speaking, writing thus comes before nature. At the same time, *poiesis* is in a sense to succeed *physis*. For the role of the poet in modern times, that is to say, under the regime of artifice, was not to seek vainly to effect a return to nature, but rather to subsume nature into his art. In this inaugural text of modern literary theory, composed at the dawn of the industrial era, literature is therefore construed as that mode of writing which begins precisely where nature ends, while nonetheless potentially anticipating the reconciliation of a liberated humanity with a reformed nature, premised upon the transformation of the actual into the ideal.

For all this talk of nature lost—an ancient *topos* recently revived by Jean-Jacques Rousseau and variously inflected by Schiller and his younger contemporaries in Britain and Germany (as well as by successive generations of romantics and neo-romantics there and elsewhere ever since)—the continued existence of nature 'out there', the earthly matrix of the living world, was never seriously in doubt around 1800. Lord Byron, enduring a bleak summer on Lake Geneva in the wake of the eruption of the Tambora volcano in Indonesia, might have been moved to imagine, in his grim poem "Darkness," the possible demise of life on earth in the absence of the beneficent light of the sun (and, searingly, without the metaphysical consolation of a divinely orchestrated new beginning) (Bate 1996). In this poetic thought experiment, there is no suggestion that humans could have brought this catastrophe upon themselves, however, even though it has the effect of disclosing the moral darkness that dwells within them. Things look very different, though, once the possible cessation, or at least catastrophic reduction, of sunlight on a planetary scale appears neither as a supernatural intervention nor as a natural disaster, but as a consequence of human prowess in artful construction, in this case, of weapons of mass destruction. Since the end of the Cold War, the threat of 'nuclear winter' has receded from public concern (although, as the recent bout of sabre rattling between Iran and the US indicates, the possibility of nuclear devastation, if 'only' regionally rather than globally, remains undiminished). In the meantime, we have become conscious of a less spectacular wave of destruction sweeping across the planet as an unintended consequence of the revolutionary changes in human production, consumption and reproduction that got underway in Schiller's day.

As the 'natural philosophers' of that time, notably F. W. J. Schelling and G. W. F. Hegel well appreciated, change, whether great or small, sudden or slow, is endemic to the natural world, which was already beginning to look more like a dynamic process of transformation than a static artefact crafted once and for all by a distant deity (Rigby 2004a, 24–45). Still, the incredibly complex and diverse matrix of life into which scientists now believe modern humans evolved some forty thousand years ago currently appears to be changing in ways that cannot but seem privative. Pollution, habit loss, global warming: none of this might spell the end of life on Earth; but the tidal wave of extinction that such anthropogenic factors is now engendering surely threatens the particular *oikos*, the planetary community of living beings into which humanity was born, and to which we owe our evolutionary emergence. Are we then in the midst of our own endgame? Certainly, Clov's matter-of-fact assertion in Samuel Beckett's play of that name, "There is no more nature" (1958, 16) no longer looks as 'absurd' as it did in the 1950s. If, as Bill McKibben has argued, nature is already at an end since there is no longer any corner of the globe that remains untouched by the effects of human technology, is it not altogether too late for 'nature writing'? In times such as these, we must ask once more, what on earth are poets for?[3]

By some accounts, of course, it was 'always already' too late for nature writing, to the extent, that is, that 'nature' is itself arguably a product of writing. According to Jacques Derrida's deconstructive reading of Rousseau in *Of Grammatology*, "the absolute present, Nature, that which words like 'real mother' name, have always already escaped, have never existed; [. . .] what opens meaning and language is writing as the disappearance of natural presence" (1997, 159). Ecocritics are wont to recoil in horror from statements such as these. Coming hard on the heels of the infamous *il n'y a pas de hors-texte* ("there is no outside-text,"

158), Derrida's rhetoric certainly sounds infuriatingly Idealist; that is, until we pay attention to the capitalisation of Nature (something that is more readily done, incidentally, if we are reading the written page, rather than listening to the spoken word). Far from denying the existence of a more-than-human material reality—the diverse realm of "stuff," in Chris Cuomo's felicitous phrase (1998, 29)—Derrida is actually problematising the ideations by means of which we name, and in so doing tame, constrain and lay claim to it, whether in the name of knowledge, power or (inevitably, perhaps) both. What has never existed 'outside the text' is not nature, but Nature: a metaphysical construct borne of a particular intertextual history and projected onto certain kinds of stuff in a variety of contexts, with a range of potentially very material effects.[4]

By this stage in Derrida's discussion (again, infamously), 'writing' has come to name an aspect of human language in general, in that the structure of supplementarity that Rousseau attributes to writing in a restricted sense is shown to inhabit the spoken word as well: the phoneme no less than the grapheme is a sign that stands in for a referent which is thereby invoked precisely as absent, or at any rate, other than the sign itself. On one level, this is irrefutable. As Hegel observed in the *Jena System Programme* (1803/04), the biblical preroga- tive bestowed upon the mythical first man of imposing names of his own choosing on the rest of creation "annihilated" his Edenic earth others by substituting for the particularity of their embodied being something ideational that could henceforth exist, virtually, in their absence (1975: 288): a primary negation, which is ultimately affirmed by the Idealist philosopher as necessary to the progressive unfolding of the Spirit in history. While I would beg to differ from Hegel regarding the privilege that he accords the concept and the telos that he imparts to history (along with his assumption that speech is exclusively human), I would nonetheless like to join him, to some extent contra Derrida, in insisting that something new does come into play with the invention of writing, and especially perhaps alphabetical writing. Hegel, once again, puts a positive spin on this development. While he objects to the materiality of writing in general as an exteriorization of the Idea, and to alphabetical writing specifically as second degree exteriorization, since it consists of "signs of signs" (that is, arbitrary represen- tations of the spoken word), he nonetheless applauds the alphabet as a means of "infinite education" or "cultivation" (*unendliches Bildungsmittel*): "because thus the mind, distancing itself from the concrete sense-perceptible, directs its attention on the more formal moment, the sonorous word and its abstract elements, and contributes essentially to the founding and purifying of the ground of interiority within the subject" (trans. cit. Derrida 1997, 25). It is precisely this tendency of alphabetic writing to direct consciousness away from the materi- ality of the more-than-human world around us towards the ideational world that the spoken word had ('always already') opened up within our minds, which today renders it the target of ecophilosophical critique, notably in the work of David Abram (1996). I will return to status of nature within alphabetic writing in due course. First, though, I would like to dwell for a moment on the historicity of writing in general.

Postdating the appearance of *Homo sapiens* (himself a notorious late-comer to the biotic community) by nearly 35,000 years, writing is a product of that epochal shift in humanity's relationship with the earth that attended the creation of towns in the major agrarian civilisa- tions of the ancient world, first appearing in Mesopotamia around 3,500 BCE, then around 3000 BCE in Egypt, 2,600 BCE in the Indus Valley, 1,600 BCE in China, and 500 BCE in Mesoamerica (Gaur 1987; Fischer 2001). Unlike speech, writing is not an anthropological constant: its creation was contingent upon a revolutionary (albeit extremely gradual) trans- formation in the means and relations of production, which was itself contingent upon the emergence in some parts of the world of climates, soils, and biotic communities that lent themselves to the development of agriculture. For farming is not an anthropological constant either, although it is certainly cast as such in some of the earliest surviving written creation narratives. The Sumerians, for example, 'naturalised' their own irrigation canals in the fertile valleys of the Tigris and Euphrates by construing them, along with the great rivers themselves, as the work of the gods. "So far were the Sumerians from imagining a preagricultural humankind," observes Evan Eisenberg, "that they saw humankind itself as a crop" (1998, 83).

Created in the context of a whole new phase in the human domination of the earth through the domestication of plants and animals, the cultivation of the soil, and the construction of cities set apart from the surrounding countryside, writing also came to bear witness, however obliquely, to the environmentally destructive potential of the civilization that brought it into being. In the Sumerian tablets that lie behind the later Akkadian and Babylonian *Epic of Gilgamesh* (c. 2000 BCE), the hero, ably assisted by his once wild soul mate Enkidu, seeks to defy death by making a name for himself as a legendary logger. Crossing seven mountains, which were evidently already denuded, he found the trees that he was after in "The Land of the Living," only to lose his friend as a consequence of slaying the *genius loci* of the forest, the demon Huwawa (Pritchard 1969, 47–50).[5] In the surviving version of the epic, there is no indication that Gilgamesh draws any ethical consequences from this with regard to his treatment of the earth. Recognising the futility of his quest for immortality, he responds by returning to the city and building its walls yet higher: the logs, meanwhile, continue to float down the river "like the bodies of the dead" (Harrison 1992, 18).

The deforestation that is recalled in this inaugural work of written literature was integral to Sumerian civilisation, as to every civilisation since, and it comprised but one of the major ecological impacts of the agricultural revolution. More immediately worrisome for the ancient Mesopotamians (as for present day Australians) was the salinisation of their once fruitful fields as a result of irrigation, a problem that seems to have begun to bite at precisely the time that the oldest surviving clay tablets were inscribed with cuneiform script. Analysis of the marks left by the grain stored in Sumerian pots indicates that from about 3,500 BCE, the proportion of wheat to barley, a more salt-tolerant crop, begins to decline steadily, such that by 1700 BCE, wheat has disappeared entirely (Eisenberg 1998, 124). Over the millennia, Eisenberg speculates, salinisation might also have been a major factor in the gradual shift of power and population upriver: from Sumer to Akkad to Babylon to Nineveh. In his reading, a faint suspicion "that their greatest triumph, irrigation, was bringing about their greatest disaster, salinization" (121) can be traced in another Sumerian poem, "Enki and Ninhursag," which turns upon a conflict between the tricksterish water deity and the awesome earth mother, as well as in the "Atrahasis," which recounts how the gods punished humans for making too much of a racket by causing the salty sea below to rise up through the earth: "During the nights the fields turned white. The broad plain brought forth salt crystals, so that no plant came forth, no grain sprouted" (Pritchard 1969, 104–6).

Within the world of cuneiform inscription, then, the integral space of the *oikos* is ruptured through the constitution of discrete zones and orders of being, sundering the wild from the cultivated and the countryside from the town. The separation of the truly human and his works from other-than-human spaces and entities is already implicit here. However, an abstract concept of 'nature', at least as it has been articulated in the Western tradition, whether as cosmic whole, indwelling principle, moral guide, virgin territory, or antithesis of culture, to name but some of the major usages of this infamously slippery term, only emerges within the world of fully alphabetical writing, beginning with classical Greek (Glacken 1967; Soper 1995; Coates 1998). Let me stress here that I do not want to imply a causal connection between alphabeticisation and abstraction: after all, the use of a pictographic-ideographic script did not prevent the Chinese from developing a concept of nature, at least along the lines of the first two meanings given above, as is already evident in early Confucian and Taoist texts from the sixth century BCE (Marshall 1994, 9–23). It is nonetheless striking that the "theorisation of a strictly intelligible realm of pure Ideas resting entirely outside of the sensible world," according to David Abram (1996, 197), finds its earliest articulation within the entirely arbitrary sign system of classical Greek. Even if this connection is purely contingent, rather than causal, as Abram controversially assumes, what it surely discloses is that Nature, as Derrida insists, does indeed follow writing: as an ideation, it is the creation of a long history of textual inscription, the precise contours of which have shifted and diversified in association with changing regimes of domination, both within human society, and between humanity and the earth.

Granted. But what of nature? The significance that the deconstructionist philosopher attributes to the grammatological genesis of Nature, the spin that he puts on it, and the implications that most literary theorists have tended to draw from it, clearly pertains to a different agenda from that of the ecocritic. From an ecocritical perspective, it is equally important to emphasise the secondariness of writing, not only temporally but also normatively, in relation to the vastly longer and more complex history of the unfolding of life on earth. This is, moreover, a history of the emergence of a myriad of interconnecting systems of communication, without which there would be no humanly produced texts, whether written or oral, at all. As Judith Wright reminds us in "Scribbly-Gum," there is a 'writing' far more ancient than that of human words:

> The gum-tree stands by the spring.
> I peeled its splitting bark
> and found the written track
> of a life I could not read.
> (Wright 2003, 131)

While the markings on the Scribbly Gum can only be thought of as writing in a highly figurative or extended sense, namely with reference to the phenomenon of the trace, systems of coded information transfer abound in the natural world. We are ourselves 'written' into being (through evolution, ecology, and genetics, for example, as well as through the more parochial codes of human culture) whether or not we become writers in turn. "The human process actualises semiotic processes that it did not make and that it did not shape," avers Robert S. Corrington: "Our cultural codes, no matter how sophisticated and multi-valued, are what they are by riding on the back of this self-recording nature" (1994, ix). It is, as Laurence Coupe puts it, to defend *this* nature that Green Studies "debates 'Nature'" (2000, 5).

Yet can we speak of nature without thereby also invoking Nature? Does this term not carry altogether too much Western metaphysical baggage to serve us well in a contemporary context? Heidegger, in his day, already thought so. The philosopher of being and dwelling disavowed 'nature', not because he had no time for the other-than-human (although his hierarchy of beings was notoriously anthropocentric), but rather in order to safeguard the *autopoiesis*, or self-unfolding and self-revealing, of the manifold phenomena of earth and sky, by liberating them from earlier metaphysical constructs, whether as an artefact of divine manufacture, as in the dominant Judeao-Christian concept of creation; a set of knowable laws of cause and effect, as in scientific positivism; or, under the regime of modern technology, as mere 'standing reserve', passively awaiting extraction, manipulation and commodification. It is, among other things, Heidegger's disavowal that stands behind Derrida's deconstruction, although the urbane French philosopher suspected the forest-dwelling Swabian sage of succumbing to metaphysics anew in his very attempt to escape it. Meanwhile, however, there is reason to suspect, as Val Plumwood does, that "the deep contemporary [. . .] scepticism about the term 'nature' may play some role in the contemporary indifference to the destruction and decline of the natural world around us" (2001, 3). In my own experience, this nature-scepticism has certainly rendered it difficult to champion the more-than-human in the academic arena of literary and cultural studies in the wake of the (post) structuralist 'linguistic turn'. In Plumwood's view, we cannot afford to do away with 'nature' at this juncture: rather than puritanically evicting this loaded term from our lexicon, we should, she argues, endeavour to deploy it otherwise. This is, I believe, a crucially important under-taking: without doubt, non-dualistic and anti-colonial talk of nature can be strategically valu-able in defending the agency and interests of the other-than-human. But we must bear in mind that we are never entirely in control of the meanings attributed to the words we use, however guardedly, and some of the cultural connotations that 'nature' carries in its wake are arguably part and parcel of the eco-social crisis in which we find ourselves today.

In recent years, various attempts have been made to find alternatives to 'nature' within ecologically oriented literary and cultural studies. Lawrence Buell, for example, prefers the term 'environment', as better approximating "the hybridity of the subject at issue-all 'envi-ronments' in practice involving fusions of 'natural' and 'constructed' elements," as well as reflecting the broadening of ecocritical concern to encompass urban and/or toxified land-scapes, rather than the more wild and/or pastoral places favoured by early ecocriticism (Buell 2005, viii). This seems to me a sound move, although this term too is problematic, in that it presupposes a topology of centre and surroundings that implicitly prioritises human agency and interests. In this respect, Ernst Haeckel's coinage seems preferable, the concept of 'ecology' implying an endeavour to understand the multiple interrelationships between living entities in the 'whole household' of the earth in its varied regions in a manner that does not centralise Homo sapiens. In practice, however, as Donald Worster (1994) has demon-strated, the pursuit of ecological understanding has always been ambivalent in its orientation and ends, historically manifesting both 'arcadian' and 'imperial' tendencies. Some cultural ecologists have been drawn to Bruno Latour's concept of 'culture-nature' in order to fore-ground the 'hybrid' quality of the world inhabited by '(post)modern' and 'non-modern' peoples alike (Latour 1993). I have myself deployed this terminology (2004a, 117), although, as Erica Cudworth has recently observed, the trouble here is that it does not allow sufficiently for non-hybrid causality. While the impact and evaluation of tidalwaves and earthquakes, for example, might well be socially and culturally co-constructed, such phenomena can hardly be said to be hybrid in genesis. Similarly, the "migratory patterns of deer, whales and birds may be disrupted by human endeavor, but a disruption of pattern and process and hybridity are different things" (Cudworth 2005, 53). In addition, it should be noted that the very concept of 'hybridity' presupposes a distinction between 'nature' and 'culture' that emerges, as we have seen, in a particular ecosocial context, and is thus far from universally applicable. The indigenous Australian notion of 'country', by contrast, implies a rather different way of understanding the relationship between humans and others living together in the context of what Deborah Rose has rendered delightfully as a "nourishing terrain" (1996). I have endeav-oured to translate something of this Indigenous sense of place into the post-Heideggerian concept of *ecopoiesis* that I have adopted and adapted from Jonathan Bate with reference to the literary 'languaging' of dwelling (Bate 2000, 75–76; Rigby 2004b).[6] Here, too, however, there are potential pitfalls: at the very least, any notion of place-based belonging needs to be rigorously rethought in the face of the increasingly urban, itinerant and global context of human existence.

Whether we call it nature writing, environmental literature, ecopoetics or something else entirely, the question that remains to be addressed here is that of the relationship between such writing and the more-than-human others, places and histories towards which it bids us turn. To what extent, that is, can such writing be understood to be 'after nature' in the further sense of rendering a true likeness of that which it represents? As Lawrence Buell has observed in his recent reflections on the "question of mimesis," the aspiration to veracity, often coupled with a preference for realism, as is evident in much early ecocriticism has drawn considerable fire from constructionist quarters (2005, 30–32). Recalling that those marks on the page are mere 'signs of signs', conventionalised substitutes for spoken words, arbitrary signifiers with virtual signifieds, invoking a world of ideas that predetermines our perception of the material world beyond the page, must we not conclude that in this regard too, nature comes after writing? To some extent, the constructionist case can be understood positively as shielding us from the epistemological hubris of assuming that things-in-themselves (to recall the Kantian origins of this argument) can be rendered transparent to human knowledge, their essential being captured in the net of merely human words. However, if the multiple signifying systems of other-than-human entities are not thereby to be rendered mute, and their potentially resistant agency denied, we must also acknowledge at the very least that our constructions are never entirely free, but always also "constrained" (Hayles 1995) by a more-than-human material reality that precedes and exceeds whatever we might make of it. It is in the interests of safeguarding precisely that precedence and excess that I have argued elsewhere for an 'ecopoetics of negativity', emphasising the inevitable failure of the written word to restore to presence that to which it refers us (2004b). "Language never replicates extratextual landscapes," as Buell so pithily puts it, "but it can be bent toward or away from them" (2005, 33).

Recalling Wright's Scribbly Gum, we might then venture that earth and sky have their own stories to tell, and it is to those that some writers call us to attend. Rather than thinking of this primarily as a matter of mimesis, however, I suggest that such writing be considered, more broadly, as embodying a literary practice of response: as such, we can truly say that writing comes second, following on from the other's call, while becoming in turn the locus of a new call, to and upon the reader.[7] Called forth by particular more-than-human others, places and histories, our words are nonetheless cast into, and framed by, a human communicative context, necessarily responding also to the words of others of our own kind, whether written or spoken. The particular mode of written response will therefore vary in accordance with a range of cultural, social, situational and generic contingencies. This too is exemplified by Buell in his discussion of "environmentality across the genre spectrum" (2005, 44–61). In some genres, mimesis of one kind or another will surely be involved in the articulation of the response: I am certainly very taken by Mark Tredinnick's suggestion that the musical dimension of lyrical language (in prose writing, no less than poetry) can in some sense render, or at least be attuned to, the music of a place (2005). Here too it is important to qualify my earlier comments on naming as a potential strategy of domination that obliterates particularity. For naming can also be crucial in the recognition of diversity and disclosure of interconnections. While words can certainly be deployed in the service of control, when we surrender the assumption that to name is to know we might find, as Kevin Hart writes in "The River," "That every word said well is praise" (2002, 153).

Lest we are to fall prey to an idolatry of the text, however, it is also important to acknowledge, as Jean-Louis Chrétien (2004) would graciously have us do, the inevitable inadequacy of each and every response, however framed. For it is only in its glorious falling short that the text bids us to 'lift our eye from the page' (Bonnefoy 1990), calling us forth into an embodied engagement with more-than-human others, places and histories, while also encouraging us to join in the symphonic chorus of other responses, past, present and yet to come.

In our own space-time of ecological imperilment, I believe that there is an additional call on the writer of more-than-human beings, places and histories. Writing, as we have seen, was born of ecosocial rupture. Today, however, perhaps more than ever before, it might also be turned towards what, in the Jewish tradition, has been termed *tikkun olam*: 'repair of the world'. Although the antiquity of this phrase reminds us that we are by no means the first generation to experience their world as 'broken', the global character of the present threat to the flourishing of more-than-human life on earth would appear to be unprecedented, at least since *Homo sapiens* appeared on the scene. Moreover, in reinterpreting *tikkun* as extending to our relations with our other-than-human earth others, we should not overlook that to which it is more conventionally conceived as calling us: namely, to the healing and transformation of human social relations (and, thereby also, at least for the faithful, our relations with G-d). Here it is important to recall the extent to which the devastation of the earth is intertwined with the oppression, exploitation and marginalisation of subordinate humans. As Michael Bennett has argued, therefore, environmental literature and criticism must needs respond not only to the sublime alterity of the " 'black hole' of a weasel's eye," but also to "the just-closed eyes of a child of the ghetto killed by lead-poisoning from ingesting the peeling paint in his/her immediate environment" (1998, 53). It is within this horizon of understanding that I would like to return in conclusion to the Schiller essay with which I began. Reading it against the grain, we might recast his call for a new kind of (possibly postmodern) literature, beyond the opposition of naïve naturalism and sentimental yearning, as envisaging a mode of writing that, in responding to the social and ecological brokenness of our world, however inadequately, might conjoin concern with the flourishing of all life, human and otherwise, with respect for the claims of human justice and freedom.

Notes

1   Kate Rigby (FAHA) is Associate Professor and Director of the Centre for Comparative Literature and Cultural Studies at Monash University and President of the Association for the Study of Literature and Environment (Australia-New Zealand). Her most recent book is *Topographies of the Sacred: The Poetics of Place in European Romanticism* (University of Virginia Press, 2004).

2   Many thanks to Kevin Hart and my two anonymous reviewers for their invaluable comments and suggestions on an earlier draft of this article, and also to Rose Lucas for sharing with me the inestimable gift of Mary Oliver's essays and verse. All remaining oversights and errors are my own entirely.

3   "What are Poets For?" is the title of an essay by Heidegger (1971), alluding to a poem entitled "Bread and Wine" by another of Schiller's younger contemporaries, Friedrich Hölderlin, and of the Heideggerian last chapter of Bate's monograph, *The Song of the Earth* (2004).

4   For a helpful explanation of Derrida's philosophical materialism, see Cheah 1996.

5   On the eco-cultural significance of the Gilgamesh story, see Harrison 1992, 14–18; Westling 1996, 18–23; and Eisenberg 1998, 111–21.

6   See also Scigaj 1999 for a version of ecopoetics that leans more on Merleau-Ponty than Heidegger.

7   Although my understanding of the call is phenomenological in orientation, Freya Mathews (2003, 2005) makes a plausible case for a 'panpsychic' understanding of the way in which we might be addressed by material entities, whether 'natural' or 'artifactual'.

Works Cited

Abram, David. 1996. *The Spell of the Sensuous. Perception and Language in a More-than-Human World.* New York: Vintage Books.

Aristotle. 1957. *The Physics.* Trans. Francis M. Cornfield. Vol. 1. Cambridge, Mass.: Harvard University Press.

Bate, Jonathan. 1991. *Romantic Ecology. Wordsworth and the Environmental Tradition.* London: Routledge.

———. 1996. "Living with the Weather." In *Green Romanticism,* ed. J. Bate. Special issue of *Studies in Romanticism* 55, no. 3: 431–48.

————. 2000. *The Song of the Earth*. Cambridge, Mass.: Harvard University Press.

Beckett, Samuel. 1958. *Endgame*. London: Faber & Faber.

Bennett, Michael 1998. "Urban Nature: Teaching Tinker Creek by the East River," *ISLE* 5 (Winter 1998), 49–59.

Bonnefoy, Yves. 1990. "Lifting Our Eyes from the Page," *Critical Inquiry* 16 (Summer 1990), 794–806.

Buell, Lawrence. 1995. *The Future of Environmental Criticism. Environmental Crisis and the Literary Imagination*. Oxford: Blackwell.

Cheah, Pheng. 1996. "Mattering." *Diacritics* 26:1, 108–39.

Chrétien, Jean-Louis. 2004. *The Call and the Response*. Trans. Anne A. Davenport. New York: Fordham University Press.

Coates, Peter. 1998. *Nature: Western Attitudes Since Ancient Times*. Cambridge: Polity.

Corrington, Robert S. 1994. *Ecstatic Naturalism: Signs of the World*. Bloomington: Indiana University Press.

Coupe, Laurence. 2000. *The Green Studies Reader. From Romanticism to Ecocriticism*. Foreword, Jonathan Bate. London and New York: Routledge.

Cudworth, Erika. 2005. *Developing Ecofeminist Theory. The Complexity of Difference*. Basingstoke: Palgrave Macmillan.

Cuomo, Chris. 1998. *Feminism and Ecological Communities: An Ethic of Flourishing*, London: Routledge.

Derrida, Jacques. 1997. *Of Grammatology*. Corrected version. Trans. Gayatri Chakrovorty Spivak. Baltimore: Johns Hopkins University Press.

Eisenberg, Evan. 1998. *The Ecology of Eden: Humans, Nature and Human Nature*. London: Picador.

Fischer, Steven Roger. 2001. *A History of Writing*. London: Reaktion.

Garrard, Greg. 2005. *Ecocriticism*. London: Routledge.

Gaur, Albertine. 1987. *A History of Writing*. London: British Library.

Harrison, Robert Pogue. 1992. *Forests: The Shadow of Civilization*. Chicago: Univ. of Chicago Press.

Glacken, Clarence J. 1967. *Traces on the Rhodian Shore: Nature and Culture in Western Thought from Ancient Times to the End of the Eighteenth Century*. Berkeley: University of California Press.

Hayles, N. Katherine. 1995. "Searching for Common Ground." In Michael E. Soulé and Gary Lease (eds), *Reinventing Nature: Responses to Postmodern Deconstruction*. Washington D.C.: Island.

Hegel, G. W. F. 1975. *Jenaer Systementwürfe*. Hamburg: Meiner.

Heidegger, Martin. 1971. "What are Poets For?" In *Poetry, Language, Thought*. Trans. and ed. Albert Hofstadter. New York: Harper and Row, 89–142.

Lacoue-Labarthe, Philippe. 1989. *Typography: Mimesis, Philosophy, Politics*. Intro. J. Derrida, ed. Christopher Fynsk. Cambridge, Mass.: Harvard University Press.

Latour, Bruno. 1993. *We Have Never Been Modern*. Trans. Catherine Porter. Cambridge, Mass.: Harvard University Press.

Marshall, Peter. 1994. *Nature's Web. Rethinking Our Place on Earth*. New York: Paragon House.

Mathews, Freya. 2003. *For Love of Matter. A Contemporary Panpsychism*, Albany: SUNY Press.

————. 2005. *Reinhabiting Reality. Towards a Recovery of Culture*. Albany: SUNY Press and Sydney: UNSW Press.

McKibben, Bill. 1990. *The End of Nature*. Harmondsworth: Penguin.

Oliver, Mary. 2004. *Blue Iris. Poems and Essays*. Boston: Beacon Press.

Plumwood, Val. 2001. "Nature as agency and the prospects for a progressive naturalism," *Capitalism, Nature, Socialism* 12:4 (Dec. 2001), 3–32.

Pritchard, James Bennett (ed.). 1969. *Ancient Near Eastern Texts Relating to the Old Testament*. Princeton: Princeton University Press.

Rigby, Kate. 2004a. *Topographies of the Sacred. The Poetics of Place in European Romanticism*. Charlottesville: University of Virginia Press.

———. 2004b. "Earth, World, Text: On the (Im)possibility of Ecopoiesis," *New Literary History* 35:5 (Summer 2004), 427–42.

Rose, Deborah Bird. 1996. *Nourishing Terrains: Australian Aboriginal Views of Landscape and Wilderness*. Canberra: Australian Heritage Commission.

Sanders, N. K (trans. and ed.) 1972. *The Epic of Gilgamesh*. Harmondsworth: Penguin.

Schiller, Friedrich. 1985. "On Naïve and Sentimental Poetry." Trans. J. A. Elias, in H.B. Nisbet (ed.), *German Aesthetic and Literary Criticism: Winckelmann, Lessing, Hamann, Herder, Schiller, Goethe*. Cambridge: Cambridge University Press.

Scigaj, Leonard. 1999. *Sustainable Poetry: Four American Ecopoets*. Lexington, KY: University Press of Kentucky.

Soper, Kate. 1995. *What is Nature? Culture, Politics, and the non-Human*. Oxford: Blackwell.

Tredinnick, Mark. 2005. *The Land's Wild Music. Encounters with Barry Lopez, Peter Matthiessen, Terry Tempest Williams, and James Galvin*. San Antonia, GA: Trinity University Press.

Westling, Louise. 1996. The Green Breast of the New World: Landscape, Gender and American Fiction. Athens, GA: University of Georgia Press.

Worster, Donald. 1994. *Nature's Economy. A History of Ecological Ideas*. Cambridge: Cambridge University Press.

Wright, Judith. 2003. *Collected Poems*. Sydney: Angus & Robertson.

Index

Kelly, Petra 280
Kent, William 91
Kew Gardens 201
Killingsworth, M. Jimmie 172
Kilmer, Joyce 264
Kimball, Andrew 180
Kincaid, Jamaica 190, 201–2
King Lear (Shakespeare) 13, 17, 273
King, Thomas 192
Kirby, Vicki 150
kitsch 244–50
knowledge: problems of 322–9; production
    228; sharing 213, 215–16
Knutson, Roslyn 292
Kohák, Erazim 304
Kolodny, Annette 165
Krech, Shepard III 180
Kristeva, Julia 249
Kroeber, Karl 172, 251
Kuletz, Valerie 138–9
Kundera, Milan 250
Kvaloy, Sigmund 52
Kyoto Protocol 224, 255

Lacan, Jacques 249
Laclau, Ernesto 319
Lacoue-Labarthe, Philippe 358
LaDuke, Winona 137
Lake District National Park 85
Lake, Peter 327
land rights/conflicts 140, 154, 183, 204–5
"Landscape and Narrative" (Lopez) 97
landscapes: in fiction 97–8; interior/exterior
    97, 100; landscaping 91, 304; otherworld
    301–7; regional 303–7; tropical 310–19
Langland, William 37
language issues 215–16
Lankford, Scott 217–18, 220
Latour, Bruno 132, 145–6, 255, 343, 363
The Lay of the Land (Kolodny) 165
Lazarus, Neil 178
Le Guin, Ursula 125
Leal, Teresa 138, 142
Leavis, R. R. 35
Lee, Ang 159–62
Lefebvre, Henri 296–7
Leibnitz, G.W. 44
Leibniz, G. W. 271
Leland, Mickey 157
Leonardo da Vinci 20–1, 328
Leopold, Aldo 2, 56, 68, 72, 99, 114, 125–6,
    171, 196, 199
Lesser, Zachary 292
Lester, Yami 204
Levin, Jonathan 185
Levine, George 100
Levitt, Norman 166
Lewis, John 157
linguistic/discursive turn 143–4, 146, 187–8
Linnaeus, Carl 78, 215

liquid seed theory 21
literary studies 120–7
literary theory 98–100, 122, 165–6
literary/nonliterary boundary 98–9
"Literature and Ecology" (Rueckert) 123, 287
Literature and the Environment 204
Literature of Nature (Murphy) 173
Liu, Alan 90
The Lives of Animals (Coetzee) 191
Living Downstream (Steingraber) 140
living earth concept 281, 284
local-global contexts 79, 142, 202–3, 205,
    217–23, 228, 279
Locke, John 271, 274, 329
London Liberties 295–7
The Long Twentieth Century (Arrighi) 336
Longino, Helen 145
Lopez, Barry 97, 99, 125, 172
The Lord of the Rings (Tolkien) 247
Love, Glen 122, 165, 169
Lovelock, James E. 284, 286
"Love's Alchemie" (Donne) 29
Love's Labour's Lost (Shakespeare) 297
"Love's Progress" (Donne) 29–30
Lowe, Celia 216
Lucier, Alvin 244, 246
Lyell, Charles, Sir 342
Lykke, Nina 148
Lynch, Tom 140
Lyrical Ballads (Wordsworth and Coleridge)
    288–9, 293
Lyson, Thomas 155–6

Maathai, Wangari 203
Mabey, Richard 200
Macbeth (Shakespeare) 283
MacDonald, Scott 168
Mach, Ernst 338
Macherot, Raymond 164, 171
The Machine in the Garden (L. Marx) 165
Macy, Joanna 250
Malaysia 225, 227
Malcomson, Scott 204
Malthus, Thomas 78
Man's Responsibility for Nature (Passmore) 267
A Map of Glass (Urquhart) 150–1
Marcone, Jorge 173
Margulis, Lynn 284
Marshall, Peter 361
Martel, Yann 192
Martínez-Alier, Joan 168, 178
Marvell, Andrew 322, 325–7
Marx, Karl 91, 148, 268, 274, 280–1, 337, 341
Marx, Leo 1–2, 165
Marxism 187, 290, 297, 319, 338, 345
masculinity issues 108, 159–62
Maslin, Mark 343
Massinger, Philip 36–7
materialism 91, 185, 244, 290–1
materiality 83–4, 143–52